PENGUIN BOOKS

LLOYD GEORGE:
FROM PEACE TO WAR 1912–1916

John Grigg, FRSL, was born in 1924, and educated at Eton and New College, Oxford. In the period between the two (towards the end of the Second World War) he served in Holland and Germany with the Grenadier Guards. After editing a monthly magazine he became a columnist on the *Guardian* (1960–69), after which, apart from a spell on the staff of *The Times* while he was writing a volume in the paper's official history (Vol. 6, *The Thomson Years*), he was a freelance journalist. Before his death, on 31 December 2001 he had published three volumes of a projected five-volume life of Lloyd George: *The Young Lloyd George*, *Lloyd George: The People's Champion* and *Lloyd George: From Peace to War*. For the last two he was awarded, respectively, the Whitbread Prize and the Wolfson Prize. The fourth Volume, *Lloyd George: War Leader*, is to be published posthumously. He also wrote *1943* and a short life of Nancy Astor. He was chairman of the London Library committee for the period 1986–91 and from 1996 was president of the Library. He was married, with two sons and three grandchildren.

'The Golfer', Spy cartoon of Lloyd George
taken from the *World*, *c*.1913.

LLOYD GEORGE

FROM PEACE
TO WAR
1912–1916

John Grigg

PENGUIN BOOKS

PENGUIN BOOKS

Published by the Penguin Group
Penguin Books Ltd, 80 Strand, London WC2R ORL, England
Penguin Putnam Inc., 375 Hudson Street, New York, New York 10014, USA
Penguin Books Australia Ltd, 250 Camberwell Road, Camberwell, Victoria 3124, Australia
Penguin Books Canada Ltd, 10 Alcorn Avenue, Toronto, Ontario, Canada M4V 3B2
Penguin Books India (P) Ltd, 11 Community Centre, Panchsheel Park, New Delhi – 110 017, India
Penguin Books (NZ) Ltd, Cnr Rosedale and Airborne Roads, Albany, Auckland, New Zealand
Penguin Books (South Africa) (Pty) Ltd, 24 Sturdee Avenue, Rosebank 2196, South Africa

Penguin Books Ltd, Registered Offices: 80 Strand, London WC2R ORL, England

www.penguin.com

First published by Eyre Methuen Ltd 1985
First published in paperback with a new preface by Methuen 1991
Published with a new preface to the second paperback by HarperCollins 1997
Published in Penguin Books 2002
1

Printed in England by Clays Ltd, St Ives plc

Contents

Illustrations

Acknowledgments and thanks are due to Mrs Jennifer Longford for
no. 7; to Lord Bonham-Carter for no. 4; to the Press Association for
nos. 1, 2, 3, 10, 21, 23, 24, 25, 26; to the BBC Hulton Picture Library
for no. 5; to the Mary Evans Picture Library for nos. 6, 8, 11, 12, 13,
16, 27, 28, 31 and the illustrations on pp. 36, 57, 97, 252, 285, 501; to
Associated Newspapers for no. 9; to Popperfoto for no. 14; to the
National Portrait Gallery for nos. 17, 20; to the Imperial War Museum
for nos. 19, 22, 29, 30; and to Keystone Press for no. 18.
The publishers regret that they have been unable to trace an accurate
date for the frontispiece.

Acknowledgments

I am most grateful to Mr Anthony Pitt-Rivers and the executors of his mother's estate for allowing me to read the letters from H. H. Asquith to Sylvia Henley, and I owe a great debt to Lord Bonham-Carter for his permission to quote from them, as from other Asquith material of which he held the copyright.

Dr Michael Brock helped me in a number of ways, especially in supplying (with Lord Bonham-Carter's agreement) photocopies of extracts from Margot Asquith's as yet unpublished diary. I am very grateful to him.

Lloyd George's grandsons, Owen and Bill (Earl Lloyd George of Dwyfor and Viscount Tenby) continued to be most generous in their help, and I cannot thank them enough for allowing me access to their collections; also for their permission to quote words used by their fathers.

Mrs Jennifer Longford gave me invaluable information about her mother, Frances Stevenson (later Countess Lloyd George of Dwyfor), for which I am greatly indebted to her.

I have to thank Her Majesty the Queen for allowing me to work in the Royal Archives at Windsor, and for gracious permission to quote passages derived from them or of which she owns the copyright.

Others to whom I am much obliged for copyright permissions include Professor A. K. S. Lambton (Lord Robert Cecil); the Earl of Crawford and Balcarres (Crawford); the National Library of Wales (Ellis W. Davies); Dr H. Mostyn Lewis (Herbert Lewis);

Mrs D. M. Maxse (L J. Maxse); Viscount Monckton of Brenchley
(Walter Monckton); Mr Milton Gendel (Montagu); The Hon Sir
Steven Runciman and the University Library, Newcastle-upon-
Tyne (Runciman).

Special thanks are also due to Lady Olwen Carey Evans, Sir
Geoffrey Harmsworth Bart., Mr A. J. Sylvester and Miss Jean
Walton.

An Alistair Horne Fellowship at St Antony's College, Oxford,
provided a most agreeable base from which to do necessary work at
the Bodleian. I should like to record my thanks to the Warden and
Fellows, as well as to Mr Horne.

J.G.

Preface

My last volume took the story of Lloyd George's life from the end of the Boer War in mid-1902 to the end of the year 1911, one of the busiest and most fruitful of his career. This one will cover the five-year period from the beginning of 1912 until the end of 1916, when he replaced Asquith in the premiership. It will attempt to describe his last efforts as a reforming minister in a peacetime party government, and then his transformation into a dynamic war minister as the country faced an ordeal more profoundly disturbing than the civil wars of the seventeenth century, and probably more so than anything it had experienced since the Black Death.

My aim in writing a multi-volume life of Lloyd George is not to supplant all the good books that have been written about him already, but merely to supplement them. And of course I have no illusion that I am writing a 'definitive' account of his life (a term which is anyway absurd as applied to history and most other forms of knowledge). In this volume, as in its two predecessors, I would merely claim that I am letting him speak as much as possible for himself, by quoting substantially from his speeches and from his recorded words in conference or conversation; also that I am doing my utmost to be truthful about him, whether or not the truth is to his advantage.

As before, readers will be left in no doubt of my opinions, because I believe it to be right for a biographer to argue with his subject and not to stand aside in a posture of inhuman detachment. At the same time I hope I shall never fail to give the evidence on which readers can form their own opinions, which may or may not accord with mine.

By the end of 1911 Lloyd George had seen his National Insurance Bill safely on to the Statute Book, though the struggle to implement the Health Insurance scheme was still ahead of him. That struggle will not, however, be described in detail in the present volume, because the topic has been dealt with quite fully in Chapter Eleven of *Lloyd George: The People's Champion*. Another matter already covered is the Liberal government's bungled attempt to reform the franchise between 1911 and the beginning of 1913, which involved frustration for Lloyd George both as genuine democrat and genuine female suffragist. To this, too, there will be only passing allusions.

The footnote references provided throughout the book give a fair idea of the primary and secondary sources on which it is based, though of course a great many more were consulted without being quoted.

During the period covered by the book the Lloyd George Papers at the House of Lords Record Office become, for the first time, the chief documentary source for his public life. For this Frances Stevenson is to be thanked, because it was only when she came into his life that his official and political papers began to be systematically preserved. The great archive from 1912 onwards is her monument as well as his.

Lord Beaverbrook used to say, back in the 1960s, that the two most important unpublished sources for twentieth-century British history were Frances Stevenson's diary and Asquith's letters to Venetia Stanley. He had been able to make use of both, having acquired the original of the first from Frances, and earlier, from Venetia, copies of many of her letters or excerpts from them. Now both collections are substantially available in print.

A. J. P. Taylor's edition of Frances's diary appeared in 1971, and is indeed an invaluable record, though teasingly incomplete. It does not begin until 21 September 1914, and thereafter there are many gaps. In the main these occur when the author was either ill or too busy to keep a diary, but Mr Taylor suggests that parts may have been 'discarded or even lost'. His edition of the Lloyd George–Frances Stevenson correspondence (*My Darling Pussy*, 1975) is another significant source. Letters relating to the period covered by this book occupy only eighteen pages, but some of these are very interesting, as is Mr Taylor's commentary. (The full manuscripts of diary and letters can be studied in the House of Lords Record Office.)

I am extremely grateful to Mr Taylor and the Beaverbrook Foundation for the permissions they have given me, and to the staff of the House of Lords Record Office for their invariable efficiency and kindness.

A more or less full text of the Asquith letters to Venetia Stanley was published in 1981, superbly edited by Michael and Eleanor Brock. These letters, which for most of 1914 and early 1915 are the equivalent of a very detailed diary – since Asquith was then writing to Venetia most days and often more than once a day – provide an incomparable insight into the high politics of the time.

When Venetia married Edwin Montagu the flow of letters to her ceased (though the Montagus remained friends of the Asquiths, often staying at the Wharf). But very soon the Prime Minister found a new epistolary confidante in Sylvia Henley, an elder sister of Venetia and married to a serving Army officer. Asquith's letters to her, as yet unpublished, are less frequent than to Venetia during the last phase of their correspondence, though still frequent enough: well over a hundred between July 1915 and December 1916. And they are no less informative. (In one, for instance, he gives a virtually full list of all the warships at Invergordon.)

I am most grateful to Mr Anthony Pitt-Rivers and the executors of his grandmother's estate for allowing me to read these letters in 1981. But my chief debt is to the Hon. Mark Bonham Carter for his permission to quote from them, as from other Asquith material of which he holds the copyright.

Dr Michael Brock has helped me in a number of ways, but more especially in supplying (with Mr Bonham Carter's agreement) photocopies of extracts from Margot Asquith's as yet unpublished diary. I am very grateful to him.

Lloyd George's grandsons, Owen and Bill (Earl Lloyd George of Dwyfor and Viscount Tenby) have continued to be unstinting in their help, and I cannot thank them enough for allowing me free access to their collections: also for permission to quote words used by their fathers.

I have to thank Her Majesty the Queen for allowing me to work in the Royal Archives at Windsor, and for gracious permission to quote passages derived from them or of which she owns the copyright.

Others to whom I am indebted for copyright permissions include Professor A. K. S. Lambton O.B.E., F.B.A. (Lord Robert Cecil); The Earl of Crawford and Balcarres P.C. (Crawford); the National Library of Wales (Ellis W. Davies); Dr H. Mostyn Lewis (Herbert Lewis); Mrs D. M. Maxse (L. J. Maxse); Viscount Monckton of Brenchley (Walter

Monckton); Mr Milton Gendel (Montagu); the Hon. Sir Steven Runciman C.H., F.B.A. and the University Library, Newcastle-upon-Tyne (Runciman).

My special thanks are due to Lady Olwen Carey Evans D.B.E., the late Sir Geoffrey Harmsworth Bart., Mrs Jennifer Longford, Mr A. J. Sylvester C.B.E. and Miss Jean Walton.

An Alistair Horne Research Fellowship at St Anthony's College, Oxford, provided a most agreeable base from which to do necessary work at the Bodleian, and I should like to record my thanks to the Warden and Fellows, as well as to Mr Horne.

Among the many books from which I have quoted I wish to acknowledge in particular: *More Pages from My Diary* by Lord Riddell (Country Life) and *Lord Riddell's War Diary* (Nicholson and Watson); *The Supreme Command* by the 1st Lord Hankey (Allen and Unwin) and *Hankey: Man of Secrets*, Volume I, by Stephen Roskill (Collins); *War Memoirs of David Lloyd George* (Ivor Nicholson and Watson); *The World Crisis* by Winston S. Churchill (Scribners) and Martin Gilbert's *Churchill* Companion Volume III, Parts 1 and 2 (Heinemann); *Arthur James Balfour*, Volume II, by Blanche E. C. Dugdale (Hutchinson); *Asquith* by Roy Jenkins (Collins); *Four and a Half Years*, Volume I, by Christopher Addison (Hutchinson); *The Unknown Prime Minister* by Robert Blake (Eyre and Spottiswoode); *Politicians and the War, 1914–1916* by Lord Beaverbrook (Oldbourne); and *David Lloyd George and the British Labour Movement* by C. J. Wrigley (Hassocks: Harvester Press).

Five outstanding works by North American scholars should also be mentioned: *Arms and the Wizard* by R. J. Q. Adams (Cassell); *Lloyd George and Foreign Policy*, Volume I, by Michael G. Fry (McGill's – Queen's University Press); *Proconsul in Politics* by Alfred M. Gollin (Blond); *The Rise and Fall of the Political Press in Britain*, Volume II, by Stephen E. Koss (Hamish Hamilton); and *Lloyd George and the Generals* by David R. Woodward (Associated University Presses).

Mr Christopher Falkus has been a most patient and encouraging publisher, and Miss Alex Bennion a friendly, conscientious editor.

September 1984   J.G.

Preface to New Paperback Edition

This is the third of my three volumes so far published on the life of David Lloyd George. The previous one – *Lloyd George: The People's Champion* – took the story from the end of the Boer War in 1902 to the end of the year 1911, one of the busiest and most fruitful of his career. In this one I cover the five-year period from the beginning of 1912 until the end of 1916, when he replaced Asquith in the premiership. My task in the book is to describe his last efforts as a reforming minister in a peacetime party government, and then his transformation into a dynamic war minister, as the country faced an ordeal more profoundly disturbing than the civil wars of the seventeenth century, and probably more so than anything it had experienced since the Black Death.

From the moment he decided – rightly, in my view – to support British intervention in 1914, Lloyd George was the most important contributor to the war effort. Though for more than two years he did not hold the supreme position of responsibility, he was nevertheless, from the first, the man who did most towards the country's eventual victory. Asquith's contribution should not be underrated; he took many tough decisions and, at any rate until the latter part of 1916, remained formidable as head of the government. Above all, he never wavered in his determination to see the war through to a victorious conclusion. But it was soon evident that he was less suited than Lloyd George to the demands of war leadership. He lacked Lloyd George's ability to stir emotion by the spoken word, and also, more significantly, he lacked Lloyd George's genius for innovation and improvisation. The war was of a kind, and on a scale, never before known. Unconventional methods were needed to survive in it, let alone win it, and Lloyd George's approach was less conventional than Asquith's.

His commitment to the war won him the admiring support of Conservatives in the country, to whom he had previously been a bogeyman. Some Conservative leaders had long recognised that he was by no means the rabid partisan that his campaign rhetoric made him appear, but a statesman always open to compromise and willing to subordinate party interest to the national interest. In particular, two men very different from each other, who in succession led the Conservative party – Arthur Balfour and Andrew Bonar Law – had both long seen him in his true colours. It was no coincidence that both became key figures in his coalition government. But the war transformed the Tory masses' view of him. After his Queen's Hall speech in September 1914 his standing in the country was that of a national rather than a party leader.

This volume shows Lloyd George on two occasions very actively involved with the Irish Question, which was to be a growing preoccupation later, especially during his postwar premiership. His attitude to Ireland has been much misunderstood, usually in a way that does him far less than justice, though in one instance he has received less censure than he deserves (as I suggest towards the end of Chapter Thirteen).

Marconi features in the volume, and the degree of Lloyd George's offence is candidly assessed. At the same time the idea that he could easily have been disowned and jettisoned by Asquith for his role in the affair is shown to be fallacious.

The beginning of 1913 was a turning-point in his personal life, because it was then that Frances Stevenson entered it on a permanent, if clandestine, basis. Chapter Twelve describes how their romance developed from the summer of 1911 when (as recorded in the previous volume) she came to Criccieth as a holiday governess for the Lloyd Georges' daughter Megan. In later chapters the curious nature of their relationship is further explored. For Lloyd George she was no passing infatuation; she remained his close companion – as mistress and, eventually, second wife – until his death more than thirty years later. Unquestionably he loved her, depending on her for help with his work scarcely less than for human comfort. But he loved politics more, and his wife Margaret never ceased to matter to him in ways that were unique.

To a biographer Frances Stevenson is important not only because she was so important to him, but also because, after her arrival in his life, his letters and other documents were carefully preserved – having earlier been treated by him with cavalier indifference, and therefore mostly lost – and because she kept a diary which, despite large gaps, will always be a vital source for any student of his career.

As in previous volumes, I leave readers in no doubt of my opinions, because I think it right for a biographer to argue with his subject and not to stand aside in a posture of inhuman detachment. But I hope I never fail to give the evidence on which readers can form their own opinions, which may or may not accord with mine.

J.G.

ONE
Policies Old and New

Lloyd George rounded off the eventful year 1911 by spending Christmas at home in North Wales; but soon afterwards he was back in London, and on the second day of the New Year he left, without Margaret, for the sort of winter holiday he most enjoyed. Accompanied by Sir Rufus Isaacs, the Attorney-General – whose name would soon be all too closely linked with his – he stayed the first day or two in Cannes, at Rost's Continental Hotel, finding time for a brief visit to his old friend and patron, Lord Rendel, at the Château de Thorenc. No doubt he could remember being Rendel's guest there exactly seven years before, when he was still a backbencher and a relative stranger to the grand life, and when the butler, mistaking his name for 'Lord George', had addressed him as 'My Lord'.

From Cannes he and Isaacs went on to Cap Martin, where Sir Harold Harmsworth – Northcliffe's younger brother, and soon to be Lord Rothermere – had put his luxurious villa La Dragonnière at their disposal, with all expenses paid. They were joined by the Master of Elibank, Liberal Chief Whip, and Vaughan Nash, Asquith's private secretary; but not, as some have stated, by Asquith himself. The Prime Minister did, indeed, leave England a week after Lloyd George, but the nearest he came to Cap Martin was Toulon, where he boarded a ship to Naples en route to Sicily. His companion was Edwin Montagu, and they were joined in Sicily by Asquith's daughter Violet and her friend Venetia Stanley.

The party at La Dragonnière was well looked after by Rothermere's local agent, and Lloyd George, never one to shun publicity, was quite pleased to observe that the press, including even the *New York Herald*, was taking a close interest in his movements. He played a little golf, but to his annoyance the weather was very bad – mistral and rain – the worst he had ever experienced on the Riviera. On 17 January he celebrated his forty-ninth birthday, reflecting that in his youth he had never thought he would live so long. The following day, as he was leaving a concert in Monte Carlo, a well-dressed woman gave him her hand and said: 'You don't know me. You have enemies but you also have friends.'[1] They were to be found, evidently, in some rather unlikely places.

He was back in London at the weekend, complaining that Margaret was not there to welcome him, but at least comforted by the presence of two of his children, Olwen and Dick. There was plenty to occupy him, even before the new session of Parliament. His National Insurance Act was on the Statute Book, but the great scheme of health insurance embodied in it had yet to be brought into effective operation. The National Health commissions were at work, and so was the coordinating body under the chairmanship of Lloyd George's foremost ministerial aide, C. F. G. Masterman (who in February became so in form as well as fact, when he was transferred from the Home Office to the Treasury, as Financial Secretary). Yet the scheme was still under relentless attack from a powerful section of the Press, and the British Medical Association was still giving a lot of trouble – as it was to continue to do throughout the year, though with clearly diminishing support from the mass of ordinary doctors. Despite all his other labours and difficulties, Lloyd George had to give much attention to the problems of Insurance until the scheme was finally working in early 1913. He had to resist pressure to postpone both the first collection of contributions and the first payment of benefits. He judged the odds correctly, his nerve did not crack, and the key dates passed without mishap. But the nagging anxiety caused by Insurance is an aspect of his life in 1912 which should not be forgotten.[2]

On 13 February, the eve of the new session of Parliament, Asquith presided over the traditional dinner for ministers and made what one

1. D.L.G. to M.L.G., 18 January 1912 (N.L.W.). Margaret received about half-a-dozen letters from him while he was in the South of France. In one she was told of a beautiful basket of flowers sent to La Dragonnière by the prefect of Alpes-Maritimes, and chivalrously addressed to *her*.

2. The evolution of Lloyd George's Health Insurance scheme, and the passage of his National Insurance Bill, are described in John Grigg, *Lloyd George: The People's Champion*, ch.XI.

of them described as 'an unprecedented speech'. He said that rumours that he was about to retire, and that Lloyd George and Grey were rivals for the succession, were untrue. He had no intention of retiring 'until he had completed the tasks to which he had set his hand'. What seemed particularly odd was that he should thus mention two senior colleagues by name without adding any request for secrecy. 'Was it boast or was it an "official dementi" or was it a severe lesson publicly delivered . . . or was it merely a drastic way of snuffing out the mischievous rumours at once?'[1] Within a month, at any rate, the two ministers in question had a chance to demonstrate their loyalty, when they made unscheduled speeches at a public lunch in Asquith's honour, at which they, together with Morley and Crewe, were the Cabinet ministers chosen to sit at his table: a selection 'noted as significant'.[2]

The Government certainly needed to be united for the trials ahead, some of which were of its own making. Granted the Liberals' dependence upon the Irish Party, and the pledges they had given, it was obligatory for them to introduce a third Home Rule Bill; and it was scarcely less necessary for them to satisfy Wales and Nonconformity with another Welsh Disestablishment Bill. These measures were, in fact, the most predictable items in the King's Speech on 14 February, Home Rule being announced, in the familiar euphemism, as a measure for 'the better government of Ireland'. There was no way, however, of getting these bills through expeditiously, and for this the Government had only itself to blame.

The much vaunted Parliament Act of the previous year, which had supposedly curbed the power of the House of Lords, had in fact given that Chamber – and therefore, since the composition of the House was unchanged, the Conservative Party – a licence to delay Liberal legislation for more than two years, while in the process wasting an immense amount of Parliamentary time. The same power of delay, conferred by the Government itself, was sure to be used against its bill to extend the franchise and reform the system of registration, which, if carried, would come near to establishing universal manhood suffrage, and which might be amended to give women the vote as well. Since,

1. Walter Runciman to his wife, 14 February 1912 (Runciman Papers, University of Newcastle). Had Vaughan Nash made mischief on his return from La Dragonnière?
2. Lunch at the Covent Garden Theatre on 8 March 1912, attended by 'five or six hundred of the fighting army of Liberalism' (reported next day in the *Manchester Guardian*). Lloyd George said, among other things, that Asquith had won the personal affection of his colleagues as 'no political chief of modern times' had won it.

moreover, the Parliament Act had also reduced the life of Parliaments from seven years to five, the Opposition's greater freedom to obstruct could be indulged with the prospect of a relatively early general election.

The Unionists were thus given every encouragement to be militantly partisan, and their mood in 1912 fully matched their opportunity. At the beginning of the year Leo Maxse wrote in his influential monthly:

> The Cabinet are pursuing their career of anarchy with a view to beating all previous records. In obedience to the orders of Mr Redmond [the Irish leader], they are preparing to disrupt the United Kingdom and to provoke civil war in Ireland. They are following up the destruction of the Constitution by the destruction of the Church, to gratify the malignancy of Mr Silvester Horne and Dr Clifford [Nonconformist leaders]. They seriously propose to flood the electorate with an indeterminate number of women – Mr Lloyd George thinks in millions – apparently in order to convert the greatest of Sea-powers into the smallest of she-powers.[1]

In late 1911 Maxse's waspish editorials had helped to bring about Arthur Balfour's resignation as Conservative leader, and Balfour's successor, Andrew Bonar Law, was a full-blooded exponent of the view that an Opposition's duty is to oppose. There was no air of philosophic detachment about Law, and he began the year 1912 with a display of invective on which Maxse himself could hardly have improved. Speaking on 26 January at the Albert Hall he described the Liberals as 'Gadarene swine', and the Government as 'a revolutionary committee' whose record was 'an example of destructive violence' without parallel since the Long Parliament.

Actually, in most respects Bonar Law was far from being the uncompromising hard-liner that he chose, for good tactical reasons, to appear. Except on the subject of Ireland, where as the son of an Ulster-born Presbyterian minister he could hardly fail to have strong emotions, his rhetoric tended to belie a character that was essentially cautious and realistic. Yet, having become leader of a demoralised party, which had lost three general elections in a row, he could see that an aggressive style was best calculated to inspirit and unite his own people, and was anyway what they expected of him. With endearing

1. *National Review*, January 1912.

candour he said as much to Asquith himself, as they walked together in procession from the House of Lords after listening to the King's Speech. 'I am afraid,' he said, 'I shall have to show myself very vicious, Mr Asquith, this session. I hope you will understand.'

However rude he might be about the Prime Minister in debate, he always had a considerable admiration for him in fact, though Asquith did not reciprocate the sentiment. On the contrary, he somewhat despised Law on intellectual grounds, and was quite out of sympathy with him temperamentally. It was a curious irony, indeed, that the principal party of the Left should at this time be led by a man who 'loved society' and 'dined out incessantly', whereas the Conservative leader 'hated social engagements' and 'never dined out of his house unless he had to'.[1] Between Law and Lloyd George, on the other hand, friendly relations had existed for a number of years, and continued to exist in spite of growing public acrimony. They, too, had their differences of temperament, but they were alike in being outside the traditional British hierarchies of landed wealth or Oxbridge education. Their mutual understanding and distinct liking for each other formed a solid basis for the partnership which would be established between them only a few years ahead, though in drastically altered circumstances.

On the whole Law's style of controversy achieved what it set out to achieve, but in the Debate on the Address in 1912 it caused him to commit an embarrassing gaffe, when Asquith managed to trap him into agreeing, if only by a nod of the head, that the Conservatives would repeal the National Insurance Act on their return to power. Social reformers on the Tory side, who favoured the Act in principle and did not like to see their party exploiting its current unpopularity, were distressed that there should be any question of a pledge to repeal it; while many even among those who were sincerely opposed to it felt uneasy about Law's position, because it was then generally regarded as against the spirit of the Constitution for a newly elected government to seek to undo the work of its immediate predecessor. Law soon recanted, in effect, by means of an explanatory letter to the Press, drafted for him by F. E. Smith, and his supporters put the mistake down to inexperience, without seriously losing confidence in him. Reluctant though they might be to threaten legislation already on the Statute Book, they intended to do their utmost to prevent the

1. Robert Blake, *The Unknown Prime Minister*, p. 98. Law's remark to Asquith, quoted by Lord Blake, is from Asquith's *Memories and Reflections*, Vol. I, p. 202.

Government's forward programme from ever reaching it, and they counted on Law to give them a suitable lead.

Political leaders, however, are always apt to be surprised by events, and the first major bill of the new session was of a kind anticipated neither by the Government, which introduced it, nor by the Opposition. This was the Coal Mines (Minimum Wage) Act, a landmark in British industrial and constitutional history, which resulted from the gravest of all the challenges from organised labour during the turbulent years 1911–1914, a nationwide strike of coalminers. The dispute was not only over pay, though the desire for better and fairer wages, particularly for miners working the less productive seams, was a vital element in it. It was also about power: a trial of strength between the Miners' Federation of Great Britain, in which there was some syndicalist influence, and first the employers, then the State itself.

On 18 January (the day Lloyd George was accosted by his unknown female admirer at Monte Carlo) the Federation announced that a ballot of the miners showed a four-to-one majority favouring strike action in support of the demand for a minimum wage; the sums demanded being five shillings per shift for men, two shillings for boys (the so-called 'five and two'). When Parliament met there still seemed to be a faint chance that a settlement would be reached between the union and the coal owners, and hope was expressed in the King's Speech that 'a reasonable spirit would prevail on both sides'. But soon afterwards they were completely deadlocked, so the Government had no choice but to intervene.

Its intervention at first took the form of an attempt to find a solution which both sides would accept. Asquith himself and three of his colleagues – Lloyd George, Edward Grey and Sydney Buxton (President of the Board of Trade) – had meetings with miners' and owners' representatives, but failed to secure agreement on a proposal that minimum rates should be fixed by district conferences, on which the Government would be represented and would act as umpire. The owners were divided, and the union continued to insist upon a single national minimum – the 'five and two' – with the added demand that it should be legally enforceable. Meanwhile the union's time-limit ran out and on 1 March the strike began. Soon more than two million men were idle, 850,000 in the mining industry and 1,300,000 in other industries dependent upon coal. The whole country was gripped by a sense of acute crisis, and among the comfortable classes there was talk of revolution. People began to lay in large stocks of food and other provisions, and one backwoods peer armed all his servants with revolvers.

In this unprecedented emergency Asquith kept his head and showed all the resourcefulness and tact that he had failed to show during the railway dispute the previous year, when Lloyd George had had to pick up the pieces. In 1912 Asquith was very much in command; never, perhaps, were his formidable powers more effectively deployed than in his handling of the miners' strike. After a final effort, in mid-March, to bring about an agreed settlement, he decided to introduce legislation on the lines of his own proposal, establishing the principle of a minimum wage but leaving the determination of actual amounts to district boards under Government-appointed chairmen. The Bill was passed through all its stages in ten days, and became law on 29 March. Labour opposed it, because it did not meet the miners' demand for 'five and two' as the national minimum, but the Conservatives, despite a preliminary show of opposition, abstained on Third Reading in the House of Commons, and above all did not use the House of Lords to obstruct the Bill.[1] The miners themselves voted against it and for going on with the strike, but by less than a two-thirds majority, which their Executive deemed insufficient. On 11 April, therefore, they returned to work and the crisis was over. It had cost the country thirty million working days, but the authority of the State emerged substantially intact.

Lloyd George's part in the affair, though not the leading one, was nevertheless important, and his comments at the time help us to understand how his thoughts were shaping. By many prosperous Liberals, as well as by most Conservatives, he was regarded as a prime cause of the labour unrest, but it did not worry him unduly that he was so regarded, because he felt that the unrest was largely justified. When the miners came out on strike, and his friend Sir George Riddell said that the people clearly meant to have a greater share of the profits of industry, Lloyd George said: 'I for one am not sorry. Asquith's declaration of a minimum wage sounded the death-knell of the Liberal Party in its old form.' Riddell, a newspaper magnate with a legal

1. A similar self-restraint operated in favour of the Government's Trade Union Bill, which enabled trade union funds to be used for political purposes – a right threatened by the Osborne Judgment of 1909. This Bill was let through by the Lords in early 1913. It was, in fact, their normal habit to give a more or less unimpeded passage to sensitive labour legislation.

training, was very active behind the scenes during this crisis, as in many other episodes of Lloyd George's career. In particular, he kept in close touch with Vernon Hartshorn, a member of the miners' Executive and future Labour Cabinet minister, whose point of view he conveyed to Lloyd George in a letter dated 16 March:

Last night I had another long interview with my friend, who strongly represents that the Bill should provide that in no case shall the minimum for adults be less than five shillings per day. He says that the popular impression that the Executive not the men are responsible for the miners' attitude is altogether erroneous and that the leaders will have much trouble in prevailing upon the men to return to work unless they are satisfied that they have secured satisfactory terms . . . He says & with justice that a wage of five shillings per day must be, & ought to be, ensured by society to a man who risks his life by following such a hazardous occupation.[1]

Up to this point Lloyd George had been a firm supporter of Asquith's view that the Government's legislation should not include the 'five and two', or indeed any figures at all, and he was still of the same opinion on the 18th, when he said to Riddell: 'The Cabinet cannot agree to fix wages by statute . . . A vital question of principle is involved.' The following day he even spoke of having strike pay declared illegal, and of imprisoning union leaders if necessary. But in fact he was not at all impervious to Hartshorn's appeal and towards the end of the month was arguing that 'five and two' *should* be included in the Bill. That he should have wobbled to this extent is the measure of Asquith's toughness in sticking to the principle he had laid down; and his toughness was rewarded. Lloyd George was much impressed by his performance throughout the crisis, and told Riddell that they were 'the very best of friends'.[2]

While the Bill was before Parliament Lloyd George defended it in a vigorous speech. Too much, he suggested, was being made of the Syndicalist menace:

1. Viscount Tenby's collection.
2. Riddell's account of the coal strike, with the remarks quoted above, is in *More Pages from My Diary*, ch. V. While Lloyd George was in communication with Hartshorn through Riddell – and also through Masterman – Margot Asquith was trying a more direct form of diplomacy with the miners' vice-president, Robert Smillie. According to him she did not cut much ice, but he would naturally have been reluctant to admit any effect she might have had on him (*My Life for Labour*, pp. 220–4).

I have followed the matter very carefully, because I was for two or three years at the Board of Trade, and it was part of my business, almost weekly, to deal with strikes, and even since I have been at the Exchequer I have been in close touch with most of the big strikes. I do not believe Syndicalism is a real peril . . . I cannot see men of very great weight in the Labour movement who have committed themselves to it. No men of real influence and power have committed themselves to Syndicalism. Syndicalism and Socialism are, of course, two totally different things. They are mutually destructive . . . There is this guarantee for society, that one microbe can be trusted to kill another, and the microbe of Socialism, which may be a very beneficent one, does at any rate keep guard upon the other, which is a very dangerous and perilous one.

The words 'which may be a very beneficent one' were obviously added on the spur of the moment, as a gesture to Labour M.P.s who thought of themselves as Socialist. But his true meaning, surely, was that Socialism was a very harmful microbe, only less harmful than Syndicalism. In any case, there was nothing necessarily Syndicalist or Socialist about the demand for a minimum wage.

It is a demand which every Minister in charge of the Treasury has to meet constantly from civil servants. [Hon. Members: 'And doctors.'] I am glad my Hon. Friends have reminded me of that. I have been, I will not say fighting, but negotiating, a demand of that kind which has been put forward by a body of men who I think are, as a rule, ornaments of the Conservative Party. [Hon. Members: 'No, no.']

He undertook to withdraw the remark if Conservatives felt it was a reflection on them.[1]

The Minimum Wage Act was in several ways an outstanding victory for the miners, but it was certainly not a defeat for the Liberal Government. The idea that it was a symptom of 'Liberal England's' advanced morbidity, presaging its 'strange death' in the near future, has been fixed in innumerable minds by the artistry of Mr George Dangerfield. But is his baleful vision true to the contemporary facts? After giving his account of the miners' strike, he writes in a characteristic passage:

1. Hansard, Fifth Series, Vol. XXXV, Coal Mines (Minimum Wage) Bill, First Reading, 19 March 1912: Lloyd George's speech, cols. 1773–82.

And Liberalism . . . Liberalism, with its fatal trust in compromise, had evaded the issue once again. But, slide and wriggle as it would, there was a doom which it could not evade. The millstones of Capital and Labour, the upper and the nether, grind slowly but exceeding small, and Liberalism was caught between them. It might put off the evil hour, poor slippery old faith, but they would crush it in the end.

What issue had Liberalism evaded? And was Liberalism anyway a single homogeneous faith, slippery or otherwise? Were there not two distinct schools of thought in the Liberal Party, which could be reconciled in practice only by the 'trust in compromise' so deplored by Mr Dangerfield: a trust which was and is, surely, not a 'fatal' but a vital element in the British political tradition? Capital and Labour, too, hardly seem to have been the monolithic objects that Mr Dangerfield portrays. There were many different sorts of capitalist, and Labour was divided not only, as Lloyd George argued, between Socialism and Syndicalism, but also, and more fundamentally, between Utopian theory of all kinds and the pragmatic Lib-Lab reformism which still probably commanded the loyalty of most Labour people. Moreover, when the old Liberal Party was eventually crushed, it was not between the millstones of Capital and Labour, but between those of the Conservative and Labour Parties, and above all through the working of a political system loaded in favour of a two-party alternation.[1]

Intelligent observers in the spring of 1912 did not take the view that the Government had been worsted. Hilaire Belloc, for instance, even before the miners returned to work, was prepared to acknowledge that the Prime Minister's tactics had paid off.

He [Belloc] admits now that he made a mistake about the coal strike in predicting the miners would win. Asquith, he says, has been too astute for them. He amused them by his Minimum Wage Act, over which they lost their time and spent their money, and now he has them in his hands.[2]

In fact, both sides could reasonably be satisfied with the outcome: the best way for any dispute to end. The next important strike, which was in the London docks, ended less happily with the total defeat of the

1. *The Strange Death of Liberal England*, p. 288. Mr Dangerfield's famous book is so good as narrative history that its tendentiousness is apt to go unchallenged.
2. Wilfrid Scawen Blunt, *My Diaries*, Part Two, 31 March 1912.

strikers. This may have been regrettable – was, indeed, regretted by Lloyd George – but clearly does not support the argument that England was running out of control.[1]

The Government's worst problems began, or rather resumed, when the miners' strike was over; for then it had to go back to the laborious and, some might say, irrelevant task of trying to carry Irish Home Rule and Welsh Disestablishment under the time-wasting procedure imposed by the Parliament Act. Lloyd George had no illusions about what this would do to Liberal fortunes and party morale. He was sure that the effects would be disastrous unless there were also some new initiative in social reform which, he felt, it was up to him to provide. On the day the Home Rule Bill was introduced he wrote to his wife from the House of Commons:

> Home Rule launched. Went off quite well but no enthusiasm . . .
> My own opinion – *between you and me* – is that the Liberal party will
> by & bye be looking in the direction of the Welsh hills for another
> *raid* to extricate them out of their troubles.[2]

In mid-April the thoughts even of politicians were momentarily distracted from politics by the sinking of the *Titanic*. When the news came through that the ship had hit an iceberg, there was at first a rumour that she was crippled but still able to proceed under her own steam. Then the full enormity of the disaster became known – 1,500 people drowned – and Lloyd George was like everybody else in reacting with awe-struck horror. One of the victims was a journalist whom he knew and admired, the controversial W. T. Stead. He kept thinking of Stead and was sure he had met his fate bravely, only regretting, as the ship went down, that he would not be able to report the catastrophe himself.

From the shock of this tragic event Lloyd George had soon to revert to a subject which had long since lost its capacity to shock anyone: the Disestablishment of the Welsh Church. The Government's Bill was introduced by the Home Secretary, Reginald McKenna, on 23 April,

1. Lloyd George would have liked to see a minimum wage established for all dock-workers, but the employer in this case, the Port of London Authority (whose chairman, Lord Devonport, had been his junior minister at the Board of Trade) would not give way, while the strikers failed to receive the necessary support from dock-workers throughout the country. In Cabinet Lloyd George's view was shared by Haldane, but Asquith sided with the majority which felt that the P.L.A. should not be coerced.
2. 11 April 1912 (*Letters*, p.161). The words in italics were written in Welsh.

and in content was much the same as the earlier bills which had come to grief. The most hotly contested provisions were bound to be those relating to disendowment, because some Tories who might take a fairly relaxed view of changing the Welsh Church's legal status were far more concerned about any derogation from the rights of property. There were also people on the Liberal side who were unhappy about the disendowment provisions, the most notable being C. P. Scott of the *Manchester Guardian*.

In any case, the whole atmosphere had changed since Lloyd George was a young politician, when Disestablishment was a sacred cause in Wales, arousing patriotic as well as spiritual fervour, and when it also had the enthusiastic backing of English Nonconformists. By 1912 formal religion was in decline throughout the United Kingdom, and not least in Wales, though among the Welsh denominations Anglicanism was, on the whole, doing better than the Nonconformist sects. It was still a minority, but a relatively healthy one, which could no longer be described as 'alien', since it had largely re-identified itself with Wales's cultural tradition. Disestablishment was ceasing, therefore, to be a really burning issue in the Principality, and in England it was hardly an issue at all. English Nonconformity, itself a waning force, had very little stomach for a renewal of the old fight and could make only a token contribution.

Lloyd George, for his part, had never relished the role of Nonconformist crusader which the circumstances of his birth and rearing had thrust upon him. Of course he had attacked the Anglican establishment in Wales repeatedly and with zest, but his motive in doing so was only to a very limited extent sectarian. Insofar as it had to do with religion at all, it could more truly be described as secularist. He had very little time for religious dogmas or restraints of any kind, and his early experience of organised religion had left him with a taste for the Bible, Welsh hymns and good sermons, but also with the strongest possible distaste – which he had to conceal as best he might – for every other religious aspect of Welsh Nonconformity.

It was only in the social and political senses that he was a genuine Welsh Nonconformist, because it came naturally enough to him to oppose the institutions, lay and ecclesiastical, which in his youth were identified with English dominance. Much as he enjoyed denouncing religious bigotry, he was not free to denounce it impartially – or Nonconformist bigotry would have been one of his prime targets. His crypto-secularism could vent itself upon Anglicanism as it could not, obviously, upon Nonconformity – or, in any full-blooded way, upon Roman Catholicism (because of the Irish alliance). Yet the whole business increasingly bored him. He was out of sympathy with many of his supporters, and well-disposed towards some of his opponents, above all towards Bishop Edwards of St Asaph. These two men might have settled the Welsh Church question between them as far back as 1895, and again in 1903, if left to their own devices. Eventually, after much further controversy – and after a world war – they did settle it between them. Meanwhile the tedious ritual of another Disestablishment Bill had to be gone through in successive sessions, and Lloyd George had to try to think of new ways to make an old act entertaining.

Such entertainment as there was arose from the issue of Disendowment, and he certainly contributed his share. The case for Disendowment, as he and others argued it, was that the Church of England, which anyway had stolen the property of the old Church at the time of the Reformation, had since betrayed its trust by using its resources largely for its own clergy's benefit rather than for the benefit of the people of Wales. The Government's bill would ensure that these charitable funds were once again applied to charitable, or socially desirable, purposes. Among the measure's foremost critics were two sons of the late Lord Salisbury (the Prime Minister), both sitting in the House of Commons and both distinctly fond of the sound of their own voices: Lord Robert and Lord Hugh Cecil. It was from them, interacting with Lloyd George and with a history professor outside Parliament, that discussion of the Welsh Church bill briefly acquired a little entertainment value.

The fun began when Lord Robert Cecil's speech on First Reading was interrupted by Llewelyn Williams. Their exchange was as follows:

Lord Robert Cecil: . . . The Government, for a precedent in justification of their action, go back to the days of the Tudors. I thought myself it was a matter of common knowledge that one time during which this country lived under an intolerable tyranny was the reign of Henry VIII and Edward VI.
Mr Llewelyn Williams:[1] Yes, and under the Cecils.

---

1. Liberal M.P. for Carmarthen Boroughs. Friend and travelling-companion of Lloyd George when he was a backbencher. Still on fairly good terms with him, though soon (after 1914) to become very hostile.

Lord Robert Cecil: As a matter of fact, my ancestors had no share in the government of this country until the reign of Elizabeth. . . .

He went on to say that chantry was suppressed with the consent of the Church. Later in the same debate, when Lloyd George was speaking, he was interrupted by both the Cecil brothers:

Mr Lloyd George: . . . Most of the property [of the old Church] was given to laymen as bribes for selling their old faith. There are laymen now enjoying those endowments, and they are the people who when I tried to take a halfpenny in the £ called me a thief . . . There is no one more bitter against Disestablishment and Disendowment, no one condemns the spoliation and pillage and plunder of this Bill as they do . . .

Lord Robert Cecil: This is not Limehouse.

Mr Lloyd George: That is it. I thought I would get home.

Lord Robert Cecil: The Right Hon. Gentleman knows perfectly well my mouth is closed in this Debate [because he had already spoken], or he would not have ventured to make such an accusation.

Mr Lloyd George: The Noble Lord has a very high opinion of his prowess.

Lord Hugh Cecil: The Right Hon. Gentleman is habitually very courteous to me. I do not know whether his suggestion is that my family received Church lands . . . I think that is nothing but a personally offensive observation which has not any bearing on this Debate whatever. As a matter of fact, it is not true. If the Right Hon. Gentleman did mean that – which I hope for what remains of his character for courtesy and common sense he did not – then he is, as he generally is when discussing historical questions, entirely wrong.[1]

Unfortunately for the Cecils their remarks caught the eye of Professor A. F. Pollard, then as now recognised as an outstanding authority on the Tudor age, who in a letter published in *The Times* of 26 April pointed out that the brothers' 'greatest ancestor', the future Lord Burghley, was one of two principal Secretaries of State 'throughout the worst and most Protestant period of Edward VI's reign, while chantry and other Church lands were being distributed

1. Hansard, Fifth Series, Vol. XXXVII, cols. 995–6 and 1280–1. Lord Hugh Cecil got a First in History and a prize fellowship at Oxford, and had been in Parliament on and off since 1895. Lord Robert, a barrister with a more modest academic record (a Second in Jurisprudence), had been elected to Parliament at a by-election only the previous year, 1911.

among the members of the Government'. And he asked where Lord Robert had got hold of the idea that confiscation of the chantries had the Church's sanction. He also explained that he was not, in fact, a supporter of the existing Government's Disendowment plan. Undaunted, Lord Robert replied the following day that his statement about chantry was taken from another M.P., Sir David Brynmor Jones,[1] and he had 'little doubt' it was accurate. As for Lord Burghley, he had, indeed, been a Secretary of State under Edward VI (and Mary I), but 'had no real share in the government of the country in the sense of directing its policy' until the reign of Elizabeth I. Finally, Lord Robert described as 'astonishing even in a professor' the suggestion that descendants of men who received grants of Church property in the sixteenth century should be precluded from attacking Disendowment proposals in the twentieth. 'It would be as sensible to argue that no one must be a temperance reformer whose remote ancestor held shares in a brewery!' He himself owned not an acre of former Church land, and was second to none in condemning 'the tyrannical spoliation of the Church by the Tudors'.

These were just ranging shots. On 29 April *The Times* carried a longer letter from Pollard, in which he sought, first, to demonstrate that Lord Robert's idea of historical evidence was 'astonishing even in a lawyer'. He refuted with unanswerable scholarship the argument that Edward VI's Chantries Act had the sanction of the Church. Then he turned his guns on Lord Hugh, who was a more redoubtable antagonist, at any rate intellectually. He showed in detail how much Church property Burghley's father, Richard Cecil, had acquired during a single decade, though this, he said, did not include the biggest additions to the family estates, or what was gained by marriage alliances with other families enriched by Reformation spoil. Yet he was at pains to stress that he was in no way prejudiced against Burghley or the Cecils generally.

. . . but for the claims to exceptional virtue and special historical knowledge implied in Lord Hugh Cecil's interjection [during Lloyd George's speech], there would be no reason for singling out his family. Lord Burghley himself was moderate in his acquisitions as in his policy. His emoluments were not excessive considering his services to the State; they were small, indeed, compared with the

1. Liberal M.P. for Swansea District. Also an historian, though less eminent than Pollard and anyway a medievalist.

plunder secured by the pious founders of the ducal houses of Somerset, Bedford, Devonshire, Rutland, and Norfolk . . . When this Bill comes to be debated in the House of Lords, it may perchance abbreviate the 'sacrilegious' argument if noble Lords reflect that the restitution to the Church of a tithe of the property that was taken from it by their ancestors would richly compensate it for the proposed disendowment of its four Welsh dioceses, and would establish more conclusively than any eloquence the sincerity of the horror they express of 'sacrilege'.

Lord Hugh's reply appeared the following day. Tacitly conceding Pollard's historical points, he disputed their relevance to his own position, and above all challenged the relevance of any such points to any contemporary controversy.

> . . . What happened to the gifts made to Richard Cecil, the record of which Professor Pollard's industry has published, I am not sure; but I presume they descended to Lord Exeter, who was Lord Burghley's eldest son. At any rate, none of them has come my way.[1] But if they had I should have enjoyed them without scruple; for I am sure that long prescription constitutes, in morals as in law, a perfectly good title to property.
>
> As to the more important general questions whether those who are descended from persons who received lands that had been taken from the monasteries are entitled to object to Disendowment as immoral, Professor Pollard's position seems a strange and unreasonable one . . . Suppose that Mr Churchill denounced in the House of Commons some transaction as corrupt, would it be anything but childish and ill-mannered to reply that it was too late for him to talk about corruption because the great Duke of Marlborough made illicit profits on Army contracts, and Lord Sunderland [Marlborough's son-in-law] freely accepted bribes? I am surprised that a man in Professor Pollard's position should be so foolish. He might as well pick a pocket and then complain that the policeman who arrested him was descended from Robin Hood.

To this Pollard replied briefly but effectively:

> It is a question not of descent but of inheritance. I agree with Lord

---

1. The founder of Lord Hugh's and Lord Robert's branch of the Cecil family was Burghley's younger son, Robert, 1st Earl of Salisbury, who succeeded his father in most of his offices, and who also built Hatfield.

Hugh Cecil that descent from a thief should debar no one from denouncing theft. But to my mind the inheritance and retention of stolen property should. This to Lord Hugh is foolishness. His view apparently is that the guilt of theft is wiped out by prolonged enjoyment of the proceeds. No doubt there is a Statute of Limitations, but I doubt its application to the moral sphere. However, I do not wish to stray from the path of history into the labyrinth of ethics.[1]

So an interesting correspondence ended.

Lloyd George must have followed it with special interest and amusement, and Pollard's reference to sacrilegious ducal houses was sure to be very welcome to him, because in the 1909 Budget controversy dukes had become a favourite quarry of his. Now one of them yet again played into his hands, and the result was a devastating passage in his next Parliamentary speech on Disestablishment, during the Second Reading debate in mid-May:

> The Duke of Devonshire issues a circular applying for subscriptions to oppose this Bill, and he charges us with the robbery of God. Why, does he not know – of course he knows – that the very foundations of his fortune are laid deep in sacrilege, fortunes built out of desecrated shrines and pillaged altars . . . When a charge of felony is brought against a criminal, at any rate he is given a right by law to challenge the panel of the jury, and that is what I am doing . . . I am not complaining that ancestors of theirs did it, but they are still in the enjoyment of the same property, and they are subscribing out of that property to leaflets which attack us and call us thieves. What is their story? Look at the whole story of the pillage of the Reformation. They robbed the Catholic Church, they robbed the monasteries, they robbed the altars, they robbed the almshouses, they robbed the poor, and they robbed the dead. Then they come here when we are trying . . . at any rate to recover some part of this

1. *The Times*, 1 May 1912. At the time Pollard was Professor of Constitutional History at University College, London, and a research fellow of All Souls College, Oxford. His politics were Liberal – after the war he once stood, unsuccessfully, as Liberal candidate for the London University seat – but he was, as he said, opposed to disendowment of the Welsh Church, and anyway was the last man to curry favour with politicians. (When, much later, he was offered a knighthood on retirement, he refused it.) His principal motive for entering into controversy with the Cecils was almost certainly a simple desire to correct historical error, though probably this was reinforced by some resentment of what he, a man of unprivileged social origin, must have seen as moral arrogance in their attitude.

pillaged property for the poor for whom it was originally given, and they venture, with hands dripping with the fat of sacrilege, to accuse us of robbery of God.[1]

No occasion which could inspire such a phrase as 'dripping with the fat of sacrilege' should, perhaps, be regarded as entirely futile. Lloyd George had an incomparable flair for the telling image, and this was certainly one of his most telling. But from the same Second Reading debate something even better in the way of inspired fancy and verbal felicity resulted, as a by-product. It did not occur in any of the speeches delivered in the Chamber, but as a reaction to one of them by a brilliant outsider. The opening speech for the Opposition was made by F. E. Smith – whose interest in ecclesiastical matters had, until then, been a well-kept secret – and his peroration ended with the words: 'The Government will be well advised, even at the eleventh hour, to withdraw a Bill which has shocked the conscience of every Christian community in Europe.' These words gave G. K. Chesterton the theme for a masterpiece of satirical verse ('Anti-Christ, or the Reunion of Christendom') whose famous punch-line – 'Chuck it, Smith!' – linked the orator's name in perpetuity with a single thoughtless utterance.

So far as humbug went, Chesterton might almost as well have written 'Chuck it, Lloyd George!' On 28 May the Chancellor attended indoor and outdoor mass-meetings at Swansea, and as he spoke (according to a newspaper report) 'the immense audience swayed with an intensity of emotion'. Yet there must have been some, even in that audience, to whom his rhetoric seemed a little tawdry:

You will find the State in great cities like this sometimes stern and terrible, sometimes tender and beneficent. You will find courts of justice; you will find labour exchanges; you will find hospitals, infirmaries and schools. You meet the Law and the State in every street and in every square. But go up to the hills! No hospitals are there – rarely schools up there. The hand of the State has never been there, except to collect taxes [laughter]. It never carries the cup of cold water to the parched lips of a fevered shepherd in those districts. Nonconformity is there [cheers]. It has erected its infirmaries and dispensaries and sanatoria for the bruised soul [hear,

---

1. Hansard, Fifth Series, Vol. XXXVIII, cols. 1325–6. The Duke of Devonshire could hardly deny his indebtedness to sacrilegious ancestors, seeing that his grouse-shooting lodge was called Bolton Abbey.

hear]. It has erected seminaries; they are educating the young and the old in the great ideal of a life guided by faith and a death freed from fear.

These are the people . . . who patiently, for forty years, have stood at the bar of the Parliament of the United Kingdom . . . with this humble petition – that, throughout their native land, from the banks of the Severn to the shores of the Irish Sea, from the rugged hills of Arfon down to the rich valleys of Glamorgan, their faith should be freed from the bondage of the State, and that the inheritance of the poor should be restored to them [loud and frantic cheering].[1]

Lloyd George at least had the excuse that Welsh Disestablishment was a subject on which it was politically obligatory for him to speak, and to speak in the accents of passion. F. E. Smith had no such excuse.

The Breton fishermen of Chesterton's imagination certainly had no cause for premature alarm when the Welsh Church Bill's Second Reading was carried in the House of Commons in May 1912. There was, indeed, 'still Committee', which did not begin until late November and then lasted until early February 1913, during which time the Government made substantial concessions on Disendowment, much to the chagrin of some of Lloyd George's Welsh colleagues and supporters. Though the largest item, tithe, was still to be alienated, the Church would retain glebe, money from Queen Anne's Bounty and grants from Parliament since 1800, and there would be commutation of life interests. Even so, the House of Lords rejected the Bill on Second Reading, and the whole wearisome process had to be started over again, as the Parliament Act required. In the summer of 1913 the Bill was reintroduced in the House of Commons, and in due course was sent again to the Lords, only to suffer there the same predictable fate. So in the spring of 1914 the Bill was brought in a third time, and the Lords were yet again considering it – though without the power any longer to block its passage – when war supervened and Britain's order of political priorities was drastically changed.

While so much of his time was being given to Welsh Disestablishment, industrial conflicts and the continuing problems of National

<hr>

1. *Cambria Daily Leader*. The indoor Convention was held in the Albert Hall, Swansea; the outdoor demonstration in Victoria Park. The words quoted are from Lloyd George's speech in the Albert Hall.

Insurance, Lloyd George could still not neglect the traditional functions of his office. The 1912 Budget, his fourth, was presented to Parliament on 2 April, just after the Minimum Wage Bill had been enacted, but before the miners' strike had come to an end. In preparing it, he had the benefit of a memorandum written for him by one of the ablest of his Treasury officials, John Bradbury, which stated the case for Liberal finance as practised by Asquith and, more especially, Lloyd George himself, with a degree of partisan commitment that no politician could have exceeded.[1]

Bradbury justified the Liberals' very large increase in expenditure, and corresponding increase in taxation, not only on social grounds but also from the point of view of the nation's credit. Indeed, he argued that there was a direct link between the two, since a vital condition of good credit was that 'the electorate, who are the ultimate depositories of political power, should understand its value. And nothing could better convince the working classes of the value of national credit than the application of that credit to social reform, as it is applied, for instance, in the Insurance Act.' He pointed to the Government's excellent record in the redemption of debt: an average of £10,600,000 per year for the five completed years since it took office, which was more than the *maximum* achieved by any government before 1906. He also gave the Chancellor an answer to those who were complaining of the low price of Consols, and depicting it as a symptom of general economic weakness. In fact, said Bradbury, 'Consols go up when the profits on money invested in business go down, and go down when the profits on money invested in business go up.' The existing price level was, therefore, a symptom not of weakness but of prosperity.

In a separate note he suggested arguments for use against Bonar Law and others on the subject of the land value duties, which had been such a provocative feature of Lloyd George's 1909 Budget. The critics alleged that, whereas the yield of those duties had been estimated at £500,000 for the first year, £500,000 was in fact the cost of collection, and the yield only £20,000. Bradbury was able to show that these statistics were misleading, because as quoted the estimate included, while the actual figure excluded, the yield of mineral rights duty, which in 1910–11 amounted to over £500,000. Moreover, the cost of

1. This document, with marginal marks by Lloyd George, is preserved among the Bradbury Papers at the P.R.O. It is entitled 'Six Years of Liberal Finance'. Bradbury, already an Insurance Commissioner as well as a senior civil servant in the Treasury, was to become joint Permanent Secretary to the department in 1913.

collection was essentially the cost of the land valuation, which should be spread over the period until 1915 – when it was expected the valuation would be complete – and not treated as an annual cost. Finally, the valuation itself was of importance not only for the land value duties, but also for the more efficient assessment of death duties, in which respect it had already proved its worth.

With such useful polemical reinforcement from the Treasury Lloyd George was able to offer, in his Budget statement, a strong vindication of his whole system of finance. The previous year had produced the largest surplus on record, partly because there had been substantial underspending by the Admiralty, and partly because several taxes had yielded nearly £3,500,000 more than the total anticipated. For the year ahead he put national expenditure at £186,885,000, or £5,601,000 above the previous year's estimate; and he put the revenue for 1912–13 at £187,189,000. Despite the demands of health and unemployment insurance he saw no need to propose any increase in taxation, since his 1909 pattern of taxes would still cope with all demands, if the economy remained buoyant. On the whole he believed that it would so remain, but did not, all the same, feel justified in making any tax reductions.

There was only one major controversial issue, and that was his declared intention to hold the previous year's record surplus – amounting to £6,545,000 – temporarily in suspense with a view, he said, to meeting contingencies such as unforeseeable effects of the miners' strike, or overspending by the Admiralty to make up for its underspending the year before. In reality he probably wanted, above all, to have money available for further social reform, without having to raise taxes. It would be very convenient for him to have a large sum of money in hand, which could be used more or less at his discretion.

Austen Chamberlain, the Opposition's chief spokesman on finance, objected strongly to the proposed course. It would, in his view, be unprecedented for a surplus to be diverted from the Sinking Fund without explicit statements as to the purpose, or purposes, for which it would be assigned. There was a good deal of support for Chamberlain's argument, and not only on the Conservative side. At first Lloyd George stood by his policy, but in June gave way to the extent of allowing £5,000,000 to go to the Sinking Fund, retaining only about £1,500,000. No doubt this considerable setback added to his sense of frustration at the time, and to his feeling that Liberalism had to find a way of recapturing the initiative.

"As Prince Arthur [inset] used to do."
(The CHANCELLOR OF THE EXCHEQUER.)

From *Punch*, 24 July 1912

The Government had clearly been losing popularity since the last general election, in December 1910, which was anyway far too close a call. During 1911 the Liberals had lost four seats to the Conservatives, and on 5 March 1912 they lost another, at Manchester South. The news of this by-election reached Lloyd George while he was dining with the Mastermans at the Hotel Cecil, and his immediate comment was: 'That's bad, that's very bad.' But before the end of the evening he had recovered his normal cheerfulness: 'One good thing about it is that it will stiffen our people up to do real propaganda.'[1] His task, he knew, was once again – as in 1909 – to provide a cause which would arouse their enthusiasm, and for which they could unitedly campaign.

Unity was a serious problem, however, because there was no identity of interest – on the contrary, there was often a conflict of interest – between the Liberals' working-class constituency, for whose allegiance they had to compete with Labour, and their tradi-tional middle-class supporters. Well-to-do Liberals had tended to be upset by Lloyd George's 1909 Budget, and even more by the Lime-house speech in which he had counter-attacked his critics. Now, similarly, there was resistance to the idea of using the State's power to

1.Lucy Masterman, *C. F. G. Masterman, A Biography*, p. 235.

ensure that wages were raised to a decent level. On 11 June he tried to persuade the Cabinet to extend the minimum wage principle recently conceded to the miners, as one of his colleagues, Charles Hobhouse recorded at the time:

> At Cabinet yesterday Ll.G. tried very hard to induce us to agree to introduce legislation which would enforce the payment of a scale of wages on all employers in the trade within a given area, if associations of masters and men had agreed to the scale, and no matter how many masters or men stood outside the agreeing associations. Haldane, Buxton were with him, and Runciman partly. I raised the note of dissent, then Wood, and at the end of the discussion the P.M. sang a still stronger tune, and eventually we postponed further action . . . [1]

Lloyd's George's feelings after this unsuccessful attempt are reflected in a conversation between Masterman and Riddell four days later:

> *R.:* L.G. is evidently growing out of sympathy with the other members of the Cabinet.
> *Masterman:* Quite correct. He is very restless. He said to me the other day when he came from a Cabinet meeting at which he had been trying to do something for the poor dockers, 'I don't know exactly what I am, but I am sure I am not a Liberal. They have no sympathy with the people.'
> *R.:* L.G. is beginning to understand town dwellers better than he did.
> *Masterman:* Yes. That used to be the difficulty. L.G. is a country lad. All his early experiences were in an agricultural community.
> *R.:* To carry out his present-day policy he will have to come to the minimum wage or some other form of State interference – a sort of mild Socialism, although he would not admit it. I suppose the world is moving that way.
> *Masterman:* Yes, and the sooner he adopts it the better. [2]

In fact the 'country lad', baulked in his attempt to promote a

---

1. Charles Hobhouse, *Inside Asquith's Cabinet* (edited by Edward David), p. 115; diary entry for 12 June 1912. Haldane had succeeded Loreburn as Lord Chancellor two days previously. Buxton was President of the Board of Trade, Runciman President of the Board of Agriculture, and McKinnon Wood Secretary of State for Scotland. Hobhouse himself was Chancellor of the Duchy of Lancaster, having earlier been Lloyd George's junior minister at the Treasury.

2. Riddell, *More Pages from my Diary*, 1908–14, p. 69.

generalised minimum wage policy, was turning instead to a radical new policy for the land. He might have turned to it anyway, in addition to the other policy, because it was a logical development in his perennial campaign against the landed interest, and because there was a powerful faction within the Party demanding it. Already, on 27 May, he had told Riddell: 'I am convinced that the land question is the real issue. You must break down the remnants of the feudal system. I have a scheme.' Now, dining with Riddell on 19 June, he expanded further on the subject:

We discussed the political situation. L.G. turning to me, said, 'I have told the Prime Minister about my plans. He has given his consent. As I have told you before, the old boy has always treated me extremely well.' L.G. then stated his new land policy. . . .

(1) Breaking down the 'relics of feudalism'. (2) Creation of land courts to fix fair rents and tenure for agricultural land. (3) Creation of courts to fix fair terms for leaseholders who desire to improve the demised premises. (4) Creation of tribunals to fix agricultural wages in the various districts . . . (5) Establishment of a rule that in fixing agricultural rents regard must be had not to wages paid but to wages which should be paid and which are to be ascertained under (4).

He said, 'First of all we shall make an investigation to ascertain the facts accurately. We propose to start the campaign in September. . . . '

L.G. is shrewd and crafty, combining the astuteness of an attorney with a statesman's imagination, courage and foresight. This land scheme is a shrewd political move. While it deals with present-day economic troubles, it is framed to appeal to the Liberal politician who is not prepared to attack the commercial classes, but will rejoice in attacking the pockets and privileges of his traditional bugbears and enemies, the squires and ground landlords.[1]

It was most unfortunate that the Liberals shirked the issue of industrial wages in 1912, because the chief cause of labour unrest during this period was, almost certainly, that wages were failing to keep abreast of prices, let alone ahead of them. Workers could see that the economy was booming, and there was all too conspicuous evidence of the wealth that some people were able to enjoy. Yet for the majority of the population real wages were declining. Asquith's

---

1. Riddell, *op.cit.*, p. 63 and pp. 70–1. Riddell's other guests on this occasion were Masterman and Sir William Robertson Nicoll, editor of *British Weekly*.

consent to Lloyd George's plans for a land campaign is perfectly understandable; he must have been relieved to see the Chancellor's radicalism diverted from the minimum wage issue in general to an issue altogether less controversial among Liberals of the solid sort.

Though Lloyd George, as Masterman said, was now more aware than in his youth of the conditions under which most town-dwellers lived, and though he could anyway draw the rational inference, for a democratic politician, of the fact that most British people lived in towns, nevertheless his prejudice against the squirearchy was still very strong, and he was still prone, in spite of himself, to think of social conflict in rural rather than urban terms. He also cherished the fantasy of a flourishing, repopulated countryside – flourishing *because* repopulated – whereas the prosperity of British agriculture later in the century was to depend, in reality, upon its being increasingly capital-intensive. The Land Campaign upon which he was now about to embark was, therefore, from the first a slightly misconceived enterprise, though in many ways worthwhile and stimulating.

He lost no time in setting up an unofficial enquiry to discover the facts, and it was agreed that town and country should be investigated separately. In practice, however, the country had priority. The matter was first discussed in detail at a working breakfast in June, attended by Masterman, C. P. Scott, Seebohm Rowntree and C. Roden Buxton, who was to become honorary secretary of the Land Committee (with, under him, a paid secretary, J. St. G. Heath). As chairman of the Committee Lloyd George chose the experienced politician, Arthur Acland, who had been one of his supporters when he took his seat in the House of Commons in 1890, and with whom he had worked closely on Welsh education. Acland had been out of Parliament since 1899, but had remained active in Liberal politics. As a former Cabinet minister he had some prestige, and as the son of an eleventh baronet, with landed connections, he was all the more valuable for the progressive views he held. His appointment was not, however, entirely welcome to the hon. secretary, who was soon writing to Lloyd George: 'You have given us a somewhat difficult task by making Acland our chairman. I think, if I may say so, that it was a most admirable choice, and I have the greatest respect & admiration for him; and we are determined to do all we can to carry him with us. But a *Times* leading article (of all things) is enough to terrify him.'[1]

1. C. Roden Buxton to D.L.G., 11 August 1912. (L.G.P.)

The other members of the main Committee were five M.P.s, including the Welsh Radical Ellis Davies and E. G. Hemmerde.

Hemmerde, a barrister and dramatist, was returned to Parliament in May, at a by-election in North-west Norfolk. He had been an M.P. before, but had lost his seat (a Welsh one) in 1910. The Norfolk result encouraged Lloyd George to pursue the land question, because the seat might well have been lost and the fact that it was held, though with a reduced majority, was largely credited to the message that he sent to Hemmerde. There was concern on the Opposition side. The Conservative Chief Whip, Lord Balcarres, noted in his diary:

> I do not like the Norfolk by-election. It is true we have reduced the Radical majority by fifty per cent, but the Radical victory will be treated as a triumph, not for Home Rule, Disestablishment, or Insurance, but as a proof that Lloyd George's recent excursion into bucolic problems is the only method of retaining the shires. A minimum wage of twenty shillings a week for agricultural labourers, and the further promise that the towns shall pay for the country – these are the implied results of the recent policy, to be embodied no doubt in a Budget of 1913 contrived to re-establish falling Radical credit as was the case with the Finance Bill of 1909.
> But can this be successfully accomplished twice in five years?[1]

And Joseph Chamberlain's old friend Jesse Collings, president of the Rural League, wrote to Lord Milner complaining that neither Bonar Law nor the candidate on the spot had realised the importance of the land question, which was 'the only thing the men cared about'.

> How different from the action of our own Leaders was that of Lloyd George! On the eve of the poll, he wrote a stirring letter in support of Mr Hemmerde, and of his land proposals, and backing all the promises that Hemmerde had been making.
> To my mind, the lesson to be learnt and the warning to be heeded from the Norfolk election, are that a merely negative policy of opposition to Home Rule and other constitutional changes . . . will have no effect on men of poverty and in suffering unless it is accompanied by a definite constructive programme of social reform.[2]

Some of Lloyd George's ill-wishers in the Liberal Party were apt to say

1. *The Crawford Papers*, ed. John Vincent, p. 276 (2 June 1912).
2. Collings to Milner, 9 July 1912 (Milner Papers, Bodleian).

that his radical policies, and above all his manner of putting them across, were a gift to the Conservatives, but the remark just quoted suggests that they were mistaken.

The main Land Committee held its first meeting on 16 July. It was decided to issue questionnaires and to appoint local investigators, so that information could be gathered on all aspects of the subject. The enquiry was to have no official status, though it had the Government's blessing. This procedure was by no means universally welcomed even by Liberals with a commitment to social reform. For instance, Violet Markham – sister of Lloyd George's friend, Sir Arthur Markham, and a very active philanthropist – wrote a letter to *The Times* to explain why she would not cooperate with the enquiry:

> . . . . I disapprove very strongly, not of the principle of such an enquiry, but of the constitution of this particular one and the subterranean methods by which it is conducted. I do not know what you mean by an 'unofficial body appointed under the auspices of the Government . . . to collect reliable and unbiased information'. An unofficial body appointed under Government auspices is a contradiction in terms. Government is responsible to Parliament and through Parliament to the nation, and cannot authorise *sub rosa* irresponsible and self-appointed commissions in matters of this kind. . . .
>
> It is surprising to me that your committee can imagine that the nation at large would regard facts collected by a secretly constituted political association as either 'reliable' or 'unbiased'. Personally, I would attach less importance to the conclusions of such a body than I should to those of the Tariff Reform Commission, which at least published evidence . . .
>
> I must express my astonishment, shared by many members of our party, that any group of Liberals should have embarked on a course of secret enquiry, the methods of which they would have been the first to condemn if adopted by their political opponents.[1]

Since the enquiry was ostensibly unofficial it had to be financed from private sources, and one of its backers was Seebohm Rowntree's father, Joseph. Another was the enlightened paternalist soap-manufacturer, Sir William Lever. But probably the richest man of all

1. *The Times*, 20 August 1912. Violet Markham's letter was also quoted in the following day's *Daily Mail*.

supporting it was Baron Maurice de Forest, natural son of the Austrian Jewish banker Baron Hirsch (friend and money-lender to Edward VII as Prince of Wales), from whom he had inherited vast wealth. De Forest was English-educated, had taken British nationality, and was married to the daughter of an English peer; but he was never really accepted by the social establishment in England, and was regarded as even more of an outsider when, in 1911, he unsuccessfully sued his mother-in-law for slander. In the same year he was elected to Parliament, most incongruously, as the Liberal Member for West Ham North. Lloyd George and Churchill befriended him, partly from obvious cupboard-love motives, but also because they found him a diverting change from the ordinary run of British politicians.[1]

Yet he had none of the commanding talent which had enabled the exotic Disraeli to win through, and he tended, in fact, to be an embarrassment – except in the financial sense – to any cause with which he was associated. Since he was an M.P. he wanted to have a political role in the Land Campaign, and was therefore appointed both a member of the main Committee and chairman of the sub-committee responsible for conducting the urban enquiry. On this his colleagues were Hemmerde (who had, incidentally, been one of his counsel in the slander action against his mother-in-law) and Rowntree's lawyer, E. R. Cross. In practice, Cross did most of the work. The paid secretary of the main Committee wrote to Lloyd George: 'Buxton and Cross both feel that [de Forest] cannot be left to do any of the more complex work by himself and we are careful not to leave him things of importance.' And Buxton, the hon. secretary, wrote: 'Hemmerde, de Forest & Cross are, nominally, the sub-committee dealing with the urban side. This means, in effect, Cross single-handed.'[2]

At the end of September de Forest entertained Lloyd George and fellow members of the main Committee for a weekend at his country house, Gaddesby Hall, near Leicester. It was a working weekend, though a local newspaper referred to it as 'Limehousing in luxury'. Apart from the Saturday afternoon, which was a free period – spent by Lloyd George playing golf – and the Sunday evening, when the party went to the Congregational church in Leicester, all the time, including after dinner, was devoted to long business sessions.[3] But when the

1. Churchill had known him since childhood. In later life de Forest assumed Liechtenstein citizenship and took a Liechtenstein title, Count de Bendern.
2. Heath to D.L.G., 17 August 1912, and Buxton to D.L.G., 18 August 1912 (L.G.P.).
3. Ellis Davies Journal, 27, 28, 29 and 30 September 1912 (N.L.W.).

party broke up, the Land Campaign was still only in the early planning stage. September had come and gone without the start that Lloyd George had hoped for, and it was not, in fact, until October of the following year that he was able to launch the Campaign. The story of its launching and rather brief career belongs to a later chapter. Meanwhile Lloyd George had to survive an apparently deadly threat to his own career, which had its origins deep in his character as well as in the nature of British politics during the transition from oligarchy to democracy. This was the episode known to history as the Marconi Scandal.

TWO
Thin Ice

Unlike most politicians of his day Lloyd George had no capital resources, whether self-made or derived from the money-making activities of ancestors (such as those who had done well out of the Reformation). As a young M.P. he had to live off a share, perhaps unduly large, of the profits from the solicitors' firm in which he and his brother William were the founder-partners, supplemented by whatever fees he could earn from casual journalism and lecturing. From the very first his lack of financial independence was intensely irksome to him, not because he cared much about money for its own sake, but because he could see that private wealth was a key to political independence.

During the 1890s his desire to have capital and to have it quick, combined with inattention to the sort of details that bored him, resulted in a discreditable speculation in a dud Patagonian gold-mining syndicate. From this he emerged less disadvantageously than many small investors whom he had encouraged to put their money into it, because at least he was paid as a director and his firm was paid for its legal services. But as an attempt to make his fortune the Patagonian business was an utter failure, and the one piece of luck for him, in view of subsequent developments, was that it remained unknown to the world at large until long after his death.[1]

During the Boer War his financial position became more pre-

1. To be precise until 1973, when the story was first told in John Grigg, *The Young Lloyd George*, ch. 7.

carious, because his legal practice suffered on account of the brave stand that he took against the war. One day, in the House of Commons library, a particularly militant political opponent offered him a loan, which he felt obliged to turn down, though he never ceased to appreciate the chivalrous gesture. But soon afterwards help came in a form that he could accept, when the Liberal tycoon and philanthropist, George Cadbury, asked him to negotiate the purchase of the *Daily News* for a commission of one thousand guineas. The deal went through, and Lloyd George's fee enabled him and his family 'to subsist in perfect comfort for five years'.[1]

At the end of that time the Liberals were back in power and he was a Cabinet minister with a substantial income. Though as President of the Board of Trade he did not receive the normal Cabinet minister's salary of £5,000 a year, but the anomalously lower one of £2,000 a year, this was of course princely compared with anything he had had before. Even so, some of his colleagues felt that he was hard done by and ought to be helped out of party funds. Lloyd George would have nothing to do with this, because he always regarded institutional subsidies, even from supposedly friendly sources, as compromising to the essential freedom of a politician. In any case, his salary went up to £5,000 a year when he became Chancellor of the Exchequer in 1908. But the higher salary was no substitute for capital, because he was still very conscious of being at the mercy of chance. How was he to maintain his independence when he was out of office? The question continued to trouble him, and his sense of insecurity left him open to temptation.

One man of proved goodwill towards him seems to have had some inkling of danger, because in the third week of March, at the height of the miners' strike crisis, Lloyd George received this curious letter from Bournville, Birmingham:

Dear Mr Lloyd-George,

Those who hate you and your measures make themselves heard, but the millions who rejoice in your work and in the courage you have shown on behalf of labour, like myself, have no means of expressing their gratitude for what you have done – this must be my apology for writing to a man whose every moment is full of important business, but even now I would not write if I did not feel

1. Gwilym Lloyd George (Viscount Tenby), unpublished fragment of autobiography (Viscount Tenby's collection).

that I had a definite duty to convey to you my own desire which I believe represents that of millions, *that you should hold fast your integrity*. Many of us have seen that a great crisis was coming in the world's history, that the teaching of Jesus Christ should be more fully carried out as to the brotherhood of men, that in His sight the humble labourer is equally as precious as the wealthy millionaire. Those who are in the advance guard of an army must expect to bear the brunt of the battle. I trust you will not be discouraged by apparent defeat such as [the by-election at] South Manchester, and by the ingratitude of those whose cause you are pleading. Your fate is only that of every great leader whose names go down to history as the great benefactors of mankind. What you have to suffer is but little compared to the sufferings of our great Leader, Jesus Christ, Whom I believe you are desiring to follow. 'Ye build the sepulchres of the prophets, and your fathers slew them.' It is extremely difficult *when falsely accused* to remain absolutely calm and collected under a sense of duty done. May this be your experience, and 'may the peace of God which passes all understanding keep your heart and mind' and then 'at eventide there will be light' and *your life will be a magnificent object lesson to others*.

With best wishes,

Yours sincerely,

George Cadbury[1]

Beneath the pietistic unction of this letter one cannot, surely, fail to detect a note of worldly advice and warning. The words in italics suggest that Cadbury had heard rumours bearing upon Lloyd George's integrity, and was afraid that the great public causes of which he was the foremost champion might be injured by weapons gratuitously placed in his enemies' hands. The final message seems to be that he should behave in an exemplary manner, for the sake of his own conscience and reputation. So, at any rate, Cadbury's words can easily be interpreted, and it is hard to see why otherwise he would have bothered to write at all.

What were the rumours that could have prompted him to write in such a way? The Patagonian syndicate was a thing of the past, and very few influential people had known about it even at the time. There is not the slightest evidence that it was being talked about in 1912 and,

---

1. George Cadbury to D.L.G., 21 March 1912 (Earl Lloyd George's collection, N.L.W.). Author's italics.

besides, Lloyd George's financial dealings in the 1890s, when he was only a backbencher, were hardly likely to create enough of a stir to warrant Cadbury's concern.

New evidence may help to explain why he wrote as he did. As recently as February 1911 Lloyd George had been told by a correspondent of a rumour that he had made £100,000 out of Surrey Commercial Dock shares.[1] Surrey Commercial was one of the three London dock companies which had been bought out when the Port of London Authority was being established, in 1908, under a scheme prepared by Lloyd George but enacted by his successor at the Board of Trade, Winston Churchill. It would, no doubt, have been possible, though also incredibly risky, for Lloyd George to make a large sum of money out of the P.L.A. transaction. But, replying to his correspondent, he categorically denied that he had ever made any money out of the London docks; and such records as remain support his denial.[2] All the same, the rumour may have persisted, and if so it was sufficiently serious to have given Cadbury grounds for writing.

Whatever may or may not have been true about the past, it is in any case certain that Lloyd George failed to heed Cadbury's implied warning for the future. Within a month he was taking a step consistent neither with integrity nor elementary prudence. On 17 April he

---

1. Earl Lloyd George's collection (N.L.W.), which also contains a note, on Treasury Chambers paper from Lloyd George's secretary, John Rowland, reporting a letter shown to him by Northcliffe's secretary. This referred to an 'informant' who had held Port of London stock recently quoted at 44.

His brokers happen to be the Govt. brokers & he wrote to them suggesting that he should sell out & reinvest somewhere. The brokers strongly advised not selling & gave as their reason the fact that L.G. was a big buyer of the stock for his own account. They further told him to wait & sell on their advice wh. wd. be at the time that L.G. began to realise the stock he was carrying. This advice arrived when the shares had risen to no less than 77½ after wh. they rose to about 79, & the following day the P. of L. Bill was announced wh. provides for the Govt. taking over the stock at 78. The sum of £50,000 was named as L.G.'s personal gain in this connection.

Rowland's note is dated 29 December, and from internal evidence the year must be 1909. There is no trace of any comment on the note by Lloyd George.

2. In the P.L.A. Library there is a book with copies of letters from the Registrar of Surrey Commercial to a large number of shareholders in 1908–9, and Lloyd George is not among them. But there is no complete list of shareholders, and anyway he might have been holding shares through a nominee (though, to judge from his Marconi behaviour, this is unlikely). There are no lists of shareholders for the other two London dock companies in the P.L.A. Library, nor Registrars' books like the above. The P.R.O. has no records for any of the London dock companies, and there are none at the Companies' Registration Office.

agreed to buy a thousand shares in the American Marconi Company, offered to him at £2 a share by his friend Rufus Isaacs, Attorney-General and soon (in June) to be promoted to the Cabinet. One has to say 'agreed to buy' rather than 'bought', because Lloyd George was told that he could pay for the shares later. American Marconis were not yet available to the public in Britain, but when they were put on the market two days later they opened at £3.5.0 and closed at £4. Rufus Isaacs had a number of them to dispose of privately before they went on sale to the public, because one of his brothers, Godfrey, was a director of the American Marconi Company. This brother had recently returned from a visit to the United States, during which he had persuaded his colleagues there to increase the capital of the company by more than six million dollars.

As well as being a director of American Marconi, Godfrey Isaacs was also managing director of the English Marconi Company, which on 7 March had entered into a contract with the British Government for erecting a preliminary chain of wireless stations throughout the Empire. The minister who negotiated the contract on behalf of the Government was the Postmaster-General, Herbert Samuel. American Marconi did not stand to gain directly from this contract, because it was not a shareholder in the English Company, though the English Company did have a holding in the American. But it is hard to believe that news of the British Government's preference for Marconi telegraphy had no indirect effect upon the American issue, which was certainly very successful.

Lloyd George was, of course, extremely busy in April 1912. Among other things, he had just introduced a Budget and so had a Finance Bill on his hands. When Isaacs started to talk to him about American Marconi shares, he cannot have given his whole mind to the subject. But then, would he have done so at any time? His interest in the Stock Market was never deep or sustained. The attraction of Isaacs's proposal was that it could well result in a quick capital gain, because the shares were cheap and the outlook seemed favourable.[1] As

1. His speculative activity at this time was not confined to Marconis. On 15 April 1912 he wrote to Margaret: 'So you have only £50 to spare. Very well, I will invest it for you. Sorry you have no more available as I think it is quite a good thing I have got.' And on 19 April: 'I got my cheque from my last Argentina Railway deal today. I have made £567. But the thing I have been talking to you about is a new thing.' (*Letters* pp. 161–2.) The 'new thing' was presumably not the Marconis, since the first reference to it is on the 15th, two days before Isaacs produced the shares. Lloyd George's failure to mention them to Margaret at the time of the transaction is perhaps significant.

for the legality and ethics, he must have been satisfied that Isaacs, who after all was the Crown's chief Law Officer, and who was holding several thousands of the shares himself, knew what he was doing and was in no way acting improperly. Isaacs had many superlative qualities. For instance, his capacity for hard work was prodigious, and his charm and tact made him an excellent negotiator. But he had not always shown steadiness of judgment where money was concerned. During an unusually varied youthful career, before he decided to read for the Bar, he had the unpleasant experience of being 'hammered' on the Stock Exchange. Though the main reason for this was undoubtedly a sudden slump in the foreign market where he operated, one of his biographers gives as an additional reason his 'lack of caution'. Moreover he had gained admission to the Stock Exchange by making a false declaration of his age, which another biographer takes as evidence that he was 'unpredictable, rash, self-opinionated and essentially conceited'. Chastened by these experiences he became far more discreet and circumspect in later life, but can hardly have undergone a total change of character. Like Lloyd George, he remained an adventurer at heart.[1]

As well as the Chancellor and the Attorney-General, one other minister was involved in the purchase of American Marconis, and his involvement was of crucial importance, because it did not concern himself alone. This other minister was the Government Chief Whip, the Master of Elibank, who was with Lloyd George on 17 April when Isaacs offered the shares, and who also took a thousand of them on his own account. Later, both he and Lloyd George sold half of their holdings, and then bought 3,000 more shares between them. But 'The Master's' purchase of Marconis did not end there, because the following day, 18 April, he bought a further 2,500 shares, and on 14 May 500 more, *for Liberal Party funds*. These 3,000 shares obtained for the Party have received far less attention than they deserve from historians. They have tended to be mentioned, if at all, only incidentally, as a side-issue in the Marconi affair; whereas in fact they provide the key to subsequent developments, and it is very arguable that the political survival of Isaacs and Lloyd George was due to them.

'The Master', for his part, was intending to leave politics, not because he was a failure in the business – few Chief Whips have been

1. H. Montgomery Hyde, *Lord Reading*, p. 17, and Denis Judd, *Lord Reading*, p. 20. In his teens Isaacs sailed round the world as a ship's boy, visiting among other places Calcutta, which he next visited nearly forty-five years later – as Viceroy of India.

more successful – but, very largely, because of the state of his family finances. His father, Lord Elibank, had made the ancestral estates over to him, but they were in such bad order, and there was so little cash, that the heir felt a pious duty to redeem the situation. So in early August he took a highly paid job in the service of the eminent Liberal contractor, Weetman Pearson, who in 1910 had been ennobled, through his instrumentality, as Lord Cowdray; and he also took a peerage himself, as Lord Murray of Elibank. His successor as Chief Whip was the rather less effective Percy Illingworth. The need to make money, though certainly the principal, seems not to have been the only reason for Murray's withdrawal from politics. He also mentioned his health and – tantalisingly, to Riddell – 'hinted that there was a personal reason known to his colleagues'.[1] He did not specify the reason or identify the colleagues, but it is a fair guess that the trouble was Marconi.

By that time trouble was certainly in the air. Ugly rumours were going around, mainly to the effect that the contract for starting an Imperial system of telegraphy had been awarded to the Marconi Company because its managing director was the Attorney-General's brother, but also to the effect that ministers had been gambling in Marconi shares, using their inside knowledge. On 20 July, the day after the contract (signed in March) was tabled in the House of Commons, some of the rumours which until then had been circulating by word of mouth appeared for the first time in print, when a scurrilous journalist called W. R. Lawson wrote, in the weekly *Outlook*, an article containing the words: 'The Marconi Company has from its birth been a child of darkness . . . Its relations with certain Ministers have not always been purely official or political.' Soon afterwards another weekly, the *Eye-Witness*, began a series of articles of which the first was entitled 'The Marconi Scandal': a headline that lives on in the vocabulary of history.

The *Eye-Witness* was edited by Cecil Chesterton, brother of G.K. but much inferior to him in talent and spirit – though undeniably a skilful journalist – and it was formerly edited by Hilaire Belloc, who remained a very active influence throughout the Marconi affair. The bond uniting the contemptible Lawson, the mediocre Cecil Chesterton, and the brilliant but flawed Belloc, was that they were all

---

1. *More Pages from My Diary*, 10 August 1912 (pp. 91–2). Riddell adds that he 'did not care to enquire' which colleagues were privy to this secret.

victims of the disease of the heart known as anti-semitism. It was a gift to them that the Attorney-General and his brother had the name of Isaacs, and an added bonus that the Postmaster-General, who had negotiated the contract, was called Samuel. Another journalist very prominent in the Marconi witch-hunt was Leo Maxse, editor of the *National Review*, but in his case the description, 'anti-semitic' has to be qualified, because – in common with his friend Georges Clemenceau – he had been a passionate Dreyfusard. His motives in the Marconi affair were, above all, extreme Unionist partisanship and a zeal for exposure.

Rufus Isaacs told Samuel, back in June, that he, Lloyd George and Murray had bought some American Marconi shares for themselves, and Samuel then passed this information on to the Prime Minister. It is said, however, that Murray told none of his colleagues of his purchase of shares for the Liberal Party (a claim whose credibility will soon be discussed). When the 'Marconi Scandal' article appeared the pros and cons of suing the *Eye-Witness* for libel were weighed by all the ministers concerned, including (now) Asquith, and the decision was not to sue. This failure to take action was, inevitably, regarded as a sign of weakness, and the smear campaign only grew more virulent. As Lady Donaldson remarks: 'No one would be likely to believe that men with nothing to hide would be content week after week to ignore public charges of the vilest corruption.'[1]

Samuel, in fact, *had* nothing to hide. The Marconi contract was entirely sound and in the public interest; he had not been swayed by any improper considerations, nor had he touched any Marconi shares. On 7 August, just before the recess, he explained in the House of Commons his reasons for signing the contract with Marconi, and in other circumstances his speech would have disarmed criticism. But the Opposition would not now let the matter rest, and the Prime Minister felt obliged to offer a Select Committee of the House to enquire into the contract itself and the suspicions relating to it.

On 11 October, when Parliament reassembled after the summer recess, there was a debate on the Government's proposal that such a Committee should be appointed. Samuel spoke again in the debate, but by far the most important speech was Rufus Isaacs's, in which he uttered the notorious *suggestio falsi*:

Never from the beginning . . . have I had one single transaction with

1. Frances Donaldson, *The Marconi Scandal*, ch. 4, p. 58.

the shares of *that company*. I am not only speaking for myself, but also speaking on behalf, I know, of both my right hon. friends the Postmaster-General and the Chancellor of the Exchequer, who, in some way or other, in some of the articles, have been brought into this matter.[1]

The words 'that company' referred, in context, to the English Marconi Company and were, of course, artfully chosen to conceal the fact that ministers had acquired shares in another, and related, Marconi company. Lloyd George did not take part in the debate except to engage in an unnecessarily heated exchange with the Labour M.P. George Lansbury. Asquith was absent, indisposed.

In accordance with normal practice the Select Committee was constituted on party lines, with six Liberals (including the chairman, Sir Albert Spicer), two Irishmen and one Labour man providing a Government majority over six Tories (including Lord Robert Cecil). All the same its proceedings, which lasted for more than half a year, caused the Government a great deal of embarrassment and led, by degrees, to precisely the revelations that it had been hoped to avoid. The first break occurred after Leo Maxse had said, in the course of his evidence to the Committee on 12 February 1913:

One might have conceived that [the Ministers] might have appeared at [the Committee's] first sitting clamouring to state in the most categorical and emphatic manner that neither directly nor indirectly, in their names or other people's names, have they had any transactions whatsoever, either in London, Dublin, New York, Brussels, Amsterdam, Paris, or any other financial centre, in any shares in *any* Marconi company throughout the negotiations with the Government.

Clearly Maxse knew too much, and it was obvious that the ministerial dealings in American Marconis could no longer be concealed. The facts were soon given, as though innocently and casually, in a statement by counsel for Rufus Isaacs in the process of bringing an action for libel against a French newspaper, *Le Matin*. There was no possible reason for suing this foreign paper (which anyway apologised), after all the defamations that had been left unprosecuted in

1. Hansard, Fifth Series, Vol. XLII, col. 718.

British journals, except that it gave the Ministers a spurious occasion for admitting, by proxy, what they should have admitted long before. On 19 March, at all events, the public was informed that Isaacs, Lloyd George and the Master of Elibank (now Lord Murray) had bought American Marconi shares on which – it was irrelevantly added – they had made an eventual loss.[1]

Further details emerged when Isaacs, soon afterwards, appeared before the Committee. He had no choice but to explain that the shares had been acquired before they were available to the British public, that Lloyd George and Murray had sold some of their shares when the price went up, and that they had bought more when the price went down. These disclosures were not very helpful to Lloyd George, who was the next witness, and his performance can only have impressed those who were already heavily prejudiced in his favour. In particular, he was very weak in his efforts to show that he had been investing rather than speculating in Marconis. But with such a bad case, it would have been difficult for him to shine.

After his evidence and cross-examination, he was asked to produce his pass-books for scrutiny by the Committee and G. Walter Knox, past president of the Institute of Chartered Accountants. In due course the books were produced, some being sent to the Committee through its secretary, others to Knox direct. Knox seems to have shown less impartiality than befitted a professional man ostensibly helping the Committee in a crucial aspect of its work. There is a letter from him thanking Lloyd George for his hospitality, and expressing pleasure that the result of the Enquiry was what he 'expected it would be'.[2]

Before this predictable result, however, there was one more sensational disclosure. Most unfortunately for Murray, his stock-broker absconded and was declared bankrupt, so that his books were opened for examination. Thus it came to light that Murray had bought 3,000 American Marconis for the Liberal Party, which were now held in a special trust account under the joint names of his brother, Captain Arthur Murray, and the new Liberal Chief Whip, Illingworth. Summoned to give evidence, Illingworth denied having

---

1. Isaacs had wisely retained as his senior counsel the very well-known Unionist politician, Sir Edward Carson, who introduced his statement about the American shares as follows: 'There were other Marconi Companies . . . and, although what I have said . . . entirely completes the matter as regards the truth or falsity of the libel, I must, in regard to one transaction in one of the companies by the Attorney-General which it is necessary to explain, ask your indulgence, although it is a little outside the libel.'
2. G. Walter Knox to D.L.G., May 1913 (L.G.P.).

any previous knowledge of the circumstances in which the shares were acquired. Murray himself, of course, was summoned as well, but he was conveniently remote from the scene of the Enquiry, acting for Lord Cowdray in South America. His messages to the chairman, protesting his inability to be back in England until July, were sent from Bogota in Colombia, and 'Bogota' soon became a favourite Tory catcall.

It was, of course, impossible for the Committee to report unanimously. The Liberal majority gave all the Ministers unqualified absolution, with only the chairman trying to suggest that the purchasers of American shares had acted unwisely; while the Tories published a minority report drafted by Cecil, which in one or two respects was unduly harsh. Poor Samuel, who alone deserved to be completely vindicated, suffered in effect from the indiscriminate partisanship of both sides; and the country suffered from delay in implementing a good contract. On 18 June the House of Commons began a two-day debate on an Opposition motion regretting the transactions of certain ministers, and their 'want of frankness', in the Marconi affair. Isaacs and Lloyd George spoke first, and then withdrew. The Attorney's speech was not much admired, even by his supporters, but some found Lloyd George's very affecting, above all the peroration:

Every man who goes into public life knows that he must face poisoned shafts and endure their fester. I have been accustomed to it all through my life, and therefore, perhaps, it does not hurt me as deeply as it might do. Let me say this to the House. This is not what has given me most pain. What has given me most pain has been the anxiety which a heedless action of mine has given to thousands, inside and outside the House, of those who have been comrades of mine in great struggles. Nothing – I ask the indulgence of the House while I make this personal statement – has grieved me more deeply than the apprehension lest some thoughtless act should have put in jeopardy, even for an hour, causes in which I have been brought up to believe as a religious faith. I am conscious of having done nothing which brings a stain upon the honour of a Minister of the Crown. If you will, I acted thoughtlessly, I acted carelessly, I acted mistakenly, but I acted innocently, I acted openly and I acted honestly. That is why I, with confidence, place myself in the hands, not merely of my political friends, but of Members in all parts of this great assembly.[1]

Asquith was not only present this time, but spoke with powerful effect on the second day of the debate. The Opposition motion amounted, he said, to a vote of censure on the ministers concerned, and as such he rebutted it. Nobody who had heard Isaacs and Lloyd George speak the day before could, he asserted, ever have heard 'a franker or more manly explanation'. As for the far distant Murray, it was impossible that any charge of want of frankness against him could ever be substantiated. The Prime Minister drew a distinction between 'rules of obligation' and 'rules of prudence', admitting that his colleagues had – as they admitted themselves – not 'fully observed' the second sort of rule, in failing to avoid transactions which could give 'colour or countenance' to the belief that they might be transgressing the first sort. Yet he insisted that their honour, both private and public, was 'absolutely unstained'.[2] In the division at the end of the debate the Opposition motion was defeated by 78 votes, about twenty less than the usual Government majority.

To the extent that a party vote in the House of Commons can save reputations, the Ministers' reputations were now, therefore, saved; and with their reputations, their careers. In the country at large feelings about the affair had probably all along been less excited than in the political world, because ordinary people had more serious things to worry about than the high moral tone of politics, concerning which in any case there has always, perhaps, been more general scepticism than politicians like to believe. In April, three weeks after the revelation that Isaacs and Lloyd George had taken shares in American Marconi, Northcliffe found that the total number of letters on the subject received by all his newspapers was 'exactly three, one of which was printed – the other two were foolish'. In his very well-informed view, 'the whole Marconi business looms much larger in Downing Street than among the mass of the people'.[3] And while the final Commons debate was in progress, Lloyd George received this report

1. Hansard, Fifth Series, Vol. LIV, cols. 448–9. One Welsh M.P., J. Hugh Edwards, later a biographer of Lloyd George, wrote to him on 27 June: 'Never have I heard anything in the House so deeply moving and so soul-stirring as your great speech. I assure you that not only are we all proud of you, but some of us would – literally – sacrifice our all for you if it were necessary.' (L.G.P.)

2. Hansard, Fifth Series, Vol. LIV, cols. 548–60.

3. Northcliffe to W.S.C., 11 April 1913 (*Churchill*, Companion Vol. II, Part 3, p. 1740). Churchill had earlier persuaded Northcliffe to take a lenient view of the Ministers' action.

from the Birmingham agent of the Free Trade Union, who had addressed over forty meetings in the West Midlands during the previous two months:

> At these meetings I have had innumerable references made to the Insurance Act, the Land Question, and to various other subjects; but not a single mention has been made by any one of my opponents to the Marconi Enquiry! This seems to suggest that outside of London Clubs and the London Press the campaign against yourself, and some of your colleagues in the Cabinet, is exerting little influence. Nearly all my meetings were held in the open air, and the conspicuous silence of the provincial Man-in-the-Street on this particular matter is surely significant.[1]

All the same, even among his friends and sympathisers there were some who felt that he had acted, to say the least, unwisely, and that it would be fitting for him now to let bygones be bygones and avoid any recrimination against his Tory critics. But he was in no mood to listen to such advice and only a fortnight after the Commons debate he delivered at the National Liberal Club a polemic of truly Limehouse vintage, which deserves to be quoted at length because it conveys so well the force and resilience of his personality, as well as some of its less attractive features. After thanking the Party for its support, and acknowledging that 'the leading, the more powerful, Conservative journals' – meaning no doubt, more especially, the Northcliffe Press – had 'refused to lower their dignity by joining this unctuous and fatuous man-hunt', he went on:

> I wish that I could say that of them all, and I wish that I could say that of the Tory Party in the House of Commons . . . For months and months, through the dreary, dark winter, we had to sit silent when calumny was being hurled from every quarter at our heads. We, as Members of the House of Commons, felt bound by its traditions not to answer. The tribunal that we belong to was investigating the matter, and we felt our hands tied, but there were other Members of the House of Commons just as bound to observe the honourable traditions as we were. They were free. They never respected that tradition, and for months we could not answer. It is the shabbiest chapter in the history of any party. Hitting a man when he is down, hitting a man when his hands are tied and he cannot hit back – that is the Tory notion of fair play.

1. Charles Alec Fellowes to D.L.G., 17 June 1913 (L.G.P.).

BLAMELESS TELEGRAPHY.

John Bull. "MY BOYS, YOU LEAVE THE COURT WITHOUT A STAIN—EXCEPT, PERHAPS, FOR THE WHITEWASH."

From *Punch*, 25 June 1913

There is one martyrdom which I always thought was the least endurable of all. That was where the victim had his hands tied and arrows were shot into his body; and he could neither protect himself and tear them out nor sling them back. I can understand something of that now. For months every dastardly and cowardly journalist in the Tory Press shot his poisoned darts, knowing that the hands were tied behind the back by the principles of honour . . . My hands are free now – free to shield, free to smite, not for myself, but for the cause I believe in, which I have devoted my life to, and which I am going on with.

Before I do so, with your permission, I should like to sling a javelin or two at my persecutors . . . when I was looking at the list of those who voted to turn us out of public life, I wondered how many of them would have gone into that lobby if it had been a condition of being allowed to vote that they must show their pass-books for three years. . . .

I should like to say one word about politicians generally. I think that they are a much-maligned race. Those who think that politicians are moved by sordid, pecuniary considerations know nothing of either politics or politicians. These are not the things that move us . . . In politics there is no cash, and if this campaign of calumny goes on there will be very little credit, either. There is no politician I know of who has attained a high position on either side . . . by capacity and strength of character – who would not in a business or profession make ten times as much as he makes in politics or is ever likely to make in politics . . . The men who go into politics to make money are not politicians. Men go in, if you like, for fame. Men go in, if you like, for ambition. Men go in from a sense of duty. But for mere cupidity, never!

We all have ambitions. I am not ashamed to say so. I speak as one who boasts: I have an ambition. I should like to be remembered amongst those who, in their day and generation, had at least done something to lift the poor out of the mire. . . .

I have something else to say. We cannot quite leave it here. Great principles have been laid down, preached, by the Tory Party. We mean to hold to them. Someone says: 'Why not drop it?' But why drop it? When they have got all the worst out of it against us, why should we drop it when there is nothing but the best remaining? I hail this new altruism of the Tory Party. Just think of the noble declaration of Lord Robert Cecil. No man is to put himself in a position where his public duty shall conflict with his private interest. I welcome it. We shall enforce it. After all, political virtue is not a kind of prison fare with which you forcibly feed Radical evildoers. Vicarious virtue is precarious virtue. What a pity that those doctrines were not in force before! Think of the commons of England – millions of acres of common land, the inheritance of the people, bartered away by Parliament, when the landlords governed both the Upper and the Lower House. Ah, if only Lord Robert Cecil had lived in those days . . . In those days people were blind, not to their own interests, but to their obligations. The new light had not dawned upon their conscience. . . .

In fact, they were still 'at it'. He cited a number of issues in his own day to illustrate the persistent selfishness of landlords. Then he ended:

The real peril in politics is not that individual politicians of high rank will attempt to make a packet for themselves. Read the history of England for the past fifty years. The real peril is that powerful interests will dominate the Legislature, will dominate the Executive, in order to carry through proposals which will prey upon the community. That is where tariffs – the landlord endowment – will come in.

No: the principles which they intended to use as a scourge for their foes we shall insist upon making a standard for their friends. These principles are full of hope for the people, and whatever we have suffered – and we have suffered – we shall not have suffered in vain if this principle is exalted for observance by all Parties, all interests.

There is a great story in the greatest of all Books of the man who spent his life fighting the Philistines. One day he was assailed by a wild beast, which he slew. Returning to the scene of the conflict a few days later, he found the carcase full of honey. My right hon. Friend and myself have been assailed by a hideous monster which sought our lives. Not by our own right arm, but with the help of friends, we have slaughtered it and, unless I am mistaken, out of its prostrate form will come something that will sweeten the lives of millions who hitherto have tasted nothing but the bitterness and the dust of the world.[1]

1. Speech at lunch given at the National Liberal Club, 1 July 1913. Rufus Isaacs also spoke. According to Ellis Davies, who was there, 'several people cried' during Lloyd George's speech (Ellis Davies Diary, N.L.W.).

Seldom have special pleading and sheer falsification been made to sound more noble – and there was some genuine nobility in the speech, as well. Lloyd George was pleased with it, explaining to Riddell: 'It was the only course open to me. I am not a white sheet man. It does not suit me.'[1] In this case he was a whited sepulchre man.

The Marconi affair *was* a scandal: to that extent the verdict of history is right. Yet the precise nature of the scandal is even now imperfectly understood, and the accepted view of it needs to be modified in some ways. The accepted view is, broadly, that Lloyd George, Isaacs and Murray were foolish to take shares in American Marconi, and maladroit in their efforts to conceal what they had done, but not otherwise grossly culpable; while Asquith behaved towards them as a loyal headmaster towards gifted members of his staff who had become involved in a trifling but troublesome escapade. When they were attacked, as it were, by a rival school, he stood up for them and refused to allow them to pay the penalty for their misdeeds, even though the departure of at least one of them – whom many regarded as a threat to himself – might have been very much to his advantage.

The facts, surely make this commonly held view seem altogether too bland. As to the offending ministers, their initial offence was worse than foolish; it was an impropriety only a little short of corruption. If American Marconi had been a shareholder in British Marconi, the ministers' dealings would have been outrageous; as it was they can hardly be described as innocent. The contract between British Marconi and the British Government had been signed quite justifiably, and without any improper influence: of that there can be no reasonable doubt. But the contract was bound to have some beneficial effect upon the fortunes of American Marconi, and anyway it had not yet been ratified by Parliament. For British ministers to take shares in the American company at all, and more especially at such a time, would clearly have been a misdemeanour rather than a mistake, even if there had been no aggravating circumstances. But such there most certainly were, in that the managing director of the British company, who was also a director of the American, was brother to one of the ministers, and it was through him that they were able to obtain American Marconi shares, at a relatively low price, before they were put on the open market in Britain.

1. Riddell, *More Pages from my Diary*, 6 July 1913.

Conduct already bad was made far worse, however, by the lengths to which the ministers went to conceal what they had done: sufficient evidence in itself that they were aware of having behaved badly. Their failure to take legal action, during the summer of 1912, against journals that were publishing monstrous and racialist libels, was due above all to fear that in disposing of the lies they would provide an opportunity for the truth to come out. In the Commons debate of 11 October 1912 their spokesman Rufus Isaacs uttered, no doubt by pre-arrangement, a form of words that was deliberately calculated to deceive. Later, they pretended that they had not come clean to the House of Commons on that occasion because they felt that it would be more suitable to tell their story in full to the Select Committee that was being set up. But they showed no eagerness to testify to the Committee. On the contrary, they did their utmost to frustrate its work by informing two of its Liberal members, privately, of the American share purchases, so that they could act as a barrier against awkward questioning by Tory members.

So much for Lloyd George's brazen claim, in his speech at the National Liberal Club, that he and Isaacs had been unable to answer the charges against them 'for months and months', because of their deep respect for the tribunal which alone was competent to investigate the charges. When, in spite of their strenuous efforts to prevent exposure by the Committee, Leo Maxse showed that he probably knew about the American shares, they eventually made the long-delayed admission not to the Committee, but in a court of law, through counsel, as an ostensibly casual accompaniment to a trumped-up action for libel against a foreign newspaper. Even then nothing was said about Murray's involvement, and by the time that leaked out, through what (for the ministers) was a singularly malign chance, Murray was safely out of reach in South America. From first to last their intention was to reveal as little as possible, and such revelations as occurred were due to no honesty or candour on their part. It was only because the Committee reported, and the House of Commons voted, on strictly party lines, that they were able to escape the severe censure they unquestionably deserved.

Lloyd George is open to special reproach for his part in the business. It cannot be seemly for a Chancellor of the Exchequer to gamble in shares, as he did, even when the dealings are completely above board, as in this case they were not. The Minister with chief responsibility for the nation's finances is expected to maintain certain standards, and

playing the market is obviously not a proper form of activity for him.
As the *Round Table* commented at the time:

> The Chancellor of the Exchequer is, in a sense, the *ex officio* head of
> the City of London; for he is the highest financial officer of the
> British Empire. City opinion is therefore affronted by the dis-
> closure of this sublime functionary behaving for all the world like
> the poor, greedy, excited Mr Juggins of ordinary life.[1]

But what would have been reprehensible in any Chancellor was
doubly so in Lloyd George, for the reason hinted at by Cadbury and
acknowledged, in effect, by himself: that a great cause depended on
him, and the hopes of millions were reposed in him. By acting as he
did he was not only risking his career and dishonouring his office, but
betraying the trust of all those who looked to him as their champion.

Nor is that all that has to be said. His behaviour in the Marconi affair
could more easily be extenuated, if not excused, had he been, himself,
invariably generous and tolerant towards other politicians similarly
placed. But he was the man who, during the Boer War, had hurled
moral anathemas at Joseph Chamberlain on account of his family
connection with the firm of Kynoch, which was in contractual
relationship with the Government of the day. When reminded of this,
Lloyd George asserted that the two cases were not analogous, though
he declined to explain why on the absurd pretext that he did not wish
to stir up old controversies. In fact, there was a rather close analogy,
since in both cases the focus of criticism was a fraternal link (between
Chamberlain and his brother Arthur, the chairman of Kynoch's, as
later between Rufus and Godfrey Isaacs). Lloyd George had used
against Chamberlain the argument that a Minister of the Crown
should be not only pure but, like Caesar's wife, above suspicion. By
his own criterion he now stood condemned.

Moreover, if his attempts at self-vindication in the Marconi affair
seem hypocritical by reference to the past, how much more does one
passage in his National Liberal Club speech seem so by reference to the
future. There was no cash in politics, he said, and anyone with talent
and drive could make ten times as much in a business or profession as

1. June, 1913: quoted in Frances Donaldson, *op.cit*, p. 135. Of Lloyd George's alleged
'investment' Lady Donaldson writes: 'He and the Master of Elibank had done what every
tyro indulging in a half-guilty flutter does. They had bought half-way up a boom and sold
excitedly at a profit. Then at the first drop they had bought again in larger quantities, on this
occasion half-way down a slump.'

he was ever likely to make in politics. Was this to be true of himself? Though he was capable, no doubt, of excelling in almost any chosen line of work, it is not self-evident that he would have emerged any richer from a business or professional career than he did from his career in politics. Had he emerged ten times as rich, he would have been a plutocrat indeed.

His resentment of those who attacked him from the security of hereditary wealth (whether or not originally ill-gotten) was natural enough, and it was equally natural that he should wish to be free, like them, from financial anxiety. But to speak of himself as a martyr, whose sufferings in the Marconi affair, due almost exclusively to the spite of his enemies, would richly benefit the cause of social reform – this was humbug on the grand scale. The truth was that he had only narrowly escaped doing immeasurable harm to the cause he represented, and had clearly done it no good whatsoever.

Now what of Asquith's role in the affair? In one respect – perhaps the most important of all – he is certainly blameless. He did not acquire any American Marconi shares himself, nor did he encourage others to acquire any. He had no part in, nor any responsibility for, the genesis of the scandal. But how much did he know of it in its early stages, and what was the extent of his complicity in the cover-up? Is the image of him as a detached, but loyal, headmaster fundamentally accurate, or is it fundamentally misleading?

. From the moment he heard of his colleagues' dealings in American Marconi, without insisting that they seek the earliest opportunity of a full disclosure, he became, surely, an accessory after the fact. When was that moment? In his *Memories and Reflections*, published in 1928, he wrote that at the time of the first Commons debate, in October 1912, the acquisition of American Marconi shares by Isaacs and Lloyd George, 'was unknown both to their traducers and their friends': in other words, presumably, to himself among others. In this retrospective account he implied that he had known nothing of their guilty secret until it was made public on the occasion of the libel action against *Le Matin*. If it were true that he knew nothing, then he would have no responsibility for their prolonged attempt at concealment, which included a flagrantly disingenuous speech in Parliament. But it is not true. In fact, he knew of the share dealings by all three ministers (in Murray's case, at any rate, of the shares he had bought for himself) at the very latest by the beginning of August 1912, because he admitted as much quite explicitly in a Parliamentary answer on 26

March 1913. This was forgotten when he came to write his *Memories*, and it had been conveniently ignored by his apologists.[1]

His absence from the October debate was said to be due to indisposition, but political opponents treated this excuse with some scepticism at the time. It was put around that his complaint was a carbuncle on the neck, but according to one witness 'there was no symptom of any such disorder' the day before, and many assumed that he had been 'malingering'.[2] Whatever the state of his health, it must have suited him to be away from the House of Commons when the truth as he knew it was being withheld and a false impression deliberately created. It would seem that he must have been party to the deception, or he would surely have remonstrated with Isaacs after the debate. Yet by distancing himself from the actual scene he preserved the *appearance* of Olympian detachment which marked his treatment of the affair throughout, and which the factual error in his reminiscences served very much to enhance.

Though in March 1913 he did admit, under pressure, that he had known at a relatively early stage about the shares bought by the ministers as individuals, he never admitted that he had known about the shares that Murray had bought for the Liberal Party. When that secret leaked out, the line taken by Asquith and the other ministers was that Murray had kept the transaction entirely to himself; and Murray never deviated from the same line when he eventually returned to England and was questioned by a committee of the House of Lords – though we should not forget his cryptic remark to Riddell in August of the previous year, that there was a 'personal reason' for his resignation, which was 'known to colleagues'. The official version, on which all concerned later agreed, was that he had told absolutely no one of his purchase of shares for the Party until he went abroad, and that he had then told no one except his brother, Arthur. Even his successor, Illingworth, was allegedly not informed, though he was appointed a co-trustee, with Arthur, of the Party's Marconi holding.

Is this version really credible? Quite apart from the remark to Riddell it is hard to think of any reason why Murray, a naturally communicative man, should have failed to tell his friends that he had bought shares for the Party the day after he had bought some for

1. It was, however, brought out by Frances Donaldson (*op.cit.*, p. 116). Other evidence suggests that he knew at the beginning of June (Viscount Samuel, *Memoirs*, p. 75).
2. *Crawford Papers*, p. 280 (10 October 1912).

himself, at a time when they all imagined they were on to a safe, as
well as a good, thing. Riddell indeed definitely states that Illingworth
had 'known these facts for some little time'.[1] And it is virtually
impossible, in that case, to believe that he did not share his knowledge
with the Prime Minister.

It is, however, easy enough to understand why all knowledge of a
Marconi share purchase for the Party had to be disclaimed; for the man
ultimately responsible for Party funds was the leader of the Party,
Asquith himself. Dealings by individual colleagues on their own
account were of concern to him as head of the Government, to the
extent that the Government's credit might be affected. But dealings on
behalf of the Party touched him more closely, since his own personal
credit was directly involved, as well as that of the Government. If he
did, in fact, know that Marconi shares had been bought for the Party,
it would have been most dangerous and impolitic for him to admit to
the knowledge, so long as he could be confident that others would
keep the secret. On the assumption, therefore, that he felt that
confidence, it seems likely that his denial was mendacious.

The secret of his knowledge would have been confined to a very
small number of people, none of whom had any motive for giving it
away. Murray himself was a thoroughly reliable friend and colleague,
who could afford to bear the responsibility alone, since he had left
politics and was satisfactorily employed elsewhere. Isaacs, Lloyd
George, Illingworth and any other ministers who may have known
that Asquith knew about the Party shares (if he did) would also have
been well aware that his headmasterly reputation was a vital asset to
the Government, and therefore to themselves. If he had shown any
sign of abandoning *them*, they might have contemplated abandoning
him, and vice versa. But there was probably a mutual recognition of
the need for solidarity in a situation where the abandonment of one
might well have led to the ruin of all.

That Asquith was sensitive about Lloyd George as a potential rival
is evident from his curious speech at the eve-of-session dinner. But the
two men also had, on the whole, a good working relationship, unless
mischief was made by others, and in any case Asquith was too realistic
not to see how important Lloyd George was to the Government's
success, even to its hopes of survival. He had, therefore, a strong
interest in defending Lloyd George in the Marconi affair, and this

1. Riddell, *More Pages from my Diary*, 7 and 8 June, 1913, p. 159.

largely explains why he not only condoned but actively abetted the cover-up, while appearing to be detached. Yet it does not, perhaps, seem a wholly convincing explanation, except on the hypothesis that he also knew about the shares bought for the Party. Beyond question Lloyd George was on thin ice in the affair, but so was the whole Government; and the ice under Asquith's own feet may have been the most treacherous of all. The stock view of his role probably exaggerates his integrity, therefore, while doing far less than justice to his political nerve and agility.

Ethical considerations apart, it was surely very lucky indeed for Britain that Lloyd George's career was not brought to an end by the Marconi Scandal. Perhaps the public reaction, or lack of it, reflected a true sense of the national interest, as well as a shrewd understanding of the frailty of politicians.

THREE

Second Love

Some have said that Lloyd George's hair turned grey, or even white, during the Marconi affair, but photographs of him before and after show that this is untrue. He was already beginning to go grey in 1909–11, and his hair only became white towards the end of the Great War. The process was, therefore, gradual, more or less natural for a man of his age, and accelerated – if at all – by the supreme cares of wartime leadership.[1] Another sign of deterioration which, it is suggested, may have reflected the strain of Marconi is that he wore reading glasses for the first time in public while giving evidence to the Select Committee. But surely it is at least as likely that he did so to create an impression of *gravitas*, which might otherwise, in the circumstances, have been rather hard to sustain; or that his doing so was pure coincidence. In general there can be no doubt that his physical and psychological stamina was more than equal to the ordeal. Despite the anxiety which he must have felt from an early stage, and of course increasingly as the months went by and the (approximate) truth came out, there was never any noticeable loss of concentration or weakening in his performance as a politician.

His nerve was tested and not found wanting as the date approached

1. Or did his hair have magical properties? On 7 November 1915 Riddell dined with the Lloyd Georges and noted afterwards in his diary: 'His hair looks much darker than it did. I charged him with dyeing it. He said, "It is strange that you should think that; my wife has just been telling me that I am less grey than I was. I really do believe that my hair does change colour in accordance with my physical condition. I am feeling much better than I was." Mrs Lloyd George confirmed this theory and added that when L.G. was reading for his "final", a small white patch appeared in his hair, and gradually went away.' (R.W.D., pp. 133–4.)

for payment of National Health Insurance contributions to begin. The date fixed was 15 July 1912 and, since the Northcliffe Press was urging its readers not to contribute to the scheme, there were grounds for fearing that its temporary unpopularity – while its cost to individuals was apparent, and its value to them not yet tangible – might be successfully exploited for the purpose of killing it at birth. But Lloyd George faced the danger with breezy confidence and his usual keen eye for the ridiculous. On 29 June he dealt with the subject firmly, but light-heartedly, in the course of an address to Liberals at Woodford:

> The Insurance Act will come into operation on July the fifteenth. I wish to make an appeal for a fair trial for the Act from the people in this country. There are those who forget that it is an Act of Parliament. In this and in every other country there are bad-tempered people who want their own way; if they don't get it, they smash something. When these people lose their tempers they try to punish somebody; and, if they cannot punish the people responsible for the law that they do not like, they punish somebody who is near to them, somebody who is helpless, somebody who has served them faithfully. They cannot get at me, and they cannot turn the Prime Minister out; so they begin worrying the servants. They write letters to the papers threatening to reduce the wages of their servants, threatening to lengthen their hours – I should have thought that almost impossible – and, in the end, threatening to dismiss them.
>
> They are always dismissing servants. Whenever any Liberal Act of Parliament is passed, they dismiss them. I wonder that they have any servants left. Sir William Harcourt imposed death duties; they dismissed servants. I put on a super-tax; they dismissed more. Now the Insurance Act comes, and the last of them, I suppose, will have to go. You will be having, on the swell West End houses, notices like 'Not at home – her ladyship's washing day.'

In a more serious vein, he deprecated anarchical behaviour by the well-to-do, because it could so easily spread. They were setting an evil fashion, of which they might themselves become the victims.

He had more to say on this theme at Kennington on 13 July – the Saturday before the crucial date, which was a Monday – and his particular target was the Northcliffe Press, including as it did *The Times* as well as the *Daily Mail*:

> Defiance of the law is like the cattle plague. It is very difficult to

isolate it and confine it to the farm where it has broken out. Although this defiance of the Insurance Act has broken out first among the Harmsworth herd, it has travelled to the office of *The Times*. Why? Because they belong to the same cattle farm. *The Times*, I want you to remember, is just a twopenny-halfpenny edition of the *Daily Mail*.

He lamented the inconsistency of 'the poor old law-and-order *Times*', all for 'shooting, transporting, gibbeting' protesters in the past, and for forcibly feeding suffragette window-breakers in the present, yet 'when it is a question of paying threepence a week to keep workmen and their children from starving' saying 'No more law and order.' The scheme, however, would not be killed; it was triumphantly surviving the murderous designs of its enemies.

No doubt you would like to know what the position is today. Well, I have it . . . I am telling you what no newspaper knows and what *The Times* will not repeat, probably, on Monday. There are in this country thirteen millions of working men and working women who, under this Act, are compulsorily insurable – a nasty phrase, I know, but you will thank me for that exactly as we are thanking Mr Forster for making Education compulsory. . . . Well, the Act has not yet come into operation, but at this very instant there are nine-and-a-half million members of approved societies. By Monday, there will be ten millions.

And 'in three weeks or a month', he predicted, the whole insurable population would have joined societies and would be contributing – a bold claim which was, however, substantially vindicated in the event.[1]

Lloyd George's passing allusion to the forcible feeding of suffragettes was made soon after he had experienced physical force directed against himself by an over-zealous champion of the women's cause. As he was preparing to deliver his speech at Kennington a male suffragist attacked him and tried to strike him on the head. Luckily he escaped injury, though in the scuffle that preceded the man's arrest by the police Lloyd George was pulled to the ground. Afterwards he said

1. By the end of the first week after 15 July the Post Office had in hand over ninety per cent of the money estimated as due, and by 1 October contributions were running slightly ahead of actuarial expectation. Lloyd George's forecast did not, therefore, err by very much (Bentley G. Gilbert, *The Evolution of National Insurance in Great Britain*, p. 424).

that the attack had merely stimulated him, and that he would have hit the man if the police had not intervened.[1]

1912 was a year of mounting suffragette violence, provoking counter-violence by the State. In February Mrs Pankhurst had told members of her organisation, the Women's Social and Political Union, that the argument of the broken pane of glass was the most valuable argument in politics; and soon afterwards, accordingly, hammers were issued to 150 suffragettes who were then sent out to smash the windows of selected West End shops and offices. A few days later Mrs Pankhurst was arrested, joining the dozens of suffragettes already in prison – though her even more fanatical daughter Christabel soon chose to take refuge in Paris, without forfeiting her authority in the movement. In England hunger strikes and forcible feeding followed, while militants not yet behind bars kept up, and even extended, the campaign of vandalism. To window-breaking was added the more serious crime of arson in the repertoire of W.S.P.U. violence, with the result that some hitherto regarded as extremists were driven to an open breach with the Pankhursts. And so it went on, until the sex war was overtaken by European war in the summer of 1914.

Meanwhile the cause of Parliamentary votes for women was effectively blocked, but not, as is often alleged, mainly on account of W.S.P.U. methods. The narrow Second Reading defeat of another Conciliation Bill at the end of March 1912 was, indeed, probably due to Mrs Pankhurst's hammer tactics, but the Bill would have been unlikely to survive its Committee stage, in any case. Genuine suffragists like Lloyd George would have tried to widen the proposed franchise so as to make it less potentially damaging to the Liberal Party; but for the same reason, *mutatis mutandis*, the Unionists would naturally have resisted any such amendment.

The Government was altogether in no state to push women's suffrage through. For a start, it was not united on the issue, and the Prime Minister himself was among the anti-suffragists. There was also a near-prohibitive restriction on the time available for contentious legislation, because of the Parliament Act straitjacket. And the Irish Members, determined at all costs to maintain the priority of Home Rule, were suspicious of anything that might impede or delay the

1. Riddell, *More Pages from My Diary*, 14 July 1912. Margaret Lloyd George said that it was just as well her husband had not become involved in a fight, because he was 'very muscular and, when angry, very fierce'.

progress of their measure. After Speaker Lowther had ruled, in January 1913, that the Government's Franchise and Registration Bill could not be amended to include women's suffrage clauses, no further attempts even of a token kind were either made or supported by the Government during the pre-war period to secure the vote for women. One writer has argued that Lloyd George's lack of decisive influence on this issue at the time was due to Marconi,[1] but a more crippling difficulty for him was, surely, that the other leading Radical in the Cabinet, Churchill, was equivocal on Suffrage.[2] Whatever the reasons, the Liberals' failure to enfranchise women was one of the worst blots on their record, and no amount of special pleading can excuse it.

The assault on Lloyd George at Kennington was by no means his only unpleasant experience at the hands of the W.S.P.U. and its male supporters. He had had plenty of trouble from them already, and more was in store for him. In September – after a break at Marienbad, ostensibly for the sake of his health[3] – he attended the National Eisteddfod at Wrexham and was heckled there by suffragettes, who in turn were roughly treated by the crowd.[4] Soon afterwards there were even nastier scenes at Llanystumdwy, whose excessive tranquillity had so irked him as a child. The occasion was the opening there, on 21 September, of a village institute paid for out of libel damages received from the *People* in 1909. Now that Lloyd George was once again threatened by scandal, if of a different sort, this celebration of his earlier success in preserving a 'Mr Clean' image was not without

1. David Morgan, *Suffragists and Liberals*, pp. 108–9.
2. Churchill took the line that Asquith could not be expected to use the Parliament Act to promote a change which, in his view, would be disastrous. This line of Churchill's was dictated partly by opportunism and partly by his own coolness towards the cause – in which he differed from his wife. 'Clementine publicly declared that she was "ardently in favour of votes for women" and privately lobbied Winston, but she had ruefully to acknowledge that she was never able to make him support the cause, except in carefully qualified terms.' (Mary Soames, *Clementine Churchill*, p. 59.)
3. He was advised by a doctor there to go on a diet. 'No sauces of any kind – or pickles. High game to be avoided. Tomatoes to be avoided. I must take a great quantity of vegetables – not much meat – no internal organs like kidneys or sweetbread – & above all plenty of stewed fruit. I must drink between meals twice a day a bottle of mineral water.' His own kidneys, allegedly, 'wanted washing very badly – they were full of gravel' (D.L.G. to M.L.G., 17 and 28 August 1912).
4. While at the Eisteddfod, he was invited by a deputation of Welsh Americans to visit the United States, and replied that he would love to go there when he was less busy, since he had 'an amazing amount of correspondence from America'. In fact, he did not go there until 1923, after his fall from power.

irony, more especially as the honoured guests included Rufus Isaacs.[1]
Marconi, however, had nothing to do with the disturbances that
occurred when Lloyd George spoke from a platform erected in a field
near the institute. Ellis Davies, an eye-witness, wrote in his diary:

> . . . no sooner had he appealed to the crowd in Welsh to be gentle
> with any suffragettes present than one of the women quite near the
> stage shouted 'Votes for Women' & in the attempt to lead her out –
> she herself fighting & kicking those who tried to protect her – the
> crowd pressed down & an ugly rush was made for the platform. No
> sooner was one disposed of than other women cried in other parts of
> the field.

According to Press reports, two women were then attacked by the
crowd, their hair pulled and their clothes nearly torn off, before they
could be rescued by the police. Even Davies, though concerned for the
good name of his nation and sex, had to admit that 'feeling got the best
of some men'.

On a visit to Scotland in the late autumn Lloyd George had to face
further W.S.P.U. interruptions when he spoke at Aberdeen and
Kirkaldy. At Aberdeen on 29 November he made, incidentally, this
realistic comment on the Liberals' electoral triumph in 1906: that it
was two-thirds due to disgust with the Tories, and only one-third
'attributable to a genuine, deep-seated desire on the part of the people
for reform'. He also gave what might have been interpreted as a signal
to the rich that his demands on them were not prompted by vindic-
tiveness: 'Mr Chamberlain once said that wealth ought to pay ransom.
I do not say that; what I do say is that prosperity ought to pay a
thank-offering.'

Early in 1913 the suffragettes struck against him in a new way when
part of the house that Riddell was building for him beside the golf
course at Walton Heath was blown up on 19 February. If all the bombs
planted had exploded a number of workmen would have been killed,
but fortunately there were no casualties, though the material damage
was quite extensive. Lloyd George himself was in no danger, because
he was abroad at the time, on his way to the South of France, during

---

1. Isaacs was supposedly unable to take part in the proceedings until after sunset, because 21
September was the Sabbath. But in fact he was not an orthodox Jew. The evening's
entertainment at the institute took the form of a Welsh concert. Among others who attended
the opening were Sir Hugh Ellis-Nanney, Lloyd George's Tory opponent in two elections,
and David Evans, his old headmaster, to whom he paid a graceful compliment.

the short interval before a new session of Parliament was opened in March. He wrote at once to Riddell to apologise for being 'such a troublesome and expensive tenant', and to suggest that the W.S.P.U. should be made to pay for the repairs, since Mrs Pankhurst had claimed responsibility for the crime. Riddell did not act on the suggestion, but in due course Mrs Pankhurst was sentenced to three years' penal servitude.[1]

During his holiday on the Riviera Lloyd George had two rounds of golf with Bonar Law: further evidence of the strong underlying friendship between them. That the Tory leader was prepared to have comradely 'out-of-school' meetings with Lloyd George at such a time – between the revelation that he had bought American Marconi Shares and his appearance before the Select Committee – was surely a most striking example of personal affection and fellow-feeling transcending partisanship. The world as yet had no means of knowing that these two apparently bitter antagonists liked each other and understood each other so well. But before very long the truth would be out.

On 17 January 1913 Lloyd George passed the milestone of his fiftieth birthday, and the occasion was celebrated at a dinner given in his honour by Percy Illingworth at the National Liberal Club. But this public event was of trivial significance compared with an entirely private one that occurred four days later. For it was on 21 January 1913 that Lloyd George and Frances Louise Stevenson were, as they used to say to each other, 'married'. Then, indeed, he passed a really important milestone and entered a new region of his life's experience, in which he was to find many difficulties but also considerable joy and certainly much practical support.

How did he come to fall in love with a woman young enough to be his daughter, and she to accept the role of a mistress not even *en titre*? What was the background to their unorthodox romance? It would be misleading to describe him, before he met her, as an unhappily married man. He had always been very fond of his wife, Margaret,

1. In fact, the leading culprit was the crazy enthusiast Emily Wilding Davison, who remained at large and so was able to achieve, a few months later, her desired status of martyr, when she threw herself in front of the King's horse as it led the Derby field round Tattenham Corner. Mrs Pankhurst had no prior knowledge of the Walton Heath exploit, but took responsibility on principle for this and other similar acts perpetrated by members of her organisation. As before, she was soon released from prison after going on hunger strike, only to be re-arrested and locked up again under Home Secretary McKenna's Prisoners' Temporary Discharge for Ill-Health Act (nicknamed 'The Cat and Mouse Act').

despite their quarrels and incompatibilities; and he was also very fond of his children. But the children, apart from Megan, were either grown up or nearly so. Dick, the eldest, came of age in 1910, in which year he also graduated from Christ's College, Cambridge. Two years later he was a qualified civil engineer with a job in the Cowdray organisation – obtained for him, needless to say, by Lord Murray. After spending some months in Spain, at the firm's expense, acquiring fluency in Spanish, he left for South America early in 1913. Olwen, the second surviving child, had attended Roedean and a school in Dresden before coming of age in 1913; while the eighteen-year-old Gwilym was at that date leaving Eastbourne College and going up to Jesus College, Cambridge.[1] Megan, eight years younger than Gwilym, was therefore the only true child remaining in the family circle, and it was in giving holiday tuition to Megan, during the summer of 1911, that Frances Stevenson first came into Lloyd George's world.

She was recommended for this task by the headmistress of Clapham High School, where she had been a fellow-pupil of his beloved eldest daughter, Mair, whose death in 1907 was the worst bereavement he ever suffered. Frances was, in fact, only a little older than Mair, having been born in 1888, the year the Lloyd Georges were married. During the 1911 summer holidays at Criccieth, Lloyd George was clearly very conscious of her presence, and probably felt, even then, rather more drawn to her than he would naturally have been to any pretty young woman. The following term Megan was sent as a weekly boarder to the school at Wimbledon – Allenswood – where Frances was teaching, and at the weekends Lloyd George would often call there himself to collect his daughter and bring her home. On several Sundays, moreover, during the autumn of 1911 Frances was asked to tea at 11 Downing Street. She looked forward to these visits 'avidly' and retained a special memory of one when

> we went after tea to the evening service at the Castle Street chapel and since we were returning to a house empty of servants, for they were away in their own chapel, we bought delicatessen at Appenrodt's (whose existence ceased with the outbreak of war in 1914) and waited on ourselves for supper. Later, L.G. made me play some of the glorious Welsh hymns, and everyone sang lustily, none more lustily than L.G. himself. After which I took the Tube back to

1. Younger readers may need to be reminded that, until 1970, the age of majority was twenty-one.

school at Wimbledon.[1]

Thus the situation developed, and the following spring, when Frances told Lloyd George that she was planning to give up teaching, he quickly countered by asking her to summarise for him a French book on the land system. She had no hesitation in agreeing and by this step, small in itself, moved distinctly closer to him and to permanent involvement in his life.

She was able to summarise a French book because her mother was half-French, both her parents spoke the language, and she herself was therefore virtually bilingual. Her maternal grandfather was an Italian artist called Armanino, who migrated to Paris and married a young Frenchwoman, a teacher in Montmartre. These grandparents then led a typical Parisian *vie de Bohème* until, at the Germans' approach in 1870, they moved to London, where they later decided to stay. (As a foreigner Armanino could not have fought in the war.) Their daughter, Louise Augustine, married at nineteen a young man of Lowland Scottish ancestry, John Stevenson, whose parents had also moved to London – from a farm in Lanarkshire. John Stevenson had been sent to France after leaving school, and had worked there in what his daughter primly calls a 'situation', while studying the country and its language. As a result he spoke French at least as well as his wife, and got a job as secretary to a firm of French import agents.

The Stevensons lived modestly, but genteelly, in a rented house in South London, and the Armaninos lived with them. Frances was the eldest of five children: four girls and a boy. She was very fond of her parents, but was perhaps most influenced by her grandmother, who among other things taught her to play the piano and cultivated her love of music. She read a lot and was an impressionable child, responsive to beauty. One moment in her childhood, when she was about twelve, stayed vividly in her consciousness:

My mother had sent me on an errand on coming home from school, and as I walked down the road in the dusk I saw an almond tree in full blossom against a lavender sky, with a silver crescent moon faintly appearing. The beauty of it made me catch my breath. My spirit seemed to soar, and I whispered to myself, 'I will never grow old!'[2]

1. Frances Lloyd George, *The Years that are Past*, p. 49.
2. *ibid.*, p. 18.

Soon afterwards, when the Stevensons' fifth child was born, they were so far compelled to lower their standards of respectability as to send the older children to a council school. But it was not long before Frances and her brother, Paul – who were the clever ones – obtained scholarships to good independent schools, he to Christ's Hospital, she to Clapham High School (where she met Mair Lloyd George). From there in due course she won a London University scholarship and went as a classical student to Royal Holloway College. At Holloway the sense of emancipation was 'like wine' to her, and again – as in her mystical vision of the almond tree – her 'spirits soared'. This generalised enthusiasm was not, however, altogether helpful, from the academic point of view. She was, on her own admission, 'too full of the joy of life' to be an ideal student, and at the end of three years she faced her final examination with great misgivings, because she knew she had not done enough work. All the same, she somehow managed to pass, and was awarded her degree in 1910, by Lord Rosebery.

Now a young woman of twenty-two, she was a relatively moderate, though in her parents' eyes rather alarming, exponent of what a later generation came to know as Women's Lib. She took pride in the fact that her Christian name meant 'free', and she sympathised with the Pankhursts and their movement, while contenting herself with actual membership of the non-militant suffrage organisation. She joined the Fabian Society, and read novels thought unsuitable for young women, such as H. G. Wells's *Ann Veronica* – whose reputation as a feminist manifesto is, incidentally, one of the more piquant ironies of literature.[1] For employment she turned to teaching not because she wanted to do it, but because it was just about the only sort of work she could do without further training, which her parents could not afford.

---

1. The book can more truly be regarded as a manifesto for male chauvinism, since its ultimate message is that the sexes will be unequal to the end of time. Talking to herself in prison, Ann Veronica says:

'A woman wants a proper alliance with a man, a man who is better stuff than herself. She wants that and needs it more than anything else in the world. It may not be just, it may not be fair, but things are so. It isn't law, nor custom, nor masculine violence settled that. It is just how things happen to be. She wants to be free – she wants to be legally and economically free, so as not to be subject to the wrong man; but only God, who made the world, can alter things to prevent her being slave to the right one. . . .'

And after A.V. has eloped with Capes, when they are together in the Alps: 'One of the things that most surprised him in her was her capacity for blind obedience. She loved to be told to do things.' Wells sent an inscribed copy of *Ann Veronica* to the aged Tolstoy, who died the year after it was published. He was a worthy recipient.

So it came about that she was offered a resident teaching post at Allenswood, which had the advantage of being within easy reach of her home. She liked the children and claims to have been a good storyteller, using this technique for teaching them history and literature – as Lloyd George had done with his children. Some of her pupils gave her the nickname which stuck to her afterwards, and which he used: Pussy. It was aptly chosen, both for the sense of softness that it conveys, and for certain other feline qualities that she might be said to have possessed.

Among her colleagues she made friends with the music teacher, who was Welsh, and she also got on well with the Welsh housekeeper at the school, whom she would accompany on Sunday afternoons to the Welsh Baptist chapel in Castle Street (perhaps rather oddly, since she was herself a confirmed member of the Church of England). It was there that she first saw Lloyd George, and on the last Sunday in June, 1911, heard him address the congregation, 'instantly' (so she tells us) falling 'under the sway of his electric personality'.

I listened to his silver voice, observed his mastery over his audience. He seemed to establish a personal relationship immediately with every member of it, and although he spoke almost entirely in Welsh, I felt myself in some mysterious way drawn into the orbit of his influence.[1]

So, when, only a month later, she went to 11 Downing Street to be interviewed by him personally for the holiday job at Criccieth, she expected to find him almost godlike and was not, apparently, disappointed.

My nervousness was dispersed in a few moments by the warmth of his voice and the kindliness of manner which put me entirely at my ease. His image as I saw him then is graven on my mind: the sensitive face, with deep furrows between the eyes: the eyes themselves, in which were [sic] all knowledge of human nature, grave and gay almost simultaneously – which, when they scrutinised yours, convinced you that they understood the workings of your heart and mind, sympathised with all your difficulties, set you in a place apart. The broad brow; the beautiful profile – straight nose, neat insolent chin, and a complexion as young and fresh as a child's.[2]

1. Frances Lloyd George, *op.cit.*, p. 40.
2. *ibid.*, p. 42.

As we know, she got the job, Lloyd George's interest was aroused, and by the following spring she was not only preparing to give up teaching but also starting, in a small way, to work for him.

More important, however, than merely translating and summarising a French book was her decision, at about the same time, to learn shorthand. It is not clear whether the idea of doing so was her own, or whether it was suggested to her by him, but in any case we may be sure that he was quick to see the possibilities that it would open up. Through the summer and autumn of 1912 they were seeing more and more of each other. Later she recalled that it was one Sunday in July that 'both of us realised for the first time that something serious was happening – when I asked him to come to the garden party the following Saturday & he said he would'.[1] She would often visit him at the House of Commons to be given more Land Campaign chores to do, or to listen to debates from the Gallery. They began to correspond almost every day (unfortunately burning the letters) and would sometimes dine together at a restaurant. As the year's end approached he made her the proposal that she should come to him as private secretary and even more private mistress, explaining that he could not propose marriage because his career would be destroyed if he were divorced.

When she went to stay with friends in Scotland for Christmas, she took with her Katharine O'Shea's book on Parnell – a gift from Lloyd George to help her to understand why a politician on whom the hopes of many depended should never sacrifice his public duty to the love of a woman. While in Scotland she had a proposal of marriage from Stuart Brown, a 'highly intelligent, musical . . . civil servant with a future'; but when she received from Lloyd George an 'urgent letter' saying that 'something terrible had happened', she went back to him at once and soon accepted his terms. The terrible thing was, she says, the Marconi scandal, but – as A. J. P. Taylor has pointed out – the first phase of this had passed during the autumn, and the 'real storm' only blew a little later. In his view, Lloyd George probably 'used the affair as the clinching argument for sweeping away Frances's doubts'.[2] Her

1. *Lloyd George: A Diary*, by Frances Stevenson, ed. by A. J. P. Taylor; 24 May 1921, p. 217.
2. *My Darling Pussy: The Letters of Lloyd George and Frances Stevenson 1913–41*, edited by A. J. P. Taylor, p. 2.

Stuart Brown's department was the India Office, in which eventually he rose almost to the top, retiring – with a knighthood – shortly before Britain retired from India. He continued for a time to write to Frances, though in a comradely rather than amorous vein. (The letters are in the L.G.P.). Later he married a friend of hers.

doubts, however, may not have amounted to very much by then, because she was clearly under his spell and enraptured by the prospect of sharing his life and work. As she says herself, referring to the time *before* she went away for Christmas: 'The point of no return had been reached – and passed.'[1]

At any rate their relationship was secretly formalised on 21 January 1913, and thereafter remained on the same footing for thirty years – until, after Margaret's death, they were officially married. During most of their time together Lloyd George was, in reality, a bigamist. He genuinely loved Frances, and needed her as a companion, but he also continued to feel much of his old affection for Margaret, while naturally giving Frances the opposite impression. In different ways he needed both women, and with characteristic nerve and resourcefulness he got what he wanted.

His love for Frances was much more than the infatuation of a middle-aged man for an attractive young woman. Certainly he was always very susceptible to female charms, and her charms were very considerable. Certainly, too, there is a well-known tendency in some vigorous men who feel their youth receding to seek to preserve it, or win it back, through amorous involvement with a much younger person. These factors, however, could never fully account for the depth and permanence of Lloyd George's love for Frances; nor were they, indeed, the crucial factors. One powerful additional element in her appeal to him was that she had known Mair, and that she reminded him of the favourite daughter whom he never ceased to miss. Two years after their 'marriage' he told Frances, with what may have been disconcerting candour, that she had 'taken the place *somewhat* of Mair', for whose loss she made up '*a little*'.[2] A more self-assertive character might well have resented such words, and shown her resentment. But – and this was another of Frances's vital qualities for the role she had undertaken – she had a marvellously accommodating disposition. Her manner was quiet and comforting even to those who met her casually; to Lloyd George it was that of an adoring slave. Making it her business at all times to sustain his morale and ease his burdens, she paid him an

---

1. Frances Lloyd George, *op.cit.*, p. 51. She also records that when she gave notice of her intention to leave Allenswood, the headmistress raged: 'The man has upset me enough with his Insurance stamps, and now he takes away one of my staff.' (*ibid.*, pp. 51–2.) The reason Frances gave for leaving must, therefore, have been that she would be working for Lloyd George.

2. F.S.D., 21 January 1915, p. 23 (author's italics).

unremitting tribute of admiration and service, adapting herself to his imperious needs and erratic moods. Megan described her as 'like a thick pile carpet into which one's feet sank gratefully',[1] and anyone who spent any time in her company could appreciate the description. To Lloyd George she combined, therefore, some of the sweetness of Mair with the readiness to provide endless praise and reassurance which had made Uncle Lloyd indispensable to him. But whereas Uncle Lloyd was ageing and distant, Frances was young and constantly by his side.

Her constant presence was due, of course, to the fact that she was also able to perform – and very efficiently – the functions of a private secretary. Without her professional competence, her other qualities would not have been enough to win her the place that she came to occupy in his life. And her professional competence consisted of far more than shorthand and typing, and the systematic filing of documents (for which historians must ever be grateful to her). More significantly, she also had the intelligence and education to act as private secretary to a senior Cabinet minister, and before long to a Prime Minister. By the standards of her day she was a woman of most unusual accomplishments, and in more than one respect she had the advantage of Lloyd George himself. He, for instance, could not speak French, and had never attended a university.

Another point should be noted about her double role. Lloyd George was a man of strong sexual appetite, but the ruling passion of his life was politics. He gave more time and energy to his work than any other contemporary politician except Churchill, and he did not like to be distracted from it for long even by those pleasures and recreations that he most enjoyed. A serious love affair involving a lot of to-ing and fro-ing would not have suited him at all, and would have imposed a strain upon him that would soon have become intolerable. Beyond question such an affair would have had to be sacrificed to his work. Yet it did suit him to be in love, and to have a regular outlet for his affections. The romance with Frances was, to be sure, very important to him emotionally, but it was also very convenient practically, because he could see her almost every day without having to waste time going to visit her somewhere, or having to arrange a surreptitious meeting under his own roof. Even at weekends he could often have her

1. Said to author. Before Megan found out about her father and Frances, and then turned against her implacably, she was on close terms with her and had plenty of opportunity to observe her character.

company without prejudice to his work, by taking her with him to Walton Heath ostensibly – and up to a point actually – on business.

In hardly any sense can Frances be seen as a young edition of Margaret. It was because the two women he loved were so different that they were both necessary to him. They were, indeed, rather similar in their attitude to money, for both were distinctly keen on it. But that was just about the only resemblance. Margaret was wholly Welsh; Frances, though Celtic on her father's side, had not a drop of Welsh blood but, on the other hand, an heredity that was half Latin. She consoled herself for having no natural affinity with Lloyd George's Welshness by believing that he was really more like a Frenchman than a Welshman. In some ways this was true, but it was also true that in other ways he was very Welsh indeed; and in those ways he was, obviously, much closer to Margaret than to Frances. Margaret and he spoke the same language, were bred in the same culture, and grew up in the same inspiring neighbourhood. They had been married for a quarter of a century; indeed, their silver wedding anniversary fell only three days after he and Frances were 'married'. They had brought up their children in a Welsh-speaking home. Such bonds are not easily broken, and in any case he did not wish to break them.

Margaret, moreover, was on the level with him as Frances never quite was. This was partly because she had the status of wife, while Frances lacked even the status of mistress. But there was more to it than that. When Lloyd George was courting Margaret he was a young man unknown to the outside world; with a local reputation for cleverness, industry and ambition, but also for rather loose behaviour; with no money and uncertain prospects; and belonging to a Nonconformist denomination which her family regarded as inferior. By local standards she was a cut above him, and when she agreed to be his wife it could be felt that it was he rather than she who was making the 'good' marriage. By temperament, too, she was as proud and self-willed as he was, and she was never dazzled by his success. Both were spoiled as children by their families, and both went through life expecting to have their own way. Unequal though they were in talent, they were nevertheless equal in the freedom of spirit which they shared, and which each recognised and respected in the other.

To Frances, on the other hand, he was from the first a much older man who was also a world-famous politician. Inevitably she looked to him as father-figure as well as lover, and the disparity was never bridged, even when they had been together for many years. This was in the nature of the case, but her own character had quite a lot to do with it as well, because whereas Margaret's outward conventionalism masked an inner freedom, the opposite was true of Frances. In her – as in Ann Veronica – the New Woman was largely on the surface, concealing a woman of primordial instincts, naturally accepting a state of subjection to the male. Her relative tolerance of Lloyd George's casual infidelities, which to Margaret were a pain and outrage, may be seen, at least partly, as a by-product of her acceptance of inequality. And though she did not remain faithful to him, in the sexual sense, throughout the whole of their association, her love affair with another man when she was middle-aged did not alter her subordinate, not to say servile, relationship to Lloyd George in any other respect. Eventually she became his wife, and later still a countess; but nothing could make her the equal partner that Margaret was.

All the same, what Frances did for Lloyd George should on no account be underrated. It was brave of her to give her life to him, on his terms, in 1913; and the fact that she was far more conventional than she seemed makes her decision all the more courageous. She says herself that the terms on which he insisted 'were in direct conflict with [her] essentially Victorian upbringing', and that in her heart she 'wanted to marry and have a home and children'. Her parents, too, were understandably shocked by the affair; when she confessed to her mother, Mrs Stevenson quoted to her 'the classical words: "I would rather see you dead at my feet." ' To Frances's horror, her parents asked to see Lloyd George, and he – with typical boldness – asked them to dinner at 11 Downing Street. The party must have been one of the stickiest ever held there, and even his persuasive arts failed to move the Stevensons.[1] But they did not sever all contact with Frances. Perhaps, in spite of themselves, they could not help sharing a little of her excitement at being so close to the heart of things.

There was, of course, a large admixture of hero-worship in her love for Lloyd George, and she was also, to an indefinable degree, in

1. Frances Lloyd George, *op.cit.*, p. 52 and p. 56. According to Frances (p. 30), Mrs Stevenson was strangely Puritanical for a Frenchwoman, more especially in discouraging her daughters from making themselves attractive to the opposite sex. This was the more surprising since her own parents had led a Bohemian existence in Paris under the Second Empire. But one should perhaps remember that they had led it as husband and wife, not in the style of Rudolph and Mimi – or of Frances and Lloyd George.

At the end of her life Frances was a conspicuously pious and active laywoman in the diocese of Guildford.

love with the job he gave her, which in no other circumstances could she have hoped to obtain. But she also loved him for himself, and was on the whole more solicitous than Margaret in her ministrations to him. Like Mrs Timothy Davies ('Mrs Tim') – with whom he had, earlier, a quite protracted though altogether less profound affair, and with whom he remained on friendly terms – she knew how to create an atmosphere of comfort, and how much such an atmosphere meant to him. Margaret was in some ways an unsatisfactory wife. It was not her fault that she became very matronly with the passage of time, and so presumably lost much of her physical appeal to him. But it *was* her fault that she often failed to provide him with harmless luxuries that he liked, and that she so manifestly preferred her own life in North Wales to their life together in London. When he was a young M.P. she had often abandoned him for months on end, and though for the last ten years or so she had spent most of her time with him, at least while Parliament was sitting, it still seemed that she regarded Criccieth as her one true home, even if she had to be there without him.

In addition to the cover provided by Frances's appointment as a private secretary, Lloyd George's affair with her was further assisted by the cooperation of two other people: his housekeeper Sarah Jones, and a new Welshman in his office, J. T. Davies. Frances says that Sarah was a friend to her from the first, by whom her position in Downing Street was 'greatly eased and abetted'.[1] A very independent character, who had a mind of her own and did not hesitate to speak it, Sarah had been with the Lloyd Georges since 1901. Though she often scolded Lloyd George as a wayward child, she was, in fact, devoted to him and evidently felt that he deserved more looking-after than Margaret gave him. Not only in Downing Street, but at Walton Heath and, later, at Churt, she protected the lovers' interests and presided over her employer's alternative home. Near the end of his life there was a quarrel between them and she transferred her allegiance to Megan. All the same, she was among those who stood by his bedside when he was dying.

J. T. Davies succeeded John Rowland as Lloyd George's Welsh private secretary in April 1912, at the age of thirty, and remained associated with him until his own, rather premature, death in 1938. Like Rowland, he was Welsh-speaking and had earlier been a

1. Frances Lloyd George, *op.cit.*, pp. 72–3.

schoolmaster; but how and why he came to be appointed is not known. What is certain is that he became very useful to Lloyd George, not least because he was willing to handle business that a more scrupulous man might have found distasteful. Frances shared a room with him at the Treasury, and says that he 'took [her] under his wing from the first moment and was for ever afterwards [her] friend'.[1] This no doubt further commended him to Lloyd George.

Even with such inside help, however, the affair with Frances would have been impossible if the code governing the private lives of public men, and Press attention thereto, had been in Lloyd George's day what it later became. While he was in active politics, State and Press turned a blind eye to the extra-marital activities of politicians, so long as they were careful to keep out of the Divorce Court. This code was based upon two clear principles: that marriage was an institution whose maintenance was in the public interest, and that public men should therefore set an example by upholding it in their own lives. If a politician broke his own or somebody else's marriage, he knew that his career would be broken. But unless he was sued by his wife for divorce, or cited as co-respondent in another man's divorce suit, he could commit adultery with impunity, and without fear of publicity. It was lucky for Lloyd George that he lived when he did.

Sarah Jones and J. T. Davies may have been the first to know what was going on, but in the course of time a number of other people working with Lloyd George must have had, at least, some inkling of the truth, though remarkably few seem to have been fully aware of it. To Lloyd George's colleagues it must have seemed quite in character that he should appoint a woman secretary, and that he should like to have a pretty woman around to brighten the scene of his official labours.[2] But it probably never occurred to most of them that he was seriously in love with her; still less that he and Frances were living together. One likely exception was Riddell, who may well have perceived the essential facts at a very early stage. According to Frances, he had an 'insatiable curiosity, and he simply had, if possible,

---

1. Frances Lloyd George, *op.cit.*, pp. 57–8.
2. On 23 June 1907 a Mr Widdons of the War Office wrote to John Rowland, enclosing a copy of the Regulations regarding the appointment of lady typists to his department, and saying: 'I am afraid that even if the lady in whom Mr Lloyd George is interested possesses the necessary qualifications it is impossible to hold out any hope of early employment' (Earl Lloyd George collection). The lady in question is not named, but Mr Widdons's phraseology suggests that Lloyd George's reputation in Whitehall as a minister specially interested in ladies was already well established in 1907.

to get at one's private life, more, I think, because he liked to be able to form a complete picture of the person in question than from any morbid motive'. But he was a discreet man, and thoroughly loyal to Lloyd George.[1]

How soon Margaret really knew about the affair, it is impossible to say. She had learned to take her husband's roving eye for granted, and was painfully accustomed to his infidelities. Knowing him as she did, and being in any case a shrewd woman, she could hardly have failed to sense that something was going on between him and Frances even before their liaison was secretly formalised. She may have hoped, however, that it would prove to be no more than a passing fancy. If so, she had clearly ceased to entertain this hope three years later, for on 12 March 1916 Frances records in her diary:

> D. got into trouble the other day at W[alton] H[eath]. Mrs Ll.G. was outside the door while he was talking to me on the telephone, & took him severely to task. 'I know very well whom you would marry if anything happened to me', she said. D. tried to laugh it off, but he says she knows very well that his affection for me is real.

And in the entry for 13 January 1917 there is the first evidence of Margaret's total awareness:

> D. returned from W.H. very fit after weekend, though we had both been very miserable without each other. D. said he would have sent for me, only that he felt it would not quite be playing the game with Mrs Ll.G. 'She is very tolerant,' he said, 'considering that she knows everything that is going on. It is not right to try her too far.'

Margaret may have tolerated the relationship – while resenting it heart and soul – not only because she loved her husband and believed in his political mission, but also because she may have preferred a regular well-camouflaged affair within the household, as it were, to the sort of philandering outside affair that he had had before and would otherwise be all too liable to have again. One such was his affair with Julia Henry, which came to an end with significant abruptness in the autumn of 1911, after Frances had made her début at Criccieth and

1. Frances Lloyd George, *op. cit.*, p. 58. Riddell had been a solicitor before becoming a newspaper tycoon, and in his dealings with Lloyd George behaved more as a confidential adviser than as a journalist on the look-out for scoops.

Megan had been moved to Allenswood.

Julia was the wife of Sir Charles Henry (made a baronet in the 1911 New Year list), who was an Australian-born copper magnate and Liberal M.P. Her name before she married was Lewisohn, and her family was American Jewish. Lloyd George had known the Henrys since 1907. They had been very attentive to him at the end of that year, when he was staying in the South of France after Mair's death, and had since entertained him often in England, both at their London house and at their luxurious house near London, at Henley-on-Thames. They had also accompanied him on some of his more recent trips abroad. He certainly relished the creature comforts that they were able to provide, which before long included the personal favours of his hostess. But so far as he was concerned there was never any question of a serious romance. He found Julia attractive and was very willing to indulge in what seemed, to him, no more than an uninhibited flirtation. But that was all. Unfortunately her attitude was a good deal less light-hearted, and there were signs, even before the counter-attraction of Frances appeared, that he was beginning to regard their affair as an embarrassment. With the first appearance of Frances he was quick, therefore, to sever such amorous ties as had existed between himself and Julia.

Hers was the classic reaction of a woman scorned. After scenes with her husband which were evidently most unpleasant, she left for America in a near-hysterical state and, while crossing the Atlantic, poured out her indignation in a long letter to him, from which a few extracts should be quoted:

You know quite well how for so many years Mr Lloyd George valued our friendship, how in the hour of his sorrow he came [to] us for comfort. . . . You knew his attention to me, how he came to my box at the Opera, to lunch & dinner incessantly, even reading his speeches to me for my opinion. All this greatly flattered me as it would have *any* woman & he always said it was our kindness to him during his grief that enabled him to pull through. I have all his letters full of the greatest regard & gratitude. I do not wish to shield myself for any wrong I have done in allowing myself to be fascinated with his company. That was my misfortune that we ever met & that he admired me, & now unfortunately as you always say we cannot job backwards, it is the present situation that has to be dealt with. Without a word to me all of a sudden he shirked coming round & the humiliation I received from his treatment would be impossible to describe. It was not a question of his coming in to see me alone he could have come back with you to dinner. . . . During my illness you remember he never called once himself to enquire or sent any message. All this was the greatest pain to me. . . . Then although I implored of you not to do so you sent that letter giving him right on a matter you knew nothing about & refused to listen to, ridiculing women & their vagueries [sic] & hoped he would not allow such trivial things to upset him, & that my grievances were all imaginary. . . . I think that a man who is going to be ruler of England, one who is the idol of his colleagues & all those he comes in contact with should treat me with such discourtesy after all the kindness he has extracted is past my endurance. . . . I never wish to see him alone, but he owes me that respect & regard to come round with you once in three weeks or so. . . . We must let all bygones be bygones, & as an honourable woman & one who has cherished you & loved you dearly all these years I must demand at all sacrifice Mr Lloyd George's respect & regard, until I am assured of this I can never face England again. No harsh words or reproaches dear will have the slightest effect. I can write no further, I am too broken-hearted. . . .[1]

It is clear from this letter that Henry did not sympathise with his wife's fury against Lloyd George, and that her own wounded feelings were mixed with a desire to maintain at least the appearance of continuing friendship with him. So the makings of a reconciliation were there, and in due course Lloyd George reverted to visiting the Henrys at home, though much less frequently. Henry was useful to him, and a Parliamentary colleague whom he anyway rather liked; but

1. Julia Henry to Charles Henry, written on R.M.S. *Mauretania* and posted in New York on 21 November 1911 (N.L.W.). The first of Lloyd George's surviving letters to Julia, dated 16 August 1907, shows the bantering superficiality of his approach, which she apparently mistook for something deeper:

My dear Mrs Henry . . . How often have I meant to write but alas the cares of State have been unusually insistent & obtrusive. And moreover writing is so unsatisfactory a medium of conversation. There is so little you dare write which you would unhesitatingly say! . . . There is no knowing when we can get away. . . . Your glowing description of your balcony with the view to be enjoyed from it is very enticing – & full of all sorts of delightful possibilities which I dare not dwell upon lest I break away from this horrid convict establishment & escape there. Mr Henry & I are off to a theatre tonight – then an all night sitting – then to Porchester Gate [the Henrys' London house]. But we will miss the hostess – oh so much . . . With all best greetings, Ever sincerely D. Lloyd George. (N.L.W.)

it was over a year before he wrote again to Julia, when their relations were re-established on a more or less formal footing.

FOUR

Frustrated Campaigner

At the turn of the year 1912–13 there was a secret correspondence between Asquith and Lloyd George on the arguments for and against an early appeal to the country. The opposition was in temporary disarray on the issue of food taxes, and this encouraged the Prime Minister to suggest that a dissolution in April might be desirable. 'We should be free in the new Parlt to deal with the House of Lords, & Land questions, & Free Trade would be safe for another five years.' On the other hand he could see that the course would be risky, and that their supporters might not be keen 'to face the bother & expense of a new election so soon'. Lloyd George in his reply conceded that there were obvious advantages to be gained by dissolving 'before the present trade boom cracks up and the working classes drop into unemployment or low wages'. But he expected trade 'to remain good for another 12 months', and felt it would be a mistake to hold an election before the benefits of the Insurance Act were properly appreciated. 'There ought to be a carefully organised campaign on the Govt. record, Free Trade, Insurance, and our future programme. April allows no time for that to develop.' His view prevailed, partly no doubt because the crisis in the Conservative Party proved short-lived.[1]

---

1. H.H.A. to D.L.G., Christmas Day 1912, and D.L.G. to H.H.A. (copy), 28 December 1912 (L.G.P.) The threat of a disastrous split in the Opposition ranks, and of another leadership struggle, was ended early in the New Year when Bonar Law gave way, in effect, to the Free Fooders – showing that he cared more about party unity and the fight against Home Rule than about Imperial Preference.

True to his belief that the general economic climate would remain favourable, Lloyd George proposed no addition to the tax burden in the Budget which he introduced on 22 April 1913. Despite criticism, he relied upon the natural growth of revenue from existing taxes to cover a growth in expenditure estimated at £7,500,000; and his judgment was vindicated in the event. The total amount to be spent in the coming year he put at £195,640,000, describing the figure as 'colossal' and 'startling' – not only as an affectation of Gladstonian virtue for the benefit of old-fashioned Liberals, but because there was always in him a certain hankering for Retrenchment, which cohabited uneasily with his zeal for social reforming activity by the State. He deplored the 'sterile' expenditure on armaments, while stressing that this was 'dependent not on the will of Government or the House of Commons so much as on the concerted or rather competitive will of a number of great nations'. But he also referred proudly to the 'larger sums spent upon objects which give a promise of strength and happiness to the nation', such as an additional £20,000,000 during the past year to help the aged poor, the sick, the infirm and the unemployed.

During discussion of the Finance Bill he was attacked by Philip Snowden, on behalf of Labour, for allowing the cost of living to rise without a corresponding increase in wages, and for maintaining indirect taxes which bore most heavily upon the poor. Some Labour speakers even advocated an income tax on wage-earners as an alternative to taxes on food. This would certainly have been fairer but, as Lloyd George was quick to point out, politically hazardous; and as for Snowden's argument, he thought it would be wrong for any large section of the community to be exempt from taxation altogether.[1]

The shadow of the Parliament Act was to be seen in a decision to give effect to the Budget in two separate bills: a Finance Bill sufficiently narrow in its scope to incur no risk of being disqualified as a money bill within the meaning of the Act, and a Revenue Bill containing fiscal provisions of wider import. This dichotomy was to have baleful consequences the following year, but it was a dichotomy for which the Government itself was responsible, resulting from the unfortunate distinction between money and non-

1. Mallet and George, *British Budgets*, Second Series, pp. 3–19.

money bills enshrined in the Parliament Act. Another by-product of the conflict with the Lords was a measure put through by Lloyd George in 1913 to enable taxes to be collected, for a limited period, before a Finance Bill became law. From this, too, trouble would soon flow.

It was, indeed, rather absurd that Asquith should have been writing to Lloyd George about the necessity to 'deal with the House of Lords' only two years after an election had been fought and won on the issue of dealing with it, and less than eighteen months after the passage of a bill by which it should have been rendered innocuous to Liberal legislation. But such was the mortifying reality. In 1911 Lloyd George had talked privately of abolishing the House of Lords and getting along without a Second Chamber of any kind. Now he was prepared to speak openly of abolishing the existing House and substituting an entirely different sort of body:

> There is one reform which the action of the House of Lords has made essential, and that is the abolition of the present Second Chamber. The Prime Minister has already announced that next year he will introduce a measure for a new Second Chamber. It is not for me to say what it will be. One thing I can predict; it will be a Chamber in which all parties, all sections, all creeds will have equal treatment.[1]

This was not one of his more successful predictions.

The 'future programme' referred to in his letter to the Prime Minister was, however, above all the programme of comprehensive land reform on which he had set his heart, and to which the Cabinet was, in principle, committed. The urgent need now was to give this a detailed and persuasive content. It was easy enough to say, as he said at the end of January, addressing an audience of well-wishers:

> Foremost among the tasks of Liberalism in the near future is the regeneration of rural life and the emancipation of the land in this country from the paralysing grip of a rusty, effete and unprofitable

1. Speech at Caernarvon, 31 July 1913.

system. The land is the greatest, the most essential, of our national assets.[1]

But it was less easy to translate such rhetorical flourishes into hard policy. Even without the distraction of the Marconi enquiry during the first half of 1913, and the predictable distraction of the Budget, there would have been many obstacles to the formulation of specific proposals for the land. The subject itself was complex, more especially in its urban aspects. Lloyd George was well aware of the difficulty of changing British institutions and British ways, for however manifestly good a cause. When introducing Old Age Pensions in 1908 he had referred to the problem of hacking a path 'through the inextricable tangle of an old society like ours'. Yet Old Age Pensions was a simple and straightforward affair compared with National Health Insurance, and even that was perhaps less involved, less bedevilled by competing interests, less fraught with hidden snares, than a national programme for land reform.

The virtual impossibility of dealing with the land on an integral basis was, in effect, conceded by Lloyd George himself when he appointed separate committees to investigate the problems of town and country. Even so, he might have been able to present something that could have passed as an integrated programme if the two committees had completed their work at the same time, and if the Liberal Party had been united on the various issues subsumed under the general heading of 'the land'. But there was no such synchronisation, and no such unity. Both committees took much longer over their work than Lloyd George had originally intended, but whereas the Rural Report was published in early October 1913, the Urban Report did not appear until April of the following year.

This delay reflected not only the greater complexity of the matters under investigation, but also human and financial difficulties in the

1. Speech at the National Liberal Club, 31 January 1913. The occasion was the presentation to the Club of Lloyd George's portrait by Christopher Williams, paid for by Welsh members of the Club and a few other Welshmen. He began his speech by saying that when he had first visited the Club twenty-five years before he had been particularly impressed by 'the stately and solemn figures which adorned the walls'. But 'had I any notion at the time that, twenty-five years later, my own would be there, I do not think that they would have inspired me with quite the same awe'. Presiding at the dinner was Lord Lincolnshire, Lord Privy Seal and a large landowner, who – Lloyd George was 'delighted to hear' – agreed with his approach.

conduct of the inquiry.[1] As for opinion within the Party, there was, first of all, a basic conflict between radicals of all kinds and those Liberals who, to put it mildly, felt no enthusiasm for higher taxation of the rich or further extensions of State power. But the radicals themselves were divided, some favouring site-value taxation, not least as a means of breaking the 'land monopoly' and forcing land on to the market, others preferring land purchase by the State. Those, moreover, to whom land ownership seemed the principal issue could not ignore the fact that, although rural freeholders were overwhelmingly Tory, many urban freeholders were Liberal – as were the holders of many urban long leases. There were differing views on tenancy, on wages, on housing, and on the machinery for enforcement or arbitration. Lloyd George had no precise idea what he wanted to achieve, but knew the direction in which he wanted to move, and anyway had learned from his experience with National Health Insurance that even a planned reform might have to undergo drastic alteration before it could be implemented. He was therefore very hopeful that, once his new campaign had been launched, the necessary changes would gradually take shape and would constitute, in the end, a most beneficent whole.

An advance copy of the Rural Report was in his hands in mid-August, and confirmed most of his hunches, or prejudices, about the conditions of life and work on the land. Most agricultural labourers were shown to be receiving less than 18s. a week, and many less than 16s. a week. Standards of housing were appallingly low, and the incidence of disease high. The Report recommended that a decent wage should be enforced by tribunals, though no indication was given as to how the tribunals should be composed. It was also suggested that there might be land courts to which tenant farmers could appeal against wage awards which they considered unfair, or against landowners threatening them with unfair eviction.

Armed with this Report, and with evidence gleaned from other sources, Lloyd George finally launched his long-heralded Campaign on Saturday 11 October, at Bedford. He made two speeches that day, both at the Skating Rink, and both to entirely Liberal audiences. The first was in the afternoon, lasting over two-and-a-quarter hours, and

1. De Forest withdrew his support when it became apparent to him that he was only needed for his money. New backers for the Urban Enquiry included the American-Jewish soap millionaire Joseph Fels, who was also a generous patron of Keir Hardie.

addressed to 2,500 Liberal delegates; the second, in the evening, lasting about thirty-five minutes, to a less select audience of 4,000. The chairman, Lord Beauchamp (who, as First Commissioner of Works, was a member of the Cabinet), explained at the outset that Lloyd George would be speaking on behalf of the Government, and with the Prime Minister's authorisation.

By far the largest part of both speeches was devoted to attacking the existing system, with special chastisement for landowners who were also peers. One-third of the land of England belonged to the House of Lords, he said – with a pleasant smile, no doubt, to the chairman as he said it. He also spoke with his usual indignation of the way so much of the land was reserved for sport, but on this occasion added a colourful detail – that the mangold-wurzels of hard-working farmers were eaten by hungry pheasants – which earned him the derision of most countrymen and was used against him, if only in fun, for the rest of his life.

The constructive part of his remarks was as brief as it was vague. There had to be a living wage for labourers, and fair hours of work. Cultivators, large and small, had to be protected against the confiscation of improvements. They must also have access to good professional advice, and be helped with the marketing of their produce. Greater facility must be given to the State for the acquisition of land. Finally there was this significant hint of a major reform of local taxation: 'The present system of rating, in so far as it discourages improvement by either owner or cultivator, and rewards the indolent or unenterprising or overcrowding owner who declines to put his land to the best use, must be reconsidered and recast.'

All in all, Bedford cannot be numbered among Lloyd George's triumphs. Neither the tone nor the balance of his oratory was right for the occasion. The *Times* report the following Monday was damning:

Disappointment was undoubtedly the feeling of many, even of the selected Liberal delegates, who were present. Mr Lloyd George spoke with all his accustomed skill, and made his points effectively. He was not personally vituperative (except when he referred to Mr Leo Maxse as 'the cat's meat of the Tory Party'), but his address was inspired throughout by what it is only possible to call a savage rancour against the landowners, the House of Lords, and 'the Tories' . . . all of whom he assailed collectively, indifferently, and at times, it seemed, interchangeably.[1]

And if *The Times*, as an Opposition paper, may be suspected of biased reporting, this account sent to Walter Runciman, Minister of Agriculture, is harder to impugn:

I will jot down my impressions of the Bedford meeting before they can be distorted by reading newspaper reports. I am glad I went, and still more glad that you did not. For . . . George's speech was certainly not a triumph. Has his magnetic power left him? I saw no signs of it yesterday. He had a fine reception, but during his long speech the audience was almost bored; there was applause certainly but never very hearty, nothing like what I have heard at much smaller meetings in 1904–5. There was no wild enthusiasm. He stated the case on insufficient wages and bad housing well and convincingly, but he spoilt it by omitting the argument that a sufficiently paid and decently housed labourer is a more efficient labourer, and by wandering off the main point. Crofters and deer-forests have nothing to do with agricultural land in England and Wales, and no one was interested to hear that labourers were better paid in the time of Henry VII than now. He spent an hour and a half telling us what we either knew very well before or did not want to know . . . The impatient voices asked – what are your remedies? and I don't think they were quite satisfied with the answer. There was little applause, and when at the end he suggested that they should

1. *The Times*, 13 October 1913. That Leo Maxse should have been singled out for personal asperity is perhaps understandable in view of this letter from him to Lloyd George dated 10 October 1913:

Sir,

I trust that when you are inside your fortifications at Bedford you will answer the following questions of public interest upon which there is widespread curiosity. . . .

1. Did the Master of Elibank, with whom you had a 'common venture' in American Marconis at £2 on April 17th 1912, conceal from you the fact that he was purchasing the same as Trustee of the Radical Party funds at £3.5.0 per share on the following day, April 18th?

2. Were you aware that while you and your colleagues were engaged in settling the Coal Strike in March 1912 the Master of Elibank was investing some £20,000 of Party funds in Home Railway Stock – securities peculiarly liable to be affected by the course of ministerial negotiations?

I beg to remain,
Yours faithfully,
L. J. Maxse

(Earl Lloyd George collection, N.L.W.)

read in Monday's papers what he had said there was not a very sympathetic laugh. Of course he was in a difficult position having to make the opening speech of the campaign without a clearly defined policy of reform; but I think he would have done better if he had refrained from back-handed hits at the landlord class. There are plenty of landlords who admit the case for reform. I believe you are more likely to get your reforms carried . . . using for political purposes at the next General Election the Old Age Pensions argument that Liberals are doing what Tories said they wanted to see done but did not do. . . .[1]

'There are plenty of landlords who admit the case for reform' – this was, indeed, a prime weakness in Lloyd George's polemical stance by the time his Land Campaign came to be launched. We saw earlier how the first signs of his intention to highlight the land as an issue caused apprehension among Unionist politicians, and during the sixteen months or so which had elapsed since then they had not been idle. They had conducted a private inquiry of their own and had produced a statement of policy. Nor was their motive simply defensive; they had a genuine interest in reviving agriculture, and some of them were prepared to contemplate quite radical measures. When Lloyd George attacked landowning dukes at Limehouse in 1909 he could reasonably claim to be counter-attacking in defence of his Budget, which the Conservatives were threatening to destroy by means of their exclusive weapon, the House of Lords. Moreover, he was then attacking landowners from an urban point of view, and in an urban setting. The political and other circumstances of the Limehouse speech justified its character – though even then it would have gone down considerably less well had it been delivered in a country town. What is certain is that oratory of a similar character, deployed four years later, and at Bedford, was quite inappropriate and a serious error of judgment on his part.

The rural land problem was now susceptible of a large degree of inter-party agreement, and in his heart Lloyd George knew that this was so. He had shown that he knew it, in his speech at the National Liberal Club, back in January:

A great Conservative landowner said to me: 'I have no doubt that, when your proposals come out, I shall condemn them. I have no

<hr>

1. Arthur Gage to Walter Runciman, 12 October 1913 (Runciman Papers).

THE LAND "CAMPAIGN."

Scoutmaster Asquith (to Scout George of the "Pheasant" Patrol). "WHAT HAVE YOU TO REPORT?"
Scout George. "THE ENEMY IS ON OUR SIDE, SIR."
Scoutmaster Asquith. "THEN LET THE BATTLE BEGIN!"

["Whatever can be done to improve the lot of the agriculturist will have the Opposition's cordial support."—*Pall Mall Gazette.*]

From *Punch*, 17 December 1913

doubt that I shall be very angry with your methods and that I shall find your language intolerable. All the same I am glad that you have taken this in hand.' It will create in politics [Lloyd George said] what this landowner called an agricultural atmosphere, which is what he has been waiting for for some time.

And even at Bedford – in his shorter, evening, speech – he gave the show away when he admitted, in a flurry of mixed metaphors, that 'the land had been manured with Tory programmes', and that 'before a shot was fired they had run four-fifths of the way', adding, in the same speech: 'If they like to agree to settle this problem, we will work with them. But it must be a real agreement and a real settlement.' It was hard to reconcile such language with the language of denunciation and commination of which his two Bedford speeches largely consisted. The rural Land Campaign suffered at the outset from being – on its author's own implied admission – essentially rather a sham fight.[1]

Yet he persevered with it, and on 22 October, at Swindon, announced that the Government was planning to set up, in place of the Ministry of Agriculture, a new Ministry of Lands and Forests, which would assume responsibility for small-holdings, land purchase and the development of land-based industries, as well as for the land valuation instituted in his 1909 Budget. Land Commissioners would be appointed to arbitrate in matters of wages, rents and tenure, and to authorise loans for housing and development. They would also have the power to acquire land, which they could begin to exercise when the valuation was complete in 1915.

Before his next big speech, at Middlesbrough, Lloyd George was sharply reminded of the need to explain the relevance of his campaign to town-dwellers. Charles Trevelyan, a leading member of the land reform group in Parliament, wrote to him on 2 November:

I see that you are going to speak at Middlesbrough at the end of this week. I suppose that you intend to deal with the land question in

1. Much of the hard thinking on the Unionist side was done by Lord Milner, whose approach to agricultural problems was no less radical than Lloyd George's. Before long they would be tackling such problems, and many others, together as War Cabinet colleagues. Another intriguing pointer to the future was that the Duke of Bedford contributed £1,000 to the Conservatives' agricultural enquiry. This cannot have been done without the knowledge, and may well have been done at the suggestion, of the Duke's agent-in-chief, R. E. Prothero – who within a few years was to be Lloyd George's Minister of Agriculture.

urban districts. I want to urge you very strongly not to delay any longer declaring yourself in general terms at least in favour of land values as the proper basis of local rating . . . To masses of Liberals this is now an essential part of their creed.

Even without such a reminder Lloyd George would hardly have been likely to talk about mangold-wurzels at Middlesbrough. But when he spoke there on 8 November he certainly tried hard to make his Campaign appealing to an urban audience, while insisting that town and country were interdependent. The rural policy was vital to the towns, he said, and the urban policy equally vital to the country. The land was 'the key to all social reform'. Municipalities must be enabled to acquire it easily, not below its value, but at its value. Trevelyan was partially satisfied, writing next day to another land campaigner that Lloyd George was 'beginning to realise fully the overpowering evil of the high prices of land', and that he had 'grasped as clearly as any of us the evil of rating on improvements'.[1]

His most successful speech of the Campaign was made in the unlikeliest of places: the Oxford Union Society. On 21 November he spoke there against the motion that 'This House has no confidence in the Land Policy of His Majesty's Government'. As he entered the building a large pheasant was thrown at him and hit him on the head. Inside, he had to sway an audience made up, very largely, of the sons of political opponents. He told them that land was selling at a higher price than it had commanded for years, despite his 1909 Budget. And he allowed them to perceive the moderation and desire for united action that underlay his apparently bitter polemics:

I am represented as a very violent partisan, making partisan speeches simply drenched with partisanship. Let me say this to you, speaking as an old man to young men; this country is governed by party. Party has become an essential part of government. Many men have tried to get their ideas through without associating themselves with party, and they have always failed, because party government is an essential part of the government of this country.

1. As at Bedford, Lloyd George made two speeches at Middlesbrough, one in the afternoon, the other in the evening; both at the Hippodrome. One argument that he used was that some industrial workers, at least, should live in the country and commute (a word not yet used, however, in this sense). He cited the example of Belgium, no doubt with Seebohm Rowntree's *Land and Labour, Lessons from Belgium* (1911) in mind. The letters from Trevelyan are quoted in A. J. A. Morris, *C. P. Trevelyan: Portrait of a Radical*, p. 94.

You might as well try to cross from here to Vancouver without using the machinery of transport – the railway or sea provided for you – as try to get anything through in this country without party government. *I sometimes honestly deplore it. There are many things which, if you could get a party truce for five years, you could get through and transform this land.*

The undergraduates listening to him were not to know that in 1910 he had tried, secretly, to bring a coalition government into being for just such a purpose. But they were so influenced by his speech that at the end of the debate the motion condemning his policy was defeated by a majority of sixty-eight. The seconder of the motion, a future Conservative Cabinet minister, wrote to him afterwards:

Lest I should seem ungrateful, let me thank you at once for your extremely generous and kindly treatment of my speech. Although I have not yet fulfilled your prophecy by becoming a Radical, I must admit that now that I have met you, I shall have to make considerable alterations in my platform perorations.[1]

Another who attended the debate and heard Lloyd George with admiration was a future Conservative Prime Minister, Harold Macmillan (who, incidentally, voted against the motion[2]).

The penultimate major speech in the Land Campaign was at Holloway on 29 November, when Lloyd George raised for the first time the idea of leasehold enfranchisement. Finally, on 3 February 1914, in Glasgow, he announced that the Government had decided on the principle of rating site values, to which it would give effect in legislation. This announcement marks, if not the end of the Land Campaign, at any rate the beginning of another process into which it gradually became merged: the preparation of, and the struggle over, Lloyd George's 1914 Budget.

Hopes that the Land Campaign would give a quick boost to the Liberal Party's fortunes were certainly not fulfilled. Somehow it never quite caught on, and as a means of diverting public attention from the Irish question it failed almost totally. On 8 November, about a month after the Bedford meetings, there was a by-election at Reading, caused by Rufus Isaacs's controversial appointment as Lord Chief Justice.

1. Walter Monckton to D.L.G., 23 November 1913 (L.G.P.)
2. Private information. He was a Liberal at the time.

The result was a heavy defeat for the Liberals, with the Conservatives winning the seat, and with evidence, too, of many Liberal voters defecting to Labour. Three more Liberal seats were lost during the winter: South Lanarkshire in December, Bethnal Green and Leith in February. At Bethnal Green the casualty was Charles Masterman, whose promotion to the Cabinet – as Chancellor of the Duchy of Lancaster – was his undoing. Obliged (by a rule in force until after the Great War) to re-contest the seat, he lost it by a narrow margin. This began a run of bad luck which effectively destroyed his career. In May he lost again, at Ipswich, and in February 1915, after further attempts to find a seat had come to nothing, he resigned his office.

The Land Campaign was very little discussed by the Cabinet as a whole, and the Prime Minister himself considered it only intermittently. Lloyd George, for the most part, improvised it as he went along, in accordance with sketchy guidance from his colleagues or, quite often, going out ahead of them and trusting that they would follow. There had been no meeting of the Cabinet during the two months before he spoke at Bedford, though he had travelled all the way to Arran to tell the Prime Minister what he proposed to say and to obtain his general approval – on the strength of which Beauchamp was able to describe what he would be saying as a statement of Government policy. Between Bedford and Swindon the Cabinet twice discussed the subject and concluded that agricultural wages, the protection of tenants and other such matters could only be dealt with by commissioners acting under the existing Board of Agriculture or a new Land Ministry. No firm decision, however, was taken in this sense, and Lloyd George's announcement at Swindon that there would be a new Ministry, and that there would be land commissioners, was typical of his way of forcing the pace.

The Cabinet was divided on the merits of the Land Campaign. Harcourt was thoroughly opposed to it, and some others regarded it without enthusiasm. But the majority, including the Prime Minister, Grey and Haldane, gave it broad support. (The idea of land commissioners, as an alternative to wages boards, was in fact Haldane's.) Though there was no further formal discussion of the issue in Cabinet until the following spring, it came up, of course, at informal meetings of ministers; and on 9 December, at the National Liberal Club, Asquith endorsed the principles of a living wage for farm labourers and the compulsory acquisition of land by public authorities.

To make any significant impact in the countryside the Land

Campaign had to appeal to tenant farmers as well as farm labourers, so isolating the landowners. But this it largely failed to do. The tenant farmers were content enough to be offered increased security of tenure, but they had no wish to see the traditional pattern of owner-ship changed. On 6 February 1914 a deputation from the National Farmers' Union told Lloyd George that their members were in accord with the Government's policy 'except on the question of State-aided land purchase'. In their opinion, said the union's secretary, 'no farmer was better off than the farmer who was a tenant under a good landlord'. If Lloyd George had been at all serious when he once remarked to Isaacs that the country districts were ripe for revolution, the N.F.U's attitude must have helped to undeceive him.

Meanwhile, as we have seen, he was being pressed to give more attention to the needs and interests of urban voters, and he had also to turn his mind to the preparation of a Budget for 1914. On 12 November 1913 Asquith, Grey, Crewe and Haldane were his guests for a working dinner at 11 Downing Street, at which the financial and political outlook was discussed. Lloyd George submitted estimates for the following year, showing that there would be a £10 million deficit if Churchill's naval programme went through uncut, and if the Board of Education got the £2 million it wanted for grants. His colleagues expressed 'very strong feeling' against increased taxation before the next election. As to the timing of this, Asquith and Grey favoured a dissolution in 1914, but Lloyd George 'urged that it was a question of tactics that could not be determined so many months in advance'.[1]

The New Year began with a struggle between Lloyd George and Churchill over the naval estimates, from which Churchill emerged the winner. As a result, the Budget had to allow for naval expenditure more than £5 million up on the previous year's. This was one reason why Lloyd George's colleagues found, when they were given a rough idea of his Budget plans towards the end of April, that he would be asking for nearly £9,800,000 in new revenue, additional to the expec-ted increase through natural growth: a figure obviously very close to the £10 million he had mentioned back in November. So much for his colleagues' desire that there should be no tax rise. On the civilian side,

1. Lloyd George's note of points discussed at the dinner (L.G.P.). When the party broke up at midnight, Grey and Haldane described it as 'the best and most useful discussion we have ever had as a Cabinet' – an illuminating comment, perhaps, on ordinary Cabinet meetings at the time.

however, Education was not to be such an important factor as he had then suggested. The main reason, apart from the Navy, for his big revenue requirement was that he had decided on a bold scheme for altering fundamentally both the rating system and the relation between central and local finance.

Site-value rating was recommended by the Urban Report, published at long last in April; but Lloyd George had already committed himself to this measure in his Glasgow speech. The purpose of it was to make the ground landlord carry a fair share of the burden, and to give some relief to the improving tenant. It was not proposed that the whole burden of rates should be transferred from premises to sites, but that 'the taxation of site value should henceforth form an integral part of the system of local taxation'. At the same time Lloyd George's scheme provided for Exchequer grants to a total of £11 million in a full year, which would reduce the amount that local authorities had to raise in rates by, on average, 9d. in the £. One effect would be to compensate them for the partial derating of improvements. Moreover, these grants would be differentiated according to the wealth or poverty of an area, so that authorities with limited rating resources would not thereby be handicapped in the provision of services. Temporary grants of £2,500,000 were to be voted for 1914–15, so that the scheme could come into operation before the next financial year. The valuation set in train by the 1909 Budget was to be adapted so that site value and development value would be separately recorded, and it was Lloyd George's optimistic belief that the process could still be completed by 1915.

To meet the new demands he planned to rely exclusively upon direct taxation, carrying further the principle that the rich should pay proportionately more. Income tax was to be graduated from 9d. in the £ for earned incomes under £1,000 to 1s. 4d. for earned incomes over £2,500. 1s. 4d. was also to be the general rate for unearned income: an increase of twopence. Supertax, introduced in 1909, was now to be graduated as well. Starting at the lower level of £3,000 a year (compared with £5,000), the scale would rise from 5d. in the £ to a top rate of 1s. 4d. on incomes above £8,000: all, of course, in addition to income tax. Finally, there was to be steeper progression in the scale of death duties, with the maximum rate, on estates in excess of £1 million, rising from 15 to 20 per cent. And the distinction, for tax purposes, between settled and non-settled estates was to be abolished.

These changes were meant to produce £8,800,000 of additional revenue, or £1 million short of the required amount. For the extra £1 million Lloyd George proposed to raid the Sinking Fund, arguing that the rate of debt redemption since the Liberals returned to power had been unprecedented, and that he did not feel justified in imposing fresh taxation merely to maintain such a high rate. He introduced the Budget on 4 May, in a speech whose lack of clarity reflected the complex nature of his proposals and the haste with which they had been put together. His Budget speech in 1909 had been a poor performance, as a speech, but in 1914 he did even worse. Moreover, the Budget itself, for all its merits, soon ran into even more serious trouble than its famous precursor.

The trouble was of two kinds. First, there were the procedural toils resulting from the Parliament Act, and therefore self-inflicted by the Government. Lloyd George knew that he could not get his reform of local government finance carried in a separate Revenue Bill (techni-cally not a 'money bill') within the existing Parliament, because it would almost certainly be blocked by the House of Lords and would not then have enough time to pass in spite of the veto. Yet if the scheme were included in the Finance Bill (a 'money bill'), its effect might well be to invalidate the bill as such. A further complication, for which he was more directly responsible than for the flaws in the Parliament Act, was that because of his own Provisional Collection of Taxes Act of the previous year it was necessary for the Finance Bill to be enacted by 5 August, long before there could be any possibility of passing legislation to authorise the new Exchequer grants. In voting for the Bill M.P.s would, therefore, be voting for taxes to finance a scheme as yet unsanctioned by Parliament. Faced with this difficulty, Lloyd George suddenly changed course and included his local govern-ment scheme in the Finance Bill. This was then challenged by a Conservative backbencher as unconstitutional, and the Speaker ruled that it was so.

Already, however, the Cabinet had decided to retreat in face of the other kind of trouble which the Budget had aroused – trouble from an influential group of Liberals in Parliament. The 1909 Budget, once agreed in Cabinet, had encountered little resistance from the Govern-ment's own ranks. Such opposition as there had been – mainly to the land clauses – had been relatively small-scale and half-hearted. But the Budget of 1914 was opposed by about forty Liberal M.P.s, who not only disliked the rating of site values but also objected to the whole trend of financial and social policy as promoted by Lloyd George. The leader of this group was a Liverpool shipowner, Richard Holt, and it consisted largely of other rich men – among them, ironically, Baron de Forest. Their opposition, combined with the procedural problems, was too much for the Government, and on 22 June it was decided to drop the local government scheme from the Finance Bill. The temporary grants were abandoned altogether, the permanent grants 'postponed'. As a further sop to the rebels the new rate of income tax on unearned incomes was brought down from 1s. 4d. to 1s. 3d.

These drastic concessions were, of course, a great disappointment to the Government's radical supporters, and to Labour. But the Finance Bill remained a far-reaching measure, still comparable with that of 1909; and on 31 July, after much use of the guillotine, it became law. During his six years as Chancellor before the outbreak of war Lloyd George had been true to his intention to broaden the State's sphere of responsibility, to use the Budget unashamedly as an instrument of social reform, and to make sure that the heaviest burden was borne by those who could bear it most easily. Whereas direct and indirect taxation used to account for roughly equal shares of the revenue, under his stewardship the proportion contributed by indirect taxes had been reduced until, after the 1914 Budget, it represented less than 40 per cent of the total. And the more than 60 per cent that was being paid in direct taxes was being paid, preponderantly, by the rich. It was not, moreover, only the poor who benefited; the middle classes benefited as well. Even after the 1914 Budget the large majority of income-tax payers were less heavily taxed than they had been when the Liberals came into power.[1]

In March, faced with a particularly daunting Budgetary task, while also – as we shall see – deeply involved in the growing Irish crisis, Lloyd George had a recurrence of the throat trouble which had plagued him before in times of frustration and stress. But his natural resilience soon prevailed over what was, it seems, essentially a nervous complaint. After spending Easter at Criccieth, he returned to

1. Bruce K. Murray, *The People's Budget 1909/10: Lloyd George and Liberal Politics*, pp. 310–11. Middle-class taxpayers were favoured by the effects of graduation. When the Liberals took office income tax stood at 1s. in the £, and was undifferentiated.

Speaking on 26 June 1914, at a dinner to celebrate the Budget – *after* the local government scheme had been dropped from it – Haldane could still describe it as 'the greatest Budget which Mr Lloyd George has yet produced'. In his own speech at the dinner, Lloyd George said that Haldane deserved much of the credit. He also made this comment: 'Disraeli boasted that he had educated his Party; I can boast that I have educated the Opposition.'

London for the first round of the Parliamentary struggle over the Budget. At Whitsun he was at Criccieth again, and Asquith was staying nearby, at Penrhôs in Anglesey, where he was the guest of Lord and Lady Sheffield, parents of his young confidante, Venetia Stanley. From there he wrote to his wife, Margot, on Wednesday 3 June:

> [Edwin] Montagu drove over to Criccieth to see Ll. George yesterday with one or two messages from me. The result is that Ll. George has invited himself here and arrives this evening: perhaps till Friday. I didn't want to see him particularly, as it rather spoils the holiday atmosphere, and all he has to say can keep till London.

But Lloyd George came, and seems not to have spoilt the holiday atmosphere, for Asquith wrote again on 4 June:

> Ll. George arrived here yesterday in time for lunch, & afterwards we went to the links & played a foursome. . . . We had quite a good game. Ll. George drives quite well & is not bad with his iron, but is an execrable putter. He is in very good conversational form and made himself agreeable to the Sheffields after his fashion. They did not know him before & old S. has a considerable aversion for him politically.

He and Asquith could nearly always get on well if left to themselves. Though never kindred spirits, they had an easy and friendly working relationship so long as others did not interfere and make mischief between them.

It has been said that Lloyd George's partial defeat over the 1914 Budget was a sign that the Liberal Government had come to the end of its tether as a reforming force. Certainly, the loss of the rating and grants scheme was a most unfortunate setback, but there is no reason at all to assume that it would have been permanent if the War had not supervened. (In the event, it did prove permanent, and the rating system remains a very live political issue nearly seventy years later, with site-value rating a principle in which many still believe.) The Liberals did not have to go to the country until the end of 1915, so in normal circumstances one more Budget would have been available to Lloyd George before an election. Apart from the temporary grants for 1914, his idea was only that his scheme should be postponed. The rich Liberals who helped to sabotage it in Parliament were by no means, he thought, representative of opinion in the Party at large; and the evidence suggests that he was right. If the scheme had been reintroduced at leisure, as it were, in a Revenue Bill, and then rejected by the House of Lords, it might well have given the Liberals a good issue on which to fight the next election. And if they had won, by however small a margin, the impulse would surely not have been lacking for a further burst of reforming activity.

To have a fair chance of winning, however, they needed a continuation of prosperity. If trade had turned bad, or if the economy had been damaged by massive strikes, they would have been most unlikely to win the election. Above all, they needed an Irish settlement, or at least some accommodation in the Irish quarrel, for without this their regime would have perished, not through any loss of reforming vigour, but as a consequence of having led the country into the agony of civil war. Ireland was the domestic issue that most threatened to destroy them, and it was an issue to which, in the immediate pre-war period, Lloyd George had increasingly to give his attention.

FIVE

First Involvement with Ireland

After the Lords' rejection of Lloyd George's 1909 Budget, Asquith had committed himself and his Party more or less unequivocally to Irish Home Rule; and after the election of January 1910 the Liberals were, in any case, dependent upon the Irish National Party for a majority in Parliament. But until the House of Lords was reformed, or its absolute veto removed, there was no way of giving the Irish what they wanted, and it turned out that the January election had not, after all, decided that issue. Another had to be fought at the end of the year to give the Liberals a mandate for limiting the veto, and even then it was not until August 1911 that the Parliament Act was passed, under threat of a mass creation of peers. Early in the next session the Asquith Government's Home Rule Bill was, therefore, introduced, and in the ordinary course of events under the Parliament Act it was hoped to get it through by June 1914. But with such a bill, and on such an issue, the course of events could not be ordinary.

The Unionists' zeal in defence of the veto had been due far less to their belief in hereditary privilege than to their passionate opposition to Home Rule. This was a cause which united them, whereas their other major policy, Tariff Reform, tended to divide them. They also knew that Home Rule was definitely unpopular in Great Britain, whereas Tariff Reform would only be popular if there were a trade recession. The Liberals, for their part, were markedly less united in support of Home Rule than the Unionists were against it. During their decade in the wilderness between 1895 and 1905 they had come to regard it as an insuperable obstacle to their return to power, and in the

1906 election they were not committed to introducing it in the next Parliament. But when the Lords rejected the Budget at the end of November 1910, the Irish, who were by no means enamoured of the Budget, were suddenly placed in a very strong bargaining position. The Liberals' extremity became their opportunity, and their leader, John Redmond, was able to insist upon a firm commitment to Home Rule. Hence Asquith's declaration at the Albert Hall, on 10 December, that it was Liberal policy, 'while explicitly safeguarding the supremacy and indefeasible authority of the Imperial Parliament', to 'set up in Ireland a system of full self-government in regard to purely Irish affairs.'

Asquith was far from being an ardent Home Ruler. It was very much under his influence that Campbell-Bannerman refrained from pledging the party to Home Rule in 1906, and earlier, in 1901, Asquith had stated publicly that the Liberals should never again take office if they had to depend upon the Irish for a majority. He was, therefore, a Home Ruler by necessity rather than conviction, and convinced Unionists had some reason to feel indignant against him, more especially when, in the second election of 1910, he delayed repeating his Home Rule pledge until many of the election results were declared. He was, moreover, one of 188 (out of 272) successful Liberal candidates in that election who had not mentioned Home Rule in their election addresses. All the same, the Unionists certainly played Home Rule up in the election, even if many Liberals tried to play it down, and there could be no denying the existence of a substantial Home Rule majority in the new Parliament, since, in addition to 272 Liberals and 74 Redmondites, the 42 Labour M.P.s had also to be counted as supporters of the Irish cause.

Among those Liberals who did not mention Home Rule in their election addresses, another was Lloyd George. Yet at heart he was more of a Home Ruler than Asquith, partly because he was a Celt, but also because he strongly favoured local autonomy within the United Kingdom and Empire. He was, it is true, repelled by the narrow tribalism which seemed too prevalent in the Irish national movement, and by the hint of separatism in Parnell's celebrated speech at Cork in 1885, when he had said: 'No man has a right to fix the boundary of the march of a nation. No man has a right to say, "Thus far shalt thou go and no farther." And we have never attempted to fix the *ne plus ultra* to the progress of Ireland's nationhood, and we never shall.' Lloyd George was very proud of Wales's distinctness and cultural identity, but never carried his Welsh patriotism to the point of suggesting that Wales might become a separate nation-state. To him, the British Empire and the United Kingdom did not restrict, but on the contrary enhanced, Welsh nationality. Of course he claimed a full and equal share for Welshmen in the life of the larger communities, but he accepted that there was a *ne plus ultra* to Wales's progress as a nation, and saw no reason why what was good enough for Wales should not be good enough for Ireland.

Nevertheless he genuinely wanted Home Rule for Ireland, within the pattern of 'Home Rule All Round'. And he wanted it, if possible, for a united Ireland. The only time he ever set foot in the country, when he visited Belfast in 1907 as President of the Board of Trade, he attacked separatism while asserting the Imperial role of Ireland as a nation:

> Ireland has a great and distinguished part to play in maintaining in peace that great commonwealth of nations which we refer to as the British Empire. . . . To sever the bonds – why, it would be a loss to Ireland. It would be a greater loss to the Empire. The greatest loss would be to humanity, if you confine the brilliant genius of Ireland within the bounds of an island, when you have hundreds of millions of the human race who would be benefited by your taking a full share in the direction of the British Empire. Do not be deluded by extravagant talk into the belief that anybody means to cut the painter between Britain and Ireland'.[1]

His intention was, no doubt, partly to reassure Protestant Ulstermen that the Union was in no danger from a Liberal Government, but the sentiments were authentically his own, and deeply felt. He was saying what he believed, and always would believe.

It is sadly noteworthy, by the way, that he visited Ireland only once in his life, and that he had to say, in Belfast, that he was the first Cabinet Minister to be visiting Ulster for more than twenty years. One of the most lamentable absurdities of the British record in Ireland during the time that the Act of Union was in force was that so few leading British politicians had any first-hand knowledge of the country. Even Gladstone only went there once, for a visit of three weeks, during which, as J. L. Hammond has to admit, he 'stayed in

---

1. 9 February 1907. The phrase 'commonwealth of nations' was still quite a novelty, and few politicians would have used it at the time, though it was first used by Rosebery in January 1884, in a speech at Adelaide, S. Australia.

the houses of Whig lords' and never 'went below the surface of the society in which he found himself'.[1] Lloyd George was widely travelled by the standards of his day. Even as a backbencher he crossed the Atlantic twice, paid numerous visits to the Continent, cruised in the Mediterranean, and spent holidays in the Scottish Highlands. But he never crossed the Irish Sea until, as a minister, he went to Belfast in 1907; and thereafter he never crossed it again. At least, in his case, the absence of first-hand knowledge was to some extent made up for by an exceptionally lively imagination and the quality, most rare in a politician, of being a good listener. All the same, it was unfortunate that he had so little direct contact with a country in whose history he was to play a vital part.

It should not be thought that he was prejudiced in favour of Protestant Ulster on sectarian grounds. In his Belfast speech he was appealing to his audience as Irishmen, without distinction of community or creed, to join in the task of bearing the White Man's Burden. He was, it must again be said, very little influenced by the dogmatic Protestantism which had surrounded him during his childhood in North Wales. His attitude was far more secularist than sectarian, and he had always been fundamentally bored by the sectarian politics in which he was forced, by his origins, to indulge. Contrary to what might be supposed, he was not repelled by Roman Catholic ritual, but if anything rather attracted by it. Once, when visiting Rome during his early years in politics, he had attended a mass conducted by Pope Leo XIII, and later described it to his friend Herbert Lewis as 'the most impressive service he had attended in his life'.[2] And in May 1917 Maurice Hankey noticed how fascinated he was by a service in Amiens cathedral.[3]

On the other hand, he had no time at all for confessional politics, or for the sort of religious control of education that would tend to divide communities on sectarian lines. When, in February 1898, John Dillon moved an amendment to the Address calling for the establishment of a Roman Catholic University, Lloyd George spoke against the amendment, and one passage in that speech should be quoted here:

If I understand the history of Ireland aright, its greatest curse has been this division of the people into two distinct peoples, whose

1. J. L. Hammond, *Gladstone and the Irish Nation*, p. 159.
2. Herbert Lewis Diary, entry for 22 October 1920 (N.L.W.)
3. Stephen Roskill, *Hankey: Man of Secrets*, Vol. I, p. 387.

differences have been intensified by religious disagreements. You have two separate camps . . . and I say it is the policy of the great prophets of Nationalism to break down these barriers between Catholics and Protestants, to weld them together into one nation with a common patriotism. It is against their interests to set up an institution which renders permanent these religious differences, which gets hold of the children at a most susceptible part of their career, because the men you turn out of these universities will be the future governors of Ireland. The proposal will separate them into two distinct and hostile camps.[1]

There is surely nothing in those words to suggest crude anti-Popery, and nothing indeed to suggest any lack of sympathy for the ideal of Irish unity. They assert very strongly the principle of secularism as indispensable to the realisation of a common Irish nationhood.

Significantly, the man he most admired in the Irish national movement was Michael Davitt, land agitator, collectivist and fervent advocate of secular education. The admiration was mutual, dating from the day in 1886 when the youthful Lloyd George had proposed a vote of thanks to Davitt at Blaenau Ffestiniog, to be told, in return, that he would one day shine in Parliament. In that year Lloyd George might, in fact, have become M.P. (for Merioneth) nearly four years before his first election, and had he been a candidate in 1886 he would have stood as a supporter of Joseph Chamberlain rather than Gladstone. Though he later stood as a Gladstonian, in deference to overwhelming popular sentiment in Wales, he never ceased to believe that his countrymen would have been wiser to follow Chamberlain in 1886. Had they done so, in his view Gladstone would 'have given way and Parnell would have accepted a different sort of [Home Rule] Bill, which would have fitted into a pattern of Home Rule All Round'.[2]

It would be quite wrong to regard Lloyd George as a crypto-Unionist; his commitment to Home Rule was genuine, though he disliked the exclusiveness of Gladstone's policy and thought it should

1. Hansard, Fourth Series, Vol. LIII, cols. 979–80. In 1908 Dillon's dream was substantially realised when Ireland's National University came into being, federating the university colleges of Dublin, Cork and Galway. This was not strictly a Roman Catholic university, since it was not under the Church's direct control. But Roman Catholics could enter it freely, whereas to become students at Trinity College, Dublin they needed episcopal permission. The Irish language was soon made compulsory for matriculation at the National University, though Dillon did not at all approve of this shibboleth, which he opposed in vain.
2. Conversation with Herbert Lewis, recorded in Lewis's diary 3 October 1898 (N.L.W.).

have been part of a larger whole. He was also frequently irritated by the narrow-mindedness and, as he saw it, the monomania of most Irish Nationalists. For instance, it annoyed him that they did not support the Welsh Nonconformists over Balfour's Education Bill in 1902, and they also gave him a lot of trouble over the liquor duties in his 1909 Budget – because in Ireland the drink trade was as much a vested interest of the National Party as, in England, it was of the Conservatives.

Such was the background to his serious involvement in Irish affairs, which began with the introduction of the third Home Rule Bill in April 1912. Between then and the outbreak of war the subject made ever-increasing demands upon his time and his resources as a negotiator, despite all the other things he was trying to do.

Together with Churchill, but in common with no other member of the Cabinet, Lloyd George was of the opinion that the Home Rule Bill should be introduced with provision for individual Ulster counties to opt out. He took this view not because he shared Ulster Protestant feelings about Home Rule, but because he had the perception and realism to appreciate their strength. Unlike some of his colleagues, he could see that 'the Orange card' which Lord Randolph Churchill had chosen to play in 1886 was 'the ace of trumps' rather than 'the two' chiefly for the reason that Ulster Protestant opposition was inherently formidable. Lord Randolph's son had a similar insight. Of course, he and Lloyd George were also aware that Ulster resistance became still more formidable when encouraged from outside by British Unionists, but they were under no illusion that without such encouragement it would cease to exist. Their plea for a concession to Protestant Ulster in the Bill itself was rejected, however, partly because illusions about Ulster were so prevalent among Liberal politicians and their Irish allies, and partly because some members of the Cabinet thought it wiser to hold concessions in reserve for bargaining at a later stage.

Months before the Bill was even introduced there was abundant evidence of Ulster's determination to resist. On 23 September 1911 the first of many mass demonstrations was held, at the home of the Unionist Member for East Down, Captain James Craig. Craig was the organiser, but not the star, for it was at this meeting that the leading Irish Unionist in the House of Commons made his rallying call to Ulster, in anticipation of the coming crisis. His words were as solemn as they were seditious: 'I now enter into compact with you, and with the help of God you and I . . . will yet defeat the most nefarious conspiracy that has ever been hatched against a free people. . . . We must be prepared . . . the morning Home Rule passes, ourselves to become responsible for the government of the Protestant Province of Ulster.' The speaker was Sir Edward Carson.

Ironically, Carson was not an Ulsterman. On both sides his family was Southern Irish, he had been educated in the South, and he sat for Dublin University (Trinity College). Though a sincere Irish patriot, his loyalty was to Ireland as an integral part of the United Kingdom. It was his profound belief that Irish Home Rule would lead to the disintegration of those larger unities – of the British Isles and Empire – which mattered to him even more than Ireland. When he became Parliamentary leader of Irish Unionism in 1910, his aim was to defeat the policy of Home Rule absolutely, not just to fight a rearguard action on behalf of Protestant Ulster. Circumstances, however, confined him to the lesser role, which he then espoused with total dedication.

He was not at all ambitious in the ordinary sense. Though he had held office as Solicitor-General in the last Conservative Government, he always insisted that he was in politics only for the sake of Ireland, or to defend the Union – objectives which he regarded as inseparable – and there could be no doubt that he meant what he said. There was a streak of Quixotism in him, which showed itself even in his career at the Bar, most conspicuously in his defence of Cadet George Archer-Shee ('the Winslow Boy'); and the same quality was manifest in his political career. As leaders of the Ulster revolt he and Craig formed a most potent partnership, with Craig doing the staffwork and, as a Scots-Irishman, more truly representative of Ulster, but with Carson providing the inspiration and charisma, bringing to the cause of a rather inarticulate community all the eloquence of a Dubliner.

Soon the movement took a para-military form, since it was found that licences for drilling could be obtained from any magistrate if the stated purpose was to maintain legal rights and liberties. On 9 April 1912, just before the Home Rule Bill was introduced, 100,000 men paraded in a suburb of Belfast, and the saluting-base which they marched past was ominously occupied by Bonar Law as well as Carson. Addressing the gathering, Law – son of an Ulster-born Presbyterian minister – pledged 'help from across the Channel' when 'the hour of battle' came. The following month Law was urging the King to refuse his assent to the Home Rule Bill, and on 29 July, at Blenheim Palace, he described the Government as 'a revolutionary committee which has seized upon despotic power by fraud'. He then also repeated a statement which he had made before becoming Leader of the Opposition, in a passage which, his biographer admits, went far 'to break the conventions upon which Parliamentary democracy is based':

> I said that, in my belief, if an attempt were made to deprive these men [the Ulster Protestants] of their birthright – as part of a corrupt Parliamentary bargain – they would be justified in resisting such an attempt by all means in their power, including force. I said it then, and I repeat now, with a full sense of the responsibility which attaches to my position, that . . . if such an attempt is made, I can imagine no length of resistance to which Ulster can go in which I should not be prepared to support them, and in which, in my belief, they would not be supported by the overwhelming majority of the British people.[1]

Lloyd George does not seem to have been unduly perturbed by this speech, because he wrote to his wife the following day without mentioning it. The reason for his lack of reaction is probably that he knew the Irish crisis would not come to a head until the Home Rule Bill was nearing the end of its lengthy course under the Parliament Act. He may also have detected the first signs of an eventual compromise, in the support Bonar Law and Carson had given, in May, to a Liberal backbencher's amendment to the Bill, proposing the exclusion of four Ulster counties, Down, Derry, Antrim and Armagh. The amendment was opposed by the Government, and Carson indicated that, though a step in the right direction, it did not go far enough for him. But it seemed that he might be prepared to accept the exclusion of a somewhat larger area, and Lloyd George could feel that there would be room for negotiation later on, if only the Nationalists could be brought to accept the necessity for some form of exclusion.

This, however, posed great difficulties, because most Irish Nationalists – including their Parliamentary leader, John Redmond, and his lieutenant, John Dillon – knew virtually nothing of Protestant Ulster and were, therefore, convinced that Carson and his followers were only bluffing. Redmond and Dillon had been on opposite sides in the split over Parnell, but had been working together well since Redmond became chairman of the Nationalist M.P.s in 1900. Of the

---

1. Robert Blake, *The Unknown Prime Minister*, p. 130.

two, Dillon was the more closely in touch with ordinary opinion in Southern Ireland, and seemed to British politicians the more intransigent. Redmond was a noble and honest, but also rather blinkered, character, to whom F. E. Smith's *mot* about Austen Chamberlain – that he always played the game and always lost it – could equally well be applied. He was a staunch Parliamentarian and, though a Roman Catholic, no less of a British imperialist than Carson himself. The difference was that Redmond believed Home Rule would strengthen the Empire, whereas Carson was sure it would have the opposite effect. Both men were fanatical in a distinctively Irish way, but Carson had the advantage of knowing both parts of Ireland. If Redmond had been anything like as familiar with the North as Carson was with the South, their quarrel would have been easier to resolve. Even Joseph Devlin, the Nationalist leader in Ulster, did not at first fully grasp what was happening on the other side of the communal divide, and so failed to shake his Southern colleagues out of their perilous complacency.

At the end of September 1912 there was another impressive show of Ulster Protestant feeling when Carson led nearly half a million men and women in signing a Covenant to resist Home Rule; and early in the New Year the Ulster Unionist Council began to raise a Volunteer Force, so giving coherence and formal shape to the para-military activity already widespread. In mid-January 1913 the Home Rule Bill completed its first circuit in the House of Commons, and was then summarily rejected by the House of Lords. The second circuit was more rapid, and by the time Parliament rose for the summer recess the Bill had been passed and rejected for the second time. It was, therefore, in the autumn of 1913 that the Irish crisis entered its acute phase, since everybody knew that the Bill had only to be passed again through the House of Commons in the next session, and it would automatically become law despite the Lords' veto.

Partly under pressure from the King, Asquith decided to make an overture to Bonar Law, and as a result the two leaders met secretly at Cherkley, near Leatherhead in Surrey, the country house of Law's friend, Sir Max Aitken. Their meetings (three in all before the end of the year) caused some misunderstanding, though on the whole they served to make Asquith and Law more aware of each other's difficulties. But they could not remove those difficulties. Many Unionists still hoped that the Government would break on the Home Rule issue, and that the whole project would, once again, be wrecked; while many Liberals, and above all the Irish Nationalists, were still unwilling to see any derogation, even temporary, from the principle of a United Ireland.

Lloyd George, who had always regarded this attitude as unrealistic, felt that the Government now had to take an initiative in the direction of compromise. On 12 November, soon after Asquith's second meeting with Bonar Law, he proposed to the Cabinet that an area of Ulster, as yet unspecified, should be allowed to opt out of Home Rule for a period of five or six years. The merit of this proposal was that two general elections would have to occur before the threat of inclusion could be implemented.

There was a good deal of support for the proposal in Cabinet, and Asquith was authorised to discuss it with Redmond. But one who did not support it was Augustine Birrell, Chief Secretary for Ireland since 1907. So much did he dislike it that he offered his resignation, which unfortunately was not accepted. Birrell was a barrister and a man of letters, distinguished in his way and an engaging companion, but by temperament utterly unsuited for any office requiring hard work and the power of decision. As Chief Secretary he carried very little weight, but was nevertheless in a position to do considerable harm (later, indeed, terrible harm). Very close to Redmond, he encouraged the Irish leader not to take Lloyd George's proposal too seriously. Redmond's only idea for a compromise was that there might be an Ulster Council, subject to the Dublin Parliament but with some special powers: a sort of 'Home Rule within Home Rule'. Dillon did not fancy this idea at all, preferring Lloyd George's, which at least would involve no permanent separate organisation for the Ulster counties. But he, like Redmond, was entirely opposed to any initiative on the part of the Government at that stage; and both men were equally prone to underrate the seriousness of Protestant Ulster's defiance. Since, on the Opposition side, neither Bonar Law nor Carson was prepared to make the first move, the year ended in deadlock – though with Government proclamations forbidding the import of arms into Ireland or their transport along the Irish coast.

During the recess there was a correspondence between Bonar Law and the King's private secretary, Lord Stamfordham, which established the King's unwillingness, on reflection, to act as Law had suggested, in the sense of asking Asquith to recommend a dissolution or be dismissed. Meanwhile extreme Unionists, with Milner as the moving spirit, were planning an alternative strategy for the defeat of

Home Rule, which amounted to nothing less than an Army plot to frustrate the will of the elected House of Parliament. The scheme was to amend the annual Army Act in the House of Lords in such a way as to force the Government either to delay Home Rule until after an election, or to hold an election in order to have an Army Act, without which there could be no military discipline. The country's most famous and revered soldier, the veteran Lord Roberts, was implicated, and so was another Anglo-Irish military man, whose career was more in the future than the past, the Director of Military Operations at the War Office, Major-General Henry Wilson. Wilson was not only in close touch with Law and the even more drastically seditious Milner; he also found it consistent with his duty to give advice to the Ulster Volunteers.

The new session of Parliament was opened on 10 February, with the Cabinet still undecided. Anodyne words about 'the spirit of mutual concession' and 'the foundations of a lasting settlement' were written into the King's speech, but they seemed remote from the immediate realities. A few days earlier Asquith had proposed to Redmond that Protestant Ulster should have sweeping powers of veto within a Home Rule Ireland, which was a variant of the 'Home Rule within Home Rule' formula. But the King told the Prime Minister, at his next audience, that he was sure this would not be acceptable to the Ulstermen. The Cabinet reverted, therefore, to the idea of temporary exclusion, and on 4 March it was agreed that individual counties should be given the freedom to opt out for a period of three years. After a newspaper leak which caused a further intervention by the King, the period was extended to six years, as Lloyd George had proposed in November, and Redmond was forced most reluctantly to agree to this. On 9 March, as the Home Rule Bill began its third and last Parliamentary circuit, Asquith announced that the Government would also be introducing an Amending Bill to give effect to the concession to Ulster.[1] Carson rejected what he called 'sentence of death with a stay of execution for six years', but left the door open to possible agreement on exclusion without a time-limit.

Events were now moving swiftly towards a fundamental showdown. Carson's rejection of the Government's compromise had a galvanising effect on Churchill, who in December had said he would resign if there were any question of coercing Ulster without first

---

1. A separate bill was needed, because if the Home Rule Bill were to pass against the Lords' veto it had to be re-submitted without amendment, as the Parliament Act prescribed.

making a reasonable offer. Lloyd George commented at the time that, if such an offer were made and rejected, no one would take a tougher stand than Churchill, and he was proved right. In reply to Carson, and with Lloyd George's encouragement, Churchill uttered fighting words at Bradford:

> We are not going to have the realm of Great Britain sink to the condition of the Republic of Mexico . . . if all the loose, wanton and reckless chatter we have been forced to listen to these months is in the end to disclose a sinister revolutionary purpose, then I can only say to you 'Let us go forward and put these grave matters to the proof.'[1]

Not to be outdone in histrionics, Carson two days later delivered a scorching attack on Churchill in the House of Commons, at the end of which he announced that his place was in Ulster, and left to catch his train at Euston with twenty-five minutes to spare. Some naturally feared, while others may have hoped, that he had gone to proclaim a rebel government in the Province.

It was now Lloyd George's turn to make a strong speech. At Huddersfield on 21 March he dealt faithfully, but also wittily, with Carson:

> Sir Edward Carson owes everything to the law. He made his fame by prosecuting people for defying laws which are now acknowledged to have been unjust. That is the foundation of his fame and fortune. He came over here and attained one of the finest positions as an advocate at the British Bar. If people had anticipated his action and had taken the law into their own hands, there would have been nothing for Sir Edward Carson to do. He would have been looking forward to the advent of Old Age Pensions – which, by the way, he voted against.

He also echoed Churchill's warlike tone: 'We are confronted with the gravest issue raised in this country since the days of the Stuarts. Representative government in this land is at stake . . . I am here this afternoon on behalf of the British Government to say . . . that they mean to confront this defiance of popular liberties with a most resolute, unwavering determination, whatever the hazard may be.' But he, like Carson, did not slam the door, saying at an overflow

---

1. 14 March 1914. The contemptuous reference to Mexico is, incidentally, eloquent of the prevailing attitude towards such countries at the time.

meeting: 'When we have exhausted the means of conciliation, we shall have a perfectly free conscience' – which obviously implied that the means of conciliation were not yet exhausted.

Even as he spoke, however, the incident often described as the 'Curragh mutiny' was occurring, which threw doubt upon the Government's 'unwavering determination' and suggested that there were strict limits to its power to enforce the will of Parliament in Ireland. For some time there had been talk of disaffection among Army officers there, and the King had warned Asquith that, if the Irish negotiations broke down, many might resign their commissions rather than fight a civil war against Ulster. But matters came to a head in the third and fourth weeks of March, when the Secretary of State for War and the Commander-in-Chief in Ireland between them precipitated a crisis.

Neither was a very intelligent man. The minister, Colonel J. E. B. Seely, who succeeded Haldane in 1912, had nothing to recommend him for the post except that he was a jolly fellow with a good fighting record in the Boer War, and with the political cachet of being an ex-Conservative. The commander, Sir Arthur Paget, was a typical well-connected officer of the old school. On 19 March Seely briefed Paget on necessary troop dispositions in Ireland and the problem of officers' loyalty. It was stated that officers with homes in Ulster were not to be compelled to take part in any operations there which might compromise them in their personal lives, but that any others who refused to obey orders should be dismissed. This briefing, already harmful in that it seemed to anticipate acts of insubordination which, in an Army, should never even be contemplated, did more harm as transmitted by Paget to a group of his senior officers in Dublin the following day, since he contrived – probably through maladroitness rather than any mischievous intent – to give an alarmist twist to what Seely had said, suggesting that the whole of Ireland would be 'ablaze' within twenty-four hours.

As a result, the commander of the 3rd Cavalry Brigade at the Curragh, Brigadier-General Hubert Gough, an Ulsterman, soon announced that he and sixty of his brother-officers in the Brigade would accept dismissal rather than be involved in 'the initiation of active military operations against Ulster'. Other military figures in Ireland, notably the commander of the 5th Division, Major-General Sir Charles Fergusson, behaved sensibly and correctly, but Gough's 'mutiny' was allowed to steal the show. Recalled to London for discussions, he received a written assurance from Seely that the Government had 'no intention whatever of taking advantage of the right to crush political opposition to the policy or principles of the Home Rule Bill'. Not content even with this, he persuaded the Chief of the Imperial General Staff, Sir John French, to confirm in writing that he took the assurance to mean that the Army in Ireland would not be used to impose Home Rule upon Ulster. Instead of being sacked or severely disciplined, Gough was allowed to return in triumph to Ireland, while in London Henry Wilson quietly rejoiced at the turn of events.

It was, of course, quite wrong to negotiate with Gough at all, and the pledge given to him was disgraceful. Asquith had no choice but to repudiate it, and to accept the resignations of Seely and French. He also decided, in order to steady the Army and reassure the public, to take over the War Office himself. Still, the Curragh incident had damaged the Government's credit in a most sensitive area, and the damage could not be undone.

Worse was soon to follow. Despite the Government's ban on the import of arms into Ulster, early in the morning of 25 April a total of 24,600 rifles and about three million rounds of ammunition were landed at the ports of Larne, Donaghadee and Bangor, and then spirited away in a fleet of cars. The consignment had been shipped from Germany, and the principal organiser of the operation was Craig, though with Carson's full complicity. The Government, after talking for a day or two about arresting Ulster leaders and starting criminal proceedings, was forced to conclude that nothing effective could be done. The gun-running was, therefore, a spectacular demonstration of Protestant Ulster's invincible power. Even Dillon had to admit that any move against the Ulster Volunteers would be – and, for that matter, would always have been – disastrous.[1] Yet there was a most significant reaction to Protestant para-militancy, in the swift expansion of the rival Irish Volunteer movement, which increased its membership from fewer than 2,000 at the end of 1913 to 160,000 by mid-1914, about one-third of whom were in Ulster. This development was unwelcome to most of the Irish Parliamentary

1. The day after the gun-running, C. P. Scott suggested to Dillon that the Ulster Volunteer movement should have been checked earlier, but Dillon 'dissented and strongly deprecated any action even now which might lead to actual conflict between Army and Volunteers – fearing effect on future of Ireland' (*The Political Diaries of C. P. Scott, 1911–1918*, edited by Trevor Wilson, 26 April 1914, p. 84).

leaders, and to Redmond above all; but in view of the scale of armed preparedness on the Protestant side, and the Government's manifest impotence, it was hardly surprising.

After a relative lull in Irish affairs during May, at any rate so far as British politicians were concerned, the Government's promised Amending Bill was introduced, in the House of Lords, on 23 June. The Bill contained the provision already rejected by Carson, that each Ulster county should have the right to vote itself out of Home Rule for a period of six years. The previous weekend Lloyd George, though in the thick of his Budget difficulties, spoke again at some length on the Ulster issue. His tone was more reasoning than assertive – a change from his bellicose tone at Huddersfield. Referring to the minority of Irishmen who were standing out against Home Rule, he asked:

What is the nature of their protest? They say that they are called upon to submit to a Government which they loathe and abhor. Well, we have all had to do that in our time. . . .

We may even yet have to submit to Governments which we loathe and abhor. We will take it philosophically; we will not arm; we will not drill; we will not organise ourselves into battalions; we will not salute; we will not gun-run; we will not have generals and colonels and captains – not even gallopers. [F. E. Smith had described himself as Carson's 'galloper']. What we will do is bide our time and vote them down when we get the chance. That is the very essence of democracy.

Let us examine a little further the character of their protest. They say: 'We must protest because we have been driven from under the British flag.' Who has driven them from under the British flag? What do they mean by it? They will have representatives at Westminster when Home Rule has been established. They will have a voice in the control of the Army, of the Navy, of our foreign affairs, and of every great Imperial question. They will have just the same voice as Englishmen, Scotchmen and Welshmen.

They talk as if we were going to force them to join Germany, France, Italy or Japan. They will be British subjects just as much as before. They will have the same interest in Imperial questions, the same direction of Imperial affairs, as they have now. As a matter of fact, they will have much more say on Imperial questions than our kith and kin in Canada, Australia and New Zealand. . . .

They demand, some of them, exclusion from the new Government in Ireland. On what grounds? Ulster has always been an integral part of Ireland. It is being governed with Ireland at the present moment. Ireland has quite a separate system of laws, a separate administration of her laws, and a separate judiciary to interpret her laws. Ulster has exactly the same laws as Munster, Leinster and Connaught. . . .

This is not the first time that Ulster has had Volunteers. When you go home, turn up your history books and read up the history of the Volunteer movement at the end of the eighteenth century in Ireland. It was largely a Protestant movement . . . to force Great Britain to recognise and establish an independent Parliament for the whole of Ireland. . . .

The Government, he said, could not recognise permanent exclusion. But

I will tell you what we are prepared to do. Next week you will have introduced into the House of Lords, on behalf of the Government, a Bill which will give to every county in Ulster the option to vote itself out of Home Rule until two general elections have passed in this country. Just see what that means. Mr Bonar Law has stated that, if the electorate of this country are given an opportunity of pronouncing their judgment upon the question of Home Rule, and if they decide in favour of it, then the Unionist Party will cease to support the Volunteers of Ulster in their resistance. . . .

But Home Rule could not be abandoned for Ireland as a whole:

. . . whilst they think it an intolerable act of oppression to force Home Rule upon a corner of Ireland where sixty per cent of the inhabitants protest against it, they think it great Imperial statesmanship to refuse Home Rule to a part of Ireland where ninety per cent of the inhabitants do ask for it. There we cannot agree with them.[1]

Unmoved by such arguments, the House of Lords gave the Amending Bill short shrift. Without being formally rejected, it was amended so as to exclude all the Ulster counties without plebiscites and without a time-limit, which was tantamount to rejection. Know-

---

1. Speech in the grounds of Bessemer House, Denmark Hill, 20 June 1914. Lloyd George was much interrupted by 'Votes for Women' enthusiasts, several of whom, including a clergyman, were thrown into the lake by members of the audience.

Under Home Rule, Ireland would not have been represented at Westminster on the same basis as England, Scotland and Wales, but on a reduced scale.

ing that Ulster could not be coerced, the Government now had to enter into further direct negotiation with the Opposition, and it was decided to do so in the form of a conference rather similar to that which had been set up in 1910, though the precedent was hardly encouraging.

The idea of a conference had been in the air for some time. On 11 September 1913 a letter appeared in *The Times* from Lord Loreburn, the former Liberal Lord Chancellor, in which he argued that there should be 'a Conference or direct communications between the leaders'. Later the same month, when Lloyd George was visiting Asquith on the isle of Arran, before launching the Land Campaign, he received a 'secret and confidential' letter from F. E. Smith, who had been seeing the King and Churchill. In it Smith mentioned four ways in which a settlement might be promoted, and one was a conference. 'I am strongly of opinion', he wrote, that 'the Conference shd be summoned by the King', and he added that it might be extended to cover House of Lords reform and the Land.

Before replying, Lloyd George discussed the letter with Asquith and Churchill, and his eventual answer was positive but vague: 'You know how anxious I have been for years to work with you and a few others on your side. I have always realised that our differences have been very artificial & do not reach the 'realities'.[1] Smith had been a party to his secret coalition scheme in 1910, and the idea of all the talents combining could never lose its appeal to Lloyd George. But there was no returning to such a wide-ranging project in 1913, and for the time being Asquith did not even want a formal conference on the single subject of Ireland, preferring to try the other method suggested by Loreburn, that of direct communication between leaders. Hence his informal meetings with Bonar Law during the autumn and early winter of 1913.

Even when, in May 1914, Speaker Lowther and the King separately pressed him to hold a conference, he was still reluctant to commit himself to what seemed a procedure of last resort. But by the middle of July he was ready, at length, to try it. From 21 to 24 July eight politicians, two from each of the parties concerned, met under the Speaker's chairmanship at Buckingham Palace. They were: for the Government, Asquith and Lloyd George; for the Conservatives, Bonar Law and Lansdowne; for the Irish Nationalists, Redmond and

1. F. E. Smith to D.L.G., 26 September 1913; D.L.G. to F. E. Smith, 6 October 1913, copy in Frances Stevenson's hand (L.G.P.).

Dillon; and for the Ulster Unionists, Carson and Craig.[1] The King opened the conference with a short speech in which he called for 'generous compromise', and then left the politicians to get on with their work. There was some indignation in the Labour Party and the Liberal Press that the leaders were meeting thus in an extra-Parliamentary setting, and under the Sovereign's auspices. But this would not have mattered at all if only they could have reached agreement. Unfortunately they could not.

The conference applied itself, above all, to the task of defining the area to be excluded, and it was on this issue that the talks broke down. For months it had been deferred or fudged, but sooner or later it had to be faced. The historic province of Ulster consisted of nine counties, of which four – Down, Derry, Antrim and Armagh – had Scots-Irish (Protestant) majorities of varying strength, and three – Cavan, Monaghan and Donegal – had strong Gaelic-Irish (Roman Catholic) majorities. In the remaining two – Fermanagh and Tyrone – the communities were closely balanced, though not in concentrated blocks. It was, therefore, exceedingly hard to find any way of partitioning those two counties, quite apart from the difficulty of persuading either side to agree to their being partitioned.[2]

Carson proposed that the whole of Ulster should be excluded, putting to Redmond the disarming argument that the larger the Nationalist majority in the excluded area, the better the chance of eventual reunion. But Redmond, though tempted, had to reply that, if he were to agree to exclusion of the whole of Ulster, he would lose all support in the rest of Ireland. On the third day Asquith proposed a formula whereby the six north-eastern counties, less South Armagh, South Fermanagh and North Tyrone, would be excluded without a time-limit. But Bonar Law greeted this with scepticism, and Redmond rejected it. The detailed problem of territorial definition was, therefore, never solved, and the time-limit question was never even discussed. On 24 July the Speaker issued a brief statement reporting that the Conference had failed.

Immediately after its last meeting Asquith told the Irish leaders that the Amending Bill would have to go forward without a time-limit for exclusion; that all the counties of Ulster should have the right to opt out, as counties, for an indefinite period. Redmond and Dillon agreed,

1. Birrell's lack of standing is well illustrated in his absence from the Conference.
2. Lloyd George suggested that Tyrone might be divided according to Poor Law districts, but the suggestion found no favour with Redmond or Carson.

two days later under protest, to submit this new concession to their colleagues. But two days later the Irish Volunteers staged their riposte to the Ulster gun-running, when a consignment of arms – much smaller than that brought to Ulster, though also from Germany – was landed at Howth, near the northern entrance to Dublin Bay. Through bad judgment on the part of a police chief, acting on his own initiative, an unsuccessful attempt was made to disarm Volunteers who had collected some of the rifles and ammunition. Later in the day, as a detachment of the King's Own Scottish Borderers was marching back into Dublin, it was subjected to much jeering, stone-throwing and abuse, and at Bachelor's Walk – one of the quays beside the Liffey – shots were fired into a crowd, killing three and wounding thirty-eight. Though the Government was not strictly to blame for this tragic incident, Irish opinion was naturally outraged by the contrast between what had happened in Dublin and what had *not* happened in Ulster. The Amending Bill had to be postponed, and before it could be brought on again the Irish crisis had yielded to one of far greater and deadlier import.

It is hard to conjecture what would have happened if there had been no European crisis at the end of July. Asquith seemed determined to impose the Amending Bill in its final form upon the Nationalists and, subject to that, to impose Home Rule upon the Unionists. But would Carson and Law have accepted county option, even without a time-limit? The structure of a Provisional Government was fully prepared in Ulster, and would have been put into operation as soon as Home Rule was enacted, unless and until Ulster demands were satisfied. Granted the attitude of the Army, the tough mood of Protestant Ulster, and the Opposition's readiness to exploit the situation, the Government might well have had to choose between civil war and further concessions at the expense of its Irish allies. The Unionists' bargaining position was enormously stronger than the Nationalists'.

After the Curragh affair, and the unimpeded gun-running in Ulster, Lloyd George could see that the Irish needed to build up a countervailing force, even telling C. P. Scott that he thought the Irish Volunteers should be armed.[1] Above all, his experience of Irish affairs during the pre-war period confirmed him in the view that a united Home Rule Ireland could only be achieved by agreement between North and South; it could never be imposed from England.

1. 17 June 1914 (*Scott Diaries*, ed. Trevor Wilson, p. 87).

SIX

The Approach to War

Until the Great War Lloyd George was only occasionally concerned with foreign, Imperial or defence questions. Though he often went abroad for holidays, he had to be largely home-orientated in his work. It was not that he lacked, before 1914, a general view of the world and Britain's place in it. On the contrary, he began his career with a strong opinion on the essentials of policy, to which he remained remarkably faithful to the end of his life. His first newspaper article, written when he was seventeen, was not on any parochial subject, but on Lord Salisbury's foreign policy; and it contained these striking words:

> Toryism has not been barren of statesmen – real and not charlatan – statesmen who prized the honour of England above the interests of party – who really hated oppression and demonstrated their detestation of it . . . by the laudable assistance which they rendered to weak nationalities in their desperate struggles for Liberty – for freedom from the yoke of inhuman despots – for very existence.[1]

In that passage we see, surely, prefigured the Lloyd George of later years. To regard his career as a gradual progression from tribal, sectarian politics to world statesmanship is to misunderstand it fundamentally. In his beginning was his end.

Both by temperament and democratic conviction he was drawn to France, and during the Fashoda crisis in 1898 he took a line which

1. *North Wales Express*, 5 November 1880.

conflicted most notably with the prevalent Jingoism and Francophobia. Speaking of the risk of war with France, he expressed confidence in a British victory, but added:

> If we defeat France, we shall be defeating the only power on the Continent with a democratic Constitution. Emperors, kings and aristocratic rulers will mock at the whole thing – two great democratic Powers at each other's throats, the only countries where you have perfect civil and religious liberty in Europe quarrelling with each other to make sport for the titled and throned Philistines of Europe.[1]

Lloyd George was never an Entente or balance-of-power politician, in the sense of being opposed to the idea of a Concert of Europe. But is the antithesis, in any case, really valid? Lloyd George was always a Concert of Europe man; he wanted the nations of the Continent to live in a state of peace and growing harmony. But he was also a realist, who could see that the maintenance of peace might depend upon an approximate balance between potentially warring powers, and who recognised that vital national interests had to be defended. To him, the Anglo-French Entente Cordiale, like the later and even looser British understanding with Russia,[2] was not an alliance aimed at Germany or any other country, but the model for similar understandings which together could help to promote a general European concert. Despite his natural preference for France, he was not at all anti-German and would have welcomed a friendly bilateral relationship between Britain and Germany, which would have supplemented, not supplanted, the Entente. In the summer of 1908 he called for just such a relationship in an interview which he gave to the Vienna *Neue Freie Presse*.

Meanwhile his famous stand against the Boer War had caused his attitude on two key issues to be profoundly misinterpreted, and in some quarters the misinterpretation persists. Even now, there are some who would describe his opposition to the Boer War as that of a pacifist and anti-Imperialist, with which his support for the Great War is, therefore, starkly contrasted. But in fact he was never a pacifist, and was always an enthusiastic upholder of the British Empire, more especially of the maritime supremacy on which it was based. He was

---

1. Speech at Haworth, 24 October 1898.
2. Signed August 1907. Its primary purpose was to reduce tension between the two Powers in Asia.

against the Boer War not because he had any *a priori* objection to war in any circumstances, but because he regarded that particular war as unnecessary and damaging – not least to the true interests of the British Empire. He could sympathise with the Boer republics as small nations struggling for liberty, because they were not threatening anything that he could perceive as a vital British interest. Had they been a threat to, for instance, British sea power, he would have favoured coercion rather than conciliation.

His sensitivity to any naval challenge was demonstrated in 1911, when his intervention during the Agadir crisis took by surprise all those, at home or abroad, who had misread his underlying attitude. In his *Neue Freie Presse* interview in 1908 he had insisted that the friendship he sought with Germany would be impossible so long as the Germans were trying to rival British sea power. At the time of Agadir he was not only prepared to go to war with Germany if the Kaiser's apparent pretensions in Morocco were maintained; he also believed that, in that event, Britain would not be able to limit herself to a sea war, but would have to send an expeditionary force to the Continent as well. Though in long retrospect he suggested that he was indignant to hear of Staff talks with the French, and most reluctant to agree to them, at the time he supported them vigorously.[1]

After the Agadir crisis Lloyd George felt that Germany had learnt a salutary lesson, and that France had been encouraged to withstand German pressure. He was, therefore, well disposed to an attempt to improve relations with Germany and, if possible, negotiate an agreement with her, more especially to end the naval arms race. The attempt was entrusted to Haldane, and carried out in circumstances of secrecy and deception which did nothing to assist its chances of success, but much to discredit the unfortunate emissary.

Haldane was still War Minister at the time of his mission to Germany in February 1912. His valuable Army reforms had antagonised powerful elements on the Right – since his Territorial scheme was a blow to the privilege and prestige of local commanding officers

---

1. The first Anglo-French Staff talks occurred soon after the Liberals took office, in January 1906. These were sanctioned by the Prime Minister, Campbell-Bannerman, though never brought before the Cabinet. In 1911, when the existence of talks became known, and when isolationists in the Cabinet made an issue of them, Lloyd George ranged himself with Asquith, Grey, Churchill and Haldane in support of the talks as a precautionary measure, though not as implying any commitment to intervene on France's side whatever the circumstances. His own account (*War Memoirs*, Vol. I, pp. 49–51) does not exactly mis-state the facts, but does give a rather misleading impression.

– without, of course, endearing him to Radicals, who had long regarded him with suspicion as a prominent Liberal Leaguer. Love of German philosophy and culture made him dangerously naïve about the German State and its ambitions. When the Kaiser was visiting London in May 1911 Haldane gave a lunch party for him, to which several leading politicians and Service chiefs were invited, as well as J. A. Spender, Edmund Gosse, J. S. Sargent and Robert Baden-Powell. This sort of gesture could only confirm his reputation as an extreme Germanophile. Yet he was not anti-French and by no means opposed to the Entente Cordiale. Recalling later the thinking behind his 1912 mission, he wrote that his cardinal principle had been

> that the size of the German navy made it impracticable to quit the Entente. As Grey always said among ourselves, the real reason for the Entente is that it was one way of retaining command of the sea. If we could not at least neutralise the navies of France and Russia, Germany could add to the power of a smaller fleet by making naval alliances. Thus we must stick to the Entente. But Grey . . . was willing to try – if Germany would check her shipbuilding – . . . to enlarge this Entente [so] as to bring it to the form of a real Concert of Great Powers and so secure Germany as well as France and Russia.[1]

Haldane's attitude was, in fact, very similar to Lloyd George's, though sentiment inclined him towards Germany, Lloyd George towards France.

The chances of an Anglo-German entente, anyway slight, were prejudiced by the Kaiser's announcement of a new naval programme on the eve of Haldane's arrival in Berlin. Even if the War Minister had been more gifted than he was for diplomacy, and even if he had gone with an open remit to negotiate on behalf of the British Government – instead of going ostensibly to discuss university affairs, which was a transparent fiction – it is most unlikely that any positive results would have been achieved. The Germans would only consider limiting their neutrality in the event of conflict between Germany and another Power, whereas Britain was only prepared to offer neutrality in a case where Germany was the victim of unprovoked aggression, together with colonial concessions in central Africa at the expense of Belgium and Portugal. In other words, Germany wanted either to press ahead

1. Haldane to H.H.A., 1 September 1922 (quoted in Stephen Koss, *Lord Haldane: Scapegoat for Liberalism*, p. 77).

with building a navy to rival Britain's, or freedom to attack France in the sure knowledge that Britain would not intervene. When Haldane reported to the Cabinet after his trip, Lloyd George was emphatic that there could be no negotiation with Germany unless the new naval programme was scrapped. But soon he was deeply involved in the coal-mining dispute, and then introducing a Budget; so he had no time to give serious attention to foreign affairs.

Despite the failure of the Haldane mission, the international atmosphere was fairly relaxed during the spring and summer of 1912, and when Lloyd George addressed the City merchants and bankers at the Mansion House on 12 July, he commented on the very different circumstances in which he had spoken there the previous year, when he had used the occasion to make his Agadir pronouncement:

> I am glad to be able to feel that the disturbing element in our foreign relations has been settled – that great question which has always been rather an irritant and a menace to the relations of the Great Powers . . . the question of Morocco, the gathering ground of thunder clouds. What is more, it has been settled in a way which has been satisfactory to all the parties concerned. That is very important. There is no feeling of resentment. There is nothing that rankles. All the parties are pleased at the settlement, and that means that the era of goodwill has begun.

His peroration was full of glowing hope for the future.

Within a few months, however, there was war in another 'gathering ground of thunder clouds', the Balkans, as Montenegro, Serbia, Greece and Bulgaria together attacked Turkey, whose rule in Europe had been even less tolerable since the Young Turk revolution in 1908. The Balkan League was everywhere victorious, and by the end of October the Turks had been almost completely evicted from Europe. But they managed to hold the Bulgarians in front of Constantinople, and in December there was an armistice. For various reasons the Great Powers wished, at the time, to bring about a settlement, and a conference of ambassadors under Grey's chairmanship led to the Treaty of London in May 1913.

After this the Balkan League soon disintegrated. Bulgaria, feeling hard done by, attacked Serbia and Greece, and was in turn attacked by Roumania. At the Treaty of Bucharest in August the Bulgarians lost territory all round, and the Turks were allowed to keep Adrianople, which they had recaptured in the second war. While the fighting was going on Lloyd George spoke again at the Mansion House, on 11 July, observing with satisfaction that general war had been avoided, as over Morocco, and exulting in the Great Power cooperation that had been manifest throughout the crisis:

> So long as the Balkan States now at war with each other do nothing to upset the decisions which have already been agreed upon by the Great Powers . . . we hope that no Great Power will find it necessary to take any action which will give rise to difficulties between the Great Powers.

We can now see that it was more by luck than good management that the Balkan crisis of 1912–13 did not anticipate, in its effect, the crisis of July 1914. The impression widely created of a Concert of Europe alive and in working order was, alas, illusory. According to one authority, what prevented war in the earlier crisis

> was not respect for any Gladstonian concert but the fact that on each occasion the power wavering on the brink of action felt that the time was not quite ripe or was influenced by its ally's plea for temporary restraint. This in turn meant that, although resisting mobilisation and war over that particular incident, preparations for the future were hastened.

This was particularly true of the leaders of Germany, who were prepared 'to let a conflict begin if the right cause cropped up'.[1] Lloyd George was one of many who were lulled into a mood of false optimism by the apparent emergence of a partnership for peace in Europe. It was, moreover, very convenient for him that the radicals' dream of international accord should seem to be nearing realisation at a time when he needed their enthusiastic support for his Land Campaign. In the winter before Armageddon we find him, therefore, at his most dove-like, and one consequence was his row with Churchill over the naval estimates for 1914.

Churchill had been transferred to the Admiralty in October 1911, since when he had been characteristically preoccupied with his new task and prone to talk relentlessly about what Lloyd George called his

---

1. Paul Kennedy, *The Rise of the Anglo-German Antagonism, 1860–1914*, p. 456.

'blasted ships'.[1] Lloyd George was – it must be repeated – as keen as anyone on preserving Britain's naval supremacy, but as Liberal Chancellor of the Exchequer he was bound to make at least a show of keeping Service expenditure under control. There was, too, a certain residue of old-fashioned 'retrenchment' Liberalism in him, despite his willingness to use the Budget for costly social projects of which no true Gladstonian could approve. But above all it was as the Cabinet's leading radical, seeking once again to carry his party to victory with a programme of domestic reform, that he opposed Churchill's naval estimates for 1914–15, which amounted to well over £50 million and involved the building of four new Dreadnoughts.

In 1909, when similarly poised for a major political effort at home, Lloyd George had fought McKenna's naval estimates for the coming year, and on that occasion Churchill, as President of the Board of Trade, had been his ally. Even so, McKenna and the Sea Lords had come, on the whole, very well out of the encounter. Now Churchill was on the other side. The radical combination of him and Lloyd George had disturbed the equilibrium of the Cabinet, and might have developed as a threat to Asquith's position as Prime Minister. He took steps, therefore, to exploit the rivalry that always accompanied, without ever quite destroying, their friendship, first by appointing Churchill to the Home Office in 1910 – which made him more or less equal with Lloyd George in the ministerial hierarchy – and then, after the Agadir crisis in 1911, by moving him to the Admiralty, where he could be expected to clash with the Chancellor.

In the latter part of 1913, while Lloyd George was leaning towards the Left, Churchill was leaning no less ostentatiously towards the Right, even to the extent of attending a private dinner of the Conservative shadow cabinet on 8 December. There were rumours that he was planning to rejoin his old party, and a number of his colleagues wanted to push him into resigning. Lloyd George at first did not share their view, and it would anyway not have suited him for Churchill to resign on the Irish issue – which was a possibility – since on that the two of them were in substantial agreement. But the naval issue was a

1. Masterman, *op.cit.*, p. 234. 'Winston was taking less and less part in home politics, and getting more and more absorbed in boilers, as George complained. Soon after his appointment he was really a perfect terror to his colleagues, and anyone standing alone used to find him bearing down on them. . . .'

In the same reshuffle, McKenna was moved to the Home Office, Haldane succeeded Loreburn as Lord Chancellor, and his place at the War Office was taken by the unfortunate Colonel Seely.

different matter. If he gave way to Churchill on the 1914 estimates, he would be putting his leadership of the radicals at risk, not for the principle of naval supremacy, but for a margin of naval superiority which seemed to him excessive. The prospects for peace would be jeopardised just when, in his opinion, they were brighter than at any time in recent years, and the Liberal Party, no less than himself, would be thrown into quite the wrong posture. With these considerations in mind he decided that a showdown with Churchill was necessary, even though it might result in one or other of them having to resign.

On New Year's Day 1914 the *Daily Chronicle* published an interview with Lloyd George, in which he launched what was both an attack on Churchill's estimates, and, in effect, a peace offensive. The moment had come, he said, for overhauling Britain's expenditure on armaments. The strain in Anglo-German relations was, 'owing largely to the wise and patient diplomacy of Sir Edward Grey, completely relaxed'. Both countries now realised that they had nothing to gain and everything to lose from a quarrel.

The Agadir incident served a very useful purpose in bringing home to these two great countries the perils involved in the atmosphere of suspicion which had been created and maintained by the politicians, the Press and certain interests. The realisation of the imminence of the danger came as a great shock, and sanity has now been more or less restored on both sides of the North Sea.

Another reason for optimism, and for checking the rate of naval construction, was that Continental nations, including Germany, were now thinking less of building up their naval power than of strengthening their land forces.

The German Army is vital, not merely to the existence of the German Empire, but to the very life and independence of the nation itself, surrounded as Germany is by other nations each of which possesses armies almost as powerful as her own.

The country has so often been invaded, overrun and devastated by foreign foes that she cannot afford to take any chances in that direction. We forget that, while we insist upon a sixty per cent superiority, so far as our naval strength is concerned, over Germany being essential to guarantee the integrity of our own shores, Germany herself has nothing like that superiority over France alone, and she has, of course, in addition to reckon with Russia on her eastern frontier.

THE APPROACH TO WAR 135

That is why I feel convinced that, even if Germany ever had any idea of challenging our supremacy at sea, the exigencies of the military situation must necessarily put it completely out of her head.

He therefore deprecated 'feverish efforts' to increase Britain's naval superiority, and said that 'if we went on spending and swelling [the Navy's] strength we should wantonly provoke other nations'. For good measure he recalled the protest by Churchill's father, Lord Randolph, against bloated and profligate naval estimates when he was Chancellor of the Exchequer.

This was not one of Lloyd George's happiest efforts. Unlike his Agadir speech, it was made off his own bat without prior consultation with Asquith or Grey. Beyond doubt it was an unwarrantable intrusion into a colleague's departmental sphere, which that colleague had all the more reason to resent seeing that the views expressed appeared to call his own policy in question: a fact which the polite reference to him could hardly conceal.[1] Without doing anything to appease German ambition, the interview did indeed 'wantonly provoke' Russia and France, who were made to feel that, so long as Britain's supremacy at sea went unchallenged, she would look with equanimity upon the growth of German military power, even though this must obviously represent an ever-increasing threat to them on land. At a time when it was most important that the British Government should seem united in foreign affairs, a serious division was advertised. In its domestic effects the interview was maladroit, since it weakened Lloyd George's hand in Cabinet vis-à-vis Churchill. Internationally the effects were mischievous.

While his words were reverberating throughout Europe, Lloyd George was on his way to Algiers, where he arrived on 4 January after a deservedly stormy passage. Next day he wrote to Margaret:

They are all making a great fuss of us here . . . the Algerian daily paper has a photo – not at all a bad one. The Governor of Algeria happened to be crossing at the same time. He offered me his Cabin de luxe. I lunch with him today. Last night we had his private box at

1. Grey, it is true, was also trying to cultivate better relations with Germany, having been encouraged to do so by the supposed success of Concert of Europe policies during the recent Balkan crisis. But he certainly did not wish to upset Britain's Entente partners, or to imply that the German danger no longer existed.

the Opera. . . .

The French papers published copious extracts from my *Daily Chronicle* interview.

A few days later the tone is slightly less bland:

I ran away to get peace & quietude from politics & here I am pursued by journalists and officials. . . .

France is agitated about my interview.

To satisfy his imaginary craving for seclusion, he disappeared for five days into the Sahara desert, in a special train provided by the Governor. But on the 13th he was in Paris on his way home, lunching there with the French Finance Minister, Joseph Caillaux, who had been Prime Minister at the time of the Agadir crisis.[1]

By the end of the month the naval estimates row was over, with Churchill the out-and-out winner. His detailed arguments, solidly backed by the professionals, had impressed those of his colleagues whose minds were relatively unprejudiced on the issue, and he was further helped by the suspicion, which the *Daily Chronicle* interview had done much to aggravate, that Lloyd George was engaged in an attempted left-wing takeover of the Government. Asquith, sensing that his authority was on trial, reacted with all the toughness and skill that he had shown during the 1912 miners' strike, and that he was soon to show again in even more momentous circumstances. He gave Churchill his full support and, when Lloyd George threatened to resign, countered with the threat that he would recommend a dissolution and go to the country.

By using this weapon, so often one of the most effective in a Prime Minister's armoury, he called Lloyd George's bluff – if indeed the Chancellor was consciously bluffing. It is hard to be sure of his state of mind at the time. The dispute between him and Churchill was more tactical than ideological. Both men believed in a strong Navy, and both were by temperament patriotic radicals, acting habitually with an empiricism which could easily be mistaken for opportunism. They also enjoyed each other's company, and felt instinctively akin. One would guess that Lloyd George was partly influenced by the force of Churchill's arguments, and that this made him more amenable to

---

1. Soon after his return Lloyd George had to deny German reports that he had said, 'France is our insurance against Germany; but we should much prefer to have an understanding with Germany.' Such were the distortions to which his *Daily Chronicle* interview laid him open.

Asquith's show of strength. At all events, he accepted his defeat with a good grace, and did not suffer too much loss of face, because public attention was soon diverted to the growing crisis in Ireland, which brought him and Churchill once again into close cooperation.

Unfortunately it was not only the British people, but even more their leaders, whose attention was diverted; and Lloyd George was perhaps the most preoccupied of all, having a contentious and complicated Budget to introduce, while also spending a lot of his time in Irish negotiations. Altogether, during the past eighteen months, his interest in foreign affairs and defence had been more tenuous than ever. Between the beginning of 1913 and the outbreak of war he attended only one meeting of the Committee of Imperial Defence, and at that – on 5 August 1913 – he merely commented sharply on Admiralty plans for strengthening the defences of the Shetlands. His thoughts were concentrated upon home politics; even the *Daily Chronicle* interview was above all a reflection of his domestic concerns. He did not feel that there was any imminent danger of European war, and when he spoke again at the Mansion House, on 17 July – nearly three weeks after the assassination of the Archduke Franz Ferdinand, and less than a week before the Austrian ultimatum to Serbia – he expressed a confidence which was only very slightly guarded:

Last year at this time I think we were in the middle of a great war in the East; at any rate the times were very troublesome, very anxious. One can realise now how very anxious the situation was, and it is a matter of pride for us that, amidst all that tangle, which might have led to one of the greatest disasters that have ever befallen civilisation in Europe, it was this land, under the able guidance of Sir Edward Grey, which took the lead in re-establishing peace.

There are always clouds in the international sky. You never get a perfectly blue sky in foreign affairs. There are clouds *even now*; but, having got out of the *greater difficulties last year*, we feel confident that the common sense, the patience, the goodwill, the forbearance, which enabled us to solve *greater and more urgent problems last year*, will enable us to pull through these problems at the present moment.

It is sad that so much of the capital of the world should be wasted in war and in preparations for war. During the last ten years alone the nations of the world have spent £4,500 million in war and in preparations for war – £1,000 million more than Britain has

advanced in fifty years to civilise the world. It is a sad reflection . . .
and I repeat now that I do not believe that this *creeping* catastrophe
which is coming upon the nations will be effectively resisted until
finance takes the matter in hand and saves the world from this
disaster. [Author's italics.]

He ended with an appeal for industrial peace at home, and a prayer that
'civil strife' would be averted in Ireland.

The catastrophe of general war was, in fact, no longer creeping, but
galloping. The crisis precipitated by the Archduke's murder was very
much greater and more urgent than the Balkan crisis of 1912–13,
although this was not yet apparent to Grey, and still less to Lloyd
George. In fairness to Grey, one should admit that he took the
situation seriously from the first, but for nearly a month he worked on
the false assumption that procedures which had been effective before
would be effective again. He hoped that the Germans would restrain
the Austrians, the Russians the Serbians, and that a four-power
conference would produce an accommodation. But the Germans,
unknown to him, far from restraining the Austrians, were on this
occasion exerting the maximum pressure on them to start a war, and
guaranteeing total support if they did. The Austrians, therefore,
presented a virtually unacceptable ultimatum to Serbia and, when the
Serbians gave a satisfactory answer, lost no time in declaring war all
the same.

Until the Austrians delivered their ultimatum – news of which was
conveyed to the Cabinet when it met after the Buckingham Palace
conference on Ireland had broken down – Grey's colleagues had been
unaware that anything really dangerous was afoot in Europe. Eleven
days later the country was at war. The steps from total detachment to
total involvement were so swift that politicians had great difficulty in
adjusting their thoughts. At first Ireland was still competing strongly
for attention; the gun-running at Howth, followed by the Bachelor's
Walk incident in Dublin, occurred on 26 July, two days after the
Austrian ultimatum. But as the true nature of the foreign crisis became
apparent Ireland receded into the background. On 27 July the Germans rejected Grey's proposal for a four-power conference, and the
Cabinet was told that Germany might attack France through
Belgium. Yet there was no agreement at all that France should be
supported in that event. On the contrary, as Churchill later wrote:

'The Cabinet was overwhelmingly pacific. At least three-quarters of its members were determined not to be drawn into a European quarrel, unless Great Britain was herself attacked, which was unlikely.'[1]

On the 29th Grey tried to persuade his colleagues to give conditional backing to France, but without success. Even so, he told the German ambassador, Lichnowsky, that if France were attacked Britain would not be able to stand aside. At about the same time the German Chancellor, Bethmann-Hollweg, was virtually informing the British ambassador, Goschen, of Germany's intention to invade France through Belgium, and appealing for British neutrality. On the 31st there was a move by two members of the Cabinet (Morley and Simon) to secure a declaration that in no circumstances would Britain intervene. Grey said that he would resign if the proposal were adopted, and it was known that if he went Asquith would go too. The proposal therefore lapsed, but there was still no question of any decision the other way. Grey could give the French no encouragement to believe that they would have British support, in the increasingly probable and imminent event of German aggression. His unauthorised remark to Lichnowsky was not repeated to the French ambassador, Cambon, who was in despair at Britain's uncommitted stance:

Meanwhile Austria had gone to war with Serbia, and general mobilisation had been ordered in Russia. The Russian government did not want to be dragged in and had, in fact, influenced the Serbs' disconcertingly conciliatory response to Austria's provocative demands. But when Serbia was attacked the Russians had to act. Britain tried to delay their mobilisation by means of a personal message from George V to his cousin, the Tsar, sent on Asquith's advice in the small hours of the morning. But this arrived too late, and on 1 August Germany declared war on Russia.

On the 2nd the British Conservatives became unequivocally interventionist, when Bonar Law wrote to Asquith that 'it would be fatal to the honour and security of the United Kingdom to hesitate in supporting France and Russia at the present juncture'. Yet the Cabinet still hesitated. At its first meeting that day, in the morning, Asquith read Law's letter to his colleagues, but most of them still hoped that Britain could stay out of the conflict. They were only prepared to

1. *The World Crisis*, ch. VII.

agree – at the price of John Burns's resignation – that the Royal Navy should take responsibility for defending the French Channel coast; further than that they would not go.

By the time they met again, in the evening, they knew that the Germans had marched into Luxemburg, and it was obvious that Belgium would be invaded within a matter of hours. A significant change of mood resulted, and the Cabinet then agreed that Britain would have to take action if there were a 'substantial violation' of Belgian neutrality. Next morning the Cabinet was faced with the news that Germany had sent an ultimatum to Belgium, which King Albert and his government had rejected, appealing to Britain for help. British public opinion, as manifested by huge, demonstrative crowds in central London, now seemed ready for war. All the same, the Cabinet took no decision at its morning meeting, but merely discussed what Grey was to say in the House of Commons that afternoon.

His famous speech there crystallised a view that was already forming. After he had spoken, there could be no doubt that Parliament, like the country, would wholeheartedly support intervention. Redmond followed Bonar Law in pledging the support of his party, and though Ramsay MacDonald spoke in the opposite sense he soon had to resign the Labour leadership to Arthur Henderson. On the 4th, while German troops were marching through Belgium, a British ultimatum to Germany went unheeded, finally expiring at 11 p.m. British time. The Liberal Cabinet thus led the country into war, with the loss of only one more minister, the veteran John Morley.

What was Lloyd George's role in the crisis? Though he opposed intervention until a late stage, he did so without fervour or conviction. Naturally pro-French, and never a true isolationist, he was at first somewhat uncertain how to react, as C. P. Scott found on 27 July:

> As to European situation [he had been speaking before about Ireland] there could be no question of our taking part in any war in the first instance. Knew of no Minister who would be in favour of it. . . . But he admitted that a difficult question would arise if the German fleet were attacking French towns on the other side of the Channel and the French sowed the Channel with mines. He also evidently contemplated our going a certain distance with France and Russia in putting diplomatic pressure on Austria. Then if war

broke out we might make it easy for Italy [nominally in alliance with Austria and Germany] to keep out by as it were pairing with her. This would be a service to Italy, who hated Austria much more than she did France and no more wanted to be in the war than we did; also a service to France by relieving her of one antagonist.

As to the prospect of war he was very gloomy. He thought Austria *wanted* war – she had wanted it before during the Balkan crisis – and not an accommodation. . . . Germany did not want war, but would be bound to support Austria. He thought that if there was to be war it would come quickly so that Germany which could mobilise in a week could gain the initial advantage over France which took a fortnight and Russia which took a month. Germany would probably seek to strike hard at France and cripple her in the first instance, then swing back and strike at Russia. By sea she might use her superiority in order (1) to land a force behind the French force advancing to meet the German invasion across Belgium, (2) to join the Austrian fleet in the Mediterranean and cut the French communications with Algeria where she has a large force of very serviceable native troops.

I [C.P.S.] pointed out the danger of bluffing – of pretending to stand by the 'Triple Entente' in order that we might claim as a price for retiring from it the corresponding retirement of Italy from the Triple Alliance, but he defended it on the ground of serviceableness to France, remarking 'You know I am much more pro-French than you are.'[1]

That conversation goes far to explain Lloyd George's initial non-interventionism, and his eventual acceptance of the necessity to intervene. When he spoke to Scott he was still under the illusion that Germany wanted peace, and that the warmonger in the case was Austria. Had he known that Austria was, in fact, being pushed by Germany, his immediate reaction would, no doubt, have been clearer and more forceful. As it was, he feared that Germany would become involved willy-nilly, and his prime concern, significantly, was for the maritime implications. He said nothing, moreover, of any British obligation to defend the neutrality of Belgium, but emphasised the need to help France.

1. *Scott Diaries*, ed. Trevor Wilson, pp. 91–2. The idea of a German move through Belgium can have come as no surprise to Lloyd George when Grey raised it in Cabinet on 27 July. It had been discussed at some length at a meeting of the Committee of Imperial Defence which he attended on 23 August 1911, during the Agadir crisis.

Until the evening of 2 August he remained associated with those in the Cabinet who believed with varying intensity that British should stay out. But he never sought to lead a peace party, though he alone could have made such a party effective. Judging the issue according to the criterion of British interests as he saw them, he could not agree with out-and-out neutralists that it must always, and in all circumstances, be folly for Britain to take sides in a Continental quarrel. Yet he needed to be satisfied that the existing quarrel called for British intervention, and for some days the evidence did not satisfy him. His attitude is well caught in a letter from Asquith to Venetia Stanley on 1 August:

> We had a Cabinet wh. lasted from 11 to ½ past 1. It is no exaggeration to say that Winston occupied at least half of the time. We came, every now & again, near to the parting of the ways: Morley & I think the Impeccable [Simon] are on what may be called the *Manchester Guardian* tack – that we shd. declare now & at once that *in no circumstances* will we take a hand. This no doubt is the view for the moment of the bulk of the party. Ll. George – all for peace – is more sensible & statesmanlike, for keeping the position still open. . . . The main controversy pivots upon Belgium & its neutrality. We parted in a fairly amicable mood, & are to sit again tomorrow (Sunday) an almost unprecedented event.[1]

At the Cabinet's morning meeting on Sunday the 2nd – at which it was decided to defend the French Channel coast – Lloyd George managed to give Asquith a different impression, that he was with Morley and Harcourt in opposing 'any kind of intervention in any event'.[2] But in fact that had never been his view, and was by then less so than ever. His mind was rapidly moving the other way. He supported the naval decision, as one would expect from what he had said to Scott, and at the evening Cabinet did not dissent from the decision that Britain would have to act if there were 'substantial violation' of Belgian neutrality. He still had reservations, but they were mainly of a long-range political and strategic kind, as can be seen from his remarks that evening after the Cabinet, when he and others were dining with Riddell:

> While we were at dinner, Simon took a paper out of his pocket and, handing it to Lloyd George, said, 'Those are my views'. Lloyd

1. V.S.L., p. 140.
2. *ibid.*, p. 146.

George read it carefully and handed it back to him without comment. Simon showed it to me before he left. It was a draft letter of resignation.

A long discussion took place regarding the rights and wrongs of the situation. Lloyd George brought out the official war map and, putting it on the edge of the dinner table, graphically described the position of the various forces. He said that as a compromise the Government had determined to tell Germany that England would remain neutral if Germany undertook not to attack the coast of France or to enter the English Channel with a view to attacking French shipping. He said that if the Germans gave this undertaking in an unqualified manner and observed the neutrality of Belgium, he would not agree to war but would rather resign. He spoke very strongly, however, regarding the observance of Belgian neutrality . . . . L.G. strongly insisted on the danger of aggrandizing Russia and on the future problems that would arise if Russia and France were successful. I [Riddell] suggested that it would be well to let the future take care of itself, and that we had got to think about the present. How should we feel if we saw France overrun and annihilated? In reply, Lloyd George said, 'How would you feel if you saw Germany overrun and annihilated by Russia?' I said, 'Well, the Germans would have brought it on themselves by their action. The war is due to them. Austria would not have acted as she did if she had not had the support of Germany.' L.G. said, 'Yes, but in 1916 Russia will have a larger Army than Germany, France and Austria put together. . . . No doubt the Germans think they must strike before their enemies are ready to annihilate them. No doubt they have been stimulated by extravagant and erroneous reports regarding the state of affairs in Ireland. In fact the Foreign Office are quite convinced of this.' . . .

Lloyd George was in a difficult position. He was bombarded with letters from friends like Scott of the *Manchester Guardian*, who had wired saying that any Liberal who supported the war would never be allowed by Liberals to enter another Liberal Cabinet.[1]

1. Riddell, *War Diary*, pp. 4–6. The others dining with Riddell were Simon, Masterman and Ramsay MacDonald. MacDonald noted afterwards: 'Masterman jingo, George ruffled, Simon broken. George harped on exposed French coasts & Belgium but I gathered that excuses were being sought for.' (David Marquand, *Ramsay MacDonald*, p. 164.) But Riddell 'understood Ramsay MacDonald to agree that if Belgian neutrality were infringed, this country would be justified in declaring war upon Germany.' Perhaps he, too, had not yet quite made up his mind.

When the Cabinet met the following morning, 3 August, three ministers – Morley, Simon and Beauchamp – were threatening to resign (Burns having gone the night before). But Lloyd George, far from joining in their threat, appealed to them to stay in the Cabinet at least until after Grey's speech in the House of Commons that afternoon. They agreed, and in the event only Morley later resigned. The same day Lloyd George wrote to Margaret at Criccieth:

> I am moving through a nightmare world these days. I have fought hard for peace & succeeded so far in keeping the Cabinet out of it but I am driven to the conclusion that if the small nationality of Belgium is attacked by Germany all my traditions & even prejudices will be engaged on the side of war. I am filled with horror at the prospect. I am even more horrified that I should ever appear to have a share in it but I must bear my share of the ghastly burden though it scorches my flesh to do so.

He stressed the Belgian issue to C. P. Scott, when they met briefly on the 4th. The violation of Belgian territory, he said, had 'completely altered the situation', though he also referred to 'the provocative attitude of German diplomacy [which] the despatches when they were published would prove up to the hilt'. And he mentioned again the maritime issue. The Government 'could not have tolerated attacks on the French coast of the Channel'; had they done so, 'public opinion would have swept them out of power in a week'. He had done his best for peace, but 'events had been too strong for him'.[1]

In Margaret's absence, Frances Stevenson was able to spend the whole of the fateful weekend before Britain entered the war at 11 Downing Street with Lloyd George, and she later gave this account of his views at the time:

> He was certainly no pro-German, but he felt in the first place that we were not prepared for war, and secondly his instinct was against war. He was pressed all the time by his colleagues who *wanted* war with Germany (e.g. Churchill, who was for war at any time, and Asquith who realised probably that war was inevitable). And the anti-war people were certainly not amongst his friends – Simon, for instance, and John Burns, and John Morley. . . .
>
> My own opinion is that L.G.'s mind was really made up from the first, that he knew we would have to go in, and that the invasion of

1. *Scott Diaries*, ed. Trevor Wilson, pp. 96–7.

Belgium was, to be cynical, a heaven-sent excuse for supporting a declaration of war. He was fully aware that in taking the side of the pro-war party in the Government he would offend a large section of his supporters. . . .[1]

A Cabinet colleague, Charles Hobhouse, recorded in his diary: 'At first Ll.G. was very strongly anti-German . . . but as the Liberal papers were very anti-war, he veered round and became peaceful. Churchill was of course for any enterprise which gave him a chance of displaying the Navy as his instrument of destruction.'[2] This comment was thoroughly unfair to both men. Hobhouse and Frances Stevenson alike did Churchill a grave injustice in suggesting that he wanted war. Though his temperament was combative, and his spirit naturally roused by war's excitement and drama, he was also in the position – most rare for a politician at the time – of having witnessed its horrors, and he would definitely have preferred peace, if he had judged it consistent with the country's safety and honour. As in the row over the naval estimates, the difference between him and Lloyd George had much to do with their respective offices. If Lloyd George had been First Lord of the Admiralty in July 1914, and Churchill Chancellor of the Exchequer, it is quite possible that their roles in the crisis might have been reversed. In temperament they had more in common with each other than with any of their colleagues. Lloyd George, though genuinely against war, had always been fascinated by the subject, studying campaigns as eagerly as the young Cromwell. And he too, of course, relished the challenge of great events.

His activities during the past two years or so had been absorbing and at the same time remote from foreign affairs, so it had been all too easy for him to fall into a state of wishful thinking about Germany. His mind was orientated towards the next election, which he hoped the Liberals would be able to win on a programme of peace abroad and further radical reform at home. Many of those Left-wingers whose enthusiasm he needed for his domestic policies were, unlike him, isolationist and neutralist in regard to the outside world, and this was bound to be an embarrassment to him in any serious international crisis. When such a crisis arose in July 1914 his desire to retain their support doubtless increased his reluctance to take an interventionist line in the early stages. But he was reluctant anyway, and did not,

1. Frances Lloyd George, *The Years that are Past*, pp. 73–4.
2. *Inside Asquith's Cabinet*, ed. Edward David, p. 179.

therefore, veer round against his natural inclination. Quite apart from wishing to avoid giving offence to 'a large section of his supporters', he was not yet clear in his mind where Britain's true interest lay.

From his remarks to C. P. Scott we can see that his strong instinct to back France was, even at the outset, competing with other instincts. But there is no sign that he was much concerned, then, about the fate of a 'small nationality'. The importance of Belgium was borne in upon him as the crisis developed, and there were strategic as well as political reasons for this. Anxiety about possible German naval action in the Channel led to anxiety about potential German control of the Belgian coast and the Scheldt estuary – a traditional British concern, but apparently new to him. Moreover, he began to reflect that, if Belgian neutrality could be assured, there would be less need for Britain to intervene on behalf of France, because the French army should then be able to hold the comparatively short line between Belgium and Switzerland despite Germany's superiority in manpower. By the same token, if France were attacked through Belgium, the need for British intervention would be that much greater. Above all he sensed that Belgium would provide, for Britain, the most unifying *casus belli*. There would be far more sympathy for a small country bullied and trodden down by a mighty neighbour than for a country which was not only large but also, until very recently, Britain's historic enemy.

Both at the time and subsequently the belief that Britain went to war for the sake of Belgium was a convenient myth, because to a nation which always likes to feel virtuous it made the decision seem more idealistic than it actually was. But at least this myth was less absurd than to believe, as some did at the time and many more have done since, that Britain was trapped into war against its own interests by a network of secret commitments and the diabolical machinations of Grey. Britain emphatically did not go to war on account of any obligations, legal or moral, to its Entente partners or, for that matter, to Belgium. The Entente relationship with France, and still more Russia, in no way constituted a military alliance, and it was repeatedly explained that staff talks did not restrict or prejudice Britain's freedom of action in the event of war on the Continent, whatever the rights and wrongs. As for Belgium, the Cabinet interpreted the 1839 Treaty as imposing a duty to defend Belgian neutrality upon all the signatories collectively, but not upon Britain in the absence of any of the others. The question of moral obligation was, of course, rather more nebulous, but Cambon found to his chagrin that the British Cabinet recognised no such obligation to support France even as the victim of imminent and flagrant aggression. Finally, it is manifest that the moral claims of Belgium provided not the reason, but rather the pretext, for Britain's decision to intervene.

The *reason* for intervention was that the Cabinet, faced with the fact of a formidable German onslaught in the West, came round to the view that Britain's vital interests were threatened; and the Cabinet's view was shared by Parliament. The peace-at-any-price school, whose strength may have been overrated from the first, dwindled to insignificance when the Germans attacked. It is often argued that if British policy had been less equivocal the war might have been avoided, and it is indeed possible that a clear warning at the beginning of the crisis that Britain would not remain neutral if France were attacked might have deterred the German warlords. When Grey did give his secret and unauthorised warning on 29 July, the effect in Berlin was noticeable, though by then matters had probably gone too far.

It will always be tantalising to speculate what might have happened if Britain's attempt to delay Russian mobilisation had succeeded, but the genuineness of Germany's apparent change of course at that moment is open to considerable doubt. The only time when a warning from Britain might have had a good chance of preventing war was much earlier, but then Grey himself was trying to keep the peace by Concert of Europe methods, rather than by balance of power methods. Had it not been so, he would have been acting in a manner repugnant to the opinion of most of his colleagues, and to British public opinion. The country and its representatives were capable, as they showed, of reacting powerfully when the German threat materialised, but their attitude towards a hypothetical threat was always likely to be uncertain.

The decision to intervene was taken by Britain's leaders with open eyes. It was an unsentimental decision, though the Belgian issue appealed to mass sentiment and so consolidated mass support for the war. Whether or not it was the right decision can never be proved either way, but those who maintain that it was *not* have to ask themselves how long France could have survived as an independent state without British help, and how long – if France and the Channel coast had fallen under German control – Britain could have escaped an even greater and more perilous struggle. No one can fairly accuse the Liberal Cabinet of going to war in any spirit of reckless jingoism.

Those few ministers, including Asquith and Grey, who concluded at a relatively early stage that Britain would have to intervene, did so with much sadness, while the majority, including Lloyd George, came to the same conclusion only after a period of heart-searching which was, if anything, unduly prolonged.

Some will always take the view that, in agreeing to the policy of intervention, Lloyd George sold his soul to the Devil. In fact he made a very hard choice, but one that was both honourable and consistent. For all his eagerness to push ahead with social reform, he could not ignore a threat to the country and its power in the world, upon which, according to his lights, all progress at home ultimately depended. Without having any romantic illusions about war, in the last resort he did not shrink from it, because he knew that 'the same arts that did gain/A power must it maintain'. His decision cost him more time and travail than any other in his life, but once his mind was made up there was no faltering or looking back. For the next four years of unexampled strain and destruction all his creative energies were devoted to ensuring that the struggle ended in victory for Britain.

If he had gone the other way, denouncing intervention, Britain would still have entered the War, though probably under a Coalition or even a Conservative government. The people were in no mood to support a peace party, even if he had been minded to lead one. But although they would have decided to fight without him, it is unlikely that they could have won without him. His commitment to the war does not seem to have been necessary for the country's participation, but was almost certainly necessary for its survival.

SEVEN
Changed Utterly

The Great War which began in August 1914 was an ordeal without precedent in history. Never before had so many nations, or such vast armies, been brought into conflict, and never before had the human and other costs been so enormous. Not all of the world's major powers were involved at the outset. Within a fortnight Japan came in on the side of the Entente, and in November 1914 the Ottoman Empire joined the other side. But it was not until April 1915 that Italy entered the war as an Entente ally, and not until April 1917 that the United States became a 'co-belligerent'. Only then could the struggle be truly described as a world war, though from the first it extended far beyond the confines of Europe.

Hardly anyone foresaw the kind of war it would become. Since the fall of Napoleon Europe had experienced wars which, however large-scale, were of relatively short duration. The only warning of what might happen was in the New World, where the American Civil War lasted for four years, was fought by citizen armies, and cost the lives of more than 600,000 men. But few in Europe heeded the warning. America was a long way off and its example of modern warfare seemed less relevant than the Franco-Prussian war, which was, indeed, a massive trial of strength, but all over within a single year. Most of the leaders who committed their countries to war in 1914 believed that the issue would be decided as quickly as in 1870–1.

For the British, the experience was peculiarly new. Their power in the world had been built up over three or four centuries by naval rather than military means, and they had a deep instinctive prejudice against large standing armies such as their Continental neighbours possessed. Even before their recent period of isolation from the Continent, their military interventions there had been sporadic and limited. They preferred to fight on land by proxy, making the fullest use of allies and mercenaries. At the battle of Waterloo there were more foreign than British troops in Wellington's army alone, quite apart from Blücher's Prussians. The only Continental war that the British had fought since then, the Crimean, was costly in life but all the same undeniably a peripheral affair. Between the Crimea and 1914 they conducted no further operations in Europe, but put down revolts among their subject peoples and fought a number of Imperial wars, of which the most serious was the South African at the turn of the century. This meant that they had more recent experience of fighting on land than the other principal belligerents in 1914; but obviously neither the terrain nor the type of warfare in South Africa was relevant to the struggles awaiting them in France and Flanders.

Most members of the Cabinet did not at first envisage any really substantial British involvement on the Continent. Indeed, the country went to war without any decision to send even a token expeditionary force to France, though the French had good reason to believe that one would be sent as a matter of course. Even when, on 6 August, it was decided that troops should after all be sent, the initial contribution amounted to no more than 120,000 men, while the French were deploying front-line forces a million strong to face a German invading army numbering at least a million and a half. Few in Britain imagined that the B.E.F. sent over in August would be only the advance-guard of what would become a gigantic army. The general assumption was that the war on land would essentially be fought, on the Entente side, by the Russians and French, and that Britain's share in the war would mainly consist of keeping control of the sea, thereby subjecting the Central Powers to a blockade which would help to ensure their swift defeat.

This idea soon had to be abandoned, but meanwhile Britain had to face and overcome its first crisis of the war, which was neither naval nor military, but financial. As such it was, of course, Lloyd George's special concern, and his handling of it showed to the full his capacity for rising to an emergency, which was to be tested again and again during the years immediately ahead.

The financial crisis began as soon as war appeared to be imminent, and resulted from Britain's unique position in the world economy. London was not only the world's principal foreign exchange market; it was also paramount in the spheres of deposit banking, acceptance and discount. At the mere prospect of war the system more or less broke down. By 1 August 'the foreign exchange market had practically ceased to operate, the Stock Exchange was closed, it was impossible to get bills accepted or discounted, the accepting houses and bill-brokers were both in grave danger of having to stop payment, the joint-stock banks were faced with perils of unknown magnitude, and the Bank of England itself found the demands upon it increasing alarmingly, and its reserve very near exhaustion.'[1]

Reflecting on this phenomenon years later, Lloyd George derided the theory that the war was provoked by financiers to serve their own interests. Nothing, to judge from his observation, could have been further from the truth. 'I saw Money before the war; I saw it immediately after the outbreak of war; I lived with it for days, and did my best to steady its nerve, for I knew how much depended on restoring its confidence; and I can say that Money was a frightened and trembling thing.'[2] By common consent his own nerve remained steady. On 1 August, which was a Saturday, the Bank of England was authorised to exceed the legal maximum fiduciary issue, and the Bank rate was raised to 10 per cent. Monday was, conveniently, a Bank Holiday, and it was then proclaimed that the following three days, 4, 5 and 6 August, should also be Bank Holidays. Over the weekend, and throughout the week, Lloyd George worked incessantly on measures to restore credits and revive the system. By Friday 7 August matters were sufficiently under control for the banks to open again for business, and for the Bank rate to be brought down to 5 per cent.

Other measures taken to meet the crisis involved a drastic increase in State intervention. A Bill was rushed through Parliament enabling the Treasury to issue notes for £1 and ten shillings, in case the supply of currency should dry up as a result of the possible hoarding of gold coins. A short-term moratorium on contractual payments was legalised, subject to a list of exceptions designed to protect the poor. Types of payment that could not be postponed included wages, sums not exceeding £5, rates and taxes, National Health Insurance and workmen's compensation. The Treasury guaranteed the Bank of England in action to rescue the discount market, and in advancing

1. E. V. Morgan, *Studies in British Financial Policy, 1914–25*, p. 10.
2. W.M., Vol. I., p. 74.

sums to acceptors. A little later it gave massive support to the Stock Exchange, and it assumed major responsibility for the insurance of shipping in wartime. Though at first Lloyd George invoked the spirit of 'business as usual', to reassure the nervous leaders of commerce and finance, in fact he was introducing almost revolutionary changes.

His methods were as unconventional as his measures. Austen Chamberlain was invited to join the Chancellor's group of advisers, and on one occasion – when Lloyd George had to go off to attend a Cabinet meeting – was even asked to preside in his absence. It was unheard-of, Lloyd George claimed, for an Opposition leader thus to take the chair at a Government conference, and he privately regarded it as a foretaste of coalition. Another Unionist to whom he turned for advice was the veteran Lord St Aldwyn, now a leading banker but formerly, as Sir Michael Hicks-Beach, Chancellor of the Exchequer – a post which he had held when Lloyd George was a young M.P.

But above all, the Chancellor relied upon his friend Rufus Isaacs, now Lord Reading and Lord Chief Justice. Reading, already bored by the high legal office which he had assumed, amid bitter controversy, less than a year before, was only too glad to desert it for more congenial work; or rather to retain it, while neglecting its duties. From his experience as a young man he knew his way about the City of London, and with his combination of knowledge and tact was able to give Lloyd George immense help in his dealings with the banks and other City institutions. It was a tribute to all concerned that his record in the Marconi affair did not prejudice his work, or cause any serious murmurings when he was added to the Treasury team. (There may, however, have been some smiles around the table when, at one meeting, he had to explain the procedure for 'hammering' a member of the Stock Exchange.[1])

Lloyd George made good use of his official advisers, too. He had an excellent working relationship with the Governor of the Bank of England, Sir Walter Cunliffe, whose dour and taciturn manner contrasted piquantly with his own. He continued to be well served by his Permanent Under-Secretary, Sir John Bradbury, whose name became a nickname for the £1 Treasury notes. Sir George Paish, joint editor of the *Statist*, had joined the Chancellor's staff, and his recommendations for dealing with the crisis were very closely followed.[2]

1. Conference at the Treasury, 11 September 1914.
2. George Paish to D.L.G., 1 and 2 August 1914.

J. M. Keynes, though not yet formally recruited to the Treasury, submitted a memorandum in which he advised against the suspension of specie payments, and his advice on this point was taken.[1]

Until August 1914 Lloyd George had no familiarity with the inner workings of the financial system. During his six years at the Exchequer his mind had been absorbed by the social-reforming potential of public finance, rather than by its technical mysteries. Yet his was the sort of mind which could very quickly get the hang of almost any subject, however complicated, and over a few days people who had regarded him as incurably ignorant of finance came to acknowledge, with a certain awe, his growing mastery of its details. According to one Treasury official: ' . . . he promises now to reach the front rank of financial experts, if his present knowledge makes him retain a taste for the pure finance side of the Treasury work which he has hitherto entirely neglected.'[2] And Runciman told a Cabinet colleague: ' . . . the way Lloyd George has picked up financial questions is marvellous. He knew nothing originally of commerce and trade, and bills of lading or exchange, holders, drawers, acceptors had no meaning for him. Notwithstanding all this he has mastered these problems, and captivated the bankers, and the measures taken have been wise, prudent and far-seeing.'[3]

From the official record of many meetings held to discuss the crisis we can see how he kept the experts on their toes, while remedying his own ignorance. Here, for instance, is an exchange with Sir Algernon Firth – president of the Association of Chambers of Commerce – at a meeting with traders' representatives on 3 September:

C. of E.: Just give me what is happening with regard to one or two markets. Take the Canadian market. Take the business which Yorkshire transacts with Canada. [Firth was a Yorkshireman.]

1. 3 August 1914. The memorandum has markings and underlinings in Lloyd George's hand, and one sentence that clearly struck him reads: 'The recent heavy drain of gold from the Bank of England has been mainly due to a fit of hoarding on the part of the Joint Stock Banks.' Another passage marked, though not heeded, expresses doubt about the issue of Treasury £1 notes, rather than Bank of England notes. Keynes joined the Treasury formally in January 1915.
2. Basil Blackett's Diary, 1–8 August 1915, quoted in Cameron Hazlehurst, *Politicians at War*, p. 173.
3. Hobhouse, *Inside Asquith's Cabinet*, entry for 21 August 1914, p. 182. Runciman had recently moved to the Board of Trade, and Hobhouse was Postmaster-General. In 1909, as junior minister at the Treasury, he had written scathingly of Lloyd George's 'absolute contempt for details'.

Supposing you sell goods to Canada, would you mind telling me what the old process was. You drew bills first of all?

A.F.: We drew a bill first of all.

C. of E.: On whom?

A.F.: On the buyer, the merchant in Canada.

C. of E.: Who was the acceptor?

A.F.: The merchant in Canada.

C. of E.: Was there any accepting house that intervened?

A.F.: No, none; it was direct to the merchant; his name and ours were on the bill. It may be a perfectly good firm, which has the funds, but it cannot buy exchange at a reasonable price without losing 5 or 6 per cent; in selling its goods it cannot buy exchange in Canada on London to meet the bills.

C. of E.: Do you know where the machinery has broken down in Canada?

A.F.: No.

C. of E.: You cannot tell me that?

A.F.: No, I should very much like to know myself.[1]

Throughout the discussions he treated the various interested parties as, in the emergency, servants of the State, so long as they showed that they wished to act in the same spirit. But he was quick to rebuke anyone who seemed to be thinking sectionally, as he did at a meeting with businessmen on 11 August, when Sir Alfred Mond and Lord Mersey were firmly reminded of their duty:

A.M.: We are working for the interests of our workpeople, and if the Government think that we have no interest . . . they can feed our 2 million workmen instead of our doing so.

C. of E.: That is beside the point, if I may say so. We are all labouring to the same end, but at the same time you cannot treat the Government as a sort of separate concern; the Government for this purpose is the country, and therefore, when we are going into a concern of this kind [a scheme for financing trade in wartime], we have to do something which is in the interests of the whole country, and we could not blindly give a sort of *carte blanche* to the bankers and financiers of this country to finance anyone whom they thought fit, without any sort of check on them: we should be bad business-

1. P.R.O. This meeting was, typically, attended by a number of other ministers, as well as by officials and the Governor of the Bank. The traders' representatives numbered sixteen.

men if we did that.

M.: I think you overstate the case, if I may say so, from your point of view. The Treasury is not going to finance anyone at all. It is asked to make an advance upon specific goods. If the goods are really worth the 100 per cent, whatever it may be, there can be very little risk in advancing up to 80 per cent and the charge that the Government will make, whether it be 4 per cent or 5 per cent . . . is from the point of view of the gentlemen whom I have been presiding over a sufficient guarantee that the Government cannot possibly lose. That is the way they looked at it.

C. of E.: I quite agree, but do you not think that the bankers are the proper people to make these advances?

M.: You must not ask my opinion about these things.

C. of E.: I am afraid I must.

M.: I do not express any opinion at all.

C. of E.: But you are here, if I may respectfully say so, to advise the Government. . . . You are not merely representing the traders; you are advising the Government.[1]

In retrospect, some of the measures that Lloyd George took in August and September have come in for criticism. Keynes among others argued that the 10 per cent Bank rate imposed on 1 August was unduly high, and there have been suggestions that the moratorium was more wide-ranging than it need have been. It has also been alleged that Lloyd George – despite what he said to Mond – gave too much support to the banks, and was altogether too much under the influence of bankers. But no one denies that, faced with an unprecedented crisis, he succeeded in counteracting a loss of confidence that might soon have led to panic; or that he made it possible for the British financial system to continue to operate, in however limited a form.[2] That was his first vital achievement in the War.

Politically, the country was united behind the decision to fight, and in its determination to win, though not in the actual process of government. There was, at first, no coalition. The Liberals remained in power on their own, with full responsibility for conducting the War.

---

1. P.R.O. Mond, in addition to his great business interests, had been a Liberal M.P. since 1906. Later he was to be a minister under Lloyd George (see chapter 18). Mersey, whose business connections were with Liverpool, had been a Unionist M.P. and a senior Judge.
2. The Stock Exchange did not reopen until 4 January 1915.

Normal party conflict was, in theory, suspended for the duration, though there was an unpleasant revival of it in September, when Irish Home Rule and Welsh Disestablishment were put on the Statute Book, with an accompanying Act postponing their implementation until the war was over. Bonar Law made a most intemperate speech attacking what his biographer describes as 'a fair enough solution',[1] and the Unionist Members then walked out of the House. But on the whole an uneasy truce was established, with the opposition wishing to be patriotic yet keeping a sharp eye on the Government for any signs of failure – of which, before very long, there would be plenty.

Unionist hostility was to some extent disarmed by certain gestures of a quasi-coalitionist kind. One was Lloyd George's invitation to Austen Chamberlain to help him tackle the financial crisis. Another was the fact that Arthur Balfour, who ever since 1906 had retained his seat on the Committee of Imperial Defence, was asked to attend meetings of the War Council. But by far the most important was the choice of a national hero to take the office of Secretary of State for War, which Asquith himself had assumed at the time of the Curragh incident. The hero, of course, was Field Marshal Lord Kitchener. Though in the strict sense apolitical, he was admired and trusted by nearly all Unionists, and his appointment was deeply reassuring to them, as to the nation at large.

Apart from Lord Roberts (who would anyway soon be dead) Kitchener was Britain's most illustrious living soldier. Thanks to good logistics and the Maxim gun he had overwhelmed the Dervishes, recaptured Khartoum and avenged Gordon. Thanks to a strategy of herding Boer families into concentration camps he had brought the war in South Africa to what seemed a victorious, if not exactly a glorious, conclusion. As commander-in-chief in India he had quarrelled with that most imperious of Viceroys, Lord Curzon, and had emerged from the quarrel a clear winner. Most recently he had been serving as agent and consul-general in Egypt, to which post he had been restoring the prestige that it used to have in Cromer's day. His reputation, aided by a tall erect figure and impressive moustache, gave him an aura of almost godlike authority.

Since June he had been home on leave, and was about to return to Egypt as the country became committed to war. On 3 August – the day of Grey's fateful speech in the House of Commons – he was due to

1. Blake, *The Unknown Prime Minister*, p. 229.

leave from Dover, and had actually boarded the cross-Channel steamer when he was recalled to London by a message from the Prime Minister. Asquith was reluctant to offer him the War Office, and had already decided that he would continue to hold the post himself, while delegating the work to Haldane, who would remain Lord Chancellor. But the issue was forced by the sheer weight of political and press opinion, as well as by Kitchener's refusal to serve in any other capacity. On 5 August Asquith yielded, but made out to Venetia Stanley that he had acted spontaneously, in accordance with his own judgment: 'I have taken an important decision today to give up the War Office and instal Kitchener there as an emergency man, until the War comes to an end. . . . It was quite impossible for me to go on, now that the war is actually in being; it requires the undivided time & thought of any man to do the job properly . . . there was none of my colleagues that I could put in my place. . . . It is a hazardous experiment, but the best in the circumstances, I think.'[1]

The experiment was certainly hazardous, and before long turned out to be disastrous. Kitchener was a very remarkable man but also a very awkward one. His strange assortment of qualities and defects would have made him a difficult man to place in 1914, even within the limits of his own profession. But whereas his unfitness to be a warlord was only partial, his unfitness for the collegiate role of a Cabinet minister was total. Even as a soldier he was excessively aloof and self-sufficient; how much more so, therefore, when he was required to cooperate with a group of Parliamentary politicians. Asquith affected to think that it would be 'amusing' to see how he got on in the Cabinet, but in the event there was little cause for amusement.[2] Kitchener did not cooperate; he did not even keep his colleagues informed; and, worse still, it soon became apparent that his autocratic methods were unlikely to win the war. Civilian power had virtually abdicated in favour of military power, without the justification of probable military success.

Yet it is hard to see how Asquith could have avoided making him War Minister. The demand for his appointment came not only from Unionists, and reflected much more than a partisan distrust of Liberals. Above all, it reflected a general popular view – which was to persist throughout the Great War – that civilians should leave the

1. V.S.L., p. 157.
2. *ibid.*, p. 158.

conduct of warlike operations to those who were trained to conduct them. As Churchill wrote, later, with delightful irony:

The foolish doctrine was preached to the public through innumerable agencies that Generals and Admirals must be right on war matters, and civilians of all kinds must be wrong. These erroneous conceptions were inculcated billion-fold by the newspapers under the crudest forms. The feeble or presumptuous politician is portrayed cowering in his office, intent in the crash of the world on Party intrigues or personal glorification, fearful of responsibility, incapable of aught save shallow phrase-making. To him enters the calm, noble, resolute figure of the great Commander by land or sea, resplendent in uniform, glittering with decorations, irradiated with the lustre of the hero, shod with the science and armed with the panoply of war. This stately figure, devoid of the slightest thought of self, offers his clear farsighted guidance and counsel for vehement action or artifice or wise delay. But his advice is rejected; his sound plans put aside; his courageous initiative baffled by political chatterboxes and incompetents. As well, it was suggested, might a great surgeon, about to operate with sure science and the study of a lifetime upon a desperate case, have his arm jogged or his hand impeded, or even his lancet snatched from him, by some agitated relation of the patient. Such was the picture presented to the public, and such was the mood which ruled. It was not however entirely in accordance with the facts; and facts, especially in war, are stubborn things.[1]

In 1914 politicians themselves were largely under the illusion that the professionals must, of necessity, know best. Whereas in the Second World War many political leaders had been exposed to shot and shell in the Great War – had, indeed, been through martial experiences as harrowing as any that the Service chiefs, or most of them, had endured – in the Great War few leading politicians had any first-hand knowledge of life in the armed forces even in peacetime, and Churchill alone had been on active service. The psychological balance in the Great War was, therefore, drastically to the politicians' disadvantage, and for a time they tended to agree with the public that naval and military matters were outside their competence. Even when their own faith in the professionals began to be shaken, they were in

1. W.S.C., *The World Crisis*, Part I, Ch. X.

varying degrees inhibited from trying to shake the public's faith, partly because they were very doubtful of being able to shake it, and partly because the supposed infallibility of commanders was thought to be an almost vital factor in morale.

Kitchener was the most formidable, as well as the first, of the professional 'gods' created by and for public opinion in the Great War. Yet he was far from being a typical specimen of the pre-1914 British officer class. Educated, during his teens, at a French school in Switzerland, he had the unusual accomplishment of being able to speak French fluently; and when he joined the Army, he did not join a smart infantry or cavalry regiment, but the Royal Engineers. Before receiving his commission, and at the risk of forfeiting it for indiscipline, he had enlisted as a private in the French Army during the Franco-Prussian War. Such was the incongruous background to a career of Imperial generalship and proconsulship.

Despite his memories of 1870–1, Kitchener did not believe that the new war in Europe would, like the Franco-Prussian, be over quickly. In his view, it would last at least three years, and he could see no chance of its being won by the Entente unless Britain was prepared to raise a mass army within the shortest possible time. He felt this to be necessary because the French were so heavily outnumbered in the West, and because he had no confidence in the war-winning potential of the Russian 'steam-roller'. His sombre prognosis, and the conclusion that he drew from it, were alike deeply disturbing to his civilian colleagues. But they accepted both, and soon his famous recruiting poster was placarded throughout the land. It was some comfort that the new armies were to be raised by voluntary recruitment, since opposition to conscription was still a principle to which most Liberals religiously adhered.

Lloyd George was to have many rows with Kitchener over the next eighteen months or so, while they were serving as members of the same Cabinet though with utterly different mentalities and notions of government. No other civilian was to stand up to the Field Marshal as Lloyd George did, or to make such deep inroads into his power. But the two men did not immediately clash. Though Lloyd George at first probably shared the general optimism about early victory, hoping that Germany would be swiftly defeated in the war on two fronts, he accepted the need for raising a larger army and did not challenge Kitchener's view of the war's duration as stated at his first Cabinet meeting on 7 August – when he sat, pointedly, on the Prime Minister's right.

Yet it was some weeks before Lloyd George publicly endorsed the concept of a long war, or brought his oratorical talents into play on behalf of the war effort. This silence was due not to any second thoughts about the decision to go to war, but rather to his extreme preoccupation with departmental work, combined with an unwillingness to put on 'war paint' prematurely, or even – as it might turn out – unnecessarily.[1] Such were his gifts as a speaker that a rousing war speech from him would, he knew, inexorably change his character in the eyes of the public from that of a peace minister reluctantly supporting a war to that of an embattled war leader. And if, after all, the war were soon to be over, he would then have changed his image for no good cause. When, therefore, Riddell suggested to him on 19 August that he should 'make a speech explaining the reasons why we were at war and appealing to the patriotism of the people', he replied that 'he did not feel like speaking'.[2] He was still, surely, hoping that patriotism would do its work without any artificial assistance from him, and that he would soon be able to resume the role of a social reformer without having been obliged, meanwhile, to take on a quite different aspect.

By early September his view was changing, and it is easy to see why. In August the war had been going very badly for the Entente. The French High Command, infatuated by a belief in all-out offensive strategy, and failing to anticipate the breadth of the German enveloping movement through Belgium, had launched a series of mass attacks in the Ardennes and Alsace-Lorraine, with predictably catastrophic results. The British Expeditionary Force, marching into Belgium on the left of the French armies, had encountered units of von Kluck's First German Army at Mons, against which it had acquitted itself well. But, alarmed by the retreat of his allies to the South, the British

---

1. In 1903, during the Education controversy, Lloyd George had replied to an archdeacon who was incensed by a speech of his: 'That was purely a fighting speech. I had my war paint on then.'
2. R.W.D., p. 14. There is some analogy between Lloyd George's silence in the early weeks of the war and his abstention from platform polemics between the introduction of his first Budget at the end of April 1909 and his famous Limehouse speech at the end of July. In that instance, too, one reason was simple pressure of work, but another, almost certainly, was that he hoped at first his Budget proposals might go through without the necessity for a constitutional conflict. Only when he saw that there would, as it were, be a long war, because the Opposition was out to kill the Budget, did he resort to the colourful and combative rhetoric of Limehouse.

commander, Sir John French, had then decided on a retreat more headlong than theirs, with the ultimate intention of forming a defensive British bridgehead in Normandy. At the end of the month the Western Allies seemed in total disarray, while the Germans seemed poised to capture Paris. On the Eastern Front, meanwhile, a Russian army advancing into East Prussia had been destroyed at Tannenberg, and with it the comforting myth of the Russian steam-roller, though full news of the disaster was slow to percolate.

The first public indication of Lloyd George's new attitude was when he allowed the Press to report some remarks that he made to a deputation of local authority representatives on 8 September:

> I think cash is going to count much more than we possibly imagine at the present moment. Of course, if we have great victories, and smashing victories, that is all right, but then *they may not come yet*. We may have fluctuations, and *things may last long*. We are fighting a very tough enemy, who is very well prepared for the fight, and he will probably fight to the very end before he will accept the conditions upon which we can possibly make peace, if we are wise.[1]

But this was hardly a stirring utterance. It was not until 19 September that Lloyd George appeared for the first time in his war paint, for all the world to see.

The occasion was a mass meeting at the Queen's Hall, London, whose ostensible purpose was to boost Kitchener's recruiting campaign, more especially among Welshmen living in London. The campaign was already doing well enough. 120,000 men had joined up in August, in response to Kitchener's initial call for 100,000. But he had recently outlined to the Cabinet his plans for raising an army of 600,000 to 700,000 by April 1915. He did not rule out the possibility that there might have to be conscription at a later stage, but for the time being he was getting as many men as he could arm. Churchill argued for conscription at once, but his was a lone voice. Lloyd George felt that the people would not stand for it, and therefore supported Kitchener. His Queen's Hall speech was to be an overt expression of that support, but it was also to be much more: a resounding affirmation of British unity, and a vindication of the Allied cause.

---

1. Author's italics. Lloyd George went on to say that Britain had won wars before with 'the silver bullets'. But clearly he did not think that money would be enough for winning the present war.

Always a careful preparer of major speeches, he prepared this one with even more care than usual. But the day before he was in a very nervous state, which became more pronounced on the day itself, as the time of the meeting approached. Riddell's diary records this painful vigil:

> 18th – L.G. is to make his big speech tomorrow. We had tea together and a long talk. He said he was miserable and inert. His brain would not work. We discussed various suggestions, and then he left to consider them during a walk on Walton Heath. He afterwards told me that he had walked until it was dark.
>
> 19th – L.G. lunched with me at Queen Anne's Gate. The meeting was at 3 in the afternoon. He was terribly nervous, feeling, he said, as if he were about to be executed. It was a curious sight to see him lying on the sofa, yawning and stretching himself in a state of high nervous excitement.[1]

Then he went to the Queen's Hall, where, after a singing of 'The Men of Harlech', he rose to speak.

His first words emphasised the change that was occurring, and that his speech would make irreversible:

> There is no man in this room who has always regarded the prospect of engaging in a great war with greater reluctance and with greater repugnance than I have done throughout the whole of my political life. There is no man either inside or outside of this room more convinced that we could not have avoided it without national dishonour. I am fully alive to the fact that every nation who has ever engaged in any war has always invoked the sacred name of honour. Many a crime has been committed in its name; there are some being committed now. All the same, national honour is a reality, and any nation that disregards it is doomed.

We were honour bound, he said, to defend the integrity of Belgium. We had been ready to defend it in 1870, when it would have been very much in France's interest, at a moment of military crisis, to violate Belgian neutrality. But we did not then have to intervene, because 'the French on that occasion preferred ruin and humiliation to the breaking of their bond'.

Today it was in Prussia's interest, and she had done it. According to

1. R.W.D., p. 32.

the German Chancellor, a treaty was only 'a scrap of paper'.[1] This phrase reminded Lloyd George of his new paper currency:

> Have you any of those neat little Treasury £1 notes? If you have, burn them; they are only scraps of paper. . . . What are they worth? The whole credit of the British Empire.

Treaties were 'the currency of international statesmanship'. In economic matters, the Germans had so far been reliable.

> Let us be fair: German merchants, German traders, have the reputation of being as upright and straightforward as any traders in the world – but if the currency of German commerce is to be debased to the level of that of her statesmanship, no trader from Shanghai to Valparaiso will ever look at a German signature again. This doctrine of the scrap of paper . . . that treaties only bind a nation so long as it is to its interest, goes under the root of all public law. It is the straight road to barbarism. It is as if you were to remove the Magnetic Pole because it was in the way of a German cruiser.

He spoke of Belgium: of her innocence, and of what she was suffering.

> There she was – peaceable, industrious, thrifty, hardworking, giving offence to no one. And her cornfields have been trampled, her villages have been burnt, her art treasures have been destroyed, her men have been slaughtered – yea, and her women and children, too. Hundreds of thousands of her own people . . . are wandering homeless in their own land.

But he guarded himself against exaggeration.

> I am not going into details of outrages. Many of them are untrue, and always are in a war. War is a grim, ghastly business at best or at worst – and I am not going to say that all that has been said in the way of outrages must necessarily be true. I will go beyond that, and I will say that if you turn two millions of men – forced, conscript, compelled, driven – into the field, you will always get amongst them a certain number who will do things that the nation to which they belong would be ashamed of. I am not depending on these

1. The British ambassador in Berlin, Sir Edward Goschen, reported the German Chancellor, Bethmann Hollweg, as saying to him on 4 August: 'Just for a scrap of paper Great Britain is going to make war on a kindred nation which desires nothing better than to be friends with her.'

tales. It is enough for me to have the story which the Germans themselves avow, admit, defend and proclaim – the burning and massacring, the shooting down of harmless people. Why? Because, according to the Germans, these people fired on German soldiers. What business had German soldiers there at all?[1]

He then spoke of Serbia, another little nation that had refused to make the cowardly submission demanded of her by another bullying empire. And this led him into a rhapsody on the subject of small nations.

The world owes much to little nations – and to little men. This theory of bigness, this theory that you must have a big Empire, and a big nation, and a big man – well, long legs have their advantage in a retreat. Frederick the First chose his warriors for their height, and that tradition has become a policy in Germany. Germany applies that ideal to nations, and will only allow 6-foot-2 nations to stand in the ranks. But ah! The world owes much to the little 5-foot-5 nations; the most enduring literature of the world came from little nations; the greatest literature of England came when she was a nation the size of Belgium fighting a great Empire. The heroic deeds that thrill humanity through generations were the deeds of little nations fighting for their freedom. Yea, and the salvation of mankind came through a little nation. God has chosen little nations as the vessels by which He carries His choicest wines to the lips of humanity, to rejoice their hearts, to exalt their vision, to stimulate and strengthen their faith; and if we had stood by when two little nations were being crushed and broken by the brutal hands of barbarism, our shame would have rung down the everlasting ages.

Russia, with her huge territory and autocratic system of government, was clearly an embarrassment to the speaker. But he did the best he could by claiming that Russia had made great sacrifices for freedom

1. In December 1914 the British Government set up a committee, under the chairmanship of Lord Bryce, to investigate German atrocities in Belgium. Going largely on unsworn and uncorroborated depositions by Belgian refugees in England, the committee gave excessive credence to tales of sexual outrage against women. But the truth was sufficiently damning. As Professor Trevor Wilson has written: 'The German State had committed unprovoked aggression upon its neighbour. . . . Further, in pursuit of this policy the German authorities had prepared, and when it suited them put into effect, a deliberate policy of terrorism against Belgian civilians, including the cold-blooded execution of civil hostages and the destruction of towns and buildings of great historic and emotional significance.' (Article in *Journal of Contemporary History*, Vol. 14, 1979.)

– for instance, on behalf of Bulgaria – whereas modern Prussia had made no sacrifice for others. Yet he would not condemn the German people.

They are a great people, and have great qualities of head and hand and heart. I believe, in spite of recent events, that there is as great a store of kindliness in the German peasant as in any peasant in the world; but he has been drilled into a false idea of civilisation. It is efficient, it is capable; but it is a hard civilisation; it is a selfish civilisation; it is a material civilisation.

And it was against that false idea that Britain was fighting, rather than against the German people who were themselves the victims of it.

[They] are under the heel of this miltary caste, and it will be a day of rejoicing for the German peasant, artisan and trader when the military caste is broken. You know its pretensions. They give themselves the air of demi-gods. They walk the pavements, and civilians and their wives are swept into the gutter; they have no right to stand in the way of a great Prussian soldier.

Invoking a modern image, he added:

You know the type of motorist, the terror of the roads, with a 60 horse-power car, who thinks the roads are made for him, and knocks down anybody who impedes the action of his car by a single mile an hour. The Prussian Junker is the road-hog of Europe.

The speech ended in a spirit of growing and almost mystical exaltation, but with stress upon the price that would have to be paid.

They think we cannot beat them. It will not be easy. It will be a long job; it will be a terrible war; but in the end we shall march through terror to triumph. We shall need all our qualities . . . prudence in counsel, daring in action, tenacity in purpose, courage in defeat, moderation in victory; in all things faith!

I envy you young people your opportunity. They have put up the age limit for the Army, but I am sorry to say I have marched a good many years even beyond that. It is a great opportunity, an opportunity that comes only once in many centuries to the children of men. For most generations sacrifice comes in drab and weariness of spirit. It comes to you today, and comes today to us all, in the form of the glow and thrill of a great movement for liberty, that impels millions throughout Europe to the same noble end. It is a great war for the emancipation of Europe from the thraldom of a military caste which has thrown its shadows upon two generations of men, and is now plunging the world into a welter of bloodshed and death. Some have already given their lives. There are some who have given more than their own lives; they have given the lives of those who are dear to them. I honour their courage, and may God be their comfort and their strength. But their reward is at hand; those who have fallen have died consecrated deaths. They have taken their part in the making of a new Europe – a new world. I can see signs of its coming in the glare of the battlefield.

The people will gain more by this struggle in all lands than they comprehend at the present moment. It is true they will be free of the greatest menace to their freedom. That is not all. There is something infinitely greater and more enduring which is emerging already out of this great conflict – a new patriotism, richer, nobler, and more exalted than the old. I see amongst all classes, high and low, shedding themselves of selfishness, a new recognition that the honour of the country does not depend merely on the maintenance of its glory in the stricken field, but also in protecting its homes from distress. It is bringing a new outlook for all classes. The great flood of luxury and sloth which had submerged the land is receding, and a new Britain is appearing. We can see for the first time the fundamental things that matter in life, and that have been obscured from our vision by the tropical growth of prosperity.

May I tell you in a simple parable what I think this war is doing for us? I know a valley in North Wales, between the mountains and the sea. It is a beautiful valley, snug, comfortable, sheltered by the mountains from all the bitter blasts. But it is very enervating, and I remember how the boys were in the habit of climbing the hill above the village to have a glimpse of the great mountains in the distance, and to be stimulated and freshened by the breezes which came from the hilltops, and by the great spectacle of their grandeur. We have been living in a sheltered valley for generations. We have been too comfortable and too indulgent, many, perhaps, too selfish, and the stern hand of Fate has scourged us to an elevation where we can see the great everlasting things that matter for a nation – the great peaks we had forgotten, of Honour, Duty, Patriotism, and, clad in glittering white, the great pinnacle of Sacrifice pointing like a rugged finger to Heaven. We shall descend into the valleys again; but as long as the men and women of this generation last, they will carry in their hearts the image of those great mountain peaks whose foundations are not shaken, though Europe rock and sway in the convulsions of a great war.[1]

Despite a big rush of men to the recruiting room immediately after the speech, Lloyd George was under the impression, at first, that it had not been a success. According to Frances Stevenson he found the audience 'far too stodgy' and felt that he had not penetrated their complacency.[2] D. R. Daniel, who was in the audience, described the meeting as only 'fairly enthusiastic', but then he was unhappy about the war policy and may have been influenced by wishful thinking.[3] One twelve-year-old boy who heard the speech – later himself a famous politician – remembered its impact upon him to the end of his life.[4] In any case Lloyd George was soon reassured beyond his most sanguine hopes. The following day, a Sunday, the newspapers carried full reports, and in Monday's papers the editorials vied with each other in effusiveness. Soon letters and messages were pouring in, and it was clear that the speech had created a more profound sensation among people at large than any speech of Lloyd George's since Limehouse, though this time the effect was unifying rather than divisive.

Praise came from all sides. Liberal politicians and journalists were on the whole rapturous. Asquith congratulated Lloyd George 'with tears in his eyes', Grey said that 'he wept when he read the peroration', and Masterman called the speech the finest in the history of England.[5] J. A. Spender of the *Westminster Gazette* thought it 'wonderful', and Robertson Nicoll of the *British Weekly* hailed it as 'most noble and magnificent'. William Brace, a Labour M.P. and president of the South Wales Miners' Federation, told Lloyd George that Wales was 'proud of her most brilliant son'.[6]

But the response of Conservatives was even more remarkable. There was symbolism in the fact that, at the Queen's Hall, the chair

1. Quotations from the 'authorised edition' of the speech issued, as a pamphlet, by the Parliamentary Recruiting Committee, under the title 'Through Terror to Triumph'. Parentheses indicating applause, laughter etc. omitted. The printed text itself omitted a tactless reference to Mahomet, comparing him with the Kaiser in 'boastful effrontery': hardly good for recruiting in some parts of the British Empire.
2. F.S.D., 21 September 1914, p. 2.
3. D. R. Daniel, unpublished memoirs (N.L.W.).
4. R. A. Butler, *The Art of Memory*, p. 82.
5. F.S.D., same entry as above. On Sunday, the day before he spoke so affectingly to Lloyd George, Asquith wrote to Venetia Stanley: 'Ll. George seems to have made a very characteristic speech, with some excellent "purple patches".' (V.S.L., p. 250).
6. Letters in L.G.P. Nicoll wrote on Saturday; Spender and Brace on Monday.

was taken by Lord Plymouth, a Tory peer who was also a large landowner in Wales: just the sort of man whom in the past Lloyd George had regarded, and who had regarded him, as a bogey-man. It was also symbolic that, the previous day, the Irish Home Rule and Welsh Church Bills had received the Royal Assent despite Bonar Law's extraordinary display of partisanship in the House of Commons on the 15th. The country could no longer afford the bitterness of traditional controversies; there had to be unity at a time of national danger, and Lloyd George was ideally suited to be the agent of catharsis. Rank-and-file Conservatives, who had hitherto been blinded to his true nature by their own prejudices and his colourful polemics, suddenly saw him for what he was: as robust a patriot as any of their own leaders, but with a grander vision and a more inspiring eloquence. The Northcliffe Press, in its fulsome praise of the speech, merely reflected the feelings of its readers.

Among the letters which Lloyd George received from Conservatives, that from Wilson Noble typified the new attitude towards him:

> May an old Tory who sat opposite to you for some years in the House of Commons thank you from the bottom of [his] heart for your splendid speech? Nothing since this brutal war began, hardly even excepting the accounts of gallantry & chivalry of our troops, has done so much good as its perusal. . . .
>
> > yours with intense admiration, etc.

And James Hawthorn, who said that he had been a Conservative all his life, wrote from Brighton:

> I have read the speech which you delivered yesterday, and for the first time in my life have really admired you. Your clearness and aptness of expression and illustration were always undeniable, but your politics and electioneering methods have hitherto been execrable. . . .

One Conservative who had come to admire Lloyd George when he was President of the Board of Trade was Lieutenant-Colonel Mark Lockwood, who now wrote: 'I always said that when you spoke it would be worth hearing. I loved your speech.'[1] He also mentioned that his only nephew and heir had been killed in action. A fortnight or so later Lloyd George replied:

1. 8 October 1914.

I was so sorry to hear the news about your nephew's death, but I know you are too good a patriot to grudge even the life of one to whom you are attached in the service of your country. . . .[1]

Such a sentiment might have come better from him had he not written to his wife a week after the war began:

They are pressing the Territorials to volunteer for the War. [Gwilym] mustn't do that just yet. We are keeping the sea for France – that ought to suffice her for the moment especially as we are sending 100,000 men to help her to bear the first brunt of the attack. That is all that counts for Russia will come in soon. I am dead against carrying on a war of conquest to crush Germany for the benefit of Russia. Beat the German Junker but no war on the German people & *I am not going to sacrifice my nice boy for that purpose. You must write Wil telling him he must on no account be bullied into volunteering abroad.*[2]

With that letter in mind, what are we to make of the Queen's Hall speech? Was it a masterpiece of genuine patriotism, or a masterpiece of hypocrisy? It is important to realise how much Lloyd George's assessment of the task facing the country had changed before he spoke on 19 September. In the second week of August he was still, obviously, hoping that the war would be short and would not require a massive effort by Britain on land. Five weeks later he knew that victory could only be achieved after a long ordeal, and at heavy cost.

On any view, there is surely much to admire in the speech. In its indictment of German policy – of the amoral foreign policy for which Bismarck, above all, was responsible – it stands the test of time. And it has the great merit of distinguishing between German policy and the German people. There is no blanket condemnation of Germany as a nation, nor any failure to recognise the universality of original sin. The vision of a better world to follow the War is splendid, and the fact that it did not, in the event, materialise is no reason for impugning the vision, or for doubting its sincerity. Lloyd George truly believed that ordinary human beings deserved a fuller life, and he truly hoped that 'the War might lead to the making of a new Europe – a new world.' The passage in which he referred to the 'consecrated deaths' of those who fell echoed the famous address by Abraham Lincoln, whom he

1. 8 October 1914.
2. 11 August 1914 (N.L.W. and *Letters*, p. 169). Author's italics.

had always revered, on the battlefield of Gettysburg.[1]

Yet there were two serious flaws in the Queen's Hall speech. First, disproportionate emphasis was given to Belgium and the small nation issue. Of course the violation of Belgian neutrality was a grave offence, and of course Lloyd George had a natural sympathy for small nations. But he must have known in his heart that it was not essentially for the sake of Belgium that Britain had gone to war, or that he personally had felt intervention to be necessary and inescapable. In the speech he almost bracketed Belgium with Serbia, asserting that 'if we had stood by when two little nations were being crushed and broken by the brutal hands of barbarism, our shame would have rung down the everlasting ages'. Yet there would have been no question of British involvement, shame or no shame, if Serbia alone had been attacked; and the decision to intervene on behalf of Belgium would never have been taken if that country's geographical position had been different, or if the German advance had not been sensed as a direct threat to Britain.

There was so much popular feeling for the Belgians, stirred by their brave resistance and their sufferings, that Lloyd George would have been bound to make a good deal of them in his speech, even if he had not shared the feeling, as in fact he very largely did. He would also have been bound to make a good deal of German vandalism in Belgium, and it is to his credit that he did so with a measure of caution, and with the implied admission that atrocities were always liable to occur in the 'grim, ghastly business' of war. He had not forgotten what he said about British concentration camps in South Africa, and did not pretend that Britain's record was entirely clean. But he did suggest that Britain's sole motives for entering the present war were to vindicate the sanctity of treaties and to defend the liberty of small nations. In other words, it was not enlightened self-interest or fear for the security of Britain and her empire, but pure chivalry, that had brought the country into conflict with Germany.

The political advantages of this line were considerable, because it appealed to the ever-potent desire of the British to feel virtuous, and made a special appeal to those who would never have supported the War if they had felt that Britain, too, was merely continuing balance-of-power politics by other means. It also helped to reconcile those

---

1. ' . . . we cannot dedicate, we cannot consecrate, we cannot hallow this ground. The brave men, living and dead, who struggled here, have consecrated it far above our power to add or detract. . . .'

who believed that Britain should hold aloof from Continental wars and rely upon the Navy for her defence. The argument of honour was a handy alternative to the more controversial argument of strategy and geo-politics. Moreover, since national unity was vital, and Lloyd George's aim in making the speech above all to unify the country for a long, hard struggle, he could be forgiven for using some rhetorical licence. Unfortunately he used too much of it in relating the concept of honour so exclusively to the case of Belgium, and to Britain's duty to defend small nations. Britain was a great Imperial power, whose tenderness towards subject nationalities was not always apparent to foreigners; and there was potential embarrassment for the future in playing up the small nation theme as Lloyd George did. National honour was indeed, as he said, a reality, which could not safely be disregarded. But the true point of honour in 1914 was that Britain should contribute fully to the war in which her own survival, as well as that of others, was at stake. To the extent that this point was obscured, the Queen's Hall speech was undeniably flawed.

But there was another and worse defect in it, for which Lloyd George can less easily be excused. If the small nation theme was overplayed, the theme of Sacrifice was grossly exploited, and in a way that does not, somehow, ring quite true. Did he really 'envy' the young men he was addressing their 'opportunity'? For all his moral courage, he was not altogether brave in the physical sense. It would be wrong, certainly, to describe him as a physical coward – no coward would have faced the murderous mob that he deliberately faced at Birmingham in 1901 – but there were limits to his physical courage, and in particular he was frightened of high explosives. He was not, as we have seen, in any hurry to sacrifice his own son Gwilym, and in fact both Gwilym and his elder brother, Dick, were soon serving as A.D.C.s to generals, through their father's influence.[1] Yet in his speech, as in his letter to Lockwood, he was proclaiming death in battle as an end to be met proudly if not actually sought by young warriors, and ungrudgingly accepted by their next-of-kin. For most generations, he said, sacrifice came 'in drab and weariness of spirit', but for the present generation with a 'glow and thrill'. Such a hard-selling tone in recruiting oratory seems distasteful when used by a non-combatant speaker, and distinctly false coming from Lloyd George.

It was also rather odd, surely, for him to be speaking of the British

1. Both, however, later served in positions of danger.

people as having been 'too comfortable and too indulgent', when the ordinary people had been living in conditions which he had denounced in countless speeches as a disgrace to the country. The people to whom his remarks at the Queen's Hall applied were the prosperous classes, but it was not only, or even mainly, from them that the recruits he was calling for would come. Most of those who joined Kitchener's army were leaving mean, cramped homes and stunted lives in Britain to find even greater wretchedness and probable mutilation or death on foreign battlefields. Whereas the well-to-do had, indeed, been running few risks in pre-war Britain, except in financial speculation, rough games or the hunting field, many working-class men had been risking their own and their families' livelihoods in collective action to win marginally improved conditions of work and pay. The waves of strikes before the War anticipated, in the heroism of those who took part in them, the waves of infantry thrown against enemy positions in France or Flanders. And many of the people involved were the same. Sacrifice was no new experience for the poor, who were already sufficiently 'scourged' by the 'stern hand of Fate'. Young working-class men who joined up were not exchanging luxury for sacrifice, but the more or less involuntary sacrifices of peace for the as yet voluntary sacrifice of war. To them what Lloyd George said about sacrifice might well have seemed a cruel mockery, though in fact they appear to have been no less inspired by it than those to whom it more properly applied.

There was one further, and very regrettable, aspect of Lloyd George's peroration, which only time would reveal. Catching the mood of the moment, as expressed by Rupert Brooke and other articulate members of the privileged élite, he gave the idea of Sacrifice a sub-Christian twist by confusing it with the idea of atonement for sin. Whereas the French, for instance, knew that their men were fighting and dying for France, the British were encouraged to feel that they were performing a sacrificial act which would purge the world, once and for all, of the evil of war. This idea became a distinctive feature of the British war mystique, and Lloyd George's speech did much to establish and popularise it. The ultimate result was that, after 1918, Britain succumbed to the tragic illusion that the war had ended war, and that no continuing effort was needed to preserve the peace. Without the distorting motif of atonement, the linking of patriotism with a broader idealism would have been wholly salutary. As it was, Britain's wartime idealism prepared the way for a disastrous post-war fallacy.

But whatever the merits and defects of the Queen's Hall speech, its formidable impact is beyond question. As well as changing the atmosphere in Britain, it changed Lloyd George's position utterly. Willy-nilly, he became the country's civilian war leader in fact, if not yet in name. The speech was not only read by millions in their newspapers; it was also reproduced as a pamphlet under several imprints, and translated into fourteen languages. Subsequent major speeches of his were likewise disseminated, and the effect was to give him a readership similar in scale to the audience for Churchill's broadcasts in the next war. In the pre-radio age no other politician had such a following.[1] While Kitchener was mesmerising the masses as an august figure and a 'great poster',[2] Lloyd George was reaching them with dynamic words. Asquith, still the Prime Minister, enjoyed for a time more general respect than he had known in the last, intensely partisan, days of peace. But he was not cut out to lead a nation at war, and admitted himself that it was not his role 'to carry round the fiery cross'.[3] Besides, as Prime Minister he was bound to incur most of the odium for setbacks and deficiencies in the war effort.

The only other civilian with qualifications for war leadership comparable with Lloyd George's was Winston Churchill; but, though comparable, they were not quite equivalent. Churchill had the energy, imagination and resourcefulness, and he also had one advantage which Lloyd George lacked, that of having taken part in military operations. But his eloquence was not yet, if it was ever, quite as electrifying as Lloyd George's; his speeches seemed more literary and contrived. In any case, he did not have Lloyd George's breadth of appeal, and still less could he compete with it after the Queen's Hall speech. Conservatives had not forgiven Churchill for leaving their party in 1903, or for his wounding attacks on it since his defection, while Liberals could never be sure that he would not, in turn, leave them in the lurch. By contrast, Lloyd George had never changed sides, and his new-found popularity with Conservatives was not yet signifi-

1. An enthusiastic French reader of the speech was the Governor-General of Algeria, who wrote to the British Consul-General on 11 December 1914: 'Lloyd George a un genre bien particulier d'éloquence. Chaque phrase ressemble à un coup de fouet . . . infaillible sur les masses populaires – et quand on y ajoute la logique, l'ordonnement, on est sure également de soulever l'approbation d'une assemblée d'élite.' (L.G.P.)

2. The phrase, often attributed to Margot Asquith, was in fact coined by her daughter Elizabeth.

3. V.S.L., p. 201.

cantly at the expense of Liberal goodwill; he was altogether a more adroit and sensitive politician. As First Lord of the Admiralty Churchill had a direct share in running the war, and this might be thought to have given him a great advantage over other civilian ministers, including Lloyd George. But in fact it worked to his disadvantage, because his many valuable achievements were less obvious than the things that went wrong within his sphere of responsibility, for which he was indiscriminately blamed.

After the Queen's Hall speech, then, Lloyd George was Britain's war premier in waiting, though without having any conscious designs on the position. Unfortunately for the country, he had more than two years to wait.

EIGHT

Coming to Grips with the War

After appealing to the patriotism of London Welshmen at the Queen's Hall, Lloyd George was soon preaching the same message in Wales. At a meeting in his constituency he was preceded by a local man, wounded in action, who said that he had kept his nerve at Mons and in other battles, but that to speak in front of the Chancellor of the Exchequer 'unnerved him completely'. Lloyd George, after expressing his conviction that the war was righteous, used the technique of invidious comparison:

> In recruiting, Scotland comes first in numbers; England is second; Wales is third. Mr Asquith will be in Dublin tomorrow; if Wales does not wake up, we shall be last. That is not the position for a nation which has turned out more soldiers than any in the Continental wars of the past. At Crécy and Agincourt, where the British were eminently successful, half the soldiers were Welsh.[1]

A few days later, at the Park Hall in Cardiff, he spoke to a representative gathering at which the raising of a Welsh army corps was discussed. Lord Plymouth, who again was in the chair, may have had mixed feelings when he heard Lloyd George compare his own recruiting efforts with 'the great voluntary recruiting for the French Revolutionary army' which was also 'done by a lawyer' (presumably

1. Criccieth, 24 September 1914.

Danton). Lawyers, he said, had their uses in a national emergency. And he went on:

> In proportion to our population it is incumbent upon us to raise at least 40,000 or 50,000 men in the Principality of Wales as a contribution to the new army. If every able-bodied man in this country were liable to military service as they are in Germany, in Russia, and in France, the number of men who would at the present moment be under arms from the Principality of Wales would be at least a quarter of a million. All we are asking is to escape conscription . . . a volunteer army of 50,000 is just as good as a forced army of 250,000.

It was important, too, to recruit the brightest and best, because they could be trained more quickly and effectively. But such people had to be convinced that the war was just.

> They have to face wounds, dismay, death, and more. They have to face something which wears down the nerves and the endurance of troops. They have the wet, cold nights in the trenches, and their courage must be sustained by a sense that they are fighting for a righteous cause.

The new army had to make up in morale what it lacked in training. While paying due tribute to those who enlisted in peacetime, he emphasised the high quality of the new recruits. And he was glad that Wales's identity was being recognised for military purposes. The Junkers, with all their faults, knew the importance of territorial inducements when forming an army, and Britain, at least in that respect, must follow their example.

He ended with a muster-call of Wales's two most populous counties.

> I have been looking at the lists – 20,000, I believe, from Glamorganshire. [A voice: '24,000'.] That is better . . . is it 8,000 from Monmouthshire? [Sir Ivor Herbert: '12,000'.] 12,000 and 24,000! Who say that Welshmen are faint-hearted? If they do, Glamorgan and Monmouthshire, at any rate, are prepared to answer. We have almost got our army corps. We might start another today.

in the capital they found it empty-looking and grim.
oung men were at the front, while the politicians apart
ceau and Briand were still at Bordeaux, whither they had
aris seemed likely to fall.[1] Next morning, Sunday, the
a meeting with General Deville, inventor of the famous
, who was accompanied by Captain Cambefort, a fluent
ker and, in normal times, a captain of industry. Deville
sed by the French Government to tell Lloyd George
e wanted to know about the French system of arms
e, and during an hour and a half many questions were
nswered. At lunch, when the party was joined by Briand,
rge asked him if there was any danger of a peace party
France if, as many expected, the Germans were soon
of the country. Briand replied that there was no such
e shall go through to the end.' Another distinguished
seen that day in Paris was the military governor, General
ithout whose initiative the Marne victory would probably
een won.

Monday morning the British party drove to Amiens,
rman Uhlans had been only a month before, but which was
eadquarters of a French army commanded by General de
. On the way they passed through Montdidier, which had
air raid. Lloyd George found bomb fragments there 'hardly
heard, for the first time in his life, 'the crack of shells fired
derous intent against human beings': an experience which,
vn admission, made him shudder. Castelnau took him up to
line within 1,500 yards of the enemy, and during the day he
among others, General de Maudhuy, another army com-
and General Foch, deputy to the commander-in-chief,
offre. After leaving the French generals the visitors looked in
. Headquarters at St Omer, but Sir John French was not there;
een called away because there was fighting on the British
his was the beginning of the first battle of Ypres, in which over

ges Clemenceau was the outstanding Radical veteran of the Third Republic, who had
eputy since 1875 and prime minister from 1906 to 1909. In 1914 he was already well
seventies, but as formidable as ever and a scourge of the weak-kneed. Aristide Briand,
years his junior, was an ex-Socialist who shared with Lloyd George a Celtic
ound (he was a Breton), extraordinary eloquence and a gift for negotiation. At the end
ust, when Viviani had broadened his government to give it a more national character,
had joined it as Minister of Justice. But Clemenceau had stayed out; for him, it was
hip or nothing.

36,000 in two months rallying to the flag! It is a great story.[1]

Lloyd George's determination that military units composed of
Welshmen should have a suitably Cymric character led to his first
brushes with Kitchener. There was a preliminary row about Nonconformist chaplains in the army, Lloyd George maintaining that they
should be allowed to go to the front along with chaplains of the
Established Church, and pointing out that Sikh and Gurkha troops
had priests of their own faith. Despite initial resistance, Kitchener
soon gave way on this issue.[2] But he was harder to budge on the
creation of specifically Welsh units, and on permission for Welsh
soldiers to speak the vernacular on parade or in their billets. These
matters became the subject of what Asquith described as 'a royal row'
between Lloyd George and Kitchener, during which Lloyd George
told the Field Marshal that he was only one member of the Cabinet and
must stand criticism like the rest.[3] The result was a further climbdown by Kitchener, and his agreement that an all-Welsh army corps
should be raised.

The task was not so easy as Lloyd George's euphoria at Cardiff may
have suggested. Of those so far recruited in Wales many had been sent
to reinforce the three existing Welsh regiments – the Royal Welsh
Fusiliers, the South Wales Borderers and the Welsh Regiment, which
consisted of two battalions each and were already in action abroad –
while many had joined a variety of other units, not specifically Welsh.
A further difficulty was that the relatively short stature of Welshmen
caused many to be disqualified by the Army's minimum height
requirement. But when this was reduced for their benefit to 5ft 3ins (or
5ft for special 'bantam' battalions) the numbers began to flow in again.
By the end of the year an all-Welsh division, the 38th, had been
formed, but with mounting casualties and the general demand for
reserves it proved impossible to make up one all-Welsh corps, let

1. 29 September 1914. Asquith spoke in Cardiff a few days after Lloyd George and wrote to
Venetia Stanley: ' . . . we had all the appropriate humours & accompaniments of a Welsh
meeting – "Land of my Fathers", "Men of Harlech" . . . cheers for Lloyd George, cries of
"Clwch" (if that is the way to spell it) xc xc . . . happily we were spared the usual speech or
speeches in the vernacular.' (V.S.L., p. 260.) Sir Ivor Herbert was Liberal M.P. for
Monmouth, and Lord Lieutenant of the county.
2. F.S.D., pp. 3–4. Kitchener had been attracted in his youth to High Church ritualism, so it is
hardly surprising that he had a distaste for Nonconformity.
3. V.S.L., p. 291, and F.S.D., p. 7, corroborated by Hobhouse, op. cit., pp. 203–4. Asquith
wrote: 'K. is much the most to blame: he was clumsy & noisy: he has spent so much of his life
in an Oriental atmosphere, that he cannot acclimatise himself to English conditions.'

alone two. All the same by March 1915 80,000 Welshmen had volunteered for the armed forces, and Lloyd George was able to claim, at the National Eisteddfod on St David's Day, that Wales was then contributing more in relation to its population than any other part of the United Kingdom.[1]

Far more serious than quarrels over the rights and status of Welsh soldiers, which caused no permanent ill-will between Lloyd George and Kitchener, were the differences that began to develop over the war itself, and more especially over the supply of munitions for the army. Once he became aware that the country faced a long struggle, Lloyd George started to give his mind to every aspect of it, without regard to departmental boundaries or the supposed unfitness of civilians to meddle in Service matters. During September the battle of the Marne had saved Paris and frustrated the original German plan of campaign. By the end of the month the spotlight had shifted from France to Flanders, where the Germans were preparing to reduce the Allied position at Antwerp and thereafter, they hoped, to seize the Channel ports. This they had mercifully failed to do when the ports had been theirs for the taking at the time of the precipitate Allied retreat in August. In early October Antwerp fell, but the Belgian army fell back along the Channel coast, while the B.E.F., transferred northwards from the Aisne, was deployed between La Bassée and Ypres.

Lloyd George had already sensed that the war in the West was about to enter a new phase, in which movement and manoeuvre would give way to fixed lines. In his speech at Cardiff he had referred prophetically to 'cold nights in the trenches'. At about the same time he became convinced that the War Office was not equal to the task of providing or procuring arms in sufficient quantities for the enormous army that was being raised. He therefore suggested that a Cabinet committee should be appointed to look into the question. Kitchener was resentful of this idea, and at first his opposition prevented its being acted on. But Asquith's own anxiety about munitions soon overcame his reluctance

1. By the end of the War 280,000 Welshmen had served in the forces, or 13.82 of the male population – a higher percentage than for England or Scotland, and substantially higher than for Ireland. (Kenneth O. Morgan, *Rebirth of a Nation: Wales 1880–1980*, p. 160.) Wales provided twenty-five infantry battalions for Kitchener's armies, as well as Territorial battalions, and many Welshmen served in other units, including the various technical corps. Wales's enhanced military standing, much due to Lloyd George, was further enhanced when, in early 1915, the Welsh Guards were created as the fifth regiment of Foot Guards. (Incidentally, the spelling 'Welch' was not commonly used for the R.W.F. and the Welsh Regiment during the Great War.)

to defy the Field Marshal, and on
committee of the Cabinet, ostensi
supply side. Kitchener himself was
its members were to include Lloyd

After the committee's first two
Lloyd George decided to go at once
committee gave him the pretext tha
system of war production, though in
could about the general state of the w
have been entirely his own. There i
anything to do with it, though presum
then the only Cabinet ministers who h
outbreak of war were Kitchener and
Service departments. Kitchener had tra
of September to steady Sir John Frenc
retreat from Mons and threatening to
altogether. Churchill, more recently
supervise and inspire the defence of tha
was soon talking sarcastically about Cl
we may be sure that he was also rathe
Lord's example contributed to his desire
Above all, since he was now determined
war, he needed all the first-hand informa

He took with him to France Lord
General, Sir John Simon. Reading was
reasons for taking Simon are less clear. T
difficulty been dissuaded from resignin
deciding to go to war, and he was much
Lloyd George. But these very facts may a
his inclusion in the party. Lloyd George ma
involving him more fully in the war, and in t
who might, on their return, help to exer
Minister for more effective action.

The party crossed from Newhaven to Di
16–17 October in a destroyer quaintly (but
ately) named the *Flirt*. From Dieppe they were
towns which had been in the line of the Germ

1. The other members were Runciman, McKenna and Lu
Agriculture).

they arrived
Most of its y
from Clemen
fled when P
visitors had
75-mm gun
English-spe
was author
anything h
manufactur
asked and a
Lloyd Geo
forming in
driven out
danger: 'V
Frenchma
Galliéni, v
not have b

Early o
where Ge
now the
Castelnau
just had a
cold' and
with mu
on his ov
the front
also met
mander,
General
at B.E.F
he had
front. T

1. Geo
been a
into hi
twenty
backg
of Aug
Brian
leader

the next three weeks or so Allied troops managed to save the French Channel ports. By Tuesday morning, the 20th, Lloyd George and his companions were back in London.

What had the mission accomplished? Its most important effect was to educate him in the realities of the war. As he wrote to Margaret on the day of his return: 'Had a great time. Gave me a new idea of what is happening. It is *stalemate*. We cannot turn them out of their trenches & they cannot turn us out.' This was a view he had already been moving towards, but all that he had seen and heard in France tended to confirm it. Even the dashing and aggressive Foch, when asked if there would be any more advances, had replied that that would depend upon the quantity of men and material that Britain would be able to throw into the line. Maudhuy, reputedly also a bold general, had spoken of the terrifying effect of German artillery fire.

As for the declared purpose of the visit, Lloyd George certainly returned with much valuable information about arms supply. Deville and Cambefort told him that at the beginning of the war the French War Office had called together engineers and manufacturers to discuss the problem. The country had then been divided into districts, with selected employers at the head of each, responsible for directing plant and resources as might best serve the national interest. As a result, many private industrial concerns had been converted from producing peacetime consumer goods, such as automobiles, to war production. In the Paris area, for instance, Renault was giving the lead. There had, at first, been an acute shortage of skilled workmen, because so many of them had been indiscriminately called up; but efforts were now being made to correct this mistake.

Asked by Lloyd George if private enterprise in Britain could be used, as in France, to manufacture arms, in particular artillery, Deville replied that he believed it could, though he warned that artillery presented greater problems than any other type of arms, because there were parts of a gun so delicate that only very skilled men could make them. Britain, he said, had an immense number of splendidly equipped engineering works, with every variety of machine and machine-tool, and this should make possible a swifter increase of supply than was occurring in France. Besides, France was short of steel, though he hoped the British would help with that. He would be coming to Britain in a few days' time, and he wanted the British Government to know that he was at their disposal for any technical advice that he could give.

In his memoirs Lloyd George said that he passed this offer on to the War Office, but 'never heard if it came to anything'.[1] In fact, Deville was in London a few days later, lunching at 10 Downing Street and having afterwards what Asquith described as 'quite a good talk'.[2] But it does not follow that the War Office paid much attention to the French expert. Kitchener himself was not hidebound about war production – in this as in many other matters he was strikingly open-minded. Yet his willingness to contemplate change was largely offset by his weakness as an administrator. Even in South Africa, when he was the commander of an army which should have been automatically responsive to his will, he became known as 'K. of Chaos'. In Whitehall, as the head of a department of State, with bureaucrats and politicians to handle, he was at a fatal disadvantage. He had no idea how to delegate, or how to make sure that his orders were carried out. Yet he wanted to run the show himself, and was particularly loth to share any of his power with civilian colleagues.

During the early months of the war the system of military arms supply was still, as in peace, based largely upon the State-owned workshops, of which the Royal Arsenal at Woolwich was the most important. In addition, the War Office had a list of private armament manufacturers, such as Vickers Armstrong and Beardmore, who were considered fit to be awarded contracts. But after the outbreak of war these firms began to be severely handicapped by the shortage of skilled labour, which caused much delay in the carrying out of contracted work. Moreover, the War Office was most reluctant to extend the list of approved firms, because it feared that inexperienced manufacturers would be unable to produce material up to the required standard. Neither Kitchener nor his subordinate most responsible for arms supply – Sir Stanley von Donop, Master General of Ordnance[3] – was competent to meet the vastly increased demand for weaponry. But this did not deter them from insisting that the system should

1. Lloyd George's visit to France in October 1914 is described in W.M., pp. 150–61. There is also a diary of the trip kept by Reading, and a contemporary note on the meeting with Deville written by Simon (L.G.P.).

While at the front Lloyd George asked a young French officer whether stories of German cruelty to women were true. 'No', was the reply, 'they leave them alone as a rule.' And the officer added with a shrug: 'They do not appreciate women.' Could he have sensed that the man he was addressing did? (W.M., p. 160.)

2. V.S.L., p. 283.

3. It is one of the minor miracles of the war that a man with such a name, occupying a key post, escaped victimisation in the wave of Germanophobia that was sweeping the country.

continue to be operated exclusively by the War Office. The struggle between their restrictive attitude and Lloyd George's urgent and anxious interest in the subject was not to end even with the setting up of the Ministry of Munitions the following spring.

Meanwhile his relentless pressure, from September 1914 onwards, did have a considerable effect on the working of the old system. The first munitions committee of the Cabinet, established at his instigation on 12 October, may have met only six times before Kitchener put an end to it by refusing to attend; but while it lasted it brought some notable changes. Finding that von Donop had ordered only 900 18-pounders for delivery in June 1915, the committee forced him to increase the order to 2,100 for delivery in May. After talking to leaders of the largest armaments firms, it enlisted their cooperation in the task of expanding production. Above all, it managed to persuade the Ordnance Department that more firms should be brought into the process. A group was then formed, representing Government and the big manufacturers, whose job was to distribute sub-contracts for the making of arms components. As a result 2,500 additional firms were involved by May 1915.

If the Ministry of Munitions tended, later, both to claim and to receive an invidious monopoly of credit compared with the old system, it is only fair to recall how much Lloyd George had already done to boost arms production before he became directly responsible for it. The output of munitions may have risen nearly twenty-fold in the first six months of the War, but it would not have risen by anything like that amount if the War Office had been left to its own devices. In any case, the improvement that did occur was still very far from adequate, and the need for a fundamental change became increasingly apparent.

On 10 November Lloyd George delivered another major speech on the war, this time to an audience of Nonconformists at the City Temple in London – where, four years before, he had made one of his best peacetime speeches. It was a symptom of the pressure under which he was working that he decided to read the speech, rather than to memorise it and speak from notes as he normally did. But his oratory seems to have lost none of its power to excite, because the speech was a great success.

He began, as at the Queen's Hall, by stressing his lifelong hatred of militarism:

I think this is the second meeting I have ever addressed in my life in support of a war. [He was ignoring his two recent speeches in Wales.] I have addressed scores and hundreds against war and preparations for war. I recollect a meeting which I addressed with my friend, Dr Clifford, in opposition to a war, but it was not as peaceable a meeting as this – and by no means as unanimous.[1] It was a meeting convened to support exactly the same principle, the principle of opposition to the idea that great and powerful empires ought to have the right to use their might to crush small nationalities. We might have been right. We might have been wrong. But the principle which has drawn me to resist even our own country is the one which has brought me here tonight to support my country.

After quoting what a French general had said to him about the war's horrors, he insisted that Britain was not responsible. 'We are in this war from motives of the purest chivalry to defend the weak.' He attacked Germany and Austria as birds of prey. But, he went on:

It may be said it is not enough to prove that Germany is in the wrong. We have to justify Great Britain in embarking on a gigantic war which will tax to the utmost her resources – material, money, men – and leave her impoverished at the end of the struggle . . . we had no right to have gone into this war without the most over-whelming reasons. The sacrifice of human life is appalling. The suffering is impossible to estimate.

There are men who maintain that war is not justifiable under any conditions . . . I am afraid that I shall never be able to attain in this world quite that altitude of idealism . . . I never read a saying of the Master's which would condemn a man for striking a blow for right, justice, or the protection of the weak. To carry those pacifist principles too far is just the way to destroy the possibility of their ever becoming realised. To precipitate ideals is to retard their advent. We are all looking forward to the time when swords shall be beaten into ploughshares and spears into pruning hooks . . . But as long as there are nations and empires that beat ploughshares into swords and pruning hooks into spears in order to prey upon nations of ploughers and pruners living alongside them, to disarm would be to delay a period that we are all praying for.

1. Dr John Clifford, the veteran Baptist leader, had been an ally of Lloyd George in his controversial stand against the Boer War.

As Turkey had entered the war on the enemy side at the beginning of the month, Lloyd George naturally devoted a few scathing words to the bugbear of all good Gladstonians. 'We have been assailed by another national exponent of the higher culture – Turkey . . . and the hour has struck on the great clock of destiny for settling accounts with the Turk.'[1] But soon he was quoting Kitchener as having said, the night before, that the country's supreme need was for more men, and this led him into what was becoming the familiar routine of handing white feathers, as it were, to the hesitant:

There are honest pacifists who disapprove of all wars, and who are prepared to endure the contumely, the scorn, the anger, and the fury of their neighbours for their opinions. Those I respect. But those who approve of the war, and think it the duty of others to make all the sacrifices to bring it to a triumphant end, those men I crave leave to despise. It is only the minority of people who are cowards . . .

He even invoked, in support of his challenge, orthodox Christian beliefs which he had personally discarded long ago, when he was a boy in North Wales:

In days when we were winning the battles of religious persecution in this country there were shirkers. Their cowardice did not save them from the tomb. It is appointed that men should once die, after that the Judgment. Brave men have died, but they need not fear judgment. I think we are too ready to scoff at creeds that promise the glories of their Paradise to those who die for the cause of the country they are devoted to. It is but a crude expression of a truth which is the foundation of their great faith, that sacrifice is ever the surest road to redemption.

The speech ended with a passage in which the mixed fortunes of war were freely admitted:

Sometimes when I read the reports I feel perplexed and baffled. I see accounts of advances here and retirements there, of victories in this spot and mishaps in another, but through it all I think I can see the hand of justice more sure, gradual, slow, but certain, gripping the victory. 'Watchman, what of the night?' It is still dark, and the cries

1. The three Entente powers declared war when Turkey closed the Straits, so cutting the main supply route to Russia.

of rage and anguish still rend the air, but the golden morrow is at hand, and the valiant youth of Britain will return from the stricken fields of Europe, where their heroism has proclaimed to the world that justice is the best sustenance for valour, and that their valour has won a lasting triumph for justice.

With Lloyd George on the platform were all the recognised leaders of English Nonconformity. Robertson Nicoll was in the chair, and said in his speech that, whereas the Devil would have counselled neutrality, Christ had put the sword into their hands. Lady Nicoll, according to the reporter for the *Baptist Times*, 'brought her knitting, and was working away as unconsciously as if by her own fireside' (or, he might have added, at the foot of the guillotine). The City Temple minister, R. J. Campbell, proposed a resolution, which Dr Clifford seconded, pledging Nonconformity to the goal of victory.[1] The occasion was clearly all that Lloyd George could have wished, and he must have felt satisfied as he dined afterwards with Campbell, Clifford and Riddell.

Yet, again, there are aspects of the speech that jar, when read in the light of what we know about his true opinions and motives. Even allowing for the emphases almost mandatory in any speech to a Nonconformist audience, we can still hardly fail to be struck by the hypocrisy of some of the sentiments quoted. It may have been necessary for him to repeat his claim that Britain was fighting solely to defend the weak, and that it was only 'the purest chivalry' that had driven the country to war. Nonconformists as a body were squeamish about 'power politics', and bound to welcome the suggestion that Britain's moral position in the war was qualitatively superior to that of her allies. But did he have to go out of his way to castigate cowards, when his own physical courage was less than complete, and when he was showing – or rather concealing – a marked reluctance to sacrifice his own sons? And did he have to make so much of a belief in the joys of Paradise which he did not himself share? He chose his words carefully so as to avoid any direct statement of personal belief in an afterlife; but they were equally effective in disguising the absence of it.

Lloyd George's actual reasons for supporting the war, and his actual emotions at the time, were sound and honourable. But they differed in some ways from the reasons and emotions that he chose to express,

1. Stephen Koss, *Nonconformity in Modern British Politics*, p. 130.

and his war speeches therefore, for all their power and eloquence, lack the total sincerity that would clinch their right to immortality. At the City Temple he was at his best in the peroration. But even there he was carried away, when saying that the 'golden morrow' was at hand, into forgetting what he had said earlier about Britain's inevitable impoverishment at the end of the struggle. Did anyone notice the contradiction?

While he was beating the drum as a recruiting sergeant, and beginning to interest himself in the wider problems of the war, Lloyd George was still Chancellor of the Exchequer with a work-load that would have been more than enough for any normal minister. In the early days of the war he had restored confidence and enabled the all-important British financial system to keep working. But he was left, of course, with the immense and continuing task of paying for a war whose duration and demands were as yet incalculable.

It was not only that huge sums of money had to be found for the armed forces and their equipment; in addition, the social consequences of the war imposed great new burdens on the Exchequer. For instance, separation allowances had to be paid to the wives of men on active service, and pensions to the widows of those who were killed. On the question of separation allowances, Lloyd George carried the Cabinet with him in disregarding the Archbishop of Canterbury's objection to the treatment of 'Common Law wives' on a par with ordinary married women. He took a conservative line, however, on the rate of pension to be paid to childless war widows, maintaining that it should be only 5/- a week, whereas a majority of the Cabinet voted for 6/6. His attempt to keep the rate down need not be ascribed to heartlessness, but rather to the fact that he, unlike his colleagues, was responsible for finding the money.

Immediately after the outbreak of war the House of Commons had passed a vote of credit for £100 million, and at the end of August a War Loan Act permitting the Government to borrow as it thought fit, for war purposes, on the security of the Consolidated Fund. (A ceiling of £100 million was later placed on this freedom to borrow without fresh authority.) On 16 November a further vote of credit for £225 million was sought and obtained, and the following day Lloyd George introduced his first war Budget, which was, of course, his second for the year 1914. The weekend before he was at Walton Heath, staying there over Monday because he was feeling a bit out of sorts: suffering, according to Asquith, from 'one of those psychological "chills" which always precede his budgets, when he does not feel altogether certain of his ground'. But he seemed confident enough when he rose to present the Budget, and his general performance as Chancellor, in peace and war, hardly seems to justify Asquith's further comment, in the same letter, that he had 'a terrible lack of the best sort of courage'.[1]

He began his speech – which lasted an hour and a half – with a vivid explanation of what the war already entailed financially, and why. Two million men were already in the armed forces, and the figure was likely to rise, in a matter of months, to three million. Britain's expenditure in proportion to the number of men under arms was higher than that of any other country, partly because we had to maintain 'a huge Navy' as well as the 'very considerable Army' already raised. As for the social cost, he estimated that, on the basis of two million men in the forces, separation allowances alone would be costing £65 million a year. For obvious reasons the anticipated revenue for the current financial year would not, under war condi-tions, be fully realised, while to the anticipated expenditure for the year a sum, due to the war, of about £328 million had to be added. This meant that the year's total expenditure would be about £535 million – compared with a maximum ever before spent by the nation on a whole year of war of £71 million. Less the revised estimate of revenue, the amount to be raised before 31 March 1915 was nearly £340 million.

Looking back over the past, he noted that Pitt the Younger during the French war, Gladstone during the Crimean war, and St Aldwyn (Hicks Beach) during the Boer War, had all acted on the principle that war expenditure should so far as possible be met out of taxation. He intended to follow their example. Nobody could tell how long the War would last, but the longer it lasted the worse would be the ultimate consequences of relying too much on borrowing. 'Every twenty millions raised annually by taxation during this period means four or five millions taken off the permanent burdens thereafter imposed on the country.' He proposed, therefore, to double the rates of income tax and super-tax, and – so that all classes should contribute their share towards paying for the war – to increase the duties on beer and tea. The last measure he particularly regretted, but said it was necessary in order to catch 'the elusive teetotaller'.

Since the new taxation could only apply for a third of the year, its

1. V.S.L., p. 316.

impact on the revenue could not, at first, be very significant. In 1914–15 it was estimated to produce no more than £15½ million, though for a full year the expected yield was £65 million, which would represent a forty per cent increase on the total pre-war revenue from tax. Despite Lloyd George's reluctance to borrow, therefore, borrowing was the only way to cover the immediate deficit – and in fact, as the War went on, it remained the principal source of war finance, even though taxation continued to be substantially increased. Having Treasury bills outstanding to the amount of £91 million, he had to find an additional £230 million to close the gap in the current year. So he announced that a War Loan would be floated, and for a sum a good deal larger than was needed for 1914–15. He asked for £350 million, which should be enough to see the country through to July 1915. It was to be issued at 95, redeemable at par in 1928, and to bear an interest of 3½ per cent. Moreover, it was to have the support of the Bank of England, in the sense that the Bank undertook to lend on the security of War Loan, at one per cent below the Bank rate.

The Budget was on the whole well received, and it went through in record time. Lloyd George made a second speech on 17 November, replying to the debate, and he spoke on the Budget again two days later. By the 27th it had passed into law as the Finance Act, 1914 (Session 2).[1] In retrospect, Lloyd George has been criticised for not taking advantage of the prevailing sacrificial mood to ask for much larger increases in taxation, and who is to say that it might not have been possible to strike a better balance, at that time, between taxation and borrowing – a balance more closely in accordance with the principle he had laid down?

On the other hand, one has to remember the abnormal and still very uncertain conditions under which he was working. The Stock Exchange was still closed, and the moratorium had only just been lifted. Credit had been restored by his emergency measures, but it was still potentially shaky, and the outlook for trade and industry was full of imponderables. In these circumstances he had to float a loan which, even if it had been for much less than £350 million, would still have been of unprecedented magnitude. And the people he needed to

---

1. That day he made another big speech in the House of Commons, on the War Obligations Bill. In substance this speech was a description and justification of all that he had done to keep the financial system in working order since the outbreak of war. But the House was ill-attended, as for an equally important speech by Churchill on the work of the Navy, no doubt because the session was coming to an end. (C. Addison, *Four and a Half Years*, Vol. 1, p. 47.)

subscribe to it were, on the whole, people who already felt they had been excessively taxed by him in recent years, and on whom he had already imposed higher direct taxation earlier in the current year. His fiscal demands in November 1914 may have been unduly cautious, but with so much at stake it was surely better to err on the side of caution than of recklessness.

In any case, the Loan was a spectacular success. When Lloyd George announced it in Parliament £100 million had already been pledged by the banks, and the rest of the Loan was soon oversubscribed. He was proud of it himself, and felt that his successor as Chancellor, Reginald McKenna, was wrong to float the next War Loan at 4½ per cent. In Lloyd George's view, it was a bad principle that the British Government should pay the commercial rate for money needed for national defence, and the fact that the precedent was followed in subsequent borrowing cost the country dear.[1] Among those who congratulated him on his Loan, Walter Runciman senior, shipowner and father of the President of the Board of Trade, was particularly warm in his praise. 'This will reflect on Germany with greater force than a military defeat,' he wrote. 'But it is the sound finance that I am so pleased with, and of course I am pleased for your sake.'[2]

The relatively sound finance which Lloyd George was, indeed, practising was not at all evident in the way Britain's allies were trying to meet the cost of the War. At a War Council meeting on 16 December the Chancellor reported that France wanted to borrow money in London.

The French financiers . . . were embarrassed. Before the war they had shirked raising the money for increased military expenditure by taxation, and had resorted to a loan for 32 millions. The issue of this loan had not been completed before the War, with the result that it could now only be obtained on unsatisfactory terms. Now they wished to borrow £12 millions from us, this paltry sum being required in order to reassure their own financiers that this country had sufficient confidence in the stability of French credit.

He also reported that Russia wanted to borrow £100 million in the London market, but Lord Revelstoke had informed him that the

1. W.M., pp. 121–3.
2. Walter Runciman Sr. to D.L.G., 27 November 1914 (Viscount Tenby's collection).

market would not be able to manage more than £3 million unless the loan were placed under the authority of the British Government. Lloyd George's reaction had been that the Government could give backing only for the £40 million specifically required for the war effort (the rest being for internal industries and municipal loans in Russia), and then only if a suitable amount of gold were sent to Britain and interest were charged at the rate of 6 per cent.[1]

A rather different, and more painful, financial problem concerning an ally was that posed by the Belgian government's request for money from Britain to feed the population in occupied Belgium. Lloyd George handled this with brutal clear-headedness, telling the Belgian finance minister on 10 December that not one penny would be made available for the purpose, since the effect of it would be to relieve the Germans of their responsibility for feeding the people, and so to prolong the war. He even dismissed a suggestion by Seebohm Rowntree that Britain should go half-and-half with Germany in feeding the Belgians.[2] To his mind blockade was an essential element in British grand strategy, which had to be maintained uncompromisingly; and his tender feelings for a small nation were easily subdued by his realism.

At the same War Council meeting at which the French and Russian applications for loans were considered, Churchill gave an intensive report on the bombardment of Hartlepool, Scarborough and Whitby by German raiders, which had just occurred. And later in the day he had to tell his colleagues that the German ships had escaped. These raids came as a shock to the British public, but they were not much of a surprise to Lloyd George, who had drawn attention to just such a possibility at the first War Council meeting, on 25 November. According to him, on 16 December Colonel Maurice Hankey arrived at the Council, of which he was secretary, with the words 'Well!

1. Of the French request Asquith wrote to the King: 'Owing to the vicious character of their recent finance and the distrust which is consequently felt by their investing classes, they wish to start the necessary borrowing operations by a loan here of some eight millions [sic] at 5 per cent, which would be, in effect, guaranteed by the British Government. They appear to think that, if this were successfully floated, it would go some way to restore the confidence and open the pockets of their own people. It is a very singular request, coming as it does from one of the richest countries in the world, the amount suggested being little more than, if as much as, the cost of the war for a single week. The Cabinet thought it politic to assent. . . .' (Quoted in Spender and Asquith, Vol. II, p. 129.)

2. F.S.D., pp. 14 and 15–16.

Lloyd George's raid has come off!'¹ And soon the word was going round that 'the inner circle of the Defence Committee' was 'coming to have a high regard for the uncanny foresight of L.G. in military matters'.²

His natural instinct for looking ahead, and for trying to grasp a problem in its entirety with a view to finding ways of solving it, was never more active than at this time, as he brooded on the general state of the war. The Western Front was now consolidated from the Channel coast to Switzerland. The German attempt to break through in the first battle of Ypres had failed, if only narrowly, and Joffre's nibbling attacks after the Marne victory had made no headway. In the East, the Russians had not only been defeated and driven back by the Germans, but had also now fallen back on the Austrian front, where they had won early success. It was known too that they were running desperately short of arms and ammunition. Moreover, Turkey's entry into the war had compelled them to open yet another front in the Caucasus, as it had forced the British to strengthen their garrison in Egypt and to land troops in Mesopotamia. Serbia, despite brave resistance and the recapture of Belgrade, could not be expected to hold out indefinitely without substantial help.

In mid-December Lloyd George was as near as he could ever be to feeling pessimistic, because it seemed to him that the Germans were better trained and better led than the Allies. Though the quality of British soldiers was unsurpassed, they were being wantonly sacrificed because those in authority did not know how to use them properly. A strategy of relentless attrition in the West was 'too horrible to think of'.³ He therefore applied his mind to the task of evolving alternative ways by which the war could be won. After spending Christmas at Criccieth, he returned to London on 29 December, and on New Year's Eve wrote to Asquith:

My dear Prime Minister,
    I am uneasy about the prospects of the War unless the Government take some decisive measures to grip the situation. I can see no signs anywhere that our military leaders and guides are considering

1. F.S.D., pp. 17–18, and R.W.D., pp. 45–6. Lloyd George told Frances Stevenson that Hankey had originally 'laughed at the idea', but the official record (which Hankey prepared) does not bear this out. On the contrary, he seems to have taken the warning seriously, as did Balfour and Kitchener.
2. Addison, *Four and a Half Years*, pp. 52–3.
3. F.S.D., p. 17.

any plans for extricating us from our present unsatisfactory position. Had I not been a witness of their appalling lack of prevision I should not have thought it possible that men so responsibly placed could have so little forethought. . . .

No real effort has been made until this week to ascertain the Russian position. Now [Kitchener] has invited a Russian officer to come over to confer with a view to helping Russia with ammunition. Two months ago I pressed it on the War Office. Had it been done then we could have helped Russia, whilst Archangel was still open, and saved her from the peril of exhausted caissons.

Could we not have a series of meetings of the War Committee . . . at an early date? Occasional meetings will end in nothing.

Forgive me for intruding on your well-earned rest, but I feel that a continuation of the present deadlock is full of danger.

Sincerely yours,
D. Lloyd George

He had also written a longish memorandum to serve as a basis for discussion at the meetings which he was asking Asquith to call. This was circulated to fellow members of the War Council as a secret, printed document on New Year's Day. Unknown to him another memorandum had been written shortly before his, which was also circulated for the same purpose. Its author was Maurice Hankey, about whom a word should now be said. He had been associated with the Committee of Imperial Defence since 1908 – first as assistant secretary and then, since 1912, as secretary – and he combined the mechanical efficiency of a super-bureaucrat with the imagination of a master-strategist. Being half Australian, he did not share the social assumptions of most British officers of his day, and being an officer of the Royal Marines he was able to think of warfare in amphibious terms. Gifted with a formidable memory and a flair for dealing with politicians, he was already quite a key man when the war started. As it went on, his reputation and influence steadily increased.

A copy of Hankey's memorandum reached the Prime Minister on 30 December, and on the same day he received a letter about the war from Churchill. These two documents, and Lloyd George's letter and memorandum, should be considered together, because they are similar in many ways. Yet they seem to have been composed independently. Hankey wrote later of his own memorandum and Lloyd George's: 'The resemblance between them is the more curious as we had never exchanged a word on the subject and of all the members of the Council he was the one I knew least. This coincidence of ideas led to closer contact and was the foundation of an association and friendship that was destined to stand the test of many years of strain and effort.'[1]

The major point on which Churchill, Hankey and Lloyd George agreed was that the war could not be won – or could be won, if at all, only at intolerable cost – by conventional frontal assaults in the West. Some new approach had to be found, they all felt, though there were differences between them on what precisely should be done. Churchill favoured a course of action in which the power of the Navy could be brought more directly to bear on the enemy. As a preliminary he recommended seizure of the island of Borkum, to block the Heligo-land debouch. Thereafter Schleswig-Holstein should be invaded, so that the Kiel canal could be threatened and Denmark encouraged to come in on the Allied side. With the resulting control of the Baltic the Navy could then enable a Russian army to land within ninety miles of Berlin.

Hankey, in his memorandum, mentioned the idea of an invasion of Schleswig-Holstein, but only to dismiss it. Since the area in question could be reached only through Denmark or Holland, and since neither country was likely to enter the war voluntarily, the invasion would be 'inconsistent with our attitude towards the German violation of Belgium'. He was far more interested in action in the eastern Mediter-ranean, particularly against Turkey. But Hankey gave most promi-nence to suggested technical devices for breaking through even a modern system of entrenchments, including one suggestion which clearly foreshadowed the tank.

Lloyd George's memorandum held out no hope of decisive action on the Western Front unless and until the Central Powers were weakened by successful operations elsewhere.

> After three or four months of the most tenacious fighting, involving very heavy losses, the French have not at any one point on the line gained a couple of miles. Would the throwing of an additional half-million men on this front make any real difference? To force the line you would require at least three to one; our reinforcements would not guarantee two to one. . . . Is it not therefore better that we should recognise the impossibility of this particular task, and try

1. Hankey, *The Supreme Command 1914–1918*, Vol. I, p. 250.

and think out some way by which the distinct numerical advantage which the Allies will have attained a few months hence can be rendered effective?

He went on to offer his own solution, after first casting doubt on the northern project outlined in Churchill's letter, which he ascribed to Lord Fisher, the First Sea Lord, rather than to Churchill.[1]

> This proposal is associated with the name of Lord Fisher. For the moment I cannot venture to express any opinion upon it, as I should like to know more about the military and naval possibilities of such an enterprise. It strikes me as being very hazardous, and by no means certain to fulfil the purpose which its originators have in view. Schleswig-Holstein, with its narrow neck, could be easily defended by a comparatively small German force, strongly entrenched against a hostile army seeking to advance into Prussian territory, and there is no room for flanking operations.

He did not mention the political and moral difficulty raised by Hankey, which had probably not occurred to him.

Lloyd George's own idea was that there should be two independent operations in the Mediterranean theatre, which would have 'the common purpose of bringing Germany down by the process of knocking the props from under her, and the further purpose of so compelling her to attenuate her line of defence as to make it more easily penetrable'. The larger of his two proposals was that 'our new forces should be employed in an attack upon Austria, in conjunction with the Serbians, the Roumanians, and the Greeks'. The cooperation of these nations would, he thought, 'be assured if they knew that a great English force would be there to support them'.

How was the great English force to be composed? His figures are a little confusing, but he somehow managed to deduce from them that Britain could make '600,000 available for the Austrian expedition'. 200,000 of these would be experienced troops withdrawn from the Western Front, leaving 100,000 there to stand beside the French and Belgians holding the line, and a reserve of 400,000, partly in England, partly in France, 'to be at hand in case of emergency'. Together with the Serbs and the new Balkan allies, an army of 'between 1,400,000

---

1. 'Jacky' Fisher had been recalled in October to the post which he had already held from 1904 to 1910. He succeeded Prince Louis of Battenberg, who was forced to resign as a victim of anti-German sentiment. *The Times* welcomed Fisher's appointment as a means of restraining Churchill's impetuosity. But it was dangerous for two such egos to be in double harness.

and 1,600,000 men, could be assembled to attack Austria on her most vulnerable frontier.'

Here the population is almost entirely friendly, consisting as it does of Slavonic races who hate both the Germans and the Magyars. We could send our troops up either through Salonica or, as I believe, by landing them on the Dalmatian coast. We would seize islands there which might make an admirable base for supplies not far removed from the railway through Bosnia into Austria. This operation would force the Austrians to detach a considerable army from the defence of Cracow, and thus leave Silesia undefended. The Austrians could not withdraw the whole of their army to face this new attack, because in that case the Russians could pour through the Carpathians and capture either Vienna or Budapest. The front which would be developed would be much too lengthy for the Austrian forces to entrench and hold. The Germans would be compelled either to send large forces to support their Austrian allies or to abandon them. In the first case the Germans would have to hold an enormous length of extended front, in the aggregate 1,200 miles, and the Allies would, for the first time, enjoy the full advantage of the superior numbers which by that time they can put into the field.

A further dividend would be that Italy would be forced to enter the war on the Allied side, in her own interest.

The second, and secondary, operation that he envisaged would be against Turkey. It should, he argued, be such as to enable the troops involved to operate 'not far from the sea', while compelling the Turks to fight on unfavourable terrain and a long distance from their base of supplies. The object should be to win 'a dramatic victory which would encourage our people at home', and he added that it would help if the operation could be in territory which would appeal 'to the imagination of the people as a whole'. His suggestion was that it should be in Syria, by which of course he meant Greater Syria, including the Holy Land. A force of 100,000 landed there could both inflict a local defeat and cut off the Turkish forces deployed against Egypt.

Without such new departures in strategy Lloyd George could see only 'eternal stalemate'. Tough though he was about enforcing the blockade, he did not believe that it alone could win the war.

The process of economic exhaustion alone will not bring us a triumphant peace as long as Germany is in possession of . . . rich allied territories. No country has ever given in under such pressure, apart from defeat in the field. Burke was always indulging in prophecies of victory as a result of France's exhaustion. The war with France went on for twenty years after he indulged in his futile predictions.

Now as then, the enemy had to be beaten by force of arms, in circumstances advantageous to the Allies, allowing sea power and superior numbers to prevail. But plenty of time would need to be given to planning, since expeditions organised without sufficient care usually ended disastrously. He therefore urged his colleagues to take counsel and press forward to a decision without delay.

NINE

'More True Insight and Courage than Anyone Else'

The New Year thoughts of Lloyd George, Churchill and Hankey had the immediate effect of convincing Asquith that the future course of the war ought to be discussed urgently and thoroughly, and by a group of people more select than the Cabinet. At midnight on 1 January 1915 he wrote to Venetia Stanley: 'I am summoning our little "War Council" for Thursday and Friday [7th and 8th] to review the whole situation.' The inverted commas are significant, because they show how unfamiliar a body the War Council still was. Since its constitution in late November it had met only three times. Even in political circles it was not yet regarded as any sort of rival to the Cabinet, while most members of the public were completely unaware of its existence.

The Council had many affinities with the Committee of Imperial Defence, with which, indeed, it tended to be confused. Both bodies had the Prime Minister as chairman, and Hankey as secretary. Both met at irregular intervals, and both were attended by politicians and service chiefs in about equal numbers. Membership of the Council was limited, at first, to Asquith, Lloyd George, Grey, Balfour, Churchill, Fisher, Kitchener and Wolfe Murray (the Chief of the Imperial General Staff), who counted for nothing and never opened his mouth. But soon the Secretary for India, Crewe, was added: a mediocre and colourless man, yet Asquith's favourite minister, presumably because he was equable, mildly literary, and no conceivable threat to the Prime Minister. In time for the January meetings Haldane and Admiral Sir Arthur Wilson were brought in. Haldane's qualifications were obvious. Wilson, a former First Sea Lord, had as such been at loggerheads with Churchill, but he was now back in favour and his function was merely to reinforce the Admiralty's presence in the Council. In March McKenna, Home Secretary, and Harcourt, Colonial Secretary, brought the strength of the Council up to thirteen. Apart from actual members, various other people, such as the commander of the B.E.F., might be summoned to attend *ad hoc*.

Like the Committee of Imperial Defence the War Council had the advantage, not shared by the Cabinet, that its proceedings were minuted. But unlike the C.I.D. it did not work to a fixed agenda, and by meeting in the Cabinet Room at 10 Downing Street, rather than at the Committee's offices in Whitehall Gardens, it was denied easy access to records and maps. Conclusions of the Council were sent to the political heads of departments, and normally treated as executive decisions, though the Cabinet remained the ultimate authority. As a result there was no clear-cut system for running the war. The large peacetime Cabinet was weakened and circumvented, but never, while Asquith was Prime Minister, explicitly superseded. As even his official biographers comment: 'It may be said generally of the next eighteen months . . . that the abdication of the Cabinet did not go far enough. Too many subjects were discussed by too many people with results which troubled the peace of the Government even when they did not affect the conduct of the War.'[1]

Such discussions in the War Council, during the early weeks of 1915, had consequences equally damaging to the Government and to the Allied war effort. From the welter of cross-purposes and competing ideas there emerged an operation in the eastern Mediterranean which nobody had envisaged in the form it eventually took, and which was to turn into a catastrophe of the first magnitude. The Dardanelles campaign was entered into largely by default. Those who wanted to find an alternative to attrition on the Western Front were quite unable to agree among themselves. Some were navalists who believed that the war could be more or less won by sea power, and therefore opposed any substantial commitment of British troops, whether in France or in any other theatre. But even among those who accepted the need for decisive action on land, there was no agreement

1. J. A. Spender and Cyril Asquith, *The Life of Lord Oxford and Asquith*, Vol. II, p. 127.

as to what it should be or where it should take place. If the new armies were not to be used against the German forces massed in the West, then how could they be used more effectively? In an amphibious descent on the north German coast? Against Austria–Hungary, and in support of Serbia? Or in action to weaken the Ottoman Empire, possibly even to knock it out of the war? Whereas the case for playing safe was simple, the adventurous options were complex and contradictory.

It was in these circumstances that the idea of a naval attack on the Dardanelles, put forward by Churchill at the War Council on 13 January, met with general approbation. At the end of a long day, and after two days of fruitless discussion the week before, this proposal seemed almost an answer to prayer. In its suggestion that the Navy could force the Straits, and so achieve a major strategic triumph on its own, it was attractive to most navalists – though not, it must be said, to Fisher, who had grave misgivings about it from the first.[1] It appeared to offer a means of helping Russia, and of making a demonstration of strength which would impress neutrals. 'Westerners' could support it as an operation which, as they thought, would preclude any movement of troops away from the West, while 'Easterners' could support it as action in what they regarded as the right theatre. To Kitchener, under pressure from the B.E.F. and its commander (as well as from the French), yet himself instinctively drawn to the East, the project was seductive. Even Lloyd George gave it his blessing on the spur of the moment, because he wanted some sort of action to be taken against the Turks, and above all because he felt that it left the larger strategic question open.

Even before the preliminary naval bombardment of the Dardanelles forts on 19 February, Churchill had modified his original proposal to the extent of asking that troops should be made available to assist the naval operation, and to exploit its success. It was no longer, therefore, to be a purely naval affair, though the Navy's role was still to be predominant. Kitchener at first agreed to send the 29th division from Britain, but went back on the decision three weeks later. Meanwhile

1. Churchill gave the impression that he was speaking for the Admiralty, whereas in fact he had consulted neither Fisher nor Wilson. These two did not speak against the proposal at the War Council on 13 January, because (as they later argued) it was not their place to speak there unless invited to give their expert opinions. Fisher disliked the proposal partly because it threatened his own Borkum scheme, and he was afraid that it might lead to a diversion of naval strength from the North Sea, but also because he did not think a purely naval attack on the Dardanelles could succeed.

some other troops were moved to the area, including the ANZAC units which had not yet completed their training in Egypt.

On 18 March Admiral J. M. de Robeck, who had assumed naval command off the Dardanelles only two days before, when his predecessor suddenly collapsed, tried to force the Narrows and break through into the Sea of Marmara. But he stopped the action after two of his own battleships, and one from a French squadron under his command, had been sunk by mines, and three more ships disabled by mines or gunfire. This setback was witnessed by General Sir Ian Hamilton, who had just arrived as the overall military commander. Next day the War Council authorised de Robeck to renew his attack if he thought fit, but he and Hamilton agreed that no further attempt should be made to force the Narrows unless and until the Army had gained possession of the Gallipoli peninsula. The roles of the two services as laid down in Churchill's modified plan were thus reversed, and the naval operation became wholly dependent upon the success of a military landing.

Churchill wanted the Navy at least to maintain pressure by continued bombardment and mine-sweeping, but de Robeck was unwilling to risk losing any more ships, and since he had Fisher's backing Churchill felt unable either to overrule or replace him. Consequently the Army had to undertake the appalling task of trying to storm a naturally strong position which, far from being softened up, had been considerably reinforced by the time the Allied assault began on 25 April. By 8 May it was clear that the gamble had not come off. At a cost of 20,000 casualties the troops under Hamilton's command had advanced only a few hundred yards, and had failed to secure the heights from which they might have shelled the Turkish forts protecting the Narrows.

Yet the campaign was not abandoned. British troops, in growing numbers, were kept on the peninsula until the end of the year, engaged in just such a struggle against well-prepared defences as had already proved so heart-breaking on the Western Front. When the decision to leave was eventually taken, the total of killed and wounded was 115,000; and in addition there had been 100,000 casualties from illness during the campaign. Instead of providing an escape from the war of attrition, Gallipoli became just another gruesome example of it. Such was the ultimate consequence of the War Council's flurry of activity between January and March. We must now consider more carefully Lloyd George's part in it, and the merits of his advocacy at the time.

At the first meeting of the year, on 7 January, he drew attention to the conflicting statistics of enemy fighting strength produced by the military chiefs. Whereas Sir John French, in a memorandum designed to promote the case for an offensive in Flanders, suggested that the Allies were superior in manpower on both the main battle fronts, East and West, a War Office memorandum of the previous day gave the German armies a superiority over all the Allies of nearly a million men. How was this discrepancy to be explained? Kitchener could only admit that at the present stage of the war all figures were extremely unreliable. By his searching questions and sharp comment on the balance of forces Lloyd George did more, perhaps, than anyone else to turn opinion against French's proposed offensive, though he could not secure general agreement that the Allies should, for the time being, adopt a purely defensive strategy in the West.

On 8 January he gave the Council a strong statement of his own preferred course of action. This, as he had already explained to Asquith, was to send our surplus troops to join in the fight against Austria, which was the weakest part of the hostile combination and had already suffered heavily. If a British expeditionary force were to land in southern Austria, it could expect a sympathetic greeting from the largely Slavonic population. It would also encounter a nation inferior to Germany in military efficiency. Such action would encourage other nations to come in to obtain their share of the spoils. Austria would then have to withdraw troops from the Russian front, and the Russians would be able to invade Silesia. If Austria were completely knocked out, Germany would be weakened, isolated, and cut off from her supplies of Hungarian wheat and Roumanian oil. The difficulty, as he saw it, was mainly one of lines of communication. The railway from Salonica was good, but only single-track. He therefore suggested that there should also be an approach from Ragusa, to supplement the Salonica approach.

Lloyd George made little headway with his proposal. Asquith, though interested when it was first put to him, did not support it at the meeting. If anything he appeared to be supporting French, when he said that his memorandum was 'a very able statement of the case against action outside France'. Churchill remarked that careful Staff examination should be given to the alternatives; but he had other alternatives in mind, besides Lloyd George's. In fact there was no proper Staff to consider any strategic ideas. Kitchener was virtually working without one at the War Office, since he was applying there, as a most friendly biographer has written, 'the same single-handed methods that had carried him through the Sudan and South Africa'.[1] When he claimed to be giving the Council the results of a preliminary examination of Lloyd George's proposal in the War Office, he was really only giving his own views, which were adverse. Ragusa would be impossible as a base. Salonica could only be used if Greece were an ally, and even then would present many difficulties. To him, the Dardanelles seemed the most suitable objective, both militarily and politically, though he made it clear that he was thinking of an amphibious operation, while in no way suggesting that the troops for it would necessarily be available.

Despite the lack of response from his colleagues, Lloyd George did not give up. On the contrary, he was so convinced that he was right that he redoubled his efforts. Nor did it worry him that the Council, at its next meeting, fell for Churchill's proposed naval attack on the Dardanelles. Indeed, he gave the idea his backing, because he favoured action against the Ottoman Empire as a secondary task in the East, and was pleased that it would not apparently, in this case, divert substantial military force from what he regarded as the primary task of fighting the Austrians. Some troops might be needed to occupy Turkish territory if the Navy's attack were successful, but the bulk of the forces that he hoped would be assembled in the eastern Mediterranean would be available for use against Austria.

The efforts that he made to win acceptance for his idea are lyrically described by Frances Stevenson in her diary:

> In all this I see more clearly than ever the *thoroughness* with which C. [Chancellor: one of her abbreviations for him] sets about accomplishing a plan. . . . He is indefatigable in his efforts, probing every source from which he may gain information which may be of some use to him, scrutinising every difficulty which might present itself, and adopting flanking movements, so to speak, when a frontal attack is not likely to prove successful, 'roping in' persons whose influence is likely to prove helpful or whose opinion counts for something, seeking out those who are 'on the fence' and whose opposition would be dangerous, and then talking them round, using all the arts of which he is a pastmaster. He seems sometimes to the casual observer to be impulsive and impatient, rushing at things

1. George H. Cassar, *Kitchener: Architect of Victory*, p. 295.

in his desire to get 'something done', but no one who has watched him tackling such a weighty project as this can fail to abandon that first impression.[1]

The truth lies somewhere between her uncritical homage and the view imputed by her to superficial observers. He did take immense trouble in developing an argument, applying himself to details without losing sight of the main objective, and all the time exerting his powers of persuasion to the full. He did not slacken his pace, and was undaunted by obstacles. In the equestrian phrase, he would throw his heart to the other side of the fence, and in doing so was rather prone to assume that he had cleared it before he really had. But superabundant optimism was natural to him, and without it he would have achieved little.

After his initial setback Lloyd George was soon making considerable progress, at any rate for a time. The decision of the War Council on 13 January in favour of a *naval* attack on the Dardanelles did not seem to prejudice his Balkan strategy. Moreover, at the end of the same meeting it was decided that, if there were stalemate on the Western Front in the spring, British troops should be sent to some other theatre. Within a few days anxiety was growing about the fate of Serbia, and opinion began to swing Lloyd George's way. Asquith became convinced that help for Serbia was the paramount need, and so apparently did Kitchener. On 20 January he told Lloyd George, in the Prime Minister's presence, that he would find troops to send at once to the Balkans; Lloyd George understood him to promise an army corps. But this hopeful development was scotched by the French commander-in-chief, Joffre, through the instrumentality of the French war minister, Alexandre Millerand, who was little more than Joffre's mouthpiece. Millerand, in London a few days later, persuaded Kitchener that help for Serbia should be delayed until attacks that Joffre was planning in the West had been carried out. As a result, Kitchener told the War Council on 28 January that although Salonica was the first choice as a destination for British troops in the eastern Mediterranean, it was impossible to spare any at the moment. Besides, there was no desperate urgency after all, because snow would prevent any early Austro-German invasion of Serbia.

At the beginning of February Lloyd George tackled the French head-on, in an unauthorised bout of personal diplomacy. His excuse

1. F.S.D., 17 January 1915, p. 21.

for going to Paris was that he had to confer with his French and Russian opposite numbers, MM. Ribot and Bark.[1] But he had no intention of confining himself to financial business, and much of his time was spent discussing grand strategy with leading French politicians. On 3 February he went to the Elysée to expound his Balkan scheme to the President of the Republic, Raymond Poincaré. Also present there was the British ambassador, Bertie, who recorded:

The President said that he saw certain advantages, diplomatic and political, in the suggestions put forward by Mr Lloyd George, and the French Government would consult General Joffre whose views were shared, he understood, by General Foch and Sir John French, but he evidently did not anticipate that the General would be willing to detach any contingent from his armies, and said that the diplomatic and political considerations must be very strong to justify the French Government in disregarding the views of their Military authorites. *Lloyd George also called the President's attention to the advisability of setting up a Council in France, with representatives from the French, Russian and British Commanders-in-chief, so that the latter may be kept informed of the intentions and operations of their colleagues, there being at present a lack of co-ordination between the Armies of the Allies – which is an advantage to the German Commander.* M. Poincaré appeared to approve the suggestion.[2]

The following evening Briand, whom Lloyd George regarded as 'much the ablest man in the Ministry', dined at the British Embassy, and after dinner they talked in the library, with Bertie acting as interpreter:

Lloyd George is by way of understanding some French, but not an appreciable quantity; what was said and re-said and repeated between the two Ministers might have been said in about twenty

1. The British party included Montagu, Cunliffe and Keynes, and the purpose of the talks was to arrange further help for the Russians in paying for war material, while at the same time making the burden more equitable as between the Allies. With some difficulty the French were persuaded to release £160 million worth of gold, and both they and the Russians each agreed to send £7 million of gold to London. Lloyd George got on well with Bark, and when the Russian minister was in London soon afterwards Asquith described him as 'quite a good type of Russian of German rather than Mongolian features, who intermingles English & French in his conversation'. (V.S.L., p. 418.)

2. *The Diary of Lord Bertie,* ed. Lady Algernon Gordon Lennox, Vol. I., pp. 107–8. Author's italics.

minutes, but the conversation lasted for over an hour and a half. On the part of Lloyd George it consisted of much the same arguments which he had used to the President in favour of an expedition to Salonica. Briand said that he had, nearly three months ago, advocated such a measure to relieve the German pressure in Belgium and France . . . but the French Military authorities were against it, and the Cabinet rejected the idea. Yesterday, as a result of the representations made on behalf of the British Government, and after telegraphic consultation with General Joffre, they had come back on its previous rejection and accepted the suggestion in principle.

Briand went on to say that, in his view, an Anglo-French expedition to Salonica, in conjunction with the Greek army, and with some pressure from Russia, would certainly bring Roumania in, and probably Bulgaria as well.[1]

Lloyd George also discussed his ideas with the French Prime Minister and Foreign Minister, Viviani and Delcassé, and he was sure that they, as well as Briand and Ribot, had never been told by Millerand that the British Government wanted to mount an expedition in support of Serbia. Briand was not the only Frenchman to have come earlier to the same view as Lloyd George; two senior French officers, Generals Galliéni and Franchet d'Esperey, had also expressed it. But Joffre was of the opposite opinion, and it was Joffre who determined France's war policy. The French Cabinet took indeed, on 4 February, a decision in favour of sending an Allied force to Salonica, but it was only taken in principle and subject to Joffre's discretion in the matter of timing and the provision of troops. Before returning to England Lloyd George visited Sir John French, and also met for the first time the B.E.F.'s chief of staff, General William Robertson, with whom he felt – ironically, in view of their later relations – that he had established a good rapport on strategy.

Back in London he wrote on 7 February a long letter to Grey, giving an account of his various talks and suggesting that French be asked to attend an early meeting of the War Council. If he could be made to agree to the despatch of at least one division, preferably two, to the Balkans, and if Briand were 'successful in the mission which he promised to undertake to General Joffre', then there would be 'no

---

1. Bertie *op. cit.*, Vol. I, pp. 108–9. Lloyd George told Riddell that Briand had a beautiful voice and talked so distinctly that he was able to follow what he said. (R.W.D., p. 60.)

reason why the expeditionary force should not start within a week or ten days at the outside'. Meanwhile a joint note should be sent to Greece and Roumania.

French came to the War Council meeting two days later, but would not assent to the diversion of a regular division to the East, and further stressed Joffre's opposition to the whole idea of a Balkan campaign. All the same, Asquith summed up in favour of Salonica, and the Council in effect overruled the commander-in-chief. Lloyd George's suggestion of a joint note was adopted so far as Greece was concerned, but it was not until the 15th that the British and French envoys in Athens actually delivered the note to the Greek Government. Then, despite the pro-Allied sympathies of the Greek prime minister, Venizelos, it was turned down, mainly because he was not prepared to move without the collaboration of Roumania, which had not been approached by the Allies at the same time, as Lloyd George had suggested it should be. Another drawback was that the Russians had offered only token assistance for the Balkan campaign, and it was also unfortunate that the preliminary bombardment of the Dardanelles was postponed for various reasons from the 11th to the 19th, so that the Allied *démarche* in Greece was not made, as it might have been, to the accompaniment of a show of strength in the area.

Greece's refusal put an end, for the time being, to any chance of a Salonica expedition. Lloyd George still persisted in his efforts, but the Dardanelles affair soon acquired a fatal momentum of its own, and the 29th division, when eventually moved to the East, was committed to the Dardanelles rather than to Salonica. In the War Council Lloyd George alone warned clearly against large-scale military involvement on the Gallipoli peninsula without a prior forcing of the Straits by the Navy, but his warning went unheeded. At the Council's meeting on 24 February this exchange occurred between him and Churchill:

L.G. agreed that a force ought to be sent to the Levant, which could, if necessary, be used *after the Navy had cleared the Dardanelles* to occupy the Gallipoli peninsula or Constantinople. He wished to know, however, whether in the event of the naval attack failing (and it was something of an experiment) it was proposed that the Army should be used to undertake an operation in which the Navy had failed.

Churchill said this was not the intention. He could, however, conceive a case where the Navy had almost succeeded, but where a military force would just make the difference between failure and success.

L.G. hoped that the Army would not be required or expected to pull the chestnuts out of the fire for the Navy. If we failed at the Dardanelles we ought to be immediately ready to try something else i.e. Salonica. In his opinion we were committed . . . to some action in the Near East, but not necessarily to a siege of the Dardanelles. [Author's italics.]

In the event, after the Navy's failure to force the Narrows on 18 March, the Army was asked to do precisely what Lloyd George apprehended.

Meanwhile he tried to ensure that whatever was attempted in the eastern Mediterranean would be preceded by a political initiative. At the end of another long memorandum circulated to the Cabinet on 22 February he put forward the suggestion that 'a special diplomatic mission, based on our readiness to despatch and maintain a large expeditionary force in the Balkans, should immediately be sent to Greece and Roumania to negotiate a military convention'. And at the War Council on 26 February he proposed, more widely, that a special envoy should be sent to the Balkans and Russia, to concert political and military plans. Grey's comment at the council was that, whereas it would be useless 'to send one diplomatist rather than another', if Lloyd George himself could be spared that 'might achieve something'.

But in fact he was against the idea, as can be seen from what Asquith wrote to Venetia Stanley a few hours later: 'Ll. George is (between us) really anxious to go out as a kind of Extra-Ambassador & Emissary, to visit Russia & all the Balkan States, & try to bring them into line. Grey is dead opposed to anything of the kind.'[1] At another meeting soon afterwards, when the carve-up of the Ottoman Empire was being discussed, and it was reported that Delcassé wanted a conference on the subject in Paris, Lloyd George suggested that the foreign ministers – for it had to be they, not ambassadors – should meet either at Salonica or Lemnos, or on board a British man-of-war in those waters; also that a hint should be given to Italy, Greece and Bulgaria that their fate would probably be settled at the conference. Again Grey did not like to veto Lloyd George's suggestions outright, but saw to it

---

1. V.S.L., p. 449. The Council meeting was in the morning, Asquith's letter written in the afternoon.

that no such conference ever took place.[1]

The Foreign Secretary was wedded to the idea that foreign policy should be conducted at long range, through the established machinery, and there was much to be said for this in normal times. But by 1915 the times were far from normal, and Lloyd George was surely right to think that in a modern war international negotiations could no longer be left to the slow and stately routines of traditional diplomacy. He did not, however, propose a special mission or a summit conference quite as soon as might be inferred from his memoirs. It would have been natural for him to make such a proposal immediately after his visit to Paris, and in his memoirs he suggests that he did.[2] But in fact he seems not to have pressed for any new style of diplomacy in the Balkans until he wrote his memorandum of 22 February, after the Allies' failure to secure Greek cooperation by means of an old-fashioned diplomatic *démarche*. This failure is not referred to in the memoirs, perhaps because he knew that he was to some extent responsible for it, through an uncharacteristic error of omission.

Beyond question he began the year 1915 with an over-simplified view of Balkan politics, which caused him to be too sanguine about forming a coalition of Balkan states. Such a coalition had briefly existed in 1912–13, for the purpose of fighting the Turks, but had soon broken up when its members started to quarrel over the territory they had reclaimed. Wounds from this quarrel had not yet healed, and it would have been very hard to bring Bulgaria into the war as an ally of Serbia, Roumania and Greece, which had scored off Bulgaria in the second Balkan war and the resulting Treaty of Bucharest. There was plenty of hostility to Austria–Hungary, as well as to the Turks, but also much mutual hostility, of which Lloyd George took too little account at the outset.

1. War Council, 26 February 1915. Grey had never travelled in Europe, and by 1915 it was rather late for him to start. His only experience of the outside world had been in the Empire, though even there limited. (The Imperial orientation of the family is bizarrely epitomised in the fact that two of Grey's brothers were killed by wild animals in Africa, one by a lion, the other by a buffalo.)

2. After quoting his letter of 7 February to Grey, he begins the next paragraph: 'In the conversations which I had subsequently with the Prime Minister and the Foreign Secretary, I strongly urged that a conference should immediately be summoned . . . which the Foreign Ministers of France, Russia, Serbia, Greece and Roumania should be invited to attend.' (W.M., p. 413.) The vagueness of the word 'subsequently' may or may not have been intentional.

Soon he realised how tough the political problem was, but refused, all the same, to regard it as insoluble. It seemed to him that Bulgaria could be persuaded to come in if northern Macedonia, taken from her by the Serbs, were given back; and that Serbia would probably agree to this if she were promised Bosnia and Herzegovina as a spoil of victory. These were not idle fancies. Much the same basis for a settlement was being suggested by competent British observers on the spot.[1] It was essential, above all, that the Allies should be in a position to influence, encourage and if necessary arbitrate. In other words, they had to have the largest possible force in the Balkans, and to have it there as soon as possible. With such an asset much might be achieved; in the absence of it, even friendly states could hardly be expected to throw in their lot with the Allies and one at least might join the other side.

Military intervention in the Balkans could not have been attempted without risk in the spring of 1915; but it would have been no more risky then than it was later. And anyway it would have been less hazardous than what was, in fact, attempted at Gallipoli. Moreover the political complications, great as they were, were less than those involved in the Dardanelles campaign; because the supposedly imminent collapse of the Ottoman Empire led to discussions about the future disposal of its territory, in which the Western Allies felt obliged to agree that Constantinople should go to Russia. This immediately cost them Greek participation in the campaign, which might have made all the difference.[2]

On the whole Lloyd George emerges from the strategic arguments in early 1915 more creditably than anyone. His perception that help for Serbia was the most urgent need, and Austria–Hungary the enemy

1. On 15 January 1915 G. M. Trevelyan wrote from Sofia to Francis Acland, Under-Secretary at the Foreign Office: 'We have today telegraphed to Grey urging that every diplomatic and military effort should be made to save Serbia . . . we can say from numerous conversations with Serbians from the Crown Prince downwards that the more Yugo-Slavia and Adriatic [i.e. Bosnia and Herzegovina] expansion are dwelt upon, the more Serbians will be willing to concede to Macedonia [i.e. Bulgaria]. And that Serbia will only concede at the friendly dictation of the Great Powers her Allies.' Trevelyan was travelling with Robert Seton-Watson, already an acknowledged expert on the area, and clearly expressing a view which he shared. Similar advice was being sent from Bucharest by Charles and Noel Buxton. (V.S.L., pp. 380–1.)

2. The Greeks had offered to come into the war on the side of the Entente in late August 1914, but the offer had been refused for fear of provoking Turkey, which was then still neutral. In March 1915 they offered to send troops to help the Allies take Constantinople, but this was precluded by the commitment to Russia.

most profitable to attack, was surely correct. His claim that the Allies should have acted more promptly in the Balkans – that they delayed until the best opportunities were lost – seems substantially justified. His attempts to promote an expedition to Salonica, and thereby a Balkan alliance against the Central Powers, were soundly based in principle, if at first rather cavalier in regard to detail. He was right to try to convert the French to his view, and his personal diplomacy in Paris was successful so far as it went, though he failed to see, let alone convert, the one Frenchman who really mattered at the time: Joffre. His suggestion to Poincaré that there should be a supreme Allied war council in Paris shows impressive realism and prescience.

No less striking is his clear-sightedness about the Dardanelles, and he did not make the mistake, which many others made, of underrating the Turks. At the War Council on 26 February Balfour asked 'whether the Turks were likely, if cut off, to surrender or to fight with their backs to the wall', and Kitchener replied that they would probably surrender. But Lloyd George said he 'thought it more probable that they would make a stand, as they had done in the Russo-Turkish war and at Chatalja in the recent Balkan wars'.

During the general discussion of war aims to which the Dardanelles plan gave rise, he made two observations which seem very significant in retrospect. On 10 March he said that he doubted the expediency of occupying Alexandretta – a course strongly urged by Kitchener – but 'suggested Palestine as an alternative owing to the prestige it would give us'. And on 19 March, when Haldane raised the question 'whether we intended to leave the Germans and Turks crushed at the end of the war', Lloyd George was for dealing generously with the former: 'We ought not to rule out the possibility of giving Germany a bone of some sort. She would always be a very powerful nation, and it might eventually be desirable to have her in a position to prevent Russia becoming too predominant.'

Reflecting on the blighted hopes of early 1915, Hankey wrote many years later: 'Tremendous driving power, energy and tact were required, first to unite the Allies and then to deal with the Balkan States. Fisher put his finger on the spot when he said: "You want *one* man." A Chatham, a Pitt or Lloyd George at his best might have been equal to the task, but Lloyd George's time had not yet come.'[1]

When his time did come – when, as Prime Minister, he had the fullest scope for initiating policy and for carrying it through – conditions in the Balkans, and in the war generally, were far less favourable to the Allies. During the opening weeks of 1915 the most promising options were still open and he seems to have been just about at his best. It was at this time that Churchill wrote of him: 'L.G. has more true insight and courage than anyone else. He really sticks at nothing – no measure too far-reaching, no expedient too novel.'[1] Unfortunately he was not yet at the top.

Of course, it was inevitable that he should be most strictly limited in what he could achieve, and should suffer the worst frustration, in the fields of foreign policy and strategy, because in those others were supposed to be expert. But he could not so easily be baulked in matters relating to the home front, because there his reputation was similar, *mutatis mutandis*, to Kitchener's as a warlord. With the fading of his hopes for prompt action in the Balkans he concentrated, therefore, increasingly upon the domestic side of the war. In his Cabinet memorandum of 22 February he argued that full powers should be taken to mobilise Britain's manufacturing strength for the production of war material, to commandeer all factories and, if necessary, 'to deal with labour difficulties and shortcomings'. And on the last day of the month he gave dramatic emphasis to the home front in another major public speech, delivered this time in his constituency, at Bangor.

A cathedral city and, relatively speaking, a Tory stronghold, Bangor had never been his favourite among the Caernarvon Boroughs. During the Boer war he had been almost knocked out there by an over-demonstrative opponent who struck him in the street with a bludgeon. But in the present war his image was very different, and Bangor must have seemed a good place to advertise the new political ecumenism. He told Riddell that he dictated his speech on the train to Bangor, but Frances Stevenson's diary suggests more careful preparation; and it would, indeed, have been out of character for him to be slapdash in his approach to such an important test.

The test was made rather tougher by the fact that he chose to speak on a Sunday (and, to make matters worse, in a theatre). But he lost no time in justifying this violation of the Sabbath. Ministers were so busy, he said, that Sundays were the only days they had to spare. Moreover, he had been told by an eminent Scottish divine that the

1. W.S.C. to his brother Jack, 26 February 1915.

Shorter Catechism allowed works of charity or necessity to be performed on a Sunday:

> . . . and those who tell me that this is not work of necessity do not know the need, the dire need, of their country at this hour. At this moment there are Welshmen in the trenches of France facing cannon and death; the hammering of forges today is ringing down the church bells from one end of Europe to the other. When I know these things are going on now on Sundays as well as on weekdays, I am not the hypocrite to say 'I will save my own soul by not talking about them on Sundays.'

He wondered if the British people did yet really understand the sort of war they were in, or the effort that would be needed to win it. The French understood well enough, as he could testify:

> A few weeks ago I visited France . . . Paris is a changed city. Her gaiety, her vivacity is gone. You can see in the faces of every man there, and of every woman, that they know that their country is in the grip of grim tragedy. They are resolved to overcome it, confident that they will overcome it, but only through a long agony. But no visitor to our shores would realise that we were engaged in the same conflict. . . . We are conducting a war as if there was no war.[1]

He was sure that the Allies would win in the end, because they had superior natural resources and the better cause. But the struggle would be long and hard. War was no longer a simple business:

> In the old days when a nation's liberty was menaced by an aggressor a man took from the chimney corner his bow and arrow or his spear, or a sword which had been left to him by an ancestry of warriors, went to the gathering ground of his tribe, and the nation was fully equipped for war. That is not the case now. Now you

1. There may have been a subsidiary motive for his evocation of a Paris transformed and woebegone. While he was there at the beginning of the month the Central News Agency had reported a visit by him to the Quartier Latin 'after a busy day in conference'. Though it was stated that his object in going there had been to see the Quartier 'under war conditions', Lloyd George contradicted the story angrily and demanded an apology (which he received). It may still, however, have seemed worth mentioning several weeks later that the war had extinguished all fun in a city popularly supposed in Britain, and more especially among Nonconformists, to be dedicated to sinful pleasure. He must have been rather annoyed, therefore, if he noticed in *The Times* of 1 March, on the page opposite the report of his speech, a story with these headlines: 'Reviving Paris. A New Interest in Clothes. The Short Skirt.'

fight with complicated, highly finished weapons, apart altogether from the huge artillery. . . .

There was a wonderful spirit, uniting all classes, which had produced the great surge of volunteers. But

Much as I should like to talk about the need for more men, that is not the point of my special appeal today. We stand more in need of equipment than we do of men. This is an engineers' war, and it will be won or lost owing to the efforts or shortcomings of engineers. . . . We need men, but we need arms more than men, and delay in producing them is full of peril for this country. You may say that I am saying things that ought to be kept from the enemy. I am not a believer in giving any information which is useful to him. You may depend on it he knows, but I do not believe in holding from our own public information which they ought to possess, because unless you tell them you cannot invite their cooperation. The nation that cannot bear the truth is not fit for war. . . .

Hope was the mainspring of efficiency; complacency the rust. But how were the engineering resources of the nation to be mobilised?

Here I am approaching something which is very difficult to talk about – I mean the employers and workmen. I must speak out quite plainly. . . . For one reason or another we are not getting all the assistance we have the right to expect from our workers. Disputes, industrial disputes, are inevitable; and when you have a good deal of stress and strain, men's nerves are not at their best . . . some differences of opinion are quite inevitable, but we cannot afford them now; and above all we cannot resort to the usual methods of settling them.

He had plenty of experience of labour disputes, and under normal conditions the best way to settle them was to be patient and not try to rush things.

But, you know, we cannot afford these leisurely methods now. Time is victory; and while employers and workmen on the Clyde have been spending time in disputing over a fraction, and when a weekend, ten days and a fortnight of work which is absolutely necessary for the defences of the country has been set aside, I say here solemnly that it is intolerable that the life of Britain should be imperilled for the matter of a farthing an hour.[1]

It was immaterial who was to blame. Employers might ask, were they always to give way, and workmen might say that they were entitled to their 'share of the plunder' when employers were making fortunes out of the war. Both were right, and both were wrong.

> The whole point is that these questions ought to be settled without throwing away the chances of humanity in its greatest struggle . . . during the war the Government ought to have the power to settle all these differences, and the work should go on.

He touched upon the 'difficult and dangerous' subject of trade union restrictive practices:

> There are all sorts of regulations for restricting output. There are reasons why they have been built up. The conditions of employment and payment are mostly to blame for those restrictions. The workmen had to fight for them for their own protection, but in a period of war there is a suspension of ordinary law. Output is everything in this war.

Then he ventured on to even more controversial ground:

> Most of our workmen are putting every ounce of strength into this urgent work for their country, loyally and patriotically. But that is not true of all. There are some, I am sorry to say, who shirk their duty in this great emergency. I hear of workmen in armaments works who refuse to work a full week's work for the nation's need. . . . They are a minority. The vast majority belong to a class we can depend upon. The others are a minority. But, you must remember, a small minority of workmen can throw a whole works out of gear. What is the reason? Sometimes it is one thing, sometimes it is another, but let us be perfectly candid. It is mostly the lure of the drink. They refuse to work full time, and when they return their strength and efficiency are impaired by the way in which they have spent their leisure. Drink is doing us more damage in the war than all the German submarines put together.

Near the end of the speech he returned to the theme, so strongly proclaimed already at the Queen's Hall and the City Temple, that the Allies were fighting a necessary and just war. But he went out of his

1. For the causes of this and other disputes see below.

way to indicate that there was a good side to Germany:

> There has been a struggle going on in Germany for over thirty years between its best and its worst elements. It is like the great struggle which is depicted, I think, in one of Wagner's great operas between the good and the evil spirit for possession of the man's soul. . . . At each successive general election the better elements seemed to be getting the upper hand, and I do not mind saying that I was one of those who believed they were going to win. I thought they were going to snatch the soul of Germany – and it is worth saving, a great, powerful soul – I thought they were going to save it. But a dead military caste said 'We will have none of this', and they plunged Europe into seas of blood. . . . Those worst elements will emerge triumphant out of this war if Germany wins. . . . We shall be vassals, not to the best Germans, not to the Germany of sweet songs and inspiring, noble thoughts, not to the Germany of science consecrated to the service of men, not to the Germany of a virile philosophy that helped to break the shackles of superstition in Europe – not to that Germany, but to a Germany that talks through the raucous voice of Krupp's artillery. . . . I make no apology on a day consecrated to the greatest sacrifice for coming here to preach a holy war against that.

This passage is also notable for the clear implication that Britain was fighting to save *herself*, as well as others, from vassalage to a militarist Germany. The speech ended with a parable about ants, told in Welsh.

Reactions, again, were enthusiastic. *The Times* described the speech as 'a new departure on the part of Ministers', and praised Lloyd George's 'courage and imagination'. According to Frances Stevenson, many were saying that he had made the greatest speech of his life. Next day – St David's Day – he attended an eisteddfod at Llandudno, and the day after inspected Welsh troops at Colwyn Bay and Rhyl.

With Lloyd George rhetoric was nearly always accessory to action, not, as with many politicians, a substitute for it; and it was very soon apparent that he meant what he said at Bangor about priorities on the home front. On 9 March he introduced another Defence of the Realm bill, enabling the Government to take over any factories or workshops needed for war production, and to cancel any contracts that stood in the way. He asked that it should be rushed through, and the House of Commons proved surprisingly tractable. Afterwards he told Riddell that his colleagues had expected 'a terrible row' over the bill, and had therefore given him the job of introducing it.[1]

Whatever they may have thought, no row in fact occurred. Bonar Law's only criticism was that the proposed action had not been taken in August or September, and he urged the Government to make better use of 'the organising capacity of the business community'. This was right up Lloyd George's street, and he replied that he wanted manufacturers to be summoned together in the various industrial districts of the country, so that they could be consulted about the work to be done and how to do it. (He had in mind, obviously, what he had heard about the French system during his visit to Paris in October.) He also suggested that there might be a central directing organisation with a business man at its head; and the words that he used in making the suggestion brought into currency the phrase 'man of push and go', which became associated with his style of government.[2]

Labour's spokesman in the short debate on Second Reading, John Hodge – who would later hold office under Lloyd George – showed as much keenness as Bonar Law that the country's industrial resources should be properly mobilised. But he also argued strongly that workers' representatives should be called into consultation as well as employers, and that fair wages should be enforced in factories that were taken over.

There was, indeed, a serious problem about wages. During the first six months of war the cost of living had risen by more than twenty per cent, while wages had remained more or less static. This would have been quite enough in itself to create a sense of grievance among workers, but ill-feeling was aggravated by the knowledge that higher costs were to some extent due to profiteering by industrialists. The dispute on the Clyde, referred to by Lloyd George at Bangor, was caused by the employers' inadequate response to a wage claim which the Clyde engineers had been pressing since before the war. The men's demand for an increase of 8s. a week may have been rather ambitious by pre-war standards, but it was thoroughly reasonable in view of wartime inflation; and when the employers offered less than half the

1. R.W.D., p. 68.
2. His actual words were: 'It is possible that we could get a business man at the head of the organisation. We are on the look out for a good, strong business man with some go in him who will be able to push the thing through and be at the head of a Central Committee.' (Hansard, Fifth Series, Vol. LXX, col. 1277.) The Bill was disposed of by the House of Commons in two days. Lloyd George calls the resultant measure D.O.R.A. III, but in fact it was D.O.R.A. II.

amount claimed, the men naturally turned to militancy.

Lloyd George's attitude towards trade unions was seldom wholly sympathetic. At the best of times he was bound to have mixed feelings about organisations which might present a sectional challenge to the power of the State, and when the nation was at war he could hardly fail to regard them with suspicion, if not with outright hostility. Whatever might be the rigours of life for civilian workers, they were as nothing, in his view, compared with the hardships that British soldiers were enduring; and however underpaid men in factories might feel themselves to be, they were far better paid for what they were doing than the men in the trenches. Hence the severity of his remarks about alleged slackers, about 'the lure of the drink' (of which more in the next chapter) and about trade union restrictive practices. It seemed to him that discipline on the home front should be comparable with that in the armed forces, even though it could not be subject to the same sanctions. Trouble-makers in industry were in his eyes virtually traitors, or at any rate saboteurs, and he was particularly indignant that the Clyde workers were led by an unofficial group of shop stewards.

Their action drew attention, however, to the need for a deal with labour before the Government took over factories for war production, and on 11 March the Cabinet decided to 'try to get some sort of an understanding' with labour representatives, Lloyd George being given charge of the negotiation. Even Kitchener was aware that his great expansion of the army had created problems which the War Office alone could not solve. Commenting on Lloyd George's memorandum of 22 February he had written: 'the real crux of the situation is . . . the organisation of the skilled labour required to man the machinery, and, if the Chancellor of the Exchequer could help us in this *and in the many labour difficulties with which we are confronted*, I have little doubt that in time an increased number of men, up to a total of 3,000,000, may be recruited and trained fit to take the field.'[1] Though not yet willing to surrender control of arms supply to a civilian, Kitchener did at least recognise that the human aspects of the matter were best left to Lloyd George.

As a result trade union leaders were invited to confer with the Chancellor on 17 March, and after three days' discussion the so-called

1. Remarks on the Chancellor of the Exchequer's Memorandum on the Conduct of the War, 25 February 1915. Author's italics.

Treasury Agreement was signed. But there were some hitches. Through an oversight the Lancashire cotton unions, who were concerned in war production as manufacturers of thread for equipment, were not included in the invitation. More seriously, the Miners' Federation and the Amalgamated Society of Engineers withdrew from the conference, and another had to be held a week later before the A.S.E. was satisfied. The miners did not return and were never a party to the agreement.

Its main provisions were that the unions would accept compulsory arbitration as an alternative to strikes, and would suspend traditional workshop regulations so as to permit male *and female* dilution, while the Government guaranteed that these concessions would be limited to the period of the war, and gave a rather vague assurance on the control of profits. Since there was, as yet, no statutory backing for the agreement, its significance was largely symbolic. But it was certainly important that the Government was seen to have negotiated with the unions independently of the employers, so treating them as an estate of the realm; and from that point of view the National Labour Advisory Committee, brought into being under Arthur Henderson's chairmanship to help make the agreement effective, was a further notable innovation.[1]

Seventeen years later Lloyd George described, in his memoirs, the scene from which the Treasury Agreement emerged:

The Conference was held in the gloomy board room of the Treasury, with the gilt throne of Queen Anne at one end of the room. There was a tradition that once upon a time it had been occupied by kings and queens who came to discuss their finances with the Lords of the Treasury. The last sovereign who sat upon it was the first Hanoverian George. Since he understood no English and the Lords of the Treasury understood no German our sovereigns ceased to go through the formality of attending these meetings at the Treasury to arrange their finance, and that once glistening and plush throne has now a sad look of tarnished and torn neglect. The room was so crowded with the representatives of

1. Henderson, who had succeeded MacDonald as chairman of the Parliamentary Labour Party, and had recently become a Privy Councillor, was one of the two trade union signatories of the Treasury Agreement. The other was William Mosses, general secretary of the Federation of Engineering and Shipbuilding Trades. Lloyd George and Runciman signed for the Government.

workers in many trades that some of them had to lean against this rickety throne of the last of the Stuarts.

He had invited Balfour to attend the meetings, so giving him his first experience of conferring with workers on a basis of equality. His face expressed 'quizzical and embarrassed wonder'.

He was surprised to find the workmen's representatives talked so well. They put their points clearly and succinctly, wasting neither time nor words. On the other hand, there was just a note of aggressiveness in manner and tone to which he was not quite accustomed from such quarters. For the moment it almost quelled him, and he was silent throughout. . . . He liked new experiences, but not of this sort. This was a portent which had for the first time appeared in the quarter of the sky where he had shone for a generation, and it came uncomfortably near. His ideas of Government were inherited from the days when Queen Anne sat on that throne. They were only changed to the extent that the fact of her being the last occupant constituted a triumph for the subject and thus modified the Constitution in a popular direction. But this scene was fundamentally different. He saw those stalwart artisans leaning against and sitting on the steps of the throne of the dead queen, and on equal terms negotiating conditions with the Government of the day upon a question vitally affecting the conduct of a great war. Queen Anne was indeed dead. I had watched his mood for years from an opposing bench. In looking at him now I felt that his detached and enquiring mind was bewildered by this sudden revelation of a new power and that he must take time to assimilate the experience.[1]

Lloyd George's retrospective account of the trade union leaders should not be taken as an entirely faithful reflection of his view of them at the time. Frances Stevenson's comments in her diary, obviously influenced by what he was telling her, give a less flattering picture of the men with whom he had just been negotiating:

They were here for 3 days last week, overrunning the Treasury. . . . They are a very unsatisfactory lot of people . . . and one cannot help feeling that it is a danger for the working classes to be in the hands of such incompetent and narrow-minded – for they *are* essentially narrow-minded and selfish – men. . . . I suppose the working classes

1. W.M., pp. 295–7.

will work out their own fate; but one cannot help feeling that their unpatriotic attitude in the present crisis will deprive them of sympathy when the war is over, and when the working classes will be in need of consideration owing to the effects of the war.[1]

It is undeniable that Lloyd George's attitude at the time was more indulgent to the employers than to the unions. His idea of profit limitation was that it should be confined to firms engaged on war work, which left out many whose excess profits were increasing the cost of living to all workers. Moreover, the agreed level of profit within war industry was generously fixed at twenty per cent above the average for the two previous years, which had been abnormally profitable. Trade unionists in such firms were, therefore, being asked to make an absolute, if temporary, surrender of their rights and interests in return for a rather modest sacrifice by the employers, and while the general grievance about living costs was hardly being met at all.

The principal reason for Lloyd George's apparent bias in favour of the bosses was that he regarded their willing cooperation in the task of winning the war as more essential, if possible, than that of organised labour. He had a natural liking and respect for self-made businessmen, which contrasted with his contempt for hereditary grandees. He wanted to encourage men of push and go, and found that many more captains of industry than trade union leaders could be so described. He was concerned to keep the basic economic system working even in the emergency of war, and was persuaded that any too drastic profit limitation would threaten the system.

One further important reason for his attitude should be mentioned. Lloyd George cared profoundly for the authority of the State – in this there was no difference at all between him and Balfour – and it was on the whole easier for the State to deal with industrialists than with trade unionists, because the former were freer to act independently. A trade union leader tended to be more closely accountable to his members than a captain of industry to his shareholders, even when the direction of an enterprise was not combined, as it often was, with financial ownership and control. Whatever the personal inadequacies of the men who spoke for unions, they had an obstinate strength deriving from their function. Though they might be almost negligible as individuals, the collective interest that they served was potentially

1. F.S.D., 25 March 1915, pp. 35–6.

formidable. With bosses it was the other way round. Many had great ability, especially those who had built up their own businesses; but as individuals they were more amenable to the various forms of State pressure and cajolery, precisely because they could answer for themselves. Lloyd George felt that capital would defer to the State so long as it was not gratuitously antagonised, but he feared that too many concessions to labour might make the State subservient.

The Treasury Agreement was a considerable success for him, if only as the first step along a new road. As a contribution to the industrial war effort it was valuable and timely. But it did not portend an altogether happy relationship between him and organised labour in the future. On the contrary, it marks the beginning of a period of mutual wariness and intermittent conflict, from which he was to emerge the long-term loser. Ironically, when he came to write his description of the scene in the Treasury Board Room the trade unions' own party was the official opposition, having already twice formed the government of the country, while the Liberals were in a state of disintegration and Lloyd George himself almost completely isolated. If the quizzical Balfour had lived to read Lloyd George's words, he would have had the last smile.

TEN
New Government, New Job

Lloyd George had now got into the habit not only of going to Walton Heath at weekends, but also of sleeping there as often as possible during the week, even if it meant driving down after dinner. He was finding (so he told Riddell) that he could not sleep properly at 11 Downing Street. Why? We can only speculate. Perhaps his deep underlying fear of aerial bombardment made him feel uneasy in the centre of London, though it was not until April that the first Zeppelin raid on the capital occurred. In any case he was always physically drawn to the country, despite the many attractions of town life to a man of his temperament, and though his work – all-important to him – required him to spend most of his time in London. Having grown up far from the noise and dirt of big cities, he could never quite rid himself of the urge to escape.

But another motive is suggested by this undated note to Frances Stevenson: 'Go *now* a little beyond House of Lords. I am off to Walton.' He could pick her up by Victoria Tower Gardens, they could drive down together, and once there could enjoy a degree of privacy obviously unattainable in Downing Street. Walton Heath was a refuge for them both as lovers. It was also, for a time in March, a convalescent home for Frances, who had become rather mysteriously ill at the end of February. According to A. J. P. Taylor, this happened while she was still living with her parents.

She thought she was pregnant. Her mother, who had hitherto persuaded herself that Frances was merely working for a peculiarly kind boss, exploded in the conventional way: 'I would rather have you lying dead at my feet.' Frances, though loyally defending her relations with Lloyd George, agreed not to have a child and noted: 'The idea of our love-child will have to go for the time being,' as though a baby could be conceived or unconceived at will. Frances may have had a miscarriage or perhaps she was merely out in her reckoning. At any rate she was ill and wretched; yet in the circumstances she could not bear to remain in her parents' house. Lloyd George had to take responsibility for her. Mrs Lloyd George was down in Wales. So Frances could be despatched to . . . Walton Heath with Sarah to look after her.[1]

The ferocious remark attribubed to Frances's mother on this occasion was also allegedly made by her two years earlier, when Frances first confessed her intention to live with Lloyd George, so revealing that he was more than 'a peculiarly kind boss'.[2] Did Mrs Stevenson really say the same thing twice, or have the two occasions been confused? To a woman of her puritanical outlook the news that Frances was expecting an illicitly conceived child may well have been even more traumatic than the original confession.

But in any case what really happened about the pregnancy, actual or supposed? Mr Taylor mentions two possibilities, either of which may be correct. But there is also a third, on the face of it more consistent with Frances's statement 'The idea of our love-child will have to go for the time being.' Though a baby cannot be conceived at will, it can surely be unconceived at will by means of abortion; and it is rather hard to see what Frances can have meant by saying that the idea of a child would 'have to go', unless she was thinking of having it aborted. She believed herself to be pregnant, and can hardly have imagined that a miscarriage would occur simply because she wanted it to occur. If we accept her belief as well-founded, then it seems most likely that she resorted to abortion as the only way out of a painful dilemma. Long afterwards she told her daughter Jennifer that she had had two abortions in her early years with Lloyd George.[3]

More even than a miscarriage this would account for her extraordinary physical and mental prostration at the time. It would also account for Lloyd George's extraordinary care and solicitude. On 11 March

1. *My Darling Pussy*, ed. A. J. P. Taylor, p. 5.
2. Frances Lloyd George, *The Years that are Past*, p. 56 (already quoted p. 82 above).
3. Private information from Mrs Jennifer Longford.

she wrote:

> I do not think I can ever repay him for his goodness to me the last fortnight or three weeks. He has been husband, lover & mother to me. I never knew a man could be so womanly & tender. He has watched and waited on me devotedly, until I cursed myself for being ill & causing him all this worry. There was no little thing that he did not think of for my comfort, no tenderness that he did not lavish on me. I have indeed known the full extent of his love.[1]

As a rule Lloyd George was very squeamish about illness. His instinct always was to recoil from it and leave others to deal with it. Moreover, during the weeks that Frances was ill he was under a pressure of work that would have overwhelmed most men, even if they had nothing at all to worry about in their private lives. The way he ministered to her is, therefore, all the more striking, and suggests that he was behaving not only as a man very much in love, but also as a man who felt deeply in her debt. If, as well as sacrificing respectability (in her parents' eyes) and the chance of a normal married life, she had also sacrificed the immediate prospect of motherhood, his slavishly attentive behaviour would be easier to understand. On the evidence at present available there can be no certainty, but it seems most probable that she had an abortion.

She returned to work during the period of the Treasury Agreement, but soon she was ill again and he sent her to Brighton to recover properly in the sea air. She stayed at the Bedford Hotel and on 7 April he wrote to her there:

> My own sweet,
>
> I have already read your darling letter twice over & it is yet but the eleventh hour of the morning. I write now lest I fail to find time later on as I have a bustling day in front of me.
>
> I am glad you are at the Bedford. A boarding house or rooms would have been so dull but there is always life – of a sort – at a hotel. I am always interested in people – wondering who they are – what they are thinking about – what their lives are like – whether they are enjoying life or finding it a bore.
>
> I envy you that stormy sea. Nothing fills me with such a sense of

---

1. F.S.D., pp. 33–4. The previous diary entry is for 23 February.

wild exhilaration as a raging boiling tumbling sea.

REST for 2 days without any exertion at all. . . . Should not be at all surprised that now you are away from the artificial stimulants & excitements of your life here that you might feel weaker & more depressed. That is the first stage of real rest. . . .

Look after yourself – for my sake sweetheart mine. I love you so fondly tenderly *fiercely*.

Ever & Ever,
your
D.[1]

No letter could be more revealing of Lloyd George. He writes with obvious passion, and the romantic side of his essentially realistic and practical nature is clearly inspired by her, while it also responds, as always, to the idea of a great storm. At the same time he has a subtle and sensitive awareness of her needs, and of the likely state of her mind. With a candid egotism that is nevertheless flattering to her, he urges her to look after herself for his sake.

Above all he shows in the last sentence of the second paragraph the quality which, allied to his formidable talents, made him uniquely effective as a politician: his genuine interest in people. It is hard to imagine Winston Churchill looking at ordinary, anonymous fellow-guests at an hotel and wondering who they were, what they were thinking, what sort of lives they were leading, and whether they were happy or bored. Lloyd George lived largely for himself and for the very important public causes in which he believed. He was no more unselfish than Churchill or most other individuals conscious of superior powers and determined to use them to the full. Yet he also had a rare capacity to project himself into the thoughts and feelings of others, and to relish the experience. Had his creative faculties been for literature rather than politics, this intense, unlimited curiosity might have made him a great novelist.

When Frances received the letter just quoted she was reading Meredith's *The Egoist*, which Lloyd George feared might lessen her love for him, because it threw 'such clear light on the male character'. He regarded Meredith's insight into character as analogous to that of a physician 'when he puts the electric light arrangement on his fore-head'. In his view, Meredith 'was the first person to conceive the revolt of woman – the revolt against the accepted relations of husband and

1. *My Darling Pussy*, pp. 7–8.

wife'; or at any rate the first person to write about it. Yet it was, he
said, Ibsen's *A Doll's House* which had converted him to women's
suffrage.[1]

By mid-April Frances was more or less restored to health, and on
the 22nd she and Lloyd George drove down together in the evening to
Walton Heath.

> There was no-one there to prepare a meal, so we collected refresh-
> ments of various kinds at Sutton for an impromptu supper. We left
> the car at Kingswood & went for a long walk on the Heath. C. was
> quite mad, & improvised mock sermons for my benefit, taking
> idiotic subjects for his texts. I love to see him in these mad moods;
> he is like some wild boy broken loose from school. Moreover, I
> know when he is like that that he has thrown off all worries and
> cares for the time being & that his mind is having a rest. It was dark
> by the time we got to Walton. We passed such a happy evening
> together.[2]

No doubt his tearing spirits owed much to the fact that she was well
again, and that the crisis through which they had passed – whatever its
precise cause – had left their 'marriage' and working relationship
unimpaired. But he was always resilient; in the worst of times there
were deep reserves of vitality and cheerfulness on which he could
draw.

An unexpected nuisance to him in March 1915 was the sudden revival
of controversy over the Welsh Church. Although the Government's
disestablishment measure had, along with Irish Home Rule, been
suspended for the duration of the war, it was found that the commissioners responsible for the process of disendowment were already at
work, and this was causing trouble with the Opposition. The Government therefore decided to introduce a Bill postponing all the effects of
disestablishment until six months after the end of the war. This

---

1. F.S.D., p. 43. Lloyd George's enthusiasm for Meredith may have gained a little from the
somewhat remote Welsh origins of the author's family. The enthusiasm was not shared by
Asquith, who wrote some years later to his friend Hilda Harrisson: 'I wonder how you like
The Egoist? It is supposed to be what that phrase-maker, President Wilson, called "the acid
test" of the pure Meredithian: a test I have never been able to pass.' (*H.H.A., Letters from Lord
Oxford to a Friend*, first series, p. 169.) Raymond Asquith was even more damning, describing
Meredith as 'a kind of unhealthy mixture between a snob and a contortionist thinly veiling
adulation of the upper classes by the disingenuous obscurity of his style.' *Raymond Asquith:
Life and Letters*, ed. John Jolliffe, p. 116.)
2. F.S.D., pp. 45–6.

provoked even worse trouble with the Government's Welsh supporters, which was needlessly aggravated by the failure of the Home
Secretary, McKenna, to consult the Welsh M.P.s in advance. They
were afraid that the Church would use the time to create new life-
interests, which would then have to be compensated, and they were
even more afraid that disestablishment might be lost altogether if a
Conservative government were returned at the end of the war,
committed to repeal.

When the House of Commons debated the postponement Bill on 15
March, Lloyd George had to defend it against his former colleagues.
He did not hesitate to blame McKenna by implication:

> I am not going to say a word about the question of consultation with
> Welsh Members. I am heartily in accord with everything that has
> been said about that . . . not a word have I to say in deprecation of
> any criticism which has fallen from my Friends from Wales upon
> that topic. But they will remember . . . that we have been worked in
> a way that no Ministers have been worked in my time. We are
> engaged in very anxious work, working constantly, and we were
> under the impression that there had been consultations. I, as well as
> the Prime Minister, certainly thought that the same consultation
> had taken place with Welsh Members as had taken place with the
> leaders of the Opposition.

On the danger that a Conservative government might repeal
disestablishment during the post-war period of grace allowed by the
Bill, he argued that magnanimity was the surest protection:

> I ask my hon. friends quite seriously . . . are they helping the temper
> of the country in considering the question of repeal by refusing to
> give fair consideration to proposals for granting an extension of six
> months to the Church when some of its leading men are engaged in
> the War? I say they are not. I should be more afraid of repeal under
> these conditions. I do not think the party opposite, when the time
> comes, will pledge themselves to repeal. The country will have its
> mind on other things. When this War is over they will be tired of
> domestic controversies. The War has raised issues never thought of
> – deep, searching, permanent issues that will affect the whole life of
> this country and the destinies of humanity for generations. Those
> questions – great questions of reconstruction – those are the ques-
> tions which will occupy the minds of the nation of every class, great
> and small, when the War is over. They will be impatient of sectarian

controversies. They will not tolerate them. They will want to get something bigger.[1]

Asquith was much impressed and wrote the same evening to Venetia Stanley:

I have rarely heard a more courageous speech – quite impromptu – with all those attractive, histrionic modulations of tone & gesture which only the Celtic and Slavonic races have at command. It would have given you real artistic pleasure to listen to it. Afterwards, at my invitation, the whole Welsh party came to my room, where I was fortified by the presence of Ll.G. & McKenna: their feathers had been a good deal ruffled by L.G.'s pronouncement; and I addressed them like a Father. . . . I hope & believe they have gone back to their mountains & vales with the fear of God in their consciences: and a certain apprehension of fiery vengeance if they don't 'toe the line' (what a phrase!) of reason & common sense.[2]

In fact, neither his fatherly admonitions nor Lloyd George's artistry succeeded in making the Welshmen toe the line, and in due course the bill had to be withdrawn. But disestablishment was, as Lloyd George perceived, a dying issue, and after the War he was able to dispose of it once and for all.

Another traditional Welsh and Nonconformist issue, which had always meant more to him, was that of temperance; and temperance, unlike disestablishment, seemed to have an urgent bearing upon the War. He had said at Bangor that drink was doing the country more damage than 'all the German submarines put together'; and it was indeed true that the easy availability of drink, combined with somewhat higher wages and the strain of war, was one reason – though by no means the only one – why war production was not all that it might have been. Much of the evidence on the subject was vague and anecdotal, but there was nevertheless a considerable residue of truth. Lloyd George, naturally inclined to assume the worst where drink was concerned, was rather too ready to accept all the evidence at face-value. But there were many others who did the same, and who

1. Hansard, 5th series, Vol. LXX, cols. 1814–1819.
2. V.S.L., p. 481. Frances Stevenson shows what an effort the speech was for Lloyd George. 'C. must have been extraordinarily excited when he sat down, for when he came to me half an hour later he was still shaking with excitement, & it was a long, long time before he calmed down. When he did become more calm he almost collapsed with exhaustion.' (F.S.D., p. 40.)

felt that Britain should follow the example of France and Russia in taking drastic action to control, if not to prohibit, the consumption of alcohol.

Shortly after negotiating his Treasury Agreement with labour, Lloyd George gave an interview mainly devoted to the opening of this 'great new chapter in the history of labour in its relations with the State'. But he also said that, to judge from official reports coming 'from every quarter where Government work is being done', it was clearly essential that 'excessive drinking' should be made impossible in wartime.[1] He did not, however, reveal to the reporter that his own solution to the problem would be the creation of a State monopoly of drink, which would have the additional merit of depriving the Conservative Party of one of its principal vested interests. Yet a few days later he was discussing details of this project with 'a lot of brewers' and '2 skilled accountants'.[2]

While working on his plan for State ownership and control, he did not, however, think it inconsistent to encourage the voluntary approach to temperance; and it occurred to him that patriotic abstemiousness could usefully begin at the top. On 29 March he suggested to the King, at an audience early in the day, that he might set an example to his people by giving up strong drink for the duration. Immediately after the audience Lloyd George received, at the Treasury, a deputation from the Shipbuilding Employers' Federation, and later the same day reported to the King's private secretary, Lord Stamfordham:

> . . . It was a very powerful deputation and represented practically all the great firms engaged in turning out munitions of war and ships for the Admiralty. The statements they made were of a very sensational character. . . . So far from working harder now than they did before the war, the men are giving less time and the slacking is on the increase. The employers are in utter despair. Mere restriction of hours they regard as quite inadequate and they are firmly of opinion that unless the drink is suppressed altogether for the period of the war they will be unable to perform their contracts.
>
> There was not a teetotaller amongst them, but as they were of the opinion that it was most important that the workmen should not imagine that drink was to be forbidden them whilst the rich were to

1. *Daily Citizen*, 22 March 1915.
2. V.S.L., 25 March 1915 (pp. 508–9).

be permitted still to indulge in it, they proposed that rich and poor alike should be deprived of liquor during the war.

It was altogether a most impressive but depressing deputation. They attributed the shortage entirely to drink.[1]

We see here a classic instance of Lloyd George being carried away by his eagerness to get something – anything – done to remedy a defect in the system. He had not clarified his own thoughts before plunging into feverish activity. At one moment he was saying that excessive drinking must be curbed during the war; at the next suggesting that drinking should be stopped altogether, either voluntarily or compulsorily. To argue thus was to blur the crucial distinction between judicious restraint and total abstinence. Moreover, if there was to be prohibition or a tough measure of State control, then why was it necessary for the King to start a movement of voluntary self-denial? Lloyd George seems not to have asked himself this question.

The King, though not normally an impulsive character, responded with undue alacrity to the appeal made to him. On 30 March Stamfordham wrote to Lloyd George:

> If it be deemed advisable, the King will be prepared to set an example by giving up all alcoholic liquor himself and issuing orders against its consumption in the Royal Household, so that no difference shall be made, so far as His Majesty is concerned, between the treatment of rich and poor in this question.[2]

Apart from making his decision subject to ministerial advice, the King imposed no further conditions, such as that other prominent figures, including members of the Cabinet, should undertake to follow his lead. Ministerial assent to his offer was swiftly forthcoming. Lloyd George took Stamfordham's letter to the Cabinet and replied to Stamfordham the same day:

> I read your letter and they were all very gratified at the indication of His Majesty's intention. . . . The Cabinet are convinced that very strong action must be taken . . . and they felt that if the King took the lead in the matter the nation would follow him. Such an announcement is in the opinion of all of us almost essential in order

1. Letter in Royal Archives. George V did not record in his diary that Lloyd George had invited him to take the pledge, but Frances Stevenson states that it was so in hers, and from the King's later remarks on the subject we can infer that the idea was not his own.
2. Quoted in H. Nicolson, *King George V*, p. 262.

to induce the working classes to accept drastic measures. If the letter which you wrote me this morning were published it would I feel certain have an extraordinary effect and all classes would hasten to follow the fine lead thus given by the Sovereign. . . .[1]

The King's letter was accordingly published, but all classes did *not* hasten to follow. Though Lloyd George told Stamfordham that there should be 'declarations from Judges, Cabinet Ministers, Clergy, the Medical Profession, and the great Manufacturers, and if possible the Trades Union Leaders', no such declarations were made, and he added rather ominously 'I am trying to find someone who will take this in hand.'[2] Stamfordham was quick to reply: 'Will you allow me to express a hope that you will not depute this delicate duty to anyone.'[3] Lloyd George neither deputed it nor assumed it himself; the duty was simply neglected. On 5 April Stamfordham travelled up from Windsor to tell Lloyd George that 'the King proposed to wait to give any definite orders about the prohibition of drink in the Royal Household until the Government had taken action towards general prohibition'. But by then it was too late for such bargaining. Lloyd George replied with brutal firmness that the Prime Minister had 'consented to the publication of the King's letter and ipso facto to the King's Prohibition being enforced'. Indeed he 'felt that rightly or wrongly the public view was that His Majesty had actually issued the order.'[4] So that was that. The order was given the following day, and the King and his Household were left, in Harold Nicolson's words, 'high and dry' for the rest of the war. Among Cabinet ministers only Kitchener joined his sovereign in taking the pledge.

Lloyd George may have felt, in retrospect, some discomfort about his less than glorious part in the business, because in his war memoirs he does not admit that the King's decision was prompted by him.

1. Royal Archives. Frances Stevenson suggests that Asquith, for one, was not immediately gratified by the King's offer and that he took a little convincing that it ought to be accepted. 'Later in the day [30 March] the P.M. sent for C. & said "About that King thing – I would not play that card yet if I were you. . . ." C. then explained – for he saw what was troubling the old boy – that you would be able to get alcoholic drink if you could produce a doctor's certificate to the effect that it was necessary for you to have it. At that the P.M. brightened up. "Oh, well," he said strutting up & down the room, "there will be any amount of doctors' certificates!" He seemed more resigned after this piece of information. . . . ' (F.S.D., p. 39.) The King, in fact, had a brief dispensation on medical grounds after his accident in France in October 1915, when he was thrown from his horse and severely shaken.

2. D.L.G. to Stamfordham, 1 April 1915 (Royal Archives).

3. Stamfordham to D.L.G., same date.

4. Memorandum for the King from Lord Stamfordham, 5 April 1915 (Royal Archives).

Indeed he indulges in a little *suggestio falsi* when he writes:

> The House of Commons flatly declined to pass any self-denying
> ordinance for its own observance, and this attitude on the part of the
> nation's legislators helped to prevent "The King's Pledge" from
> becoming the starting point which King George and his advisers
> had hoped it might prove for a big voluntary movement of national
> sobriety.[1]

He does not choose to mention that the King's chief adviser in the
matter was himself, or to consider how the nation's legislators might
have acted if they had been given an exemplary lead by the Cabinet, to
reinforce that of the King. But he claims that the King's pledge at least
strengthened the Government's hand for the measure which it had to
take. When all allowances are made, it does seem rather unworthy of
Lloyd George to have persuaded the King to make a sacrifice that he
was not prepared to make himself. Though at all times a very
moderate drinker, he never renounced drink altogether and was not,
therefore, morally qualified to urge total abstinence upon others.

So much for the voluntary approach to solving the national drink
problem. But what of Lloyd George's parallel, and inconsistent, plans
for action by the State? Replying to the deputation of shipbuilding
employers on 29 March, Lloyd George said:

> Having gone into this matter a great deal more closely during the
> last few weeks, I must say that I have a growing conviction, based
> on accumulating evidence, that nothing but root and branch
> methods will be of the slightest avail in dealing with this evil. . . .
> We are fighting Germany, Austria and drink; and, as far as I can see,
> the greatest of these three deadly foes is drink . . . the words which
> you have addressed to my colleagues and myself will be taken into
> the most careful consideration by my colleagues when we come to
> our final decision on this question. Coming as they do from those
> who know what the facts are . . . they will, I am certain, carry very
> great weight in these quarters.[2]

In these remarks, which were given at once to the press, he seemed to
be going far towards endorsing the employers' demand for total
prohibition, though the idea of a State monopoly on which he was
already working could hardly be reconciled with such a course.

---

1. W.M., p. 330.
2. Verbatim record of deputation (L.G.P.).

Moreover, trade unionists were indignant that he accepted the employers' statements as wholly valid, and protested against the collective defamation of workers. On 31 March more than one newspaper carried a letter from the chairman and the general secretary of the Boilermakers' Society, in which the employers' statements were vigorously challenged:

> The tales told by the Shipbuilding Employers' Federation are the same old misrepresentations, exaggerations and contradictions that we have heard from them many times. They are the tales they usually give us instead of money. . . . On the few occasions when drinking loss of time has been reported to us investigations have been made, sometimes with a joint court of employers' and workmen's representatives. Eighty per cent of the charges have been unwarranted and untrue. . . . We are therefore grieved that the Chancellor, on an *ex parte* statement, should have come to conclusions and permitted himself the grave statements which he made. . . . The wholly unjustifiable attack of the Shipbuilding Employers' Federation will do more than all the drink in the country to diminish output.[1]

Faced with such a riposte, Lloyd George felt obliged to enquire more closely into the facts, having hitherto gone largely on hearsay. Factory inspectors were asked to report on the state of affairs in the Clyde and Tyne areas, and at Barrow-in-Furness. In addition, Lloyd George arranged with the Home Secretary that thirty-three experienced police officers should investigate locally and send in reports. (McKenna must have taken a malicious pleasure in being asked to collaborate in checking statements which Lloyd George had too readily accepted.)

The detailed evidence showed, not surprisingly, that each side in the argument had been overstating and oversimplifying its case. For instance, the factory inspector reporting from Barrow said that, while much loss of time was due to drinking, another cause was that many workers were earning good enough wages to be able to maintain their ordinary standard of living with four or five days' work a week. The inspector from the Clyde wrote:

> The whole question has arisen because of the action of a few men in the more important shipbuilding yards, and there is a feeling that

1. Letter signed by R. W. Lindsay (chairman) and John Hill (general secretary).

the mass of workers throughout the country should not be penalised because of the dissipated and unpatriotic behaviour of a small minority of overpaid men in one or two specific callings.

More comfortable working conditions improve time-keeping; for instance, during the last three weeks of fine bright weather distinctly better time has been kept. Again, much time lost . . . is due to wet and windy weather; work outside is difficult and almost impossible under such conditions unless the building berth is a roofed one. . . .

Figures showing percentage of hours lost by outside workers are valueless unless allowance is made for the periods in which work was impossible owing to weather conditions. It is not uncommon for men to work on piece work until their clothing is wet through, and the experience of employers is that, in this condition, if they hang about afterwards, colds and chills supervene, with perhaps the loss of a week or fortnight's employment. These facts I mention so that the men's position can be given full justice.[1]

The general summary of the police reports drew a distinction between the drinking habits of workmen on the Clyde and in England. On the Clyde the popular drink was 'half-a-gill of whisky, quickly followed by a schooner of beer (about ¾ pint)' and the beer was 'of a heavier quality than English beer'. This might not have much immediate effect on hardened drinkers, but was 'not calculated to improve the capacity of the men for sustained work'. It was also noted that many men ate too little, which both increased the temptation to drink and made the effect of doing so more injurious. And the summary concluded:

The evils of excessive drinking were readily admitted by some of the better workmen, who considered that the action of a minority was bringing unmerited discredit on the workmen as a whole. Others considered that the part played by drinking had been exaggerated, that the workmen had been subjected to too great a pressure and were suffering from the strain, and that the deficiency of output was largely due, especially on the Clyde, to the withdrawal of skilled men who should be recalled from the colours.

The question of drinking and its remedies is freely discussed by the workmen among themselves. Many of them believe in further

1. Reports from W. Sydney Smith (Barrow) and Harry J. Wilson (the Clyde) 3 April 1915 (L.G.P.).

restriction . . . and their minds are prepared for some drastic measures. There was, however, a general consensus of opinion that complete prohibition would be bitterly resented by a large number of the workmen, and that if it were adopted as a policy it would lead to retaliatory measures on their part.[1]

In the light of such evidence it would have been crazy for the Government to try to impose an absolute ban on drinking, nationally or locally, and support for this policy was anyway extremely limited. But Lloyd George's scheme for a State monopoly had more to commend it, and he continued for a time to press its claims with the utmost energy. Though Asquith was dead against it from the first, several Cabinet ministers supported it, and Lloyd George was also able to secure the backing of a number of newspaper editors and some Labour leaders. Outside Parliament, Joseph Rowntree's approval was a formidable asset, mitigating the opposition of many other Nonconformists and Temperance reformers. But above all Lloyd George managed to obtain the written acquiescence of Bonar Law, who privately regarded the Tory Party's connection with the Trade as an incubus of which it would be well rid. In his letter he stipulated only that there should be adequate compensation to the brewers and distillers, and Lloyd George was advised by an expert committee that the cost of the operation for England and Wales would be about £250 million.[2] But by the middle of April it was apparent to him that he would not be able to get his scheme through the Cabinet, let alone Parliament, so he turned to the consideration of a less sweeping, though still sufficiently drastic, measure.

The Defence of the Realm Bill (No. III), which he introduced on 29 April and which became law within three weeks, provided for the setting-up of a Central Liquor Control Board, independent of both government and magistracy. This body was given power to impose any restrictions it liked in any area it chose, and if necessary to run its own breweries, pubs and canteens. There was to be no appeal against its decisions. The composition of the Board was widely representative

1. General Summary of police reports on drinking in the shipbuilding trades, followed by detailed reports, 12 April 1915. (L.G.P.) Lloyd George also had the benefit of replies from various armament works to a request for information from the Master-General of Ordnance. These gave a mixed impression of the effect of drink on production, some reporting that it was serious, others that it was almost negligible. (L.G.P.)

2. Law's letter is quoted in Blake, *op. cit.* p. 239. The expert committee, presided over by Herbert Samuel, included among others Lord Cunliffe, Sir John Bradbury and Sir William Plender (report in L.G.P.).

of parties and interests, and it commanded general confidence. By the end of the year half the population was feeling the effect of its restrictive orders, and by December 1916 most places were subject to the shortest licensing hours in British history. It also took steps to dilute the strength of liquor. The areas for which it assumed direct responsibility, notably the fifty square miles stretching from Dumfriesshire to Maryport in Cumberland (the so-called 'Carlisle experiment') produced results which were both morally and financially gratifying. Despite some grievances and anomalies the Board was on the whole a success, and its establishment effectively disposed of drink as a serious threat to the war effort.

Its chairman, Lord D'Abernon, was a Conservative whose views on the harm that alcohol could do were all that Lloyd George could have wished. As well as the control to be exercised by his board he also favoured increased taxation of drink, and in Lloyd George's eighth and final Budget, presented on 4 May, there were indeed proposals for doubling the duty on spirits, quadrupling the wine duty, sextupling the tax on sparkling wines, and also raising tax levels on the heavier types of beer.[1] He knew that the Tories would oppose these increases, because Bonar Law had told him as much the day before; and it was clear to him that he would not therefore be able to carry them, granted the ecumenical requirements of wartime politics. All the same he wanted the country to know his intentions, and the Tory Opposition to bear the full responsibility for frustrating them. In the event his liquor tax increases were opposed not only by Austen Chamberlain and Bonar Law for the Tories, but also by Redmond – since in Ireland the Trade was the National Party's vested interest – and by Henderson on behalf of Labour. So the proposals had to be abandoned with some ignominy.

In other respects the Budget was, as Asquith said, 'a humdrum affair'.[2] Lloyd George informed the House that the war had cost Britain £360 million to the end of March, and that the cost was escalating. If the war were prolonged throughout the coming financial year he foresaw a net adverse balance of about £400 million, on the basis of existing taxes. Yet he made no provision for covering the deficit, arguing that it would be inappropriate to do so until the likely

1. Advance notice of these proposals was given when he introduced D.O.R.A. (III) on 29 April – a most unusual procedure.
2. V.S.L., p. 582.

duration of the war could be more accurately judged. 'This is not', he said, 'a suitable moment to attempt a forecast of the probable expenditure upon the war or to submit proposals for that purpose.' He therefore left the general pattern and incidence of taxation unchanged, while hinting at the possibility of a tax on excess profits if the war lasted a further two or three years.

This was widely regarded at the time, and has been regarded since, as a surprising failure on his part to match the country's needs and the mood of the people. A tough Budget was expected and would have been almost welcomed, because the magnitude of the task of defeating Germany was becoming more apparent every day, not least as a result of his own speeches. His Budget seemed to contradict the grimly realistic tone of his utterances on the war. It also contradicted what he was saying privately at the time. Only two days before the Budget he told Riddell that he thought the war would be a long affair. 'I fear that eighteen months or two years hence we shall be in just the same mess – trenches blown up – air raids – destroyers sunk. In fact, I am confident that the war will last a long time – perhaps three years.'[1] Holding this view, how could he have introduced such a miserable anti-climax of a Budget? How, more especially, could he have failed to honour the spirit of his agreement with labour by doing something at once about excess profits?

The most charitable explanation is that he was too engrossed in other work during the early months of 1915 to give proper attention to the problem of war finance. He had indeed mighty preoccupations outside his own department, and it would be hard to deny that most of them were justifiable in the national interest. Perhaps he devoted rather more time than was strictly necessary to the drink question, but few would reproach him for his efforts to improve the central direction of the war, or for his labour on behalf of a sensible policy and strategy in the eastern Mediterranean, or for his negotiations with the trade unions, or for his anxiety about the supply of arms which (as will be seen) absorbed him increasingly as the months passed. Though it is still hard to understand the inadequacy of his 1915 Budget, the circumstances in which it was prepared should not be forgotten.

Before the end of May, and before the Finance Bill even received its Second Reading, he left the Treasury. His successor promptly set about raising a new War Loan, and before long an excess profits tax

1. R.W.D., 2 May 1915, p. 84.

was introduced. It was unfortunate that this was not brought in by Lloyd George as Chancellor, and that his last Budget should have been just about his worst.

The Cabinet committee set up in October 1914 to coordinate arms production came to an end early in the New Year, when its chairman, Kitchener, announced that he would no longer attend its meetings. But to Lloyd George it was unthinkable that such a vital function should be left under the exclusive control of the War Office and its Ordnance Department, and he did not relax his pressure for a more efficient system. In his Cabinet memorandum of 22 February he said that 'the Germans and Austrians between them had, even at the commencement of the war, much larger supplies of war material and more extensive factories for the turning out of further supplies than the Allied countries', and had 'undoubtedly since made much better use of their manufacturing resources'. It was necessary for all Britain's engineering works to be converted to the production of war material. In his Bangor speech at the end of February he made public his deep concern about the supply of munitions, and proclaimed, 'This is an engineers' war.'

On 5 March there was a conference on the subject at 10 Downing Street, with the Prime Minister presiding. Lloyd George, Kitchener, and General von Donop (Master General of Ordnance) were among the eight others who attended. Lloyd George opened the proceedings by saying that he was dissatisfied with the figures for rifle production given by Kitchener at the previous day's War Council meeting. Von Donop replied, with astonishing complacency, that enough machinery had been ordered 'to meet all possible requirements' in the production of rifles and small arms ammunition. When Lloyd George later pointed out that 'the number of rifles mentioned by General von Donop would not suffice for three million men', Kitchener said that three million was 'a new figure to him'; he had 'only been trying to obtain sufficient rifles for two million'. But, Asquith reminded him, the House of Commons had recently been asked to vote for an army of three million men. Lloyd George appealed for the supply of rifles to be 'extended almost indefinitely so that we could arm these additional numbers', and he also argued that the rate of production should be considerably accelerated.[1]

1. L.G.P. Though Asquith wrote three letters to Venetia Stanley on 6 March, in none of them was this conference mentioned.

The problem was how to break the War Office's executive monopoly in the matter. For a time Asquith played with the idea of an Army Contracts directorate with a minister in charge. This was strongly advocated by Edwin Montagu, who was also the man first considered for the post. Montagu had recently joined the Cabinet as Chancellor of the Duchy of Lancaster, after serving for a year as Lloyd George's junior minister at the Treasury.[1] Still only in his middle thirties, he had risen in politics as Asquith's protégé but was far from being a mere hanger-on. He was also in the curious position of being the Prime Minister's rival in love. (He had already proposed once to Venetia Stanley, and would soon succeed in persuading her to marry him.) Rich and privileged, intellectually a late-developer, sensitive and emotional yet capable of a certain ruthlessness, he was now becoming a rather important figure. But since he did not yet carry enough weight for a job which would involve standing up to Kitchener, Asquith soon turned to Lloyd George as the only man likely to be able to do it. Lloyd George, however, would not take it on without a degree of control that the Field Marshal was still unwilling to concede. So for the time being the idea lapsed.

Instead, a second attempt was made to solve the problem by means of a committee, but this was doomed to be largely unsuccessful because the new Munitions Committee had no effective power and because Kitchener had so little intention of deferring to outsiders that he appointed a War Office Armaments Output Committee of his own. In theory, the Munitions Committee (or Treasury Committee, as it was often called) had 'full authority to take all steps necessary', but in practice it could do very little without detailed information from the War Office, which was provided grudgingly if at all.

The most significant difference between the new committee and the earlier one was that Lloyd George rather than Kitchener was chairman. As such, he was able to fix the agenda and initiate enquiries. For instance, he obtained expert reports on arms production in France and

1. In both offices he succeeded Masterman, who at the end of January was forced to resign, having failed to secure re-election to Parliament after his appointment as a Cabinet Minister, as was then obligatory. His fall was a public, and even more a personal, tragedy. It was due partly to flaws in himself, but above all to the fact that he was picked on by Northcliffe as a sacrificial victim for National Insurance. His bitterness was understandable, and embraced Lloyd George who, he felt, could have done more to help him. To some extent this was true, though not to the extent that Masterman believed. The muddle that occurred over his possible candidature at Swansea was not really Lloyd George's fault. All the same, he deserved rather more general support from Lloyd George than he got in his adversity.

the United States. He also established good working relations with the War Office Output Committee, and gave strong backing to the efforts of its chairman, G. M. Booth (shipowner and son of Charles Booth), to involve more of British industry in the manufacture of arms. Some progress was thus made, but the main value of Lloyd George's committee was that it helped to prepare him for the great task that he was soon to undertake.[1]

Events meanwhile were occurring on the Western Front which were to have a decisive bearing on the struggle in Whitehall. Despite Lloyd George's plea that the Allies should adopt a defensive strategy in the West, while seeking to outflank the Central Powers through the Balkans, the military commanders could not be restrained. In February and March Joffre carried out futile attacks in Champagne, which cost the French army 50,000 men, and in April he sacrificed a further 64,000 in an equally pointless attack against the St Mihiel salient. On 10 March the British attacked at Neuve Chapelle and suffered, in three days' fighting, over 10,000 casualties. In April the Allies lost some ground in the Ypres sector, when the Germans made the first use of gas – 'labelled an atrocity by a world which condones abuses but detests innovations'[2] – but they soon recovered from the surprise and stabilised the line, so demonstrating yet again the inherent superiority of defence in the current war. Not heeding the lesson, the Allied commanders resumed offensive action in May and incurred further huge casualties for no remotely commensurate gains. The British attacks were again in the Neuve Chapelle sector, towards Aubers ridge and a little to the south around Festubert. The opening of the Aubers ridge battle was witnessed by Churchill and later described by him in a memorable passage, full of disgust and compassion, which should be taken to heart by anyone who may be tempted to think of him as a warmonger.[3]

One reason for the failure at Neuve Chapelle in March was that artillery support proved inadequate after the attackers had achieved initial surprise. Even if there had been no shortage of guns or ammunition the operation would still have been misconceived, but might have resulted in rather more ground gained and substantially

1. Booth was also a member of Lloyd George's committee, which included among others Montagu, Balfour, Henderson, von Donop and representatives of the Admiralty, though not Kitchener or Churchill.
2. B. H. Liddell Hart, *History of the First World War*, ch. V.
3. *The World Crisis*, ch. XXXI.

fewer lives lost. In any case, the deficiencies of supply gave French an excuse of which he availed himself to the full. It was galling to him that the political head of the War Office should be, not a civilian, but a soldier of far greater prestige than himself, and senior to him in the list of field marshals. He had resented Kitchener's intervention to stop him pulling the B.E.F. out of the line during the battle of the Marne, though he had no further cause to complain of being overruled. To a fault, Kitchener 'left him a free hand to make, in conjunction with General Joffre, such plans as he deemed fit'.[1] On the supply side his grievance was legitimate, though knowledge that his artillery was below the necessary strength did not, unfortunately, restrain him from launching attacks. His failures were due largely to his own recklessness, but he was able to put the blame on Kitchener.

The War Minister's parsimonious attitude towards the expenditure of ammunition in battle was, in Lloyd George's view, a hangover from his triumphant campaign in the Sudan, which 'was waged on the basis of a tender for the total cost of the operation . . . submitted to that most austere of all Chancellors, Sir Michael Hicks-Beach.'[2] Kitchener had then kept within his estimate, and Lloyd George felt that he continued to look at every military project from the same angle, though he was now dealing with a very different sort of Chancellor and a very different sort of war. From the first Lloyd George had made it clear that the War Office could have all the money it needed for munitions. Yet Kitchener, instead of telling French not to attack until he had better artillery support, seems to have criticised him only for not making more economical use of his available resources. After Neuve Chapelle the War Minister's complaint was that French had been 'far too extravagant', using 10,000 shells when he had said he would only need 5,000. The human losses were less serious, because they could be more easily replaced.[3]

On 15 March Kitchener did say in the House of Lords that arms production was 'not equal to our necessities', and this statement helped Lloyd George to negotiate his Treasury Agreement with the unions. But a month later the War Minister was assuring Asquith that

1. Sir William Robertson, *Soldiers and Statesmen 1914–1918*, ch. II. As French's chief of staff Robertson was in a good position to judge.
2. W.M., p. 192.
3. F.S.D., p. 40. Frances Stevenson records Kitchener's chilling remarks as having been made to Lloyd George and Balfour, though in his memoirs Lloyd George says they were made at a Cabinet meeting. (W.M., p. 193.)

French had as much ammunition as he would need for his 'next forward movement' – French having indeed changed his tune for a time, probably because he was so eager to attack at Aubers ridge and avenge the reverse inflicted on his men in the second battle of Ypres. On the strength of Kitchener's assurance Asquith spoke about supply in dangerously complacent terms at Newcastle on 20 April, and even Lloyd George went beyond the line of duty in defending the War Office's record in a Commons debate the following day. But whatever these speeches may have done to bolster public confidence was soon undone, when news of the Ypres battle came through. It seemed to people at home, as to troops at the front, that there should have been precautions against the Germans' use of gas, and more powerful artillery, with a better supply of shells, to strike them as they advanced.

The public had been kept in a state of false optimism by the absence of any serious discussion of the war in Parliament, and by the effects of censorship on the press. M.P.s had been tamed and muted by the party truce, while the newspapers had been prevented from printing disturbing reports or letters from the front. But by the early spring of 1915 the conspiracy of silence was cracking. A group of back-bench Conservatives called the Unionist Business Committee was showing signs of mutiny on the question of arms supply, and there was also considerable restiveness, mainly for the same reason, among Labour and Irish Nationalist M.P.s, upon whose support the Government depended. At the same time the Press was beginning to feel that it had a duty to give the public a more realistic picture of the war, and to exert itself more strenuously to bring about the changes necessary for winning it. In Churchill's words, 'the sun of newspaper power' now began 'to glow with unprecedented and ever-increasing heat'.[1]

If any one man could be said to embody that power it was Alfred Harmsworth, Lord Northcliffe, who had revolutionised British journalism and created in the popular press – his more or less single-handed invention – a new force in British politics. Since 1908 he had also been chief proprietor of *The Times*, towards whose proud traditions and self-consciously Olympian staff he felt a mixture of respect and exasperation. His undoubted genius was above all for journalism, but the patriot and frustrated politician in him craved a

1. *The World Crisis*, III, part 1, p. 242 (quoted in *The History of The Times*, 1912–1948 pp. 371–2).

role of decisive importance in the State, which on occasion he achieved. Spring 1915 was one such occasion. Whereas the Cabinet was kept largely in the dark by Kitchener, Northcliffe was singularly well informed about conditions on the battle fronts. His *Daily Mail* received thousands of letters from soldiers in the trenches, and the staff of its Continental edition, published in Paris, collected information about French politics and the French army which could not be obtained through official channels. For months past he had been concerned about the technical and industrial side of the war, and his remarkable flair for applied science made his anxiety all the more acute.

Though he had done much to mobilise the public opinion which brought Kitchener to power, now he did not hesitate to turn against the War Minister. On 1 May he wrote to Sir John French, inviting him to make 'a short and very vigorous statement' about the arms shortage, which would 'render the Government's position impossible'. French was already in close touch with *The Times*'s military correspondent, Charles à Court Repington – a very intelligent man, who also had become estranged from Kitchener – and after the disasters of Aubers ridge and Festubert Repington was allowed to report that 'the want of an unlimited supply of high explosive shells was a fatal bar to our success'.[1] These words, appearing in *The Times* on 14 May, caused the profound sensation that they were intended to cause, and a week later Northcliffe himself wrote a leader for the *Daily Mail* in which he delivered an all-out attack on Kitchener.

Meanwhile French had sent two of his staff officers, Brinsley Fitzgerald and Frederick Guest, to give Lloyd George, Balfour and Bonar Law personal briefings on the shortage of shells; and on 17 May Law was told that the Unionist Business Committee would soon force a debate on munitions. These various moves together made the 'shell scandal' a great national issue. As such it merged with, and contributed to, the crisis which destroyed the last Liberal government.

---

1. Repington claimed that the words were 'not suggested by Sir John French', perhaps rather more from vanity of authorship than any desire to defend French against the charge of complicity. Even if the report was not written in strict collusion with the commander-in-chief, and even if he 'never saw' it before it was sent, Repington knew very well that it would have his wholehearted approval, as indeed it had. Moreover, since details of casualties and weapon, as distinct from ammunition, shortages were cut out by the censor, it seems unlikely that an obviously sensational comment was allowed through without authorisation from the highest quarter. (Repington, *The First World War*, Vol. I, pp. 36–7.)

Much has been written about this crisis, and rather heavy weather made of it. But the paramount fact, surely, is that political reconstruction had become more or less inevitable because the war was going badly. If the Dardanelles campaign had been a success there would have been no pressure for fundamental change; and it is possible that the Liberal government might have survived, even without success at the Dardanelles, had there not also been failure and heavy losses on the Western front. But the combination of disasters was bound to have drastic results, and it only remained to be seen exactly what they would be and how they would come about.

Lloyd George always liked the idea of coalition. In 1910 he had tried very hard to promote one, at considerable risk to himself, when he felt that party controversy was threatening the country's vital interests. But that experience had been chastening to him, and he now had mixed feelings about a national government. Though still fully alive to the potential advantages, he had become rather more aware of the dangers and difficulties; so that, whereas Churchill clearly favoured a wartime coalition, Lloyd George was at least resigned to the continuance of party government, provided there was also an effective party truce. There is no evidence that he was plotting to force his colleagues into coalition with their traditional opponents, though of course he believed – and made no secret of his belief – that there had to be changes.

Was he looking for a change in the Premiership, and was he more especially intriguing to replace Asquith by himself? Some thought so at the time, and a vague suspicion has lingered on. Should it on balance be credited or dismissed? That he was increasingly disillusioned with Asquith's performance as war leader is beyond question. During the transition from peace to war he had been greatly impressed by the Prime Minister's toughness and skill. In October 1914 he told Riddell that Asquith was 'a very strong man', who possessed 'the rare combination of a tough-fibred, strong body with a fine delicate mind'. Even in November he was telling the same confidant that, whereas Grey lost sleep when there was bad news, 'the old P.M. [had] not turned a hair' and was 'as strong as a horse'. But in the New Year he showed growing signs of exasperation as the defects in Asquith's style of war leadership became apparent to him. No one had better reason than he to deplore the lack of steady direction in the War Council, from which the Dardanelles calamity and, in his view, enormous missed opportunities in the Balkans had resulted. He could also justifiably feel that a lot of work was being done by him which the Prime Minister ought to be doing himself. In early March 1915 he expressed his dissatisfaction to Riddell: '[Asquith] lacks initiative and takes no steps to control or hold together the public departments, each of which goes its own way without criticism. This is all very well in time of peace, but during a great war the Prime Minister should direct and overlook the whole machine.'[1]

Yet he still had much respect for Asquith's political gifts, and did not underrate his prestige which, though naturally strongest among Liberals, was by no means confined to them. In complaining of him to Riddell and others Lloyd George was almost certainly letting off steam rather than making any deliberate attempt to supplant his chief. Unfortunately it was always too easy for people to make mischief between them, by suggesting to Asquith that the Chancellor was in sinister cahoots with the Press. At the very beginning of Asquith's Premiership ill-wishers had persuaded him that Lloyd George had leaked the composition of the new Cabinet to the *Daily Chronicle*. The charge then was substantially false and Asquith was unwise to give it any countenance. Of course Lloyd George was on friendly terms with many journalists and inclined to talk to them very freely, treating them as responsible men with as much concern as any politician for the interests of the State. It would be absurd to pretend that he was a stickler for Cabinet secrets or that he was notably loyal to Cabinet colleagues. But in politics secrecy and loyalty are at the best of times more widely professed than practised. Lloyd George was a disturbing colleague mainly because he was so dynamic, and because his zeal for public business was so tireless. These characteristics made him seem more self-servingly ambitious than he really was, and caused every impatient outburst of his to be interpreted as calculated subversion or conspiracy.

With the growing evidence of military failure the Prime Minister came under attack in the right-wing Press, and on 29 March a Liberal newspaper – again the *Daily Chronicle* – condemned the 'innuendos and suggestions' against him. Before lunch that day McKenna went to him and accused 'Ll.G. & perhaps Winston' of being involved in the Press campaign. Asquith was susceptible to such Iago-like talk, and at 3 p.m. wrote to Venetia Stanley that McKenna had 'a certain amount of evidence as to Ll.G. to go upon'. Later the same day he confronted

1. R.W.D., entries for 11 October 1914, 22 November 1914, and 7 March 1915 (pp. 34, 42 and 65).

Lloyd George with the charge, and at 7 p.m. reported his reaction to Miss Stanley:

> I have never seen him more moved. He made a most bitter onslaught on McKenna whom he believes, through his animosity against Winston, to be the villain of the piece & the principal mischief-maker. He vehemently disclaimed having anything to do with the affair: Kitchener, he said, is the real culprit because, in spite of every warning, he has neglected up to the 11th hour a proper provision of munitions: & K. being a Tory, or supposed to be one, the Tory press, afraid to attack him, are making me the target of their criticism. As for himself (Ll.G.) he declared that he owed everything to me; that I had stuck to him & protected him when every man's hand was against him; and that he wd rather (1) break stones (2) dig potatoes (3) be hanged & quartered (these were metaphors used at different stages of his broken but impassioned harangue) than do an act, or say a word, or harbour a thought, that was disloyal to me. And he said that every one of our colleagues felt the same. His eyes were wet with tears, and I am sure that, with all his Celtic capacity for impulsive & momentary fervour, he was quite sincere.[1]

The following day Lloyd George took much the same line in conversation with Riddell:

> I shall not let this rest. I have never intrigued for place or office. I have intrigued to carry through my schemes, but that is a different matter. The Prime Minister has been so good to me that I would never be disloyal to him in the smallest detail. I may criticise him amongst ourselves, as I have no doubt he criticises me, but we are absolutely loyal to each other.[2]

He did not, indeed, let the matter rest, but insisted on a face-to-face encounter with McKenna in the Prime Minister's presence. This took place on 30 March, and the quarrel was then effectively resolved in Lloyd George's favour, McKenna denying that he had ever accused his colleague of plotting against Asquith.[3]

1. V.S.L., pp. 517 and 519. Asquith gave no details of the 'evidence' produced by McKenna.
2. R.W.D., p. 70. Riddell comments that Lloyd George 'looked quite ill', and quotes him as saying that Asquith (too) was in tears at the interview.
3. V.S.L., p. 522. Another account of the row over McKenna's insinuations is to be found in Frances Stevenson's diary (p. 42 – entry for 8 April, written while she was convalescing at Brighton).

Of course Lloyd George was protesting too much. As Beaverbrook says, he 'always had too ready and too complete answers to every possible objection which might be brought against his conduct, as though he had considered in advance that his actions might lay him open to charges of selfishness or insincerity'.[1] Yet it was in large measure true that he cared for his 'schemes' rather than for office as such, and that his schemes were essentially altruistic and patriotic. Fiercely ambitious though he was, his ambition was of no mean or narrowly personal kind. In intriguing for his schemes he could not help intriguing to some extent for himself, because he believed that he was best qualified to carry them through. His motives, therefore, were less pure than he claimed, though purer than his critics supposed. In the spring of 1915 he could see that the war effort was suffering from a lack of driving force at the top, and he wanted to supply the required force. But it does not follow that he coveted the office of prime minister, and from his behaviour in the crisis it would seem on the whole that he did not.

By the middle of May the shell scandal was threatening the Government and would surely have been enough to destroy it within days, or at most weeks, even if no further trouble had arisen. According to Repington, his sensational report in *The Times* on 14 May caused Lloyd George to tell the Prime Minister that 'he would be unable to go on', and this, though uncorroborated, is a credible story.[2] Beyond question Lloyd George was furious at the way he and Asquith had been misled by Kitchener before the recent battles. This he already knew privately from the emissaries sent to him by French, but when the scandal became public, with the appearance of Repington's report, it would have been natural for him to indicate at once that the Government's position was no longer tenable. Bonar Law and Balfour, who also had been briefed by the officers, could hardly be expected to keep their party under control now that the truth was out. Lloyd George had every reason to conclude, on the 14th, that there would have to be big changes.

Next morning, however, the shell scandal was overtaken by another issue, which forced the pace of change in a manner that no one could have foreseen. As Lloyd George was entering 10 Downing Street he happened to run into Admiral Lord Fisher, who announced

1. *Politicians and the War*, ch. XV.
2. Repington, *The First World War*, Vol. I, p. 39.

grimly, 'I have resigned.' Fisher had been opposed to the Dardanelles operation (though without at first saying so at the War Council), and he was anyway resentful of being subordinate to a civilian minister, while Kitchener at the War Office was his own boss. Now into the bargain he was becoming unhinged, through a combination of vanity and senility. Yet his prestige remained immense, and it was obvious that his resignation would be a devastating blow to the Government. Every effort, therefore, was made to dissuade him, but to no avail. His decision to go was inflexible, and as soon as it came out there was sure to be a tremendous row.

Meanwhile he sent Bonar Law a hint of what was impending, with the result that, early on Monday the 17th, Law called on Lloyd George to ask if it was true that Fisher had resigned. When told that it was, he said at once, 'Then the situation is impossible', and Lloyd George could only agree with him. It would have been difficult enough for the Tory leader to keep his backbenchers in check on the issue of shells, even for a short time ahead, though at least on that issue their hostility was to some extent mitigated by protective feelings towards Kitchener. But on the issue of Fisher's resignation their wrath would be compounded by hatred of the renegade Churchill. In the circumstances any doubts that Lloyd George may still have had about the necessity for coalition – and it is unlikely that he had many after the 14th – were instantly dispelled. He went straight next door to speak to Asquith, and in 'an incredibly short time' the Prime Minister came round to the same view. Law was then invited to join them in the Cabinet Room, and in 'less than a quarter of an hour' agreement was reached on procedure for ending the Liberal government and substituting a coalition.[1]

It was considered vital to forestall any renewal of party conflict in Parliament, not only because the spectacle of it would damage national morale and give comfort to the enemy, but also because Italy, which had recently signed a secret treaty to join the Entente, had still not actually declared war and might yet be deterred from doing so.[2] After a week of intense negotiations the new government was submitted to the King on 25 May, and it was Asquith who submitted it. The Conservative leaders accepted him as Prime Minister, though many of

1. W.M., pp. 227–9.
2. The secret Treaty of London was signed on 26 April, and on 4 May Italy denounced the Triple Alliance. But she did not declare war until 23 May, and then only against Austria–Hungary.

their supporters in Parliament and the Press were against him, and though Law and Balfour at any rate might have preferred to serve under Lloyd George, who told intimates at the time that one or both of them had suggested he should have the premiership.[1] If the offer was made, it was certainly refused, and Asquith relied heavily on Lloyd George in the awkward business of constructing the government.

While the Prime Minister's own position was secured, two outstanding colleagues were in varying degrees sacrificed. Conservatives demanded as part of their price for entering into coalition that Haldane and Churchill should be cast out. Of the two, Haldane was perhaps the less deserving of such a fate. Without his Army reforms Britain would have been unable to send an expeditionary force to France when the war began, and in many other ways would have been unequal to the emergency. Yet his great service as War Minister counted for nothing against the prejudice of those who condemned him as 'pro-German' merely because he loved German culture and philosophy. He was Asquith's oldest friend in politics, with even more claims on the Prime Minister's loyalty than Grey, who was anyway no longer fit for his job. Yet Grey remained while Haldane was dropped altogether. Churchill, for all his genius, and for all his good work at the Admiralty, had committed grave errors and contributed in no small way to the Liberal government's downfall. To the extent that he suffered, he suffered at least partly for his own mistakes; and he was not thrown completely overboard like Haldane. Though to his bitter indignation he had to leave the Admiralty – being replaced there by Balfour – he stayed in the Cabinet as Chancellor of the Duchy of Lancaster.

Apart from Churchill, the other man with clear ministerial responsibility for setbacks and failures in the war was Kitchener, and there were many in political and governing circles who would have liked to see him go, including some prominent Conservatives – Bonar Law for one. But any chance there may have been of getting rid of him was blasted by Northcliffe, whose *Daily Mail* leader on the 21st, violently attacking him, only produced a massive reaction in his favour. Copies of the paper were burnt at the Stock Exchange, to loud cheers, and its circulation fell (for a time) by more than a quarter of a million. Asquith's original idea was that the War Office should be taken over by Lloyd George, who showed considerable, if not quite

1. F.S.D., p. 51 and R.W.D., p. 94. According to the first source both made the suggestion; according to the second Law alone made it, when he visited Lloyd George on the 17th.

wholehearted, interest in it. But eventually the question did not arise, because it proved impossible to dislodge Kitchener.

At the same time the case for a separate department of State to control the whole process of arms production had become irresistible, now that the public was aware of the supply deficiencies in France. The case had long been argued by *The Times*, and many individuals in the know had recognised the weaknesses of the existing system. But now at last there was a consensus in favour of change, to which the King gave expression when he advised Asquith, on the 18th, that there should be 'a Minister to superintend manufacture of Munitions of War'.[1] For several days the Prime Minister hoped to be able to avoid creating a new department, by appointing Lloyd George War Secretary and so giving him control of supply. But when it became clear that Kitchener would be staying on at the War Office, the next idea was that Lloyd George would take charge of arms production while remaining Chancellor of the Exchequer; and it was hopefully imagined that the job might be done in three months. An alternative solution, put forward by Lloyd George, was that the Prime Minister might look after the Treasury during his temporary absence, but the Conservatives rightly objected to an arrangement which would be too onerous for a wartime premier. So at length it was settled that Lloyd George would indeed leave the Treasury to set up and run the new Ministry of Munitions, and that another man would meanwhile hold the office of Chancellor of the Exchequer. But Lloyd George was to continue to live at 11 Downing Street, and it was understood that he would return to his old job when the work on munitions was completed.

In agreeing to coalesce with the Liberals the Conservatives demanded parity of representation in the new government: more especially, that they should have ten Cabinet posts. Asquith appeared to concede this demand in principle, but then went about forming the government in such a way as to ensure effective Liberal dominance. In this he had the indispensable support of Lloyd George. The Conservatives got their way about Haldane, and up to a point about Churchill. They also scored in obtaining the office of Attorney-General for Sir Edward Carson, and that of Solicitor-General for F. E. Smith. But in other respects they were worsted by the Liberals.

When the Cabinet was finally formed they had only eight places in it, and of the most important offices only one – the Admiralty – was

1. Stamfordham to Prime Minister's private secretary, Maurice Bonham Carter.

REINFORCED CONCRETE.

John Bull. "IF YOU NEED ASSURANCE, SIR, YOU MAY LIKE TO KNOW THAT YOU HAVE THE LOYAL SUPPORT OF ALL DECENT PEOPLE IN THIS COUNTRY."

From *Punch*, 2 June 1915

held by a Conservative politician, Balfour. (Kitchener was no politician, even if privately a Tory.) Haldane's successor as Lord Chancellor was another Liberal, Buckmaster. The new Chancellor of the Exchequer, supposedly as a stand-in for Lloyd George, was McKenna, and his place at the Home Office was taken by Simon. In all, the Liberals had eleven seats in the new Cabinet, out of a total of twenty-one. As well as the Liberal and Tory members, plus Kitchener, there was one representative of Labour, Henderson, who became President of the Board of Education. Asquith tried to persuade Redmond to join, but the Irish leader declined, while protesting strongly against the inclusion of Carson.

The Conservatives, apart from Balfour, occupied positions that were either senior but non-executive, or executive but without the highest rating and prestige. In the first category were Curzon as Lord Privy Seal and Lansdowne as Minister without Portfolio; in the second, Austen Chamberlain as Secretary for India, Bonar Law as Colonial Secretary, Walter Long as President of the Local Government Board, Selborne as President of the Board of Agriculture, and Carson as Attorney-General.

Most surprising was Law's comparatively modest place. As leader of the party he might have expected, and indeed did expect, to be given one of the offices that mattered most. He was a rival to Lloyd George for the War Office, and then for the Ministry of Munitions. When it was decided that Lloyd George should leave the Treasury he felt, understandably, that he should be Chancellor, all the more so as Asquith had offered him the job at the outset of their negotiations. But in the end he was excluded from all three posts, on plausible though disingenuous pretexts. It would not, allegedly, be right for Tories to hold both Service departments, still less both Service departments and the Ministry of Munitions (Kitchener being counted as a Tory for the purposes of this argument). As for the Exchequer, it would arouse Liberal fears and violate the spirit of the party truce if a Tariff Reformer were to go there.

Such were the reasons given, but they were not the decisive ones. Asquith had always underrated Law and doubted his competence. Moreover, he was determined to keep the Tories in their place and to establish none of them as a potential challenge to his own leadership. It suited him, as Lord Blake convincingly suggests, to give the Tory leader a somewhat 'depressed status'. His own position 'might be strengthened if the principal Conservatives had no definite leader to represent them, if in fact the whole question of Tory leadership seemed to be thrown open'.[1] During the crisis Asquith was at his most ruthless and resourceful, showing no sign of any loss of nerve, or of the will to rule, as a result of losing Venetia Stanley as his confidante (with her announcement to him, on the 12th, that she would be marrying Edwin Montagu). For the country's sake it would probably have been better if he *had* cracked up, because his great political talents were not of the sort required for winning a war. But, far from cracking up, he formed a new government with himself as its undisputed leader, and he also dealt most effectively with a threatened revolt of Liberal backbenchers. The outcome of the crisis was a notable victory for him, if not for the Allied cause.

Yet it is unlikely that he could have won through as he did without Lloyd George's staunch cooperation. Despite a personal liking for Bonar Law, and an assessment of his ability less contemptuous than Asquith's, Lloyd George helped to restrict his power within the coalition, as well as that of the Conservatives as a body. When at a late stage Law seemed ready to have no coalition at all unless his terms were accepted, Lloyd George faced the prospect calmly and thought how the Liberal government might carry on with a leavening of non-party peers.[2] Throughout he acted as a good Liberal and loyal lieutenant, though he also had motives of his own for blocking Law's appointment to key posts. So far as the Ministry of Munitions was concerned, he could reasonably feel that Law's quiet efficiency would not be enough to bring the new department to life, and that his temperament would not equip him for the necessary tussle with the War Office. Similar objections could be made to him as a candidate for the War Office, where he might well have been too much in the hands of the soldiers.

But Lloyd George's reluctance to see him appointed to the Treasury had more to do, surely, with the need to secure his own position. He was determined to retain the second place in the Government, which his reversionary right to the Treasury symbolised. Law could not have become Chancellor as a mere stand-in; his appointment would have threatened Lloyd George's authority, which was vital to him not least for his impending work at Munitions. Far more than personal ambition was at stake, and of course infinitely more than mere protocol.

1. Blake, *The Unknown Prime Minister*, pp. 251–2.
2. Stamfordham, memorandum for the King, 25 May 1915.

But Lloyd George's attitude was resented by Law, and caused a temporary cooling in their relations.

On the 25th, when the crisis was over, Asquith wrote to Lloyd George with an emotion seldom shown in his letters to men:

My dear Lloyd George,

I cannot let this troubled & tumultuous chapter in our history close without trying to let you know what an incalculable help & support I have found in you all through. I shall never forget your devotion, your unselfishness, your powers of resource, what is (after all) the best of all things, your self-forgetfulness.

These are the rare things that make the drudgery and squalor of politics, with its constant revelation of the large part played by personal & petty motives, endurable, and give to its drabness a lightning streak of nobility.

I thank you with all my heart.

Always your affect^e

H. H. Asquith

It was Asquith's turn to be protesting too much. Yet he was genuinely grateful to Lloyd George, and not without reason. Next day the new Minister of Munitions received a shorter and less flowery letter from his old friend, Herbert Lewis (who, incidentally, would be joining the new government as junior Education minister): 'There was only one man for the most important job of all. No one is better able to blow people up when they deserve it – & if ever a nation has deserved it, that nation is Germany.'[1]

1. Viscount Tenby's collection (N.L.W.).

ELEVEN

'The Heaviest Burden'

Lloyd George was Minister of Munitions for a little over thirteen months, and during that short time he achieved a feat of creative improvisation which even his harshest detractors have been forced to admire. Few phases of his controversial career have suffered less from the scrutiny of revisionist historians, and in few, if any, did he have more scope for the exercise of his distinctive talents. Though as Prime Minister he had, of course, a much wider field of responsibility, he was also subject to more restraints and often found it more difficult to get his way. At Munitions he came to acquire almost dictatorial powers for carrying out his allotted task, and he used them not only to produce necessary types and quantities of arms, but also, while doing so, to change the relationship between the British State and British industry, involving them with each other as never before, and in many ways accelerating the process of social change. His work at Munitions was, therefore, of great importance for the future of the country in peacetime, as well as vital for winning the war.

The success of his efforts owed something, even at the time, to propaganda, and has tended in retrospect to be somewhat exaggerated in the more fulsome accounts. Not all of the increased war production after May 1915 was due to the Ministry of Munitions, since much had already been put in hand; and of the credit unquestionably due to the Ministry under his leadership not all was strictly due to him personally. Yet it is hard to deny that he deserved the paramount share. In accepting the post he risked his whole reputation. If the new department had turned out to be a flop he would have got most of the blame –

he would have suffered as Churchill did over Gallipoli – so it is only fair that he should get most of the praise for its success, which was not only apparent but largely real. Moreover, one should not forget how outstanding his contribution had been to the supply side of the war before he took executive charge of it himself. But for his relentless nagging and many useful interventions matters would have been considerably worse than they were in the spring of 1915.

It suited his temperament to be building a new institution rather than having to adapt himself to an old one. Just as he always found the atmosphere of old buildings oppressive, so he disliked the atmosphere of traditional departments of State. At the Board of Trade and, even more, at the Treasury he had to deal with established rules and an established hierarchy. At the Ministry of Munitions he was able to establish his own. He seems to have thought at first of running the new department from 11 Downing Street,[1] but in fact settled for an office on the ground floor of a fine house, 6 Whitehall Gardens, recently vacated by Lockett Agnew, the art dealer. Later he would describe with relish the circumstances of his early days there. His office was an Adam drawing-room 'where every panel glittered with long pier-glasses'. These distracted his visitors, who saw themselves reflected from every angle; so he had the glasses covered over. Furniture in the room consisted only of a table and two chairs which, according to him, the Office of Works tried to remove; and he had 'a greater struggle over getting a carpet than over getting 50 millions for munitions'. Details in the story varied, and of course it lost nothing in the telling.[2]

Essentially he was, indeed, starting from scratch. The new Ministry had to be given substance and a legal framework, but he was wise enough to see that it could not be formed entirely of new elements, nor achieve at once the full scope and authority he desired for it. There had to be continuity as well as innovation, and its assumption of powers

---

1. R.W.D., entry for 26 May 1915, p. 96.

2. The pier-glasses are mentioned in Lloyd George's War Memoirs (p. 244) and the carpet in his address on leaving the Ministry, as reported in its official history (vol. II, part I, chap. II p. 45). In his memoirs he says there were *two* tables and *one* chair, and he quotes Colonel House, President Wilson's confidant – who apparently visited him on his first day in the office – as saying that Lloyd George insisted he should have the chair, though he in turn insisted that Lloyd George should occupy it while he (House) sat on a table (W.M., pp. 242-3). Frances Stevenson records that the adjoining office, to be occupied by herself and J. T. Davies, had two chairs and a table, which on the first day two men attempted to remove. (*The Years that are Past*, p. 77.)

would have to be gradual. As a first step he recruited Sir Hubert Llewellyn Smith as his chief adviser. Llewellyn Smith had been his permanent secretary at the Board of Trade, and they had worked well together because Smith, though a civil servant, was independent-minded and a social reformer at heart. In moving temporarily to Munitions he retained his post at the Board of Trade, and his standing in Whitehall as well as his personal qualities were of great value to the new enterprise. His very first act was to meet his opposite number at the War Office, Sir Reginald Brade, and to convince him that a large transfer of powers should be made.

Even so, the problem of demarcation was hard to resolve. Kitchener seems to have thought, at the outset, that Lloyd George's department would be subordinate to the War Office, as its equivalent was in France. On 26 May he wrote to Lloyd George, 'Delighted to hear you are coming to help me', which implied a misunderstanding of their future relationship.[1] Lloyd George did not intend to be a mere supplier of requirements laid down by the War Office, because he had no confidence in the generals' capacity to assess the army's needs in the matter of weaponry. His aim was to control the ordering as well as the production of arms. But he had to be content with achieving this aim by stages. At first it was agreed that the new Ministry should take over the staff of the War Office's Armaments Output Committee, and the explosives department; but there was no clear agreement as to who should control the contracts and finance departments, or the royal arsenals. In the Order in Council of 16 June, which brought the Ministry formally into existence, it was stated that the Minister's duty was to ensure the supply of munitions 'as may be required by the Army Council or the Admiralty *or may otherwise be found necessary*'. The words in italics could have read 'or may be found necessary by the Minister, forming his own judgment'.

As parliamentary secretary Lloyd George chose Dr Christopher Addison, who had given him important help in his fight with the doctors over health insurance, and whom he regarded as a capable, resourceful man of proven loyalty to himself. Attempts by the Prime Minister to secure a political niche in the Ministry for Harold Baker, a close friend of the Asquiths but not otherwise qualified, were firmly resisted. Baker was a good classical scholar but a thoroughly incompetent minister, and Lloyd George must have suspected that his

1. L.G.P. The letter is dated simply '26th', but the more precise dating can reasonably be assumed.

role – like that of Charles Hobhouse at the Treasury in 1908 – would have been to keep an eye on his chief. Addison was the Minister's, not the Prime Minister's, man. He was the sort of radical who looked to Lloyd George for leadership and, being honourably ambitious, also looked to him for patronage. As a physician and former professor of anatomy he might have been somewhat embarrassed by his new job. For one who had started his career ministering to the sick and promoting public health it was certainly rather odd – almost a violation of his Hippocratic oath – to be organising the manufacture of lethal weapons. But he did not allow this apparent incongruity, which some were disagreeable enough to point out, to weaken his self-confidence.

Lloyd George had the idea that Addison, the civilian, should be joined by a second junior minister, who would represent the military side and facilitate dealings with the War Office. For this post his choice was Major-General Sir Ivor Philipps, a rich Welshman and Liberal M.P., on whose divisional staff Gwilym Lloyd George had been serving as an A.D.C. But he did not last long. The ruling that even temporary ministers had to give up all their directorships was not acceptable to him, and in any case he was not much of a success in the job. In September he returned to his division.

With the staff of the armaments output committee Lloyd George acquired the services of Sir Percy Girouard, whom he rashly appointed director-general of munitions supply in the new Ministry. It was an appointment he soon regretted. Girouard was a very able man, who during his brief period of working on the problems of arms supply under Kitchener had taken some initiatives of lasting value. But his temperament and background unfitted him to work with strong-minded colleagues, or under a chief like Lloyd George. Originally a railway engineer, he had risen to quite high rank in the Army (under Kitchener), and had then been a colonial governor (in west and east Africa), before becoming a director of Armstrong's munition works at Elswick in 1912. Naturally bossy, he had got into the habit of being obeyed more or less without argument, and he did not have the tact to make his authoritarian ways acceptable.

Tact was certainly needed in a position which seemed to challenge that of Llewellyn Smith, not to mention that of Lloyd George himself. But instead of underplaying his hand, Girouard from the first over-played it. On 27 May he attended a meeting in Lloyd George's office, at which Addison and Llewellyn Smith also were present. According to Addison:

> Much discussion took place as to [Girouard's] functions and those
> of Llewellyn Smith. No doubt Girouard is a man of brains and
> ability but I was not favourably impressed with him today. He
> appeared too anxious to get control into his own hands. However
> L.G. put him down pretty vigorously and, as he explained to me
> afterwards privately, he had done so deliberately. He probably felt
> it was necessary to let Girouard see at once who was to be master in
> the department. L.G. can do this as effectively as anyone I know and
> this time he did it superbly.[1]

Girouard did himself further damage in Lloyd George's eyes by
insisting that the directors of the various branches of his department
should all be munitions experts. Lloyd George was by no means
indifferent to the value of experts; he was always ready to make use of
them in the ways that he thought appropriate. But he did not regard
them as necessarily the right people to run an organisation. As he later
exclaimed to the American Ambassador, Walter H. Page:

> The Government has experts, experts, experts, everywhere. In any
> department where things are not going well, I have found . . .
> boards of experts. But in our department at least I've found a
> substitute for them. I let twenty experts go and I put in one Man,
> and things begin to move at once.[2]

The sort of man he looked for was one endowed with a general talent
for executive action and with a keen sense of priorities.

The last straw was when Girouard arranged for the King to visit
Coventry, and accompanied him as representative of the Ministry,
without even informing Lloyd George in advance. This led swiftly to
Girouard's departure after only two months as director-general, and
Lloyd George's statement in the War Memoirs that he did not replace
him was morally, if not technically, true. For a short time Ivor
Philipps acted as nominal successor, and then the post was given to a
civil servant, Sir Frederick Black, whom Lloyd George persuaded
Balfour to release from the Admiralty. But in reality it was not the

1. *Four and a Half Years*, p. 83. Soon afterwards Addison was commenting that Girouard, 'like
a good many military men was greatly concerned about his status and title', but that
Llewellyn Smith was 'big enough not to worry about that sort of thing'. In a letter to Lloyd
George, however, Llewellyn Smith stressed the importance of not letting it appear that
Girouard was 'head of the whole office'. (15 June 1915, L.G.P.)
2. *The Life and Letters of Walter H. Page* by Burton J. Hendrick, Part II, p. 259.

same post. Overall direction of munitions supply could be exercised only by Lloyd George himself. Black was a discreet official who knew that the title of his office was not to be taken literally.

One major figure from the previous regime who survived in the new Ministry was Lord Moulton, who came to it with the explosives department. Moulton was a formidable man, one of the most gifted of his generation, though now almost totally forgotten. He was a brilliant mathematician who turned to law and became an outstandingly successful barrister, specialising in patents. At the same time he engaged in electrical researches which earned him fellowship of the Royal Society. From 1885 he was on and off a Liberal M.P., but in 1906 was appointed a Lord of Appeal. Soon after the outbreak of war Haldane suggested him to Kitchener as chairman for a committee to advise the War Office on propellants, and for the rest of the war his superb scientific mind was concentrated on this subject which, though new to him, he completely mastered. Such was his concentration that he shut himself off from all other interests, seldom even reading a newspaper.[1]

Until the Ministry of Munitions came into being Moulton's powers were circumscribed. His committee evolved into a branch of the War Office, of which, as a civilian, he was not allowed to be the sole head. His authority had to be shared with a brigadier-general. But when the explosives department was transferred to Lloyd George he gave Moulton undisputed control of it, with direct access to himself (bypassing Girouard, while Girouard lasted). The department remained in the Institute of Mechanical Engineers' building at Storey's Gate, while the main establishment of munitions supply was at Armament Buildings, Whitehall Place. This physical separateness emphasised Moulton's relative independence within the organisation.

Though he was not Lloyd George's discovery, most of the Ministry's star performers were. By the end of July he could claim to have 'at least ninety men of first-class business experience', most of them working 'without any remuneration at all'.[2] Probably the luckiest find of all was Eric Geddes, a forty-year-old Scotsman of sturdy build and rigorous self-discipline, who in his teens had worked on an American railroad and as a very young man had gone out to run a forestry estate in India. The estate included a light railway, and this

1. H. Fletcher Moulton, *The Life of Lord Moulton*, p. 180.
2. House of Commons, 29 July 1915. Quoted in W.M., p. 254. Another who was kept on was George Booth.

led him into the business of railway management. By 1914 he was a top executive of the North-Eastern Railway in England, and on 26 May 1915 his immediate superior recommended him to Lloyd George for employment in the Ministry of Munitions, citing his exceptional drive and also his tact, which should enable him to 'get on well with military men as well as civilians'.[1] Two days later he was interviewed by Addison, who 'thought him first-rate' and introduced him to Lloyd George.[2] He was at once appointed deputy director-general under Girouard, with special responsibility for the production of guns. This was only the first of many assignments over the next few years, culminating in Cabinet office.

Geddes was the paradigm of a Lloyd Georgian man of push-and-go. Though his particular forte was transport, he had the capacity to grasp administrative problems in any sphere, and to find solutions to them. One who worked with him described him as 'after L.G. . . . the greatest driving force in the Ministry'. He was 'like an unruly schoolboy' with 'a big and loyal heart'.[3] Above all he was loyal to Lloyd George. Though never a yes-man, he knew who was the boss and respected what he knew. In Lloyd George he saw a dynamism surpassing his own, and he was glad to be able to serve such a chief, whatever the incidental travail. His work in any case was a therapeutic release from almost unbearable distress at home, where the wife he loved had gone out of her mind after giving birth to one of their children.

Other notable recruits to the Ministry in the early days were Ernest Moir from Pearson's, Glyn West from Armstrong's, James Stevenson from the whisky firm of John Walker, Leonard Llewellyn from the Cambrian Coal Combine, Charles Ellis from John Brown and Company, Alfred Herbert from the machine-tool firm bearing his name, Samuel Hardman Lever from the City of London, William Beveridge from the Board of Trade, and Walter Layton from the University of Cambridge. All were to emerge from the experience with honour, and some were destined for higher things.

In the Minister's private office J. T. Davies and Frances Stevenson were joined by William Sutherland, a civil servant who had worked on Old Age Pensions and National Insurance, and who had also

---

1. Sir Alexander Kaye Butterworth to D.L.G. (L.G.P.) Butterworth was general manager of the N.E.R., Geddes his deputy and designated successor.

2. *Four and a Half Years*, p. 84.

3. *A Good Innings, the Private Papers of Viscount Lee of Fareham*, ed. by Alan Clark, p. 144.

helped Lloyd George with his Land Campaign. More recently he had been secretary to the Cabinet committee on munitions supply. In the years ahead he was to serve his master in a variety of ways, not all equally reputable, and in the process would make a good many enemies. Hankey, for instance, once described him as 'an odious fellow . . . some sort of political parasite of Ll.G.'s'.[1] His main function was dealing with the Press, and according to Beaverbrook he was 'exceedingly talkative, often revealing secrets, cunning and never disloyal to his master. Like every court favourite he suffered derision, scorn and hatred.'[2]

Soon after the move to Munitions Frances heard that her brother Paul had died of wounds in France. Lloyd George himself broke the news to her after they had been to Barrie's new play, *Rosy Rapture: The Pride of the Beauty Chorus*. (J. T. Davies had brought him the news during the last act.) He then took her home to be with her parents. But she was soon back at work, and it was probably due only to the extreme pressure under which she and everybody else in the office were working that she stopped keeping her diary from the end of May to the beginning of September, apart from one entry recording a memorial service for Paul and others in his regiment. She felt that a shadow had been cast over her life which would never disappear.

Lloyd George used to say that, though always a hard worker, he had never in his whole life worked harder than when setting up the Ministry of Munitions. It is easy to believe him. Within three weeks of his appointment, and despite all the other claims on his time, he had delivered a series of powerful speeches in the country. In the first, at Manchester on 3 June, he addressed himself boldly to the question of compulsion, which he defined as one 'not of principle but of necessity'. Even if compulsion were not yet necessary for the armed forces, it might all the same be necessary for mobilising the country's industrial strength. There had to be greater mobility of labour, and greater subordination of labour to the requirements of the State. The army, after all, might consist of volunteers, but their actions once they were in ceased to be voluntary.

The enlisted workman cannot choose his locality of action. He cannot say, 'I am quite prepared to fight at Neuve Chapelle, but I

1. Roskill, *Hankey: Man of Secrets*, Vol. I, p. 329.
2. *Politicians and the War*, p. 284 (footnote).

264 LLOYD GEORGE: FROM PEACE TO WAR

won't fight at Festubert, and I am not going near the place they call
"Wipers".' He cannot say, 'I have been in the trenches ten hours and
a half and my trade union won't allow me to work more than ten
hours.' He cannot say, 'You have not enough men here, and I have
been doing the work of two men. My trade union won't allow men
to do more than their own share.' The veteran who has been seven
years at the job, seven years in the army, can't say, 'Who is this
fellow by my side, this mere fledgling? He has only just a few
weeks' training; it is against my union's regulations, and I am off.'

When the house is on fire, questions of procedure, of precedence,
of etiquette, of time, and division of labour, disappear. You cannot
say that you are not liable to service at three o'clock in the morning
if the fire is proceeding. You don't choose the hour; you cannot
argue as to whose duty it is to carry the water bucket and whose
duty it is to tip it into the crackling furnace. You must put the fire
out. There is only one way to do that. That is everything must give
way to duty, good-fellowship, comradeship and determination;
you must put the whole of your strength into obtaining victory for
your native land and for the liberties of the world.

This speech made a big impression, though the reactions were not
all favourable. Some Liberals were alarmed at Lloyd George's
apparent backsliding towards compulsion, and at several other signs
of his willingness to abandon traditional Liberalism. One passage
must have been particularly disturbing to those who regarded
wartime politics as a necessary, though regrettable, distraction from
the true order of things.

Party politics are gradually vanishing. We hear occasionally a
lingering growl, and we are looking forward to the days when we
will hear the roar of the party politician again. It will be a proof that
peace has returned. I am not sure that the same men will quarrel
with the same men; in fact, I am fairly certain that they will not; but I
hope it may be that when the hour for reconstruction comes all will
be for the State, all will be for the nation.

It must have seemed that the reference to party politics was bitterly
ironical, the preference for coalition manifest.

At the same time Labour hostility was aroused by what seemed to
be a threat to vital trade union liberties. In the last speech of the series
he took account of this feeling to the extent of showing that he was no
stranger to trade unionism – that he could understand it from the

inside.

> I happen to belong to about the strictest, the most jealous, trades
> union in the world. If any unskilled man – and by an unskilled man
> we mean a man who has not paid our fees – if any man of that sort,
> however intelligent he was, tried to come in and interfere with our
> business, we would soon settle him. But if during the period of the
> war there were any particular use for lawyers, if you found that
> upon lawyers depended the success of the war – I know it requires a
> good deal of imagination . . . do you suppose that even the
> Incorporated Law Society, the greatest and narrowest of all trades
> unions, could stand in the way of bringing in outside help in order
> to enable us to get through our work?[1]

Thus he returned to his point that trade union restrictive practices
must give way to the national interest.

Between these two speeches in Lancashire he spoke at Cardiff on 11
June, and at Bristol the following day. Before leaving for Wales and
the West Country he received a delegation of trade unionists and
challenged them to find a way of putting the right men in the right
places without compulsion. The delegation, representing unions
party to the Treasury agreement, accepted a scheme put forward by
the National Advisory Committee (established under that agreement)
that there should be a voluntary system of transfer for workmen, with
compulsion only as 'a last and unavoidable resource'. But the corol-
lary was that the standard of living of workmen should be safeguarded
'by eliminating the element of excessive profits or exorbitant prices of
the necessaries of life'. On 16 June Lloyd George met the trade union
leaders again and showed them a synopsis of his proposed Munitions
of War Bill, the stated intention of which was to provide legislative
back-up for the Treasury agreement.

A week later he introduced the Bill in the House of Commons,
devoting much of his speech to the problems of labour, and reporting
what the trade unions had undertaken to do:

> We had a very frank discussion . . . and I was bound to point out that
> if there were an inadequate supply of labour for the purpose of
> turning out the munitions of war which are necessary for the safety
> of the country, compulsion would be inevitable. They put forward
> as an alternative that the Government should give them the chance

1. Liverpool, 14 June 1915.

of supplying that number. They said 'Give us seven days, and if in seven days we cannot get the men we will admit that our case is considerably weakened.' They asked us to place the whole machinery of Government at their disposal, because they had not the organisation to enlist the number required. We have arranged terms upon which the men are to be enlisted, and tomorrow morning [24 June] the seven days begin. Advertisements will appear in all the papers. An office has been organised and the trade union representatives are sitting there in council directing the recruiting operations.

In his reply to the debate he explained further the philosophy behind his measure. He was not, he said, threatening the working classes, but

. . . if we cannot, by voluntary means, get the labour which is essential to the success of this country in a war upon which its life depends, we must use, as the ultimate resort, the means which every State has at its command to save its life. You have got to save the life of Britain. We talk about the State as if it were something apart from the workman. The workman is that State. He is a living ingredient in it. Do not separate him and say, 'There is the State.' He is the State, and after all it is universal suffrage . . . which has decreed these powers.

In fact, the franchise in Britain was still far from universal. Women did not have the vote at all and only fifty-eight per cent of men had it. A large part of the working class was still disfranchised. Besides, the electorate was only decreeing the powers in the sense that they were being endorsed, vicariously, by a Parliament elected in December 1910. The appeal to democratic right was, therefore, morally rather specious.

All the same the Bill received general support, not least from Labour, and was swiftly passed into law. It gave the Government a more or less free hand in the munitions industries, where there were to be no strikes or lock-outs, no trade union restrictive practices, and (in theory) no excess profits. The burden of sacrifice was, beyond question, more on labour than on the employers, but for reasons already explained Lloyd George felt that this balance was justified. His relatively indulgent attitude towards employers was revealed in one passage of his opening speech, when he said that 'such questions as the profits of employers and *whether they be limited or not*, or the prejudices of workmen as to abandoning their old traditions and practices in connection with trade unions', were, compared with the task of winning the war, 'not worth a moment's consideration' (author's italics).[1] But on the whole the patriotism of workers, stimulated by his oratory, tended to overcome any sense of social injustice.

The campaign of public indoctrination with which he launched his new Ministry was certainly effective, but he was well aware that its effect would wear off unless the results were good, and seen to be good. He did not believe in salesmanship without a saleable article, but he also knew that public relations were important, and not only for meretricious reasons. He made a point of involving his Parliamentary colleagues in the work of the Ministry, by arranging for M.P.s to visit munitions factories, where they would normally be asked to address the workers. This was useful both in giving politicians first-hand knowledge of what was going on, and in bridging the gulf between rulers and ruled. By the end of 1915 more than a thousand such visits had taken place. He saw to it, also, that the business of arms production was well covered in the Press. Parties of journalists from colonial and foreign, as well as British, newspapers were invited to tour industrial areas and given every facility for doing so. Throughout his time as Minister publicity was never neglected, though of course it was incidental to the substantive work of the department.

From early in the war Lloyd George had been deeply concerned about inter-Allied cooperation, or rather the lack of it. He was sickened by the failure of the various Entente governments and high commands even to keep each other informed of their plans, let alone to concert them. More than once he had taken the initiative in an attempt to establish closer communication, particularly with the French, and in February had suggested to President Poincaré that an Allied war council should be set up in France. He had also, in the same month, proposed to his Cabinet colleagues that a special envoy should be sent to the Balkans and Russia, to coordinate Allied policy and strategy in the eastern theatre, and soon afterwards that there should be a conference of Allied foreign ministers in the area. But nothing came of those ideas at the time.

As Minister of Munitions he was more fortunate. Within his own departmental sphere remarkable cooperation developed with Britain's principal ally. Two days after his appointment he had a letter from

1. Report of debate on Introduction of Munitions of War Bill, 23 June 1915 (Hansard, Fifth Series, Vol. LXXI, cols. 1183–1276).

Albert Thomas, under-secretary in the French War Ministry with special responsibility for armaments, welcoming him to his new post and saying that nothing would be more useful than meetings and discussions between them to enable the joint needs of the British and French armies to be more satisfactorily met.[1] Thomas was an out-standing man. Still only in his middle thirties, he looked rather older because of a corpulent figure and luxuriant black beard which gave him, to English eyes, the appearance of a caricature Frenchman. He might have passed for a professor and had, indeed, been one. His standing in French politics was far more considerable than the rather modest title of his office suggested, in that he was a Socialist, in some ways the heir of Jaurès, and wholly dedicated to winning the war. In 1917 he was a rival to Clemenceau for the premiership, but could not find enough support for a government of the Left and went into temporary eclipse. After the war he became the first head of the International Labour Organisation set up under the auspices of the League of Nations, and it is possible that he might again have played an important part in the affairs of his own country, as it moved towards another supreme crisis, had he not died prematurely in 1932.

When circumstances brought him and Lloyd George together they were barely acquainted. But soon there was a strong rapport between them. Both were humorous, both were eloquent, but both believed that action counted for more than words. They also tended to see eye-to-eye on strategic issues. Though neither could speak the other's language, they were able to converse freely through an interpreter, who as a rule was either Frances Stevenson or the red-bearded Paul Mantoux (destined to give eminent service in the same capacity at the Peace Conference). In the desperately crowded month of June 1915, when Lloyd George was recruiting staff for his new Ministry, making speeches in different parts of the country, negotiating with trade union leaders and introducing his Munitions of War Bill, he also managed to fit in a trip to Boulogne for meetings with Thomas and various officers on the 19th and 20th. The following month they met again, in London, and after this visit Thomas wrote: 'At the Ministry of Munitions I had the joyous impression of a young and new organisa-tion which will be able to mobilise all the nation's resources for War. . . . I must also express the very cordial and very deep sympathy that I have for you personally, and my hope that our collaboration will

1. Albert Thomas to D.L.G., 30 May 1915 (L.G.P.).

Lloyd George with his wife at the foot of Moel Hebog, North Wales, 1913

Land campaigning, 1913. At Swindon

At Sutton-on-Ashfield

Asquith and Lloyd George conferring at the Wharf

Edward Carson,
September 1913

Lloyd George unveiling
his portrait by
Christopher Williams
at the National
Liberal Club,
3 January 1913

Frances Stevenson early in the war

Two Field Marshals: Kitchener receives his old chief, Lord Roberts, at the War Office, 1914 (*War Illustrated*)

Two First Lords:
Churchill and his successor, Balfour

Lloyd George in his study at
11 Downing Street, 1914

With Herbert Samuel, reviewing the women munition workers'
procession, 22 July 1916

What they saw

The Coalition Cabinet, May 1915.
From left to right (standing):
Arthur Henderson, Austen
Chamberlain, McKinnon Wood,
Churchill, Bonar Law, Kitchener,
Asquith, Crewe, Lloyd George,
Harcourt, McKenna, Buckmaster,
Grey, Simon, Runciman, Birrell,
Long, Selborne; *(seated)* Balfour,
Carson, Lansdowne, Curzon
(Illustrated War News)

Bonar Law: 'He always took the only
comfortable armchair in the room'
(Beaverbrook)

Certificate signed by Lloyd George for
a badged munition worker (*Liddle
Collection, University of Leeds*)

'I do not know whether I am in order,
Mr Speaker, in showing this': Lloyd
George holds up a fuse during a speech in
the House of Commons, 23 July 1915
(*Illustrated London News*)

Arthur Henderson

Eric Geddes

General Robertson

Colonel Hankey

Lloyd George with Lord Derby, inspecting the dockers' battalion, 1915

Meeting at Beauquesne, 12 August 1916.
From left to right: General Joffre, President Poincaré, King George V, General Foch, General Haig

Asquith arriving at Kingstown on his way to Dublin, May 1916

Lloyd George, walking near Criccieth with his son Dick, on leave from the Front

'The blinds of Britain are not down yet':
Lloyd George at the National Eisteddfod, Aberystwyth, 17 August 1916

With Megan on the same occasion

In conference with Briand, Paris, 11 August 1916

With Albert Thomas, viewing the ruins of Verdun, 7 September 1916

With Albert Thomas and Reading (*second from right*) near Fricourt, September 1916

On St George's Hill, near Fricourt, 12 September 1916
(Reading is on the extreme left)

Lloyd George in December 1916

become more effective with every day that passes.'[1]

They met again on other occasions, and between meetings were in constant touch by letter or messenger. And their collaboration was indeed fruitful. Even before he became Minister of Munitions Lloyd George had obtained from France valuable advice bearing upon the problem of arms production in Britain. Now he was far better placed to do so. With Thomas as his French counterpart he could count on a prompt response to any request for information, and substantial benefits resulted. For instance, in September 1915 Thomas sent Lloyd George drawings of certain types of French mortars, and the following month arranged for British experts to study their use in France, and to borrow specimens. At about the same time a British mission was studying French methods of shell-filling, with useful consequences. If the relationship of trust and mutual assistance established by Lloyd George and Thomas had been matched in other spheres, the Anglo-French war effort would have prospered more swiftly and less painfully than it did.

In November 1915 Lloyd George tried to extend arms cooperation to the other main Entente allies, Russia and Italy. At a four-power conference in London it was agreed to set up a central munitions office, whose function would be to collect information about programmes, orders, raw material reserves, machinery and labour. After the conference Lloyd George wrote cheerfully to Thomas claiming that it had been 'a great success', because 'you and I settled questions with Russia and Italy in the course of a couple of days which otherwise might have taken weeks or even months'.[2] But his optimism was misplaced. The central munitions office came to nothing, mainly because the general staffs would not disclose their secrets.

At least he was able to exercise a large measure of control over Allied arms purchases in North America. Early in the war there had been a chaotic scramble there, with the different governments and all sorts of commercial agents competing for arms contracts. As well as forcing prices up this naturally produced very poor results. Deliveries were erratic, if they occurred at all, and standards of manufacture varied wildly. In January 1915 the firm of J. P. Morgan and Co. was appointed sole purchasing agent for Britain and the other Entente powers. Morgan's had branches in London and Paris, but none in

1. Albert Thomas to D.L.G., 14 July 1915.
2. D.L.G. to Albert Thomas, 1 December 1915. The conference was on 23–24 November.

Germany, and they were very pro-Entente (particularly pro-British). Thus a single channel was established for negotiating contracts in the New World, and Britain's financial primacy in the Alliance gave her control over the placing of orders, even France becoming ever more dependent financially as the war went on.

But the Morgan's contract did not solve all the problems of supply from North America, and when Lloyd George became Minister he saw that vigorous action was needed to make the system more efficient. His first step was to send his old rival D. A. Thomas to report on the causes of delay. Thomas, the future Lord Rhondda, was a powerful industrialist and politician from South Wales, with whom Lloyd George had clashed over certain aspects of Welsh nationalism in the 1890s, but whose ability he admired. A very recent survivor (with his young daughter) of the *Lusitania* sinking, Thomas was understandably reluctant to risk another Atlantic voyage so soon. But as a patriot he overcame his qualms and crossed to America, taking with him an artillery expert; while his namesake, the French armaments minister, appointed a mission to work closely with him. He advised that Morgan's role should be confirmed, but that there should also be an organisation for watching deliveries and speeding up production. This was accordingly established, under a soldier at first but later, as the American branch of the Ministry of Munitions, under E. W. Moir, which soon became a large organisation with a staff running into hundreds.

In Canada the task of expanding the production of arms was entrusted to W. L. Hichens, chairman of the shipbuilding firm of Cammell Laird. Hichens had been a member of the Milner Kindergarten in South Africa, and he was the first Milner disciple, though by no means the last, to be recruited for state service by Lloyd George. At his instigation an Imperial Munitions Board was set up, and by the end of the War Canada was contributing almost as much as the United States in supplies for the British army. This suited Lloyd George and was his deliberate intention, on political as well as financial grounds. It was also of great significance to Canada in accelerating its industrial development.

Overseas sources of supply were important, but subsidiary. They were also very expensive. Basically the job of producing arms for the forces of the Crown had to be executed at home, in Britain, and nobody at the time doubted that it was a formidable job. Northcliffe, who thought that the Government as a whole had the greatest responsibility of any for a hundred years, praised Lloyd George for having 'cheerfully accepted the heaviest burden of all'.[1] Addison described the task as 'almost appalling in its magnitude'.[2] Yet a biographer of Kitchener has written that 'in fact the Ministry of Munitions was largely an agency for the distribution of munitions ordered by Lloyd George's predecessor'.[3] How can such contradictory statements have come to be made?

It is true that the first components ordered by the Ministry of Munitions did not arrive until late October 1915. But this is not to say that orders previously placed by the War Office would have been fully carried out if the Ministry had never been created. On the contrary, one of the chief complaints against the old system was that deliveries were so badly in arrears. The main reasons were that supervision was inadequate and the production of arms on too narrow an industrial base. All the evidence suggests that without the general control exercised by the Ministry, and the vast expansion of production that it initiated, even the War Office's own orders would not have been met.

Besides, the orders were far below the requirements of the growing army and the prospective scale of operations. At the Boulogne conference soon after his appointment Lloyd George heard a French artillery expert argue the case for more heavy guns and high-explosive shell. He also asked General John Du Cane, representing Sir John French, how many guns of all natures, and how much ammunition, would be needed to enable an army of a million men to have any chance of breaking the German lines. It became clear that the amount of heavy artillery ordered by the War Office was grossly insufficient, and the supply of ammunition already deplorably low.

At the end of June the War Office asked for additional guns to equip an army of seventy rather than fifty divisions, and the Ministry revised the existing orders accordingly. But Lloyd George was not satisfied even with this enlarged programme. It seemed to him that an army of a hundred divisions would have to be catered for, and in August he further increased the orders, on his own responsibility, to match the size of the army he foresaw. The War Office strongly opposed his ambitious programme, but the Cabinet supported him and he was justified in the event.

1. Northcliffe to D.L.G., 29 May 1915 (L.G.P.).
2. *Four and a Half Years*, Vol. I, p. 86, 30 May 1915.
3. George Cassar, *Kitchener: Architect of Victory*, p. 359.

In this and other respects his deliberate policy was to budget for a surplus, with the dual purpose of stimulating production and ensuring a margin of safety. His aim was to give the army enough weaponry for defensive operations in 1915, and possible offensive operations from March 1916. As the official history records: 'The most striking feature in which his policy contrasted with the policy of the War Office was in the length of his vision. . . . He gave orders spreading over two years, and was prepared – as in the case of big guns – to order in excess even of the maximum programme laid down by the War Office, if by that means he could induce contractors to undertake extensions which gave earlier deliveries.'[1] Broadly, his aim was achieved.

In building his organisation he combined systematic planning with the flexibility and pragmatism that came naturally to him. At the centre he worked through departments responsible for different aspects of the Ministry's work, such as explosives, munitions supply (which soon spawned a number of further departments for specific tasks), trench warfare, statistics, finance, and (later in the year, when they were taken over from the War Office) inventions and munitions design. In the country he was determined that the Ministry's writ should run, yet he also wanted to make full use of local enthusiasm and knowledge. On his first wartime visit to France, back in October, he was much impressed by what he heard of businessmen grouping together to promote war production in their own districts; and when he got back used them as an argument against the War Office's exclusive policy. By the spring of 1915 the idea had begun to catch on in Britain. A pioneering group in Leicester led to the establishment of similar groups elsewhere, and the one in Leeds took the important step of setting up a national shell factory, which was copied in several other places. Girouard and Booth deserve much credit for encouraging these schemes, while they were acting for the War Office through its armaments output committee. But the large degree of control still exercised by the Ordnance Department would surely have hindered the development, if the Ministry of Munitions had not come into being when it did.

Lloyd George welcomed the local initiatives, as one might expect, and proceeded to build on them rapidly. The national shell factories were multiplied, and in addition national projectile factories were started to manufacture heavier types of shell, and national filling

1. H.M.M., Vol. II, Part I, ch. II, p. 12.

factories to break the bottleneck caused by the concentration of filling work at the Royal Arsenal, Woolwich – control of which, in any case, passed to the Ministry in August. All national factories were built with public money; they belonged to the State and were subject to ultimate control by the Ministry, which provided the money for paying their staffs. But the method of local management varied from factory to factory, and from place to place.

Many were administered by new district boards of management, appointed by the Ministry to supplant the original Leicester-type local groups, whose role became purely advisory. The boards were smaller and more amenable to Ministry control, although, like the others, unpaid. Labour as a rule was not represented on the boards, but in each district labour advisory boards were formed to balance the advisory groups of manufacturers. Above the district bodies were area offices, acting on behalf of the Ministry in the ten areas into which the United Kingdom was divided by James Stevenson, Lloyd George's choice as director of area organisation. In each area office there would normally be a superintending engineer and staff, a representative of the Admiralty, a division dealing with labour matters and a secretary.

From the first Lloyd George set much store by having comprehensive, up-to-date and reliable information to go on. In early June he obtained reports from Addison and the newly appointed head of the statistics department, Walter Layton, on the actual state of munitions orders and deliveries. These were so disturbing that it was thought too risky even to circulate them to the Cabinet. Colleagues who wished to read them had to do so in the privacy of Addison's room.

Towards the end of June Stevenson's department sent questionnaires to 65,000 workshops throughout the country, with a view to discovering what machinery they already had, how many hours a day they were working, and what sort of contracts they were fulfilling. By the middle of July 45,000 replies had come in, and the detailed information so obtained was almost the equivalent of an industrial Domesday Book. Without it the huge expansion of arms manufacture that the Ministry put in hand would never have been possible.

Soon afterwards a system of weekly progress reports was inaugurated for all factories working on armaments. Cards had to be sent in, on which would be stated, for instance, the maximum deliveries to be expected under the contract, the number of shells (or whatever the product might be) that had passed inspection during the week, the amount of necessary raw material in stock, the estimated deliveries for the following week, and any reasons for failure to reach a promised level of output. According to the official history this progress card system was 'anything but popular at the factories', but was found to be 'extraordinarily useful', producing a 'weekly avalanche of information' which enabled causes of delay to be swiftly identified and rectified.[1]

These reports enabled Layton to give Lloyd George weekly budgets for each of the supply departments, on the basis of which he would send minutes to the directors concerned that could be very sharp and probing. In addition he took pride in having an established routine of weekly meetings with his heads of department, at which their budgets and his comments could be discussed. 'It was a great advantage,' he wrote later, 'to have them all together for these meetings. For when one of them was asked why his output was failing to keep up to the level estimated for it he might give the explanation that he had not been supplied with some raw material, semi-manufactured product or other component which was essential for the output of his particular section. In such a case, as the officer responsible for the supply of that missing component would also be present, the matter could be thrashed out without delay and a great deal of time and paper saved.'[2]

The official history suggests that these meetings were held at irregular intervals until the end of 1915; from then until the middle of February they were held weekly, with unsatisfactory results. They were not conducted 'in any systematic fashion'. Though a tentative agenda was circulated beforehand, 'discussions of important topics were commonly introduced without previous notice of any kind. No shorthand minute was taken and only the scantest records were kept.'[3] Lloyd George's recollection of them seems to have been unduly flattering, but such is often the effect of hindsight.

Though one of the greatest executives in British history, Lloyd George was not in the conventional sense a good administrator. His achievements were due, above all, to his ability to look ahead; his judgment of priorities; his close, if fitful, attention to detail; and the urgent spirit with which people who worked with him and for him became infused. But he did not have a tidy mind, and in the process of getting things done he habitually caused a fair amount of incidental confusion. His genius was for animating, rather than administering,

1. H.M.M., Vol. X, Part III, ch. I, pp. 15–16.
2. W.M., Vol. I, pp. 281–2.
3. H.M.M., Vol. II, Part I, ch. VI, p. 158.

an organisation, but since the Ministry of Munitions was new what it particularly needed was a chief who could give it the breath of life. Tidying and consolidation could come later.

The results during the first year were remarkable, both in scale and quality. Despite agonising difficulties the essential work was done and Britain's enormous 1916 army was, in the event, well supplied. Of course much that was achieved owed little to any direct intervention by Lloyd George. In a Ministry which, by the time he left it, had a headquarters staff of 12,000 there must obviously have been unsung heroes – and heroines, for over 40 per cent were women. At a higher level, some of the best work of those whom he appointed to key posts was done on their own initiative, and they deserve the principal credit for it (though he also deserves a large share, since it was precisely because they were men of initiative that he had chosen them). In any case there were numerous ways in which his direct personal impact was decisive. Some have already been mentioned, most notably his overruling of the War Office on the size of the big-gun programme, but a few more should now be described.

One concerns the provision of trench mortars. The British army entered the war with no weapons at all in this category, and even in 1915, before the Ministry of Munitions was set up, only three hundred British-made mortars had been issued to the troops in France. These were of four different types, none wholly satisfactory, and anyway they had obviously to be spread very thin. For the rest the men had to make do with obsolete mortars provided by the French, or even with contraptions made by themselves from iron water-pipes or other such materials.

They wanted and needed a weapon to counter the deadly German *Minenwerfer* which was one of the worst torments they were exposed to in the line. Robert Graves found that there was 'nothing to equal the German sausage mortar-bomb',[1] and Lloyd George received a vivid description of it two months after his appointment, in a letter from the front. The author was the son of the Bishop of Winchester, Gilbert Talbot, whom he had met when visiting the Oxford Union in November 1913. The letter could hardly have failed to impress him deeply, and in more ways than one:

I think you would be moved by the amount your name is on men's

1. *Goodbye to All That*, ch. 13.

lips out here. 'I wonder if Lloyd George is getting us shells.' 'I suppose we shall be able to advance when Lloyd George can produce the shells' etc. etc. . . . I think you would be amused at the number of military men who so short a time ago could hardly bring themselves to mention your name – but who now gratefully recognise how much you have done. . . . The chief features of this bit of the line are undoubtedly bombs and trench mortars. We want quite unlimited bombs. They're much the most effective things in this trench warfare. . . . The Germans have got a new trench mortar up here – a vile thing that throws a huge torpedo-shaped projectile by compressed air. It rises slowly to a great height and then falls spinning slowly and explodes with an ear-splitting and most demoralising din. It doesn't do much material damage – we've had relatively few casualties from it – but the moral effect is enormous. We've had a great many cases of nervous breakdown from it and it's most awfully hard to keep the men steady while it's going on . . . our own trench mortars are at present much smaller & less powerful. . . .

The fight in the crowd that night at Oxford among the turnips was really quite a good preparation for the trenches & the bombs.

Gilbert added that he was by no means the only young man on the Unionist side who had been inspired by Lloyd George's leadership during the war and who hoped to be able to follow it afterwards. A few days later he was killed.[1]

Lloyd George did not need this letter to alert him to the mortar problem, though it must have further stimulated his efforts to find a solution. On 30 June he had witnessed at Wormwood Scrubs a demonstration of the Stokes mortar, which had been rejected by the War Office; and his immediate response was to decide that a thousand of these weapons should be ordered. Wilfrid Stokes was the chairman and managing director of Ransomes and Rapier. He was an engineer of proven originality, who had already made a name for himself with rotary kilns for cement-making, break-down cranes, railway rolling-stock, and sluices of a type used, for instance, in the construction of the Aswan dam. His mortar was revolutionary in that it consisted of an unrifled steel tube, and that the bombs it fired needed no breech or trigger mechanism, but were activated by contact with a striker when

1. The letter was written from a dug-out, 28 July 1915. After hearing of Gilbert's death Lloyd George sent it for his father to read.

dropped down the barrel. The first characteristic meant that it could be manufactured quite easily by firms without previous experience of making arms; the second, that it could be fired very rapidly.

Since new weapon designs were still meant to be approved by the Ordnance Department of the War Office before being put into production by Lloyd George's Ministry, he had to arrange for the preliminary thousand Stokes mortars to be manufactured with the backing of money subscribed by an Indian prince. Some of these were available for use in the battle of Loos in September, firing smoke shells. But it was some time before Stokes guns and their ammunition were supplied in bulk to the army in France. The delay was caused by trouble in devising a simple, safe and efficient fuse for the bombs. Eventually one was evolved, and in early January 1916 approval was given by the Ministry's own department of munitions design, now at last the responsible body and under the direction of General Du Cane, who had favourably impressed Lloyd George when he attended the Boulogne conference as French's representative.

Meanwhile bombs as well as mortars were being manufactured pending the trials, so that when both were finally approved there was the minimum further delay. At the end of March French wrote that 'all reports agree as to the efficiency of the 3-inch Stokes gun', and said that he would be substituting it for the existing types of light mortar.[1] Thereafter it became, according to one historian, 'the outstanding and ubiquitous trench weapon of the war'.[2] In addition, the army was equipped with a medium mortar, and a heavy 9.45-inch mortar based on the French 240-mm, whose design was communicated to Lloyd George by Albert Thomas. By May the mortar problem was effectively solved, and during the second quarter of 1916 two million rounds of mortar ammunition were supplied for good mortars, compared with 50,000 in the same quarter of the previous year for unsatisfactory models.

There was some loss to set against this immense gain. Since it would have been imprudent to cancel production of and for existing weapons until the superiority of others had been demonstrated, the Ministry was left with hundreds of unwanted mortars and about half a million unwanted bombs. Money and time were thus wasted, but the waste was more or less inevitable and, surely, a small price to pay for

1. H.M.M., Vol. XI, Part I, Ch. III. p. 43.
2. B. H. Liddell Hart, *History of the First World War*, ch. V.

equipping the army with the right trench weapons; in particular with one which was to hold its own for the rest of the current war and throughout the next.

If mortars were important, machine-guns were even more so; and, during the early phase of the war, in similarly short supply to the British army. When the war began only two were allotted to each battalion. By June 1915 the need for a larger provision was recognised by the War Office, though estimates of the need were still too conservative there. In any case the War Office's requirements were not being met, not only for the obvious reason that productive capacity was still very limited, but also because the War Office was on the whole placing only short-term contracts for machine-guns, which did not encourage firms to tool themselves up for larger-scale production. In other words, not enough was being done to increase the capacity for producing these weapons, and deliveries even on the orders that had been placed were seriously in arrears. On 1 June the number of machine-guns in service with the British army in all theatres was 1,330, which was sixty per cent below the required number. A week later the Ministry of Munitions was given to understand that the number ultimately needed would be in excess of 13,000; yet only about 7,350 had so far been ordered.

Lloyd George acted promptly to make good the deficiency. In the sober words of the official history: 'As soon as the Ministry was formed a vigorous and extended programme for securing the numbers of guns required was undertaken.'[1] In his War Memoirs Lloyd George quotes his own more colourful words at the time to Eric Geddes, who, as deputy director-general of munitions supply, was immediately put in charge of machine-guns. When Geddes reported a conversation with Kitchener, in which the War Secretary said that four machine-guns per battalion would be the maximum and anything more a luxury, Lloyd George replied: 'Take Kitchener's maximum . . . square it, multiply that result by two; and when you are in sight of that, double it again for good luck.' This well-known remark is certainly misleading to the extent that it suggests Lloyd George's programme would equip every battalion in the army with sixty-four machine-guns. In fact, as John Terraine has pointed out, sixty-four became the standard equipment of *machine-gun* battalions of which,

1. H.M.M., Vol. XI, Part V, ch. II, p. 10.

later in the war, one was assigned to every infantry division. Yet Lloyd George is perhaps more justified in claiming that 'before the end of the War the total number of machine-guns issued to the fighting forces and kept in reserve for contingencies exceeded a figure equivalent to an average of 64 per battalion.'[1] What is beyond question is that his programme provided enough machine-guns, and to spare, to satisfy the army's needs.

How was it done? Three firms were making machine-guns for the British forces: Vickers, Lewis and Hotchkiss, the last two foreign-owned. (The famous Maxim gun was in the process of being phased out.) Vickers guns were produced at two factories in the south-east suburbs of London, at Erith and Crayford, but their capacity needed to be much expanded and their productivity much improved. By July they had turned out only about a thousand of the nearly 1,800 guns promised. Lloyd George and Geddes realised that to get the required results they had to give the firm a large, long-term contract; so on 19 July they ordered 12,000 guns to be delivered by June or August 1916, at a steadily rising rate of delivery. Government assistance was to be given for the necessary expansion of plant, and the firm was also to be helped in securing skilled machine-setters from the forces; to whom, moreover, bonuses would be offered for instructing others in their trade. These measures were largely successful, and in 1916 the factories were producing guns in large quantities for the French army as well as for the British. By the end of the war their weekly output was over a thousand.

Lewis guns were manufactured by the Birmingham Small Arms Company, by agreement with the Belgian owners. The foreign connection caused difficulties on the financial side, but essentially the method of increasing output was the same as with Vickers. Whereas fewer than 2,000 Lewis guns had been ordered by the War Office and Admiralty combined before the Ministry of Munitions came into the picture, thereafter 4,000 more were immediately ordered. It was found, however, that a decision had to be taken between expanding the B.S.A. plant for further rifle or machine-gun production, and Lloyd George decided that machine-guns should have priority. The order for them was then increased to 10,000, to be delivered in mid-1916. Again, the Ministry advanced a proportion of the capital for

1. W.M., pp. 605–6. John Terraine's critique of Lloyd George's machine-gun programme, and how he writes about it in his memoirs, is in *The Smoke and the Fire*, ch. XIV.

new building and equipment. In return the company undertook to maintain the plant for twenty years in a condition to manufacture Lewis guns at a rate of 500 per week, if necessary. By the end of the war the rate of output was 1,400 per week.

The French firm which made the Hotchkiss gun did not work in England through an established English firm, like B.S.A., but brought over its own plant and skilled workmen from France to manufacture the gun at Coventry. This process began in February 1915, and the French government was to take up to fifty a month of the guns produced. Lloyd George sanctioned a scheme for doubling the factory's output, even though the British military authorities still did not accept Hotchkiss guns for use in the British army. (Only the Admiralty was in the market for them at first.) By November the rate of production was 690 monthly, and the army did after all make considerable use of them, though there was competition between Hotchkiss and Lewis guns for the arming of tanks, in which the Lewis was for a time preferred.

The only other machine-gun to be considered was the Danish Madsen, originally a British design but rejected by the War Office some years before the War. Its great merit was that it was lighter than the other three, and capable of continuous fire. On the other hand it was very noisy, and tended to give its position away by a flash. In May 1915 four hundred were ordered by the Navy, and five hundred by the Army, to be delivered from Denmark; but the problems of export proved insuperable. It was then proposed either that the Danish factory should be transferred to England, or that Madsen guns should be manufactured in England by Rolls-Royce. The second of these projects seemed to be materialising, but in the end had to be cancelled, because there were long delays in obtaining the necessary drawings from Denmark, and meanwhile the demand for Madsens lapsed. The reason for this, illustrating the general success of the machine-gun programme, was that production of the other models was so buoyant.

Lloyd George's approach to his task as shown in his handling of the mortar and machine-gun problems was matched by his handling of many others, but it would be tedious to go through his work on the technological side weapon by weapon. Something must, however, be said about his contribution to bringing the first tanks into service, and about his part in overcoming serious difficulties concerning explosives and fuses.

It cannot be claimed for him that he was the prime godfather of the tank as he was, surely, of the Stokes gun. At the high official level Hankey and, indeed, Churchill have stronger claims to the title. All the same, without Lloyd George's involvement the first tanks would not have been in service as soon as they were. When Churchill left the Admiralty he asked Lloyd George to take over responsibility for 'landships', and his successor, Balfour, agreed. The development of the tank thus continued under the aegis of the Ministry of Munitions. In February 1916 the Army gave an order for a hundred prototype tanks, but in April Lloyd George himself sanctioned, in anticipation of a formal War Office demand, the provision of fifty tanks of a new type, carrying guns. Tank supply was made one of the three most urgent priorities in the work of the Ministry. On 15 September tanks were first used in battle and, whether or not the occasion was ill-judged and premature, it was certainly a credit to the Ministry that they were available for use then at all.

The massive gun programme that Lloyd George put in hand despite War Office hostility required a corresponding growth in industrial output, particularly of ammunition, which he obtained above all by building national factories for making and filling shells. But no less important was the provision of explosive for the shells, and the means to detonate them safely and surely. When the war began T.N.T. was replacing lyddite as the standard explosive for shells in the British army, but it was evident to Lord Moulton that all the available raw material for T.N.T. would be insufficient for the army's probable needs. He therefore urged the military to use a mixture of T.N.T. and ammonium nitrate known as amatol, and by the time the Ministry of Munitions came into being amatol was recommended for use in some types of shell, though not on the whole in the larger types. But the mixture recommended was 45 T.N.T. to 55 ammonium nitrate, whereas Moulton was convinced that amatol could be mixed in the ratio 20/80 without loss of explosive force. In any case the decision in favour of amatol was being 'completely disregarded' by those responsible for filling shells, and soon after Lloyd George's appointment Moulton wrote to complain of this.[1]

Arguments about the nature of the explosive charge for shells led to a shortage at the battle of Loos, fought in September. Granted the supply position the battle should not have been fought at all, and Haig

1. Moulton to D.L.G., 16 June 1915, quoted in W.M., pp. 577–80.

for one was against it. But there was no public scandal, because the military themselves were clearly to blame. Lloyd George was able to use the occasion to clinch control of Woolwich Arsenal, already formally transferred to his Ministry. But the problem of combining the right explosive with a suitable detonating mechanism proved hard to solve and, despite the growing output of shell cases, prevented the completion of shells on anything like the required scale. The trouble was that the 20/80 mixture of amatol, combined with the method of filling and type of fuse then in use, resulted in a high proportion of prematures and blinds.

Lloyd George was convinced that his Ministry could have solved the problem more quickly if it had assumed control of munitions design while taking over Woolwich, but design remained under the War Office until the end of the year. Meanwhile, Lloyd George sent his mission to France to study French methods of shell-filling, and one member of the party was the 8th Viscount Chetwynd who, most unusually for a man of his background, was an enterprising and resourceful industrialist. Chetwynd was given a more or less free hand to run what became the largest of all the national filling factories, at Chilwell near Nottingham. Here he evolved a method, based on French experience, of pressing 20/80 amatol into large shells. This enabled the supply of ammunition at last to keep pace with Lloyd George's gun programme, though it was still some months before the system of detonation was considered satisfactory.

For reorganising Woolwich and directing the whole process of shell-filling throughout the country Lloyd George employed Geddes, fresh from his work on machine-guns. He also made good use of the services of Arthur Lee, whom he had appointed, in October, to succeed Ivor Philipps as joint parliamentary secretary to the Ministry. Lee was a Conservative M.P. who had held junior office at the Admiralty in the Balfour government, but who, even then, deserved something better. His record was exciting and varied. After joining the army as a young man he had volunteered for service in the Far East, and had performed a remarkable feat of espionage at Vladivostok. Then, as military attaché with the U.S. forces in Cuba during the Spanish–American war, he had been made an honorary member of the 'Rough Riders' and became a close friend of Theodore Roosevelt, soon to be President. Next, as military attaché in Washington, he had met and married the daughter of a leading New York banker. With her wealth to buttress his talents, and still only in his early thirties, he was ready for a political career.

But Lee was never quite at home in the Conservative Party. To many traditional Tories he seemed too obviously ambitious, and the fact that he was also an aesthete tended to make him even more suspect. He was quarrelsome, too, and a row with Lord Charles Beresford forced his resignation from the Carlton Club. As the editor of his private papers has written: 'He had neither the hearty cunning of the Birmingham businessman, nor the "form" – the tacit recognition of common interests and colouring – of the hereditary governing class.'[1] Being a bit of a misfit and social outsider was, however, no impediment at all to getting on with Lloyd George, and over the next few years Lee's fortunes became increasingly identified with those of a leader whom he had strongly attacked in the climate of uninhibited partisanship before the war. The public act for which Lee is best remembered (perhaps alone remembered) – the gift of Chequers to the nation by his wife and himself – occurred during Lloyd George's premiership, and Lloyd George was the first prime minister to benefit from it. Meanwhile he came to the Ministry of Munitions in October 1915 from British headquarters in France, where his work had earned him the thanks of Kitchener.

One incident under the heading 'explosives' should be mentioned in passing, because Lloyd George makes so much of it in his memoirs. This is the alleged deal with Dr Chaim Weizmann over the production of acetone which was necessary for the manufacture of cartridges of all sizes. According to Lloyd George, when there was a danger that the supply of acetone might fail, because it could only be distilled from wood and Britain's timber resources were limited, he was advised by C. P. Scott to seek the help of 'a very remarkable professor of chemistry in the University of Manchester'. Lloyd George therefore turned to Weizmann, who in a few weeks found a way of obtaining acetone from maize. Wishing to show his appreciation, Lloyd George then suggested recommending Weizmann for some honour, but was met with a firm refusal.

He said: 'There is nothing I want for myself.' 'But is there nothing we can do as a recognition of your valuable assistance to the country?' I asked. He replied: 'Yes, I would like you to do something for my people.' He then explained his aspirations as to the repatriation of the Jews to the sacred land they had made

1. Alan Clark (ed.), *A Good Innings*, p. 2.

famous. That was the fount and origin of the famous declaration about the National Home for Jews in Palestine.

A vivid story – but not to be taken too seriously. The policy expressed in the 1917 Balfour Declaration had other founts and origins, compared with which Weizmann's request counted for little.

All that Lloyd George did to create a suitable framework for arms production, to set the right priorities, to anticipate the scale of future demands, and to stimulate technological developments, would of course have been worthless had he not also dealt effectively with the many-faceted problem of labour. The Munitions of War Act gave him unprecedented powers over industry. He had the right to take control of any factory felt to be necessary for war purposes, and in such controlled establishments, as in the national factories where he was the ultimate employer, his regulations overrode the normal processes of profit-making and collective bargaining. Appeals could be made only to two classes of tribunal set up by the Ministry, of which the second-class adjudicated in small disputes, with power merely to impose fines, but the first-class adjudicated in all disputes and had power to send offenders to prison for brief terms as well as to fine them.

Yet the intractable difficulty remained of organising and deploying the potential work-force to the best national advantage; in particular of laying hands on all available skilled workers, seeing that they were used where they were most needed, and making sure that they were not wasting any of their time through outmoded practices. Under the Munitions of War Act no worker engaged on a government contract could be taken on elsewhere without a leaving certificate. This provision, denounced as serfdom by trade union militants, was thought necessary to safeguard essential war work and to prevent competition for skilled men between rival contractors. But whatever its merits and demerits it could not increase the total of skilled workers available for war industry, nor could it ensure that those actually employed in such industry were working as efficiently as possible.

Ever since it became apparent that the war would not be over quickly, and that winning it would require a huge industrial as well as military effort, the folly of allowing thousands of skilled men to enlist in the early weeks had been growing more and more obvious. But how was the harm to be undone? At the end of 1914 Churchill initiated a scheme for issuing badges to men working in the Royal Dockyards

DELIVERING THE GOODS.

From *Punch*, 21 April 1915

or on Admiralty contracts, and this was later copied, in a smaller way, by the War Office. But the badging system affected only about half a million men who moreover were not prevented by it from joining up, but merely given the State's outward and visible blessing for not doing so. In addition, in May 1915, the War Office sent a circular to all recruiting officers advising them that workers within certain specified trades should not be accepted for enlistment. This, too, was helpful so far as it went, but did not go far enough. Some important categories were omitted, and in any case the 'advice' was liable to be disregarded by officers and would-be recruits.

As Minister of Munitions Lloyd George had some success in extracting skilled men from the armed forces. Under various schemes devised by his Ministry about 43,000 were placed in controlled establishments, while remaining servicemen. And he followed Churchill's example in protecting his workers with badges. But the numbers were still entirely inadequate for the vastly expanded war industry that he was promoting. More skilled workers had to be found or trained at home, and there had to be more rational use of the available skill. That was the essential need, but how was it to be met?

In theory the answer was industrial conscription, but when Lloyd George hinted at this in his first major speech as Minister there was, as we have seen, a prevalently hostile reaction from Labour as well as from many Liberals. He therefore decided to give the trade unions a chance to find their own alternative solution, and we left them trying to raise, with the Ministry's help, an army of War Munitions Volunteers who would be prepared to work wherever they were sent, provided they would be doing so at trade union rates of pay and subject to trade union conditions.

The response to this appeal seemed rather encouraging at first and was, indeed, quite substantial. But the practical results were disappointing, as Lloyd George already knew when he made a statement to the House of Commons before the summer recess:

We have enrolled nearly 100,000, the great bulk of them skilled men in the engineering and ship-building trades. The difficulty has been that they are not all available for Government work. Nearly all of them are engaged on work of some degree of importance; sometimes indirectly, and without the workman's knowledge, engaged on Government work. For instance, we have men who are engaged in making screws and bolts, which are used in shipbuilding. . . . Another illustration is that of men who are engaged on work which . . . is essentially work for the life of the nation such as making machinery for turning out Army biscuits.[1]

He had to admit that he would be lucky if he could use one-fifth of the men who had enrolled, and even that proved to be an over-estimate. 'By the close of his tenure at the Munitions Office there were more than 120,000 names on the rolls and yet the total number transferred to munitions work was only about 12,000 men. In brief, the War Munitions Volunteer scheme had failed to live up to the expectations of its creators.'[2]

Probably Lloyd George never expected quite as much of it as he allowed to appear. What is certain is that he was able to turn its failure to excellent advantage. The initiative was now back with him, and he acted firmly though also wisely. While keeping compulsion well in view as the ultimate sanction, he did not propose to introduce it but turned instead, with redoubled insistence, to the question of restrictive practices. The moment was opportune to force the trade unions to rationalise their working rules, at any rate for the duration of the war, and above all to accept a very large measure of dilution. This meant that skilled workers would have to be prepared to admit many thousands of unskilled, both to acquire the same skills by training and to do that part of existing jobs which did not need a high level, or perhaps any level, of skill. It also meant that male workers would have to see many jobs supposedly exclusive to men done by women as well, or even mainly by women. It was his belief that a full-blooded programme of dilution would increase productivity by twenty-five per cent.

Though the trade unions were in a relatively weak position he knew how important it was to carry them with him. He wanted to implement his programme with their leaders' full cooperation, and with the sympathetic understanding of as many as possible of the rank-and-file. On 9 September he spoke to the T.U.C. at Bristol. His audience there was the biggest gathering of trade unionists since the outbreak of war, and the speech he made was worthy of the occasion.

He came, he said, as 'the greatest employer of labour' in the country, and suggested that it might be the first time a great employer had been allowed to address the T.U.C. He then repeated his joke

1. Hansard, Fifth series, Vol. LXXIII, cols. 2359–60, 28 July 1915.
2. R.T.Q. Adams, *Arms and the Wizard*, p. 93.

about being a trade unionist himself, giving it a topical twist: 'The barristers' trade union regards any trade union with a sort of supercilious contempt like that with which the coppersmith looks at the plumber.' This oblique reference to a current demarcation dispute at Fairfields works on the Clyde got him a laugh.

Noting that they had passed a resolution pledging themselves to help the Government to the uttermost in prosecuting the war, he said that he took them at their word. 'The Government can lose the war without you; they cannot win without you.' Why had the Germans been doing so well lately against the Russians? 'The German workmen came in . . . they worked and worked, quietly, persistently, continuously, without stint or strike, without restrictions, for months and months, through the autumn, through the winter, through the spring. Then came that terrible avalanche of shot and shell which broke the great Russian armies and drove them back. That was the victory of the German workmen.' The war had 'resolved itself into a conflict between the mechanics of Germany and Austria on the one hand and the mechanics of Great Britain and France on the other'.

Then he came to the main point of his speech:

We have set up sixteen national arsenals . . . within the last few weeks. We are constructing eleven more. We require, in order to run these, the old and the new, to equip the works which are engaged at the present moment in turning out the equipment of war, and we require many more skilled men. . . . This country at the present moment is not doing its best . . . and it is almost entirely – not entirely – a labour problem. You alone can assist. [A voice: 'With the employers.'] I am not going to spare them. I am going to tell what I am doing with the employers, but you have to allow me to develop in my own way.

I want to put before you quite candidly the whole of the facts. . . . The machinery of this country which could be employed for war material is not working day and night. You have only got 15 per cent of the machines which you can use for the turning out of the rifles, cannon and shell working night shifts. If you could get plenty of labour to make these machines go night and day, just think of the lives that would be saved. It is a problem not of destroying life, but of saving the lives of our own men.

. . . The first fact that I want to get into the minds of trade unionists is that, if you employed every skilled workman in the

Kingdom, you would not have enough labour for the task which we have in mind. Therefore, when it is a question of our diluting skilled labour with unskilled labour, it is not a question of turning out the skilled workman in order to put a cheaper workman in his place. We have plenty of work for that skilled workman. There are not enough skilled workmen to go round. . . .

The second point that I want to put to you is that there is a good deal of work which is being done by skilled workmen – highly skilled – who have had years of training, but which can just as easily be done by those who have only had a few weeks' or a few days' training. Therefore what we have to do is this. We want to turn the unskilled on to work which unskilled men and women can do just as well as the highly skilled, so as to reserve the highly skilled for work which nobody can do except those who have had great experience.

Another thing that we want to do is this. You cannot have the unskilled to do the work alone without having skilled people to look after them. For instance, take shell making. Instead of putting people to do that work, what we should like to do would be to put on, say, ten or eleven unskilled men or women with one skilled man to look after them. We have women working on fuses at Elswick and at other places; and they are doing their work uncommonly well. There are skilled men looking after them, and it requires very skilful men to look after them [laughter]. But they are doing the work admirably.

He demonstrated what he meant with a 4.5-inch shell which he had brought with him.[1] Such work, he said, was done by women in France and Germany. Intelligent men and women could be trained to do it within a few days, but they had to do it under expert supervision.

Much of the remainder of the speech was devoted to giving instances of restrictive practices. But he also spelled out the State's bargain with trade unionists and employers. On the workers' side all restrictions would be waived that inhibited the best use of skilled labour, or that had the effect of preventing men from producing to the limit; and there were to be no stoppages in essential work. In return, the Government guaranteed that the workers' sacrifices would not 'inure to the enrichment of individual capitalists, but entirely to the benefit of the State'; that traditional customs and practices would be

---

1. He had produced a fuse to illustrate a point during his Commons speech on 23 June.

restored after the war; that increases in output would not be used as an excuse for lowering the piecework rate; and that unskilled men and women should be paid exactly the same wages for piecework as skilled workers for the same class of work.

On the control of employers he had this to say:

We have declared 715 establishments producing munitions of war to be controlled establishments. . . . Those represent 95 per cent of the labour engaged in that market. Don't forget this – we have not asked any trade union to suspend any regulation except in an establishment where we control profits. . . . What have we done about controlling the profits? We have controlled them by Act of Parliament.

[A voice: 'What about the shipping?'] You don't make shells with ships. I am talking about those shops which are making guns and rifles and machines and tools for turning out shells and guns. We prepared our regulations for restricting profits. We submitted them to the Labour Advisory Committee. . . . We are restricting them on the basis of what they were before the war.

We insisted upon their submitting all accounts to us. They are only to get a standard based upon the profit made before the war, with any allowance made in respect of increased capital which they put in. What do we do with the balance? We put it into the Treasury to carry on the war. It is the first time that it has been done in the history of any country. You have taken over nearly the whole of the engineering works of this country, and they are controlled by the State. I have seen resolutions passed from time to time by trade unionists about nationalising the industries of this country. We have done it. The whole of the engineering industry of this country which is engaged in doing anything for material of war is now State-controlled, and the profits which they make out of the war are annexed for State purposes. That is better than any resolution that you have carried.

How convincing was this argument? Profits in controlled establishments – of which there were to be 2,000 by the end of the year – were limited to one-fifth above the average for the two years immediately before the war. This was quite a generous margin. As for other firms, the questioner had a point, to which Lloyd George's glib reply was no proper answer. He had failed, in his May budget, to do anything about excess profits in general, even though they were clearly contributing to the rise in the cost of living from which workers and their families were suffering. But within a fortnight (on 21 September) McKenna's first budget imposed a fifty per cent tax on excess profits in firms other than those already covered by the Munitions of War Act; and this tax was to rise to eighty per cent in 1917. Even so workers could legitimately feel that they were making a larger relative sacrifice than their employers.[1]

Lloyd George's peroration at Bristol was very powerful, if in one respect slightly disingenuous:

Do not forget that the future of labour depends largely on what happens during this war. There are impressions made on the minds and hearts of the people today which you would not make in a thousand years under ordinary conditions. The whole country is a molten mass in the great blast-furnace of war. Any impression which you make now will be deep, deep, deep, indelibly deep. Labour has not yet won its rights. The higher the ideals you put before labour the longer the road you have to travel and the more difficult the fight; you cannot do it without friends. Believe me, the strongest cause in the world, the strongest class in the world, and the strongest Empire in the world cannot do without friends. The vast majority of the people of this country are neither capitalists nor trade unionists; you must get them with you.

After the war there will be things that you can do, if you win the heart of the country, which you could not achieve in generations. The country will want a re-settlement and reconstruction. It feels in its conscience that things are wrong, and it will want to do right. Don't put the country against organised labour. Why should I pretend? I was brought up in a workman's home. There is nothing that you can tell me about the anxieties and worries of labour that I did not know from the first twenty years of my life. The first and greatest nobleman I ever met was an old working man. He writes to

1. While McKenna's 1915 budget was being discussed Lloyd George privately floated an idea which, according to him, 'received a very considerable measure of acceptance from the Cabinet', for taking half of everybody's income to finance the war, partly in tax and partly as loan for the more prosperous classes, and as a deduction from wages for the working class. In the event this idea was clearly not accepted by the Cabinet, and there is no evidence that Lloyd George made any attempt to revive it when he was Prime Minister. (Memorandum and correspondence with Sir Leo Chiozza Money, quoted in C. J. Wrigley, *David Lloyd George and the British Labour Movement*, p. 88). Wrigley comments 'In some respects his proposals were a very drastic forerunner of the Post-War Credits, introduced in 1941, and Pay-as-You-Earn (P.A.Y.E.) introduced in 1943' (p. 261).

me every day, at eighty-two years of age; I get his letter every morning, telling me how to put the world right. And, if you will allow me to say so, however busy I am – and I am not a good letter-writer – there is one letter that I do not miss; it is the one to the old British workman.

No, I know the workman, and the tenderness that I received from the old workman's household would make me a friend of labour, even if there were no other reason. I beg you, as a man brought up in a workman's home, do not let the sympathy of the country be against labour by holding back its might by regulations, fetters and customs, when the poor old land is fighting for life. I beg of you to put these sentiments on one side. Let us be one people, and we shall emerge with the greatest triumph that labour ever achieved in any land.

It was true that Lloyd George had experienced poverty, or near-poverty, in his early years. His home in North Wales had been very simple, and his way of life there frugal. But it was not 'a workman's home' as those he was addressing would have understood the term, because Uncle Lloyd was not a workman in the generally accepted sense. He was a minister of religion who was also, as a master-cobbler, in his small way an employer of labour. Whatever Lloyd George may have wished to claim for rhetorical purposes, he had no cultural identity with the English working class. To the extent that he can be labelled in class terms at all he was a product of the petty bourgeoisie. But in fact as a Welshman, and more especially as a product of the nineteenth-century Welsh revival, he stood outside the conventional British class categories.

Among those who put questions to him after his speech one was a 34-year-old official of the Dockers' Union attending his first T.U.C. conference (the first of many). His name was Ernest Bevin. Bevin asked whether Lloyd George thought it would effect an improvement in the manipulation of labour if organised labour were represented on the actual directorate of controlled factories. Lloyd George's reply was guarded. Labour was represented on 'the general body which was advising the Government', but in the national arsenals 'they had to get men who had experience in management, and they had to get the best managers of concerns'.

This exchange, interesting enough in itself, is all the more fascinat-ing in the perspective of history. The young official who so addressed the mobiliser of labour and industry in the First World War was to mobilise them himself in the Second, wielding even more comprehensive power than Lloyd George was able to secure. He was also, unlike Lloyd George, a genuine proletarian, who was to become, thirty years later, the first true representative of the working class effectively to get to the top in British politics.[1]

Soon after the Bristol meeting a Central Munitions Labour Supply Committee was set up, with the worthy Henderson as chairman. Its task was to help in applying the principle of dilution, while safeguarding the rights of workers. The Committee held its first meeting on 22 September, and on 13 October Lloyd George sent a circular to all controlled establishments instructing them 'to take immediate steps to replace skilled men wherever possible by less skilled labour, either men or women, and to employ the skilled men so released in establishing night shifts or upon machinery hitherto standing idle in their shops'.[2] It was his intention that skilled men should only do work which others could not do, that labour-saving machines should be introduced wherever possible, that unskilled labour should be trained and up-graded, and that work should be reorganised so that more of it could be done by unskilled or semi-skilled labour. He wanted to recruit, as well as women, men who were unfit for military service, men over age, soldiers invalided home but still capable of work, and juveniles.

At first it was hoped that dilution schemes could be worked out locally without undue delay, and the labour advisory boards in each district were asked to negotiate on behalf of the Ministry with local trade unionists. But this procedure proved too slow, and in 1916 the Ministry began to operate a more centralised system, with its own inspectors visiting factories to make sure that dilution was being properly applied. If they were not satisfied with what was being done they might produce plans of their own for laggard firms.

1. One has to say 'effectively to the top' rather than simply 'to the top', because he was never Prime Minister. But as Foreign Secretary in the 1945 Labour Cabinet he was more dominant than many prime ministers have been. Attlee depended upon him entirely, and would almost certainly have had to give way to him if he had ever wanted to be the top man in form as well as fact.
   In 1915, though not a pacifist, he was critical of the undiscriminating enthusiasm with which most labour leaders – including his own leader, Ben Tillett – were supporting the war. (Alan Bullock, *The Life and Times of Ernest Bevin*, Vol. I., pp. 47–8).
2. Quoted in Adams, *Arms and the Wizard*, pp. 103–4.

In gaining acceptance for the idea of women as munitions workers Lloyd George was considerably helped by his old tormentors, the Pankhursts. At the beginning of the war Christabel had returned to England and made a speech which bewildered and alienated many of her followers in the W.S.P.U., but at the same time won her the support of many who had previously regarded her as a power of darkness.[1] She preached a holy war against Germany, and went so far in pandering to the current Germanophobia as to suggest that stewards who had manhandled suffragettes at pre-war meetings had spoken with suspiciously guttural accents. In the German nation she saw the collective embodiment of everything that was most detestable in the male sex, whereas Belgium and France represented the feminine ideal. (The sexual character of her own country was apparently less easy to define.)

Christabel was a very odd woman, but she was also very intelligent and had a touch of genius. By exchanging the militancy of the sex war, which had caused so much trouble in the last years of peace, for patriotic militancy in wartime, she made the case for women's suffrage finally irresistible. It is often said that the vote was conceded because women proved their right to it by their contribution to the war effort, but that is surely only half of the truth. The other half is that the all-male political establishment remembered the harassment inflicted by the suffragettes before the war and had no wish to return to it afterwards. Admiration of women's war work might not in itself have been enough to do the trick, but combined with fear of renewed suffragette violence it *was* enough. How far Christabel's dramatic change of front was calculated, how far determined by instinct and flair, is bound to be an open question, but the consequences of it can hardly be doubted.

If she was the prophetess of the movement, her mother was the more active leader for practical purposes. As well as keeping men up to the mark, with ready denunciation of shirkers or slackers, Mrs Pankhurst devoted herself to making women more aware of their duty and opportunity, and the State more aware of their willingness to serve. Thus she became a convenient ally for Lloyd George, and a demonstration in London by 30,000 women on Saturday 17 July was partly financed by the Ministry of Munitions. This 'war pageant' (as it was called) moved along the Embankment and waited while a

1. London Opera House, 8 September 1914.

deputation led by Mrs Pankhurst called on Lloyd George at Whitehall Gardens.

Addressing the deputation, Lloyd George said that the number of women employed on munitions in Britain was between one-fifth and one-tenth of the number employed in France. (He had obtained the French figures from Albert Thomas.) It was vital for women to do all the work that they were physically capable of doing, so releasing men for work that women could not do. But prejudice had to be overcome: not only that of trade unionists, but also that of businessmen. And they had to reckon with the apprehension of the working man that if women were trained to do jobs that they had formerly not done, those jobs would be permanently lost to men. The answer was that the work in question was war work, for which there would be no need when the war was over.

He conceded Mrs Pankhurst's demand that women should be paid the same rates as men for piece-work, though not for time-work. Since women would be new to it, they could not be expected to turn out quite as much as men. But there would be a fixed minimum wage for women in controlled establishments and no question of any sweating. After receiving the deputation, he walked with Mrs Pankhurst to a platform from which he repeated to the great crowd of women the pledges just given to its leaders.

The ensuing results in the way of female dilution were impressive. During the first year of war fewer than 400,000 women had taken jobs in industry (additional to those already there). But between July 1915 and the end of the war 1¼ million more were recruited. This global figure tells only part of the story, moreover, because the most striking increases were in industries where the tradition was against female employment. In metals, for instance, the percentage of women employed went up from 11.4 in 1915 (9.4 in 1914) to 17.8 in 1916 and 24.6 in 1918; in chemicals from 23.0 (20.0) in 1914 to 33.0 and 39.0 in the two later years; in Government establishments, including of course arsenals, from 3.8 (2.6) to 26.5 and 46.7 respectively. Even in textiles, where women were already a majority of the work-force, there was a nearly six per cent increase between 1915 and 1918.[1]

On the whole Lloyd George's dilution programme went through with a remarkable lack of obstruction or conflict. This was due above all to the staunch cooperation of those leading trade unionists who

1. Adams, *Arms and the Wizard*, pp. 125–6.

took responsibility for commending it to their members, and of course to the patriotism of the members themselves. But it also owed a good deal to the characteristic blend of firmness and flexibility with which Lloyd George handled the matter. As in other big initiatives during his career – National Health Insurance, for example – he kept the main objective steadily in view while manoeuvring to the full extent necessary to avoid disaster.

Despite his formidable array of statutory powers he knew that there were limits beyond which he could not safely go in defying rank-and-file trade unionists. And if he had any illusions on the point the South Wales colliery dispute of July 1915 would have removed them. This took place within a fortnight of the enactment of the Munitions of War Bill and revealed the unenforceability of one of its main provisions, at any rate against one group of workers. There is no need to go into the details of the dispute. What concerns us is that on 1 July the South Wales miners were presented with 'final' terms for a settlement, which on the 12th they rejected. The following day Lloyd George issued a proclamation under his new Act to the effect that the impending strike would be illegal, but on the 15th miners nevertheless came out to a man. Since coal stocks were low and the need for coal desperate, and since it was scarcely feasible to prosecute 200,000 men, the Government had to climb down. Lloyd George did not at all mind putting pressure on the owners to disgorge more money – he knew they were making large profits – but it was embarrassing to have his own and the State's weakness exposed so soon after an ostensibly tough measure had been passed.

There were, however, some mitigating factors. The miners' union had not been a party to the Treasury Agreement, to which the Munitions of War Act was intended to give legislative force; and it was a union in which leaders and rank-and-file were singularly united. Lloyd George had tried very hard to avert a clash with it, precisely because he knew how strong it was. But when negotiations broke down he felt obliged to proclaim that a strike would be illegal, because failure to do so would have been virtually to admit that the newborn Act was, in one major respect, atrophied. With a different union he would have acted more confidently, and he could still hope that the outlawing of strikes would work in other industries involved in munitions. Moreover, it was some solace that the South Wales dispute had been about pay and conditions, not about dilution. A dangerous precedent had been set of union resistance to the Government, but not, fortunately, on the issue that mattered most.

All the same Lloyd George did have some problems on that issue, notably on Clydeside. The trouble there was by no means exclusively caused by the dilution programme. Among other causes were wretched housing, high rents, bad industrial relations in many firms, and a local tradition of extremism. The unofficial Clyde Workers' Committee largely consisted of advanced radicals and a few outright revolutionaries. These men were popular with their fellow-workers because of their militancy and effectiveness against the bosses, rather than because their theories were widely shared. As socialists some of them favoured dilution, provided it did not mean undercutting wages; yet the shopfloor opinion which sustained them tended to be principally anti-dilutionist. As one student of the subject has written: 'Although the "unofficial" leaders of the Clyde workers did not oppose dilution *per se*, there is no doubt that their hold over the rank-and-file rested on the latter's opposition to dilution. And that opposition was both deep and widespread.'[1] At the same time the workers had no comparable interest in transforming society or usurping the functions of management. These confused motives as between leaders and led contrasted with the solidarity of the miners' union, and helped Lloyd George to master the situation in the long run.

But for a time he did not seem to be mastering it at all, and his reception on the Clyde at the end of 1915 was among the most daunting experiences of his career. After a more or less successful visit to Tyneside, where dilution had been encountering similar though less rugged resistance, he arrived on Clydeside shortly before Christmas and had, first, an uncomfortable meeting with the Clyde Workers' Committee on the premises of Sir William Beardmore's Parkhead works. The trade unionists were kept waiting for three-quarters of an hour before Lloyd George appeared with, among others, Beardmore, Arthur Henderson, and Murray of Elibank (who had been brought into the Ministry as head of the labour department, though ill health soon forced him to resign). Murray did his best to break the ice, and having been introduced to David Kirkwood, the leading trade unionist at Parkhead and a member of the Committee, he then introduced Kirkwood to Lloyd George.

In his memoirs, written twenty years later, Kirkwood describes

---

1. Samuel J. Hurwitz, *State Intervention in Great Britain: A Study Of Economic Control and Social Response 1914–1919*, ch. XVI 'The Great Dilution Struggle', p. 271.

what passed:

> He held my hand and looked straight into my eyes. 'How do you do?' he said.
>
> 'No' sae bad at a',' I answered.
>
> He still held my hand; then his eyes shone, his face changed with a smile and he was radiant. I felt he was trying to master me. He might have done it. I don't know. He is a natural hypnotist. The struggle ended by Lord Elibank [sic], as gracious as a queen, asking me to act as chairman.[1]

In this capacity he went out of his way to show that he had not been hypnotised, telling Lloyd George that he was regarded with suspicion because his Munitions Act had 'the taint of slavery about it'.

Worse was to follow at a mass meeting in St Andrew's Hall, Glasgow, held on the morning of Christmas Day. This was badly mismanaged from Lloyd George's point of view, because the local trade union officials, piqued that he had not found time to see them first, decided to boycott the meeting, and the unofficial leaders were therefore able to pack it with their own supporters. Moreover the way the meeting was staged, presumably without Lloyd George's detailed knowledge, could hardly have been more maladroit. What happened is, again, vividly recalled by Kirkwood:

> The hall was packed [i.e. crowded, though it was also packed in the other sense]. More than three thousand were in it. Hundreds were outside. Everything went wrong. Girl workers dressed in khaki were brought up from Georgetown and set on the platform. The Union Jack covered the table. A choir sang patriotic songs. Dozens of police were in the hall. Everything which the men regarded as 'kidding' was there.
>
> As Mr Lloyd George entered, the choir started 'See the Conquering Hero comes'. Then pandemonium broke loose. The audience started 'The Red Flag'. . . . As Mr Lloyd George sat down, a lock of hair strayed over his brow. Shouts of 'Get your hair cut!' came from all quarters.
>
> Uncle Arthur Henderson, as chairman, spoke in his most paternal manner, and far too long. We were all keyed up about the Munitions Act, but Uncle Arthur spoke about the neutrality of Belgium and the origins of the War. He had a bad time.

1. David Kirkwood, *My Life of Revolt*, pp. 107–8.

Mr Lloyd George began badly. He looked unwell, very tired. The audience was pitiless . . . from the body of the hall I called on the men to give him a hearing.

They were quieter, and, seizing the chance, Lloyd George showed them what speaking could be like. He held them by describing quarrels about Trade Union conditions at such a time as 'haggling with an earthquake'.

Then he rolled off burning sentences about love of country and the awful struggles against the enemy. There was nothing of the problems which we were concerned about, and the row started again.

The meeting ended as a fiasco and made things worse instead of better.[1]

But Kirkwood knew that Lloyd George was not beaten.

I had seen him face to face. He was not the kind of man to be put off his stride by a rowdy meeting. I felt that his coming among us, working folk, was a master-stroke. . . .

It was the first time that a Cabinet Minister had come to the people informally, to talk to them man to man. He had taken a big risk to make peace with us, and we had given him a sword with which to smite us. *I knew that he had captivated the country, including the Trade Unionists.*[2]

Lloyd George's chief anxiety about the St Andrew's Hall meeting was lest reports of it should give an impression to the world that Clydeside was implacably opposed to him and his policy. Newspapers on the whole printed the anodyne official account, which gave the text of his speech in full and referred to the row only in these words: 'At the outset, attempts were made to disturb the proceedings, and syndicalists sang "The Red Flag". The interrupters were in a minority; the meeting was, on the whole, good-humoured.' But the extreme socialist weekly *Forward* came out, on 31 December, with a very different sort of account, suggesting that the opposition to Lloyd George had been overwhelming, and stating, for instance, that when he had said the responsibility of a Minister of the Crown in a great war was not an enviable one, he had been answered with cries of 'The money's good' and ribald laughter. This was considered intolerable,

---

1. *ibid.*, pp. 111-12. Georgetown was a recently built national factory named after the Minister.
2. *ibid.*, p. 113. Author's italics.

and on 2 January 1916 unsold copies of the offending issue of *Forward*, and the machinery of the Civic Press which printed it, were seized on Government orders.

The editor, Tom Johnston, was certainly against the war and, though he claimed that his reporter's story was accurate, there is good reason to believe that it was, in fact, as misleading as the official version. According to the secretary of the Civic Press, himself a socialist, 'the row was made entirely by from 300 to 500 people out of 3,000 present. On the whole the feeling of the meeting was with Lloyd George.'[1] If this could be said even of a meeting packed by the Clyde Workers' Committee and boycotted by local union officials, it is easy to understand why Kirkwood felt that trade unionists in general were 'captivated' by the Minister. Even in an unrepresentatively hostile gathering only a minority tried to shout him down, while the majority silently agreed with him. Within that silent majority there were probably many who resented dilution, but who were prepared, after all, to face it for the country's sake. Thus Lloyd George was able to get his message across in the least promising circumstances, and despite much noisy evidence to the contrary.

All the same he moved forward gradually and carefully, waiting for the right moments to be tough, and then showing selective toughness. It was not until late January that he sent commissioners to the Clyde (and the Tyne) to carry out dilution. By then he was satisfied that the country had a large enough stockpile of munitions to withstand a strike of six weeks on the Clyde. The first important trial of strength occurred when four hundred men at Lang's works went on strike essentially in protest against the introduction of a substantial number of women workers. The Clyde commissioners gave police protection to those who stayed at work, and Lloyd George arranged that the cost should be borne by the Treasury rather than by the local ratepayers. Within a week the strikers were back at work.

On the day they returned (7 February) he had three leading members of the Clyde Workers' Committee – including its president, William Gallacher – arrested. The pretext was an article in the Committee's organ, the *Worker*, which was misread, accidentally or on purpose, as an incitement to violence. The three men were allowed bail, while a sympathetic strike by 2,000 men in various Clydeside works collapsed; but in due course they were sentenced to terms of

1. Quoted in Wrigley, *D.L.G. and the British Labour Movement*, p. 155.

imprisonment ranging from six months to twelve. When further strikes in March showed that the Committee's power was still not completely broken, Lloyd George took action against six more of the leaders, deporting them from the Glasgow area to other places in Scotland. Kirkwood was one of them, and he had to spend a little over a year in Edinburgh. While the strikes continued there were further prosecutions and deportations, which had the support of official union leaders and, it would seem, of most of the Clyde workers. By early April the struggle was over, and the cause of dilution triumphant.[1] In 1916 the number of trade disputes was the lowest for nine years.

Lloyd George's success in persuading trade unionists to accept his programme for expanding and diluting the work-force owed much to his concurrent programme of welfare in factories. Through this he was able to achieve within months highly significant measures of social reform, which in peacetime would have been delayed for years, even decades.

One day in November 1915 he was walking on Epsom Downs with his old friend and associate Seebohm Rowntree, and they discussed the urgent need to improve welfare conditions in munitions works, more especially in view of the growing number of women employed in them.

'We shall have to have a million women in industry before the war is over,' Lloyd George commented, to which Rowntree replied, 'It is time enough to talk like that when you are treating properly the women who are already in industry.' 'I told him', Rowntree

1. Six weeks after banning *Forward* Lloyd George saw the editor Tom Johnston, at the Ministry of Munitions and allegedly said to him 'I am the last man on God's earth to suppress a Socialist newspaper'; to which Johnston claims to have replied 'You are . . . and no one has done it since.' Lloyd George allowed the paper to reappear but refused to pay any compensation. (Thomas Johnston, *Memories*, pp. 38–9.) Johnston was in general hostile to the Clyde Workers' Committee – a good example of the cross-purposes among Clyde rebels. In the Second World War he served as Secretary of State for Scotland under Churchill.

Kirkwood was a strong patriot and a dilutionist at heart, but trapped into fighting a Minister whom he really admired. Later he was for many years an M.P., and later still a peer of the realm.

Gallacher was subsequently a distinctive figure as the Communist M.P. for East Fife. He gave his own account of the St Andrew's Hall meeting in *Revolt on the Clyde*, pp. 97–9, which substantially agrees with the Kirkwood version, without being quite so vivid or, in certain details, quite so convincing. A leading authority has written that the Government 'did not fail to respond to the challenge and when it did so it was able to exploit the weaknesses of the Committee to devastating effect'. (James Hinton, *The First Shop Stewards' Movement*, p. 139.)

recalled, 'of a factory in the North of England where conditions were unspeakably bad. A foreman in that factory said that he would rather his daughter went to hell direct than through that factory.' Lloyd George was not surprised. 'You can't tell me anything worse than I already know,' he remarked. 'I have tried to get someone to deal effectively with these bad factories but I have not found anyone suitable. Why don't you have a shot at it? If you do I will start a Welfare Department at the Ministry of Munitions and make you the Director of it.'[1]

Rowntree agreed and the department was created.

Preparatory work had already been done before he and Lloyd George had their talk on Epsom Downs. In September Lloyd George had set up a committee to advise him on the health of munition workers. The chairman was Sir George Newman, a leading authority on public health, and the committee had produced two reports by November. These dealt with Sunday labour and industrial canteens. A third, on welfare supervision, was submitted before the end of the year. Rowntree respected Newman (they had known each other since school-days), and what his committee had to say about conditions in factories was taken very much to heart by the new welfare department and its chief.

Rowntree started work at the beginning of 1916, armed with powers conferred in a Munitions of War (Amendment) Act, put through by Lloyd George mainly to meet some of labour's grievances about the earlier measure. Being a successful as well as socially enlightened industrialist he carried more weight with employers than any civil servant could have done; and in his proposals for factories controlled by the Ministry of Munitions he drew heavily on the experience of his own cocoa business at York. His philosophy appealed alike to conscience and self-interest. 'Real betterment of conditions springs in the last analysis from the conviction in the mind of the employer that here lies his plain duty, a duty which does not conflict with his business interests but promotes them, since it is obvious that workers who are in good health and are provided with the amenities of life are more efficient workers.'[1]

Dilution helped to force the pace of improvement, because the influx of women into types of factory previously more or less monopolised by men made the case for higher standards of welfare hard to resist. A questionnaire was sent to all munitions factories employing twenty or more women, so that Rowntree could discover what workers' amenities had already been installed. And, not content with evidence that might not always be reliable, he appointed women investigators to visit factories and report to him on the conditions they found, while also spreading the gospel of welfare wherever they went. A further and still more effective step was to have women welfare supervisors inside the factories, and to train hundreds of people for welfare work – a hitherto virtually non-existent form of activity within the State's sphere. As well as looking after women workers, the department also organised care for young boys employed in munition works. By the end of the war there were a thousand women supervisors and 275 supervisors for boys.

Rowntree aimed to ensure that those working on arms production did so in clean, wholesome conditions, with reasonable hours of work and at a proper level of wages, with decent provision of cloakrooms, lavatories and rooms for relaxation, with facilities for obtaining good food on the premises, with every possible precaution against accidents and contamination, and with medical services freely available. His department did not invent such things – they were already to be found in a few establishments – but under his influence and direction what had been rare became almost normal. For instance on the Ministry's initiative canteens were provided in nearly all the 150 national factories, and nearly 750 more were approved in controlled establishments, where it was agreed that the capital cost could be written off. In due course the department took direct responsibility for the supply of food to these canteens, in which about a million people could, if they wished, eat daily.

The example that the department set in the munitions industries was followed in others, such as textiles, laundries and potteries. The *Factory Inspectors Annual Report* for 1917–18 was able to state: 'The whole spirit of management has quickly changed in many factories and industries where no new welfare order runs, and where State control of profit has not entered.' The standard of wages laid down for munition workers also had a wider beneficial effect. 'In its control of wages the outstanding work of the department was . . . its contribution to the principle of standardisation . . . its establishment of rates of payment which should be common to the women in all the munition trades, and its sanction to the elimination of many of the local differences in wage rates which had outlived the conventions or the economic causes to which they owed their origin.'[1] Employers generally were impressed by the practical results of welfare, and the multitude of temporary munition workers did not easily forget the conditions enforced by the Ministry or consent, later, to any reversion to inferior conditions.

Apart from all that was done to improve life for workers at their places of work – with the primary aim of achieving less illness, less absenteeism and, therefore, more output – attention was also paid to their life outside the factory, and more especially to their housing. The Ministry built, or financed the building, of nearly 11,750 flats and houses for munition workers, and provided hostels in which 23,500 could be accommodated. One way and another, it impinged upon their lives comprehensively, with hardly the smallest detail neglected. The official history gives a random list of matters considered by the welfare department:

> The provision of a factory herd of cows (for T.N.T. workers); the relative merits of cocoa and milk as beverage for such workers; the energy value contained in suet puddings; the cost of hockey sticks and boxing gloves; the erection of swings; the purchase of flower seeds; the establishment of play centres for children; the choice of models, utilitarian and aesthetic, for factory caps and overalls; the requirements of a boys' holiday camp; the pros and cons of 'mixed clubs'; the area of washing trough required per worker; the merits of different kinds of soap and soap boxes; the comparative advantages of crèches and of their own older relatives for the care of babies whose mothers were employed in munition factories; the overcrowding of tramcars and the supply of ferry boats; the equipment, down to the last saucepan and floor mat, of hostels . . . the degree of fatigue produced by housework or by shell production respectively (as a factor in decision as to the length of the day or night shift); the influence of holidays and of works cinemas as stimuli to output.[2]

All this was, of course, a far cry from the self-help and rugged individualism of the traditional Victorian, and more especially Liberal, ethic. But to Lloyd George it seemed a heaven-sent by-product of the exigencies of war. As he said in February 1916:

1. H.M.M., Vol. V, Part III, ch. IX, pp. 173–4.
2. H.M.M., Vol. V, Part III, ch. IX, p. 176.

It is a strange irony, but no small compensation, that the making of weapons of destruction should afford the occasion to humanise industry. Yet such is the case. Old prejudices have vanished, new ideas are abroad. Employers and workers, the public and the State, are all favourable to new methods. This opportunity must not be allowed to slip. It may well be that, when the tumult of war is a distant echo and the making of munitions a nightmare of the past, the effort now being made to soften asperities, to secure the welfare of the workers, and to build a bridge of sympathy and understanding between employer and employed, will have left behind results of permanent and enduring value to the workers, to the nation, and to mankind at large.[1]

Those who believe in the concept of a Welfare State will regard the social consequences of Lloyd George at the Ministry of Munitions with favour, while those with the opposite belief will tend to deplore them. Either way, the process largely begun by him before the war was much accelerated.

Technologically, too, the Ministry's influence was wide-ranging. In order to expand the output of iron and steel greater use had to be made of scrap, and this meant that arc furnaces had to be developed as an alternative to the Bessemer process. Throughout the munitions industries automation and standardisation of equipment were encouraged, with results that outlived the war. The Ministry also gave a big boost to electrification. In the new arms factories ninety-five per cent of the machinery was driven by electricity, and as the demand for this form of power grew financial help was given to municipalities to increase their generating capacity. At the same time progress was made in linking up generating stations. The Ministry's emphasis on research and development in every aspect of its work had an exemplary, though of course unquantifiable, effect throughout British industry.[2]

But Lloyd George's thoughts at the Ministry of Munitions did not dwell very much upon Britain's industrial future, any more than they dwelt upon social reform for its own sake. His overriding concern there was to provide the material means for winning the war. If other

1. Quoted *ibid.*, p. 175.
2. Chris Wrigley, 'The Ministry of Munitions: an Innovatory Department', in *War and the State*, ed. Kathleen Burk, pp. 47–8.

benefits accrued, so much the better, and he naturally welcomed such as were clearly consistent with his peacetime aims of improved national efficiency and a juster social order. But meanwhile the country was in mortal danger and he felt that everything should be subordinated to the struggle to survive and win.

It was his conviction that the fighting qualities of the Allied armies, and the excellence of their cause, had to be backed by not just a sufficiency, but a superiority, in material equipment. At Bangor in February 1915 he had proclaimed that the war was 'an engineers' war', and at the Ministry of Munitions he mobilised the engineering resources of the country to the full. In December he defended his policy of ambitious or, as some thought, extravagant planning:

The machine spares the man. . . . What we stint in materials we squander in life; that is the one great lesson of munitions.

It is too early to talk about over-production. The most fatuous way of economising is to produce an inadequate supply. A good margin is but a sensible insurance. Less than enough is a foolish piece of extravagance. . . . You must have enough ammunition to crash in every trench where the enemy lurks, to destroy every concrete emplacement, to shatter every machine-gun, to rend and tear every yard of barbed wire, so that if the enemy want to resist they will have to do it in the open, face to face with better men than themselves. That is the secret – plenty of ammunition. I hope that this idea that we are turning out too much will not enter into the mind of workman, capitalist, taxpayer or anybody until we have enough to crash our way through to victory. You must spend wisely; you must spend to the best purpose; you must not pay extravagant prices. But, for heaven's sake, if there are risks to be taken, let them be risks for the pocket of the taxpayer, and not for the lives of the soldiers.'[1]

The success of his policy can be seen above all, perhaps, in the figures for big gun and shell production. He reduced the output of lighter-calibre guns in order to increase the supply of medium and heavy artillery (while compensating for the lighter guns in his urgent development of trench mortars). During his time as Minister the capacity for the manufacture of medium guns rose by 380 per cent,

1. House of Commons, 20 December 1915 (Hansard, Fifth Series, Vol. LXXVII, cols. 95–122).

and of heavy guns by 1,200 per cent. When he left the Ministry in July 1916 deliveries of medium artillery were running at 34.5 times the rate in June 1915, and of heavy artillery at 94 times. As for the output of shells, the equivalent of a year's supply of medium shells at the rate they were being turned out in June 1915, could, by July 1916, be obtained in eleven days, while the comparable period for heavy shells was four days.[1] Despite the hugely increased demand for guns and ammunition in the last two or three years of the war, the organisation created by Lloyd George proved more than adequate to meet the demand.

Winston Churchill, who inherited the organisation in July 1917 when he became the fourth Minister of Munitions, wrote in *The World Crisis*: 'Munition production of every kind was already on a gigantic scale. The whole island was an arsenal. . . . The keenest spirits in British industry were gathered as State servants in the range of palatial hotels which house the Ministry of Munitions. The former trickles and streamlets of war supplies now flowed in rivers rising continuously.'[2] When the war ended the Ministry had a staff of 65,000, and three million workers under its control. But Lloyd George's successors, including even Churchill, knew that they were merely administering and extending an organisation that he had created. The vital work had already been done, and it is as hard now as it was then to imagine who else could have done it.

1. Adams, *Arms and the Wizard*, pp. 172–3.
2. Ch. XLVII. One of the hotels taken over was the Metropole in Northumberland Avenue. The building is still (1985) under Government occupation as part of the Ministry of Defence.

TWELVE

Tormented Government

The 1915 coalition came into being to improve Britain's performance in the war, and to restore the people's faith in victory. Unfortunately it failed on the whole to do any better than its predecessor. Indeed, after a year its record seemed in most respects worse. The one great exception was Lloyd George's triumph at the Ministry of Munitions, but even that did not become fully apparent until the spring of 1916. In other ways the Government had only further humiliation and frustration to show for its stewardship. Moreover it did not give the country the political unity which was the most obvious benefit to be expected from coalition. From the first it was split on major issues relating to the conduct of the war, and these divisions were envenomed by intra-party as well as inter-party rancour.

The two most contentious issues were the Dardanelles and conscription, but underlying both was the issue of Asquith's leadership. He and Kitchener were the big survivors of the crisis which had forced the change of government. Kitchener was saved by public opinion, outraged by Northcliffe's attack on him; but he had lost his authority with his colleagues and, during the next year, was increasingly nudged aside and by-passed. Asquith on the other hand owed his survival not to any outside power, but to his own adroitness and will to rule. Despite his many disqualifications for the role of national leader in time of war, he remained a formidable politician who had lost, as yet, none of the skill needed to hold the supreme place to which he felt himself entitled. Others might despair of his methods but *he* remained satisfied with them, and they were certainly effective for some purposes: above all for the purpose of keeping him in office.

Coalition involved a change in the personnel of government, but not in the machinery for running the war. The government still had the same head, with the same preference for working through the traditional Cabinet. Smaller bodies were set up, but even when they met often enough they never had the necessary autonomy. The War Council of pre-coalition days gave way, at first, to a group which became known as the Dardanelles Committee, because of the problem which demanded most of its attention. Towards the end of the year this was replaced by a smaller group, known simply as the War Committee, which lasted for the rest of Asquith's premiership. But the basic flaw of divided responsibility remained. In Hankey's words:

> . . .the greatest weakness of the new system was this existence, side by side with the War Committee, of the old-time Cabinet, working to no agenda, and keeping no records. For, while the Cabinet knew exactly what the War Committee was doing, the converse did not apply. Ministers, being members of both bodies, of course possessed a general knowledge of what the Cabinet had decided, but this knowledge was often of a vague and contradictory kind. The previous decisions were not on record for the secretary to produce at the psychological moment in the discussion, as were those of the War Committee.

Hankey goes on to say that the inconvenience of the dual system 'made itself more and more felt – until a reformer came and swept it away'.[1]

That reformer was almost totally preoccupied with his own departmental work until the following spring. We have seen how Lloyd George's intense interest in the general direction of the war at the beginning of 1915 turned, willy-nilly, to concentration on the home front, even before he became Minister of Munitions. While he was in that post he had little time for anything else. Nearly all his energy was devoted to the tremendous task in hand, and he became a conspicuous absentee from committees, Cabinets and Parliament itself. Yet being the man he was he could not help thinking about the wider problems

---

1. Hankey, *The Supreme Command*, ch. XLI. The words 'Ministers, being members of both bodies' are misleading, because they could be taken to mean that all ministers were members of the War Committee, whereas in fact only a few were. A clearer wording would be 'Those ministers who were members of both bodies . . .'

of the war, and his comments on them were all the more impatient for being, perforce, intermittent.

The fortunes of the Alliance reached a very low ebb in 1915. On the eastern front the Russians began the year with costly gains in Galicia but a severe defeat at the hands of Ludendorff in East Prussia (the battle of the Masurian Lakes). In May the Germans and Austrians launched offensives which drove the Russians out of Poland and far back into their own territory, even the fortress of Brest-Litovsk falling to the enemy. Russian losses were appalling: about four million men in the first year of the war. The Tsar's soldiers fought with glorious courage, but with a desperate inferiority of equipment. At least they kept large enemy forces busy and prevented what might otherwise have been a decisive concentration in the West.

By contrast, the efforts made by Russia's Western allies did little to weaken the onslaught in the East. The Italians, attacking towards Trieste with odds of two-to-one in their favour, advanced only six miles while sustaining well over a quarter of a million casualties. In late September the French attacked again in Champagne and there was a Franco-British offensive in Artois. These battles resulted in no significant gain of ground and further massive loss of life, on a scale almost twice that inflicted on the enemy.

The British had strongly opposed any renewal of offensive operations on the Western front, after the bloody and fruitless attacks earlier in the year, and they were under the impression that their view was shared by the French. On 6 July there was an Allied conference at Calais attended – for the first time in the war – by the British and French prime ministers. Asquith was accompanied by Balfour, Kitchener and Crewe. Lloyd George was not there, though Albert Thomas was (and travelled on the following day to confer with Lloyd George in London). Though no formal minutes were taken of the Calais meeting, it was definitely understood by the British that the French had agreed to a period of standing fast in the West while pursuing the attempt to break through at the Dardanelles. But Joffre, who was more important in France than any minister, never took the decisions of the conference seriously and went ahead with plans for his next Champagne offensive.

Kitchener, who had seemed a confident and dominating figure at Calais – arguing the case for caution with all the advantage of his fluency in French – in August completely changed his position after a visit to Joffre's headquarters. It was chiefly bad news from the Russian front, where the Germans had just captured Warsaw, that convinced Kitchener there would, after all, have to be offensive action in the West; but his opinion was reinforced by bad news from the Dardanelles. He no longer needed any indoctrination from Joffre but, on the contrary, was urging him to act as soon as possible. At meetings of the Dardanelles Committee and the full Cabinet on 20 August he expounded his new belief and secured the solid, if not unanimous, agreement of his colleagues. It was at this Committee meeting that he made a famous remark, too often quoted fatalistically by historians as a justification for strategic follies: 'Unfortunately we have to make war as we must and not as we should like to.'[1]

Lloyd George was not present at the meetings on 20 August, and in his absence the only serious resistance to Kitchener's proposal came from Churchill and Carson. But there can be no doubt at all that Lloyd George shared their view, which was consistent with all that he had been saying about strategic priorities since the beginning of the year, and to which his intimate knowledge of the supply situation could only add force. He may have asked for a record of the discussion, because the following day the Prime Minister's secretary, Maurice Bonham Carter, wrote giving him an extract from Asquith's letter to the King:

> At the Cabinet yesterday Lord Kitchener reported on his recent visit to France. General Joffre is quite determined, both on political & military grounds (the main element in the former being the situation in Russia) to take the offensive without delay & on a considerable scale. Sir J. French is agreed with him as to the urgency of the step from the military point of view. Lord K, though far from sanguine that any substantial military advantage will be achieved, is strongly of opinion that we cannot without serious and perhaps fatal injury to the Alliance refuse the cooperation which Joffre expects.
>
> The drawbacks & dangers of the proposed operation were pointed out with great force by Churchill, & other members of the Cabinet – including the Prime Minister, Lord Lansdowne & Lord Kitchener himself – expressed their concurrence with some at least of his apprehensions. After much consideration the Cabinet adopted Lord K's view & the necessary steps will be taken. No disclosure

1. Churchill, *The World Crisis*, ch. XXXV.

was made of the locality or precise nature of the operations.[1]

On 10 September the Cabinet was told that the attack would be taking place in a fortnight's time. Lloyd George was able to attend this meeting and, according to Frances Stevenson,

> . . . asked whether Sir J. French had enough ammunition for the purposes of this attack. The P.M. assured him that he had. D. [Lloyd George] expressed surprise, as according to all previous estimates given by Sir John, D. did not think he could possibly have enough. He suggested that he & French should have an interview on the matter, to clear up matters. . . . This was agreed to, & the interview took place on Friday evening [10th]. French said that what he had told the P.M. was that *on a certain estimate* he had enough ammunition – say if the attack lasted six days, & a normal amount was consumed – but that if it lasted longer, & an abnormal amount was consumed, then he certainly would not have sufficient. D. says that is the whole point – that at Neuve Chapelle they had sufficient for a few days, but that the whole thing came to nothing because they were unable to go on for lack of ammunition.[2]

The battle of Loos, as the British part of the Allied offensive was called, was more disastrous than it need have been, mainly because of French's mishandling of his reserves on the first day. But in view of the still incomplete training of the new armies – units of which had their baptism of fire at Loos – and the still inadequate supply of arms and ammunition, it was likely to be disastrous anyway. By mid-October, when the attacks came to an end, the British had suffered even worse than the French by comparison with the enemy. British casualties at Loos totalled at least 50,000, whereas the German figure was at most 20,000. As for the motive behind Kitchener's conversion to an offensive strategy in the West, there is no reason to suppose that the Alliance would have suffered any more than it actually did if he had stuck to his original view. Joffre, for his part, wanted to attack because he believed the Allies could drive the Germans beyond the Meuse, and

---

1. 21 August 1915, quoting Asquith's letter of the day before (L.G.P.). Until Lloyd George's time the only official record of Cabinet meetings was the letter written, normally weekly, from the Prime Minister to the Sovereign.

Asquith's letter makes no specific mention of Carson, but in another letter written the same day, to Sylvia Henley, he says: 'Winston argued vehemently (& very well) the other way, & was backed up by Carson: but all the rest took the opposite view. So the die is cast.'

2. F.S.D., 15 September 1915, p. 58.

possibly win the war, in 1915. But Kitchener had no such facile optimism. He reached a conclusion, which he knew to be untenable on military grounds, for speculative reasons of policy.

The War Secretary's change of mind and its depressing consequences gave the *coup de grâce* to what little remained of his colleagues' faith in his judgment. At the end of October Lloyd George and Bonar Law jointly threatened to resign unless Kitchener was removed; so Asquith took the ingenious course of sending him on a mission to the eastern Mediterranean, and while he was away assumed personal control of the War Office, as after the Curragh incident. In this capacity the Prime Minister gave substantial help to Lloyd George, by transferring to him a number of key functions to which the Ordnance Department was still clinging. Moreover, since French's reputation was finally blasted by Loos, he was asked to resign and to accept, instead, the command of Home Forces, while the command in France was offered to Sir Douglas Haig (who had assisted in French's downfall by complaining of his dispositions in a letter to Kitchener).

There had been hopes that the War Secretary's tour might be indefinitely prolonged: that he might remain as a sort of generalissimo in the Near East. But in fact he returned at the end of November, and although he offered his resignation there could be no question of allowing him to go, because his standing with the public was still as high as ever. Instead, it was arranged that he should stay on as a virtual figurehead, while most of his power was transferred to other hands. During his absence Asquith decided that Sir Archibald Murray should be replaced as Chief of the Imperial General Staff by Sir William Robertson, Chief of Staff in France, and that Robertson should become the effective controller of military strategy, as Lloyd George had become of military supply.[1] Kitchener was persuaded not just to accept, but himself to implement, the change. On 27 January 1916 an Order in Council proclaimed that the C.I.G.S. would, in future, 'be responsible for issuing the orders of the Government in regard to military operations'. Robertson was to deal direct with the Government, and was to be the sole channel through which command was exercised.

For the next few months this arrangement worked remarkably smoothly. Kitchener and Robertson got on well, despite the

---

1. Sir Archibald Murray had been C.I.G.S. only since September, when he succeeded his namesake, Sir James Wolfe Murray.

invidiousness of their formal relationship. But Robertson's extraordinary status was full of danger for the future. In their desire to be rid of one over-mighty subject the politicians had created another. Meanwhile Kitchener was deprived of the substance of his office by an act of State. Of the office itself he could be deprived only by an act of God.

Important as were the operations on the Western front to which the British became committed in 1915, the theatre that mattered more to them in the second half of that year was the eastern Mediterranean. The arguments that had led them into action there had lost none of their cogency; indeed they were now even more pressing. Serbia was in desperate peril, the Russians in greater need of help than ever and the advantages to be gained from victory over the Turks ever more obvious.

In August a further and, as it turned out, final attempt was made to break the deadlock on the Gallipoli peninsula. With new divisions sent out from Britain Hamilton staged a landing at Suvla Bay, a few miles north of Anzac Cove. His aim was to cut most of the Turkish army off from Constantinople, to win ground from which his artillery could dominate the Straits, and to enable the Royal Navy at last to force them and to enter the Sea of Marmara. Complete surprise was achieved, and for thirty-six hours the high ground behind Suvla Bay was defended by only one and a half Turkish battalions. But during that time the British corps commander, Sir Frederick Stopford, did not order his men to advance from the beaches and seize the heights. He was an elderly invalid who had been through the South African war but was now, for the first time, commanding a large force in battle. While he dawdled the Turks, under the redoubtable Mustapha Kemal, brought up reserves, and when the British eventually advanced they were checked with heavy losses. Of course there can be no certainty at all that the operation as a whole would have succeeded even if there had been a dashing commander at Suvla and the heights had been seized. But beyond question the failure at Suvla was calamitous, and with it the best chance of victory disappeared. To those in the know it was apparent that in choosing Stopford for such a key role the War Office had committed another astonishing blunder.

After Suvla the case for withdrawal from Gallipoli naturally gathered strength, though there was an unexpected cross-current when, in early September, the French offered to send four divisions there. This did not represent any conversion on Joffre's part to an eastern strategy, and indeed he soon drastically qualified the offer by explaining that the troops could not be spared until the results of his forthcoming Champagne offensive were known. The main reason for the proposal was that it was politically expedient in France to give a separate and conspicuous command to General Sarrail, who was rare among senior French officers in being an anti-clerical. As Churchill drily remarks: 'Whatever dispute there might be about his military achievements, his irreligious convictions were above suspicion.'[1] In fact he had shown some military initiative in 1914 and was also to show a limited competence in his new command – though not at Gallipoli.

For the scene of action was about to shift, belatedly, to Salonica. In the early part of October the Austrians, with German help, struck again at Serbia, and were joined this time by Bulgaria, whose sly King, Ferdinand, had come to the conclusion that he had more to gain from the Central Powers than from the Entente. While these events were clearly impending Grey gave an unequivocal pledge of support to Serbia, which the Allies were in no immediate position to honour. An Anglo-French advance guard of two divisions was landed at Salonica, but it was too small to have any decisive effect. By the time more substantial forces were transferred from Gallipoli Serbia had been overrun and the Germans had established a direct rail link with Turkey. To make matters worse, the Greek King Constantine, far from helping Serbia as treaty obligation required, had dismissed his pro-Allied premier Venizelos and adopted a menacing attitude towards the Allies.

Lloyd George could reasonably argue that this was the very catastrophe he had warned against at the beginning of the year, and which he had sought to prevent by timely action in the Balkans, including a diplomatic offensive and a landing at Salonica, with improvement of the railway from there into Serbia. No doubt he had underrated the complexities and perversities of Balkan politics, but it remains a plausible surmise that if he had been sent to negotiate with the Balkan States he might have persuaded Serbia and Greece to make the necessary concessions to Bulgaria in Macedonia in return for equivalent benefits elsewhere, and so have put together an effective alliance against both the Austro-Germans and the Turks. To achieve this it would also have been necessary for the major Allies to be present

1. *The World Crisis*, ch. XXXV.

in the area in convincing strength, and it was Lloyd George's conten-
tion that they should be. An outright victory at Gallipoli would
probably have had the same result, but he was from the very first
doubtful of such a victory, being more aware than his colleagues of the
difficulty of beating the Turks when they were defending their own
homeland. Hence his preference for Salonica.

The crisis in the Balkans intensified debate within the British
Cabinet on future strategy in the eastern Mediterranean. While few
ministers favoured, like the General Staff, complete withdrawal and
concentration in the West, the bulk of opinion was divided between
Gallipoli and Salonica, with Asquith, Balfour, Curzon and, of course,
Churchill still supporting the first; Lloyd George, Law, Chamberlain,
Long and Carson pressing for the second. At a meeting of the
Dardanelles Committee on 11 October the 'decisions' arrived at
reflected the prevailing disunity. It was agreed that 150,000 men
should be sent to *Egypt* – i.e. leaving their ultimate destination open –
when the current operations in France were over; also that a specially
selected general should be sent out to report as to which sphere and
which objective should be given priority in future.

The following day Lloyd George circulated a long memorandum in
which, after some remarks in the 'I told you so' vein, he argued that
Allied drafts on their way to the Dardanelles should be immediately
diverted to Salonica, and that Greece should be forced to 'redeem her
treaty obligations to Serbia'. As for Gallipoli, the idea of making
another attack there was, to his mind, 'an insane one'. He ended with a
withering comment on the proposal to send a general out to report.
'We are now not merely to send out a general to trawl the eastern
Mediterranean for a new policy, but before he reports we are to send
150,000 men away from France – from the only objective which the
General Staff are prepared to stake their reputation upon
recommending.'[1]

In a simultaneous memorandum Law argued strongly that troops
should be sent at once from Gallipoli to Salonica, and that any further
reinforcement of Gallipoli would be 'quite indefensible'. But one
member of the same ministerial group wrote a letter of resignation.

---

1. The suggestion that a request to Greece should, if not complied with, be followed by a
'demand', is not to be compared with Germany's treatment of Belgium, since Venizelos,
who wished to work with the Allies, had a democratic mandate, whereas the King who
dismissed him was acting arbitrarily. (The King's pro-German tendencies were naturally
increased by the fact that he was married to a sister of the Kaiser.)

This was Carson, and when, after desperate attempts to dissuade him, his resignation was announced on 19 October, it was a political event of the first importance. Carson was a man nobody could ignore. As leader of the Ulster revolt he had successfully defied government, Parliament and the armed forces of the Crown. And if the feat of organisation behind this achievement had been Craig's rather than his, it was nevertheless his figure that dominated the public mind. Now, with his charisma and forensic power, he was a most dangerous man to be returning to the back-benches. Opposition in the House of Commons would inevitably find in him the leader it had lacked since the coalition was formed.

His immediate reason for resigning was that he had taken Grey's pledge to Serbia seriously and could not in conscience be a party to abandoning that country to its fate. But soon he expanded his ground of complaint to include the machinery of war direction. In the House of Commons on 2 November he said: 'What is wanted for carrying on the war is a small number – the smaller the better – of competent men sitting, not once a week, but from day to day, with the best expert advisers they can get, working out the problems that arise in the course of the war. . . . The whole question is one of concentrating responsibility'.[1] Thus he was challenging not just a particular course of policy, but the whole Asquithian method of running the war.

Lloyd George was like-minded on the points at issue, and so was Bonar Law. To both men Carson's resignation was an embarrassment and, in some ways, a reproach. Yet both decided that they had to soldier on in the Government. Law, though insecure as leader of the Conservative Party, and well aware that Carson would now become a magnet for backbenchers' loyalty, nevertheless felt that resignation would be almost tantamount to desertion in face of the enemy. Lloyd George was chiefly concerned to see his work on munitions through; but he, too, would have felt uneasy about breaking ranks at the time. Later he came to doubt the wisdom of their self-denial. 'Mr Bonar Law and I shared [Carson's] opinion . . . but on the whole decided that we could not withdraw from the Ministry at this critical juncture. I am not sure that we were right.'[2]

Ultimately Law and Lloyd George would combine to destroy Asquith and his system, but the time for such a combination was not yet. Neither was yet ready to work with the other for such a purpose,

1. Hansard, Fifth Series, Vol. LXXV, col. 533.
2. W.M., p. 513.

or quite convinced that anyone would be capable of replacing Asquith as prime minister. Indeed, despite their underlying rapport, relations between them had been distinctly cool since they became colleagues in government. Law resented his exclusion from any office befitting his status as party leader, and rightly felt that Lloyd George was partly responsible for this. Lloyd George also was feeling rather isolated in the autumn of 1915. While his affronts to the voluntary principle had lost him a good deal of Liberal support, he was far from having won the unqualified trust of Conservative politicians. It still seemed quite possible that he might fail as Minister of Munitions, and he knew that his failure would be greeted with considerable *Schadenfreude* in both political camps.

A small incident in mid-September illustrates the edginess of both men. Asquith, having offended Law the previous month by leaving him off an important Cabinet committee to which, however, he appointed Curzon, then angered Lloyd George by offering Law the deputy leadership of the House of Commons. On the face of it, this was a sensible suggestion. Lloyd George's departmental work was making it increasingly difficult for him to attend the House, so he was unable to give Asquith as much relief as formerly. Law, on the other hand, would have had time to spare from the Colonial Office. But Lloyd George saw the offer as a threat to his recognised position as second man in the Government, and he protested against it strongly to Asquith. He also wrote in some bitterness to Law, whom he suspected of having raised the matter with the Prime Minister behind his back, though Law denied having done so.

Where the initiative lay is of no consequence now, and the whole affair seems very trivial in retrospect. Asquith was willing for Law to have the job, and Law to take it: that much is certain. As for their motivation, it was probably more innocent than Lloyd George imagined. Asquith may well have desired only to make amends to Law for the earlier slight, while easing his own burden a little; and Law, apart from a straightforward desire to serve, was surely more interested in his precedence *vis-à-vis* Conservative colleagues than in stealing a march on Lloyd George. At all events, when Lloyd George protested, the idea was immediately dropped and no more was heard of it – until he became Prime Minister himself and appointed Law Leader of the House of Commons.

As the Balkan crisis was looming up Lloyd George and Asquith discussed the formation of a small group to take the place of the Dardanelles Committee, and Lloyd George fancied that he had persuaded the Prime Minister to have 'a small Cabinet of 6 or 8 members'.[1] But there is no evidence that Asquith ever thought of superseding the traditional Cabinet. He did, however, jot down eight names for a 'suggested War Conduct Committee'. The names were himself, Kitchener, Grey, Balfour, Lloyd George, Bonar Law, Churchill and Curzon. He showed the list to Law who commented, 'Admirable if not too large, but I hardly think any could be left out.'[2]

Nothing was done to give effect to this proposal until after the fall of Serbia and Carson's resignation. Then, in the debate on 2 November when Carson explained why he had resigned and made the demand, already quoted, for a small War Cabinet, Asquith outlined what he himself would and would not be doing:

> I do not propose to change the size of the Cabinet; but of course there is a great deal to be said in time of war for having one, or it may be more – at any rate one – comparatively small body of men who will deal with the daily exigencies of the State . . . we have had since a very early period of the war a body fluctuating in number from time to time, and which has varied in name. . . . It is a body to which either general questions of State or questions of strategy in particular areas and arenas have, by the consent of the Cabinet, been referred. I have come to the conclusion . . . that it is desirable to maintain that system, but to limit still further the number of the body to whom what I may call the strategic conduct of the war is from time to time referred. I think . . . that the Committee, or by whatever name it may be called, should be a body of not less than three, and perhaps not more than five, in number, but with this important proviso that, whether it be three or five, it should, of course, have power to summon to its deliberations and to its assistance the particular Minister concerned with the particular Department whose special knowledge is needed, or is desirable, for the determination of each issue as it arises.[3]

No announcement of the new Committee's membership was made

1. F.S.D., 5 October 1915, referring to a conversation between H.H.A. and D.L.G. 'about a fortnight ago' – i.e. in the early 20s of September (p. 63).

2. H.H.A. to Sylvia Henley, pencilled note; dated 24 September 1915, so clearly at least roughly contemporary with the conversation referred to in note 1 above.

3. Hansard, Fifth Series, Vol. LXXV, col. 526.

until nine days later, and meanwhile there was much jockeying behind the scenes. Though in his speech Asquith had seemed to favour a body smaller than the '6 or 8' originally mentioned, he was unable to hold to this in the event. The first meeting after the speech was attended only by himself, Kitchener and Balfour, but Law threatened to resign if Kitchener remained a member, and Lloyd George backed him in a letter to the Prime Minister. It was after this that Asquith decided to rid himself of Kitchener, at least temporarily, by sending him to the Near East. The next proposal was that the Committee should consist of the Prime Minister, Balfour, Lloyd George, McKenna and Lansdowne, but, as Asquith wrote on 11 November to Sylvia Henley, 'dear old Lansdowne refused to serve', so he 'was obliged to take on B. Law'. That day he announced the final revised list of five names in the House of Commons. But the number of those more or less regularly attending soon grew to nine.[1]

Asquith's attempt to have Lansdowne on the Committee rather than Law is almost incomprehensible. Though an adroit diplomat when he was Foreign Secretary in the Balfour government, Lansdowne had been a failure as War Minister during the Boer War. Now he was seventy years old, and soon to show that he lacked the will to see the war through to a finish. He was entirely unfit for a Committee whose ostensible purpose was to help in making the higher direction of the war more dynamic, and in preferring him to Law for such a task Asquith showed erratic human judgment and a strange attitude towards the new Committee.

Another mistake was the inclusion of McKenna, which was bound to infuriate Lloyd George, as indeed it did. According to Frances Stevenson, Asquith told McKenna at a Cabinet meeting that he would not be on the Committee, but then changed his mind as a result of spending the weekend before its announcement with the McKennas (or 'McKennae', as he mock-classically called them). Frances Stevenson was undoubtedly reflecting Lloyd George's view when she wrote that this appointment would 'destroy the usefulness' of the Committee 'to a large extent'.[2] In fact it was more effectively impaired by the

---

1. Grey was always present, and Kitchener could not be kept off the Committee after his return. The First Sea Lord and Chief of the Imperial Staff attended regularly after the first meeting. Curzon established a right to come as chairman of the Shipping Control Board, and Austen Chamberlain came as Secretary for India and, later, chairman of the Manpower Board. (Hankey, *op.cit.*, p. 442).
2. F.S.D., 15 November 1915, pp. 72–3.

basic flaw already mentioned, that it was only a committee of the Cabinet and not a fully responsible body. It met every two or three days between its creation and the end of the year, but Hankey explains that this was not an unmixed blessing. 'The frequent meetings of the Committee and the Cabinet took up so much of their time that Ministers found it difficult to devote sufficient time and attention to their departmental and Parliamentary work. In the long run this told on nerves and tempers and was an important contributory cause of the eventual breakdown of the system.'[1]

Notably absent from the new Committee was Winston Churchill, and it was evident to him that his omission from it portended doom for the Dardanelles strategy. The general sent to report on the state of affairs in the eastern Mediterranean, Sir Charles Monro, who was also appointed to succeed Hamilton as commander-in-chief at Gallipoli, had promptly reported in favour of evacuation. It was clearly only a matter of time before the campaign with which Churchill was identified was brought to an end, and he therefore resigned from the Government on 12 November, the day after Asquith announced the composition of the new Committee. For the next six months he served on the Western Front, while keeping a vigilant eye on the course of politics at home. He was deeply resentful of his former colleagues; and of Asquith above all, who compounded his other offences in Churchill's eyes by intervening, in December, to deny him the command of a brigade, which French was prepared to give him. (Asquith feared the political repercussions, and when Haig soon replaced French Churchill was firmly confined to command of a battalion.)

His feelings towards Lloyd George were less bitter – because Lloyd George had been candidly opposed to the Gallipoli landings from the first – and they were anyway mitigated by a shrewd sense that the Minister of Munitions was the man of the future, with whom it would be expedient to make common cause. His wife, Clementine, had her doubts. On 29 December she had Lloyd George to lunch, and the following day wrote to her husband advising him not to 'burn any boats' (i.e. with Asquith). Lloyd George, she said, was 'the direct descendant of Judas Iscariot'. Although she hated Asquith, 'if he held out his hand I could take it (though I would give it a nasty twist) but before taking LlG's I would have to safeguard myself with charms,

1. Hankey, op.cit., p. 444.

touchwoods, exorcisms & by crossing myself. I always get on with him & yesterday I had a good talk, but you can't hold his eyes, they shift away.' Churchill liked her to say what she thought, but seldom took her advice. On 1 January 1916 he wrote: 'I am very glad you had LG to lunch. Do this again: & keep in touch. It really is most important, a situation may develop at any time, wh will throw us inevitably together. Our relations are now good – & shd be kept so.' And three days later he wrote again: 'Keep in touch with L.G. His necessities will keep him straight if a split occurs. Asquith on the other hand will never have need of me again. It is *need* alone that counts.'[1]

After Churchill's departure opinion hardened in favour of withdrawal from Gallipoli, though for a time there were still doubts about it and a nagging fear that the actual process of evacuation would be a shambles. But what of the alternatives: in particular, what of Salonica? The British general staff was opposed to the operation there, while the French were more than ever keen to develop it. Since the end of October there was a new government in France, Briand having succeeded Viviani as prime minister. Among other changes the most significant appeared to be the replacement of Joffre's mouthpiece, Millerand, by General Galliéni as war minister. But in fact Galliéni was a sick man, who was disappointing in the job and did not last long. From Lloyd George's point of view it was a great relief that Albert Thomas retained his post, and Thomas was soon to make a decisive intervention in the Allies' strategic debate.

On 16 November Lloyd George travelled to Paris with Asquith, Balfour and Grey for a conference with the new French government. At this it was agreed that the Salonica bridgehead should be reinforced, but soon afterwards the British began to have cold feet, as the military position there deteriorated, and at a second conference held at Calais on 3 December the British ministers insisted on withdrawal, a decision which the French accepted under protest. Neither Lloyd George nor Thomas was present at the Calais conference, but when the French ministers, returning from it, announced sadly to their colleagues that they had been forced to acquiesce because the British Cabinet was adamant for withdrawal, Thomas said that he knew Lloyd George took the opposite view. This information caused the

1. Clementine S. Churchill to W.S.C. quoted in Martin Gilbert, *Winston S. Churchill*, Vol. III, pp. 623–4.

   W.S.C. to Clementine S. Churchill, Gilbert, Companion Vol. III Part 2, p. 1351 and p. 1357.

French Cabinet to reject the agreement and to send Thomas to London to talk the British round, which he succeeded in doing.

Why Lloyd George did not go to Calais is an open question. Frances Stevenson says he was not asked to go 'either because he was not available or (which is more likely) because he held different views from the others' on Salonica'. However that may be, Asquith went with Balfour and Kitchener (just back from his trip). On 4 December Lloyd George received a telegram from Thomas with the news that he would be coming over to explain 'the real opinions of the French'. At a meeting of the War Committee on 6 December Lloyd George clashed with Kitchener, who had lately been visiting Greece and talking to the Greek King. According to Frances Stevenson, Kitchener read a telegram received from Greece to the effect that the Germans deman- ded that the Allies evacuate the Balkans, and would allow the Greeks to cover the re-embarkation of Allied troops at Salonica. 'It is a good thing', she quotes Lloyd George as saying, 'that the British and the Germans have found something to agree upon at last. . . . Surely this must be the beginning of concord between us and the enemy!'[1]

The official record of the exchange is more prosaic:

MR LLOYD GEORGE said that as regarded the policy of evacuation both the German and the British General Staffs were in agreement, because what the Greeks (or in other words the Germans) were promising was that, if we went away quietly, they would permit us to go.

LORD KITCHENER did not agree with this view. It did not seem to him to be based on the facts. That we should leave Salonica was the wish of the Greeks, and they were very anxious about it. Both the King of Greece and the General Staff of the Greek Army wanted us to leave. To his mind there was nothing to show that this was the wish of the German General Staff.

MR LLOYD GEORGE said that, according to what had been arranged, we apparently got nothing. He understood that the arrangement would be that, if we vacated Salonica, the Germans and the Bulgarians would not attack. If no assurance to that effect had been given, i.e. that we should not be attacked, he thought we were in a very dangerous position, and that the Germans would take the opportunity to attack us while we were embarking our force.

1. F.S.D., pp. 84–6.

The minutes also record Lloyd George's statement, quoting Albert Thomas, that 'the unanimous feeling in the French Council of War on the receipt of the decision come to at Calais was one of consternation'.[1] Next day Thomas lunched with Asquith (who found him 'a delightful shaggy creature, full of esprit and good sayings'), and afterwards had an hour's talk with the Prime Minister, Grey and Lloyd George, in the course of which he convinced his host that the Briand government would not survive agreement to withdraw from Salonica.[2] At a War Committee meeting the following day there was less talk of withdrawal, and Kitchener agreed in principle when Lloyd George cited Thomas's view that 'to keep Salonica open for the Allies was a good military proposition'.

At this meeting Lloyd George proposed that the French should take control of the Allied force at Salonica. 'Some authority must decide how those troops should be protected, and in his opinion the French should do it, whether it was a question of coercing the Greeks or not . . . the one thing that was important was to assure unity of responsibility and direction'.[3] Asquith privately dismissed this as 'a really insane proposition', but told his correspondent that the War Committee had 'agreed to send K. and E. Grey to Paris . . . to concert, with carte blanche, a joint plan for extricating our troops'.[4] He may have been referring only to the need to extricate them from their immediate tactical difficulties, rather than to pulling them out of Salonica itself, because the policy of evacuation had virtually been dropped before Kitchener and Grey left for France. While they were there it was dropped completely and the Calais decision reversed.

The crisis which had caused the British to press for withdrawal gradually passed, and the Allied bridgehead at Salonica was consolidated. Although no break-out from it was achieved until 1918, and the Germans derided it as their largest internment camp, at least an Allied presence in the Balkans was maintained and the port of Salonica denied to the enemy as a U-boat base. Moreover units of the Serbian army, which at first had taken refuge on Corfu, were able to regroup and fight again as part of the Allied force at Salonica. Lloyd George was surely right to argue that withdrawal from there would have been 'regarded throughout the East as a token of weakness and irresolu-

1. Secretary's Notes of War Committee meeting, 10 Downing Street, 6 December 1915.
2. H.H.A. to Sylvia Henley, 7 December 1915.
3. Notes of War Committee meeting, 8 December 1915.
4. H.H.A. to Sylvia Henley, 8 December 1915.

tion', and would have meant 'the utter loss of the Balkans'.[1] Yet no one could have been more bitterly aware than he that the right time for landing at Salonica had been earlier, when neither the French nor his own colleagues had been willing to do it.

In the final arguments over Salonica he was, however, supported by Bonar Law, who had meanwhile also been forcing a decision to withdraw from Gallipoli. On 4 December he replied effectively to a memorandum from Curzon in which the perils of evacuation were luridly depicted. His firmness put an end to vacillation and, on the day that Thomas lunched at 10 Downing Street, the Cabinet decided to evacuate Suvla and Anzac while continuing for a time to hold Cape Helles. Accordingly troops were withdrawn from the first two places during the night of 19 December, with hardly any loss, and on 8 January Helles was evacuated also, with equal success. The only theatre where the British were now seriously engaged against the Ottoman Empire was Mesopotamia; but there an enterprising force under General Townshend had recently been surrounded at Kut-el-Amara – the prelude to a long siege and eventual disaster.

While the Asquith coalition was wrangling over strategy and the system of war direction, an even more divisive issue was coming to the fore. This was the issue of compulsory military service, which divided the Government largely on party lines. Most Conservatives wanted conscription (though among the leaders Balfour and even Law had some reservations), while most Liberals tended, with a greater or lesser degree of moral fervour, to oppose it, as did also the Irish and Labour. Asquith himself did not oppose it on principle, though he was certainly not drawn to it temperamentally and had intellectual doubts about its necessity. His attitude was that it could be introduced only if and when the military case for it was overwhelming, and seen to be so. Without clear evidence from the competent authorities that enough manpower could no longer be raised by voluntary means, he would do nothing to promote conscription.

His immobilism on the issue was sustained by the man who to the public at large, if not to his colleagues, still seemed the most competent authority of all: Kitchener. If Kitchener had turned against the voluntary system, Asquith would have felt free – indeed obliged – to turn against it too. But Kitchener was most reluctant to depart from it.

1. W.M., p. 525.

No doubt he took some proprietorial pride in a system through which he had conjured up a vast army simply by pointing his finger. But there was more to it than that. He had seen the number of recruits far exceed the Army's capacity to clothe, arm or train them, and was slow to accept that a time might be approaching when the demand would be greater than the supply. According to Hankey, moreover, he was in no hurry to commit Britain's reserves of manpower to what might be premature action on the Western Front. 'He had now realised that artillery and ammunition on a much larger scale than had ever been conceived in the past was essential to support any offensive movement, and he was concerned at the rate at which France was squandering her manpower. . . . He wished to keep in hand a reserve against the time when both the French and Germans had exhausted themselves by the prodigality of their efforts.'[1]

Lloyd George could hardly be accused of any partiality for suicidal offensives with insufficient weaponry or artillery support. Yet by the middle of 1915 he was convinced that the voluntary system of recruitment had served its turn and must give way to compulsion. If the war could have been won quickly by the 1914 volunteers all would have been well, but as the country faced the prospect of a long war the voluntary system was manifestly inefficient and inequitable. At its best, in the early days, it had worked largely through spontaneous patriotism, though even then, as he well knew, there had been an element of moral blackmail in the call for volunteers. By 1915 the system had lost much of its original virtue. In the words of an acute, though admittedly partisan, observer:

> Every effort was made to whip up the flagging recruiting campaign. Immense sums were spent on covering all the walls and hoardings of the United Kingdom with posters, melodramatic, jocose or frankly commercial. In many districts a regular system of 'peaceful picketing' was set up, and wounded heroes in mufti found white feathers thrust upon them by well-meaning females. The continuous urgency from above for better recruiting returns, and the interest of recruiting sergeants and doctors, led to an ever-increasing acceptance of men unfit for military work. . . . Throughout 1915 the nominal totals of the Army were swelled by the maintenance of some 200,000 men absolutely useless for any conceivable military

1. Hankey, *The Supreme Command*, pp. 426–7, recalling conversations with Kitchener at the time.

purpose.[1]

Though conscription now seemed to Lloyd George a military necessity, if Britain were to establish and keep up to strength a field army of seventy divisions, nevertheless as Minister of Munitions he was more immediately dissatisfied with the industrial implications of voluntaryism. Hence his speech at Manchester on 3 June, in which he flew a kite for industrial conscription ('We cannot afford ten months to enlist the great industrial army.') The alarm that this provoked was by no means wholly negative in its effects, and he continued to believe that the threat, if not yet the reality, was justified.

In July a National Registration Act was passed, despite fears that it would be (as indeed it was) a first step towards conscription. The Register was taken in mid-August, and at about the same time Asquith appointed a Cabinet Committee to consider the manpower problem. (This was the Committee which Bonar Law, to his annoyance, was neither consulted about nor asked to join.) Testifying before the Committee on 18 August Lloyd George made his attitude very plain. When the chairman, Crewe, asked him if he would go to the point of placing every citizen at the Government's orders the following exchange occurred:

MR LLOYD GEORGE: If you ask me whether personally I think it would help the efficient conduct of the war I say at once that it certainly would. I would say that every man and woman was bound to render the services that the State required of them, and which in the opinion of the State they could best render. I do not believe you will go through this war without doing it in the end; in fact, I am perfectly certain that you will have to come to it.

THE CHAIRMAN: When one says 'The State', you and Kitchener cannot choose the work to which individuals are to be put; somebody has to select how a particular man is to be employed. . . . Somebody has to say to John Smith, 'You have to work in a coal mine, or go on board ship, or to the trenches.' That, of course, would require a very large organisation. But what I understand is that you think that ought to be quite generally applicable.

MR LLOYD GEORGE: That question is not involved in that of military compulsion. It raises quite another issue.

THE CHAIRMAN: You can have purely military and naval

1. L. S. Amery, *My Political Life*, Vol. II, p. 64.

compulsion.

MR LLOYD GEORGE: I think to make a nation absolutely efficient for war you ought to have a general compulsion, but I do not think it is essential. I think if you have a system of compulsory military service—

THE CHAIRMAN: In which you would include the making of Army material?

MR LLOYD GEORGE: No. I think if you had compulsory military service you could work the rest all right.[1]

In other words, he was interested in military conscription not only as a means of finding manpower for the army, but even more, perhaps, as an inducement to men to work on munitions instead of being sent to the front. Knowing what prejudice there was against industrial conscription as such, he felt that this might be a roundabout way of achieving much the same result.

The news of Suvla and Loos, soon to be followed by the entry of Bulgaria into the war, and then by the fall of Serbia, aggravated a general feeling of discontent and anxiety which expressed itself most clamantly in the demand for compulsory service. The issue was symbolic as well as practical. On 13 September Lloyd George released to the Press, in advance of publication, the preface to a collection of his war speeches, which ended with these words:

If we are not allowed to equip our factories and workshops with adequate labour to supply our armies . . . if practices are maintained which restrict the output of essential war material; *if the nation hesitates, when the need is clear, to take the necessary steps to call forth its manhood to defend honour and existence*; if vital decisions are postponed until too late; if we neglect to make ready for all probable eventualities if, in fact, we give ground for the accusation that we are slouching into disaster as if we were walking along the ordinary paths of peace without an enemy in sight; then I can see no hope: but if we sacrifice all we own and all we like for our native land; if our preparations are characterised by grip, resolution, and a prompt readiness in every sphere; then victory is assured.[2]

1. Report of meeting printed for use of the Cabinet, 11 September 1915.
2. *Through Terror to Triumph* ('Speeches and Pronouncements of the Right Hon. David Lloyd George M.P. since the beginning of the War', arranged by F. L. Stevenson B.A.), Preface, p. IX (author's italics.) On 11 October Frances recorded 'the sale of our book has reached 30,000 copies!' (F.S.D., p. 66.)

He was thus identifying himself openly with the conscriptionists.

Since the coalition was formed its leading Parliamentary critic had been Lord Milner, whose undoubted talents as an administrator Asquith would have been wise to harness. At the end of July Milner became chairman of the National Service League, and on 20 August he announced that the League would no longer merely be advocating national service for home defence, but universal and compulsory military service for the duration of the war.'[1] His campaign, which was only part of a comprehensive onslaught on the Asquithian system of government, was strongly supported by the Northcliffe Press and other Unionist journals. In the House of Commons the opposition lacked leadership until Carson resigned in October, though of course it was clear from Lloyd George's preface and other signals that the demand for conscription and more resolute government was growing within the Cabinet.

The case for voluntary recruitment was, meanwhile, further weakened by evidence that the numbers raised by it were falling off. In May 135,000 had volunteered, but for August the figure was 95,000, and for September 71,000. Asquith realised that some action would have to be taken, but felt that the time was still not ripe for outright compulsion. The device through which he managed to avert the smash that seemed to be inevitable in mid-October was the so-called Derby scheme. He appointed the Tory magnate Lord Derby, himself a compulsionist, to carry out a final canvass under the voluntary system, with the title director-general of recruiting. The National Register suggested that about one and three-quarter million able-bodied men of military age were still neither in the armed forces nor in essential civilian work, and the Derby scheme was a last attempt to tap this reserve by a method that could still pass for voluntary. All men between the ages of eighteen and forty-one were invited to 'attest' in forty-six groups, twenty-three for married men and twenty-three for unmarried; and an assurance was given that the unmarried would be taken first. The scheme was to have six weeks' trial.

The immediate effect on recruitment was good, because those who attested were free, if they wished, to enlist at once, and a considerable number did. Moreover by the end of the year the first four groups of single men had been called up. The recruiting figure for October rose to over 113,000, and that for November to nearly 122,000. But the

1. A. M. Gollin, *Proconsul in Politics*, p. 279.

results of the scheme as a whole were fatal to the voluntary system. Only 840,000 unmarried men attested, compared with 1,345,000 married, and nearly two million men did not come forward to attest at all. It was obvious that married men had been the readier to attest because they had been assured that they would not be taken before the unmarried, and there was every reason to assume that the two million non-attesters included a substantial number of single men who were fit for combatant service but keen to avoid it. The conscription crisis had, therefore, merely been postponed, though the Derby scheme did provide a handy organisational basis for the compulsory system that was now bound to come.

In facing the issue again, at the turn of the year, Asquith had certain advantages that he had lacked earlier. Kitchener now accepted the necessity for compulsion, and in any case a balancing military authority was being built up in the person of Robertson, who was a strong compulsionist. With the decision to evacuate the Dardanelles, one of the Cabinet's most controversial issues had been laid to rest: all the more so, since Anzac and Suvla had already been evacuated with none of the terrible carnage that had been feared. Above all, the Prime Minister could point to the evidence of the Derby scheme, and could use his pledge to the married men to justify abandoning the voluntary principle; even, indeed, by an ingenious stroke of casuistry, to pretend that the principle was being, in a sense, upheld. For his argument now was that all single men should be forced to attest so that his pledge to married men – itself given within the framework of a voluntary scheme – could be honoured.

For a time it seemed that this limited measure of conscription would cost him the resignations of Simon, Runciman, McKenna and Grey, which would have been a formidable defection of Liberals. But in the event only Simon resigned. He alone took his stand on unwillingness to accept the principle of compulsion for military service. The other three objected to conscription for economic reasons. In their view Britain could not afford an army of seventy divisions, with the distortions of manpower and other resources that it would entail. If the country's financial power were to be maintained the army could not be expanded to a scale matching that of France or Germany; and its financial power was no less vital to the Alliance than to itself. Asquith had much sympathy with this argument, but very little patience with the cussedness of his three colleagues. As Roy Jenkins says: 'Perhaps the best way for a minister to irritate his chief is stubbornly to advocate a policy which the Prime Minister would half like to follow, but knows he cannot.'[1] The three were, after all, persuaded to stay, in return for the face-saving appointment of a Cabinet committee to investigate the competing military and economic claims on Britain's resources. Asquith also fended off a threat that Henderson and two junior Labour ministers would have to resign after Labour's National Executive Committee pronounced against the bill.

His decision to introduce compulsion for single men (and childless widowers) was surely inevitable in the circumstances. Anything less would have destroyed the Government at once, and might have led to a general election in which the grievance of the married men would have been a powerful factor. The sanction of an appeal to the people was available to the Unionists, because the life of Parliament had to be extended and the Lords could have withheld consent. The bill passed the House of Commons with only 105 voting against it, among whom only about fifty were Liberals (compared with thirty who had voted against the National Registration Bill six months earlier). But the question was not settled. Asquith had won another breathing-space, that was all.

Lloyd George certainly brought heavy pressure to bear during the New Year crisis. On 20 December he had given vent, in the House of Commons, to his fury at the way vital decisions had been deferred and opportunities missed on the Allied side. 'The footsteps of the Allied forces have been dogged by the mocking spectre of "too late", and unless we quicken our movements damnation will fall upon the sacred cause for which so much gallant blood has flowed.'[2] These words were taken to refer not only to the Balkans and other foreign theatres, but also to the home front. The day after Boxing Day, just back from his bruising visit to the Clyde, he gave Asquith what was both an ultimatum and a valuable offer of support.

When he arrived home on Sunday [27 December] he found that there was a good deal of wobbling on the question of giving effect to the P.M.'s pledge to married men. . . . On Sunday night L.G. wrote to the P.M. and told him that, so far as he was concerned, unless the pledge were kept in the letter and in the spirit, he would go. If the P.M. would keep it, he would stick to him as leader and, if

1. *Asquith*, p. 390.
2. Hansard, Fifth Series, Vol. LXXXVII, col. 121. Frances Stevenson listened to the speech which, she says, 'created a sensation' (F.S.D., p. 87).

necessary, carry on a campaign up and down the country and do any dirty work required and generally back him with all his power.[1]

He also said that 'under no circumstances would he take office in a Conservative Government'.[2]

This message was delivered to Asquith by Reading who, with Montagu, was dining at 10 Downing Street. The Prime Minister then decided, with their full agreement, upon a course which was 'unpalatable', and which might 'lead to schism and disruption', but which seemed to him 'fairly clearly . . . the right course'.[3] In other words, he decided to compel all single men to attest, and the following morning he put the proposal to the Cabinet. In his ensuing struggle with Grey, Runciman and McKenna he knew that he had Lloyd George's backing, as in May 1915, for staying on as Prime Minister. There was also Lloyd George's assurance that despite his cooperation with the Tories on some issues, he had no intention of joining them. Of course the attitude of the Liberal dissenters meant more to the Prime Minister than to the Minister of Munitions. It would hardly have broken Lloyd George's heart if Grey and co. had carried out their threat to resign, and he did not care much about the loss of Simon. But there is no evidence that he wanted Asquith to go, when it came to the point. The two men were still linked by a sense of mutual indispensability, however thin the feeling might wear at times.

Their views on the conscription issue remained, however, so different that peace was bound to be short-lived. Lloyd George was intent upon achieving a comprehensive system, and regarded the bill just passed as an inadequate and illogical half-measure, justifiable only as a means of weaning Liberals away from their old orthodoxy. Asquith, though not himself a Liberal purist on the issue, had doubts about the military necessity and the economic expediency of conscription, which reinforced his reluctance to face any further unpleasantness on its behalf. His desire was that the compromise scheme should last indefinitely; Lloyd George's that it should be superseded as soon as possible.

1. Addison, op.cit., 30 December 1915, Vol. I, p. 156.
2. F.S.D., 31 January 1916, p. 89.
3. H.H.A. to Sylvia Henley, 27 December 1915. From this letter it is clear that Reading was dining with Asquith that evening, rather than lunching with him the following day, as stated by Frances Stevenson in her diary a month later. And Asquith's next letter (28 December) shows that the Cabinet met on the Monday morning, and not, as Frances suggests, after lunch that day.

Events favoured the compulsionists. Though the recruiting rate went up in the first three months of 1916, the increase was insufficient. According to an estimate supplied by the Board of Trade – Runciman's department – 340,000 men could have been spared from civilian life during that period without great disturbance of trade, or as many as 530,000 at a pinch. But the number actually to come forward was only 212,000. Meanwhile the Army reported a shortage of manpower almost as acute as at the beginning of the year, with the infantry abroad 78,000, and Territorial units at home 50,000, below strength. Yet the scale of operations planned for the Western front in 1916 called for much larger forces and a larger reserve, not just for maintaining the existing establishment.

On 21 February a further consideration arose with the first German attack on Verdun, starting a battle which was to last until December at stupendous cost to both sides. Now the French could argue more persuasively than ever that there had to be a substantial increase in the British contribution on land. The Russians on their side, mauled and debilitated as they were, were still willing to make big sacrifices in support of the French. Were the British to be less staunch allies to their sister-democracy across the Channel?

The news from Verdun had a very swift effect on Lloyd George, reviving all his smouldering choler at the way the war was being run in Britain. On 26 February Riddell had tea with him at Walton Heath and noted:

He is perturbed at the progress of the battle at Verdun and thinks the French are losing ground. He is evidently dissatisfied with the conditions of affairs here. He says the P.M. never moves until he is forced, and then it is usually too late. He fears we shall not improve matters until we get another leader. He says that at a time like this the P.M. should lead, not follow.

He added that Bonar Law did not take a strong enough line with Asquith, but admitted that his position was difficult because he had no support from members of his own party in the Cabinet.[1]

Lloyd George at this time was feeling intermittently under the weather, as quite often happened during a period when he was anxious and perplexed. He was spending much of his time at Walton Heath. On 11 March Frances Stevenson wrote in her diary:

1. R.W.D., pp. 157–8.

Everyone tells the same tale – that the country is sick of the present Government & loathes & despises Asquith. And yet, now that there is no Opposition, it is very difficult to turn them out. There are signs, however, of a row in the country. The married men say that they have been tricked by the Government, & they say that many of them will refuse to come when they are called. Many people are asking: Why does not Lloyd George make a stand & turn the rotters out? I asked D. this morning why he did not. He replied that it was a very difficult thing to do; that it would immediately be put down to personal motives. 'It would be much easier', he said, 'were I not in the running for the Premiership – if I could point to someone else and say: Put *that* man in Asquith's place. But who is there who would make a fitting Prime Minister? Bonar Law is limp and lifeless; Balfour can never make up his mind about anything. There *is* no one.'[1]

Soon afterwards Asquith went abroad for ten days, visiting Paris for a conference first and then travelling on to Rome. He said that Lloyd George had declined to accompany him 'on various pretexts', but Lloyd George maintained that he was merely asked to join the party in Rome, which seemed to him pointless.[2] In fact he did, after all, attend the conference in Paris, and according to him this was because Albert Thomas came over from Paris specially to entreat him to attend; whereas Hankey was under the impression that Asquith had insisted on his attendance.[3] Whatever the true reason, he found the conference interesting and spoke of it soon afterwards to Riddell:

It was a success – not because anything definite was accomplished, but because of the goodwill engendered. L.G. says, however, that the feeling in France concerning England is not happy. The French think they are making all the sacrifices and we are endeavouring to preserve our trade and carry on as usual. This he thinks may prejudice the alliance. He feels we should make strong efforts which will dispel this feeling.[4]

The most appropriate gesture would be the universalising of

1. F.S.D., p. 102. On 19 March Lloyd George told Riddell that he 'would not be prepared to replace Asquith by Bonar Law'. He thought 'Asquith much superior to B.L. in every way – a much bigger man' (R.W.D., p. 165).
2. H.H.A. to Sylvia Henley, 23 March 1916; F.S.D., 27 March 1916, pp. 104–5.
3. F.S.D., p. 105; Roskill, *Hankey: Man of Secrets*, Vol. I, p. 258.
4. R.W.D., 1 April 1916, p. 168.

compulsory military service, for which the Army was anyway pressing with ever greater urgency. The final crisis on this issue was now impending. For most of the first fortnight of April Lloyd George absented himself from the War Committee on the plea of illness. He was in a brooding state, nerving himself for another showdown. On 14 April he came to the Cabinet 'in a most furious rage' and demanded, with Bonar Law's support, that the Cabinet Committee set up in January – to which he had not been appointed – should clear its findings with the Army Council. This was tantamount, in Hankey's view, to giving the Army the role of arbiter in a dispute to which it was party, and when the Cabinet agreed he felt that the voluntary cause was lost.[1]

Three days later Frances Stevenson recorded:

Things have come to a head over general compulsion . . . the question of men must be settled one way or another, & the Cabinet is divided. D. was the first to take the stand of general compulsion, & it was naturally thought that he would be backed by the Unionists in the Cabinet. They have, however, ratted almost to a man (F. E. Smith being the exception) being afraid of losing office apparently. When this happened D. was torn between inclination & expediency. Fortunately the Army Council took the same view as D., & they are making a firm stand. If Asquith will not accept compulsion wholeheartedly, then they will resign, & D. with them. The doubtful point is whether the Unionists, or which of the Unionists will resign. D. came up to town last night and dined with Bonar Law & he says he has never seen anyone in such a state of abject funk. He (B.L.) does not know which way to turn or what to do. If D. goes out, it is almost impossible for B.L. to stay in without becoming an object of contempt; & yet he is very loth to resign.[2]

On 19 April Asquith had to appear in the House of Commons and admit publicly that the Cabinet was split on the issue of conscription. But behind the scenes the trend was towards acceptance of the inevitable. Next day the Cabinet agreed on another compromise, proposed by Henderson, and Asquith then suggested that both Houses of Parliament should debate the matter in secret session after

1. Roskill, op.cit., p. 264 (quoting Hankey's diary for 14 April 1916).
2. F.S.D., 17 April 1916, pp. 105–6.

Easter. That evening he wrote to Mrs Henley:

> Things have now straightened out, as they generally do, if you give
> them time, & don't strike before the hour. (This, I suppose, is the
> philosophy of 'Wait and See' – that much abused formula.) At any
> rate the Crisis (with the biggest of 'C's) is over. Ll.G. at heel, and
> the rest acquiescent, & even a little more.

But it had, he said, been 'a hellish experience', and he wisely, if rather
contradictorily, added that he was too old a hand to think the trouble
was over.[1]

It was not over, indeed. After the Easter break, which Lloyd George
spent at Criccieth, Parliament met in Secret Session and Asquith
announced the new compromise. The intricacies of this are irrelevant,
because the House of Commons revolted and two days later the
proposals were withdrawn. It was Carson and the Unionist War
Committee who led the revolt, though a number of Liberal compulsionists played their part. On 2 May Asquith introduced a bill making
compulsory service universal, and within a month it was law.
Opposition was negligible. The bill passed its Second Reading
without a division, and on Third Reading only twenty-seven Liberals
and ten Labour M.P.s voted against it. The Irish, to whose country the
measure did not apply, abstained.

Ireland had meanwhile contributed, in a most significant way, to a
national mood more than ever ready for tough measures. If Asquith
needed an extraneous crisis to help him carry his government through
the final conscription crisis, he was certainly provided with one on the
last day of the Easter holiday. Returning to London from the Wharf
(his country house at Sutton Courtenay near Oxford) late at night on
Easter Monday, 24 April – or, to be precise, early in the morning of
the 25th – he was given the first news of the republican rising in
Dublin. With the terse comment (to Hankey, who had driven up with
him), 'Well, that's something,' he went off to bed.[2] Next day he had
the Secret Session.

The gravity of the war situation was further emphasised by the
news which came through on the 29th, that the British troops
besieged at Kut-cl-Amara had been forced to surrender. This was a
serious humiliation, though censorship for a long time concealed the

1. 20 April 1916.
2. Hankey, *The Supreme Command*, p. 475, quoting diary entry for 24 April 1916. For more
about the Easter rising, and its consequences, see next chapter.

appalling sequel – that seventy per cent of the British prisoners died on their way to Baghdad or in captivity. Nor did the public at home know that a million pounds, offered as a bribe to secure the garrison's release, had been spurned by the Turks.[1]

The atmosphere of general crisis helped Asquith to abandon with impunity his commitment to the voluntary system, and to win the support, however grudging, of most Liberal M.P.s for his measure of universal military service. They did not at all like it but felt that it had to be, and in any case knew that if they did not vote for it the Government would fall. The Conservatives, who did like it, did not like Asquith and were annoyed that he had once again managed to hang on to power. But most of them had no clear idea who could or should replace him. He thus emerged from the episode with his reputation badly damaged, but his government and power intact.

Compulsionists rightly gave Lloyd George much of the credit for the triumph of their cause. One of the most important of them gave him the sole credit. On 2 May Sir William Robertson wrote:

> Dear Mr Lloyd George,
>   The Bill introduced today should more than compensate you for the rubbishy Press attacks of the last week or two. The great thing is to get the Bill, and for it the Empire's thanks are due to you – alone.
>   Yours very truly,
>   W. R. Robertson[2]

But he had indeed been subjected to bitter attacks from some outraged Liberals, and the most vitriolic had come from A. G. Gardiner, editor of the *Daily News*, in the form of an open letter appearing in that paper on 22 April, and reprinted the same afternoon in the *Star*. In this he accused Lloyd George of being 'one of the chief architects of the fall of the Liberal Government and of the establishment of the Coalition', and of now engineering the conscription crisis in order to substitute himself for Asquith as leader of the country.

On 6 May Lloyd George replied to his critics, and strongly vindicated his record, in a speech to his constituents at Conway. When he had spoken at Bangor in February 1915, he said, the country had more men than equipment.

---

1. The surrender was negotiated by the maverick Conservative M.P., Aubrey Herbert. (Margaret Fitzherbert, *The Man Who Was Greenmantle*, pp. 178–81.)
2. 2 May 1916 (L.G.P. and quoted in W.M., pp. 733–4).

Therefore I dwelt rather upon munitions at that date. Men were coming in such numbers that we had no equipment for them. . . . Later in the year there was a falling off. The flood tide seemed to have abated. But meanwhile the achievement of the nation in raising by voluntary methods those huge armies was something of which we might very well be proud.

In about August or September, however, it had become obvious that if the war were to be won 'we should have to resort to other methods'. And he stated again the somewhat paradoxical case for compulsion in a free country.

Compulsion and voluntaryism are not inconsistent. In a democratic nation compulsion simply means the will of the majority of the people, the voluntary decision of the majority. Unless you had a majority, and an overwhelming majority, compulsion would have been impossible: so compulsion is simply organised voluntary effort. You must organise effort when a nation is in peril. You cannot run a war as you would run a Sunday school treat, where one man voluntarily brings the buns, another supplies the tea, one brings the kettle, one looks after the boiling, another takes round the tea-cups, some contribute in cash, and a good many lounge about and just make the best of what is going. You cannot run a war like that.

He reminded his audience of the totality of France's war effort, while admitting that Britain's could not be organised in quite the same way.

I do not say that we can make the same contribution in men, in proportion to the population, as France has done. . . . Why? We are supplying France with steel, with coal, with material for explosives. We are supplying other Allies with munitions of war. We are supplying them generally with transport on the seas. In addition to a great Army we have the greatest Navy in the world. Well do our Allies know that, and still better do our foes know that. The number of men engaged in equipping the Navy with munitions is almost as great as the number engaged in France in producing munitions for their Army. We must take all that into account.

With those words he showed that he was mindful of the economic arguments that had been used against conscription, and was prepared to concede them a limited validity, though not at the expense of the principle of a universal obligation to serve.

Every effort had been made to save the voluntary principle by means of the Derby scheme. But that scheme was not really voluntary.

> If you say to a man 'You come down from there: I will give you five minutes and if you don't I shall ask a policeman to fetch you down', would that be voluntary? . . . the Derby campaign had a great many of the disadvantages of compulsion and voluntaryism without the advantages of either. However I do not want to go back upon that.

He had no shame in declaring for compulsory enlistment, 'as I would for compulsory taxes or for compulsory education, or, if you allow me, for compulsory insurance'. In doing so he was as good a Liberal as ever.

Yet he had been 'subjected to a cloudy discharge of poison gas', and in a way he was glad.

> These things had been going on clandestinely and surreptitiously for months, and I could not deal with them. My difficulty was that no self-respecting man or newspaper could be found to give publication to these attacks, and therefore I could not answer them. I am not surprised. We are, after all, a country that has produced millions of fighters, but in history very rarely an assassin. They found one at last, and I am glad of it.

He dealt head-on with the charge of disloyalty to Asquith.

> I have worked with him for ten years. I have served under him for eight years. If we had not worked harmoniously – and we have – let me tell you here at once that it would have been my fault and not his. I have never worked with anyone who could be more considerate, and I disdain the things that they have said. But we have had our differences. Good heavens, of what use would I have been if I had not differed from him? . . . Freedom of speech is essential everywhere, but there is one place where it is vital, and that is in the Council Chamber of the nation. The councillor who professes to agree with everything that falls from his leader betrays him.

Near the end of the speech he made a plea for more effective and combined planning within the Alliance.

> We must have unity amongst the Allies, design and coordination. Unity we undoubtedly possess. . . . Design and coordination leave

yet a good deal to be desired. Strategy must come before geography. The Central Powers are pooling their forces, all their intelligence, all their brains, all their efforts. We have the means; they too often have the methods. Let us apply their methods to our means, and we shall win.

A small but notable figure on the platform while Lloyd George was speaking was W.M. (Billy) Hughes, Prime Minister of Australia, who had spent five years of his boyhood in nearby Llandudno. Afterwards both men addressed the crowd outside in Castle Square, Lloyd George introducing Hughes as 'one of the most distinguished champions of liberty in the Empire', of whom he was proud to be a fellow-countryman. On 18 May the two spoke again at a dinner of the London Cymmrodorion Society at the Trocadero restaurant in London. Robert Graves, home on leave from France, was there with his father.

Hughes was perky, dry, and to the point; Lloyd George was up in the air on one of his 'glory of the Welsh hills' speeches. The power of his rhetoric amazed me. The substance of the speech might be commonplace, idle, and false, but I had to fight hard against abandoning myself with the rest of his audience. He sucked power from his listeners and spurted it back at them. Afterwards, my father introduced me to Lloyd George, and when I looked closely at his eyes they seemed like those of a sleep-walker.[1]

Perhaps, so soon after the strain of making a speech, he was failing to show his usual lively interest in a new acquaintance.

Gardiner's attack did Lloyd George more good than harm. Bonar Law said that the result could not have been more favourable to him if he had paid Gardiner to write what he did. Many years later Addison – by then no longer a Lloyd George adherent, but a leading member of the Labour Party – told Gardiner how mistaken he had been:

I was myself at that time in daily contact with what was going on and had participated, particularly in connection with the crisis over recruiting, on several occasions in conversation with L.G. and others, and the line he was taking and the substance of conversations was quite different from what was suggested in your article; and although I myself have suffered at his hands, I felt then, knowing

1. *Goodbye to All That*, ch. 19. Hughes was to encounter enormous difficulties as a champion of conscription in his own country.

the facts as to the line he was taking, that the article was seriously unjust and on re-reading it today I am still of the same opinion.[1]

Lloyd George never wavered in his belief that conscription had to come when it did, because if it had been delayed any longer we should have been overwhelmed by the vicissitudes of later 1916 and 1917, to say nothing of the ultimate trial of spring 1918. Some have argued, however, that the compulsory system kept more men out of the armed forces than it brought in, and it is certainly true that for the first six months of the fully compulsory system the average monthly enlistment ran at less than half the previous rate. 'Instead of unearthing 650,000 slackers, compulsion produced 748,587 new claims to exemption, most of them valid.[2] Yet the total raised for the forces during the last part of the war, after the change of system, was almost as large as that raised during the early part, when the spontaneous urge to join up was at its height, and when the competing claims of war industry were as yet relatively modest. Since the rate of voluntary recruitment was already in decline in the late summer of 1915, it is scarcely rational to suppose that that system would have been equal to the military and psychological demands of the last two years or so of the war.

To Lloyd George the economic by-products of conscription seemed more important than the direct military consequences, though he welcomed the assistance of the military in getting the measure through and, as we have seen, earned their cordial gratitude for helping them. But above all, in early 1916, he was convinced that conscription was necessary to show allies and enemy alike that Britain's dedication to victory was wholehearted; and therefore also to create in Britain itself a sense of total involvement in the war.

1. Addison to Gardiner, 2 February 1934, quoted in Stephen E. Koss, *Fleet Street Radical*, p. 191.
2. A. J. P. Taylor, *English History 1914–1945*, p. 55.

THIRTEEN
Ireland Again

The next phase of Lloyd George's career was shaped by two tremendous unforeseen events. The first, briefly mentioned in the previous chapter, was the Easter rising in Ireland. This involved him in another attempt to negotiate an Irish settlement, which alas came to grief through errors of his own and through the folly and perversity of colleagues, but which may incidentally have saved his life. The second was the death of Kitchener, when the cruiser *Hampshire* in which he was travelling to Russia hit a mine and sank off the Orkney coast on 5 June. Between these two events the British public had to absorb the shock of another, the battle of Jutland, whose ulterior strategic significance was at first rather less obvious than the fact that the Royal Navy had lost more ships than the enemy. Lloyd George reacted to the news with excitement and some alarm. He was critical of Balfour for not having stronger men around him at the Admiralty, and of Asquith for not calling a meeting of the War Committee to consider the battle's implications.[1] But Jutland was of only momentary concern to him, and in his memoirs he hardly mentions it.

The Easter rising was not a national rebellion like that of 1798. The number of insurgents was very small, and very little happened outside Dublin. To the vast majority of Irishmen in 1916 the enemy was Germany, not Great Britain. About 90,000 Roman Catholic Irishmen were serving in the British army, and attempts by Sir Roger Casement to raise a brigade from Irish prisoners-of-war to fight on the German

1. R.W.D., entry for 3 June 1916, p. 186.

side ended in ludicrous failure. Out of two thousand or more prisoners in Germany only fifty-five responded to his call, and among them barely ten were genuine Irish nationalists. The Germans could see that the loyalty of Irishmen to the British empire compared very favourably with that of Slavs to the Austro-Hungarian.

Casement was an Ulster Protestant with a strangely divided personality. In 1911 he was knighted for his services over many years as a British consular official, and he wrote a fulsome letter to the Foreign Secretary expressing gratitude for the honour. Yet at the same time he was committed to Irish separatism and soon afterwards was implicated in the Howth gun-running. At the outbreak of war he went to America and thence, in November 1914, to Germany. On Good Friday 1916 he was put ashore from a German U-boat in Tralee Bay, Co. Kerry, with a German railway ticket in his pocket, and was arrested by two members of the Royal Irish Constabulary. On the same day a German arms ship, sailing under Norwegian colours, was intercepted in the same area, though the captain managed to scuttle it while being escorted into Queenstown.

The arms that it was carrying were intended for use in the rising, whose chances of physical success, negligible in any case, were made even more so by the loss of the ship. But the man who above all was determined that the rising should take place was indifferent to its physical success. The young schoolmaster Patrick Pearse believed that the blood of martyrs would be the seed of Irish independence, and that the apparent defeat of a rising would be turned to victory through the miracle of blood-sacrifice. He said that 'the old heart of the earth needed to be warmed with the red wine of the battlefields' – a sentiment by no means entirely absent from the general British attitude towards the war, as revealed in many poems and speeches of the time, and as institutionalised later in the Armistice Day cult of sacrifice and atonement. But to Pearse the only battlefield that mattered was Ireland; it was Irish earth that he wished to warm with his blood. He was a fanatical patriot whose obsession with the idea of separating Ireland from England was doubtless intensified by the galling fact that he was English himself on his father's side.

The men whom he was to lead into action on Easter Monday represented a small splinter of the militant Irish Volunteers led by Eoin MacNeill – a former civil servant from Ulster, and co-founder of the Gaelic League – who in turn represented a relatively small splinter of the original pre-war Volunteers. The movement had split when

Redmond gave his support to the war, but out of 188,000 Volunteers only about 13,500 went with MacNeill. They became known as Irish Volunteers, while the main body was known as National Volunteers. MacNeill rejected Redmond's policy of collaboration, but was opposed to the use of force except in circumstances that might offer a good chance of military victory. Since there was manifestly no chance of any such thing at Easter 1916, the rising had to be planned by Pearse and his associates behind MacNeill's back. They were joined in the conspiracy by the labour leader, James Connolly, who on 8 April wrote in the *Workers' Republic*: 'Is it not well that we of the Working Class should fight for the freedom of the Irish nation from foreign rule as the first requisite for the free development of the national power needed for our class?' His tiny Irish Citizen Army, founded in 1913, was to fight alongside the extremist breakaway Volunteers in the Easter rising.

At this stage the political party Sinn Fein ('Ourselves Alone'), which as it turned out was to be the chief beneficiary of the rising, was playing very little part either openly or clandestinely. Fervent republicans regarded it as unsatisfactory because, since 1910, its policy had been to give Redmond a fair chance to obtain Home Rule by his methods, and because its leader, Arthur Griffith, was not a republican but favoured a dual monarchy for the British Isles. Though formerly a member of the Irish Republican Brotherhood, a secret society pledged to achieve its aim by violence, he had left it in 1906. Nine years later its military committee included Pearse, and it was planning armed insurrection.

The arrest of Casement and the interception of the German arms ship provided a good enough excuse for detaining known extremists, and under pressure from the Viceroy, Lord Wimborne, the permanent under-secretary, Sir Matthew Nathan, agreed on Easter Sunday morning that a number of key figures should be pulled in. Had this step been taken the rising would never have occurred, and the future course of Irish history might conceivably have been very different. But Nathan felt that he could not act without authority from the responsible Cabinet minister, the Chief Secretary for Ireland, Augustine Birrell. And Birrell had to be consulted by telegraph, because he was in London.

An alert and dynamic minister would surely have returned to Dublin after hearing of the events of Good Friday. But Birrell was not a minister of that sort. He was, as already noted, an easy-going man of letters, temperamentally unfitted for decisive action. When the Coalition was formed he had made some show of trying to be released from his office, but Asquith was fond of him and persuaded him, most unfortunately, to stay on. A few days before the crisis in Ireland he told a journalist that he looked forward to his retirement from politics. 'Doing is death,' he said. 'Dreaming is the real thing!'[1] In the circumstances he could hardly have been more wrong; his inertia was to mean death for a lot of people. Instead of hurrying to Dublin when he heard about Casement and the German ship, he remained in London reading, apparently, a book 'about the Chevalier de Boufflers and his enchanting lady-mistress and wife'.[2] Nathan compounded the delay by sending his cipher telegram so late that it did not reach Birrell until Monday morning. By the time Birrell's reply reached Dublin Castle the rising had already begun.

Indeed the Castle itself had been attacked by a detachment of Connolly's Citizen Army, and if the attackers had realised how weak its defences were at the time the nerve-centre of Irish administration would have been captured. But they missed their opportunity and retreated to some buildings opposite. While this was happening another group of rebels occupied the Four Courts; yet another under the mathematics professor, Eamon de Valera, took possession of Boland's Flour Mills on the road to Kingstown; and a group including the flamboyant Countess Markiewicz (Constance Gore-Booth) established itself on St Stephen's Green until forced back into the building of the College of Surgeons.

But the most important act in the drama was the seizing of the General Post Office in O'Connell Street (then Sackville Street) in the heart of the city. Two flags were hoisted over it – the green flag with golden harp and the new tricolour of orange, white and green – and from its steps the Irish Republic was proclaimed by Pearse. Robert Kee describes this scene with a fine sense of all the attendant ironies and contradictions:

> ... amazed bystanders saw Patrick Pearse emerge on to the steps of the portico and read a proclamation from 'the Provisional Government'. This stated that in the name of God and of the dead generations, from which Ireland 'received her ancient tradition of

1. The remark was reportedly made to Sir William Robertson Nicoll, editor of *The British Weekly* (R.W.D., 16 April 1916, p. 174.)

2. Birrell to Nathan, 22 April 1916, quoted in Leon O'Broin, *The Chief Secretary*, p. 170.

nationhood', she was summoning her children to her flag and striking for her freedom. The proclamation spoke of the long usurpation of Ireland's right to control her own destinies by 'a foreign people and government', and stated most inaccurately that in every generation the Irish people had asserted their right to national freedom and sovereignty. . . . It referred to 'gallant Allies in Europe' who were supporting Ireland, thereby blandly dismissing the fact that the flower of Ireland's manhood had been fighting those allies in Europe for the past twenty months. Indeed, almost within the hour Irish men of the 3rd Royal Irish Rifles and the 10th Royal Dublin Fusiliers, themselves the product of the most recent British Army recruiting drive in Ireland, were the first to move against this self-styled republic in the Post Office. Small wonder that Pearse's words fell among a largely uninterested crowd and that the principal sounds to greet them were not cheers but the crash of breaking glass as a Dublin mob, taking advantage of the absence of the police, began to loot the fashionable shops in O'Connell Street.[1]

By the following Sunday, 30 April, it was all over. To the relief of the population all the rebel groups had surrendered and order had been restored. Apart from the rising in Dublin there had been very few incidents; the country as a whole was peaceful. Among the fifteen hundred Dublin rebels only sixty-four were killed and about two hundred wounded, including Connolly whose ankle was shattered by a bullet during the Post Office siege. Casualties among the forces of the Crown were heavier: 134 killed and 381 wounded. But those who suffered worst, numerically, were the civilians, of whom at least 220 were killed and six hundred wounded, though precise figures were never ascertained. Yet it was not the fate of rank-and-file rebels, of soldiers or policemen, or of ordinary people caught in the crossfire, that was to matter historically, but rather the subsequent fate of the brave but crazy ideologues who had launched the escapade. Between the 3rd and the 12th of May fifteen of the rebel leaders were condemned by court martial and shot, among them Connolly and Pearse, and their deaths signalled the birth of Yeats's 'terrible beauty'.

It is easy to say, with hindsight, that there should have been no executions, and even at the time a few people took this view. But they were few indeed, and even so devout an Irish patriot as Dillon seems, at first, to have assumed that the leaders would have to be shot.

1. *The Green Flag*, p. 549.

Writing from Dublin to Redmond in London on 30 April, Dillon said:

> You should urge on the government the *extreme* unwisdom of any
> wholesale shootings of prisoners. The wisest course is to execute *no
> one* for the present. This is *the most urgent* matter for the moment. If
> there were shootings of prisoners on a large scale the effect on public
> opinion might be disastrous in the extreme. . . . I have no doubt if
> any of the well-known leaders are taken alive they will be shot. But,
> except the leaders, there should be no court-martial executions.[1]

This is a rather muddled letter, though in the circumstances some
confusion of thought was only natural. But it is surely clear that even
Dillon, despite the near-Fenianism of his youth, by implication
admitted that the leaders might deserve to die. His plea was that the
death penalty should be confined to them, and that even against them
it should not be applied too hastily.

In fact it was not the haste of the executions that caused the revulsion
of popular feeling, but rather the piecemeal and seemingly random
way in which they were carried out. Over a period of nine days men
were shot singly or in batches of two, three or four. One of the last was
Connolly, who had to be shot sitting in a chair, because of his injury.
A number of leading rebels were not executed, while some who were
not leaders were. For instance de Valera's death sentence was com-
muted, whereas Pearse's brother was shot, for no obvious reason
other than that he *was* Pearse's brother. A similar capriciousness
marked the penal treatment of others rounded up after the rising.
About 3,000 people were arrested, and more than half of these were
either detained in a special camp in Wales or given prison sentences.
MacNeill received a life sentence and was sent to Dartmoor, though
he had known nothing about the rising and would have opposed it if
he had. He thus was treated with as much severity as Countess
Markiewicz, and there were many comparable injustices.

What made the penal measures more odious in Irish eyes was that
they were inflicted by a military regime. Immediately after the rising a
vacuum was created in the civilian government of the country. Birrell
and Nathan resigned; Wimborne was temporarily recalled. To fill the
vacuum a new commander-in-chief, Sir John Maxwell, was sent to
Ireland with instructions to rule the country under martial law.
Maxwell arrived at the end of Easter week, and it was on his authority

1. Quoted in F. S. L. Lyons, *John Dillon*, p. 373.

that the summary trials and executions took place. He was an old friend of Kitchener, who had appointed him governor of Omdurman after the battle there and had later found him a useful subordinate in South Africa. Most of Maxwell's career had been in Egypt, and his previous experience of Ireland amounted to less than two years (in 1902–4). Though quite a sensible man according to his lights, he had neither the knowledge nor the intuition required for a task which called for a superabundance of both.

To him the issue was straightforward. At a time of national emergency and peril, when major operations were impending on the Western front, a treacherous blow had been struck by subversive elements in league with the foreign enemy. Loyal and innocent lives had been lost, military resources diverted and much damage done. Why, then, should any mercy be shown to the guilty? He could hardly have been expected to understand that the course on which he was embarking was likely to do far more harm than the rising itself, and to turn into holy Irish martyrs leaders who, till then, had incurred mainly indignation and obloquy from their compatriots. Possibly he should have realised that to try them by court martial, and to execute them by firing squad rather than by hanging, was to confer upon them the status of genuine warriors, and therefore to give the impression that he was killing prisoners-of-war. But however they had died, so long as it was at the hands of the British, the result would have been much the same.

Pearse had correctly judged the effect of his wild gamble. His willingness to die, and the failure of the British to let him live, brought posthumous victory to him and his cause. The other provocative features of the military regime were incidental. To a nation deeply indoctrinated with the concept of redemption through blood-sacrifice the death of the fifteen leaders was transforming, ennobling, inspiring. Maxwell handed them crowns of glory that they could never otherwise have won.

Meanwhile the politicians in London, troubled by the news from Ireland but also preoccupied with the Conscription crisis, were slow to recognise the dangerous implications of what the military were doing in Dublin. On 3 May Redmond urged Asquith to stop the executions, but it was not until five days later that the Prime Minister sent Maxwell a telegram expressing the hope – he did not give an order – that they should cease, unless the cases were quite exceptional. This qualification sealed the fate of three more rebels, including Connolly.

On the 12th Asquith arrived in Dublin to assess the situation for himself and to provide that element of civilian control which had been lacking for nearly a fortnight. Thereafter there were no more executions. The Prime Minister stayed in Ireland for nearly a week and looked into many aspects of the government there with his usual quick and masterful intelligence. He did not spend all his time in Dublin, but visited Cork and Belfast as well. When he returned to London he was convinced that there needed to be a new approach to the Irish problem which should be put in hand at once. It was urgently necessary both to strengthen the shaky position of the Redmondites in Ireland and to prevent the spread of anti-British feeling in America.

The obvious arrangement was to appoint a new Chief Secretary with the task of making the new approach, and Asquith began by thinking on this line. But various candidates for the job were, on reflection, discarded as unsuitable. His first preference was for Lord Robert Cecil, who had been under-secretary at the Foreign Office since the Coalition was formed, and who had recently joined the Cabinet with the additional title Minister of Blockade. But Redmond insisted that only a Liberal could be appointed to the post and Asquith at this stage felt obliged to defer to him (though in the end, when Redmond was estranged, a Conservative *was* appointed). Among Liberals the Prime Minister first considered Montagu, but was dissuaded by Montagu's own lengthy arguments against the idea. Other names that came up were those of Runciman, McKinnon Wood and Whitley (the Deputy Speaker). But in the end Asquith turned to Lloyd George.

The initial suggestion that he should be Chief Secretary was abandoned in favour of a temporary assignment which would not involve any change of office on his part, or any appointment of a Chief Secretary for the time being. In 22 May Asquith wrote:

> My dear Lloyd George,
>
> I hope you may see your way to take up Ireland; at any rate for a short time. It is a *unique* opportunity and there is no one else who could do so much to bring about a permanent solution.
>
> Yours very sincerely,
> H. H. Asquith

For three weeks or so Lloyd George had been toying with the idea of a trip to Russia to discover at first hand the state of munitions supply there, and when it was decided that Kitchener would be going anyway there remained a good chance that the two ministers would go together – which they might, indeed, have done in the most fundamental sense but for Asquith's proposal. Lloyd George agreed, however, to try again for an Irish settlement, and on 25 May the Prime Minister announced in the House of Commons that he would be doing so at the unanimous request of all his colleagues in the Government. As he walked out of the House he was given a great ovation, and Arthur Lee asked him 'if he thought he was going to bring it off'. 'You know,' he replied, 'I am that kind of beggar. I always do think beforehand that I am going to bring things off.'[1]

His attitude towards the task, and the way he intended to go about it, were further revealed two days later in conversation with Riddell:

> I [Riddell] said, alluding to his appointment to endeavour to settle the Irish question, 'This is a great triumph for you, but the P.M. has side-tracked himself. His visit to Ireland was a great idea, and everyone wondered what he had brought back in his bag. It now appears that the bag contained nothing but a few relics of the rebellion.'
>
> L.G.: 'He brought back absolutely nothing. He had no plan and he funked the task of endeavouring to make a settlement. They all funked it.'
>
> L.G. spoke highly of Redmond, who, he said, had many of Asquith's qualities, which would have secured him a high position in this country had it not been for his faithful adherence to the Irish cause. . . . I inquired whether L.G. would hold a formal conference in connection with the Irish settlement. He replied in the negative, and said that if the conference were once to break down it would be difficult, if not impossible, to re-establish it. He intends to carry on the negotiations by personal interviews, and said that he had already seen most of the principal actors in the drama.
>
> We reverted to Asquith's position. I said, 'This appointment gives you the reversion of the Premiership. Mr A. and the Cabinet have admitted your position.'
>
> L.G.: 'Yes, if I pull it off, it will be a big thing. They have appointed me because I have certain qualities necessary for the task, but perhaps there were other motives which led them to

COMING TO GRIPS WITH THE WAR 177

36,000 in two months rallying to the flag! It is a great story.[1]

Lloyd George's determination that military units composed of Welshmen should have a suitably Cymric character led to his first brushes with Kitchener. There was a preliminary row about Nonconformist chaplains in the army, Lloyd George maintaining that they should be allowed to go to the front along with chaplains of the Established Church, and pointing out that Sikh and Gurkha troops had priests of their own faith. Despite initial resistance, Kitchener soon gave way on this issue.[2] But he was harder to budge on the creation of specifically Welsh units, and on permission for Welsh soldiers to speak the vernacular on parade or in their billets. These matters became the subject of what Asquith described as 'a royal row' between Lloyd George and Kitchener, during which Lloyd George told the Field Marshal that he was only one member of the Cabinet and must stand criticism like the rest.[3] The result was a further climbdown by Kitchener, and his agreement that an all-Welsh army corps should be raised.

The task was not so easy as Lloyd George's euphoria at Cardiff may have suggested. Of those so far recruited in Wales many had been sent to reinforce the three existing Welsh regiments – the Royal Welsh Fusiliers, the South Wales Borderers and the Welsh Regiment, which consisted of two battalions each and were already in action abroad – while many had joined a variety of other units, not specifically Welsh. A further difficulty was that the relatively short stature of Welshmen caused many to be disqualified by the Army's minimum height requirement. But when this was reduced for their benefit to 5ft 3ins (or 5ft for special 'bantam' battalions) the numbers began to flow in again. By the end of the year an all-Welsh division, the 38th, had been formed, but with mounting casualties and the general demand for reserves it proved impossible to make up one all-Welsh corps, let

1. 29 September 1914. Asquith spoke in Cardiff a few days after Lloyd George and wrote to Venetia Stanley: ' . . . we had all the appropriate humours & accompaniments of a Welsh meeting – "Land of my Fathers", "Men of Harlech" . . . cheers for Lloyd George, cries of "Clwch" (if that is the way to spell it) xc xc . . . happily we were spared the usual speech or speeches in the vernacular.' (V.S.L., p. 260.) Sir Ivor Herbert was Liberal M.P. for Monmouth, and Lord Lieutenant of the county.
2. F.S.D., pp. 3–4. Kitchener had been attracted in his youth to High Church ritualism, so it is hardly surprising that he had a distaste for Nonconformity.
3. V.S.L., p. 291, and F.S.D., p. 7, corroborated by Hobhouse, *op. cit.*, pp. 203–4. Asquith wrote: 'K. is much the most to blame: he was clumsy & noisy: he has spent so much of his life in an Oriental atmosphere, that he cannot acclimatise himself to English conditions.'

alone two. All the same by March 1915 80,000 Welshmen had volunteered for the armed forces, and Lloyd George was able to claim, at the National Eisteddfod on St David's Day, that Wales was then contributing more in relation to its population than any other part of the United Kingdom.[1]

Far more serious than quarrels over the rights and status of Welsh soldiers, which caused no permanent ill-will between Lloyd George and Kitchener, were the differences that began to develop over the war itself, and more especially over the supply of munitions for the army. Once he became aware that the country faced a long struggle, Lloyd George started to give his mind to every aspect of it, without regard to departmental boundaries or the supposed unfitness of civilians to meddle in Service matters. During September the battle of the Marne had saved Paris and frustrated the original German plan of campaign. By the end of the month the spotlight had shifted from France to Flanders, where the Germans were preparing to reduce the Allied position at Antwerp and thereafter, they hoped, to seize the Channel ports. This they had mercifully failed to do when the ports had been theirs for the taking at the time of the precipitate Allied retreat in August. In early October Antwerp fell, but the Belgian army fell back along the Channel coast, while the B.E.F., transferred northwards from the Aisne, was deployed between La Bassée and Ypres.

Lloyd George had already sensed that the war in the West was about to enter a new phase, in which movement and manoeuvre would give way to fixed lines. In his speech at Cardiff he had referred prophetically to 'cold nights in the trenches'. At about the same time he became convinced that the War Office was not equal to the task of providing or procuring arms in sufficient quantities for the enormous army that was being raised. He therefore suggested that a Cabinet committee should be appointed to look into the question. Kitchener was resentful of this idea, and at first his opposition prevented its being acted on. But Asquith's own anxiety about munitions soon overcame his reluctance

---

1. By the end of the War 280,000 Welshmen had served in the forces, or 13.82 of the male population – a higher percentage than for England or Scotland, and substantially higher than for Ireland. (Kenneth O. Morgan, *Rebirth of a Nation: Wales 1880–1980*, p. 160.) Wales provided twenty-five infantry battalions for Kitchener's armies, as well as Territorial battalions, and many Welshmen served in other units, including the various technical corps. Wales's enhanced military standing, much due to Lloyd George, was further enhanced when, in early 1915, the Welsh Guards were created as the fifth regiment of Foot Guards. (Incidentally, the spelling 'Welch' was not commonly used for the R.W.F. and the Welsh Regiment during the Great War.)

to defy the Field Marshal, and on 12 October he set up a munitions committee of the Cabinet, ostensibly to help the War Office on the supply side. Kitchener himself was to preside over the committee, but its members were to include Lloyd George, Churchill and Haldane.[1]

After the committee's first two meetings, on the 12th and 13th, Lloyd George decided to go at once to France. His membership of the committee gave him the pretext that he would ask about the French system of war production, though in fact he wanted to discover all he could about the general state of the war. The decision to go seems to have been entirely his own. There is no evidence that Asquith had anything to do with it, though presumably he gave his approval. Until then the only Cabinet ministers who had crossed the Channel since the outbreak of war were Kitchener and Churchill, the two heads of Service departments. Kitchener had travelled to Paris at the beginning of September to steady Sir John French, who was then in headlong retreat from Mons and threatening to pull the B.E.F. out of the line altogether. Churchill, more recently, had gone to Antwerp to supervise and inspire the defence of that city. Though Lloyd George was soon talking sarcastically about Churchill's performance there, we may be sure that he was also rather envious, and that the First Lord's example contributed to his desire to visit the war zone himself. Above all, since he was now determined to take a hand in running the war, he needed all the first-hand information he could obtain.

He took with him to France Lord Reading and the Attorney-General, Sir John Simon. Reading was an obvious choice, but the reasons for taking Simon are less clear. The Attorney had only with difficulty been dissuaded from resigning when the Cabinet was deciding to go to war, and he was much closer to Asquith than to Lloyd George. But these very facts may account, paradoxically, for his inclusion in the party. Lloyd George may have seen advantages in involving him more fully in the war, and in travelling with a colleague who might, on their return, help to exert pressure on the Prime Minister for more effective action.

The party crossed from Newhaven to Dieppe during the night of 16–17 October in a destroyer quaintly (but not perhaps inappropriately) named the *Flirt*. From Dieppe they were driven to Paris through towns which had been in the line of the German advance, and when

1. The other members were Runciman, McKenna and Lucas (President of the Board of Agriculture).

they arrived in the capital they found it empty-looking and grim. Most of its young men were at the front, while the politicians apart from Clemenceau and Briand were still at Bordeaux, whither they had fled when Paris seemed likely to fall.[1] Next morning, Sunday, the visitors had a meeting with General Deville, inventor of the famous 75-mm gun, who was accompanied by Captain Cambefort, a fluent English-speaker and, in normal times, a captain of industry. Deville was authorised by the French Government to tell Lloyd George anything he wanted to know about the French system of arms manufacture, and during an hour and a half many questions were asked and answered. At lunch, when the party was joined by Briand, Lloyd George asked him if there was any danger of a peace party forming in France if, as many expected, the Germans were soon driven out of the country. Briand replied that there was no such danger: 'We shall go through to the end.' Another distinguished Frenchman seen that day in Paris was the military governor, General Galliéni, without whose initiative the Marne victory would probably not have been won.

Early on Monday morning the British party drove to Amiens, where German Uhlans had been only a month before, but which was now the headquarters of a French army commanded by General de Castelnau. On the way they passed through Montdidier, which had just had an air raid. Lloyd George found bomb fragments there 'hardly cold' and heard, for the first time in his life, 'the crack of shells fired with murderous intent against human beings': an experience which, on his own admission, made him shudder. Castelnau took him up to the front line within 1,500 yards of the enemy, and during the day he also met, among others, General de Maudhuy, another army commander, and General Foch, deputy to the commander-in-chief, General Joffre. After leaving the French generals the visitors looked in at B.E.F. Headquarters at St Omer, but Sir John French was not there; he had been called away because there was fighting on the British front. This was the beginning of the first battle of Ypres, in which over

1. Georges Clemenceau was the outstanding Radical veteran of the Third Republic, who had been a deputy since 1875 and prime minister from 1906 to 1909. In 1914 he was already well into his seventies, but as formidable as ever and a scourge of the weak-kneed. Aristide Briand, twenty years his junior, was an ex-Socialist who shared with Lloyd George a Celtic background (he was a Breton), extraordinary eloquence and a gift for negotiation. At the end of August, when Viviani had broadened his government to give it a more national character, Briand had joined it as Minister of Justice. But Clemenceau had stayed out; for him, it was leadership or nothing.

While the attempt at a solution in 1916 was foundering, the last grim episode resulting from the Easter rising was taking its course. On 29 June Roger Casement was convicted of high treason, and on 3 August was hanged at Pentonville. There could be no doubt of his guilt. Even though he had been opposed to a rising at the time, and had come to Ireland in the hope of preventing it, he had clearly given comfort to the King's enemies by what he had done, or tried to do, in Germany. The Cabinet was aware of the baleful effect his execution was likely to have in Ireland and America, but decided all the same, in the absence of medical evidence of insanity, that he would have to die. He thus became the last of the Easter martyrs and so contributed posthumously to the eventual triumph of Irish separatism.

FOURTEEN
Responsibility Without Power

Lloyd George's disinclination to resign on the Irish issue was due largely to his feeling that the war took precedence over all other issues, but also, more specifically, to the vacancy at the War Office which the death of Kitchener had caused. Asquith was in no hurry to fill the post. Once again he assumed temporary responsibility for it himself, and would probably have liked to retain it permanently, as he had reason to believe the Army Council, also, would have liked him to do. But when he had proposed this arrangement in November 1915 Bonar Law, after first agreeing to it, had after a night's sleep objected to it in the strongest terms; and there could be little doubt that he would object to it equally strongly again. On the earlier occasion Kitchener had been sent to the Near East and Asquith had taken charge of the War Office on a temporary basis, though in the private hope that Kitchener's absence might be indefinitely prolonged. But no such compromise was possible now, because Kitchener was dead and the post which he had held, however nominally in recent months, vacant.

Law himself was an obvious candidate for the post. As leader of the Conservative Party he had claims to an office more central in the work of a wartime coalition than that of Colonial Secretary. But Asquith hesitated to offer him the War Office, and one good reason for hesitating was that Lloyd George would naturally expect the post to be offered to him. Yet Asquith was far from enthusiastic about the idea of Lloyd George as War Minister. If he could not take the job himself, he would have preferred it to go to someone who would be no political threat, who could not be regarded by the public as prime-minister-in-waiting, and who could be relied on to work harmoniously with the soldiers. So he let a week pass without reaching any decision.

Meanwhile Lloyd George and Law met to discuss the matter, and the upshot of their meeting was that Law pledged himself to support Lloyd George's claims to the War Office and went straight to Asquith to press those claims. Asquith, taken by surprise, at first made a rather perfunctory offer of the job to Law, but then, when Law refused, agreed to offer it to Lloyd George.[1] But that did not dispose of the problem, because Lloyd George at first insisted, with Law's backing, that if he were to become War Minister the special powers conferred upon Robertson as C.I.G.S. would have to be withdrawn. The War Office was not, as things stood, a very attractive proposition to anyone succeeding Kitchener, except as a symbol of military control. Much of its power had been wrested from it by Lloyd George himself, and the Secretary of State had been reduced, by the elevation of Robertson, to little more than a figurehead. Lloyd George was probably quite sincere in offering Law 'his unqualified support' for the job, as he did when they met, because it was one in which there would be little scope for creative action, yet one which it would be dangerous to leave open to a 'satellite of Asquith or a weak man agreeable to the soldiers'.[2] But Law wisely declined and handed the poisoned, or empty, chalice back to Lloyd George.

It took him some time to decide whether or not to accept it. He thought very seriously of resigning, though not – as would have been most fitting – on the Irish issue. He was tempted to follow Carson's example in resigning on the general issue of war direction, though he also at one point wrote to Asquith raising as an 'insuperable' difficulty the question of votes for soldiers, on which acceptance of the War Office might 'fetter' his action.[3] But the real difficulty concerned his powers. Friends whom he consulted, including Carson, almost

---

1. The meeting between Law and Lloyd George was at Sir Max Aitken's country house – Cherkley, near Leatherhead – on Sunday, 11 June. The following morning Law drove with Aitken to see Asquith at the Wharf. (Aitken stayed outside in the car while the two leaders talked.) The story that Law found Asquith 'engaged in a rubber of bridge with three ladies' was told by Beaverbrook (Aitken) much later to Robert Blake, who reproduced it in his life of Law (p. 289) and so incurred the wrath of Lady Violet Bonham Carter. The story does not appear in Beaverbrook's *Politicians and the War*.

2. Beaverbrook, *op. cit.*, p. 208.

3. D.L.G. to H.H.A., 17 June 1916. There was disagreement in the Cabinet about extending the vote to men in the Services, who would not have it under the existing electoral system. Lloyd George naturally strongly favoured their having it.

unanimously advised him to take the job, though their advice differed as to how he could best set about regulating the position *vis-à-vis* Robertson. Some argued that he should have the Order-in-Council giving the C.I.G.S. his special powers rescinded, while others felt that that would mean too much loss of face for the General and that the authority of the Secretary of State should be asserted by more diplomatic means. Meanwhile not only the *Morning Post*, but the Liberal *Daily Chronicle*, came out with leaders demanding that there should be no change in the balance of power at the War Office. The *Chronicle* article particularly annoyed Lloyd George, because he felt that it weakened his negotiating hand.[1] But even without such interventions it would have been hard for a civilian minister to force Robertson to disclaim, explicitly and formally, powers that had been conceded to him by Kitchener.

In the end Lloyd George accepted the War Secretaryship without any formal alteration to the role of the C.I.G.S. as defined by Order-in-Council. There was an exchange of letters, but this was as much to save Lloyd George's face as Robertson's, and had no practical effect. Lloyd George fancied that he would be able to get his way with the General, who only recently had written to him so flatteringly about his contribution to the enactment of compulsory military service. In Lloyd George's view Robertson was a sound but slow-thinking man, for whose deficiencies in argument he would be able to compensate at international meetings, and whose gratitude and trust he would thus come to win. He was soon to discover that this was an illusion.

But it was true that the mere fact of being War Minister gave him a new prestige, at home and abroad, which his enemies would have been glad to deny him. Shortly before he decided, at last, to accept the post, the influential Unionist author, F. S. Oliver, wrote to his brother in Canada:

The Unionist leaders didn't mind in the least if they destroyed Carson by taking away the confidence of his followers in him. They would be delighted to destroy Redmond, Dillon and Devlin by the same means, but what would delight them most of all would be if they could destroy Lloyd George, whom they fear and detest because, for all purposes of waging war, he is immeasurably their

1. In March 1915 the same newspaper had incensed Lloyd George, and caused a blistering row between him and McKenna, with an article suggesting that he was intriguing against Asquith. The editor, Robert Donald, had been on friendly terms with Lloyd George for years, but was also a confidant of McKenna.

From the *Western Mail*, July 1916

superior in spirit, courage, eloquence and resourcefulness. Moreover, there is a prospect (which I sincerely hope will be fulfilled) of Lloyd George becoming the most important man in the Government (the Prime Minister *not* excepted). If he succeeds Kitchener at the War Office . . . he must, by virtue of his powers and his character taken together, have by far greater influence in the conduct of the war than any member of the Cabinet. This the Unionists are most anxious to prevent, not only on patriotic, but upon still nobler personal grounds.[1]

These comments illustrate the link between the Irish issue and the War Office vacancy, and help at least to explain Lloyd George's decision

1. *The Anvil of War*, pp. 152–3 (part of letter dated 22 June 1916). Oliver was most unusual in being an intellectual who was also a successful businessman (he ran Debenham and Freebody). In politics he was a disciple of Joseph Chamberlain and a member of Milner's Round Table group. His widely read book, *Ordeal by Battle*, published in 1915, was a critical study of the conduct of the war in its first phase. Until 1915 he was anything but an admirer of Lloyd George, but his attitude was transformed above all by Lloyd George's performance at the Ministry of Munitions and by his stand on conscription.

not to resign from the Government, but rather to stay on, as War Minister.

The appointment was announced on 6 July, more than a week after he had made up his mind to accept. On the same day Margot Asquith wrote a much-quoted entry in her diary: 'We are out: it can only be a question of time now when we shall have to leave Downing Street.' There was, in fact, no inevitability about this at all, and Margot's prophecy was to a degree self-fulfilling in that she was to play (as we shall see) her own characteristic part in Asquith's loss of the premiership. In accepting the War Office Lloyd George was taking another big gamble, which might well have gone against him. Certainly he was now, in the public eye, more closely associated with the conduct of the war, but this was hardly an unmixed blessing. If the war continued to go badly – on the most optimistic view, a strong possibility – it would be far more difficult for him to avoid the blame as War Minister than as Chancellor of the Exchequer or Minister of Munitions. Yet his actual control over war policy and strategy, despite what Oliver wrote, would be little more than it had been before. He had the appearance of being in charge of the army and its activities, but without much of the reality: a most dangerous and equivocal position.

Whereas at Munitions he had been able to insist upon the under-secretary he wanted, at the War Office he had to abandon his own candidate, Arthur Lee, and to accept instead the soldiers' pet, Derby, who was also a favourite of the King. (Derby was offered, along with the under-secretaryship, a seat in the Cabinet, which would have further threatened Lloyd George's authority. But he wisely declined it.) As well as Robertson in the top professional post, Lloyd George inherited as his chief civilian adviser Sir Reginald Brade, who had been an official in the War Office since 1884, and its permanent secretary since 1914; whereas at Munitions Llewellyn Smith was his own choice. But he never had any cause to complain of Brade, who had already shown flexibility and common sense over the transfer of functions from War Office to Munitions, and who believed as a matter of principle that a department should be run by its political head. Beaverbrook later wrote of him: 'He is the essence of diplomacy, and possesses an extraordinarily sound judgment of men and things. . . . He played a far greater part in the conduct of the war than he will ever get credit for. . . . He could not be promoted because he could not be spared.'[1]

Lloyd George's private office moved with him. J. T. Davies, Frances Stevenson and William Sutherland continued in their previous functions, and he was able to bring Lee, if not as political under-secretary, at least as a personal aide with the title military secretary: a role which Lee found frustrating.[2] Lloyd George also had as his P.P.S. another politician with experience of soldiering in France: Colonel David Davies, Welsh millionaire, industrialist and philanthropist. But for the rest he had to deal with an institution as different as possible from the one he was leaving. Instead of a department that was new and created by himself, he had to contend once again with an institution encrusted with tradition, and worse still with an established warrior caste. No wonder he was uncomfortable there from the first.

The day his appointment was announced Asquith wrote to him:

My dear Lloyd George,

I took farewell of the War Office this evening, with much regret on my side, & I think with corresponding feelings on theirs.

They are prepared to welcome you as their Chief, and to work cordially with you, and I wish you with all my heart all success.

It is, I need not say, all-important to work intimately with the soldiers. The C.I.G.S., Robertson, you know well; he is quite first rate.

The A[djutant] G[eneral], Macready, who deals with all questions of personnel & discipline, is in his own way equally good. . . .

The Q[uarter] M[aster] G[eneral], Cowans, is one of the great successes of the War. Perhaps a little lavish, but nothing has ever been wanting in his department.

Brade, the Sec to the Army Council, is the best type of Civil Servant, and never loses his head.

I was at the W.O. when the War began; I went there again after 12 months & more of K. in Nov 1915; and I have now been there again for a month. The development is immeasurable, and – apart from

---

1. Beaverbrook, *Politicians and the War*, pp. 326–7. One sign of Brade's diplomatic flair is that he made himself agreeable to the Prime Minister's friend, Sylvia Henley. In a letter to her dated 17 August 1915 Asquith refers to 'your friend Sir R. Brade of the W.O. whom one rarely meets in the world'.

Another inheritance from Kitchener was a Rolls Royce which Lloyd George kept until the end of his life.

2. He was also made K.C.B., but in the *civil* division of the order so as not to give offence to senior officers.

matters of detail, in which there is much room for improvement, and from the need for a firm & decisive general control – I believe that there are all the requisites of a fine fighting machine.

They have to be managed, as well as driven, but I am confident that you will establish with them the best relations.

You will find Derby *persona gratissima* to them, and (to use the old language of the Bar) the best of 'Devils'.

Yours very sincerely,

H. H. Asquith[1]

The message could hardly have been clearer: the War Office and General Staff were, in the Prime Minister's view, more or less all right as they stood, and the new Secretary of State needed to concern himself only with detailed improvements, general oversight of the machine, and above all tactful handling of the soldiers.

Lloyd George's successor as Minister of Munitions was Edwin Montagu, though he had put in a good word for Churchill (still, however, a political leper), and Asquith had considered Curzon. In appointing a Liberal Asquith tilted the balance of key posts still further in favour of his party, since Lloyd George replaced the supposedly Conservative Kitchener. Two of the three departmental offices most directly bearing upon the war were now in Liberal hands, in addition to the Exchequer, the Home Office, the Lord Chancellorship and, of course, the premiership itself. Asquith's only concession to the Conservatives was to appoint one of them, H. E. Duke, to the Irish Secretaryship, nearly three months after Birrell's resignation.[2]

Lloyd George and Montagu paid each other glowing compliments as they exchanged offices, but were soon at loggerheads. On 19 July Montagu wrote:

> . . . I hear that Lee came over to Armament Buildings yesterday and saw some of our people and said he was to act as 'liaison officer' between our two offices.
>
> Forgive me for saying I don't much like this. I will prove myself eager to assist you in every way I can and if Lee likes to come and see me on your behalf I will gladly get for you all you want.
>
> Further if you want information from any of my men, I will send it to you or get the man you want to come and see you.

1. 6 July 1916 (L.G.P.).

2. 31 July 1916. When Simon resigned as Home Secretary in January on the conscription issue, he was succeeded by Sir Herbert Samuel, another Liberal.

But don't we know one another well enough and see one another often enough to dispense with a liaison officer – usually wanted for the estranged or those who speak different languages?

If you want one by all means have one but do send him to *me*. There will be no delay but I must give instructions to my own officers.

Lloyd George's reply, written the same day, put Montagu firmly in his place:

. . . pardon a little frankness. No one wishes to interfere between you and your officers. But Ministers must not be too touchy in these days. All the business between their departments cannot be transacted between their High Mightinesses. Their subordinates must be permitted to discuss matters of common interest. When I was Minister of Munitions my subordinates constantly had direct dealings with the War Office magnates. Both K. and I encouraged it. We thought the service of the State more important than our own amour propre. There are hundreds of matters every week where direct intercourse is essential. I beg of you not to make things impossible by laying down principles which are incapable of being worked out under present conditions.

Believe me I have no desire to interfere with your officers. I have never done it with any Department I ever left, so pray be at rest on that score.

Though the suggestion that his relations with Kitchener provided a model of inter-departmental cooperation might have tempted Montagu into a little gentle sarcasm, he evidently felt it would be unwise to offer more than token further resistance. For next day he wrote:

My dear Creator and Creator of my Office,

Surely you are not going to accuse me of high mightiness – I who spend all my life in trembling before the mighty!

Surely you know that everybody in this office civilian or soldier male or female from the Minister to the latest joined youngest and most dewy messenger girl are at your service (properly speaking).

You are a jumper, I am a walker, your impetus which has alone made possible your glorious achievements ignores rules and discipline. To my misfortune whatever I can achieve depends upon industrious orderliness.

I think the use you propose for Lee is likely to cause trouble – but I have said my say and cheerfully withdraw.

Do what *you like* and you will never find me obstreperous or cantankerous so long as you don't get angry with me. God bless you.[1]

The letters illuminate the characters of both men. Montagu was still generally regarded as a political creature of Asquith; yet here he was already addressing Lloyd George as his creator, so presaging his decision, a year later, to join Lloyd George's coalition. In reality he was always a less humble and more independent politician than he liked to appear.

Robertson had this to say of Lloyd George's performance as War Minister:

Of the results of Mr Lloyd George's six [actually five] months' reign at the War Office there is nothing of much interest to record, for he was connected with no measure having any special influence on the course of the war. . . . He preferred his own strategical ideas to those of the General Staff, and of administrative work, which seemed to bore him, he left as much as possible to be done by the Under-Secretary of State, Lord Derby. He was, in fact, so much occupied with political activities . . . as to devote considerably less than undivided attention to the affairs of the Army.[2]

When he wrote those words Robertson was no longer a dispassionate judge, if he ever was. Lloyd George, as Prime Minister, had disregarded his views and engineered his removal from the post of C.I.G.S. All the same they deserve respectful attention, not only because he was undeniably well placed to observe Lloyd George at the War Office, but also because he was an exceptional man by any reckoning.

It is well known that Robertson rose from the ranks to become a field marshal, and that he was the first ranker to enter the Staff College, of which he was later commandant. But it is less well known that this

---

1. L.G.P. Unfortunately for him, Montagu had inadvertently given J. T. Davies, with some other papers, a copy of a memorandum from himself to the Prime Minister, recommending that Lloyd George should be given the War Office as a means of destroying his reputation with the public.

2. *Soldiers and Statesmen, 1914–1918*, Vol. I., p. 179.

boy from a Lincolnshire village was an outstanding linguist, who
while a young officer in India qualified in Persian and five Indian
languages, and who after his return to Europe became capable of
translating German and Austrian military handbooks into English. It
is also, perhaps, less well known that he foresaw the German attack
through Belgium and, as director of military training on the eve of
war, organised manoeuvres relevant to the B.E.F.'s likely role in that
contingency; or that, as quartermaster-general to the B.E.F., he made
logistical plans without which the long retreat from Mons would have
been impossible.

Within his limits Robertson was more organised and efficient than
Lloyd George or Kitchener, but of course he was a less big man than
either, lacking Lloyd George's resourcefulness, imagination and ver-
satility of mind, his boldness and dash, and lacking also Kitchener's
strange ability (so well described by Lloyd George) to radiate, like a
lighthouse, 'momentary gleams of revealing light far out into the
surrounding gloom'.[1] He had the defects, as well as the qualities, of a
superlative staff officer. Lloyd George, when he wrote his memoirs,
was as prejudiced against him as he, when he wrote his, against Lloyd
George. Yet the character-sketch that we find of him in Lloyd
George's account is essentially fair:

> He was industrious, steady, intelligent; all the administrative tasks
> entrusted to him, whether as ranker, N.C.O., or commissioned
> officer, he discharged competently and with distinction. He was an
> excellent organiser. He had, during his military career, few oppor-
> tunities, if any, of leading men in the field. . . . His mind was sound
> but commonplace. He was cautious to the point of timidity. There
> lay his strength – that also accounted for his drawbacks.

And Lloyd George adds a surprising comment:

> When the fighting was at its worst he did not hesitate to express his
> opinion in a discussion on Peace Terms, that a strong Germany in
> Central Europe was vital to the preservation of Peace. His
> memorandum on that subject rose in parts to the heights of
> statesmanship. After a week's reflection on his own temerity he
> withdrew the memorandum and cancelled it. He would have been

1. W.M., p. 751.

much more effective as a politician than as a soldier.[1]

Robertson would never have paid Lloyd George the same compliment in reverse. To him a civilian was by definition incapable of grasping military problems and should leave them to professionals. To say that Lloyd George 'preferred his own strategical ideas to those of the General Staff' was to damn him automatically. It did not occur to Robertson that it might be a virtue in a War Minister to delegate 'as much as possible' of the routine administration to his under-secretary, so that he could concentrate, himself, upon the issues that really mattered. Those issues, in Robertson's view, lay within the exclusive province of the General Staff, unless they happened to require political or Parliamentary action, as securing compulsory service did. Then a civilian minister might have his uses. In every other respect, however, political activities were to be regarded as a dirty game unbecoming to anybody privileged to preside over the Army, to whose affairs, strictly interpreted, he should be giving his 'undivided attention'.

Most of the points in Robertson's dismissive comment on Lloyd George's time at the War Office are surely bordering on the absurd. The only one which contains even a grain of truth is that, while there, he was 'connected with no measure having any special influence on the course of the War'. But even that is an exaggeration. His brief tenure of the War Office was, indeed, the least fruitful episode in his long career as a minister – and mainly for the reason already indicated, that he had such limited scope there. But even so he achieved quite a lot by normal ministerial standards.

His most important contribution was to bring about a drastic improvement in the system of transport behind the lines in France. His share in bringing it about was simple but vital. He persuaded Haig to talk to his star man of push and go, Geddes, and the result of direct contact between the two Scotsmen was that Geddes became director-general of transportation in France, while also holding the post of director of military railways, with a seat on the Army Council, in England. Montagu most reluctantly released him from the Ministry of Munitions ('with tears in my eyes, tears which have been flowing ever since'[2]), and by the end of the year Geddes put through a programme which included laying hundreds of miles of new railway, both light and standard-gauge, as well as extensive road building and

1. *ibid.*, pp. 778–81.
2. Montagu to D.L.G., 11 October 1916 (L.G.P.).

road repairs. Through Geddes other high-powered civilians were recruited to help in the work, and at a humbler level 15,000 Chinese labourers were recruited for service in what Lloyd George chose to call the Chinese Auxiliary Corps (since it was obvious to him that if they were referred to simply as Chinese labour, people would too easily be reminded of 'an unpleasant political controversy still fresh in party memory on both sides'.)[1] Haig deserves much credit for backing Geddes to the limit despite carping and obstruction by the military, but without Lloyd George Geddes would not, of course, have been in France at all.

When the new Secretary of State took over, perhaps the worst disaster area for the British army was Mesopotamia. By the time he left, the position there had been transformed and everything made ready for a highly successful campaign the following year. Though he doubtless made some contribution to this swift and most desirable improvement, it was largely due to Robertson and the General Staff. It was Robertson's idea that Sir Frederick Maude, who had played a notable part in the Dardanelles evacuation, should be appointed to the Mesopotamian command; and, according to him, Maude came to be the only British general of whom Lloyd George approved.[2] But he also had a very high opinion of a senior staff officer at the War Office, under whose direction the logistics in Mesopotamia were reorganised. This was the Quartermaster-General, Sir John Cowans, mentioned by Asquith in his letter as 'one of the great successes of the war' if perhaps 'a little lavish'. Lavishness was not, however, Cowans's only fault. He also had a weakness for the fashionable world, and more especially the female side of it, which very nearly cost him his job and presented Lloyd George with the nastiest scandal of his time at the War Office.

The matter was raised by Lloyd George's old friend, Sir Arthur Markham, and the essence of it was that Cowans had used very improper influence on behalf of a 'society' friend, Mrs Cornwallis-West. It was alleged that he had first procured a commission for a young sergeant called Patrick Barrett, who had taken her fancy, and later, when Barrett spurned her advances, arranged for him to be sent to France, and into the firing-line. For a time the word went round that the Mrs Cornwallis-West in question was Churchill's mother, the

1. W.M., p. 800 (footnote).
2. Robertson, *Soldiers and Statesmen*, Vol. 1, p. 179. Maude captured Baghdad in March 1917, but unfortunately died of cholera the following November.

former Lady Randolph, who had married George Cornwallis-West (a man her son's age) in 1900.[1] But in fact it was her mother-in-law – and contemporary – Mrs William Cornwallis-West. Lloyd George persuaded Markham not to make a Parliamentary issue of the case, in return for an undertaking that there would be a rigorous official inquiry. When Markham soon afterwards died, and Lloyd George at the same time was under pressure to drop the inquiry, he told Frances Stevenson that he was honour bound not to do so. 'I must keep my promise to the dead.'[2]

The promise was kept. A court of inquiry was put to work, with a former C.I.G.S., Lord Nicholson, as president; the other members being a lesser military peer (Cheylesmore), a High Court judge (Atkin) and a Liberal M.P. (Maclean). According to Frances Stevenson, Maclean asked Lloyd George how he could be expected to sit on a committee when he had no idea what it was all about and Lloyd George replied: 'Go home, get your Bible, & read the stories of Potiphar's wife and Uriah the Hittite, & they will give you the case in a nutshell!'[3] This prejudicial comment turned out to be misleading. After a long and thorough investigation, held in private, the court delivered its findings to the Army Council on 16 November, and they were damaging to Cowans without being really damning. His part in the affair was shown to have been fairly marginal, though he ought to have had no part in it at all. Barrett would almost certainly have got his commission even if Cowans's personal interest had not been enlisted, and his transfer to another unit – in Wales, not in France – would have been unexceptionable if the circumstances had been different; and was anyway not ordered by Cowans. All the same, the court did find that his correspondence about Barrett with Mrs Cornwallis-West, and a letter that he wrote, at her wish, to Barrett himself, indicated 'not merely indiscretion but a departure from official propriety'. The same court also considered an allegation that he had been involved in an attempt by the same woman to secure Brigadier Owen Thomas's command for a friend of hers; but again the facts, so far as he was

1. 'Lady Randolph Churchill (Black Jane) fell in love with a private and, at her instance, General Cowans gave the man a commission. Either another woman entered the lists and captured this man, or in any case he did not respond to Jane's passion, and spleen and pique made her induce Cowans to degrade the man to the ranks again. . . . Cowans, poor man, has the reputation of jobbery, owing to his susceptibility to "ladies" '. (Lady Cynthia Asquith, *Diaries*, 8 August 1916, pp. 201–2:)
2. F.S.D., 8 August 1916, p. 113.
3. *ibid.*, 2 August 1916, p. 111.

concerned, were rather less odious than the charge.[1]

The findings were bad enough, however, to convince Lloyd George at first that Cowans would have to go. In his view it could not be tolerated 'that a Member of the Army Council should use his position in this way & allow himself to come under the influence of such a woman'.[2] But Derby advised that he should be let off with a reprimand,[3] and by 30 November Lloyd George had relented to the extent of saying that he would be made Q.M.G. in France, vacating the higher post.[4] In the event he stayed on as Q.M.G. of the whole Army until his retirement in 1920, and Lloyd George's only victim among military members of the Army Council was his old enemy, von Donop. Cowans was saved by his undoubted efficiency and likeable personality, as well as by having powerful friends, including more especially Robertson and the King. His reputation survived more or less intact until four years after his death, when his name was dragged into one of the most lurid court cases of the post-war period.[5]

For the British Army by far the most important event of Lloyd George's time at the War Office was the battle of the Somme, which began one week before he took over and ended two or three weeks before he left. In December 1915 the Allied high commands had agreed that there should be simultaneous offensives in Russia, Italy

1. Full reports by the Court of Inquiry on both cases (L.G.P.). Mrs Cornwallis-West comes very badly out of both, and two or three officers emerge from the Barrett case with more discredit than Cowans. The most embarrassing piece of evidence against him was, perhaps, one sentence in a letter from Mrs Cornwallis-West – 'I am always bothering you, Jack' – which suggested that the matters under investigation might be only the tip of an iceberg. Barrett behaved with all the decency and honour lacking in his 'social superiors'. When the episode with Mrs Cornwallis-West occurred he had already served in France, where he had been wounded and shell-shocked, and his one desire was to get back there rather than to dally at home with an elderly predatress who also had ideas of turning him into a literary gent. 'I don't want to understand Potry [sic],' he wrote. 'I only want to live a good life, and serve my God and King.' But she succeeded, even more effectively than the Germans, in reducing him to a nervous and physical wreck.

2. F.S.D., 20 November 1916, p. 125.

3. 'Strictly confidential' memorandum from Derby to D.L.G., 23 November 1916 (L.G.P.).

4. F.S.D., 30 November 1916, p. 130.

5. Dennistoun v. Dennistoun (1925), in which Norman Birkett established himself as a forensic star. The glamorous Mrs Dorothy Dennistoun was suing her former husband, Colonel 'Tiger' Dennistoun, for alimony, and in the early stages of the case there were references to a 'General X' who had been her lover from 1916 to 1920. Allegedly her husband had connived at the affair and derived military advantages from it (though these do not seem to have amounted to much). In the witness-box she revealed that 'General X' had been Cowans (d. 1921), and this created 'a considerable sensation both inside and outside the court'. (H. Montgomery Hyde, *Norman Birkett*, p. 139.)

and France (or Belgium) in the spring of 1916. But until the Germans attacked at Verdun in February British politicians were still uncommitted to a Western offensive, and Lloyd George, with strong support from Balfour, was arguing that 'it was our business to sit tight on the Western frontier, and then take the offensive in Egypt, Mesopotamia or Salonica'.[1] Verdun decided the issue against them. By the end of March French casualties there amounted to nearly 90,000, and the pressure on Britain to take a larger share in the fighting became irresistible. On 4 April Haig reported to Robertson that Joffre expected him to take action to relieve the French, and said that he accepted the necessity for this, though any early move would have to be 'of a strictly limited nature' granted 'the comparatively weak force at his disposal'. He also reaffirmed his commitment to a general offensive in the West, though without going into details and leaving the question of timing open.

Three days later the War Committee discussed future military operations. Robertson read out Haig's letter and discussion then centred on the project for a large-scale offensive, rather than on the lesser but more urgent issue; indeed the two became utterly confused. Taking advantage of the confusion, Robertson asked for, and by the end of the meeting had obtained, a virtual *carte blanche* for Haig, who was, he said, 'perfectly alive to the situation and would not do any foolish thing'. No distinction was drawn between a limited operation to give immediate aid to the French and the more grandiose scheme on which the military had agreed in principle some time before Verdun. Lloyd George, though normally quick enough to seize a good debating point, failed to suggest that Haig's absolute discretion be confined to the first matter. At one point he said, quite correctly, that if the Committee gave Haig the general permission Robertson was asking for they (the Committee) 'would have no more to say'; and later, that 'he personally held to the plan of holding the Germans up and smashing the Turks'. Yet in the end he lamely agreed that everything should be left to Haig. It is fair to recall that the meeting occurred during a time (the first fortnight of April) when he was in an anxious and troubled state, as he braced himself for a showdown on the conscription issue. All the same, his performance at the meeting was surprisingly weak.[2]

1. War Committee, 13 January 1916.
2. War Committee, 7 April 1916.

He found himself in a somewhat false position when, not long afterwards, Joffre began to press for an offensive against Bulgaria from the Salonica bridgehead. At any other time he would have been the first to welcome such a plan concerning an area whose strategic importance and potential he had been stressing for over a year. But in the circumstances he felt obliged to oppose it. Seeing that there was no longer any hope of restricting action on the Western front to limited and localised attacks, he could only assume that the Salonica operation would be starved of the resources necessary for its success. At a special Anglo-French conference in London on 9 June he said that 'to attempt the operation with inadequate strength was to discredit it', and the French were persuaded to agree that it should be postponed until conditions were more favourable. This was a triumph of sorts, but it must have been painful for him to have to argue as an anti-Easterner, if only to ensure that the whole conception of an Eastern strategy was not prejudiced by action at the wrong time and with inadequate resources.[1]

Meanwhile the pressure was increasing for early and extremely large-scale action on the Western front. By the end of May French casualties at Verdun had risen to 185,000, and the German threat to the city – whose combined symbolic and strategic value makes it comparable with Stalingrad in the Second World War – was greater than ever. At the beginning of June the Russian commander Brusilov launched an offensive against the Austrians, which at first carried all before it. The Italians were fighting hard in the Trentino. So what were the British to do, and when would they act?

Haig was thoroughly in favour of a big attack in the West, but he was in no hurry to launch it, because he wanted the maximum time for preparing his troops and accumulating the arms that were now, at last, coming through in sufficient quantities. His idea was that the British would open their attack in August, but Joffre told him that if he delayed until then the French army would cease to exist. The British had to give way on the scene as well as the timing of action. Though Haig's preference was for an attack in Flanders, Joffre insisted that the battlefield should be in Picardy, north and south of the river Somme,

---

1. According to Lloyd George, Joffre presented the French case at the London conference 'with great force and eloquence'. Whether or not he was a good soldier, he was 'one of the most forceful and dramatic speakers' Lloyd George had heard at any conference he had attended (W.M., p. 535). Yet Churchill describes Joffre as 'slow-thinking, phlegmatic, bucolic' (*World Crisis*, ch. 111).

despite the known strength of the German positions in that sector. Moreover the French contribution to the offensive, which was originally to have been forty divisions, dwindled to sixteen because of the demands of Verdun. The Somme battle thus became a predominantly British affair, and the opening date for it was advanced to 1 July.

In effect it started a week earlier, on 24 June, when the preliminary bombardment began. No bombardment had ever lasted so long, and it was intended to create a vacuum into which the attacking troops would move when they went over the top. For this it was considered worth sacrificing the element of surprise – though in fact the Germans could not believe that it was being genuinely sacrificed, suspected a trick, and so did not at first concentrate their reserves in the apparently threatened sector. The bombardment failed to create a vacuum, however, mainly because the Germans opposite were well prepared, with deep dug-outs in which they could shelter while their trenches were being pulverised, and to a lesser extent because most of the shells fired by the British guns were shrapnel rather than high explosive.[1] Another reason was that there had not yet been time for the big gun programme, which Lloyd George had forced through, to be fully implemented. As a result, of the 1,500 guns taking part in the British bombardment fewer than 500 were heavy guns, whereas the French had 900 heavy guns on their much narrower stretch of the Somme battle-front.

But an even more significant difference between the French and the British concerned infantry tactics. In the grim fighting above Verdun the Germans had shown what could be achieved by small groups of infantry rushing forward under covering fire and infiltrating the enemy lines. The French had learned the lesson and profited from it both at Verdun and the Somme. Their attack on 1 July was on the whole successful; they captured most of the German front line at relatively low cost. By contrast the British were largely unsuccessful, and their losses staggering. Instead of following the example of the French, their commanders sent them across no-man's-land in closely packed lines; and they were unable even to move reasonably fast

---

1. A large proportion of the shells, moreover (about thirty per cent), were duds. This reflected the fact that it was not until well into 1916 that the Ministry of Munitions had evolved a satisfactory system of detonation. Inevitably, many of the shells fired at the beginning of the Somme battle were produced earlier. The preponderance of shrapnel was also partly due to technological causes, though military opinion was still sharply divided as to the relative merits of shrapnel and H.E. for softening up enemy positions before an attack. In any case many of the German dug-outs on the Somme were impervious even to H.E.

because every man was carrying about 66 lbs. of equipment (more than half his own body-weight). The slow plodding lines of heavily burdened men presented a perfect target to the German machine-gunners who emerged from their dug-outs and took up position as soon as the bombardment ended; also to the German artillery. In one terrible day the British army sustained nearly 60,000 casualties, of whom about 20,000 were killed. It was the worst day in the army's history, if also one of the most heroic.

During the remaining four and a half months of the Somme battle, or series of battles, the daily toll fell to an average of 2,500. Of the total British casualties about one-seventh occurred on the first of the 140 days of fighting. All the same the British army at the Somme, which was essentially Kitchener's army of civilian volunteers, lost about 450,000 men for the gain of at best a few miles of territory. At the end of the long struggle the Germans still held Bapaume, for instance, which had been one of the British objectives for the *first day*. The Somme was claimed at the time, and is still claimed by some writers, as an Allied victory; but it was certainly not the sort of victory that Haig and his senior commanders hoped for at the outset, and continued to hope for until the late autumn rain and mud finally compelled them to stop the carnage. The German losses were, indeed, as heavy as their opponents', but they yielded very little ground and their morale was unbroken. If the Allies won the battle, their victory was the most Pyrrhic imaginable, and it is surely truer to say that neither side won.

The Somme was Haig's first big test as British commander-in-chief, and it provides more evidence of his faults than of his virtues. Two faults in particular are most apparent: his excessive deference to the ideas of subordinate commanders, and his reluctance to admit that things were not working out as he intended. The gross tactical error which had such appalling consequences on 1 July is attributable to the first of these faults. Though his own instinct and observation told him that it would be wrong for the British to advance in line, he did not impose his view and must, therefore, take the largest share of blame for what happened – because what is a commander-in-chief for, if not to impose his view in such a vital matter? John Terraine, whose scholarly advocacy has done so much for Haig's reputation, cannot disguise the enormity of his failure:

In the first stage of planning the tactics of the Battle of the Somme

. . . [he] had suggested that the British infantry should advance in detachments, rather than waves; the three Army Commanders who were infantrymen themselves were opposed to this, and [he] had accepted their judgment. They had been shown to be seriously wrong. . . . Nevertheless, his aversion to overruling the men on the spot remained strong. . . . He knew perfectly well that those who have to carry out plans must feel identified with them. It may be felt that sometimes he allowed this belief to sway him too far; the examples of foreign armies in the same War show the equal dangers of the opposite course.[1]

And this is Mr Terraine's general comment on the first day of the Somme:

When one has said that Haig, his Staff and his chief subordinates were all involved together in a vast and tragic mistake, one has said everything.[2]

Haig was a cavalryman, and although the extent of his 'cavalry-mindedness' has been much exaggerated – not least by Lloyd George – he was undeniably given, at times, to undue optimism, and to a reckless striving for breakthrough and decision long after it should have been obvious to him that only stalemate was possible. At first sceptical of the Somme project, he became euphoric about it before the battle began and thereafter continued to believe that, if the pressure were sustained, the enemy would crack. Joffre regarded the Somme as no more than a battle of attrition, and so did Robertson; but until mid-October at any rate Haig was expecting it to turn into a decisive victory, with the result that he did what Joffre wanted him to do, though for a quite different reason. On 15 September tanks were used for the first time in an attack, but not to the best effect, and again Mr Terraine says 'it is hard to resist the conclusion that Haig should have intervened more forcefully', this time to make his army commanders devise tactics more appropriate to the new weapon.[3] But even if the tanks had been used with the utmost skill, there were only forty-nine of them and they could not have won the whole battle.

No general in the First World War should be condemned for

1. *Haig: The Educated Soldier*, pp. 212–13. The criticism is understated, and the final words suggest an attempt to cancel it out. All the same the admission is clear and – when we think of the consequences – devastating.
2. *ibid.*, p. 204.
3. *ibid.*, p. 226.

making mistakes initially. The experience was as new to the soldiers as to the politicians, and even the ablest and most senior British commanders came to it unprepared. Haig was certainly a very able man, whose seniority before the war had outstripped his age, and who was by no means hidebound. He had taken an efficient and enthusiastic part in Haldane's reforming work at the War Office, and had given careful study to the German army. But his mind, though open to innovation, was not quite quick or imaginative enough for the challenges of supreme command. Moreover his Calvinist faith could give it an inflexibility which might, in certain emergencies, be an asset, but which was more often a menace. He believed implicitly in Divine Providence, and in himself as its agent. This was all very well when he was doing the right thing, but disastrous, of course, when he was doing the wrong thing. It made him unduly slow to abandon or modify any campaign to which he was committed, because there was always an underlying assumption that his plan was destined to succeed.

The least attractive feature of his character, though one not uncommon in people of marked self-confidence and self-righteousness, was a tendency to apply double standards. While professing contempt for the 'political' vices of duplicity, disloyalty and intrigue, he did not hesitate to resort to them himself whenever necessary, and the fact that he looked every inch the officer and gentleman made his use of them all the more effective. He had a special line to the King which he exploited to the full, first against French and later against Lloyd George. Though loyal to a fault to subordinates, he was systematically disloyal to superiors. We have seen how he complained of French to Kitchener after the battle of Loos; at the same time, and indeed previously, he complained of French to the King. As George V's latest biographer observes tartly: 'Haig . . . felt uneasy at conspiring behind the back of both his Commander-in-Chief and a friend who had done much to further the younger man's career. But he overcame his scruples.' When he became commander-in-chief himself the King 'assured him of his constant support and urged him to write freely but secretly whenever he wished'.[1] Haig took ample advantage of this

1. Kenneth Rose, *King George V*, p. 192 and p. 202. Haig had served under French before and during the South African war. His connection with the royal family began when he was appointed A.D.C. to Edward VII, and became closer after his marriage to one of Queen Alexandra's ladies-in-waiting. George V's regard for him was manifested early in the new reign, when Haig was made K.C.V.O. in 1911.

channel of influence.

He was equally attentive to politicians and journalists who could be useful to him. As his private secretary he appointed a Tory M.P. with great wealth and extensive social contacts, Philip Sassoon, who served him faithfully for the rest of the war and through whom he was able to keep in close touch with the London political world. Among the powerful Press allies enlisted by Haig none was more dedicated to his cause than Northcliffe, the depth of whose infatuation may be judged from these comments:

> Sir Douglas does not waste words. It is not because he is silent or unsympathetic – it is because he uses words as he uses soldiers, sparingly, but always with method. . . . While I was with the little family party at Headquarters there came news that was good, and some that was not so good. Neither affected the Commander-in-Chief's attitude towards the war, nor the day's work, in the least degree whatever. There are all sorts of minor criticisms of the Commander-in-Chief at home, mainly because the majority of the people know nothing about him. He is probably not interested in home comments, but is concerned that the Empire should know of the unprecedented valour of his officers and men. Consequently the doings of the Army are put before the world each day with the frankness that is part of Sir Douglas Haig's own character. He is opposed to secrecy except where military necessity occasions it. He dislikes secret reports on officers. . . . [And so on in the same vein of awe-struck reverence.][1]

It was no small achievement to have so captivated and enslaved Britain's most formidable publicist. In the art of self-promotion Haig had few rivals.

The view of him expressed with such sublime naïvety by Northcliffe was, partly on that account, very widely shared, and persisted for a very long time. According to Beaverbrook, it was only with the publication of Haig's private papers in 1952 that the truth about his character became known; he then 'committed suicide 25 years after his death'.[2] Many eminent commanders have, in fact, used the methods that he did to maintain their positions, though without, as a rule, quite the same pretence of despising such methods. Haig's hypocrisy cannot fail to inspire some disgust, but should not count for too much in any

1. Contemporary report, reprinted in Northcliffe, *At the War*, pp. 60–3.
2. Beaverbrook, *Men and Power*, p. xviii.

assessment of his qualities as a leader. As such he had substantial merits, though also very serious defects.

Lloyd George's first encounter with Haig was when he visited G.H.Q. at the end of January 1916. Haig welcomed him very cordially and arranged for Dick and Gwilym to be brought from their units to meet him. Afterwards Lloyd George wrote to thank the commander-in-chief for his 'great courtesy', and went on to pay him a fulsome compliment:

> The visit, if you will permit me to say so, left on my mind a great impression of things being *gripped* . . . and whether we win through or whether we fail, I have a feeling that everything which the assiduity, the care, and the trained thought of a great soldier can accomplish is being done.[1]

In saying this Lloyd George was quite sincere. Soon afterwards he told Riddell that 'a new spirit' prevailed at G.H.Q. since Haig's appointment, and that Haig was 'very keen and businesslike'.[2] But his good opinion was not reciprocated by his host. However pleasant Haig may have been to Lloyd George's face, in reality his attitude was far from friendly: 'Lloyd George seems to be astute and cunning, with much energy and push but I should think shifty and unreliable'.[3]

The next time they met in France Lloyd George was War Minister and the Somme battle had been raging for seven weeks. There was considerable anxiety in London about the progress of the fighting and more especially about the scale of losses, some idea of which was gradually percolating. Even Robertson – who always gave Haig solid backing and defended his interests against the politicians – was at first very much in the dark and dependent largely upon press communiqués. Though he urged Haig to send him information to reassure the War Committee, he received a good deal less than he needed. At

1. D.L.G. to Haig, 8 February 1916 (copy in L.G.P.).
2. R.W.D., 11 February 1916, p. 154.
3. Haig Diary, 30 January 1916. On the other hand Haig's chief of Intelligence, Brigadier-General John Charteris, wrote of Lloyd George: 'He certainly was most attractive. D.H. alone seemed quite impervious to his allurements . . . whatever else may be said of "the little man", there is no doubt that he has genius. One strange physical feature draws one's eye when he is not talking – his curious little knock-kneed legs. When he is talking one would not notice if he had no legs . . . his face is so full of vitality and energy . . . D.H. hates everything but absolute honesty and frankness . . . but can anyone in politics be really frank and honest?' (Charteris, *At G.H.Q.*, 31 January 1916, p. 133).

the end of July he had to write:

> The Powers that be are beginning to get a little uneasy in regard to the situation. . . . In general, what is bothering them is the probability that we may soon have to face a bill of 2 to 300,000 casualties with no very great gains additional to the present. It is thought that the primary object – relief of pressure on Verdun – has to some extent been achieved.[1]

Meanwhile Lloyd George had been forming his own provisional conclusions. On 19 July he lunched with Repington and talked about the Somme:

> He did not appear to believe that we should be successful, as the casualties were already so numerous, and there was every chance for the Germans to bring guns and troops from Verdun. I told him I also doubted whether we should have great success until we were able to equip with heavy guns all our Armies. . . . I told him Foch's standard for the guns and shells, which made him look serious, and he told me that in seventeen days we had fired twice as much ammunition as Douglas Haig had reckoned to fire in a month. I told him about the defect in our artillery preparation, and he agreed on the subject.

Towards the end of their conversation Lloyd George asked Repington whom he would prefer 'if there was a change in France'. Repington suggested Allenby, 'as he combined youth, physique and character'. Lloyd George could not remember him though told that he had met him some years before.[2]

On 1 August F. E. Smith circulated to the Cabinet a devastating memorandum on the Somme written by his friend Churchill, and Hankey suspected that Lloyd George, too, had a hand in it. That night Lloyd George dined with Aitken and heard Northcliffe's brother, Rothermere, give vent to some very un-Northcliffean sentiments about the military. Frances Stevenson next day recorded an account of this outburst:

1. Robertson to Haig, 29 July 1916. It was true that the tide had turned at Verdun since mid-July, though the French could be forgiven for not yet being prepared to believe it.
2. Repington, *The First World War*, Vol. I, pp. 283–6. Edmund Allenby was, in fact, two months older than Haig, though junior to him in rank. Since October 1915 he had been commanding the Third Army, which took no part in the battle of the Somme. He and Haig were never kindred spirits.

The last offensive had been a failure, he said: 'The communiqués are full of lies. They are merely for the purpose of deluding the public. They are full of lies, lies, lies! I *know* it, he said. 'I know it from information which I have received from the spot! Your officials at the W.O.,' he continued, turning to D., 'they are trying to mislead you. They too are feeding you up with lies.' D. let him go on the other side of the case, & turned the thing off. D. says there was something in what Rothermere said. . . . Northcliffe himself, however, writes from the front in praise of everything which he has seen.[1]

The following week Lloyd George went to France. He arrived in Paris on 11 August, accompanied by Reading and Lee, and after conferring with French ministers paid rushed visits on the 12th to Haig and to Rawlinson (commander of the Fourth Army on the Somme). He returned to England next day, after what can hardly be described as a serious tour of inspection. At Haig's headquarters he clearly thought it prudent to disguise his feelings:

> Lloyd George has been out here; he was very cheery and optimistic this time, quite different from his last visit. Whatever his faults, he has amazing energy and a great flow of words. Lord Reading was with him, very learned and clever, but utterly dwarfed by Lloyd George's vitality. Neither of them seemed to be worrying much about our casualty list, at which I was greatly surprised.[2]

He put on a similar act with Rawlinson.

His position, it must be said, was extraordinarily tricky and invidious. There can be no doubt at all that he was deeply unhappy about the way the battle was going on the British side, and about the apparent inadequacy of the British high command. His conversation with Repington three weeks before (recorded by Repington in his diary the same day) showed him anything but optimistic, and it is most unlikely that his mood had changed since then. Moreover, even though he may not have had a hand in Churchill's memorandum of 1 August, it is surely significant that Hankey thought he had – because Hankey was well placed to know his true state of mind. We can

---

1. F.S.D., 2 August 1916, pp. 111–12. Not long afterwards Lloyd George appointed Rothermere head of the Army Clothing Department, and the following year made him Air Minister.

2. Charteris, *At G.H.Q.*, p. 164 (diary, 12 August 1916). It seems that the day before he left for France he was not intending to visit Haig at all (R.W.D., 9 August 1916, p. 208).

assume, therefore, that he was unhappy, but obviously he could not afford to show most people how he felt. As War Minister he had to speak up for the Army, and it was also his responsibility to maintain its morale. Hence his attempt to put 'the other side of the case' to Rothermere, and hence his forced cheerfulness with Haig and Rawlinson.

Soon after this visit he had to speak in the House of Commons in a debate on the progress of the war, and of course he had to put a confident face on what was happening in France. But he did not encourage belief that victory was near:

> . . . we ought not to treat this as if it were the end. It would be a mistake for us to do so. We are fighting a very great military power with gigantic resources; they have an enormous population to draw upon, and let us realise that . . . there are many valleys to cross, there are many ridges to storm, before we see the final victory. We shall need more men, more munitions, more guns and more equipment, and we shall need all the courage and the endurance of our race in every part of the world in order to convert the work which has been begun . . . into a victory which will be really a final and a complete victory.[1]

The following month he was in France again for a longer visit. He travelled to Paris on 4 September, with Edwin Montagu, Lee and one or two soldiers. Next day Briand gave a lunch for him, and the British ambassador gave a dinner. On the 6th there was talk and further hospitality in Paris, but on the 7th he went to Verdun where he dined, not in a glittering banqueting hall, but in the cavern below the citadel. There he made a short speech which moved not only his immediate audience but the French public generally:

> I wish to tell you how glad I am that you asked me to sit at table with your officers in the heart of Verdun's citadel, I am glad to see around me those who have come back from battle, those who will be fighting tomorrow, and those who . . . are sentries on these impregnable walls. The name of Verdun alone will be enough to arouse imperishable memories throughout the centuries to come. There is not one of the great feats of arms which make the history of France which better shows the high qualities of the Army and the people of France; and that bravery and devotion to country, to

1. 23 August 1916. Hansard, Fifth Series, Vol. LXXXV, col. 2555.

which the world has ever paid homage, have been strengthened by a *sang-froid* and tenacity which yield nothing to British phlegm.

The memory of the victorious resistance of Verdun will be immortal because Verdun saved not only France, but the whole of the great cause which is common to ourselves and humanity. The evil-working force of the enemy has broken itself against the heights around this old citadel as an angry sea breaks upon a granite rock. These heights have conquered the storm which threatened the world.

I am deeply moved when I tread this sacred soil, and I do not speak for myself alone. I bring to you a tribute of the admiration of my country, of the great Empire which I represent here. They bow with me before your sacrifice and before your glory. Once again, for the defence of the great causes with which its very future is bound up, mankind turns to France – A la France! Aux hommes tombés sous Verdun!

After the visit to Verdun he was supposed to spend the weekend at Fontainebleau, but in fact spent it in Paris, where he was joined by Reading. On the 11th they visited Foch, commander of the French Northern Army Group, at his headquarters. This meeting got Lloyd George into a lot of trouble. Over lunch, at which quite a large party was present, he questioned Foch about the Somme battle and the relative performances of French and British. Next day Foch reported the conversation to Henry Wilson (then commanding a corps some way north of the Somme):

Lloyd George asked innumerable questions about why we took so few prisoners, why we took so little ground, why we had such heavy losses, all these in comparison with the French. Foch played up well as regards Haig and would not give him away. He simply said he did not know, but that our soldiers were green soldiers and his were veterans. Lloyd George said he gave Haig all the guns and ammunition and men he could use, and nothing happened. Foch said that Lloyd George was *très monté* against Haig, and he did not think Haig's seat was very secure.

On the 13th Lloyd George, Reading and Lee visited Wilson's headquarters, and Lloyd George put to Wilson 'exactly the same questions as he had asked Foch', only to get 'the same answers, i.e. that our troops and artillery were new to the game'.[1]

Foch lost no time in telling Haig and on 17 September Haig wrote in his diary: 'Unless I had been told of this conversation personally by Gen. Foch, I would not have believed that a British Minister could have been so ungentlemanly as to go to a foreigner and put such questions regarding his own subordinates'. Talk of Lloyd George's misdemeanour was soon in circulation, for, unlike details of the battle, it was information which the military had no interest in withholding: quite the reverse. On 26 September Robertson told Hankey that 'Lloyd George had made the worst possible impression on his recent visit to France', and had 'asked General Foch's opinion of the English Generals, whom he himself criticised severely'. Foch had 'promptly telephoned the whole thing to Haig and to Joffre', with the result that when Lloyd George had asked to see Joffre the latter refused a meeting unless Haig was present.[2] Two days later Lloyd George was rebuked by the *Morning Post*: there was a dark reference to his 'gaffe' and he was warned that the facts would be given if he did not mend his ways. He had, therefore, to write to the paper praising the Army and its leaders, and denying that he had done anything amiss.

It may be worth quoting the reflections on this incident, soon afterwards, of the British ambassador in Paris, Lord Bertie:

> The *Morning Post* had been attacking Lloyd George as a result of his recent visit to the Front: he left here with Reading and the French interpreter: I don't know where he could have picked up others to make up a party of fourteen to invade Foch at luncheon. I understand that he discussed with his host how it was that the British losses so far exceeded the French casualties in the Somme fighting, given the fact that the British now have a sufficiency of shells, etc.; the answer was that the British had more difficult ground and a larger enemy force to deal with, and that probably the British exposed themselves unnecessarily and the officers of the "New Armies" were inexperienced. Lloyd George may have said something which, not Foch, but another or others present twisted, out of prejudice or mischief, into Lloyd George having spoken in depreciation of British leadership: most sensible people admit that our failing is [in] competent leadership compared with the French. The

---

1. Major-General Sir C. E. Calwell, *Field Marshal Sir Henry Wilson Bart.: His Life and Diaries*, Vol. I, p. 292. Calwell gives the date incorrectly as August.
2. Roskill, *Hankey: Man of Secrets*, pp. 300–1.

hostility of the *Morning Post* to L.G. arises partly from the Ulster Settlement, which, however, fell through.[1]

Bertie was mistaken in supposing that it was not Foch himself who had made the mischief. All the same his comment on British military leadership is of interest.

Lloyd George certainly misjudged his men in speaking to Foch and Wilson as he did. Their instinctive reaction was to protect fellow-generals and to blame the wretched troops of Kitchener's army, who had, in fact shown magnificent courage and only needed a better plan of attack. But how was Lloyd George to discover what was really happening? His chief professional adviser, Robertson, was more Haig's man than his. In asking Foch, 'a foreigner', he hoped to obtain information which the British military establishment would never give him – though he was its nominal head. Wilson he must have regarded as an exception, because he knew him to be a thoroughly political general, in regular contact with leading Unionists, including Bonar Law and Milner. But Wilson also belonged to the senior officers' 'trade union', and anyway was not to be trusted.

It was inevitable that Lloyd George should be 'ungentlemanly' in his dealings with the top military, partly because he was not a gentleman in their sense (or indeed in any sense: he was both more and less), but above all because their conception of gentlemanliness implied a conspiracy against the public, whose interests it was his duty to serve. He can be criticised for an error of judgment – which he was to repeat on a larger scale the following year – but not for acting unpatriotically.

A valid criticism, however, of his visits to the Army in the field while he was War Minister is that they were so brief and so largely confined to the headquarters of army groups, armies and corps. Whereas as Minister of Munitions he had visited every part of the country, talking to the factory directors, foremen and workers upon whose efforts the success of his arms drive depended, he failed to act analogously as Secretary of State for War. He saw very little of formations in close contact with the enemy; of officers and men facing death and danger in the trenches, or of the wounded and those who ministered to them.

Northcliffe urged him to spend 'at least two weeks' with the Army, and he also wrote to Lee (from Paris) to enlist his cooperation:

1. 5 October 1916 (Bertie, *op. cit.*, Vol. II, pp. 38–9).

I do wish you could bring him out to the war. He is not popular at the front because the Army regard him as a Winston or a Seely, and you can tell him I said so, but chiefly because he is unknown to the men except as a politician. I fought battles on his behalf all along the line.

I think it is essential that the Secretary of War should be known to the officers and men. Lies in the House of Commons for the last two years, lies that the soldiers know to be lies, have not enhanced the reputation of politicians with the Army. Regarding, as I do, Lloyd George as one of our chief national assets, it is a great pity that soldiers who will one day rule England, as they ruled the United States after 1865, should not realise his determination to win.[1]

Northcliffe's primary motive for wanting Lloyd George to see more of the rank and file was that he believed this would convince him that the Army was superbly led and full of confidence in the high command. But it was sound advice all the same, and Lloyd George would have been wise to act on it. Unfortunately, though his visit to France in September was of about two weeks' duration, most of the time was spent either in Paris or among senior officers some distance from the front.

Why did he not make it his business to see the reality of war and to be seen by as many as possible of those who were enduring it? His fear of explosives was no doubt one reason, but the main reason was his squeamishness. All his life he had recoiled from illness, injury and death, so it was inevitable that the physical consequences of war would be so abhorrent to him that he could not trust himself to contemplate them at close quarters. When he was in France at the end of January he visited a young man in hospital and Frances Stevenson describes the effect on him of his experience:

D.'s face was careworn and drawn when he arrived in London, & I could see that the visit had told on his nerves. 'You must take my mind off it all, Pussy,' were almost his first words to me. 'I feel I shall break down if I do not get right away from it all. The horror of what I have seen has burnt into my soul, and has almost unnerved me for my work.' He had been to see the son of John Hinds, M.P., lying wounded in the hospital at the Welsh headquarters over there.

1. Northcliffe to D.L.G., 6 August 1916, and to Lee, undated but probably written at about the same time (L.G.P.).

The poor boy had been shot through the head, & the bullet had torn through part of his brain. He was in dreadful agony, & was paralysed all down one side. D. insisted upon fetching two more doctors to the hospital to see if they could not do anything for him, though everyone said his case was hopeless. D. later on spoke to the Commander-in-Chief, who promised that the best doctor out there should be with the boy by 5.0 yesterday afternoon. Since he has been home, D. has managed to send a brain specialist from Etaples to see him, & still hopes that it may be possible to save the boy's life. But the incident had quite unnerved him. 'I wish I had not seen him,' he kept on saying to me. 'I ought not to have seen him. I feel that I cannot go on with my work, now that the grim horror of the reality has been brought home to me so terribly. I was not made to deal with things of war. I am too sensitive to pain & suffering, & this visit has almost broken me down.'[1]

One day his son Dick returned from the front determined to give him a very thorough account of the conditions there:

'I'll make him understand. I'll make him,' I thought. I'll tell him to go to the front and see what it's like. Why must he be protected? Why should we all baby him? Sickness, misery, death – these were the only things he feared. He could never look on the face of death. But now he would have to! I'd see to it that he did know what was happening.

When I arrived home I found father at the top of his form, full of bounce and energy. He greeted me with the greatest warmth, and at dinner was obviously trying to make me feel relaxed. He had that wonderful susceptibility to atmosphere. . . . Before the meal was over, I felt certain that without having said a word about it he knew what was in my mind.

After dinner, we were alone, smoking and sipping a whisky. For a long time we were silent. I was trying to find the words which stubbornly refused to come out.

'All right, Dick. You must tell me what it's been like.'

I had had my nose buried in my glass during my agitated period of silence. Now I summoned my resolution. I knew exactly what I wanted to say.

I looked up – and saw a face so tense and miserable, so utterly

1. F.S.D., 1 February 1916, pp. 92–3. Hinds was the Liberal M.P. for West Carmarthenshire. His son died within twenty-four hours of Lloyd George's return from France.

different from the cheerful cordiality during dinner that all the words, all the strictures, demands and warnings – they all seemed pointless. Here was a man with no need to look on the face of it to know death.[1]

No wonder such a man shrank from seeing what was happening on the Somme battlefield. Haig, to be sure, had almost as little first-hand contact with the front as he had, and one fighting officer who, in the next war, was a commander-in-chief himself would remark bitterly that he never saw Haig.[2] This was surely a fair complaint, because although some leaders in war may not need to see in order to understand, it is nevertheless important for them to *be seen* so that those they are leading should believe they understand, quite apart from the moral stimulus that their presence may give. Haig perhaps remained aloof through a lack of imagination, Lloyd George through an excess of it; but either way their aloofness represented a certain failure of leadership. By contrast with Lloyd George, old Clemenceau paid frequent and perilous visits to the front when he became France's war leader.[3]

While the German and Allied armies were fighting each other to a standstill in the West, the war in the East was characterised by movement, often of a most dramatic and unexpected kind. The offensive launched by Brusilov in June was not halted for three months and cost the Austro-Hungarian empire half a million men, many of whom were Slavs willing enough to be taken prisoner. But no progress was made in the northern sector of the front, and reserves held there in expectation of a major advance were not transferred in time to Brusilov in the south, with the result that his campaign eventually failed with the loss of a million men. This failure and loss, on top of Russia's already enormous sacrifices, probably sealed the fate

1. Richard Lloyd George, *Lloyd George*, pp. 156-7.
2. 'There was little contact between the generals and the soldiers. I went through the whole war on the Western Front, except during the period I was in England after being wounded; I never once saw the British Commander-in-Chief, neither French nor Haig, and only twice did I see an Army Commander.' (B. L. Montgomery, *Memoirs*, p. 35.) Incidentally, Montgomery would not, like Haig, have made it a point of criticism against Lloyd George that he had 'breakfast with Newspaper men and posings for the Cinema Shows' (Haig to Lady Haig, 13 September 1916).
3. 'Clemenceau's speeches had impact because they obviously came from the heart, and because his reckless visits to the front showed that he was careless of his own life, however irrational such action might seem to be.' (David Robin Watson, *Georges Clemenceau: A Political Biography*, p. 313.)

of the Tsarist regime. Certainly Brusilov's 1916 offensive was Russia's last great effort in the war. But it succeeded at least in its diversionary purpose, for the troops that the Germans had to switch from the West to deal with it might have made all the difference at Verdun or in counter-attacks on the Somme.

Another consequence of the offensive was that it encouraged Roumania, after much hesitation, to enter the war on the side of the Entente. The decision was taken at the end of August, when Brusilov's army – and Russia itself – were in fact running out of steam. But at first it seemed a promising development for the Allies. Though the Roumanian army was inefficient, ill-equipped and badly led, it at once began an invasion of Transylvania which might, if pressed, have become a grave threat to the Central Powers. Lloyd George was naturally excited by the new turn of events, but also apprehensive that once again the Western Allies would fail to give adequate support. On 2 September he sent a note to General Frederick Maurice, Director of Military Operations:

> We cannot afford another Serbian tragedy. We were warned early in 1915 that the Germans meant in confederation with the Bulgars to wipe Serbia out. In spite of the fact, when the attack came we had not purchased a single mule to aid the Serbians through Salonica. The result was when our troops landed there, owing to lack of equipment and appropriate transport, they could not go inland and Serbia was crushed. . . .
>
> I therefore once more urge that the General Staff should consider what action we could in conjunction with France and Italy take immediately to relieve the pressure on Roumania if a formidable attack developed against her.[1]

Robertson made out in his memoirs that this note was written to Asquith and that he himself had no knowledge of it until after the war. But as it was in fact sent to Maurice he must have known about it, because Maurice and his protégé and they worked very closely together.[2] Moreover he wrote to Haig three days later that Lloyd

1. 4 September 1916. Roumania declared war on Austria-Hungary on 27 August. The following day Germany declared war on her, and Bulgaria did the same on 1 September.
2. He had served under Robertson at the Staff College before the war, and there 'a close friendship began which had a marked influence on Maurice's subsequent career' (D.N.B.). In 1915 he was in charge of the operations section at B.E.F. headquarters when Robertson was chief of staff there. As C.I.G.S. Robertson at once chose him to be director of military operations at the War Office.

George had 'got the Servian fit again', which is clear evidence that he knew. He had no intention of moving substantial forces from the West to Salonica, whatever Lloyd George might wish. There seemed to him no danger that Roumania would be overrun, and in any case he could think of no better way of helping her than by continued hard pounding on the Western front. His view prevailed with the War Committee on 12 September, when Lloyd George was absent in France.

It must be said that Lloyd George himself had argued, in April, that the decision to mount a full-scale attack in the West precluded effective action in the Balkans, and he had not favoured reinforcing Salonica at that time. His warning in early September was therefore, as Churchill says, rather belated.[1] If he had been giving more attention to the Balkans he might have realised that Roumanian intervention was not necessarily desirable in the circumstances. The very mixed and uncoordinated Allied force at Salonica could not deliver the strong simultaneous attack on Bulgaria that the Roumanians were counting on, and the Russians were unable to give prompt help because there was a gap of twenty miles between their railway system and the Roumanian. The attack from Salonica was delayed until the end of September, when it achieved only limited success and did not affect the issue in Roumania. And Russia's eventual military aid was similarly useless.

Just after Lloyd George left for France a German force was invading Roumania from Bulgaria. By the third week of October the port of Constanza on the Black Sea was captured and Bucharest was under imminent threat from the south and east. Consequently the Roumanian invasion of Transylvania petered out as troops had to be brought back to defend the capital, and the defences of the country's western frontier along the Carpathians were, for the same reason, weakened.● At the end of November the Germans broke through them and Bucharest was then threatened from all sides. On 6 December the city fell and Roumanian resistance was virtually at an end.

Could this disaster have been avoided, granted the timing of Roumania's entry into the war and the balance of forces there at the time? Lloyd George remained convinced that urgent measures could have saved Roumania, and he certainly tried very hard to promote

1. *The World Crisis*, ch. XLIV. Lloyd George did, however, argue in June that the existing force at Salonica should be prepared and equipped for offensive action.

such measures after his return from France. On 26 September he wrote to Asquith suggesting that Robertson should immediately be sent to Russia to concert Allied strategy with the Russian high command, and Asquith appears to have agreed to the suggestion. No doubt Lloyd George had a double motive in making it; he found Robertson's presence in London extremely irksome and would have been glad to get him out of the way for a time. But his eagerness to achieve a more unified Allied war effort was greater than ever, and he may well have hoped that a visit to the East might have a salutary effect upon Robertson's thinking.

Robertson would not go, however, and Lloyd George could not force him to go, more especially in the atmosphere created by the *Morning Post*'s leader on the 28th – which may have owed something to Robertson's annoyance about the Russian proposal, as well as to Haig's about the conversation with Foch. Royal influence was solicited and, for what it was worth, readily forthcoming in support of Robertson. On the 29th Derby wrote to his friend the King:

> Lloyd George sent for Robertson yesterday and said he wished him (and the Prime Minister agreed with him in saying so) to go on a visit to Russia and to be away about six weeks. Robertson in confidence consulted me and I told him to absolutely refuse to go – this advice coincided with his own feelings, and he has now written to both Lloyd George and the P.M. to say that he will not go. It would be absolutely impossible for him to leave and especially at this juncture. He and I standing together can I think prevent any wildcat scheme, but alone I feel I should fail. Moreover there would be no buffer between Lloyd George and Haig which is essential. All this may never come to your Majesty's ears. The scheme may be nipped in the bud, but I felt that Your Majesty would wish me to mention it to Your Majesty.

And the King replied the same day:

> I will certainly not allow R. to go to Russia. He is first of all much too valuable a man to run risks with like poor K. and then it would be impossible to get on without him especially at this critical moment of the war. I will not hear of it. . . .[1]

This correspondence gives a good idea what Lloyd George was up against at the War Office.

1. Quoted in Randolph S. Churchill, *Lord Derby: King of Lancashire*, pp. 223–4.

His struggle with the C.I.G.S. continued throughout the autumn, and was essentially a losing struggle. Lloyd George wanted divisions sent to Salonica partly for the positive reason that they might help Roumania, but also for the negative reason that their withdrawal from the West might stop the fighting on the Somme – which was, of course, precisely why Robertson was determined that they should not be moved. He turned Northcliffe on to Lloyd George like a bravo or hit man. The Press Lord appeared in the minister's office on 11 October and, since Lloyd George happened to be out, said to J. T. Davies: 'You can tell him that I hear he has been interfering with strategy, and that if he goes on I will break him.'[1] The same day Lloyd George had a minatory letter from Gwynne, editor of the *Morning Post*, and one from Robertson himself accusing him of undermining his (Robertson's) authority in the strategical direction of the war. To this Lloyd George replied with icy sarcasm:

> It ought to be decided whether I have the same right – although I am War Secretary – to express an independent view on the War in the discussions which take place as any other member of the War Council – or whether, as long as I am War Secretary, I must choose between the position of a dummy or a pure advocate of all opinions expressed by my military advisers.... You must not ask me to play the part of a mere dummy – I am not in the least suited for the part.[2]

But verbal sallies counted for little against the fact that Robertson's authority was entrenched by Order in Council. Lloyd George could only manoeuvre to circumvent it, and he made the most of French pressure to reinforce the Salonica army, with which he associated himself at an Allied conference on 20 October, held at Boulogne. But during October the War Committee agreed only to send two divisions, which was too little and too late. Robertson's complacency about Roumania's chances of holding on, combined with his belief that the war could be won only through attrition in the West, largely prevailed during the period when an alternative strategy was still, perhaps, feasible for the late autumn.

By November Lloyd George was turning his thoughts to the following year and how to prevent yet another sell-out to the military. At the beginning of the month he intervened strongly at a War

1. F.S.D., 12 October 1916, p. 115.
2. D.L.G. to Robertson, 11 October 1916.

Committee meeting from which Robertson, conveniently, was absent. The enemy had recovered the initiative, he said, and was occupying more territory than ever. The Somme battle had succeeded in relieving Verdun, but in other respects had failed. How was victory to be achieved? In a war of attrition the hammer might be more damaged than the anvil. The Germans could afford to give ground, and so avoid losses. He referred to the Allies' growing difficulties in shipping, food supply and finance, and to the danger of public demoralisation if hopes were raised – as over the Somme – only to be disappointed. The politicians, not the generals, would be held responsible for failure, and it was therefore vital that the civilian leaders should meet to take stock of the situation. There should also be a military conference in Russia, to be attended by the principal generals from the West, including Robertson.[1]

The War Committee agreed to the two proposed conferences, but Robertson reacted indignantly when he heard what had been going on behind his back, more especially Lloyd George's renewed attempt to ship him off to Russia. Nor was he mollified by a tactful letter from Hankey seeking to persuade him with the argument that 'the visit of a great General will have more effect than that of any politician'. Even when Lloyd George offered, through Hankey, to accompany him to Russia he remained obdurate. Threatening resignation, he compelled the War Committee to drop the proposal. Lloyd George had to be content with extracting from McKenna, at a Cabinet meeting, the admission that he had tacitly confirmed Robertson's suspicions: a hollow triumph indeed.[2]

The meeting of civilian leaders proved equally frustrating. At least it took place, in mid-November, but it failed to pre-empt a meeting of the military leaders which was held concurrently. There will be more to say about this later; here it is simply necessary to observe that once again Lloyd George failed, as War Minister, to outmanoeuvre the military.

Haig's hostility to him, though no less than Robertson's, was artfully disguised. After the Minister's visit to France in September, and the row caused by his conversation with Foch, Haig was further

1. War Committee, 3 November 1916.
2. Hankey to Robertson, 9 November 1916, and diary entry of the same date, recording conversation with Lloyd George. (Roskill, *op. cit.*, p. 316, and Hankey, *op. cit.*, p. 557). Derby, on this occasion, told Lloyd George that he was advising Robertson to go if Joffre went (Randolph S. Churchill, *op. cit.*, p. 226).

392 LLOYD GEORGE: FROM PEACE TO WAR

incensed by a decision to send his predecessor, French, to report on
French artillery techniques. This was not, indeed, one of Lloyd
George's more inspired moves. Even Colonel Le Roy-Lewis, the
military attaché in Paris and a fervent admirer of his, was unmistak-
ably embarrassed by it. After French had returned home, Lewis
wrote:

> It is well known here that Lord French and General Haig are not on
> friendly terms. . . . That fact that our losses in the Picardy [Somme]
> offensive were great, and that the French losses for the same
> offensive were much smaller, has been the subject of general
> comment, and it is supposed – rightly or wrongly – that you were
> considerably interested in that aspect of the affair when you were
> last here, so that the visit of Lord French has been interpreted in the
> light of a special and secret mission not of a complimentary
> character to Sir Douglas Haig. . . .
> When Lord French was here I was careful to avoid him, so that it
> might not be supposed that his visit had any special official signifi-
> cance. . . .[1]

Haig did not protest to Lloyd George about the French mission, for
which in any case he partly blamed Robertson who had assented to it.
But he wrote to Derby: 'It was a bad mistake to send French out here
for few of us have forgotten that he told *lies* in his Despatches etc. etc.
but I have written Wully [Robertson] to tell him that he may count on
my most thorough support in his efforts to help the country to win.'
And he added: 'You must stop him from quarrelling with L.G.
because the country's business is certain to suffer whenever there is
friction.'[2] Haig believed in treating politicians with all the consideration and respect that he did *not* feel for them. After Lloyd George's

1. 17 October 1916. Herman Le Roy-Lewis was a clever, independent man, hard to place. In
the South African War he distinguished himself as a staff officer, and from 1908 to 1913
commanded a cavalry brigade in England. But he seems to have been unemployed between
1913 and his appointment to Paris in 1915. Between September and December 1916 he wrote
frequently and at length to Lloyd George. His letters are interesting, particularly about
French politics, but also about visiting British and foreign personalities. Robertson viewed
him with much disfavour, and on 22 November he wrote to Lloyd George: 'My correspondence to you seems to have excited some interest at the War Office, but I have no
intention of ceasing to write to you, until you do not wish to hear from me . . . it matters
extraordinarily little to me if I offend the competent military authority.' In May 1917 there
was some talk of his becoming joint minister or even joint ambassador in Paris, but nothing
came of the idea (Calwell, *op. cit.*, Vol. I, p. 355). In fact he received no further appointment.
2. Randolph S. Churchill, *King of Lancashire*, p. 227.

visit in September, and despite his wrath about the Foch incident, he wrote the Minister a most cordial letter saying what a pleasure it had been to entertain him. In early November he wrote another urging Lloyd George to visit him again, to which Lloyd George – in the middle of his second row with the C.I.G.S. about going to Russia – replied that he would be delighted to come for a couple of days and suggested bringing Robertson, because it was 'so important that soldier and politician should work together in this war'.[1]

The near-hopelessness of Lloyd George's position at the War Office is painfully clear from a statement by Derby in the House of Lords on 28 November, only eight days before Lloyd George left the department to become Prime Minister:

> . . . speaking with the full authority of Mr Lloyd George, [Derby] gave an emphatic denial to rumours that changes were insisted on and individuals imposed on Sir Douglas Haig without his consent and approval . . . the Army Council had complete confidence in Sir Douglas Haig. They believed that the best way of showing that they had such confidence was to fall in, as far as they possibly could, with any and every suggestion that he might make to secure the greater efficiency of the Army under his control. The reports that friction existed between the Army Council or individual members of it and Sir Douglas were untrue. 'We have a combination,' Lord Derby continued, 'of Sir Douglas Haig commanding in the field and Sir William Robertson, Chief of the General Staff, which cannot be equalled and much less improved.' It was the one desire of everybody in the War Office, from Mr Lloyd George downwards, to do what they could to help a combination which, they believed, would ensure success for our arms.[2]

It would have been hard to state more accurately the opposite of what Lloyd George in fact believed.

Some time before he went to the War Office he was discussing with Riddell the qualities needed in a great war minister, and Riddell said, 'It is a question of judgment, the power of selecting men, and energy.' Lloyd George replied, 'I agree. The capacity for judging men is most important. That is where we are at a loss. We do not know the

1. Haig to D.L.G., 23 September 1916 and 7 November 1916; D.L.G. to Haig, 10 November 1916 (L.G.P.).
2. *The Times*, 29 November 1916.

Army.'[1] His own energy was equal to any test, and his judgment of men was extremely shrewd, if at times erratic. He was never afraid to appoint strong characters to positions of authority, and was quick to make use of anyone who showed talent. Unlike some great men he never wished to be surrounded by mediocrities and yes-men. But he liked to be free to do the picking, and to be acknowledged as the ultimate boss. At the War Office he was not free; a barrier of professional exclusiveness blocked him at every turn. And ultimate power had to be shared with the department's leading professional.

'*We do not know the Army*'. Did he know it any better after five months as its political chief? Not really – and for that he was at least partly to blame. He did not use his time at the War Office to familiarise himself in detail with the service over which he was presiding: to master all its intricacies and hallowed mysteries, so that he could both flatter and bewilder the professionals with his knowledge. Yet he would have been fully capable of such a feat of assimilation, if he had put his mind to it. Above all he failed to establish personal links with a large number of soldiers at all levels, particularly fighting soldiers, who could have helped him to 'know the Army' and among whom he might have spotted a few winners. His specific work as War Minister, therefore, as distinct from his wider activities as surrogate national leader, did not enhance him; but at least it did not destroy him.

1. R.W.D., 7 November 1915, p. 135.

FIFTEEN
Private and Personal

The crisis in Frances's life during the early months of 1915, whatever its precise nature, left her relations with Lloyd George as close as ever. While he was at the Ministry of Munitions and at the War Office he continued to be indispensable to him in her joint role of secretary and mistress. In October she acquired a flat of her own at 41A Chester Square, which made her still more independent of her parents and gave her and Lloyd George a place, other than Walton Heath, where they could conveniently be together. For part of the time it was shared with a woman friend, Mary Phillips, but as a friend she no doubt knew when to make herself scarce. Lloyd George would often spend a quiet evening there after one of his habitually busy days; for instance, he dined there with Frances 'off cold pheasant & cheese' after witnessing, during the afternoon, a demonstration of the first tank.[1]

He may have helped her to pay for the flat, and certainly helped her to furnish it. In November he brought her from Paris an Empire clock and two candlesticks of the same period. Indeed he seldom forgot to buy her presents while on his travels, at home or abroad. On the same visit to Paris he also picked up for her a Cross-of-Lorraine brooch and the next time he was there bought her 'the most wonderful blouse'. Even when he was in Glasgow for his rowdy meeting with trade union militants he sent J. T. Davies to buy 'a most handsome dressing-gown' for her.[2] That Christmas she gave him a photograph of herself

1. 2 February 1916 (F.S.D., p. 94).
2. 22 November and 29 December 1915 (*ibid.*, p. 75 and p. 87).

in a leather pocket-book, which he could and did always carry with him.

The ardour of his love for her cannot be doubted, but it could not take precedence over his work, which was always his supreme passion. His feelings might be summed up in Lovelace's famous words, 'I could not love thee Dear so much, Lov'd I not honour more' – honour comprising, in his case, an exalted idealism, ordinary patriotism and, of course, personal ambition. At moments he might express impatience with the constraints of prudence and duty, even on one occasion suggesting that he would be prepared to do a Parnell and face disgrace for her sake; but such talk did not reflect his true attitude. His original declaration, that he loved her but would not sacrifice his career for her, remained the iron law governing their relationship.

In October 1915 he felt it was no longer safe to take her to Walton with him in his car, and told her she would have to go down by train, explaining why in characteristic terms:

> D. does not like taking me about in his Gov. car, in case people fix on it for a scandal. I was rather sick about it, as I love driving with him, but D. made me cheer up, saying 'never mind! We are "doing" the world in spite of its spitefulness. I have defied it for 25 years – treated it with contempt, spat upon its tinsel robes, and I have won through. If you pay homage to it in certain things, you can defy it in others as much as you like.' It is very true. If you respect certain forms and conventions, you may break others to your heart's content, and the world will say nothing.[1]

He was talking defiance, but practising discretion. The breaking of convention was more on her side than his, since she was committed to an illicit liaison without the security of being married to another man.

Lloyd George was well aware of this, and seems to have wanted her to have a less equivocal status. No doubt he wanted it for his own sake as well as hers. In his day the ideal set-up for a public man with a mistress was that she should be a married woman with a complaisant husband. This provided an even better cover than was provided, for Lloyd George and Frances, by her position as his private secretary, and above all it was more satisfactory in the event of a child's being conceived. Lloyd George must have been shaken by Frances's pregnancy, actual or supposed, which was a warning of what might

1. 19 October 1915 (F.S.D., pp. 68–9).

happen so long as she continued to be his mistress without being an 'honest woman'. And since he was not prepared to make her one himself so long as Margaret was living, the only solution was for someone else to do so without prejudice to their affair.

A definite plan took shape in his mind in August 1915. Early in the month he wrote her a letter which shows very well how torn he was between love for her, attachment to his family, and above all the claims of his work:

> My own sweet little Pussy,
>
> I am longing to be back with you. I am becoming more intolerant of these partings month by month. I cannot live now without my darling. . . .
>
> I have had the dreariest of holidays – rain mist damp. Tonight I motor to Colwyn.
>
> Now Pussy I have made up my mind to disappoint myself – & you. I have two days of most important & trying work in front of me – conferences & decisions upon which the success of the Department depends & I must reserve all my strength for them . . . my passion for you is a *consuming* flame – it burns up all wisdom prudence & judgment in my soul. . . .
>
> I feel as if during the last two months I have not given my very best to the terrible task entrusted to me. My future depends entirely on it. What is much more important – the nation's future depends on it. . . .
>
> Tomorrow night I dine with Churchill so you can make your own arrangements.
>
> Oh I do want to see you – I want *you* & no one & nothing else.
>
> > Your own
> > D. – for ever[1]

In another letter, about a fortnight later, we find the first evidence, in cryptic form, of the plan whereby he hoped to regularise her position and simplify his own life:

> My own sweet child
>
> I received both your darling letters & they were like nectar for lips parched with a great passion. I have been these 2 or 3 days thinking things of unutterable tenderness & love for my little cariad. My affection for her has deepened & sweetened beyond anything words

1. *My Darling Pussy*, ed. A. J. P. Taylor, pp. 10–11. Letter dated 8 August 1915.

can tell. Yours is the tenderest & purest love of my life Pussy bach
. . . . I could face *anything* with you. I have been thinking of you all
day & much of the night & always oh so fondly.

Returning tomorrow. No time to write anymore.

I've had a talk with D. His view is that O. is moved by a
consuming desire to *get on*. That is the line. I believe he would do it
unconditionally. There is peril & pollution in the other course. I
love my *pure* little darling.

Ever & Ever

Your own

D.[1]

The 'D' referred to in the letter is the reliable J. T. Davies, while 'O'
stands for Captain Hugh Owen, former stationmaster at Holyhead
but serving now as liaison officer between the Ministry of Munitions
and the War Office. The role envisaged for him by Lloyd George was
to be a liaison officer in a rather different sense. He was to 'marry
Frances in the full knowledge of her relations' with his chief, since 'the
other course' – presumably that of trying to keep him in the dark –
would be dangerous as well as squalid. The prospect of sharing her
with another man, even one as humble as Owen seems to have been,
and as unlikely to be a serious rival, can hardly have been congenial to
Lloyd George; and the evidence suggests that his realistic promotion
of the scheme gave way at times to very natural waves of jealousy and
disgust. To Frances the idea must have been repellent from the first,
but she went through a long charade of considering it, rejecting it, and
then considering it again, before it was eventually abandoned in early
1917.

At some point in the late summer of 1915 she must have become
engaged to Owen, because on 5 October she noted in her diary that the
engagement had been broken off:

> It did not last very long! But D. was making himself miserable over
> the idea of my belonging to someone else even in name. Several
> times he has cried & sobbed as a child when speaking of it, begging
> me all the time to take no notice of him. But I could not bear to give
> him pain, & I know he is relieved now that I have broken it off. I
> must be free to be with him always, and marriage I know would
> forge new bonds. Owen is very upset, but wishes to be friends still.

1. 23 August 1915, written from Folkestone where Lloyd George was conferring about
munitions with Albert Thomas (*ibid.*, pp. 11–12).

He is very weak, and a very little satisfies him.[1]

But if Lloyd George was relieved at the time, he soon had second thoughts. On 20 October Owen wrote to Frances:

. . . Your letter breaking off the engagement was couched in very definite language – in fact the finality was so pronounced as to cause me to absolutely despair. . . . Subsequently, however, a remark let fall by one for whom I in common with you have the deepest regard, generated the hope that some action of mine upon which you had placed a wrong construction had influenced you in arriving at the decision you had taken.

And three days later she wrote in her diary:

D. is now on the marriage tack again! He says there are many advantages to be gained by marriage *provided that Owen understands what our relations are*, & promises to respect them. Am dining with Owen tonight to discuss the matter.[2]

So it went on. In November she was once again determined not to marry Owen, but the following May there was a rumour – started by her flat-mate, Mary Phillips – that she would be getting married in the near future. Nothing came of it, however, and her professional connection with Lloyd George was soon attracting what must, to him, have been unwelcome publicity, when he and his secretariat moved to the War Office.

I am sharing some of the reflected glory. People have just woken up to the fact that Ll.G. has a lady secretary, or rather, that the Sec. of State for War has a lady Secretary. I have people calling to interview me, & I have my photograph in the papers.

A worldly-wise observer, sensing danger, was quick to offer a veiled word of warning.

Sir George Riddell came in today. He says the Asquithites are still plotting to get D. out of power. . . .'They would stoop to the trick that was played on Parnell if they thought it would bring Ll.G. down.' I think Sir G. was giving me a hint to be very careful, as D.'s enemies are always on the watch; and the publicity that has been given to my appointment will make it still more

1. *ibid.*, p. 12. This passage is not printed in F.S.D.
2. *ibid.*, pp. 13–14. The diary entry, again, not in F.S.D.

necessary for us to be wary.[1]

But her wariness was not to be carried to the length of marrying Owen, and the idea quietly lapsed. Lloyd George came across Owen at Verdun, and joked about the encounter to Frances. He was 'the very image' of her 'finance' (fiancé).[2] But gradually the impossibility of the scheme became evident to, and accepted by, Lloyd George. His aim, almost certainly, had been to establish the kind of *ménage à trois* that he had earlier enjoyed with the Timothy Davieses. Much as he loved Frances, and necessary as she was to him, he may occasionally have found the isolation and intensity of their relationship a little wearing, quite apart from the lurking threat to his career. Certainly he wanted to be her only lover, but it might well have suited him to have her looked after, more or less platonically, by a man content to be his slave as well as hers.

To Frances, however, the arrangement offered only the advantage of a domesticity which did not, on the whole, appeal to her. Though it would mean more freedom for Lloyd George, it would mean considerably less for her, since it would, as she perceived 'forge new bonds'. It would indeed, make her free to have children, and the children might be his, but even her desire for motherhood seems to have yielded to her excitement in sharing his work.

> I am happy as we are – we have our little home now, where we can spend many evenings together in solitude. . . . The only thing we lack is children, but I often think that if I were married & had children, then I should not be able to keep in touch with D.'s work to the extent that I do now. . . . I don't suppose I should see nearly as much of him if I were married to him.[3]

A scheme designed to protect his career may, therefore, have foundered partly because she sensed it as a threat to hers. If she could not quite bring herself to sacrifice, for his sake, the privilege of involvement in vital public work, it was hardly for him to complain. When she fell in love with him she also fell in love with the atmosphere of power.

While happy enough in his passionate affair with Frances, Lloyd

1. 26 July and 28 July 1916 (F.S.D., p. 110).
2. *My Darling Pussy*, p. 18.
3. F.S.D., 8 February 1916 (p. 96).

George was no less happy to be Darby to Margaret's Joan. Despite his infidelity he never ceased to feel very close to her, and he respected her as he respected no other woman. One evening when they had Riddell to dinner the behaviour of married couples was discussed.

L.G. says no couples are entitled to indulge in public demonstrations of affection until they have been married twenty years; until that period has elapsed they cannot be sure that they will not have a violent disagreement which may terminate their relationship. He added, 'we have been married for twenty-eight years so we are justified in making a public demonstration'. Whereupon he kissed 'Maggie bach', as he calls his wife.[1]

She knew that the kiss was not merely for show, though of course she also knew much that hurt and angered her.

Family life was a great bond which united them and excluded Frances. He was deeply grateful for her attentiveness to Uncle Lloyd, whose health was failing. On 26 August 1916 he writes:

I am relieved to hear that the Manchester specialist is to see Uncle Lloyd. Couldn't you persuade him to spend the fortnight at Brynawelon & force him to *rest*. . . . Do hen gariad put your back into this job & I will love you ten times as much if you pull the old boy through. . . . Tell Uncle Lloyd there is an article about him & me in the Figaro, the great French newspaper. Charming.

A few days later (1 September):

I am very pleased with Dr Brocklebank's report. . . . We were evidently on the wrong tack in assuming that [Uncle Lloyd's] digestion was weak. Olwen tells me he is to get meat. Let him have it. . . .

I am off to France on Monday. . . .

I agree it would be better for Uncle Lloyd to go down for a part of the day. . . . But I want that room made more comfortable. I have bought him a nice new chair which he can . . . rest his legs upon & read papers & books. I am sending it down addressed to you at Cric. Tell them to take it to Uncle Lloyd's office. Have a nice hearthrug for him also. You can buy it there.

And the following day:

I love you so much for looking after Uncle Lloyd. I hear it makes

1. R.W.D., 13 February 1916, p. 155.

him so happy & he has always been devoted to you – always.[1]

In London Margaret set up an organisation for supplying comforts to Welsh troops, which worked from three rooms in 11 Downing Street.

> In no time these rooms were crowded with Welsh women resident in London, all only too eager to do whatever work was assigned to them. Speedily this work developed into a sorting and packing routine, the response to [Margaret's] appeal bringing in mountainous masses of every imaginable kind of comforts for the troops. Besides knitted wear and goods of all descriptions, every post brought cheques from wealthy Welshmen in all parts of the world. And with passing time the influx of gifts of money and goods steadily increased until [she] was nearly overwhelmed with the magnitude of her task.[2]

By the end of the war she had raised £200,000 (the equivalent of about £4 million in 1985).

Olwen, who had spent a year in Dresden followed by a year in Paris before the war, joined the V.A.D. and nursed in France before becoming engaged to a gifted and independent-minded surgeon, Thomas Carey Evans, whom she married in 1917. Megan, after leaving Allenswood, was sent to Garratt's Hall, Banstead, where she was a boarder. Though as careless as her father about correspondence she kept one letter – clearly written after her return to school at the end of the 1915 summer holidays – which shows how fond he was of her:

> The sunshine has gone since you left & now we have cloudy skies & a great dismal outlook. Bring the sunshine back as soon as you can, little sweet. I am sending you the Cloister & the Hearth. It is one of the most delightful stories ever written. . . . Today I had Winston Churchill, Sir Edward Carson, Bonar Law & F. E. Smith to lunch. We had a most useful & important discussion about the war. . . .[3]

In early December 1915 Dick and Gwilym went to France, and Frances recorded that Lloyd George and Margaret were 'feeling rather miserable about it', but suggested also that Lloyd George was more miserable about Gwilym's departure than Dick's. 'I believe D. would

1. Letters, pp. 183–4.
2. Richard Lloyd George, Dame Margaret, pp. 141–2.
3. 14 September 1915 (Letters, p. 180).

be heartbroken if anything happened to Gwilym, to whom he is devoted.'[1] Something nearly did happen to Gwilym before he even reached France, because on the way over his ship just missed being sunk by a U-boat. 'It missed by a few feet and then they ran over it & it was sent to the bottom.'[2] On 5 January 1916 Lloyd George had General Philipps to lunch and afterwards reported to Margaret, 'Boys alright' (he always spelt it as one word). At the end of the month they were, as we have seen, brought by Haig to his headquarters to meet their father. Dick spent two days with him, and Lloyd George wrote to his brother William that 'Dick's work was not nearly as dangerous as it was at first'. Towards the end of February, in another letter to William, he said he had just met at No. 10 a man who had been seeing the two boys: ' . . . they were both A.1., Dick and Gwilym. They had moved somewhere behind the La Basse [sic] Canal – he thought it was about the safest place in the whole line.'[3]

In April Gwilym wrote: 'I went & had dinner with Dick about two nights ago, & he is in the most palatial billet I have seen since I have been in this part.'[4] But Dick was involved in the first days of the Somme battle. Then, on 10 July (probably), Margaret wrote to Uncle Lloyd: 'You will be glad to hear that Dick is out of the fight now and without a scratch and he said this morning "Thanks to Providence". The Welsh Division are now holding the line doing the same sort of work as they did in Winter and therefore comparatively safe.'[5] And at about the same time Lloyd George wrote to William: 'The Welsh are doing brilliantly. They have just captured the Woods which had defied attack up till yesterday. . . . Unfortunately the General has broken down in health and he returned home last night bringing with him his A.D.C. Lieut. Gwilym Lloyd George. Dick is A.1. engaged for the moment in making roads for the artillery and ammunition to pass along to the Front.'[6] During his September visit to France Lloyd George wrote to Margaret that he intended to see Dick,[7] though there is no evidence that he did. On 18 November Dick was 'back looking

1. F.S.D., 30 November 1915 (p. 81).
2. Gwilym L.G. to his parents, 10 January 1916 (N.L.W.).
3. D.L.G. to William George, 1 February and 24 February 1916 (quoted in William George, *My Brother and I*, p. 253).
4. Gwilym L.G. to his parents, 24 April 1916 (N.L.W.)
5. Letter dated just 'Monday', but from comparison with D.L.G.'s of 11 July most likely to be 10 July (*My Brother and I*, p. 255).
6. 11 July 1916 (*ibid.*, p. 255).
7. 10 September 1916, from the Hotel Crillon, Paris (N.L.W.).

well' and 'gone to the theatre with Gwilym and Olwen'.[1] At the end of the month Lloyd George wrote proudly to William: 'Will Bach [Gwilym] has the true warrior spirit which I have so far utterly failed to infuse in my colleagues. I mean to propose his name as a member of the War Committee.'[2]

Gwilym certainly did have the warrior spirit, and was to prove it as a battery commander during the remainder of the war. In politics during the inter-war period he was always known as Major Lloyd George, as C. R. Attlee was 'Major Attlee'. Dick also acquitted himself honourably as a soldier, and he too ended the war as a major – in the Royal Engineers. The brothers should not be blamed for accepting the staff posts that were offered them at the beginning of the War, nor should their parents be blamed for so clearly wishing them to be out of danger. But there was a contrast between Lloyd George's private attitude as a father and his public attitude as a recruiting orator which cannot fail to strike us now, and which did not pass entirely unnoticed at the time.

One who noticed it was Julia Henry, whose only son Cyril was killed in 1915. While he was missing but not yet known to be dead she must have written Lloyd George a bitterly reproachful letter, because he replied:

I can well understand the anguish you are passing through. I have passed through the same torture [presumably the death of Mair] & my heart goes out to you & to your husband. I wish you hadn't written me the taunting words about my boys. I am doing my best to hurry them to the front. My heart bleeds for you both & all my friends know that but it would be no help to you for me to come over to listen to these reproaches.

As you know we are in the throes of a great crisis but I shall do my best to come over to see you. When does Henry come home this evening? I want to see him also.[3]

Lloyd George had good reason not to want to see Julia Henry alone. Despite her fury in 1911, when he ended their (to him) slight affair, she continued to pursue him with letters, invitations and presents. He would acknowledge the letters briefly, if at all; occasionally accept,

1. *My Brother and I*, p. 255.
2. 27 November 1916 (*ibid.*, p. 256).
3. 11 October 1915 (N.L.W.).

but normally refuse or ignore, the invitations; and accept the presents, without always remembering to thank her for them. For instance:

> It was so kind of you to send me those luscious peaches & nectarines – 'rare & refreshing fruit' of the rarest & most refreshing.
>
> I congratulate you heartily on the success – the very brilliant success – of your party. I was sorry to have to leave early but I had an anxious day in front of me. . . .
>
> I wish I had seen Cyril to felicitate him on the attainment of his majority & to wish him a career not merely of happiness but of honourable service which I know he is capable of.
>
> Friday I am engaged otherwise I should have been delighted to lunch at Carlton Gardens.[1]

Or:

> I am literally overwhelmed with work otherwise would have written you. . . .
>
> The last glasses are far and away the best – they are a great success. . . .[2]

Or:

> I am enchanted with my new equipment. I opened the parcel before an admiring assembly of officials who were full of praise for the suitability and taste of the 'set'. Many many thanks.
>
> I am tempted now even to write letters on the glorious pad.
>
> P.S. I should like to turn in to a quiet dinner with C[harles Henry] next week.[3]

Or again:

> I am busier than ever. Only just time to breathe & hardly enough time to feed. I have had *no* meal for a fortnight at which I had not to discuss business. I am longing for a few days off.
>
> It is so kind of you to send that delicious box.[4]

Frances Stevenson gives this account of the unpleasantness over Cyril's death:

1. 8 July 1914 (N.L.W.).
2. 28 November 1915 (N.L.W.). She seems to have kept him supplied with spectacles, beginning with the pair he wore at the Marconi enquiry.
3. 17 March (year not given, but obviously 1916 because written from Armaments Building) (N.L.W.).
4. 28 July 1916 (N.L.W.).

D. was very exercised in his mind as to whether he should or should not go and see the Henrys to show sympathy in the loss of their son. When the blow first fell, Lady H. wrote him some amazing letters because he failed to go round or write at once, and D. felt that if he went round she would only take advantage of his presence to make a scene, and he felt that he could not face it. He went, however, in the end, and it appears that she was very reasonable. I must say I think she deserves a little kindness, for they have both been exceedingly kind to D., only unfortunately at one time he allowed things to go too far, and is now sorry for it. . . . She is quite mad on him, and does not seem to have any pride or self-respect where he is concerned.[1]

It was a strength in Frances that she could be magnanimous about women from Lloyd George's past, provided she was confident they were no longer rivals to herself. Significantly she was not magnanimous about Margaret, because she knew that in certain ways she could never displace Lloyd George's wife. But she could afford to take a generous, or at any rate a compassionate, view of Julia Henry, and she was even capable of tolerating 'Mrs Tim' Davies, for whom Lloyd George retained a much softer spot than for Julia. Her line was that she did not mind him seeing 'Mrs Tim' so long as he told her he was doing so.

Since becoming a minister Lloyd George had necessarily seen less of some of his old cronies, such as Herbert Lewis and Frank Edwards, because his work claimed so much of his time and there was little or no place for them in his work. His feelings for those two and most of his other old associates did not change, nor theirs for him, yet with the expansion of his sphere of activity his circle of friends, or friendly acquaintances, also expanded. The War, however, as well as making him even busier, did to a greater or lesser degree alienate him from some of his former friends, though most of them followed his lead. One who turned against him very strongly over conscription was Llewelyn Williams, who had been his companion when he toured Canada in the summer of 1899. Another who felt thoroughly unhappy about his role as a war leader was D. R. Daniel, who had known him since the late 1880s when they had founded a Welsh-language newspaper together.

1. F.S.D., 15 November 1915, p. 74.

Daniel, an opponent of the war, listened to Lloyd George's Queen's Hall speech in September 1914, and of course did not like what he heard. He was also in the gallery of the House of Commons on 15 March 1915, when Lloyd George defended against the Welsh Members the Government's bill postponing Welsh disestablishment, and was deeply pained to hear him describe disestablishment as a 'petty sectarian squabble'. At the end of the year, on 4 December, they met by chance in Parliament Street and walked together to Lloyd George's office in Whitehall Gardens. Daniel's account of their conversation is worth quoting:

. . . he was exceptionally lively and kind in greeting . . . his appearance surprised me enormously. His hair appears extraordinarily thick – rather comic; more bushy than that of any eisteddfod bard! He's also gone very grey.

'Come back this way', said G., 'I'm going to the Munitions in Whitehall Gardens. . . . Where are you now?'

'In the same place,' said I. [He was assistant secretary to the Welsh Church commissioners.]

'Oh yes yes yes. Have you your eye on any task?'

'No certainty yet!'

'Well,' said G. appealingly, to my eyes, speaking rather slowly, 'I've got some places on my hands, but I'm afraid they are mostly with the gunpowder.'

'Thank you,' said I, pointing my finger to the gutter, 'I'd rather die *there*.'

'I know that,' said G.

'There was a time when you had a great respect for conscience.'

G. turned to me suddenly, grasped my left arm or put his hand on it. 'I still do. I respect you and Ramsay [MacDonald] but I haven't a jot of respect for those M.P.s who are against the war and are too cowardly to say so for fear of their constituents. . . . That's not what I did during the Boer war. . . .'

I agreed heartily. He mentioned something about his having other places to dispose of. 'I've got to look after the liquor. . . .'

'Well, I've got more experience of that kind of work,' said I, but I did not pursue the matter. We were about at Whitehall Gardens then and I remember saying something about my intention to go back to Wales before long.

'To Wales?'

'Yes, we'll do all right so long as our son is not stolen from us.'

He looked suddenly at me. I don't know what went through his mind but I think he understood me. We were now under the trees in Whitehall Gardens and I said to him I still thought he would be better out of the Cabinet – he had enough influence in the country.

'No, no,' said G. He went back immediately to his reason or excuse. 'After Belgium came up I couldn't.' But he did not seem to speak with much conviction.

I looked deep into his eyes. I said, touching my arm, 'We've worn Belgium proudly on our sleeve, yet first and foremost, falsehood and hypocrisy.'

I'll never forget G.'s look and behaviour. He did not answer or reproach me. He just turned his head and raised his hands and shook them, like a man who had just been hit by an arrow in his breast. . . .

Before going I said, 'Well, whatever the way it started, when do we see an end to this accursed carnage?'

'Not for years – not until Europe is a desert from end to end' (with deep stress).

The conversation ended. We said farewell under the branches of the trees.[1]

There is pathos as well as human interest in this fragment of talk. Daniel no doubt felt he had touched Lloyd George to the quick, and so in a sense he probably had, though not in the sense he may have imagined. Lloyd George knew that Belgium was not the main reason for Britain's involvement in the war, and might have admitted to himself that he had played the Belgian issue up considerably for the sake of people like Daniel, though Daniel was one who did not respond. But whatever hypocrisy there may have been in the emphasis given to Belgium, Lloyd George was not at all hypocritical in insisting that Britain had to go to war and had to fight through to victory, which he believed just as sincerely as Daniel believed the opposite. He must have been sad that they were no longer in political communion, and must also have felt genuine sympathy when Daniel mentioned his son. But there is no reason to suppose that he was seriously shaken by the conversation. Not wishing to quarrel with an old friend he took refuge in a gesture vaguely expressive of resentment at the cruelty of Fate, which Daniel could interpret as he chose.

1. D. R. Daniel, unpublished memoir (N.L.W.), translated from the Welsh by Dr Prys Morgan.

When Lloyd George told Julia Henry that he had discussed business at every meal for the past fortnight he was certainly telling the truth, because he had no objection at all to talking shop at meals and was an early exponent of the 'working breakfast'. He did not divide his life into watertight compartments, work and recreation, but allowed the two to flow together. By nature convivial, he enjoyed dealing with people and drawing them out, and his approach was much the same at home, on a golf course, or in his office. When he was ostensibly off duty his companions tended to be people associated with, or necessary to, his work, and by the same token he would bring to official business the lightheartedness and unpompous ease which many politicians would show, if at all, only when they were off duty. Those who worked for him found, therefore, that the experience was not only very demanding, but also very stimulating and great fun.

He liked to be host rather than guest, partly because he had so little time, literally or metaphorically, for the elaborate lunch and dinner parties which were then such a feature of the political world, even in war-time. 'A cut of mutton and a few bright companions is all I ask for,' he would say, though he might have added a modest sufficiency – never an excess – of stimulating drink. The best part of the hospitality he offered was always himself, and it could make up for the most frugal fare. When, on 7 June 1916, Lee was able to inform him that the target of shell production had been reached, and that output would in future rise steadily, a *tête-à-tête* celebration ensued which Lee vividly recaptures:

> That night will live long in my memory. When I handed the official shell-return to L.G. about eight o'clock, he was so overjoyed and excited that he took me by the arm and insisted that we should 'celebrate' by going off to dine together. When I said 'Where?' he replied 'Oh, come over to Downing Street; we can talk better there.' Then, after dashing across Whitehall, hatless and quite oblivious of the traffic, we arrived at No. 11, only to find the house apparently deserted and no one at home but his ancient house-keeper, 'Sarah'. She was a veritable Welsh dragon; dour and cross-grained, who had been with him since the days of his obscurity and who habitually addressed him with the minimum of respect. When at last she unchained the door and L.G. informed her airily, although a little timidly I thought, that he had 'brought a friend to dinner', she broke out into a tirade, saying, 'You can't dine here;

you know there's no food in the house with the mistress away.' To which L.G. replied soothingly, 'But what about that ham we had last week, Sarah, and haven't you any potatoes?' At first she declared there was none left, but when he insisted she disappeared, still growling, into the basement and after some time re-appeared with the fag end of the almost consumed ham and a few half-boiled potatoes. It was not very tempting, but L.G. was in such tearing spirits that even this fare took on the semblance of a banquet and we despatched it with gusto, washing it down with the only wine in the cellar – a half-full bottle of claret which had evidently been opened for some time. Then, as it grew dark, we went out to sit in the garden and talked long and earnestly about past and present problems and the prospects of the future. It was a marvellous summer night, with one great planet low in the western sky and the only other light the glow of L.G.'s cigar as he sat by my side and talked as I had never heard him talk before.[1]

The Lloyd Georges continued to live at 11 Downing Street when he moved from Munitions to the War Office. But in early October they decided to close the house down for reasons of economy. His income had been reduced from £5,000 to about £4,000, under a wartime measure for pooling ministerial salaries, and income tax cut it further; while of what remained £800 had to be invested in War Loan.[2] In November a flat was taken for him in St James's Court, by his P.P.S, David Davies (who had a flat there himself), and the idea was that he would sleep there when he could not manage the journey to Walton Heath, where he preferred to be at nights. But these arrangements were overtaken by the Lloyd Georges' move to 10 Downing Street the following month.

Despite his formidable egotism and relentless pursuit of objectives, there was much humanity and sheer good nature in Lloyd George. His squeamishness was due as much to kindness as to cowardice. He hated not only the sight of suffering, but also having to inflict it. He disliked sacking people and, though he did not shrink from doing it, could be quite upset by the task. One day at the Ministry of Munitions

. . . he had to give a man 'the sack' . . . for doing an indiscreet thing.

1. *A Good Innings*, pp. 153–4.
2. R.W.D., 1 October 1916 (pp. 213–14).

The poor fellow was frightfully cut up, and that upset D. very much, though he could not go back on it, as the man had committed gross breach of discipline. 'But it was only because he was an ass,' said D. 'He never meant any harm. And I could see the pain in his face – and I *loathed* myself for causing it.' The incident upset D. for the rest of the morning.[1]

Though he failed to live up to Dr Johnson's injunction that friendship should be kept 'in constant repair', he felt genuine affection for many people outside his own family and, even though they might slip from his immediate thoughts, he was usually glad to be reminded of their existence. And he was far from indifferent to the loss of friends. When Arthur Markham died in August 1916 he was troubled by the news for days and could not get it out of his mind.[2]

Shortly before this he heard distressing news of a man by no means as close to him as Markham, but one who had worked with him and whom he esteemed: Sir George Paish. Paish had suffered a mental breakdown and was in an asylum. He was suffering from delusions which mainly took the form of imagining himself to be watched and shadowed by the Treasury, whose agents had only not arrested him because they were hoping he would commit suicide. The reason, he believed, was that Lloyd George was offended by some articles that had appeared in the *Statist*, of which he was not in fact the author, and he told a colleague that if he could be assured that Lloyd George felt no hostility to him his mind would be set at rest. The colleague informed Lloyd George, who immediately wrote:

My dear Paish,

I was so sorry to hear the other day that you had had a breakdown in health. The overwork and anxiety of the War is telling on us all, and I feel myself sometimes as if I should like to take a voyage to the South Sea Islands and squat on the most inaccessible of them, where no papers could reach me, and remain there until this terrible War is over.

You must take a thorough rest. You thoroughly deserve it. No man gave me greater help during the severe financial crisis which followed the outbreak of war, and your sagacious and well-

1. F.S.D., 16 February 1916, p. 100.
2. *ibid.*, 8 August 1916, p. 113. Markham hero-worshipped Lloyd George. At their last meeting shortly before he died he 'came into D's room & took him by the hand. "You're a white man, George," he said & turned away.'

informed counsel contributed materially to saving this country from a disaster. I shall always feel grateful to you for the help you gave me then. You always took a brave, courageous and hopeful view of the situation. Throughout the whole of the tenure of my office at the Treasury I relied more upon your advice than upon that of any of my other advisers, and in every instance your judgment of the outlook was justified by the event.

I am anxious that you should take a thorough rest, free from all care, for public as well as for personal reasons, because I feel certain that next year we shall need your counsel more than ever. But meanwhile take the advice of a friend: dismiss all care from your mind; do not bother about anything, and whatever you do, dismiss worry. You have honestly deserved a rest and you can feel that you at any rate have contributed more than most people to help your country in its greatest trouble.

Ever your sincere and grateful friend,
David Lloyd George

It would be hard to conceive of a more sensitively therapeutic letter, and it was written at a time when Lloyd George had every reason to be in a distraught state himself, as his Irish negotiation was collapsing in ruins. He received a letter of touching gratitude from Paish, and in forwarding it to him Lady Paish said that she was sure his letter had helped her husband.[1]

Since his childhood, when he had read widely in the English classics, Lloyd George had not been a systematic reader except of newspapers, and of books or documents relating to his work. He did not, therefore, find the solace in literature that Asquith, for one, did. Yet every good book that he had ever read lived clearly in his memory, and he could re-tell in detail the story of, say, a Dickens novel, using his gift of mimicry to impersonate the characters. Among new books he seems to have preferred history to fiction, and during the first two years of the war he read, for instance, Belloc's life of Robespierre, Pitt the Younger's war speeches, and Nicolai's life of Abraham Lincoln.[2]

He had always enjoyed plays, including Bernard Shaw's, and in wartime continued to go to the theatre quite often. His lively if not

1. Sir George Gibb to D.L.G., 25 July 1916; D.L.G. to Paish, 25 July 1916; Paish to D.L.G., 27 July 1916; Lady Paish to D.L.G., 28 July 1916 (L.G.P.).
2. R.W.D., 11 October 1914 (p. 35), 16 November 1914 (p. 42), 15 January 1916 (p. 149).

very sophisticated musical taste found most delight in singing Welsh hymns and traditional songs, though it also extended to opera and oratorio. On 25 November 1916, within a fortnight of his becoming Prime Minister, he went to Westminster Abbey – with Margot Asquith – to hear what he described to his brother as 'one of the finest Elijah performances [he had] ever listened to'.[1]

He never showed very much interest in the visual arts, though Frances remarked upon his good taste in the choice of furniture or decorative objects. But artists were naturally interested in him, and in December 1915 he gave sittings at Walton Heath to the most gifted of all contemporary Welsh painters, Augustus John. While working on the portrait John revealed that when his father was at school at Haverfordwest he had been taught by Lloyd George's father, and Lloyd George was eager to know what impression the schoolmaster had made upon his pupil. John in due course reported that

> Mr Lloyd George *père* was a strict but always just disciplinarian, earning the respect of all the boys, but that his wife had won their *love*. This tribute delighted Lloyd George and was all the more valuable as coming from one ordinarily in the habit of confusing the distinguished offspring of the couple in question with the Devil himself.[2]

But Lloyd George was not so pleased with the portrait, which he thought would not make him 'look nice', and when Frances saw it in its finished form, in March, she was equally disappointed.

> It is a hard, determined, almost cruel face, with nothing of the tenderness & charm of the D. of every day life. It is true that it was painted when the Germans were slowly overcoming Serbia . . . and the disgrace which the others did not feel was manifest in D.'s expression & the tragedy of it all told keenly upon him. He himself suggested that the picture should be called 'Salonica', but unless this were done I do not consider it a good portrait.[3]

At least they did not anticipate the action of a later eminent couple by destroying the picture (reproduced on the jacket of this book).

Lloyd George was not unduly concerned about his image. His attitude was closer to Cromwell's 'warts and all' than to Churchill's

---

1. *My Brother and I*, p. 256.
2. Augustus John, *Chiaroscuro*, pp. 152–3.
3. F.S.D., 6 December 1915 and 12 March 1916 (p. 83 and pp. 103–4).

refusal to contemplate unflattering aspects of himself. He took life very seriously, in the sense of wanting to achieve as much as he could in it, but he did not take himself too seriously. His humour embraced the whole of life and he was capable of making jokes at his own expense, even some that a more cautious man would have avoided. For instance, he once said to Lee: 'I have an instinctive sympathy for criminals. I could so easily have been one myself!'[1] Many people might say the same if they were honest enough, but few indeed have the nerve or spirit for such beguiling frankness.

1. *A Good Innings*, p. 155.

SIXTEEN
The Howard Interview

Though Lloyd George did not acquire any fresh prestige as War Minister, apart from what was inherent in the office itself, the reputation that he had earned as Minister of Munitions, together with his crusading zeal and the general impression of realism and vigour that he had conveyed ever since the war began, made him continue to appear to many the country's natural leader.

On 17 August – soon after his first visit to France as War Minister, and shortly before his difficult speech in the House of Commons on the progress of the War – he travelled 'at some inconvenience' to Aberystwyth to speak at the National Eisteddfod, and the impact of his speech was felt far outside the Principality. He began, as he often did, at the level of banter:

There are a few people who know nothing about the Eisteddfod who treat it as if it were merely an annual jollification which eccentric people indulge in. There was a letter appearing in *The Times* this week written by a person who seems to hold that opinion. He signs himself 'A Welshman'. He evidently thinks that the publication of his name would add nothing to the weight of his appeal, so he has – wisely no doubt – withheld it. Now *The Times* is not exactly the organ of the Welsh peasantry. That does not matter to this gentleman, because he makes it clear that he has no objection to common people attending the Eisteddfod; but he expresses the earnest hope that important people like the Welsh M.P.s will not encourage such an improper assembly by giving it their presence.

His notion of the Eisteddfod is a peculiar one, and as there might be a few people outside Wales who hold the same views, I think I must refer to this estimate of its purport and significance. He places it in the same category as a football match or a horse-race and a good deal beneath a cinema or music-hall performance. These are kept going afternoon and evening without the slightest protest in the columns of *The Times* from this egregious Welshman.

The Eisteddfod offered 'prizes for odes, sonnets, translations from Latin and Greek literature, essays on subjects philosophical, historical, sociological'. It encouraged art and did not even forget agriculture. Should all this effort be dropped on account of the War? And what about singing? It was suggested that to sing during a war was indecent. 'Hush! No music, please; there is a war on!' But

Why should we not sing during war? Why, especially, should we not sing at this stage of the War? The blinds of Britain are not down yet, nor are they likely to be. The honour of Britain is not dead, her might is not broken, her destiny is not fulfilled, her ideals are not shattered by her enemies. She is more than alive; she is more potent, she is greater than she ever was. Her dominions are wider, her influence is deeper, her purpose is more exalted than ever. Why should her children not sing? I know war means suffering, war means sorrow. Darkness has fallen on many a devoted household, but it has been ordained that the best singer amongst the birds of Britain should give its song in the night, and according to legend that sweet song is one of triumph over pain. There are no nightingales this side of the Severn. Providence rarely wastes its gifts. We do not need this exquisite songster in Wales; we can provide better. There is a bird in our villages which can beat the best of them. He is called Y Cymro. He sings in joy, he sings also in sorrow; he sings in prosperity, he sings also in adversity. He sings at play, he sings at work; he sings in the sunshine, he sings in the storm. He sings in the daytime, he sings also in the night. He sings in peace; why should he not also sing in war? Hundreds of wars have swept over these hills, but the harp of Wales has never been silenced by one of them, and I should be proud if I contributed to keep it in tune during the war by the holding of this Eisteddfod today.

Welsh soldiers were singing the songs of Wales in the trenches, and were holding little eisteddfods behind the line. They wanted to feel that, while they were maintaining Wales's honour abroad, all the institutions of Wales that meant so much to them were being kept alive at home. And so Lloyd George came to his peroration:

> But I have another and even more urgent reason for wishing to keep this Eisteddfod alive during the War. When this terrible conflict is over a wave of materialism will sweep over the land. Nothing will count but machinery and output. I am all for output, and I have done my best to improve machinery and increase output. But that is not all. There is nothing more fatal to a people than that it should narrow its vision to the material needs of the hour. National ideals without imagination are but as the thistles of the wilderness, fit neither for food nor fuel. A nation that depends upon them must perish. We shall need at the end of the war better workshops, but we shall also need more than ever every institution that will exalt the vision of the people above and beyond the workshop and the counting house. We shall need every national tradition that will remind us that men cannot live by bread alone.
>
> I make no apology for advocating the holding of the Eisteddfod in the middle of this great conflict, even although it were merely a carnival of song, as it has been stigmatised. The storm is raging as fiercely as ever, but now there is a shimmer of sunshine over the waves, there is a rainbow on the tumult of the surging waters. The struggle is more terrible than it has ever been, but the legions of the oppressor are being driven back and the banner of right is pressing forward. Why should we not sing? It is true that there are many thousands of gallant men falling in the fight – let us sing of their heroism. There are myriads more standing in the battle-lines facing the foe, and myriads more behind ready to support them when their turn comes. Let us sing of the land that gave birth to so many heroes.
>
> I am glad that I came down from the cares and labour of the War Office of the British Empire to listen and to join with you in singing the old songs which our brave countrymen on the battlefield are singing as a defiance to the enemies of human right.

His friend and former sparring partner, the Bishop of St Asaph, wrote that this speech had 'the true ring of genius – the prophetic gift of forthtelling the truth'.[1] And Lord Halifax, High Churchman and

1. 18 August 1916 (L.G.P.)

ecumenist, wrote 'as one of the public' to thank him for his 'most admirable speech' which went 'straight to the heart'.[1]

His next important general utterance on the war outside Parliament had an impact which was not only nationwide but worldwide. This was his interview with Roy W. Howard, president of the United Press of America, which was published on 29 September and in which he made the famous statement that the war would be fought 'to a knock-out'. Before taking a closer look at the interview we should consider briefly the background of discussions about American mediation and a negotiated peace, because without some knowledge of the antecedents it is all too easy to misunderstand and misjudge what Lloyd George said.

Ever since the beginning of the war President Woodrow Wilson had been attracted by the thought of achieving peace in Europe with himself as mediator, and he sent his confidant, Colonel House, on missions to European capitals to promote this ambition. His idea of a just peace was that the *status quo ante* should be restored, with the Germans evacuating foreign territory that they had occupied, in return for possible compensation outside Europe, and with their victims making no serious demands upon them, military, financial or territorial. This approach was fundamentally unrealistic, because the Germans had no intention of surrendering their European conquests unless forced to do so, and in particular were determined to retain control of Belgium; while the Entente could hardly be expected to agree to what would be no more than an armed truce on terms manifestly favourable to Germany.

All the same, it suited both sides to give some encouragement to the idea of American mediation. In Germany the Chancellor, Bethmann Hollweg, favoured it as a means of engineering an excuse for unrestricted submarine warfare. He did not share the warlords' confidence that Germany could win the war at sea whatever America decided to do. In their view, it would not matter if the United States were provoked into intervention; that would merely mean that Germany would 'finish off not only England, but also America'.[2] Bethmann Hollweg was less reckless, but hoped that if unrestricted

---

1. 21 August 1916 (L.G.P.).
2. Advice of Admiral von Holtzendorf, Chief of Naval Staff, to Bethmann Hollweg, January 1916 (quoted in Fritz Fischer, *Germany's Aims in the First World War*, p. 293).

submarine warfare were started – or rather, re-started[1] – after an American attempt at mediation which could be said to have failed on account of Allied intransigence, then the United States would not necessarily enter the war against Germany. He would be able to claim that indiscriminate sinking was Germany's only answer to the Allied blockade, whose operation was anyway repugnant to American opinion. The German ambassador in Washington, Bernstorff, was sceptical of Bethmann Hollweg's policy, advising that the United States would not tolerate all-out submarine warfare, whatever the diplomatic preparation. Yet the Chancellor persisted in his attempt.

On the Allied side the American government had to be humoured, because the United States was a potential ally and meanwhile a vital source of supplies. Besides, it was felt that at a suitable moment American mediation might be a good way to begin the process of ending the war, though for the moment to be suitable the Allies would need to be either in danger of losing or on the point of winning. The idea of a compromise peace in the form envisaged by Wilson never cut much ice with those Allied leaders who really counted, though in his conversations with British statesmen in 1916 House deceived himself into imagining otherwise.

Lloyd George was involved in the talks, as were Asquith, Grey, Balfour and Reading. He had taken no part in peace discussions with House in 1915, though he had met him more than once (House was a caller on his first day as Minister of Munitions) and had warned him that, if the Allies were defeated, Germany's next objective would be Brazil. But in any case the 1915 discussions got nowhere. In 1916 there was rather more to show, though the basic incompatibility of outlook and interest was never removed. Lloyd George's contributions enable us to see his September interview in a correct perspective.

It has to be understood that he never wanted to knock Germany out in the sense of destroying her as a power. At a meeting of the War Council in March 1915 he had argued that Germany 'would always be a very powerful nation', and that 'it might eventually be desirable to have her in a position to prevent Russia becoming too predominant'. At the end of the year he talked in a similar vein to C. P. Scott. 'It was nonsense to talk about "crushing" Germany; it was neither possible

1. It was first begun in February 1915, but discontinued in May after the sinking of the *Lusitania*, with the loss of 118 American lives, caused the United States to threaten a breach of diplomatic relations. It was, however, resumed at the end of February 1916, but stopped again a week later when the Kaiser decided to support Bethmann Hollweg's policy.

nor desirable. The best thing that could happen would be when the two sides were seen to be evenly matched America should step in and impose terms on both.'[1] This should not be interpreted as the equivalent of Wilson's idea of a compromise peace. As Lloyd George saw it, the Germans had to be beaten back before there could be any question of the two sides being 'evenly matched'. In February 1916 he told Riddell: 'I still say *we must beat the Germans*, and *when they are beaten* I would endeavour to make the peace real and lasting. A great nation like Germany must live.'[2]

Meanwhile, on 5 January, House had dined with him and Reading and there had been a free-ranging discussion of possible approaches to peace. At this time Lloyd George was in a fairly bullish mood, because he could feel that he was beginning to master the problems of armament production, and could still hope that the high command's plans for another year of massive attacks in the West would be scrapped in favour of a defensive strategy there and victorious action in the East. He spoke, therefore, of American mediation in September, by which time the Allies should have secured a clear advantage. He emphasised the future economic preponderance of the United States, but suggested that it should be reinforced by military and naval preparations. On 11 February the same trio dined again, House having meanwhile visited Germany and found Bethmann Hollweg unwilling even to consider the restoration of Belgium. Lloyd George, perhaps to leave House in no doubt of British resolution, said that peace talks would not be popular in Britain.

At a further dinner on the 14th, attended by every member of the British inner group, it was agreed that Wilson should propose a peace conference at some unspecified future date. The timing 'depended on selecting the critical moment when Germany was sufficiently discouraged and Entente opinion was not yet intoxicated by Entente success'. Grey seemed to favour an early initiative, but 'Lloyd George and Balfour preferred delay until the Allies secured an undisputed military advantage'.[3] Lloyd George also insisted, with Asquith's support, that there should be prior agreement with the Americans on minimum peace terms, but to this House was unresponsive; and in his report to Wilson he suggested that the only controversial issue was timing.

1. *The Political Diaries of C. P. Scott*, ed. Trevor Wilson, 19 December 1915, p. 165.
2. R.W.D., 26 February 1916, p. 157. Author's italics.
3. Michael G. Fry, *Lloyd George and Foreign Policy*, Vol. I., p. 225.

A few days later he and Grey drafted a memorandum which in due course was accepted by the British inner group and by the French ambassador, Cambon. The memorandum stated that Wilson would be ready, 'on hearing from France and England that the moment was opportune', to propose a conference to put an end to the war. Should the Allies accept the proposal and Germany refuse, the United States would 'probably' enter the war against Germany. But if the Allies dragged their feet, 'the United States would probably disinterest themselves in Europe and look to their own protection in their own way'. As for peace terms, House 'expressed an opinion decidedly favourable to the restoration of Belgium, the transfer of Alsace and Lorraine to France, and the acquisition by Russia of an outlet to the Sea, though he thought that the loss of territory incurred by Germany in one place would have to be compensated by concessions to her in other places outside Europe.'

The War Committee was informed and the memorandum discussed there on 22 February. Kitchener wished to be assured that Germany would reject mediation, and Law took the view that Wilson's motive was the 'quest for domestic political advantage'. Others recognised that his aim was stalemate rather than Allied victory, and Asquith stated firmly that 'to the Allies a draw was much the same as defeat'.[1] In any case the memorandum committed nobody. The Americans were covered by the word 'probably', the Allies by having the right to choose the opportune moment for mediation.

As the year progressed Wilson's desire to act as mediator increased, and very much for the reason picked on by Law. It was election year in the United States and between June and November the President was running for re-election. At the Democratic Convention in June the theme which inspired most enthusiasm among the delegates was that Wilson had kept the country out of war and would continue to do so. Moreover, in his campaign speeches he took a lofty line about the war, suggesting that there was no moral difference between the combatants and that neither side was fighting for any cause worthy of American support. One consideration in his mind was obviously the substantial

---

1. Fry, *op. cit.*, pp. 227–8. It is worth noting that Russia was not a party to the memorandum, though one important Russian interest was taken into account. The fact that Kitchener was not a member of the inner British discussion group shows his diminished status in the Government, and the presence in it of Balfour rather than Law further illustrates Asquith's attitude to the leader of the Conservative Party.

German–American vote; but quite apart from that he was largely blind to the true nature of the war.

The Allies, for their part, were failing to achieve the hoped-for decisive victory during the summer, and could see that a peace move by Wilson would be not merely inopportune but disastrous. If they entered a conference and then refused terms 'which American opinion regarded as reasonable', they would 'thereby lose American support, while they would have encouraged hopes of peace among their own peoples which they could not fulfil'.[1] Those who still believed that the Germans might crack before the end of the year were naturally opposed to any relaxation of pressure, while those who did not share their optimism feared that in the circumstances even talk of a truce would imperil Allied solidarity and morale.

On 26 July Lloyd George breakfasted at the National Liberal Club with Seebohm Rowntree. Others present were two other figures from Land Campaign days, C. Roden Buxton (now an active pacifist) and E. R. Cross; the Welsh Radical M.P., Ellis Davies; and Gwilym, just back from France and 'in the uniform of a staff officer'. Lloyd George sat between Rowntree and Davies, whom he chaffed for favouring peace. When Davies said 'Yes, on terms', he asked 'What terms?' Davies explained that he would reinstate Belgium, restore Alsace-Lorraine to France, and require Russia to agree to an independent Poland, though with the consolation of an outlet to the Mediterranean. 'Through Turkey?' 'Yes'. Lloyd George agreed: 'I see no objection to their having an outlet at the expense of Turkey – let dog eat dog.' But when Davies asked 'Then why not try to make peace now?' Lloyd George replied that the Germans had not yet had 'a sickener of war'. The war might last two more years and he would fight against peace in present circumstances. He had no animosity against the Germans, but they must be convinced that they had no chance of success.[2]

When, on 10 August, the War Committee discussed American mediation for the first time since Lloyd George became War Minister, his attitude was thoroughly belligerent. But Asquith felt that some attention should be given to peace terms and invited contributions on the subject. It was not that he anticipated early peace talks with the enemy, still less that he wanted early talks, but simply that he could see

1. Sir Llewellyn Woodward, *Great Britain and the War of 1914–1918*, p. 224.
2. Ellis Davies Journal (unpublished).

value in intelligent forethought on such a theme. Various papers were submitted, including the one by Robertson which prompted Lloyd George to say in his Memoirs that the general would have been more effective as a politician than he was as a soldier. But Lloyd George himself made no written submission. His response came a little later, and in an unexpected form.

During the early part of September the Allies' first exhilaration at Roumania's entry into the war began to turn to anxiety, as the Germans invaded that country from the south. This was also the time when Lloyd George paid his controversial visit to France. On the 19th Briand made a powerful impromptu speech in the Chamber of Deputies when an anti-war Socialist accused him of needlessly prolonging the conflict. 'Monsieur Brizon', he cried, 'I entreat you, in the interests of your own ideal, if you desire peace to reign in this world, if you want the concepts of justice and liberty to prosper, then wish for your country to triumph! Do not try to persuade your fellow-countrymen that peace can be born today. Peace today would be a humiliating and ignoble peace, and there is no Frenchman who could desire such a peace!' At these words the deputies gave him a tremendous standing ovation, and the Chamber ordered that the text of his speech should be posted throughout France. Le Roy-Lewis described the scene to Lloyd George in a letter the following day, enclosing extracts from the *Journal Officiel*.

On the 25th he had a note from Northcliffe: 'I think you ought to see Mr Roy Howard, the head of the United Press of the United States, who has told me certain disquieting things. He is only in town tomorrow (Tuesday) as he is going to Germany on Wednesday morning.' Next day Lloyd George talked to Howard in his room at the War Office, and on the 27th Northcliffe sent him the text of the interview with a covering letter urging immediate publication:

I know from a leading member of the American Embassy that a peace squeal designed to arouse world sympathy will come upon us unless headed off now. The member of the Embassy to whom I refer is so anxious about it that he has gone to the United States.

I would not alter a word of the enclosure, and I would have it sent out not only by the United Press, but *next day* to Reuter, Havas, Press Association, the Russian press, the Italian and Spanish press and also the South American. I can easily arrange all that if you do not understand how to do it. Only pray do not let your propaganda department muddle it.

Lloyd George made a few additions to the text before passing it for publication on the 28th. But he took Northcliffe's advice in releasing it on his own responsibility, without giving a preview of it to anybody outside his own private office. It appeared next day in *The Times* and was swiftly reproduced throughout the world.

Here is what he said, with Howard's introduction, questions and commentary. The words added by Lloyd George when he revised the text are in italics:

There is no end of the war in sight. Any step at this time by the United States, the Vatican, or any other neutral in the direction of peace would be construed by England as an un-neutral, pro-German move.

The United Press is able to make these statements on no less an authority than the British man-of-the-hour, the Rt. Hon. David Lloyd George, Secretary of State for War.

'Britain has only begun to fight. The British Empire has invested thousands of its best lives to purchase future immunity for civilisation. This investment is too great to be thrown away. . . .

'More than at any time since the beginning of the war there is evidence throughout England of a popular suspicion of America – suspicion which did not exist a year ago. This feeling appears to be directly attributable to a notion, generally entertained by the man in the street, that President Wilson . . . might be induced to "butt in" for the purpose of stopping the European war. . . .'

Lloyd George was asked to give the United Press, in the simplest possible language, the British attitude toward the recent peace talk.

'Simple language?' he queried, with a half smile, then thought a moment.

'Sporting terms are pretty well understood wherever English is spoken,' he said. 'I am quite sure they are understood in America. Well, then. The British soldier is a good sportsman. He enlisted in this war in a sporting spirit – in the best sense of that term. He went in to see fair play to a small nation trampled upon by a bully. He is fighting for fair play in international dealings. He has fought as a good sportsman. By the thousands he has died as a good sportsman. He has never asked anything more than a sporting chance. He has not always had that. When he couldn't get it, he didn't quit. He played the game. He didn't squeal, and he has certainly never asked anyone to squeal for him.'

The Secretary for War, who looks and acts and talks more like an American businessman than any other Englishman [*sic*] in public life, was now speaking real United States. There was scarcely a trace of the usual British intonation or accent in his voice.

'Under the circumstances', he continued, 'the British, now that the fortunes of the game have turned a bit, are not disposed to stop because of the squealing done by Germans or done for Germans by probably well-meaning but misguided sympathisers and humanitarians.

'For two years the British soldier had a bad time – no one knows so well what a bad time. He was sadly inferior in equipment. The vast majority of the British soldiers were inferior in training. He saw the Allied cause beaten all about the ring. But he didn't appeal either to spectators or referee to stop the fight on the grounds that it was brutal. Nor did he ask that the rules be changed. He took his punishment, even when beaten like a dog. He was a game dog. . . . '

Lloyd George's eyes snapped as, sitting at his desk in the big room in Whitehall, he tilted back in his chair and studied the ceiling as if seeing there a picture of Tommy's game fight in the early stages of the conflict.

'And at this time and under these conditions what was the winning German doing?' he asked. 'Was he worrying over the terrible slaughter? No, he was talking of annexing Belgium and Poland as a result of his "victory". And while he was remaking the map of Europe *without the slightest regard to the wishes of its people* the British people were preparing to pay the price we knew must be paid for time to get an army ready. . . .

'During these months when it seemed the finish of the British army might come quickly, Germany elected to make this a finish fight with England. The British soldier was ridiculed and held in contempt. Now we intend to see that Germany has her way. The fight must be to a finish – to a knock-out.'

Dropping colloquialisms, the half smile fading from his face, Lloyd George continued in a more serious vein:

'The whole world – including neutrals of the highest purposes and humanitarians with the best of motives – must know that there can be no interference at this stage. Britain asked no intervention when she was unprepared to fight. She will tolerate none now that she is prepared, until the Prussian military despotism is broken beyond repair.

'There . . . were no tears shed by German sympathisers a few months ago when a few thousand British citizens who had never expected to be soldiers, and whose military education had been started only a few months previously, went out to be battered and bombed and gassed . . . the people who are now moved to tears at the thought of what is to come watched the early rounds of the unequal contest dry-eyed.

'None of the carnage and suffering which is to come can be worse than those of the Allied dead who stood the full shock of the Prussian war machine before it began to falter.

'But in British determination to carry the fight to a decisive finish there is something more than the natural demand for vengeance. The inhumanity and the pitilessness of the fighting that must come before a lasting peace is possible is not comparable with the cruelty that would be involved in stopping the war while there remains the possibility of civilisation again being menaced from the same quarter. Peace now or at any time before the final and complete elimination of this menace is unthinkable. No man, or no nation with the slightest understanding of the temper of this citizen army of Britons, which took its terrible *hammering* [original text: "beating"] without a whine or a grumble, will attempt to call a halt now.'

'But how long do you figure this can and must go on?'

'There is neither clock nor calendar in the British army today,' was the quick reply. 'Time is the least vital factor. Only the result counts. . . . It took England twenty years to defeat Napoleon and the first fifteen of those years were black with British defeat. It will not take twenty years to win this war, but whatever time is required it will be done.

'And I say this recognising that we have only begun to win. There is no disposition on our side to fix the hour of ultimate victory after the first success. We have no delusion that the war is nearing an end. We have not the slightest doubt as to how it is to end.

'But what of France?' I asked. 'Is there the same determination there to stick to the end . . . ?'

At this question the War Secretary carefully matched each finger of one hand with each finger of the other, and as he turned his chair slowly to gaze out over the khaki-dotted throng in Whitehall it seemed that the interruption had dammed the flow of his conversation. There was a full moment's pause and as the chair swung round again the reply came in a voice and in a manner impressively grave.

'The world at large has not yet begun to appreciate the magnificence, the nobility, the wonder of France,' he said. 'I had the answer to your enquiry given me a few days ago by a noble French woman. This woman had given four sons – she had one left to give to France. In the course of my talk with her I asked if she did not think the struggle had gone far enough. Her reply without a moment's hesitation was: "The fight will never have gone far enough until it shall have made a repetition of this horror impossible."

'That mother was voicing the spirit of France. Yes, France will stick to the end.

'I suppose that America's conception of France and of the French soldier before the war was as erroneous as the British idea. I suppose that you, too, regarded the French soldier as excitable, brilliant in attack, but lacking in doggedness and staying qualities. . . . History never justified this idea. But there will be a new appraisement and a new appreciation, when the real heroism, nobility and genius of the defence of Verdun are fully understood.

'France has fought the longest wars of any nation of Europe and her history is of itself assurance enough that she will hold to the end. With the British it will be the sporting spirit that will animate the army to the last. *Fair play the motive – a fair fight the method.* With the French it will be that fiercely burning patriotism that will sustain the army to the end. . . . '

'And Russia?'

'Will go through to the death,' interrupted Lloyd George to answer the enquiry. 'Russia has been slow to arouse but she will be equally slow to quiet. The resentment of the Russian against having been forced into the war is deep, and he has neither forgotten nor forgiven the fact that this happened at a time when he was ill-prepared and unsuspecting.

'No, there are and there will be no quitters among the Allies. "Never again" has become our battle cry. *At home the suffering and the sorrow is great and is growing. As to the war zone its terrors are indescribable. I have just visited the battlefields of France. I stood as it were at the door of Hell and saw myriads marching into the furnace. I saw some coming out of it scorched and mutilated. This ghastliness must never again be re-enacted on this earth, and one method at least of ensuring that end is the infliction of such punishment upon the perpetrators of this outrage against*

428 LLOYD GEORGE: FROM PEACE TO WAR

humanity that the temptation to emulate their exploits will be eliminated
from the hearts of the evil-minded amongst the rulers of men. That is the
meaning of Britain's resolve.'[1]

The significance of this interview can hardly be exaggerated. For the
Allies it seemed to represent, together with Briand's speech, decisive
rejection of any idea of a compromise peace until the war was
unequivocally won. For Britain it expressed in vivid language what
was almost certainly the popular view of the war, and the general
determination to win it and not merely to end it. For Lloyd George
himself it was a most striking act of independence and self-assertion:
the act of one who felt uniquely competent to speak for the nation, and
who was prepared to do so, on an issue of supreme consequence,
without the leave or even the knowledge of the Prime Minister and
Foreign Secretary.

For such behaviour to be justified the cause needs to be exceptional
and the value of the act itself incontrovertible. The interview that
Lloyd George gave to the *Daily Chronicle* on New Year's Day 1914 did
not fulfil at least one of those conditions. Then, too, he was speaking
off his own bat, but by far the more serious charge is that his remarks
on that occasion were ill-considered and mischievous. If the same
could be said of the Howard interview Lloyd George would indeed be
open to censure, because the circumstances were more critical, the
subject-matter more explosive, and the harm that could be done,
therefore, much greater. But *can* the same be said of it? Was the
interview at best superfluous, at worst disastrous in its effects? Or was
it, as Lloyd George claimed, necessary and salutary?

The argument that he did not need to speak as he did rests on two
assertions: that there was no danger of a peace move by Wilson at the
time, and that in any case the Allies' attitude to the idea of a
compromise peace was already perfectly clear. The first assertion is
probably correct. The evidence on the whole suggests – though Lloyd
George had contrary information – that by early September Wilson

1. This is virtually the full text of the interview. The few words omitted are purely repetitious
or of trifling importance. In his memoirs Lloyd George quotes some passages from the
interview, though not, curiously enough, the passage containing the reference to a knock-
out. Yet the chapter dealing with the subject is entitled 'The Knock-out Blow', and Lloyd
George says that that phrase provided the theme for discussion of the interview 'in every
country' (W.M., p. 885). The Dantesque passage added at the end is another that he does not
quote.

had decided to postpone his mediation to a later date. One possible reason for such a decision was Roumania's entry into the war, which might be expected to make the Entente less willing to negotiate; but a stronger one was the difficulty of intervening effectively abroad before he was re-elected. Whatever the reasons, it seems likely, though not certain, that he had no immediate plans for a peace move at the time of Lloyd George's interview, and that the interview may, to that extent, have been unnecessary.

But was there no need to tackle American public opinion on the subject of a compromise peace? Was there already sufficient awareness of the military and moral balance in Europe, even amid the cross-currents and distortions of an election campaign? On this point it would seem that Lloyd George's instinct was sound. Without a very forthright and arresting statement of the Allied case there was, surely, a danger that it would go by default, or at any rate receive very much less attention than it deserved. Briand's speech may have come to the notice of some Americans and impressed them with France's will to win. But it was the speech of a Frenchman addressed to Frenchmen, whereas Lloyd George's remarks were those of a Briton addressed to Americans in the language that Britons and Americans shared. Not only that, but they were remarks couched in an acceptable idiom by one who seemed to his interviewer to look and talk 'more like an American business man', and to speak 'real United States'. No other British politician could have made such an impact on ordinary Americans, whose thoughts and feelings about the war mattered quite as much as their leaders' policy.

Grey was afraid that Lloyd George's words would have a bad effect in America, and said so in a letter to him on 29 September, immediately after reading the interview. Britain, he thought, would be blamed for 'warning Wilson off the course', and the door to mediation by him would be 'closed for ever'. These fears were not borne out. On 4 October the British ambassador in Washington, Sir Cecil Spring-Rice, was able to inform Grey that Lloyd George's interview had had 'a great effect', and two days later that it had 'put a stop to the peace rumours which for some [had] been prevalent' in the United States. On 20 October he reported again that the effect of the interview had been 'most excellent'. Yet the door to mediation was certainly not closed. Wilson was to make another peace move before the end of the year and Lloyd George was then, as Prime Minister, to respond to it, because he knew that the Germans had put themselves in the wrong a few days earlier, and prejudiced Wilson's action, with their 'peace offer' of 12 December. It was all a question of circumstances and timing, and Lloyd George could fairly claim that in September he had said the right things to America at the right time.[1]

But in his subsequent self-justification he claimed to have been speaking not to America alone. 'I felt it vitally important to throw out a sharp challenge to the defeatist spirit which was working from foreign quarters to bring about an inconclusive peace, and which appeared to find an echo even in some responsible quarters in our own country.'[2] At least one shrewd observer, Bertie, so interpreted his remarks at the time. 'The Ambassador has been much interested in the interview, and he wonders whether it was made either with a view to warn off Mr Wilson, or to anticipate any possible declarations of a contrary nature which might be made by your colleagues in the Cabinet!'[3] There was, in fact, very little outright defeatism among Lloyd George's colleagues, but there was a distinct lack of the sort of aggressive fighting spirit without which wars cannot be won. Asquith and Grey were both as opposed as Lloyd George to a compromise peace until the Allies were in a stronger position to negotiate, but their style did not match their convictions. On 11 October Asquith said in the House of Commons: '. . . the ends of the Allies are well known; they have been frequently and precisely stated. They are not vindictive ends, but they require that there shall be adequate reparation for the past and adequate security for the future.' And on 23 October Grey said, also in the House of Commons: '. . . if we are to approach peace in a proper spirit, it can only be by recalling, and never for one moment forgetting, what was the real cause of the war.' These were not words to set the pulses racing.

Besides, there *was* a defeatist element in the Government of which the chief representative was Lansdowne. He was a defeatist in the sense defined by Asquith's statement to the War Committee (quoted earlier), that 'to the Allies a draw was much the same as a defeat'. Lansdowne could, in effect, see no alternative to a draw. On 13 November he produced a belated reply to Asquith's request for

---

1. At the end of November Wilson tried to force the Allies to accept mediation by helping to precipitate a financial crisis, and it has been suggested that his action was partly influenced by resentment against Lloyd George (Kathleen Burk, *Britain, America and the Sinews of War, 1914–1918*, ch. 5). But Wilson was by no means the only cause of the crisis and in any case there is no evidence that the Howard interview determined what he did two months later.
2. W.M., p. 852.
3. Le Roy-Lewis to D.L.G., 29 September 1916 (L.G.P.).

thoughts on peace terms, and his paper was circulated to the Cabinet. In it he marshalled all the arguments for doubting the possibility of real victory for the Allies. The Board of Trade's experts were predicting 'a complete breakdown in shipping' well before mid-1917. Home food production was threatened by manpower shortage on the land, and in the supply of manpower generally we were 'nearing the end of our tether'. Our casualties amounted to 1,100,000, including 15,000 officers killed. And could our Allies be depended on? Italy was 'always troublesome and exacting', and the position in Russia was 'far from reassuring'. Even in France there had been times when 'political complications [had] threatened to affect the military situation'.

While ostensibly supporting Asquith's view that there had to be adequate reparation and security, Lansdowne suggested no way at all in which these aims might be achieved. He took issue with Lloyd George's 'knock-out' formula. 'To many of us it seems as if the prospect of a "knock-out" was, to say the least of it, remote.' And in his last paragraph he said:

> The interview given by the Secretary of State for War . . . produced an impression which it will not be easy to efface. . . . He said, indeed, that 'the world must know that there can be no outside interference *at this stage*' – a very momentous limitation. For surely it cannot be our intention, no matter how long the war lasts, no matter what the strain on our resources, to maintain this atti-tude. . . . Let our naval, military, and economic advisers tell us frankly whether they are satisfied that the knock-out blow can and will be delivered. The Secretary of State's formula holds the field, and will do so until something else is put in its place.

This was a far cry from Lloyd George's 'There is neither clock nor calendar in the British Army today.' Lansdowne's unmistakable message was that time was running out for Britain and the Alliance.

He was answered in a tough paper which Lloyd George asked Robertson to prepare, and to which Lansdowne in turn briefly replied. Robertson's paper concluded:

> . . . we need to have the same courage in London as have our leaders in the North Sea and in France. The whole art of making war may be summed up in three words – courage, action, and determination. In peace time half-and-half measures may not be very harmful. In war time they are deadly. We must make up our minds either to fight or to make peace. . . . My answer to the question is that I am

'satisfied that the "knock-out blow" can and will be delivered' if only we take the necessary measures to give us success, and take them in time. We shall win if we deserve to win.[1]

Lloyd George and Robertson did not, of course, agree on the measures necessary for success, but they did agree that they could not be 'half-and-half measures'.

The War Committee gave no endorsement to Lansdowne's point of view, but he remained a member of the Government until Asquith fell, and so did a number of others who, to some degree at least, shared his pessimistic outlook. If he was right in claiming that many were thinking along the same lines, then Lloyd George's second alleged motive for speaking as he did in September appears to have been justified.

But were the alleged motives the true ones? Did he, indeed, give his 'knock-out' interview partly for the reason stated at the time, that he wished to counter peace talk in America and the danger of a premature peace initiative by Wilson, and partly for the further reason suggested in his memoirs, that he wished to counter the defeatist spirit 'in some responsible quarters' at home? According to A. J. P. Taylor these reasons were invented to disguise the true one, which was that in September he believed victory to be imminent. 'In fact', Mr Taylor has written, 'he committed himself to the knock-out blow in the belief that, as secretary for war, he was about to deliver it.'[2] Is this a tenable view? Did he really have any confidence in late September that the Somme battle would end in decisive victory? It is hard to see that he was ever confident that a Western offensive would have that result, and any hope that he may have had in the early days of the battle had already faded by late July, when he asked Repington's advice on a possible change of commander in France, and when he told the Seebohm Rowntree breakfast party that the war might last another two years.

In his Commons speech of 22 August, quoted by Mr Taylor in support of his thesis, he certainly tried to be as positive as he could about the fighting on the Somme. But he was very careful in that speech – as in his Eisteddfod speech a few days before – not to

1. Robertson's paper dated 24 November 1916; Lansdowne's reply, 27 November 1916. Both were circulated to the Cabinet.
2. *English History 1914–1945*, p. 62 (hardback edition).

encourage any false expectations of early victory. He suggested that the tide might just have turned, but that victory was still a distant prospect, to be attained only after long and arduous struggle. And in the Howard interview itself he said that the Allies had only 'begun to win', adding: 'There is no disposition on our side to fix the hour of ultimate victory after the first success. We have no delusion that the war is nearing an end.' His thoughts at the time were directed, not to the fantasy of an early knock-out in the West, but to stopping the carnage there and switching forces to Salonica, in the hope of saving Roumania.

There is surely no good cause to doubt that the principal motives for his interview were those stated, though there may well have been one or two subsidiary motives. It must obviously have been tempting to him to do something congenial to Northcliffe and the military at the very time when he was under attack for his conversation with Foch. But he would not have given the interview for that reason alone, or unless he had believed it to be necessary for more important reasons. He knew that he would not be forgiven for long, if at all, for his interference in strategy, and indeed it was only a fortnight later that Northcliffe invaded his office and threatened to break him if he persisted with such interference. Perhaps Briand's speech on 17 September spurred him to emulation and made him that much more receptive to Northcliffe's suggestion that he talk to Howard. But he would almost certainly have given the interview anyway.

What he said went down very well in France, despite the invidious and misleading distinction between France's and Britain's motivation for war, which had been a regrettable feature of his Queen's Hall speech two years previously. France, he implied, was fighting only in self-defence, whereas Britain was inspired to fight by chivalry and the sense of fair play. Warmly as he praised 'the magnificence, the nobility, the wonder' of French patriotism, there was more than a hint of condescension in the tribute, since he ascribed an even higher idealism to his own country. In fact, Britain was in the war for essentially the same reason as France, that she sensed a threat to her national existence, though for France the threat was more immediate and palpable, leaving less room for self-deception.

One other flaw in the content of the interview was the reference to a 'natural demand for vengeance', and the insistence towards the end that enemy leaders should be indicted and punished after the war. It would have been better if the concepts of war guilt and retribution had been totally absent. But it should be stressed that Lloyd George was talking only of punishing leaders, not of crushing peoples. The knock-out that he sought concerned only the enemy's war machine. He had no desire to knock Germany out as a nation. Quite apart from humanitarian considerations, he regarded Germany as indispensable for a proper balance of power in Europe.

In deciding to give the interview he was backing a hunch, and the effects on the whole were advantageous to his country and the Allied cause, as well as to himself. If he had consulted anyone beforehand he would not have been free to say what he wanted even if he had been allowed to give the interview at all. He had to act rather in the manner of Nelson at St Vincent. Nobody could doubt, after he had spoken, that the British would stay in the war with victory as their sole aim, and nobody could doubt that they had, in him, an alternative war leader of faith and fire.

SEVENTEEN
The Fall of Asquith

The Asquith coalition was lucky to survive the crisis over compulsory service, and was probably saved only by the rising in Dublin, which shocked politicians into a temporary state of acquiescence. But Asquith's own authority was not enhanced; indeed it was much weakened by his undignified wrigglings on the conscription issue, and his failure to push the Irish deal through weakened it further. Opponents of his leadership were by no means reconciled to it, nor were they appeased by his agreement, under pressure, to set up commissions to enquire into the Dardanelles and Mesopotamian campaigns.

This act of self-mutilation – for such indeed it was – resulted from the Government's incoherent way of doing business. On 30 May it was announced that papers on Mesopotamia would be laid in the House of Commons, and on 1 June a similar announcement was made regarding the Dardanelles. In other words, M.P.s were to be given access to secret information about the background to, and conduct of, both campaigns. This matter may or may not have been discussed beforehand by the Cabinet (in the absence of records there is no way of knowing), but in any case the decision was ill-considered and in mid-July Asquith tried to go back on it. There was then, however, such an angry reaction in Parliament that he agreed to appoint the two commissions, to which evidence was to be given in secret but whose reports would be published.

In Hankey's view, Asquith's government 'never recovered' from this decision. For the next five months 'the function of the Supreme

Command was carried out under the shadow of these inquests', and 'a good deal of mutual suspicion was engendered'. The process also involved an enormous waste of busy people's time, especially Hankey's; he had to spend 174 hours preparing the Government's case for the Dardanelles commission. The most obvious historical precedents, Walcheren and the Crimea, should have been a sufficient warning. Those campaigns had been investigated by Parliamentary committees, whereas Asquith was giving the task to outside bodies; but the difference was not very material. Some M.P.s were anyway to serve on the commissions, but above all a British wartime government was again submitting its performance to critical scrutiny, so by implication conceding that grave mismanagement had occurred. Simply by appointing the commissions Asquith was impugning his own leadership in the eyes of the world.[1]

All the same the fact that he ceased to be Prime Minister even before they reported did not, as Hankey suggests, follow inevitably from the decision to set them up. The fate of governments and their leaders depended far more upon the course of the war than upon anything else. If the war had gone really well for the Allies during the summer and autumn, Asquith's position at the end of the year would have been secure. But in fact the year ended with the Allies on balance less well placed than in the spring. Despite official claims that the Somme was a great victory, most people could sense – and many knew – that all the immensely costly fighting on the Western front had produced only stalemate. If it was a triumph for the French to have held the Germans at Verdun, it must equally have been a triumph for the Germans to have held the Allies on the Somme. In the East, meanwhile, the enemy was clearly winning important victories of a kind that did not need to be explained by propaganda. Amid growing anxiety about the war's outcome, and even about Britain's capacity to survive, the demand for a new form of war leadership became irresistible.

Until the latter part of 1916 Asquith's remarkable powers showed no

1. Hankey, *The Supreme Command*, ch. LII. The Chairman of the Mesopotamian commission was Lord George Hamilton, a former Secretary of State for India, and of the Dardanelles commission the veteran proconsul Lord Cromer, whose last public assignment it was, and who was, in effect, killed by it. 'Assiduous in attendance at the sittings, he would summon the commission to meet at his own house if he were forbidden to go out of doors. After one such meeting he collapsed. During rallies he demanded always the draft, and in January 1917 seemed about to renew his lease of life. But the flicker was brief.' (D.N.B.) Lloyd George gave evidence to the commission on 30 October 1916.

serious sign of deterioration. Though they had never been particularly well suited to running the government of a country at war, they remained, until then, more or less unimpaired, and he continued to be a very formidable politician. His handling of the crisis in which the Liberal government was replaced by coalition showed a ruthless mastery not excelled in any other crisis of his career; and towards the end of 1915 his adroitness amazed Frances Stevenson:

> One thing I cannot help marvelling at is the way in which the old P.M. has kept his Cabinet together during all this difficult time. He has done it by pure craft and cunning, propitiating here, or pretending to propitiate, making concessions there, or pretending to make them; giving promises which he never intended to keep, but which were just sufficient to keep the person concerned dangling. . . . Always wait & see! And the extraordinary thing is that this policy seems to work so extraordinarily well, even in war time, from the P.M.'s point of view; though I am afraid the policy of Britain in this war has suffered sadly by it.[1]

Asquith himself felt that 'wait and see' was usually the right policy, for the country as well as for himself, and he even took pride in employing it in the long controversy over conscription, in which however its value to the nation was, to say the least, questionable. It was not a policy of endless delay and drift, for which it has often been mistaken, but rather of letting a situation mature until most people were ready for a particular step to be taken. In normal times, and on normal issues, it was very appropriate for the chief executive in a Parliamentary system, but even before the war there were some issues – notably Home Rule – on which swift, decisive action would have been preferable. In that case the Parliament Act unfortunately necessitated delay, but Asquith was largely responsible for that measure, which, in a sense, institutionalised the principle of 'wait and see'. In the abnormal conditions of war, it was more often than not a disastrous policy, even when practised by someone as clever and resourceful as Asquith in the full possession of his powers.

As 1916 wore on his powers visibly declined. The inept decision to set up commissions of enquiry, into which he was anyway pushed, was only one example. In general he seemed to have less grip on affairs. Crawford, attending his first Cabinet on 12 July, recorded his

1. F.S.D., 16 November 1915, p. 75.

impression of the body itself and its chairman:

> It is a huge gathering, so big that it is hopeless for more than one or two to express opinions on each detail – great danger of side conversations and localised discussions. Asquith somnolent – hands shaky and cheeks pendulous. He exercised little control over debate, seemed rather bored, but good-humoured throughout.

And at another Cabinet on 2 August he noted:

> Asquith's hand very shaky, yet he warms up always when he has to speak in H. of C. – of course the two hours before lunch are those in which his spirits and his stock of spirit are at their lowest measurement.

On 4 November he had a talk with Asquith about labour on the land:

> He wasn't very helpful. His eyes were watery and his features kept moving about in nervous twitching fashion. I thought he looked ill and frail – also weak and undecided. . . . At Cabinets he is calm and urbane – but as for ruling his colleagues or abridging idle or wasteful discussions he is hopeless.[1]

During this period even his handwriting began to lose some of its disciplined regularity, no doubt because of the shake that had developed.

At the end of August he spent a few days in the country (reading Lady Desborough's book about her sons, an American book of Shakespeare studies, and *Les Anges Gardiens* by Marcel Prévost). On 5 September he went to visit the army in France, and while there met for the last time his eldest son, Raymond, who was with the Grenadier Guards on the Somme.

> I was called up by the Brigadier and thought at first I must have committed some ghastly military blunder . . . but was relieved to find that it was only a telegram from the corps saying 'Lieut. Asquith will meet his father at cross roads K.6d. at 1045 a.m. . . .' So I vaulted into the saddle and bumped off to Fricourt where I arrived exactly at the appointed time. I waited for an hour on a very muddy road congested with troops and lorries and surrounded by barking guns. Then 2 handsome motors from G.H.Q. arrived, the

1. *Crawford Papers*, pp. 356, 358 and 363 (12 July, 2 August, 4 November 1916). When Selborne resigned during the Irish negotiation, Crawford – the former Tory Chief Whip, Balcarres – was appointed to succeed him as President of the Board of Agriculture.

P.M. in one of them with 2 staff officers, and in the other Bongie [Bonham Carter], Hankey, and one or two of those moth-eaten nondescripts who hang about the corridors of Downing Street in the twilight region between the domestic and the civil service.

We went up to see some of the captured German dug-outs and just as we were arriving at our first objective the Boches began putting over a few 4.2 shells from their field howitzer. The P.M. was not discomposed by this, but the G.H.Q. chauffeur to whom I had handed over my horse to hold, flung the reins into the air and himself flat on his belly in the mud. It was funny enough.

The shell fell about 200 yards behind us I should think. Luckily the dug-out we were approaching was one of the best and deepest I have ever seen – as safe as the bottom of the sea, wood-lined, 3 storeys and electric light, and perfect ventilation. We were shown round by several generals who kept us there for an hour to let the shelling die down, and then the P.M. drove off to luncheon with the G.O.C. 4th Army and I rode back to my billets.[1]

Next day Asquith saw the tanks which were soon to be committed to battle for the first time. At Haig's headquarters he tried, on Hankey's advice, to persuade the commander-in-chief to delay using them, but to no avail.[2] Haig reported to his wife that the Prime Minister 'did himself fairly well' at dinner, and that by the end of the evening 'his legs were unsteady', though 'his head was quite clear, and he was able to read a map and discuss the situation'.[3] On the 12th, back in England, he celebrated his sixty-fourth birthday and there was a large dinner party at which his and Margot's son, Anthony ('Puffin'), proposed his health. Five days later, while he was spending the weekend at the Wharf, the news came through that Raymond had been killed.

Beyond question Asquith was very hard hit by the loss of his eldest son, and all the more so as his natural grief was probably aggravated by remorse. As Roy Jenkins says, 'Of the four sons of his first

1. Raymond Asquith to Katharine Asquith, 7 September 1916 (John Jolliffe ed., *Raymond Asquith: Life and Letters*, pp. 293–4). In his account of the occasion, written in his diary Hankey also noted that Asquith 'was as usual quite composed', but added that 'his hand was trembling rather, and no wonder'. (Hankey, *The Supreme Command* Vol II, pp. 512–13).
2. Hankey, *op. cit.* p. 513.
3. Haig Papers, quoted in Jenkins, *Asquith*, p. 412. Mr Jenkins comments: 'For the last ten or fifteen years of his life, at least, he was a fairly heavy drinker. . . . But no one ever suggested that his mind lost its precision or that there was any faltering in his command over what he did and did not want to say.'

marriage Raymond was not the closest to him,'[1] and he may have felt that his marriage to Margot, occurring when Raymond was fifteen, had to some extent come between them. Raymond's character was very unlike his father's. Though intellectually his equal, if not his superior, and certainly a better writer, Raymond lacked his father's ambition and dominating will. He was rather like Hamlet or the doomed hero of a Russian novel. His destiny was to write marvellous letters, and to die a premature and violent death.

Asquith, too, was a compulsive letter-writer, and the war did not at all cramp his epistolary style. He wrote in particular with extreme frequency to Venetia Stanley and, after her marriage, to her sister Sylvia Henley. Yet he seems never to have written at all to his eldest son in France. In a letter to his wife written within a month of his death, Raymond said: 'If Margot talks any more bosh to you about the inhumanity of her stepchildren you can stop her mouth by telling her that during my 10 months' exile here the P.M. has never written me a line of any description'.[2] The knowledge of this strange neglect must have sharpened the pain that Asquith felt when the news reached him, and must have haunted him for the rest of his life.

He must also have been tortured by the fear that Raymond's life, like so many other lives on the Western front, had been thrown away for no good purpose. Raymond was killed in the 15 September push which achieved limited tactical success though nothing of decisive importance. It was the operation in which the tanks that Asquith had seen were first used, despite his (actually Hankey's) arguments to the contrary. The particular attack in which Raymond fell was on too narrow a front, so that the advancing troops could easily be enfiladed. Shortly before receiving the news of his death, Asquith had seen a letter from him – probably written after their last meeting – in which he said of the high command's dispositions 'I suppose Philip Sassoon knows best'. At the time Asquith felt that the words showed touching resignation,[3] but in retrospect he may have felt that they were, rather, an expression of bitter and mocking irony.

During November the feeling that there had to be a change in the system of government, if not in the person of its leader, steadily gathered strength. As people in responsible positions considered the

1. *ibid.*, p. 414.
2. 22 August 1916 (Jolliffe, ed., *R. A.: Life and Letters*, pp. 286–7).
3. H.H.A. to Sylvia Henley, 12 September 1916.

outlook their apprehension grew, and with it the conviction that the existing system could no longer cope with the problems and perils facing the country. The War Committee was busier than ever, yet vital decisions were not being taken. In Hankey's words: 'During November 1916 the pressure on the War Committee became very great indeed. The number of meetings, which from January to October had averaged about six a month, rose in November to fifteen. Yet the Committee was still failing to keep abreast of its work, and the list of subjects awaiting decision was continually increasing.'[1] These subjects included the various matters, such as shipping losses, food supply, manpower and finance, whose daunting character was emphasised by Lansdowne in his essentially defeatist memorandum.

Among politicians the strongest force for change outside the Government was Carson, who since his resignation in October 1915 had been the effective leader of opposition. He was determined that there should be not only a new system – a small committee with full power to run the war – but a new Prime Minister as well. This was also the implacable aim of Northcliffe and Sir Max Aitken. Law himself, though in many ways dissatisfied with the system, was loyal to Asquith and unwilling at first to contemplate any action which might threaten his position. Among the Service chiefs Robertson was conspicuous in arguing that there had to be better machinery for the control of 'war policy', though of course he did not mean by this that he wanted any civilian control of military operations.

In Lloyd George's view war policy must necessarily include grand strategy, which in turn was bound to involve a share in deciding where and when operations should occur, if not in their detailed planning. In this respect he was out of step with most of those with whom he had to work to achieve a reform of the system. Carson, like Northcliffe, was an out-and-out 'Westerner' and supporter of the generals. Only Law occasionally agreed with Lloyd George about strategy, though even he normally backed the professionals and was doing so in the autumn of 1916. Yet Lloyd George on the whole agreed with Law, and disagreed with Carson, Northcliffe and Aitken, in not wishing to oust Asquith from the premiership. Even if Asquith had to go, through unwillingness to make the required changes, Lloyd George was quite prepared to serve under someone else, provided he had a free hand to run the war. Always more interested in power than

---

1. *The Supreme Command*, Vol. II, p. 551.

in place he did not especially covet the office of prime minister, because he knew that it entailed troublesome and distracting chores which he would gladly leave to another man.

The principal obstacle to any concerted move to enforce change was not, however, the distinctive attitude of Lloyd George, but rather the lack of rapport between Law and Carson. Despite their former close association, the two had been driven apart by Carson's resignation and subsequent activity as a critic of the Government. The breach was not complete, but Law regarded Carson as irresponsible while Carson regarded him as Asquith's lackey. Something had to happen to bring Law once again into cooperation with Carson, and the Nigerian debate of 8 November was the crucial determining event.

In this Law, as Colonial Secretary, had to defend a scheme for selling enemy properties and businesses in Nigeria to the highest bidders, whoever they might be. Carson put down a resolution that they should be sold only to British subjects or British companies, which attracted the votes not only of Protectionists but of others who knew that Law had promised to leave the Government if he failed to hold the support of his party in the House. The resolution was therefore intended to force Law's hand, and in effect it succeeded. Though in the division a majority of Tory M.P.s voted with the Government, the majority was so narrow, and the number of abstentions so large, that Law's authority in the Party could be seen to have largely passed to Carson. This fact was noted with alarm by Aitken, and when he heard, soon afterwards, that Lloyd George had absented himself from the division his alarm increased. 'It was clear that . . . the most powerful personality in British democratic politics was actively engaged on Carson's side. All this gave food for reflection.'[1]

His thoughts led him to the conclusion that Law, Carson and Lloyd George must be made to work together, for the sake of Law, the Conservative Party and the country. On 13 November he visited Lloyd George at the War Office and heard a long exposition of his views on the supreme command and how it should be reformed. 'He said quite frankly that Carson was working with him to get a War

---

1. Beaverbrook, *Politicians and the War*, ch. XXIII. In the Nigerian division the Government won by 231 votes to 117, but the Unionist vote split 73 to 65 out of a total Unionist membership of 286. The essentially non-fiscal character of the vote is evident from the fact that Churchill, an outstanding Free Trader, voted with the opposition. Lloyd George denied, implausibly, that his absence was deliberate. He was dining with Lee, and his fellow-guests were Carson and Milner.

Council with autocratic powers.' At that moment, as if to emphasise the point, Carson arrived and the conversation was interrupted for half an hour. When it resumed, Lloyd George explained that the War Committee 'had been a failure because Asquith, as chairman . . . was as dilatory and indecisive as in the Cabinet, and because, anyhow, the Committee had not sufficient authority'. His remedy was 'a real War Council of three with practically dictatorial powers'. He also talked of his difficulties with Robertson and virtual impotence at the War Office. Aitken left even more convinced that the triumvirate he had in mind 'must at all hazards be brought together'.[1]

Next day Lloyd George accompanied Asquith to Paris for the Allied conference which he had proposed at a War Committee meeting early in the month. It had been his intention, then, that the conference of political leaders should take place before the meeting of Allied generals which was due to be held the same week at Chantilly; and the French agreed that the conference should begin on the 13th, Monday. But the previous Friday Asquith said that this would be out of the question because there had to be a Cabinet meeting on Monday afternoon, and the conference would have to be delayed until Wednesday. Hankey, like Lloyd George, would have liked the Cabinet to be called for Saturday, but this was impossible because 'Runciman was going for a day's shooting, Lord Curzon for a weekend, and Lord Crawford to address his former constituents'.[2] The English weekend was sacrosanct even in wartime.

As a result the generals' meeting coincided with the politicians', and Lloyd George later claimed that the decisions reached by the generals 'to a large extent stultified the political conference'. He also made much of another grievance. In preparation for the conference he had written a long paper on the war situation in all its aspects, full of recrimination about the past and baleful remarks about the present, which ended with the proposal that 'the statesmen and generals of the great Western Powers should confer with the statesmen and generals of the Eastern Front, taking for their programme an examination of the situation in its entirety, and more particularly the military situation in the east'. He had hoped this would be used by Asquith, with

1. ibid., ch. XXV. According to Frances Stevenson, Aitken and Carson both asked him if, in the event of Law's resigning, he would be willing to form a Ministry, but he 'flatly declined' (F.S.D., 14 November 1916, p. 123).
2. Hankey Diary, 10 November 1916. (In The Supreme Command the names are given as 'X', 'Lord Y' and 'Lord Z'.)

electrifying effect, as his opening statement on behalf of the British government, but in the event he read it, much abridged, and 'without emphasis or pause', at a preliminary meeting with the French, for which Briand anyway arrived late.

The conference proper began in the afternoon of the 15th. Russia was represented at it only by the ambassador in Paris, Izvolsky, and Italy by her ambassador and finance minister (the prime minister being ill). Next day there was a further afternoon session at which the civilians were joined by the military chiefs, their discussions at Chantilly completed. According to Lloyd George, he 'left the conference feeling that after all nothing more would be done except to repeat the old fatuous tactics of hammering away with human flesh and sinews at the strongest fortresses of the enemy'. And before dinner, he says, he and Hankey went for a walk, and as they were passing the Vendôme column Hankey

> . . . paused and said 'you ought to insist on a small War Committee being set up for the day-to-day conduct of the War, with full powers. It must be independent of the Cabinet. It must keep in close touch with the P.M., but the Committee ought to be in continuous session, and the P.M., as Head of the Government, could not manage that. He has a very heavy job in looking after the Cabinet, and attending to Parliament and home affairs. He is a bit tired, too. . . . The Chairman must be a man of unimpaired energy and driving power.' We both agreed that it was important that Mr Asquith should continue to be Prime Minister. . . . It was decided, therefore, that on my return to England I should place the proposition before the Prime Minister; but that before I did so it would be best to sound Bonar Law, whose goodwill and approval it was essential to secure. I wired from Paris to [Aitken] asking him to arrange a meeting. . . . [1]

The clear implication is that the intrigue to bring about a change in the system of war government sprang from Lloyd George's frustration in Paris, and that the form that a new system might take was suggested by Hankey.

The second part may well be true in principle if not in detail. Writing long afterwards, Lloyd George may have over-dramatised his

---

1. Lloyd George's account of the Paris conference and his preparations for it, W.M., ch. XXXII.

pre-prandial conversation with Hankey. There is no record of it in Hankey's diary, but the idea of a new and more effective War Committee was clearly discussed by them in Paris. 'Lloyd George's account is supported both by my recollection and by other evidence in my possession of the views I held at that time on the conduct of the war.'[1] Since Lloyd George had already, according to Aitken, proposed such a reform of the War Committee before he left for Paris, he can only have owed the idea to Hankey if they had discussed it earlier, in England. But it is quite possible that they did, and that while in Paris they discussed it further.

Less convincing by far is Lloyd George's retrospective attempt to attribute the demand for a new sort of War Committee to his disillusionment at the conference. The Generals' Chantilly conclusions, which were discussed at the last session of the conference, did not prejudice the strategy for 1917 quite as much as he later made out, though he certainly felt that the allocation of resources for a projected campaign in the Balkans was insufficient.[2] He questioned the generals sharply about this, but on the whole he seems to have been quite pleased with the outcome. Frances Stevenson's diary in this respect contradicts his memoirs, and the diary version must be preferred:

> D. returned safely last night from Paris. . . . He says the Conference at Paris was very satisfactory in the decisions which they came to. They decided that large numbers of troops must be sent to the Balkans & every encouragement and help given to Russia in her policy.

But she goes on to say:

1. Hankey, *The Supreme Command*, p. 563.
2. The generals did, indeed, agree that existing operations on all fronts should, even during the winter, 'be pursued to the full extent compatible with the climatic conditions on each front', and that 'the armies of the Coalition [should] be ready to undertake joint offensives from the first fortnight of February 1917'. But they went into more detail about action in the Balkans than about action anywhere else, though the army at Salonica was to be raised only to twenty-three divisions, which Lloyd George considered inadequate. Behind the actual words of the communiqué there was, however, an undeniable bias in favour of action on the Western front. As Esher (who was close to Haig) wrote in his diary on 14 November: 'There can be no question at this time of day of shifting our military objectives. Possibly we might have delivered a decisive blow in the Balkans. Possibly an attack on Sofia, well ordered, might have succeeded. But it is too late. We are committed to our offensive in the West, both through the winter and next spring. It would be folly to transpose the whole strategical objective, and still greater folly to shilly-shally and compromise.' (*Journals and Letters*, Vol. 4, p. 65.) The admission that prompter action in the Balkans might have been successful is interesting, and lends support to Lloyd George's view at the beginning of September.

D. . . . though pleased at having carried the point, feels that the decisions come to at these Conferences are never acted upon with sufficient vigour, and in any case he feels that it is too late now to do much in regard to saving Roumania. . . . He feels that we have lost our chance, and he is very, very depressed at the outlook. He says he would like to resign & be made instead President of the War Committee.[1]

In other words, the conference had been a success as far as it went, but he feared that its decisions would be overtaken and stultified by events. Meanwhile the British system of war direction was defective, conference or no conference, and he was tired of occupying a position which gave him the semblance but not the reality of power. That, surely, was the truth.

For the next week he seems to have toyed with the idea of going on 'an extensive tour', taking in Russia, India, Greece, the Balkans, Egypt, Mesopotamia, and possibly Canada. Apart from the daunting logistics of such a tour, it would obviously have involved a long absence, and Frances reasonably feared that there would be 'endless plots' against him while he was away. He proposed that she should accompany him, with another girl to act as typist – and for the sake of appearances. The idea was mooted, it would seem, in Paris. Was Asquith trying to get rid of Lloyd George as he got rid of Kitchener in the autumn of 1915? The question can only be asked, and is anyway academic. By the 22nd Lloyd George had lost any interest he may have had in the idea (and it is hard to believe that he was ever really serious about it).[2] Meanwhile his own plot to change the system had been making some progress.

On the 14th Aitken gave Law an outline of Lloyd George's War Committee scheme, and they had a further long talk on the subject on the 18th. Law's reaction was distinctly bleak and guarded. The experience of serving together in the Asquith coalition had cast a shadow over the relations between Lloyd George and Law. Fundamentally they were as capable as ever of getting on well, but there was a temporary coolness, particularly on Law's side. He felt that Lloyd George was not enough of a team player, and the affair of the Nigerian debate had done nothing to mollify his feelings.

1. F.S.D., 18 November 1916 (p. 124).
2. *ibid.*, 20 and 22 November 1916 (p. 125 and p. 127).

Moreover, while recognising the inefficiency of the Government in its existing form, he 'foresaw the probability of great trouble' if Carson were promoted to a new ruling junta over the heads of the present Unionist Cabinet ministers. All the same he agreed to meet Lloyd George to discuss the proposal.[1]

Before doing so, however, he mentioned it to Asquith, who treated it loftily. Its only effect, he said, would be to give Lloyd George more power, though probably not enough to satisfy him. As for Carson, the Prime Minister did not think much of his 'constructive abilities'. These comments were well judged to appeal to Law. Aitken was vexed with his friend for spilling the beans to Asquith, despite an undertaking (Aitken thought) that he would not do so. But Law defended his action: 'I am not going to be drawn into anything like an intrigue against Asquith. . . . Lloyd George himself would do far better to go quite openly to the Prime Minister and tell him what he has told us.' On this Aitken sensibly remarks that 'if Lloyd George had gone alone to Asquith, his visit would have had no effect whatever'. To achieve results, he had to move with Law's 'support and authority'.

On the 20th Law discussed the scheme for the first time with Lloyd George, and Carson also was present: so it was, in fact, the first meeting of the triumvirate as such. It took place, like a number of others in the ensuing days, at the Hyde Park Hotel, which was Aitken's London address at the time. Lloyd George 'stated his main case with great skill and tact', saying no more about Asquith's future position than that he would continue to lead the Commons. Law was pleasantly surprised to find that Carson would be willing to re-enter an Asquith government, provided the machinery for running the war were changed. Next day there was another meeting, at which Lloyd George 'said quite frankly that Asquith must not be a member of the projected War Council'. His reason was that if the Prime Minister was a member he must, because of his office, dominate it; and that if it was dominated by Asquith nothing would be gained in efficiency. Aitken was alarmed by Lloyd George's frankness, but afterwards came to recognise that he had been wise to make a clean breast of his scheme.[2]

There were now significant developments in the Press. Lloyd George resumed friendly contact with C. P. Scott, with whom he had

1. Beaverbrook, *Politicians and the War*, ch. XXVI.
2. *ibid.*, ch. XXVII.

quarrelled over the Howard interview.[1] On the 23rd the *Morning Post* came out with a leader praising Lloyd George as 'a power which makes for victory . . . a force to which the nation may adhere, which the nation may follow'. This reflected the alliance between Lloyd George and Carson, and was all the more noteworthy coming so soon after the same paper had berated the War Minister for interfering with the generals. (For the sake of consistency, it still said that he was 'not a strategist'.) On the 24th Donald of the *Daily Chronicle* called on Law, since he was meditating 'a critical article on the direction of the war', and had 'heard from many quarters that the War Committee . . . had become altogether unwieldy, and was most dilatory in arriving at decisions'. The article appeared five days later and was 'especially important'.[2]

On the 25th the triumvirs met at Law's house in Edwardes Square and approved a memorandum drafted by Aitken, which was to be put to Asquith as a statement for him to issue. It embodied a compromise scheme under which Asquith would be president, but Lloyd George chairman, of a new 'civilian General Staff' consisting of themselves and two other Cabinet ministers without portfolio. No names were suggested for the other two – a space was left blank – but Law and Carson were the obvious candidates.[3] This group would have 'executive authority' subject to the Prime Minister's right to refer any questions he thought fit to the full Cabinet. Law took the memorandum straight to Asquith (who was still in London, though it was Saturday afternoon). He read it at once and made a few preliminary comments, but said he would give a definite answer after the weekend.

This took the form of a letter, written at the Wharf, which he handed to Law on Monday morning. In it, he rejected the proposed scheme without qualification. After saying that he could not imagine any workable war committee of which the heads of the Admiralty and War Office were not members, he went on:

> . . . the essence of your scheme is that the War Committee should disappear, and its place be taken by a body of four – myself, yourself, Carson, and Lloyd George.

1. *Scott Diaries*, ed. Trevor Wilson, pp. 235–8.
2. Stephen Koss, *The Rise and Fall of the Political Press In Britain*, Vol. II, p. 300.
3. But Lloyd George had earlier told Hankey the membership of such a group should be himself, Law, Carson and Henderson. (Hankey, *The Supreme Command*, 22 November, p. 564).

As regards Carson, for whom, as you know, I have the greatest personal regard, I do not see how it would be possible in order to secure his services, to pass over Balfour, or Curzon, or McKenna, all of whom have the advantage of intimate knowledge of the secret history of the last twelve months. . . . It would be universally believed to be the price paid for shutting the mouth of our most formidable parliamentary critic – a manifest sign of weakness and cowardice.

As to Lloyd George, you know as well as I do both his qualities and his defects. He has many qualities that would fit him for the first place, but he lacks the one thing needful – he does not inspire trust. . . .[1] Here, again, there is but one construction, and one only, that could be put on the new arrangement – that it has been engineered by him with the purpose, not perhaps at the moment, but as soon as a fitting pretext could be found, of his displacing me.

In short, the plan could not, in my opinion, be carried out without fatally impairing the confidence of loyal and valued colleagues, and undermining my own authority.

When Law said that he would be showing the letter to his two associates, Asquith was content that Lloyd George should see the references to himself. He was thus openly acknowledging, and returning, what he saw as a direct challenge.

When the triumvirs considered the letter on the Monday afternoon, Law suggested that Lloyd George should see the Prime Minister and try to arrive at an accommodation with him. Lloyd George was prepared to do this, though he could not fail to detect some faltering in Law's resolve. But the Conservative leader certainly had his problems. So far he had said nothing of what was afoot to his party colleagues in the Cabinet, and he had good reason to expect that they would be chary of the whole business, as well as annoyed at having been kept in ignorance of it. A meeting with them could no longer be

1. The same stricture was often applied – and not least by Asquith in his private correspondence – to the only other British politician of the day with the quality vaguely though intelligibly described as genius: Winston Churchill. However just the comment, it would have been unfortunate if either had been disqualified, on that account, from ever holding 'the first place'. Besides, trust is a rare commodity in the higher reaches of politics, seldom unreservedly given or truly merited. When, in September 1916, Law told Carson that he distrusted Lloyd George more than Asquith, Carson replied: 'No, that one is a plain man of the people, and, though you mayn't trust him, his crookednesses are all plain to see. But the other is clever and polished and knows how to conceal his crookedness.' (H. Montgomery Hyde, *Carson*, p. 407, footnote.)

delayed, but before it could take place Donald's article appeared, on 29 November, under the headline 'The Trials of the Coalition', and the same day even J. A. Spender produced in the *Westminster Gazette* an article referring to the Government's 'appearance of delay and indecision'. When Law met his colleagues on the 30th, therefore, it was fairly obvious that a political crisis was brewing.

Their reaction, as foreseen, was hostile to the scheme put forward by the triumvirate, and to Law's involvement with Lloyd George and Carson. Afterwards Lansdowne wrote to Law that the meeting had left a nasty taste in his mouth. All the same, Law did not surrender his freedom of action or dissociate himself from his two partners. He went uneasily ahead, still hoping for some miraculous compromise which would reconcile all differences. And it was with his predicament very much in mind that Lloyd George drew up a list of demands to Asquith, which fell considerably short of what he himself regarded as necessary. With this summary he went to the Prime Minister on 1 December:

> 1 That the War Committee consist of three members, two of which must be the First Lord of the Admiralty and the Secretary of State for War . . . and a third Minister without a portfolio. One of these three to be Chairman.
> 2 That the War Committee should have full power subject to the supreme control of the Prime Minister to direct all questions connected with the War.
> 3 The Prime Minister in his discretion to have power to refer any question to the Cabinet.
> 4 Unless the Cabinet on reference by the Prime Minister reverses the decision of the War Committee, that decision to be carried out by the Department concerned.
> 5 The War Committee to have the power to invite any Minister and to summon the expert advisers and officers of any Department to its meetings.

A rider to the first point, which he mentioned to Asquith as they talked, was that Balfour would have to leave the Admiralty.

Despite the very large concessions in this proposal – that the Prime Minister, though not chairman of the new committee, should retain 'supreme control . . . to direct all questions connected with the War', and that the Service ministers should, as he wished, be members of the committee – Asquith lost little time in virtually dismissing it. Later the same day he wrote to Lloyd George that the Prime Minister must, in his view, be chairman of the committee and not 'relegated to the position of an arbiter in the background or a referee to the Cabinet'. He also proposed that 'the reconstruction of the War Committee should be accompanied by the setting up of a Committee of National Organisation, to deal with the purely domestic side of our problems'. This idea was plainly absurd, since there was bound to be overlapping, and in any case what was needed was more effective unity of command. But Asquith had a shrewd political reason for introducing it. The idea had originated with Lord Robert Cecil and was being run by him and other Conservative ministers as an alternative to the triumvirate's scheme.

Lloyd George's note delivered to Asquith on 1 December is often described as an ultimatum, and it has been said that while he was with the Prime Minister he threatened, or hinted at, resignation if it were not accepted. This may or may not be true. What cannot be doubted is that at about this time he resolved to see the business through whatever the consequences. He would increase the pressure on the Prime Minister and hope that he would eventually agree to a compromise which would also be acceptable to himself. But if, after all, Asquith would not give way, then there would have to be a break. Lloyd George had very often spoken of resignation before without going through with it, but now his purpose was inflexible.

Were the other two equally firm? Carson certainly was, but it was easier for him than for Law. With Carson there was no question of having to resign because he had already done so fourteen months earlier. And his responsibility as a leader was to the Tory dissidents who owed nothing to the existing regime, whereas Law's was primarily to the 'good boys' who were either in the Government or supporting it. Aitken was sufficiently worried about his state of mind during the evening of the 1st to feel that Lloyd George should be summoned to build up his morale. Knowing the War Minister's movements, he went with Law in a taxi to the Berkeley Hotel, where Lloyd George was dining with Cunliffe, Reading and the Edwin Montagus,[1] and signalled to him from a corner of the restaurant. Lloyd George left the table at once and returned with the other two to the Hyde Park Hotel. There, according to Aitken, he 'exercised

---

1. Reading was potentially valuable as a friend of Lloyd George who was also on excellent terms with Asquith. Montagu, too, had a foot in both camps, and was almost as active as Aitken during the crisis, in the capacity of go-between.

consummate tact' in not trying to browbeat Law into any particular course of action. But he doubtless heard that Law would be having another meeting with his Conservative colleagues on the 3rd (Sunday), and with this in view sent him the following morning (the 2nd) a copy of Asquith's letter with a brief covering note:

My dear Bonar,
   I enclose copy P.M.'s letter.
   The life of the country depends on resolute action by you now.
                                      Yours ever
                                      D. Lloyd George[1]

Over the weekend people were able to read more about the crisis in their newspapers. On Saturday the *Daily Chronicle* and the *Daily Express* (of which Aitken was about to become the owner) both ran stories in which the names of Lloyd George, Law and Carson were given as likely members of a new war committee or council. These stories were planted, directly or indirectly, by Aitken. The Northcliffe dailies published leaders supporting the demand from within the Cabinet for a change in the system, but their news stories were less specific. Aitken says that, although Lloyd George had not, at first, wanted to have anything to do with Northcliffe, he had been persuaded – by Lee – to see him on the 1st, but had not then given him his confidence. On the Saturday morning, however, he saw him again, and presumably as a result the *Evening News* came out with posters that read: 'Lloyd George packing up'.

On Sunday *Reynolds' News* appeared with the most revealing story so far. Under the headline 'Grave Cabinet Crisis: Lloyd George to Resign', it announced that the War Minister was planning to go if his terms were not accepted, and that if he went he would take his case to the country. He was only delaying 'the final step' at the request of several colleagues in the Cabinet. The owner of *Reynolds' News* was Sir Henry Dalziel, radical M.P. and journalist, who had been a crony of Lloyd George since their early days together in Parliament, and who had been one of his companions on a rather comical trip to

---

1. Roy Jenkins says (*Asquith*, p. 432) that Lloyd George wrote this note because he now 'felt certain enough of his man', and Beaverbrook also suggests in his printed record that Law's mind was made up by the end of the previous evening's talk at the Hyde Park Hotel. But the original narrative on which the book was based is less definite and dramatic. (See A. J. P. Taylor, *Beaverbrook*, ch. 6. In Mr Taylor's view, 'Law continued to hesitate until 5 December'.) It seems, therefore, more likely that Lloyd George's note was written because he did *not* yet feel quite certain of his man.

Argentina in 1896. Naturally it was assumed that the article came straight from him, and the Conservative ministers who gathered at Law's house on Sunday morning were very annoyed about it.

At this meeting the differences between Law and his colleagues were not bridged, but at length there was agreement on a resolution which Law was to present to Asquith. It read:

> We share the view expressed to you by Mr Bonar Law some time ago that the Government cannot continue as it is.
>
> It is evident that a change must be made, and, in our opinion, the publicity given to the intention of Mr Lloyd George makes reconstruction from within no longer possible.
>
> We therefore urge the Prime Minister to tender the resignation of the Government.
>
> If he feels unable to take that step, we authorise Mr Bonar Law to tender our resignations.

What exactly Law's colleagues wanted or expected to happen is a matter of dispute, but a good witness is Austen Chamberlain, who wrote to the Viceroy of India, Chelmsford, less than a week later:

> It seemed to us . . . that the only hope of a stable Government lay in combining somehow or another in one administration the separate forces represented by both Asquith and Lloyd George. We were all of us of opinion that reconstruction had become necessary. We did not think that with a Parliament constituted like the present, a Unionist Government, or a Government under a Unionist Prime Minister, would have any chance of success. It was not for us to say which of the rival Liberals could secure the greatest amount of support in the Liberal Party and in the Parties which habitually worked with it. But we felt that the continuance of the existing Government had become impossible.[1]

But Curzon, writing even closer to the event – on the same day, to Lansdowne (who was at Bowood, having not chosen to come up for the meeting) – conveys an impression more favourable to Lloyd George, or at any rate less favourable to Asquith:

> Had one felt that reconstruction by and under the present Prime Minister was possible, we should all have preferred to try it. But we know that with him as Chairman, either of the Cabinet or War

---

1. 8 December 1916. Letter quoted in Austen Chamberlain, *Down the Years*, pp. 115–28.

Committee, it is absolutely impossible to win the War, and it will be for himself and Lloyd George to determine whether he goes out altogether or becomes Lord Chancellor or Chancellor of the Exchequer in a new Government, a nominal Premiership being a protean compromise which, in our view, could have no endurance.[1]

There is no suggestion in either of these passages that the ministers would refuse to serve under Lloyd George, if he were asked to form a government.

While most of the leading Tories were staying, however reluctantly, in London, Asquith decided to go to Walmer Castle in Kent, leaving after lunch on Saturday. To Hankey it seemed 'very typical of him that in the middle of this tremendous crisis he should go away for the weekend! Typical both of his qualities and of his defects'.[2] According to Reading (who told Montagu) he went because he had heard that Carson would be in the neighbourhood of Walmer, and he hoped to see him there for a talk. But if he said this he must, surely, have been joking. Any idea of a worthwhile separate negotiation between him and Carson was obviously fantastic.

Before leaving for Walmer with her husband, Margot Asquith asked Hankey to get in touch with Law, from whom he heard about the party meeting called for the following day. Margot was in no danger of underrating the seriousness of the crisis. Like Frances Stevenson, she loved the atmosphere of power and hated the thought of being deprived of it. Indeed it is possible that, unlike Frances, she loved the atmosphere of power even more than she loved the man who enabled her to breathe it. Certainly she had been a harassing as well as a stimulating wife to him. Asquith once confided to his daughter, Violet: 'I have sometimes walked up and down that room till I felt as tho' I were going mad. . . . When one needed rest to have a thing like the *Morning Post* leader flung at one – all the obvious reasons

1. Letter quoted in Newton, *Lord Lansdowne*, pp. 452–3. Curzon soon afterwards wrote a loyal letter to Asquith. Clearly he was anxious to ensure that, whoever was Prime Minister at the end of the crisis, he would still be in office. His behaviour was untrustworthy even by the standards of high politics. But he can have had no ulterior motive for writing as he did to Lansdowne, who was hardly likely to pass his remarks on to the triumvirate, and who was probably more opposed to Lloyd George than any other member of the Cabinet.

2. Hankey Diary, 2 December 1916 (*op. cit.*, Vol. II, p. 565). Walmer Castle was (and is) the official residence of the Lord Warden of the Cinque Ports, an office which Asquith had declined. But the incumbent, Lord Beauchamp, had been lending him the Castle for use at weekends since 1914.

for and against more controversially put even than by one's colleagues.'[1] But Margot did not confine her political interventions to the privacy of his room; she was also very apt to meddle in public matters on her own initiative, having an ill-founded belief in her capacity for fixing people. So far as Lloyd George was concerned, she had tried both mischief-making behind his back and direct personal approaches, of which the latest and last instance may have been taking him to *Elijah* (for the idea was hers) on 25 November. But he was better at fixing than at being fixed.

By Saturday evening Hankey was convinced that Asquith would have to return next day to London, so on Sunday morning his private secretary and son-in-law, Maurice Bonham Carter, drove down to Walmer to fetch him. He travelled back in his own car with Bonham Carter, who lent his to Margot to return in alone. (The weekend guests, who included General Cowans, were left to entertain themselves.) About an hour after Asquith arrived back in Downing Street Law came to see him, and their meeting has proved one of the most controversial episodes in the crisis. What was said will always be a matter of doubt, but there is no doubt at all about one thing that was done, or rather not done: Law failed to give Asquith the copy of the resolution passed at the Conservative meeting, which he had in his pocket.[2] All the same Asquith clearly and correctly understood that, unless he took very swift pre-emptive action, the Conservative ministers would resign and so bring his Government down. The action that he decided to take was to send at once for Lloyd George.

Criticism of Law's error, or maybe sin, of omission has little point unless it can be supposed that the crisis would have had a different outcome if Asquith had seen the resolution. Roy Jenkins tentatively suggests that it might:

Had Asquith been shown the resolution, and had he, like everyone

1. V.S.L., Introduction to Part I by Michael and Eleanor Brock, p. 9 (quoting Violet Bonham Carter's diary).

2. Law claimed to have communicated the contents of the resolution to Asquith, but to have forgotten to hand him the actual document. This would be easier to believe if the text of the resolution had not been the subject of anxious discussion between him and Aitken before he went to see Asquith. Aitken, who had not been present at the Conservative meeting, was unduly apprehensive about the effect that the reference to pro-Lloyd George publicity might have on Law's relations with Lloyd George, and perhaps also (though he does not say so) of the effect that it might have on Asquith. It seems on the whole more likely that Law deliberately withheld the document than that he forgot about it, though it does not follow that he misled Asquith as to its essential contents; still less that the course of history was significantly affected even if he had done so.

else, found it confusing, and discovered from Bonar Law that it was the product of a confused meeting, a natural reaction on his part would have been a demand to see the other Unionist ministers, who were still serving under him.

A meeting later that afternoon between Asquith and the 'three C's' [Aitken's nickname for Cecil, Chamberlain and Curzon, with whom, in this crisis, Long is usually associated] might have had considerable effect. To begin with, he would no doubt have found them wavering. But he was not without influence over them. In the course of the discussion their doubts about Lloyd George would have come to the surface, and the conclusion might have been that they would have stiffened Asquith, and he would have stiffened them.[1]

The argument is that he would not then have felt obliged to send for Lloyd George, but would have gone ahead with adapting the system of war direction in his own way.

Is this a plausible hypothesis? It assumes not only that the 'three C's' would have urged Asquith to act masterfully in disregard of Lloyd George – which seems most unlikely in view of the letters from Chamberlain and Curzon already quoted – but also that they were capable, themselves, of providing the necessary countervailing strength. In fact, surely, they were not. The two Conservative members of the triumvirate carried far more weight than the 'three C's'. Carson was the acknowledged leader of a large section of the Parliamentary party, and also had popular charisma exceeded only by Lloyd George's. Law had control of the party machine and solid support from rank-and-file Conservatives in the country. The really significant aspect of his interview with Asquith was not that he neglected to hand over a resolution, but that he continued to *show* resolution, acting in the spirit of Lloyd George's appeal to him. If Asquith had tried to reconstruct his government with the support of the 'three C's', but with the triumvirate still against him, he must have failed.

Apart from Carson and Law, there was only one Conservative of major importance, and he had not yet played any active part in the crisis. Balfour was probably absent from the first meeting with Law, and certainly absent – ill – from the second. Lloyd George had insisted to Asquith that he should be removed fom the Admiralty, but in other

1. *Asquith*, p. 440.

respects he was not yet in the picture at all. When he did come into it, it was to be with the most telling effect. Meanwhile Asquith sent for Lloyd George, who drove up from Walton Heath and, after smoking a cigar with Aitken at the War Office, walked across Whitehall to Downing Street.

The meeting that followed was quite amicable, despite the tension that both men must have felt, and from it emerged a new compromise. Lloyd George was to be chairman of the new war committee, but Asquith was nevertheless 'to have supreme and effective control of war policy'. The agenda of the committee would be submitted to him, Lloyd George would report to him daily, he would be free to direct it to consider particular matters, and all its conclusions would be subject to his veto. He could also attend its meetings whenever he wished. This was, in theory at any rate, a compromise very favourable to Asquith, involving only a slight recession from the stand he had taken against Lloyd George's original so-called 'ultimatum'. Moreover the question of personalities was left open, except that Lloyd George agreed to Henderson as a fourth member for the committee (readily enough, since he already favoured his inclusion). Law joined the discussion for the last half-hour, and it was then agreed that all ministers other than the Prime Minister should resign to facilitate the task of reconstruction. On the face of it, his position remained extremely strong.

After the meeting Lloyd George went back to the War Office, where he talked first to Montagu and then to Northcliffe. Law attended another meeting of Conservative ministers (this time at F. E. Smith's house in Grosvenor Crescent) and gave them the news of the compromise which, he hoped, had ended the crisis. Asquith found relief, as so often, in writing a private letter:

I was forced back [from Walmer] . . . to grapple with a 'Crisis' – this time with a very big C. The result is that I have spent much of the afternoon in colloguing with Messrs. Ll. George & Bonar Law. . . . The 'Crisis' shows every sign of following its many predecessors to an early & unhonoured grave. But there were many wigs nearly on the green.[1]

He and Margot were to dine with the Montagus, and as he changed for dinner she remonstrated with him for not having made it clearer to

1. H.H.A. to Pamela McKenna.

Lloyd George that he, Asquith, would continue to run the war. When they got back from the Montagus' she returned to this theme and kept on at him until the small hours.[1] He had had a long enough day, but she made it considerably longer.

Next morning – Monday the 4th – the newspapers carried an announcement from 10 Downing Street, issued the night before at Law's suggestion, that 'the Prime Minister, with a view to the most active prosecution of the War, [had] decided to advise His Majesty the King to consent to a reconstruction of the Government'. There was also a good deal of Press comment. The *Morning Post* said that 'Cock Robin' was dead, and the *Manchester Guardian* referred to the humiliation of Asquith, whose 'natural course would be either to resist the demand for a War Council, which would partly supersede him as Premier, or alternatively himself to resign'. Above all, *The Times* had a leader which praised Lloyd George's stand against the present 'cumbrous methods of directing the war', and the 'alternative scheme' that he had proposed; which went on to emphasise that Asquith would not be a member of the new committee, on the assumption that he had 'sufficient cares of a more general character without devoting himself wholly, as the new Council must be devoted if it is to be effective, to the daily task of organising victory'; and which further, and most woundingly, remarked that Asquith's closest supporters must have become convinced that his qualities were 'fitted better, as they were fond of saying, to "preserve the unity of the Nation" ' – which the editorial 'we' had anyway 'never doubted' – 'than to force the pace of a War Council'.

The editor, Geoffrey Robinson (later Dawson), stated afterwards in a memorandum on the subject that this article was written 'entirely' by himself, and that it was 'absolutely' uninspired, in the sense that nobody had 'suggested' it to him. But he also said that, after returning on Sunday afternoon from Cliveden (where he had been staying with the Waldorf Astors), he spoke to Carson, who 'of course was in close touch with L.G.'.[2] According to the official history of *The Times*, Dawson's 'trenchant anti-Asquith passage' was inserted after visiting Carson on his way to Printing House Square.[3] But there is no mention of Northcliffe, to whom Lloyd George had undoubtedly talked at the

1. Margot Asquith Diary (unpublished).
2. John Evelyn Wrench, *Geoffrey Dawson and Our Times*, pp. 140–1.
3. *The History of The Times*, Part I, 1912–1920, p. 297.

War Office after his meeting with the Prime Minister. Perhaps it is true that Northcliffe added nothing to the leader, but he must surely have seen it and approved of it. Had it been less strongly worded than it was, he might well have provided some further inspiration.

To what extent was Lloyd George responsible for the general Press campaign? Of course he had a good deal to do with it, though his direct share should not be exaggerated. Much of it was organised by Aitken without reference to him or Law, and it is easy to credit Aitken's assertion that Lloyd George was reluctant to involve Northcliffe, since he knew what harm Northcliffe could sometimes do to causes that he espoused (for instance, his attack on Kitchener in May 1915). But Northcliffe did become involved, and Lloyd George did see him on several occasions during the crisis. How much he said to him can never be known, though it is likely that he was more guarded with him than with some others. His total responsibility for the piece in *Reynolds' News* can be assumed if, as is said,[1] he saw Dalziel on Saturday evening; and it is more than likely anyway. The *Manchester Guardian*'s comments on Monday were doubtless in some degree influenced by the fact that Scott lunched with him at Walton Heath on Sunday, though not insofar as they related specifically to the new compromise, which was not negotiated until the early evening.

As for the *Times* leader, Lloyd George may well have been the source from which Carson heard of the Downing Street agreement, but apart from that the tone and content of the article suggest that it was, indeed, the work of Dawson with a little help from Carson. It should be remembered that Carson, unlike his two confederates, quite definitely wanted Asquith out of the premiership. Another Conservative with the same aim was Milner, who on Sunday wrote to his friend and future wife, Lady Edward Cecil: 'My fear is – there will be another compromise and a patch up. Two to one on the patch up, but there is the odd chance of a smash.'[2] When Carson heard of the patch-up, he may well have exerted himself to improve the chance of a smash, in collaboration with the like-minded Dawson.

Whatever his share in the Press campaign, Lloyd George should not be too harshly judged for the use that he made of journalists. Though undeniably a keen exponent of the process, he was not the first nor, certainly, the last. Since his time it has become standard practice for

1. e.g. *ibid.*, pp. 295–6.
2. Quoted in Gollin, *Proconsul in Politics*, p. 363.

politicians; and in an earlier age Palmerston, for instance, was an outstandingly successful manipulator of the Press. In Lloyd George's day he was by no means the only Cabinet minister who had Press contacts, and he had been as often the victim as the beneficiary of newspaper power. Before the advent of broadcasting and opinion-polling, the Press was the only medium other than Parliament (which was still very imperfectly representative) through which the feelings of ordinary people could be reached and expressed. It was only sensible, therefore, for politicians to cultivate journalists, and those who disdained to do so – of whom Asquith was one – were seriously mistaken.

Asquith's reading of *The Times* on Monday 4 December, after what must have been a rather inadequate night's sleep, did nothing to soften his view of journalists and their trade. He immediately wrote to Lloyd George:

> Such productions as the first leading article in today's *Times*, showing the infinite possibilities for misunderstanding and mis-representation of such an arrangement as we considered yesterday, make me at least doubtful as to its feasibility. Unless the impression is at once corrected that I am being relegated to the position of an irresponsible spectator of the War, I cannot possibly go on.

This was far from being an outright repudiation of the previous evening's arrangement, though it did refer to it as having been merely 'considered', not firmly agreed. Moreover the letter went on to summarise the terms of the arrangement, which was an advance on the previous evening, when Lloyd George had vainly tried (through Montagu) to get a statement of them in writing from Asquith.

His reply was swift and conciliatory:

> My dear Prime Minister,
>
> I have not seen the *Times* article. But I hope you will not attach undue importance to these effusions. I have had these misrepresen-tations to put up with for months. Northcliffe frankly wants a smash. Derby and I do not. Northcliffe would like to make this and any other arrangement under your Premiership impossible. Derby and I attach great importance to your retaining your present position – effectively. I cannot restrain nor I fear influence Northcliffe.
>
> I fully accept in letter and in spirit your summary of the suggested arrangement – subject of course to personnel.
>
> > Ever sincerely,
> > D. Lloyd George

Derby, it should be said, was backing Lloyd George's demands, as also was Robertson, who felt that a more effective instrument was needed for the conduct of 'War policy' (as distinct from military operations), and who may also have welcomed any means of removing Lloyd George from the War Office.

At 12.30 Asquith went to Buckingham Palace where he obtained the King's blessing for a reconstruction of the Government to be carried out by himself. After lunching at Downing Street he went to the House of Commons and was visited in his room by Law, to whom he said that he was becoming less keen on the plan provisionally agreed, because his colleagues seemed to be against it, and because Lloyd George was 'trafficking with the Press'. The conversation was interrupted when he was called away to answer questions, and after Question Time he tried to avoid any further talk with Law. But Law pursued him to Downing Street where Aitken describes the scene, as reported to him by Law:

> When he got there he found Grey, Harcourt, and Runciman, waiting outside the Cabinet Room with the Premier inside. He got hold of Bonham Carter and asked him to take in a message to the effect that he wished to see the Premier urgently and in advance of the waiting Liberal colleagues. He was duly admitted, but found McKenna closeted with Asquith. He then urged on the Prime Minister very strongly the necessity of standing by Sunday's agreement on the appointment of a War Council.

After further exchanges, and after 'failing to get any satisfactory reply, Bonar Law made it clear beyond all possibility of doubt that if the War Council scheme was not adopted he would break with Asquith'.[1]

Roy Jenkins notes that 'McKenna's position of apparent privilege was not without significance'.[2] He was a very competent man, who had done the State much service. But he had become obsessively hostile to Lloyd George, and was using his considerable influence with the Prime Minister, who was fond of both the 'McKennae', to poison his mind against an indispensable colleague. In other circumstances Asquith would have been able – indeed often was able – to preserve his sense of proportion when subjected to such pressure. But he was now

1. *Politicians and the War*, ch. XXXV.
2. *Asquith*, p. 449.

tired and unequal to the task. McKenna knew that any increase in Lloyd George's power would diminish his own. He was determined to wreck the proposed reform of the system, and in a sense he succeeded, though not as he would have wished. At the same time he contributed to wrecking his friend and patron, and the Liberal Party as well.

After Law had left, Lloyd George asked to see the Prime Minister, but the request was refused. Instead Asquith wrote him a letter in which the compromise of the day before was definitely rejected:

After full consideration of this matter in all its aspects, I have come decidedly to the conclusion that it is not possible that such a Committee could be made workable and effective without the Prime Minister as its Chairman. I quite agree that it will be necessary for him, in view of the other calls upon his time and energy, to delegate from time to time the chairmanship to another Minister . . . but . . . he must continue to be, as he has always been, its permanent President.

He also found the demands that had been made about personnel unacceptable. He could not 'be a party to any suggestion that Mr Balfour should be displaced' as First Lord of the Admiralty, and he did not regard Carson as 'the man best qualified among his colleagues, past and present, to be a member of the War Committee'. That evening he dined again with Montagu, but refused to discuss the political situation, knowing that Montagu would be heartbroken by what he had done.

Next morning, the 5th, Lloyd George sent in his resignation. After a long preamble rehearsing past grievances, his letter to Asquith ended:

As all delay is fatal in war, I place my office without further parley at your disposal.

It is with great personal regret that I have come to this conclusion. In spite of mean and unworthy insinuations to the contrary – insinuations which I fear are always inevitable in the case of men who hold prominent but not primary positions in any Administration – I have felt a strong personal attachment to you as my chief. As you yourself said on Sunday, we have acted together for ten years and never had a quarrel, although we have had many a grave difference on questions of policy. You have treated me with great courtesy and kindness; for all that I thank you. Nothing would have induced me to part now except an overwhelming sense that the course of action which has been pursued has put the country – and not merely the country, but throughout the world the principles for which you and I have always stood throughout our political lives – in the greatest peril that has ever overtaken them.

As I am fully conscious of the importance of preserving national unity, I propose to give your Government complete support in the vigorous prosecution of the war; but unity without action is nothing but futile carnage, and I cannot be responsible for that. Vigour and vision are the supreme need at this hour.[1]

While Lloyd George was severing his connection with the Government, some of its Conservative members were meeting in Austen Chamberlain's room at the India Office. Aitken later described this meeting as a 'court of enquiry' into Law's conduct, but Chamberlain denied that it was anything of the kind. Whatever it was, the really important event of the morning on the Conservative side was a letter to Asquith from a leading figure who did not attend the India Office meeting. Balfour, still in bed at his house in Carlton Gardens, wrote to the Prime Minister:

My dear Asquith,

I have been in bed since the political crisis became acute, and can collect no very complete idea of what has been going on. But one thing seems clear: that there is to be a new War Council of which Lloyd George is to be the working Chairman, and that, according to his ideas, this Council would work more satisfactorily if the Admiralty were not represented by me. In these circumstances I cannot consent to retain my office, and must ask you to accept my resignation.

I am quite well aware that you do not personally share Lloyd George's view in this connection. But I am quite clear that the new system should have a trial under the most favourable possible circumstances; and the mere fact that the new Chairman of the War Council *did* prefer and, as far as I know, *still* prefers a different arrangement is, to my mind, quite conclusive, and leaves me in no doubt as to the manner in which I can best assist the Government

1. Asquith promptly replied 'with much regret', and two further letters were exchanged during the day, in which the point at issue was whether (as Lloyd George wished) the letters should be published.

which I desire to support. The fact that the first days of the reconstructed Administration find me more than half an invalid, is an additional reason (if additional reason were required) for adopting the course on which, after much consideration, I have determined.

Yours very sincerely,
Arthur James Balfour

This letter, which was sent across to Downing Street at about midday, seems to have taken Asquith very much by surprise. But why had he never consulted Balfour about Lloyd George's demands? He had talked to plenty of other people – including, the previous evening, Lansdowne[1] – but not to one whose name and office were conspicuously involved, and who was also a former prime minister. On all counts Balfour's opinion would have been worth having. Receiving it now, unsolicited, he sent Balfour a copy of his letter rejecting Lloyd George's terms, which showed him as more Balfourite than Balfour. But if he imagined that there would be any recompense for his staunch support of the First Lord he was soon disappointed, because in the late afternoon another letter came from Carlton Gardens:

. . . I still think (a) that the break-up of the Government by the retirement of Lloyd George would be a misfortune, (b) that the experiment of giving him a free hand with the day-to-day work of the War Committee is still worth trying, and (c) that there is no use trying it except on terms which enable him to work under conditions which, in his own opinion, promise the best results. We cannot, I think, go on in the old way. An open breach with Lloyd George will not improve matters, and attempts to compel cooperation between him and his fellow-workers with whom he is in but imperfect sympathy will only provide fresh trouble.

I am therefore still of opinion that my resignation should be accepted, and that a fair trial should be given to the War Council à la George.

Shortly before this second letter from Balfour reached him, Asquith had seen, at his own request, the 'three C's'; and one of them, Chamberlain, recorded three days later what passed at the meeting:

[Asquith] told us the whole story from his point of view, and we explained to him the meaning of our resolution, which he had not

1. Lansdowne saw him at 5 p.m. on the 4th (Crawford diary).

THE FALL OF ASQUITH 465

previously understood. . . . He asked us whether we should be prepared to go on with him whilst Lloyd George and Bonar Law resigned. To this we replied that our only object was to secure a Government on such lines and with such a prospect of stability that it might reasonably be expected to be capable of carrying on the war; that in our opinion his Government, weakened by the resignations of Lloyd George and Bonar Law and by all that had gone on during the past weeks, offered no such prospect, and we answered this question therefore with a perfectly definitive negative. This was evidently a great blow to him. . . .

He then asked us what our attitude would be towards Lloyd George if he attempted to form an administration. We replied again that our only object was to get a stable Government conducting the war successfully. We had come under no obligation to Lloyd George, our hands were perfectly free, but we should be prepared to support, to join or to serve under any Government which offered a prospect of fulfilling our conditions.

This account surely disposes of the idea that the 'three C's' could ever have provided Asquith with a sufficient basis of Conservative support, or that their antagonism to Lloyd George was insuperable.

The second point was strikingly illustrated when Cecil 'had the courage to suggest to Asquith that the finest and biggest thing that he could do would be to offer to serve under Lloyd George'. The Prime Minister 'would not allow Cecil to develop this idea, which he rejected with indignation and even with scorn'.[1] But Cecil did develop the idea in a letter to Asquith written the same day, probably before the meeting at 10 Downing Street:

My dear Asquith,

Please forgive me if I venture to ask you to consider if it is at all possible for you to accept office in a Lloyd George ministry. Do not think that I underrate the magnitude of the sacrifice I am suggesting. But at this time it is really of vast importance that you should do so. Nothing else can preserve the unity of the country or the respect of Europe. I know well that the merely personal aspect of the position would not affect you. If it were so I would say that such an act would give you an authority with your fellow-countrymen which even you have never had. I remember well the immense effect on his

1. Chamberlain, *Down the Years*, p. 124.

personal position produced by my father's offer to serve under Hartington. Till then he had been regarded as a mere party leader. Afterwards he grew to occupy the national position which he held till his death. But I do not put this on personal but on national grounds. Your decision may make all the difference between success & failure in the war. I mentioned the matter to my Unionist colleagues & every one of them (Balfour was away) warmly agreed with me.

> With many apologies,
> Yours very sincerely
> Robert Cecil[1]

It was tragic that Asquith could not bring himself even to contemplate the course that Cecil recommended.

After leaving the Prime Minister the 'three C's' joined their colleagues at a meeting of Conservative ministers in Law's room at the Colonial Office, from which Curzon was later sent back to Downing Street with a written resumé of their collective view signed by Law. The key point in this was that they thought Asquith should resign at once. At a lunch-time meeting with his Liberal colleagues he had been advised to resign, not as a gesture of defeat, but as a means of fighting back against Lloyd George's challenge. Only Montagu had then dissented, arguing that the King should be asked to call Asquith, Lloyd George, Law and Henderson together to find a solution. But his was a lone voice. The others were still under the delusion that a viable Government could be formed without Lloyd George, Law or Carson; and Asquith himself, at that time, must still have been similarly deluded. Why otherwise would he have bothered to send for the 'three C's'? But after talking to them, and above all after receiving both the second letter from Balfour and the message from the Unionist meeting he could see that the game was up. At 7 p.m. he drove to Buckingham Palace and tendered his resignation to a King who, early in the reign, would not have been sorry to see him go, but who was now full of regret.

1. Robert Cecil to H.H.A., 5 December 1916. The phrasing suggests that the letter was written after the morning meeting at the India Office at which he probably 'mentioned the matter' to his colleagues. He would then have raised it with Asquith in the afternoon as an idea already communicated to him in writing.

Cecil's father, Salisbury, twice offered to stand down in favour of the Liberal Unionist leader, Hartington: in 1886, before forming his second ministry, and in January 1887 after the resignation of Lord Randolph Churchill.

Did he hope that his departure would be only temporary – that nobody else would be able to form a Ministry, and that the King would then turn to him again? There is some evidence that he did. J. H. Thomas wrote that what influenced him

> was the advice of a number of close friends that it was impossible for Lloyd George to form a Cabinet. He himself told me this, and I, wanting him to continue, pointed out that this advice was sheer madness. In fact, I remember saying (and I made a note of it at the time): 'Do remember, Asquith, that anybody can form a Cabinet with the patronage at their disposal that exists in this country.' But he was resolved, believing that the King would send for him [again] before the day was out. He was mistaken.[1]

And Asquith's daughter-in-law, Cynthia, who was dining at 10 Downing Street on the 5th, recorded in her diary:

> Of course, the whole evening was spent in conjecture and discussion – most interesting. I tried to absorb as much as I could, but I am not quick about politics. I gathered that, before dinner, Mr Asquith had said he thought there was quite a chance of Lloyd George failing to form a Government at all. The Tories – in urging him to resign – had predicted such a failure. In any case, most people seemed to think that any Government he could succeed in forming would only be very short-lived.[2]

Despite these sources, it is surely unlikely that Asquith had any serious hope of pulling off what, in bridge, would be called a deep finesse. No doubt he was still intermittently a prey to fleeting, irrational optimism, but at heart he must have known that his power had passed.

As soon as they heard the news Law and Aitken foregathered with Lloyd George at the War Office. It seemed likely that the King would take the constitutional course of asking the Leader of the Conservative Party to try to form a new government, but Law did not want the job. He had no doubt that Lloyd George was the right man for it, and said at once that he would put forward his name to the King. But, according to Aitken, Lloyd George demurred:

> Those who worked on the 'personal ambition' theory of his activities would have expected him to jump eagerly to seize on the

---

1. J.H. Thomas, *My Story*, p. 43.
2. Lady Cynthia Asquith, *Diaries 1915–18*, p. 242. Cynthia, daughter of the 11th Earl of Wemyss, had been married to Asquith's second son, Herbert, since 1910.

offer. As a matter of fact, Lloyd George did exactly the opposite. 'No,' he said in effect, 'I don't want to be Premier. I have not been fighting for the Premiership, but simply to get rid of the Asquith incubus. Give me the Chairmanship of the War Council and (turning to Law) I am perfectly content and would prefer to serve under you.'[1]

There was one strong argument for Law's making the attempt – that he might be able to form a government in which Asquith would agree to serve. Asquith had treated with indignation, even scorn, Cecil's suggestion that he might serve under Lloyd George. But was there any chance that he could be persuaded to serve under somebody else? He had, apparently, told Law at their meeting on the 3rd that he 'would not dream of being Chancellor of the Exchequer or Lord Chancellor'.[2] But did that necessarily mean that he would not serve in any capacity? For the sake of national unity and because of his prestige, it seemed worth trying to keep him in. The discussion at the War Office ended, therefore, with an understanding that Law should accept the King's offer if he could persuade Asquith to serve under him, but that, if not, the task of trying to form a government should be assumed by Lloyd George.

At 9.30 p.m. Law was summoned to the Palace, and had a distinctly awkward interview with the King. They argued unnecessarily about a number of matters, but in the end Law left with the conditional commission that he had agreed to accept, though only after making it perfectly clear to the King that he thought Lloyd George would be the best choice. Later that evening he called at 10 Downing Street, and asked Asquith if he would serve under a 'neutral' prime minister. When Asquith asked what was meant by 'neutral', Law raised, presumably on the spur of the moment, another possibility. 'I said that as His Majesty had sent for me I was the natural person, but that if he thought it would be easier for him to serve under Mr Balfour I would be delighted to fall in which such an arrangement.' In saying this he was, of course, going beyond what was decided earlier at the War Office, but the point is immaterial because Asquith, 'after a moment's consideration, said that he could not agree' to serve under Balfour.[3]

Next morning, the 6th, the triumvirate met at Law's house, and it

1. Aitken, op. cit., ch. XXXVIII.
2. Crawford Papers, p. 371 (3 December 1916).
3. Law's memorandum on the crisis, quoted in Blake, The Unknown Prime Minister, p. 337.

was decided that Lloyd George and Law should visit Balfour (who had sent the Tory leader copies of his letters to Asquith, thereby perhaps creating an uneasy feeling that he ought to have been consulted earlier). The two found him still bed-ridden, but not otherwise incapacitated. It was agreed to be desirable that a government should be formed in which Lloyd George would be chairman of the war committee, and of which Asquith would be a member. It seemed quite clear to Balfour that such a government would only be possible with Law as premier. Law then said that he had 'suggested a meeting at B[uckingham] P[alace], at which both he and L.G. were very anxious that [Balfour] should be present'.[1] Balfour agreed to come, though it would mean getting up sooner than he had intended.

The conference took place at 3 p.m., though Balfour had a half-hour audience of the King before it. Those taking part were Law, Lloyd George, Asquith, Balfour and Henderson. (So Montagu more or less got what he wanted after all.) In the record kept by Stamfordham it appears that Asquith was entreated by all the others in turn to join the new government, and that Henderson said he did not believe he could get his party to support any government which did not include Asquith. After speaking with some bitterness of the trials and attacks to which he had been subjected, Asquith eventually agreed to go away and consider the proposals made to him.[2] He went, as Balfour says, 'to consider whether such inclusion was practicable or not from the point of view of his immediate friends'.[3] The conference had lasted an hour and a half.

Asquith's final discussion at Downing Street involved all his Liberal colleagues and Henderson, but not – sadly though understandably – Lloyd George. By six o'clock it was all over and he had written to Law:

They are unanimously of opinion – and I agree with them – that I, and probably they, can give more effective support from outside. They also think that we could not carry the support of the Liberal

1. Balfour's memorandum on the crisis, quoted in Blanche E. C. Dugdale, *Arthur James Balfour*, Vol. II, ch. IX.

2. Stamfordham's report of the conference is quoted in full in Nicolson, *King George V*, pp. 290–1.

3. Dugdale, *op. cit.* In his memoirs Lloyd George says that the conference broke up when he, Law and Henderson offered to serve under Balfour, and Asquith 'asked indignantly, "what is the proposal that I, who have held first place for eight years should be asked to take a secondary position?" ' (W.M., p. 997.) But there is no mention of this in the contemporary reports, and it would seem that the idea of a Balfour premiership was not seriously mooted at the conference, if indeed it came up at all.

party for any such arrangement. I have no personal feeling of *amour propre* in the matter (as I believe you know) but I am more convinced, the more I think of it, that it would be an unworkable arrangement.

In fact, the decision was not unanimous. Montagu and Henderson opposed it. But all the others either urged Asquith to stay out or endorsed this advice by their silence.

The resulting events are tersely recorded by the King in his diary:

> At seven I received Bonar Law, who told me that he could not form a Government, as Asquith refused to serve under him. So I sent for Lloyd George & asked him to form a Government, which he said he would endeavour to do.

Asquith had been Prime Minister for about a hundred days short of nine years – the longest continuous tenure of the office since Liverpool's nearly a century earlier, and for over seventy years unsurpassed by any later holder. Most long-serving prime ministers have breaks in opposition, but Asquith's premiership was a single unbroken stint. Since it was also exceptionally eventful and demanding one might suppose that, by 1915 at any rate, he would have begun to feel the need for release. But with him it seems to have had the opposite effect. The longer he stayed in the post the more natural and right it came to seem to him that he should occupy it. However tired he may have been in other ways, he was never tired of being Prime Minister. His attitude became increasingly proprietorial, and any suggestion that he should relinquish the office, or even a significant share of its power, was resented by him as a monarch might resent the threat of usurpation.

This was most unfortunate, because a large measure of self-denial on his part was desperately necessary in the national interest. More and more people could see that it was so, including people who genuinely admired him and had no wish at all to humiliate him. But he could not see it himself. He continued to tinker with the machinery while refusing to recognise that the human control of it was defective. Even if he had carried his tinkering far enough (which he never did) the problem of control would have remained. The inescapable fact was that, in certain vital respects, he was not qualified to run the war. Yet he insisted that nobody else be given a free hand to run it.

In peacetime, though not perhaps exactly a great political leader, he was certainly a great head of government, choosing and holding together a team of ministers as gifted as any in British history. Despite a few curious blind spots, and a number of bad mistakes, his record of achievement before the war was by any standards impressive; as was, most notably, his handling of the Cabinet in the crisis of July–August 1914, which resulted in British intervention. Even in wartime his stamina and political skill showed little sign of weakening until the last six months or so of his premiership, and were substantial assets to set against his obvious defects as a war leader. But by the end of 1916 he was in a general state of decline, while at the same time the war was entering a most critical phase. Change there had to be, and drastic change. But how was it to come about?

The ideal solution would have been for him to take the initiative himself, then or – better still – earlier. Lloyd George's aptitude for war leadership was clearly superior to his. Unlike Asquith, he could appeal to the imaginations of people in the mass, and stir their emotions: a quality useful (if also dangerous) in peace, but often vital in war. And it was combined, in his case, with a proven talent for the kind of large-scale organisation and improvisation that the country needed in its unprecedented emergency. It was also hard to deny that he had a flair for grand strategy and the priorities of war which enabled him, at times, to outguess the military professionals. Finally, though he had been carrying the burden of high office for eleven years, he had not yet carried the supreme burden; and he had the further advantage of being ten years younger than Asquith.

If Asquith could have made the spontaneous gesture of handing over power, the necessary result would have been achieved without unpleasantness and, above all, without schism. Probably it would always have been best for the premiership itself to be handed over; for Lloyd George to become the first man in the government and Asquith the second – with all the prestige that his long experience and patriotic self-sacrifice would have given him. But it is possible, as Lloyd George seems to have believed and desired, that an arrangement for sharing the tasks of leadership, with Asquith still Prime Minister, could have been made to work, provided Lloyd George's authority within the sphere of war direction had been firmly established and clear-cut. Any attempt to share power within that sphere was bound to fail, and it was lucky, therefore, that Asquith rejected the compromise schemes to which Lloyd George and Law, to avoid a breach with him, were prepared to agree.

Instead of an amicable and spontaneous transfer, change had to be brought about by means of an intrigue. This method should not, indeed, have aroused any sense of outrage in Asquith, nor should he have baulked unduly at the form of premiership that was being proposed to him, since both the proposal and the method might have recalled an episode in his earlier career. In September 1905 he, Grey and Haldane – another triumvirate – had conspired to refuse office in the forthcoming Liberal government unless the party leader, Campbell-Bannerman, agreed to go to the House of Lords. From there it was intended that he should serve as a more or less ornamental Prime Minister, while Asquith, as Chancellor of the Exchequer and Leader of the House of Commons, would be the effective head of the government, with Grey as Foreign Secretary and Haldane as Lord Chancellor. This scheme, known to history as the Relugas Compact (after the Highland fishing lodge where it originated), surely bears a rather striking resemblance to the scheme described in this chapter.

Certain differences, however, should be noted. In 1905 the country was not in mortal danger; indeed, it was not in danger at all. The then triumvirate's design may not have been against the national interest, but no one could seriously pretend that it was dictated by it, as the 1916 triumvirate's very largely was. Another difference is that in 1905 the proposal was never put to, or discussed with, the leader whose removal from the House of Commons was being plotted, whereas in 1916 Asquith was very promptly told what the triumvirate had in mind, by Law if not by Lloyd George. Moreover the second design, far from being a hole-and-corner affair, was soon widely publicised and became an open campaign for change: precisely the aspect of it to which Asquith most objected. Above all, the two conspiracies differed in that one failed and the other succeeded. The earlier one failed because when Campbell-Bannerman was asked to form a government Asquith immediately accepted the post offered to him, without laying down any conditions and without consulting his fellow-conspirators (rather odd behaviour in a stickler for trustworthiness). The second succeeded because the triumvirate held together, and because, in official circles no less than among the public at large, there was an overwhelming sense of the need for change.

It was a very great misfortune that Asquith refused to serve in the government that followed his. If he had shown the wisdom and magnanimity that Balfour showed at the time, and Neville Chamberlain in 1940, the future of British politics in war and peace would have benefited incalculably. His conduct during the rest of the war was on the whole responsible and tame to the point of inertia; yet he allowed the official Liberal Party to become, in effect, an anti-Lloyd George faction, which helped to condemn Liberalism to decades of eclipse. Moreover, by staying out he withheld his superb intelligence from the practical service of his country while it still had much to contribute.

He said, and doubtless believed, that there was no personal feeling or *amour propre* in his decision. But surely he was deceiving himself. Though he appreciated Lloyd George's qualities, and made good use of them, his attitude towards the man himself was a mixture of fascination, rather patronising affection, and unconscious envy. Lloyd George, for his part, was irritated and at times infuriated by some of Asquith's characteristics, but nevertheless quite fond of him and deeply respectful of his mental powers; also perhaps rather jealous of his education. Whatever their differences, the two men complemented each other and had accomplished much together. The ending of their partnership was a disaster for both, as well as for their party and country.

Their differences, moreover, though very marked in temperament and cast of mind, and even more marked in style, were in some ways more apparent than real; and their contrasted styles tended to mask underlying similarities. Both were reacting against a background of strict Nonconformity. Lloyd George's private complaints about the suffocating boredom of his early life at Llanystumdwy are matched by Asquith's about his experiences as a lodger in the Liverpool Road, Islington, while he was attending the City of London School. Both were self-made men, who owed nothing to the English social establishment. Though Asquith became in a sense part of it when he married Margot (herself, incidentally, of very recent patrician stock), he was already Home Secretary when he did so, and he was never completely absorbed into it. His country house was modest, and when he accepted a peerage he took his title from a university rather than from a landed estate.[1]

Above all both men were fundamentally bold and adventurous

1. When Asquith fell Charteris, at Haig's headquarters, wrote in his diary: 'Asquith was a Sahib; he may have been a tired-out Sahib, but he was, and is, and always will be, a Sahib, and he has been very scurvily treated.' (*At G.H.Q.*, 6 December 1916, p. 180.) In the sense of being a natural ruler of men Asquith certainly was a sahib (as was Lloyd George). But in the sense that Charteris probably intended, the term was misapplied. Like many others, Charteris was misled by Asquith's style.

characters, with a driving passion for power. This is not to say that they craved it entirely for its own sake; on the contrary, they needed it much as artists need their materials or craftsmen their tools. Desmond MacCarthy once overheard a woman asking Asquith whether he liked being Prime Minister.

This question only elicited a dubious rumble.

'Don't you enjoy having so much power?'

'Power, power? You may think you are going to get it, but you never do.'

'Oh, then what is it that you enjoy most in your work?'

'Well . . . perhaps – hitting nails on the head'.[1]

Lloyd George might have said the same, and of both men the statement is largely true.

Asquith's style derived partly from Oxford, where his academic triumphs put him on the road to political success. From early manhood he was culturally an insider, whereas until middle age at any rate (and in a sense always) Lloyd George was an outsider, as an unanglicised Welshman, who had not been to a university, and who did not belong to the posh branch of the legal profession. But there was a little more to it than that. One cannot help feeling that Asquith took to heart Disraeli's maxim that the British 'require grave statesmen'. Certainly his rather ponderous public style belied the fascinating, often flippant, character that his letters reveal (and among British prime ministers he is the best letter-writer since Disraeli). Lloyd George on the other hand never acquired, or wished to acquire, the manner supposedly appropriate to a statesman. While Asquith played it grave, he played it cheeky. Yet underneath they were not quite so different as this superficial contrast suggests. Asquith was less 'Roman', and Lloyd George less of a barbarian, than many still believe.

Whatever their respective merits and demerits, one thing is sure: they were the two men who, in turn, bore the supreme responsibility during the worst ordeal that Britain had ever known. At the end of the war they were the only civilians to be awarded the ordinary war medals that men in the forces received, and it was right that they should share this simple, sublime recognition.

1. *Portraits*, I, p. 7.

EIGHTEEN
New Model

When he returned from Buckingham Palace to the War Office after receiving his commission from the King, Lloyd George looked 'very pale' and said to Frances: 'I'm not at all sure that I can do it. It is a very big task.' It was indeed. Urgent and fateful issues awaited him, but before he could begin to wrestle with them he had first to be sure that he could form a government commanding a majority in Parliament, and also having the indispensable support of Labour. Whether or not he could do so hung in the balance for about twenty-four hours, and during that time he was not even officially Prime Minister.

From his own party he could expect little if any assistance at the highest level. According to Frances, a message was received from Asquith during the evening 'to the effect that his Liberal colleagues had refused in a body to serve under D.'. There is no indication who brought the message, and some doubt about the precise form it took. The following day Runciman denied that there had been any collective decision to refuse office in the new government, though Buckmaster said the opposite a year later.[1] Beyond question there was moral pressure on Liberal ex-ministers not to serve, though probably no explicit self-denying ordinance. In any case, with one or two exceptions Lloyd George felt that he was well rid of them. Authentic or not, the message that reached him largely corresponded with his wishes.

1. Stephen Koss, *Asquith*, p. 225.

But if he could do without most of the leaders he was by no means indifferent to the attitude of Liberal backbenchers, and among them the support for him was substantial. During the conscription crisis earlier in the year, when it had seemed that he might have to go out, Addison and the Liberal M.P. for Bedford, F. G. Kellaway, had discreetly canvassed their colleagues to discover how many would back him in that eventuality. On Monday 4 December Addison and Kellaway began a similar canvass, and by Wednesday night Addison was able to report to Lloyd George that he had 'forty-nine out-and-out supporters' and that '126 others . . . would support him heartily if he could form a Government'.[1] In other words, he could count on majority support among Liberal M.P.s as soon as his position was in other respects secure.

As a working principle in the business of government-making it was agreed that his own party and Labour would be his responsibility, while Law would deal with the Conservatives. In practice Lloyd George found that he had also to do some hard negotiating with the Conservatives himself, but on Wednesday night Law, accompanied by the Conservative Chief Whip, Lord Edmund Talbot, carried out a very important mission to Balfour at Carlton Gardens. In Law's own words:

> . . . after a general conversation of about half an hour I said to him 'Of course you understand that I have come from Lloyd George to ask you on his behalf to become Foreign Minister.' Mr Balfour rose from his seat and without a moment's hesitation said:
> 'That is indeed putting a pistol at my head, but I at once say, yes.'

And Law adds the comment: 'Under all the circumstances I think that the part played by him was the biggest part played by anyone in the

---

1. Addison, *Four and a Half Years*, Vol. I., p. 274. Kellaway had edited newspapers in south-east London before being elected to Parliament in 1910. On 4 December 1916 he wrote to Lloyd George: 'For what I am worth, I am with you through thick & thin. If you have to appeal to the people, my constituency is at your disposal for a meeting at which I would preside, if you wished it.' And he recalled that the Land Campaign had been launched at Bedford (L.G.P.). He became a junior minister at Munitions in the new government, and later was Secretary for Overseas Trade and Postmaster-General. In 1925 he became (some would say appropriately) a director of Marconi's.

whole crisis.'[1] Securing him as a member of the new government was certainly a major coup.

By all accounts Asquith was dumbfounded by it, though it is hard to see why. From Balfour's letters to him the day before he should have guessed that the First Lord would be willing to cooperate with Lloyd George positively as well as negatively. Just as he was ready to leave the Admiralty if that was Lloyd George's wish, so he would be ready to accept any other office (within reason) that he might be offered. Balfour's attitude was clearly that Lloyd George should be given his chance to run the war, and that it was the patriotic duty of himself and others to do their best to help him, in or out of government.

He and Lloyd George had respected each other for the past twenty years, ever since Lloyd George as a troublesome opposition back-bencher had exercised his debating skill against that of Balfour as leader of the House of Commons. Despite occasionally mordant remarks on both sides there was no lack of mutual admiration. Lloyd George had demanded his exclusion from the Admiralty partly to create a vacancy for Carson – while Asquith was insisting that the Service ministers should be members of the new War Committee – and partly because he did not regard Balfour as the dynamic adminis-trator needed to tackle the growing crisis at sea. But he was far from thinking that there was no place for Balfour in a wartime government. Questioned long afterwards about his reason for wanting Balfour out of the Admiralty, he replied: 'Did A.J.B. never know that I always thought he was wasted there? It was never the right place for him. I was determined to use that vast sagacity of his on the things he could do best.'[2] This was not the whole truth, but true as far as it went.

1. Quoted in Blake, *The Unknown Prime Minister*, pp. 339–40. Aitken, who was not present, gives this slightly more vivid account of the incident: 'Bonar Law went to Balfour and found him sitting in a chair in his bedroom, wearing a dressing-gown. He offered him the Foreign Secretaryship. Lord Balfour jumped up instantly and replied: "Well, you hold a pistol to my head – I must accept." ' (Beaverbrook, *Politicians and the War*, ch. XL.) But Mrs Dugdale comments: 'The dressing-gown is the most certainly accurate item in this description. Balfour's way of getting out of an arm-chair could not be called "jumping", even when he was well. When he was ill it is hard to imagine the "pistol" which would have hurried him. It is doubtful whether in fact the offer of the Foreign Secretaryship was a "pistol" at all that evening. More than once in after years Balfour pointed out to me . . . the spot near Buckingham Palace where Mr Bonar Law suggested to him, as they left the Conference together, that he should be Foreign Minister in a new Administration.' (Dugdale, *Balfour*, Vol. II, p. 181.) 2. *ibid.*, p. 183.

It was after midnight when Lloyd George left the War Office with Addison and David Davies, to walk back to his flat in St James's Court, where he had a snack consisting of tea, biscuits and fruit before going to bed. Next morning he was joined for breakfast by J. H. Thomas, Labour M.P. and assistant secretary (soon to be secretary) of the National Union of Railwaymen, in preparation for his vital meeting with Labour's National Executive at midday. Thomas was a key figure because he was pro-war but anti-conscription, and had been strongly opposed to Labour's entry into the first coalition. The Labour men who came to meet Lloyd George at the War Office numbered about forty, represented all shades of opinion within the party, and included trade union leaders as well as politicians. Lloyd George spoke to them more or less off the cuff, and his speech must rank among the most important and effective of his life.

He began by telling them that the war was going badly, and that all countries which depended upon a British victory were in great peril.

The fall of Bucharest [which had occurred two days before] is not merely a question of one city passing into the hands of the enemy; it means a good deal more than that; it means that for the moment the blockade is broken, the work of the Fleet to that extent neutralised, and that we are face to face with the grimmest and most perilous struggle in which this country has ever been engaged. . . . I hate war; I abominate it. I sometimes think 'Am I dreaming? Is it a nightmare? It cannot be fact.' But these are questions to ask and answer before you go into a war; once you are in it you have to go grimly through it, otherwise the causes which hang upon a successful issue will perish. Delay in war is as fatal as in an illness. An operation which may succeed today is no good six weeks later or, maybe, even three days later. So in war. Action which today may save the life of a country, taken a week later is too late.

The country was looking for a government that would prosecute the war efficiently, but there could be no such government without the cooperation of Labour. He proposed that Labour should be represented on the new central body running the war, and that it should also be much better represented in other departments than it had been in the previous ministry. He suggested setting up two new departments, Labour and Pensions, each to be controlled by a Labour man; and in addition, that there should be two under-secretaryships and a place in the Whips' office for Labour. (In the Asquith government there had been only one Labour Cabinet minister – Henderson – one under-secretary and one Whip.)

He spoke further of his plans for overhauling the machinery of government: of the form that his central directing body would take; of the need for the State to control the mines, shipping and food supply; and of ways by which the home production of food might be increased. 'It would be a very good thing,' he said 'to have a national Lent.'

> The Catholic religion is, I think, the most complete study of human nature that has ever been presented to the world, and when it declares its Lent there is a good deal of practical common sense in it. It is not merely good morally, but it is good physically, and I am perfectly certain that a rationing system of Lent, which would be appropriate during the horrors of war, would make us feel that at any rate we were making some contribution in suffering discomfort at home. War must be brought home to nations.

When he had finished speaking he said he would try to answer any questions that he was free to answer without consulting colleagues (a reservation which must have caused some amusement to his audience). Sidney Webb asked him whether compulsory service would apply to labour. This policy had, indeed, recently been accepted in principle by the War Committee, but he replied that there would be no change in policy, though it remained 'necessary to have a complete mobilisation of labour in order to utilise to the fullest extent the country's resources'. Asked if it was his intention to continue the war until peace could be dictated, or if he would ever be prepared to consider reasonable peace proposals, he replied that he would listen to proposals at once if they were reasonable, and that 'surely no one imagined that we wanted to go on with the war and have our own sons killed'. But we must have a clear idea of Germany's intentions before we started to negotiate, and he 'thought every sensible man who wanted a good peace would be of the same opinion'.

Frances, who was present (presumably taking the shorthand notes), describes the meeting as a great success. 'Everything depended on it, and D. was at his craftiest. . . . The majority of them came there sulky, hostile, and they went away laughing and friendly.' Ramsay Mac-Donald said of Lloyd George's performance that he was 'exceedingly amiable, but excessively indefinite. He was like a bit of mercury.' Lloyd George told MacDonald that 'he might have to put him in prison, but he hoped he would come and breakfast with him the day he came out'. The Labour men adjourned to consider how they should respond, and as they left Lloyd George felt confident that their decision would be favourable. Later in the afternoon he heard that it was. Perhaps it was at that moment that he said he thought he would be Prime Minister before seven o'clock.[1]

But there were still some difficulties to overcome on the Conservative side. After his striking success with Balfour the night before, Law had been making no further progress with his colleagues. Conscious of having treated them rather cavalierly during the past fortnight, and not wishing to risk a split in his party, he was anxious to persuade most of them to join the new government. Lansdowne was expendable, and would obviously be out of place in a Lloyd George ministry. But Law wanted the 'three C's' and Long to be included, and they were playing hard to get.

Lloyd George's attitude to them is harder to determine. In his memoirs he quotes a letter received at the time from Leo Maxse, urging him to get rid of 'useless rubbish' on the Conservative side as well as 'the debris which encumbered the late Prime Minister'. And Lloyd George implies that he would have acted on this advice but for Law's misplaced loyalty to colleagues 'who were not conspicuously faithful to him'.[2] It may have been so, but the evidence rather suggests that he, too, preferred to corral as many of the Conservative leaders as possible, even the less important ones. Having not much more than half of his own party, and (by the end of the afternoon) Labour, firmly behind him in the Commons, he might well have thought that it would be prudent to make quite sure of the Conservatives.

Whatever the reason, he exerted himself to bring the laggards in. His first approach, during the afternoon, was to Long, but that was a failure. Long was quite friendly, but said that he could not commit himself in isolation from the other Conservative ex-ministers. Very different, however, was the response of Curzon when invited to join the new central war directorate. He immediately accepted without reference to his colleagues, and the solidarity of their little group was thus broken. This was very convenient for Lloyd George and not least

1. F.S.D., 7 December 1916, p. 134. MacDonald's remark quoted in Aitken, *Politicians and the War*, ch. XL. The decision to join was taken by a majority of eighteen to twelve, though Lloyd George says in his memoirs that the margin was only one vote. Ernest Bevin was among the trade unionists present.
2. W.M., pp. 1045-6.

because Curzon was the only member of it whose intellect and ability he really respected (though he had little respect for his character).

Even so, he had to make a show of negotiating with the group before its other members would agree to serve. In the early evening. the 'three C.'s' and Long came to see him at the War Office. He told them of the support he had from many Liberal M.P.s, and from Labour; and he gave them a quite detailed account of his proposed new government and how it would work. He assured them that he was under no obligation to the Irish party, said that he had no intention of asking Churchill or Northcliffe to join the government, and also disclaimed any intention of seeking to change the Army command. With these assurances Chamberlain, Cecil and Long were satisfied.

Lloyd George was now able to report positively to the King. At 7.30 p.m. he was received again at Buckingham Palace, informed the King that he would be able to form a ministry, and kissed hands on his appointment as Prime Minister. Returning to the War Office he first suggested to Addison they might go and dine at the National Liberal Club. But, thinking better of it, he sent out for two bowls of soup, a small piece of fish, and some cold chicken and ham (which went untouched). This frugal meal was a suitable inauguration of the national Lent which he had called for earlier in the day.

It was possible for Lloyd George to combine securing a majority and forming a government within the space of a single day, because he was by no means unprepared for the task. Apart from all the thought that he had given to the system of war direction during the past two years, he and Law had been discussing the immediate practical problems since Asquith resigned on Tuesday. All the same it was a remarkable feat to establish the new regime as quickly as he did, and an impression of confident energy was thereby forcibly conveyed.

In the government that he submitted to the King there were several strikingly novel features, but the most important of all was the replacement of the unwieldy peacetime Cabinet by a War Cabinet of five. This device enabled him to solve at a stroke the problem which had bedevilled all previous attempts to create a more efficient system of war government. So long as the war committee, or whatever it might be called, had to be ultimately subject to the traditional Cabinet, there was bound to be muddle and delay. Yet how could the Cabinet, with its accepted position of supreme executive power, abdicate in favour of a mere committee? The only answer lay in turning the committee into the Cabinet for the duration of the war, and the strongest evidence that Lloyd George's solution was the right one is that it was immediately copied when Britain had to go to war again. In detail the Chamberlain and Churchill War Cabinets differed from Lloyd George's, but the principle that he had established was, as a matter of course, readopted.

The proposals discussed with Asquith for a reformed war committee had assumed a membership of three or four, and inclusion of the Service ministers. Lloyd George's War Cabinet was slightly larger, and the Service ministers were not in it. While he was War Minister himself it was natural for him to agree that the Service ministers should be included, but his preference always was for a directing body of ministers without departmental ties, and when he was Prime Minister he was free to revert to that idea. There was, indeed, one departmental minister in his War Cabinet, though not a Service minister. Bonar Law was a member as Chancellor of the Exchequer, but he was the only exception.

Law was given as well the post of Leader of the House of Commons, and thus acquired, under Lloyd George, the role of deputy leadership which he might have had under Asquith, if Lloyd George had then been willing to concede it to him. It was not Lloyd George's view, but their relative positions, that had changed. What was always a sensible arrangement in theory became acceptable to Lloyd George in practice when he was Number One in the government and no longer defending the position of Number Two against a newcomer. He and Law were to develop an extraordinarily close working relationship, and the goodwill which had long existed between them, but which in the Asquith coalition had been somewhat attenuated, was to return in full vigour. Their very different temperaments harmonised to perfection, and Law's biographer is able to say that 'throughout their joint tenure of power their friendship was never marred by a single quarrel'.[1]

The other three members of Lloyd George's original War Cabinet were Henderson, Curzon and Milner. Departmental ministers and expert advisers were to attend as required, but Balfour from the first was entitled to come not only when foreign affairs were on the agenda, but whenever he could spare the time. He was therefore in effect an additional member of the War Cabinet. A similar role might

---

1. Blake, *The Unknown Prime Minister*, p. 342.

very appropriately have been Asquith's if he had joined the Government as, say, Lord Chancellor. The two ex-Prime Ministers might thus have shared the privilege of attending War Cabinet meetings by choice rather than as a regular duty.

Henderson was appointed, obviously, because he was leader of the Labour Party. He had already deserved well of Lloyd George, and of the State. 'Uncle Arthur' was never a high-flyer, but he was loyal, solid and dependable, grounded in trade unionism and Wesleyan lay preaching. Curzon was almost at the opposite pole: a self-conscious grandee, as shifty as he was brilliant. Yet he was a zealous public servant, and Lloyd George was right to make full use of him. In the Asquith Government he had had too little to do.

The remaining place in the War Cabinet was to have been filled by Carson, according to Lloyd George's original plan, and it had been generally taken for granted that Carson would be a member of whatever body was set up for running the war. But on Saturday the 9th *The Times*, in an incomplete and unofficial, but largely accurate, list of appointments, bracketed him and Milner as candidates for either the War Cabinet or the Admiralty. And when the official list was published on Monday it was seen that Milner was in the War Cabinet as Minister without Portfolio, while Carson was outside it as First Lord. Clearly there had been a last-minute switch. But why?

One biographer of Carson suggests that Lloyd George first offered him the Woolsack, which he refused for the characteristically high-minded reason that, if he ever had to resign over Ireland, he would not like it to be said that, with a Lord Chancellor's pension, he was making no sacrifice. According to the same source he was reluctant to go to the Admiralty but himself 'used his influence to find a seat on the War Council for his friend Lord Milner.[1] Another biographer says that he at first 'demurred somewhat' to the proposal that he become First Lord, but 'eventually agreed when Lloyd George promised that he should have an able administrator to assist him at the Admiralty'.[2] Lloyd George blames the jealousy of Carson's Unionist colleagues for a decision which he knew at the time to be mistaken:

It was my original intention to make him a Member of the War Cabinet. He had no administrative experience and I thought that his great talents could be better utilised in a consultative than in an

1. Ian Colvin, *The Life of Lord Carson*, Vol. 3, p. 215.
2. H. Montgomery Hyde, *Carson*, p. 414.

executive position. Conservative Ministers, however, resented his promotion to the Cabinet that directed the War, and I had reluctantly to give way.[1]

This version does not wholly accord with the evidence of Austen Chamberlain, in the letter (already quoted) which he wrote the day after he and his colleagues had discussed the new government with Lloyd George at the War Office:

> We pressed Lloyd George to include also Milner, either in addition to or in place of Carson . . . but we were told that his addition was impossible because it would necessitate the inclusion of another Liberal – even as it stood there was only one Liberal to three Unionists – and would upset Lloyd George's agreement with the Labour Party, who had been promised one seat in a War Committee of five. As to the substitution of Milner's name for Carson's, Bonar Law who was present at part of our interview could only say that it was useless to discuss it as Lloyd George was pledged up to the eyes to Carson.

Chamberlain adds in a P.S., written three days later, that he is 'glad to find that Milner is, after all, a Member of the War Committee whilst Carson goes to the Admiralty'.[2] There is nothing in that, or in the earlier passage, to suggest that a veto was applied to Carson's membership of the War Cabinet. Moreover, in the record that was kept of the discussion with Lloyd George on the 7th, it is stated that the Conservative ministers 'strongly pressed' Milner's claims *to the Admiralty*, and there is no hint of any objection to Carson's claims to a War Cabinet seat.[3]

It seems likely, therefore, that when Lloyd George soon afterwards went to Buckingham Palace with his provisional list of ministers, he was still intending to have Carson in the War Cabinet and to send Milner to the Admiralty. No doubt he had taken due note of the strong feelings expressed on Milner's behalf, though he hardly needed to do so because he was anyway intending to give Milner an important post. But the rather confusing evidence of the War Office meeting does not, on any view, suggest that he was under overwhelming pressure to appoint Milner to one post rather than to the other. He

1. W.M., p. 1077.
2. Chamberlain, *Down the Years*, 8 December 1916 (pp. 128–9).
3. Quoted in Aitken, *Politicians and the War*, ch. XLI.

must have known, surely, that the 'three C's' and Long would acquiesce in his appointment to either of the positions discussed, though they might feel that the War Cabinet would give his talents greater scope.

The King, however, seems to have argued firmly and persuasively in favour of sending Carson to the Admiralty, because there is clear evidence that it was to *his* wishes in the matter that Lloyd George deferred. The truth emerges from a conversation between him and Stamfordham about a relatively minor appointment: that of Sir Alfred Mond as First Commissioner of Works. Stamfordham objected to Mond on the King's behalf, because as the son of a German immigrant he had a guttural accent which might be a handicap in wartime, more especially in a minister whose duties included responsibility for the royal palaces. But Lloyd George would not budge, and one of the arguments that he used was that 'he had done what the King suggested about the Admiralty and nominated Sir E. Carson instead of Lord Milner as 1st Lord, so he hoped the King would not oppose Sir A. Mond's appointment'.[1] The King's reasons for making the suggestion about Carson are not indicated, but whatever they were they seem to have been decisive.

It is curious that Lloyd George, who during his premiership showed little regard, on the whole, for George V's opinions, should have begun by yielding to him on an issue of real consequence. He might well have been glad of an opportunity to get his relations with the King off to a good start, but not, surely, at the price of making what he knew to be the wrong appointment to a key post. Perhaps at the time he was less aware of Carson's defects as an administrator than he later became – and later made out. If so, he may not have regarded the choice between Carson and Milner for the Admiralty as being all that important, and his willingness to give way to the King about it becomes, then, much easier to understand.

Milner was unquestionably an administrator of the highest class, as well as a political prophet and guru of more uneven quality. In 1905 he had returned from South Africa, after eight years of more or less

1. Memorandum by Stamfordham on talk with Lloyd George at the War Office, 9 December 1916 (Royal Archives). Lloyd George also said that Mond would be busying himself less with palaces than 'in building huts and securing accommodation for temporary offices &c'. His reason for insisting on Mond was that he was a Liberal, and more Liberals were needed in the Government; also presumably that he was a man of ability and wealth, a major shareholder in the *Westminster Gazette*, and a strong supporter of himself.

autocratic power, and for the next eleven years was an angry, frustrated figure on the far Right of British politics, anathematising the Liberal government and all its works. Before the war the issue that stirred him most deeply was that of Irish Home Rule, which he saw primarily as a threat to British imperial unity, his most cherished ideal. In opposing this he was prepared to go further than any other leading Unionist, further even than Carson or Law in whom, as Parliamentarians, the instinct for compromise was not entirely dead.

Yet Milner was not a man of the traditional British Right. Early in his career he had stood for Parliament as a Liberal, and most of his views on domestic policy were advanced Liberal, even socialist. But, like Joseph Chamberlain, he had been forced into alliance with the Conservatives on the single issue of preserving (as he saw it) the essential unity, and the life itself, of nation and empire. To this, later, the issues of Tariff Reform and compulsory military service were natural adjuncts. His character as a politician is not, therefore, at all easy to define, and the same is true of his character as a man. Though in one part of his being rigid and fanatical, in another he was warmly affectionate, simple and charming; and it was this combination that enabled him to exercise such a magnetic hold over the many gifted young men who became his disciples.

Lloyd George and Milner had, of course, been bogey-men to each other during the Boer War and for some time afterwards. Yet during the first two years of the Great War their views were tending in many ways to converge. Milner and his circle came grudgingly to perceive in Lloyd George the one minister who both understood the need for drastic action and was capable of carrying it out, while Lloyd George found much to agree with in Milner's criticisms of the country's war leadership and organisation. Besides, Lloyd George never liked to see talent wasted, and he could tell from Milner's record that he would be a great asset to any war government. In recalling him from the wilderness to the very centre of power the new premier was not, therefore, merely disarming the far Right, but adding an element of proved and positive strength to his team.

The strictly political value of recruiting Milner was not, moreover, to be judged only in relation to the Right. Milner's radical views on social policy were well known to Lloyd George. As chairman of the Board of Inland Revenue, before he went to South Africa, he had been the chief official influence behind Harcourt's death duties budget in 1894. More recently he had founded the British Workers' National

League, a body to mobilise the patriotic, pro-war and Imperialist forces within the working class, and to proclaim his own gospel of what Robert J. Scally calls social-imperialism. By December 1916 the B.W.N.L. had about seventy branches around the country. It was largely financed by Waldorf Astor, a fervent admirer of both Milner and Lloyd George. This body had some usefulness as an antidote to pacifism and other troublesome movements on the Left, and it provided an additional, though lesser, reason for bringing Milner into the Government.[1]

Because of the uncertainty about which position he should have, it was not until Saturday that he knew he was to be a minister. On Friday evening, when Lloyd George was submitting his name among others to the King, he had still heard nothing himself. 'Whether I am to be in the Government or not, I have not as yet the least idea,' he wrote. 'So far I have heard nothing since the smash, and have not myself gone near anybody. Tonight I received two mysterious summons to a "War Committee" – whatever that may be – tomorrow'.[2] He was being summoned to the first meeting of the War Cabinet on Saturday the 9th, but it was only about an hour before it met that he realised he was to be a member.

His service under Lloyd George lasted more than four years, as Minister without Portfolio in the War Cabinet until April 1918, then as War Minister until January 1919, and finally as Colonial Secretary until February 1921. Though his influence declined after the war, it would be hard to exaggerate his importance in the supreme war command, more especially in concerting the work of different ministries. His appointment was one of Lloyd George's master-strokes, and he never regretted it.

Lloyd George was the only Liberal in the War Cabinet, though probably if he had succeeded in persuading Rosebery to take the office of Lord Privy Seal, the one Liberal ex-premier apart from Asquith would have been invited to share with the Tory ex-premier, Balfour, the right to attend War Cabinet meetings if and when he wished. Rosebery had been a disastrous Prime Minister, and his Liberalism

---

1. Robert J. Scally, *The Origins of the Lloyd George Coalition: The Politics of Social-Imperialism, 1900–1918*. As a social reformer who was also an imperialist Lloyd George had some sympathy with 'social-imperialism' of the Milnerian type, but his outlook was essentially different. He was a Parliamentarian and, even more, a democrat, whereas in spirit Milner was neither.

2. Milner to Lady Edward Cecil, 8 December 1916.

had become increasingly nominal with the passage of time. But he and Lloyd George had always got on, despite their many differences, for as well as enjoying each other's company they had in common a belief in efficient government (more preached than practised by Rosebery) and a feeling that party politics often stood in its way. Rosebery's inclusion in the Government would have been resented in many quarters, but it did not occur, because, after considering the offer for an hour or so, he refused the Privy Seal. Lloyd George no doubt assumed, from all that had been said, that Asquith's objections to serving under him could not be overcome. At any rate he made no overture to him at the time of taking office, though he did make indirect approaches later, which were rebuffed.

No less significant than the creation of the War Cabinet – indeed more significant in the longer run – was the attachment to it of the old War Committee's professional staff under Hankey, which became the War Cabinet Secretariat. The War Committee had worked to an agenda, and a record was kept of its meetings. But at the same time the Cabinet continued to be run without a formal agenda and without minutes. Under Lloyd George's new model government the business-like procedure of the War Committee was applied to the War Cabinet, and in due course the Cabinet Secretariat became, in peacetime, a permanent institution. No single change was more necessary to enable the executive to function efficiently, and it is one of Lloyd George's outstanding contributions to the modernisation of the British State.

Hankey had little difficulty in maintaining his primacy within the new set-up. Lloyd George had great confidence in him and, having told him what in principle he wanted the Secretariat to do, left him largely free to work out the details. Indeed, Hankey felt that there was some danger Lloyd George might be trying to exalt him as a rival to Robertson, and was careful to give the C.I.G.S. no grounds for suspecting that he had any such ambition himself. But in his own sphere he intended to be supreme. As the Secretariat expanded there was some talk at first of dividing it into two sections, civil and military, under co-equal heads, but with Lloyd George's backing Hankey remained firmly in control.

He brought with him three military assistant secretaries, Colonel E. D. Swinton, Colonel Dally Jones and Major L. Storr (who had formerly been with Kitchener). Another member of his staff from C.I.D. days, soon to be appointed his private secretary, was A. J. Sylvester, champion stenographer and later Lloyd George's faithful secretary to the end of his life. In Hankey's own words, Sylvester 'was worth three or four ordinary typists'. On their way to conferences abroad Hankey 'often dictated to him travelling in the train and never had to stop even in the dark when going through tunnels; in those penurious days there were no lights'.[1]

The Secretariat was also endowed with two political secretaries, both Conservative M.P.s: Mark Sykes and L. S. Amery. Sykes was Hankey's own nominee. On 14 December he wrote to Lloyd George that Sykes was 'mainly an expert on Arab affairs', but 'by no means a one-sided man'; that he had 'considerable knowledge of industrial questions and an almost unique position in the Irish question as practically a Conservative Home Ruler'; and that his breadth of vision and knowledge might be 'invaluable in fixing up the terms of peace'. Amery was put forward by Milner, of whom he was a dedicated acolyte, and at first Hankey regarded him as a potential cuckoo in the nest. But before long Amery was able to convince Hankey of his loyalty, and his erudite and cosmopolitan mind made him a distinct asset to the Secretariat. As political secretaries Sykes and Amery had the status of parliamentary under-secretaries, though without any obligation to answer for their activities in Parliament: not the least of many unorthodox features in Lloyd George's new model.

On the civil side Hankey chose a shipping expert, Captain Clement Jones, to help him. Jones had been with the Booth Shipping Line before becoming secretary to the Shipping Control Board under Curzon. But the most noteworthy civilian brought into the Secretariat was another Jones, who was wished upon Hankey by Lloyd George. On 12 December Hankey wrote in his diary:

> I breakfasted alone with Lloyd George. He is very anxious to foist on me a Welshman called Thomas Jones, whom I interviewed after breakfast. Before I saw him I received a message from J. T. Davies . . . that Thomas Jones is a peace-monger and a syndicalist. Still, I rather liked the man, despite a rather sly face like Ll.G.'s and I think I could use him on the industrial side. Anyhow he had ideas. . . .[2]

Despite his compatriot's attempt to sabotage his chances, Tom Jones was appointed and soon became Hankey's trusted deputy. Differing on politics, the two men nevertheless worked together well.

---

1. Hankey, *The Supreme Command*, p. 591.
2. Quoted in Roskill, *Hankey*, p. 339. In *The Supreme Command* Hankey himself quotes the entry, leaving out the words from 'breakfast' to 'I rather liked'.

Tom Jones's father had worked in the truck shop of the Rhymney Iron Company, for which T.J. also worked for a time after leaving school. But his passionate reading enabled him to qualify for entry to the university college at Aberystwyth, and thence to progress to Glasgow where he took a first in economics. Simultaneously he was evolving from a Calvinistic Methodist preacher into a committed socialist and, for a time, an active social worker. But his main career was as an academic until, in 1910, he accepted an invitation from David Davies to become secretary of the Welsh campaign against tuberculosis. Soon afterwards he was appointed Secretary of the Welsh National Health Insurance Commission, and so moved into Lloyd George's sphere.

Yet it was as a protégé, still, of David Davies that he found himself in London during the December crisis, staying in Davies's flat next to Lloyd George's. So conveniently placed, he was able to demonstrate his usefulness in ways ranging from the highly sophisticated to the menial. (It was he who prepared the tea when Lloyd George returned late at night from the War Office after being asked to form a government.)[1] Launched into the official world he became, in due course, a most important power behind the throne during the inter-war years, having meanwhile transferred his loyalty from Lloyd George to his enemies and successors.

In establishing the War Cabinet and its Secretariat Lloyd George was not wholly revolutionary. As at the Ministry of Munitions he combined old and new, building wherever possible on existing foundations yet also adding architecture of his own. And the same pattern was followed in the formation of the rest of his Government.

The most conventional of his appointments was that of Derby to succeed him as War Minister. Derby was given the job partly as a reward for supporting the triumvirate's scheme for reforming the War Committee, partly because he was a leading Conservative with a strong territorial base in Lancashire, but above all as a gesture to Robertson, who also had backed the reformers and with whom Lloyd George could not, for the time being, afford to quarrel. All the same it was a choice fraught with trouble for the future. Derby was completely in the hands of the generals – as was Carson of the admirals – and he soon became a serious liability at the War Office.

1. T. Jones, *Whitehall Diary*, Vol. I, p. 8.

Other appointments made for old-fashioned political reasons, to secure support and maintain continuity, were those of Long as Colonial Secretary, Chamberlain as Secretary for India, Duke as Irish Secretary and Cecil as Minister for Blockade (the last three retaining posts they had held under Asquith). Similarly, Crawford was made Lord Privy Seal when Rosebery refused, and Buckmaster's place on the Woolsack was given to R. B. Finlay, a distinguished but elderly barrister, who had been a Liberal M.P. before the Home Rule split, but later served as a law officer under Salisbury and Balfour. (When Riddell congratulated Lloyd George on appointing Finlay, saying that he was 'an honest old boy and a great lawyer', Lloyd George replied: 'Well, he looks honest anyhow. That is a great asset for a lawyer.')[1]

Though he had no desire to have most of the Asquithian old guard in his Government, even if its members had been willing to serve under him, he did offer the Home Office to Herbert Samuel, but to no avail. The Home Office therefore went to a Conservative, George Cave, who had been Solicitor-General in the Asquith coalition. In his place a Liberal, Sir Gordon Hewart, was appointed Solicitor-General, while the senior Law Office was retained by F. E. Smith.

Lloyd George was keen to have Montagu in, not only for party reasons but on his own merits. He asked him to stay at the Ministry of Munitions, but with undisguised reluctance Montagu declined, while indicating fairly clearly that he would accept office after a decent interval (as indeed he did). So the deserving Addison became Minister of Munitions. Apart from him, Hewart and Mond, the other Liberals from the House of Commons who accepted senior posts were Robert Munro as Secretary for Scotland, Sir Frederick Cawley as Chancellor of the Duchy of Lancaster, and A. H. Illingworth, as Postmaster-General.

But alongside all these relatively humdrum appointments Lloyd George created an entirely new ministerial structure: new in either the character of the office or the type of man appointed, or in both. The new departments that he immediately brought into being were Labour, Pensions, National Service, Food Control and Shipping. To run the first two he appointed Labour men, as promised when he spoke to the Labour delegation. He offered the Ministry of Labour to J. H. Thomas, but Thomas refused because (as he claims to have told the King) he wanted after the armistice to be in a position to say 'I at

1. R.W.D., 10 December 1916 (p. 232).

least made nothing out of the war.'[1] The next choice was John Hodge, an experienced Scottish trade unionist and a Labour M.P. since 1906 – also, incidentally, a vice-president of Milner's B.W.N.L. – who thus became the first Minister of Labour. Another leading trade unionist and original member of the Parliamentary Labour Party, George Barnes, became the first Minister of Pensions, and he was well qualified for the post as a member of the statutory committee on service pensions, and through having been chairman of the labour pressure group which had campaigned for old age pensions before 1908.

As Minister of National Service Lloyd George made a selection which might have been an excellent one, but which in fact came quickly to grief, with very unfortunate long-term consequences. He appointed Austen Chamberlain's half-brother, Neville, who had been Lord Mayor of Birmingham but, as yet, was unknown on the national stage. Neville Chamberlain was an able man, with some of his father's zeal for radical reform; but he was also rather narrow, obstinate and inflexible. It was not wholly his own fault that he failed in his first ministerial post, but Lloyd George formed a prejudice against him which was never overcome, while Chamberlain took against Lloyd George equally implacably. With his oversimplified faith in phrenology, Lloyd George would point to the small size of Chamberlain's head as evidence of his mental limitations. But at least he gave a future prime minister his first opportunity in national politics, and the Ministry of National Service was, in itself, a useful creation.

The previous government had decided to set up a Department of Food Control, and the job of Controller had been offered to a number of people, including Milner.[2] But at the time Lloyd George became Prime Minister it was still vacant, and the very urgent task of ensuring economy in the consumption and distribution of food was, therefore, not yet in hand. Lloyd George turned to a man whose capabilities he knew from personal experience. Lord Devonport, whom he appointed Food Controller, had been his junior minister when he was President of the Board of Trade, and as such a great help to him in

---

1. J. H. Thomas, *My Story*, p. 45.

2. The offer to Milner was made at the end of November, and was a very belated attempt by Asquith to secure Milner's services (and to silence a dangerous critic). When he refused, Asquith tried to persuade him to take overall responsibility for coal supplies. But Milner was no longer available to the old regime. He would do nothing to delay the 'smash' which seemed, at last, an imminent possibility.

dealing with commercial interests, for instance in preparing the measure to establish the Port of London Authority – of which in due course Devonport became the first chairman. Since, moreover, he had made his fortune as a large-scale food distributor before going into politics, he obviously had special qualifications for his new post.

The appointment of a Shipping Controller, described by Hankey as overdue, was one of the most crucial that Lloyd George had to make; and, luckily for the country, it turned out to be one of his most inspired. Shortly before Asquith fell Esher wrote that Lloyd George had 'the invaluable gift of concentrating the attention of his fellow-countrymen upon any issue vital at the moment', and the quality needed in a wartime, as distinct from a peacetime, administrator of 'cutting away red tape and of placing reliance upon personal responsibility by bestowing extended powers upon individuals selected for their capacity, vigour and courage'.[1] There could be no doubt that shipping was a vital issue at the moment when Lloyd George took over, or that much, perhaps everything, would depend upon the individual whom he chose to be responsible for it.

In Sir Joseph Maclay he found exactly the right man for the job. Maclay was a self-made Glaswegian owner of tramp steamers, whom Bonar Law had long known and felt he could confidently recommend. Lloyd George therefore found him through Law, but showed an imagination and defiance of convention in appointing him that neither Law nor any other contemporary politician, including even Churchill, would have been likely to show. He had only spoken to him on a crackling long-distance telephone line, and had not yet met him or obtained his agreement to serve, when he told the King and the War Cabinet that he would be appointing him. It was not until Saturday morning that Maclay called at the War Office, having travelled overnight from Glasgow; and it then took the combined efforts of Lloyd George and Law to prevail upon him to accept.

He was a man who, as well as knowing all about shipping and how to make the best use of it, was possessed of an iron Calvinist will. From the first he insisted that the job would have to be done his way, and he was accordingly 'allowed to draft his own powers, and, after a sharp tussle with the Admiralty, the War Cabinet accorded him the responsibility for allocating the available shipping for all national requirements'.[2] At the same time he refused (though in fact a Liberal)

1. Esher to Murray of Elibank, 28 November 1916 (*Journals and Letters*, Vol. IV, pp. 68–9).
2. Hankey, *The Supreme Command*, p. 641.

to have anything to do with politics, and throughout his five years as Minister in charge of a Department of State he contrived to be a member of neither House of Parliament. He would not consider entering the House of Commons, and only accepted a peerage when he left office. If there was any remote precedent for such a breach of the rules, there has been no comparable case since.[1] Who but Lloyd George would have been prepared to commit such a constitutional irregularity for the sake of making the right appointment to a key post? And who but he could have got away with it?

Apart from creating five new ministries (and others were to follow), Lloyd George showed an innovatory spirit in his choice of men to fill four established posts: Agriculture, Local Government, the Board of Trade and Education. To the Board of Agriculture he sent the scholarly journalist, author, and agent-in-chief to the Duke of Bedford, R. E. Prothero. A high Tory, who sat for Oxford University and had fervently opposed Lloyd George's budgetary policies before the war, Prothero had nevertheless written to him in November 1915: 'I should like to say how greatly I respect your courageous and public-spirited attitude towards the War. You seem to me to be the one Cabinet Minister who at once appreciated the tremendous difficulties and dangers of our task. . . . In happier times we shall, no doubt, quarrel and fight. Being Welshmen, and holding different views, this is right and proper. But I honestly regret having annoyed you – even in those days – by what probably was extravagant criticism.'[2]

Prothero was a Welshman by heredity rather than environment. His father was an Anglican clergyman whose life had been spent in English parishes. But clearly a remote sense of ethnic kinship reinforced his admiration for Lloyd George in wartime. Though he could not bring to his first ministerial office the qualities of a dynamic executive – he had to be supported and underpinned in that respect – his appointment was of immense symbolic value. His personality and career were calculated to reassure the landed interest, yet he accepted Lloyd George's drastic programme for the land. No man was better fitted to preside over an agricultural revolution, and to win consent for it among landowners and farmers.

---

1. The only other case to compare with it, also in Lloyd George's government, was that of General J. C. Smuts, who for a time sat in the War Cabinet without being a member of either House of the British Parliament. But he at least was a member of the South African Parliament.

2. 27 November 1915 (L.G.P.).

To the Local Government Board Lloyd George appointed Lord Rhondda, who as D. A. Thomas had been his principal rival in Welsh politics while he was a backbencher. Rhondda was not universally loved but he was a considerable financier and businessman, whose talents Lloyd George was glad to harness. Having already used them while he was at the Ministry of Munitions, he now gave them wider scope. Rhondda was a parliamentarian, though he had never before been a minister; but Lloyd George's choice for the Board of Trade was a man from right outside politics. Sir Albert Stanley was an Englishman who had been brought up in America and had achieved early success there as a manager of street railways. While still a young man he had returned to England to run the London tube, which he had since been doing conspicuously well. After the interlude that Lloyd George gave him in high political office he went back to London transport and became, later, the first chairman of the London Passenger Transport Board.

But to many the most exciting of all Lloyd George's unorthodox appointments was that of H. A. L. Fisher to the Board of Education. Fisher was an eminent historian and Oxford don who in 1912 had moved to Sheffield University as vice-chancellor. He was also a strong Liberal, and had done some quite important public work of a non-parliamentary kind, as a member of the royal commission on public services in India. But essentially he was an academic, with no thought of a political career.

Lloyd George had met him twice: the first time years before at Oxford, and more recently, in the autumn of 1916, when he asked him to breakfast to discuss the post-war settlement of Europe. Now he summoned him again from Sheffield, and Fisher travelled up 'very miserable with a feverish influenza cold'. What then happened is best told in his own words:

At the War Office I found Lloyd George looking haggard and anxious, together with Bonar Law, whom I then met for the first time. 'I have sent to ask you', began L.G. in his most flattering manner, 'to help in the government of the country', and proceeded to offer me the Board of Education. I urged that I had no Parliamentary experience. . . . The Prime Minister replied that although he was not a highly cultivated man like Mr Asquith, he believed that, being the son of an elementary schoolmaster, he cared more for popular education, and added that we had now reached a point in our history when the country would take more educational reform from an educationalist than from a politician. I confess that this observation seemed to have real force. . . . 'Would there', I asked 'be money for educational reforms and improvements?' . . . L.G. assured me that money would be forthcoming and he would give me his personal support. And so . . . on my return to Sheffield I telephoned my acceptance.[1]

The result of this conversation was the next major measure of educational reform, the Fisher Act of 1918. Fisher was an admirable choice, and Lloyd George was as good as his word. Herbert Lewis, who stayed on as junior minister under Fisher, wrote in his diary:

During the last few years the Board of Education has been very badly treated in the matter of its Presidents. It has been made the dumping ground for people for whom no other post can be obtained. Henderson, for instance, wanted a Cabinet post without portfolio, but Asquith thought that every minister ought to be responsible for his own Department. During his tenure of the Board of Education, Henderson spent nearly the whole of his time at the Ministry of Munitions. . . . Later on Crewe, Leader of the House of Lords, was made Minister of Education, but it was understood that he was only there as a stopgap. Now a real educationalist has been appointed, and I hope that the experiment of bringing in a great man from the outside will be successful.[2]

By common consent, it was.

There were three men who, above all, felt disappointed at being left out of the Lloyd George government when it was first formed: Aitken, Lee and Churchill. Aitken's claim to office rested partly on the business ability which had won him a quick fortune, but more largely, of course, on his work for the triumvirate, and in particular for Law. Yet he had been an M.P. for only six years, was viewed with suspicion by many of his Parliamentary colleagues, and was unknown to the general public. He makes out that he had reason to expect the Presidency of the Board of Trade, but A. J. P. Taylor considers this very doubtful. He may well have hoped to receive some position in the government, and in that case must have felt some disappointment when he received none. But he probably exaggerated the scale of his

1. H.A.L. Fisher, *An Unfinished Autobiography*, pp. 91–2.
2. 14 December 1916 (N.L.W.).

hopes, and therefore also the scale of his distress when they were not realised. Certainly he exaggerated his reluctance to accept the peerage which Lloyd George offered him, and which – despite objections from the King – enabled him to assume in early 1917 the familiar name and title of Lord Beaverbrook.

Lee had more solid grounds for resentment. He was ten years older than Aitken and had been in Parliament for ten years longer. He, too, had been an important auxiliary and intermediary in the process leading to the change of regime. His house in Abbey Garden had been the scene of many meetings, and the fact that he was close to both Lloyd George and Carson made him especially useful. But after Lloyd George became Prime Minister he heard nothing, and on 11 December the list of the new government appeared without his name in it. He wrote a mildly reproachful letter to Lloyd George, to which he received no answer. He then collapsed with 'flu. Getting up prematurely, because he could not bear to languish in uncertainty, he tackled Carson who merely seemed embarrassed and said that Lloyd George, of course, had him on his mind.[1]

This was true, though there were many other things on Lloyd George's mind at the time, and in any case it would have been awkward for him to explain to Lee that, in the early days of his government, he could not afford to quarrel with Law about Conservative appointments. Law's attitude, like that of most Conservatives, was unfavourable to Lee, and he was definitely opposed to his receiving office. If Carson had interceded forcibly on his behalf, it might have been harder for Law to block him; but Carson did not fight for himself, so was hardly likely to fight for anyone else. Before long Lloyd George would find important work for Lee to do, and their former intimacy was restored. But it was not until after the war that he felt able to give him high ministerial office.

Far the most substantial of the rejects was, of course, Churchill, and he was a member of the Prime Minister's own party. But the Conservatives were as hostile to him as ever, and Lloyd George himself, though he naturally put the whole blame on them, was not perhaps too incommoded by Churchill's exclusion at the outset. In his memoirs he argues that he had to wait until he was firmly in the saddle before he could face the row that there would inevitably be if and

1. Lee, *A Good Innings* (ed. Alan Clark), p. 163. 'Flu was going around at the time. David Davies took to his bed with it, and the following week Lloyd George himself was out of action for three days.

when Churchill were brought back. This is a plausible, indeed a valid, argument and the proof is that there was indeed a tremendous row when, seven months later, Churchill was recalled. But it was also true that Lloyd George needed to be well established as Prime Minister before he could cheerfully face the prospect of Churchill as a colleague. So when he gave the 'three C's' and Long a pledge that Churchill would not be invited to join the new government, he gave it with equanimity and meant it for the time being (as he meant several other pledges that he gave that day). But he was not binding himself absolutely or for the indefinite future.

Believing as he did that great talents should not be squandered by the State, it was out of the question for him to keep Churchill a permanent exile from power. The fact that he also liked him was irrelevant; he hardly ever allowed personal feelings to sway his judgment, one way or the other, in his choice of people for serious jobs. At the time of Asquith's resignation he asked Aitken to convey a hint to Churchill that he would probably not be in the new government, whoever might be forming it. Churchill was furious, and he was still full of bitterness when, three months later, C. P. Scott asked him why Lloyd George had not offered him a post. 'Oh! he professed that he had tried, but the Tories would not let him. He did not behave well to me.' When asked if he might yet join, he replied: 'Not in any subordinate capacity – only in one of the chief posts.'[1] Yet when the call came he returned on Lloyd George's terms.

On Saturday 9 December Lloyd George wrote to his brother at Criccieth:

> Presided over my first Cabinet. Found it embarrassing to be addressed as Prime Minister by all the members. Completed my list except one or two small ones I am holding over. It is a good bit. Love to all. . . . Tell Uncle Lloyd that he is responsible for putting me in this awful job.[2]

For the old man, now ailing, who had worshipped him from childhood, and had ministered to his awakening genius, what a moment of joy and fulfilment.

Two days later, when the official list was published, the political

1. *Scott Diaries*, ed. Trevor Wilson, 16 March 1917, p. 268.
2. Quoted in William George, *My Brother and I*, p. 257.

correspondent of *The Times* wrote: 'Mr Lloyd George's Ministry is without doubt the boldest political conception of our time. Some indeed will regard it as a constitutional revolution.' The following day Beatrice Webb wrote more equivocally in her diary:

> The L. G. Government . . . is a brilliant improvisation – reactionary in composition and undemocratic in form. For the first time (since Cromwell) we have a dictatorship by one, or possibly by three, men; for the first time we see called to high office distinguished experts not in Parliament . . . labour leaders in open alliance with Tory Chieftains. . . . A Cabinet has been created, not by a party political organisation or any combination of party organisations, nor by the will of the H. of C., but by a powerful combination of newspaper proprietors. The H. of C. . . . almost disappears as the originator and controller of the Cabinet. All these momentous changes may be War measures, or they may have come to stay. . . . Whatever happens the shake-up is bound to lead to more deliberate organisation – either for the purpose of enslavement or for the purpose of enforced equality.

As usual, Mrs Webb got it a bit wrong. The Lloyd George coalition was not created by the Press alone, or even mainly by the Press. Parliament and public opinion (admittedly to some extent influenced by the Press) were the decisive forces. The Nigerian division was far more significant than any leading article. Carson and Law counted for far more than Northcliffe or any other newspaper proprietor. And without the support of at least two party organisations – Conservative and Labour – Lloyd George could not have formed his government.

Was the new regime a dictatorship? Lloyd George himself did not repudiate the term, though he put his own gloss on it. When asked at the meeting with Labour representatives if the proposed War Cabinet of four would mean that the country would have four dictators, he replied: 'What is a government for except to dictate? If it does not dictate it is not a government, and whether it is four or twenty-three, the only difference is that four would take less time than twenty-three.' He was equating the word 'dictate' with the word 'govern', and simply making the point that a government's job was to govern: to take decisions and to see that they were carried out. In that sense any government in a democratic state can be (and often is) described as an elected dictatorship.

Of course the Lloyd George government was not the product of a general election. It was elected only very indirectly, through having the support of a majority in the Parliament elected six years before. Yet in some ways it was more democratic than any previous British government. Not only was it, like its predecessor, a coalition drawn from all three parties, but it gave stronger representation than ever before to Labour and also contained ministers from outside the restricted world of professional politics. It was therefore a better reflection of the nation in all its aspects than any former government had been.

There was indeed something, if not dictatorial, then certainly presidential, in Lloyd George's style as Prime Minister. Having deputed to Law the leadership of the House of Commons, he was free to concentrate himself upon the work of chief executive. Hankey appreciated the change. 'The new plan was not popular in the House of Commons, which at first resented the frequent absence of the Prime Minister, but it worked well inside the Government, and for the first time since the outbreak of war the Prime Minister really had time to do his job.'[1] But Lloyd George did not revert to the more traditional role of Prime Minister after the war. On the contrary, his presidential style then became more rather than less marked and it was increasingly resented by politicians, if not by the public.

It was not only by reducing his commitment to Parliamentary work that he set out to strengthen his position as head of the government. Realising that a Prime Minister's power was virtually confined to the exercise of patronage, and that in other ways he was just an individual without the resources of a department to draw on, he expanded his own secretariat so that he could keep an independent check on the whole official machine. Men of (for the most part) exceptional ability, and with varied interests, were recruited for the new secretariat, which was housed in huts (provided, no doubt, by Sir Alfred Mond's department) in the gardens of 10 and 11 Downing Street, and so became known as 'the Garden Suburb'.

The man chosen to be head of this remarkable institution was the Gladstone Professor of Political Theory and Institutions at Oxford, W. G. S. Adams, who had some experience of administration in the Irish department of agriculture before doing wartime work for the Ministry of Munitions. The other founder members were David Davies, Joseph Davies – a commercial statistician – Waldorf Astor and

1. *The Supreme Command*, p. 577.

THE NEW CONDUCTOR.
OPENING OF THE 1917 OVERTURE.

From *Punch*, 20 December 1916

Philip Kerr. Kerr, one of the most intelligent of Milner's disciples, was to become a particularly close aide to Lloyd George during the rest of the War and at the Peace Conference. The membership of the Garden Suburb changed a good deal during its six years of life, but Adams remained head of it throughout.

Despite his style and the steps taken to strengthen his office, Lloyd George was not a dictator. His temperament was bold, positive and decisive, but not really autocratic. He always set much store by conciliation and liked, if possible, to carry people with him. Besides, his position as national leader, though apparently unassailable once it was established, was never in fact as firmly based as, for instance, that of Churchill in the Second World War. Unlike Churchill, he was not the head of a 'grand coalition' in the full sense, because about half of one of the major parties, which happened to be his own, was not represented in it. Churchill, moreover, belonged to the majority party in his coalition, of which, when Neville Chamberlain died, he took the precaution of becoming leader as well, whereas it was Law who led the largest component in Lloyd George's. His manifest ascendancy within his government was due to force of talent and personality rather than to the inherent strength of his position.

On 19 December he made his first speech in the House of Commons as Prime Minister, and in it he stressed the gravity of the situation facing the new government and the nation.

I must paint a stern picture, because that accurately represents the facts. I have always insisted on the nation being taught to realise the actual facts of this war. I have attached enormous importance to that at the risk of being characterised as a pessimist. I believe that a good many of our misunderstandings have arisen from exaggerated views which have been taken about successes and from a disposition to treat as trifling real setbacks. To imagine that you can only get the support and the help, and the best help, of a strong people by concealing difficulties is to show a fundamental misconception. The British people possess as sweet a tooth as anybody, and they like pleasant things put on the table, but that is not the stuff that they have been brought up on. That is not what the British Empire has been nourished on. Britain has never shown at its best except when it was confronted with a real danger and understood it.

He repeated, in a wider arena, his call for 'a national Lent'; paid a warm tribute to Asquith; and ended with a reminder that the cause for which the war was being fought was 'the rescue of mankind from the most overwhelming catastrophe that has ever yet menaced its well-being'.

He was now at the summit of British politics. In arriving there he had immediately made drastic changes to the British system of government, many of which would endure. But meanwhile there was a war on and it was going badly. The view from Lloyd George's summit was on the whole bleak and menacing. Defeat was imminently possible, and victory no more than a distant, elusive gleam.

Note on sources (up to 1985)

For the period covered by this book the Lloyd George Papers become, for the first time, the chief documentary source for his public life. For this – as mentioned in the Preface – Frances Stevenson is to be thanked, because it was only when she came into his life that his political papers began to be systematically preserved. The great archive from 1912 is her monument as well as his. After his death the papers were sold by her to Lord Beaverbrook, and held at his country house, Cherkley Court, where he gave me (and some others) very limited and selective access to them. When he died in 1964 they were made available to students at the library established in his honour in a building off Fleet Street, with his friend A. J. P. Taylor as librarian. Since the Beaverbrook Library was closed in 1975 they have been held at the House of Lords Record Office, which is likely to remain their permanent home.

Beaverbrook used to say that the most important unpublished sources for British history in the earlier part of the century were Frances Stevenson's diary and Asquith's letters to Venetia Stanley. As well as acquiring the former from Frances, he had obtained copies of many of the latter, or excerpts from them, for use in his *Politicians and the War*. By the time I came to write this book both collections were substantially available in print. *Lloyd George: A Diary* by Frances Stevenson, edited by A. J. P. Taylor, was published in 1971. (The full original manuscript, forming part of the Lloyd George Papers, can be consulted at the House of Lords Record Office). *H. H. Asquith: Letters to Venetia Stanley*, edited by Michael and Eleanor Brock, appeared in 1981.

The Frances Stevenson diary is invaluable, but teasingly incomplete. It does not begin until 21 September 1914, and thereafter there are many gaps (though not, for this period, very large ones). In the main they occur when the author was ill, or too busy to keep the diary. But the editor suggests that parts may have been "discarded or even lost".

Asquith's letters to Venetia Stanley are the equivalent of a very detailed diary for much of 1914 and the early part of 1915, since he was then writing most days and often more than once a day. They provide an incomparable insight into the high politics of the time.

When Venetia married Edwin Montagu the flow of letters to her ceased (though the Montagus remained friends of the Asquiths, often staying at the Wharf). But very soon the prime minister found a new epistolary confidante in Sylvia Henley, an elder sister of Venetia, married to a serving army officer. Asquith's letters to her, as yet unpublished, are less frequent than to Venetia during the last phase of their correspondence, though still frequent enough: well over a hundred between July 1915 and December 1916. And they are no less informative. (In one, for instance, he gives a virtually full list of all the warships at Invergordon).

Lloyd George's letters to Frances Stevenson, edited by A. J. P. Taylor, appeared in 1975 under the title *My Darling Pussy*. Letters relating to the period of this book occupy only eighteen pages, but they are very interesting, as is the editor's commentary. (All the letters, published and unpublished, can be studied in manuscript at the House of Lords Record Office).

The two relevant volumes of Lord Riddell's diary – *More Pages from My Diary 1908–1914* and *Lord Riddell's War Diary 1914–1918* – are sources of the greatest value, as are the three parts of Companion Volume II, and the two parts of Companion Volume III, in the official Life of Winston Churchill (edited in turn, by Randolph S. Churchill and Martin Gilbert). Churchill's *The World Crisis* is obviously a major contribution by a major participant, like Lloyd George's own *War Memoirs*. Both are brilliant works, but large allowance has to be made for their self-serving character. *The World Crisis* has been the subject of a masterly analysis and critique by Robin Prior (*Churchill's 'World Crisis' as History*, 1983), but Lloyd George's work has yet to receive such treatment.

I will not attempt to give a list of all the other documentary and published (including newspaper) sources drawn on for the book. Many will be apparent from the footnote references that are supplied throughout. I am impenitent, by the way, about putting references at the foot of the page, because few habits in serious modern publishing irritate me more than that of bunching references at the end of chapters or at the end of a book. If readers wish to know the source of a quotation, or the authority for a statement in the text, they should be able to refer to it easily and without wasting their time.

J.G.

Index

Miners' Federation of Great Britain,
136, 219; 1912 strike, 20–1, 35, 45;
dispute in S. Wales, 296–7
Moir, Ernest (from 1916 Sir), 262, 270
Monaghan, Co., 125
Monckton, Walter (later 1st Viscount
Monckton of Brenchley), quoted,
100
Mond, Sir Alfred, M.P. (later 1st Lord
Melchett), 154–5 and 155n.1, 491,
500
Money, Sir Leo Chiozza, M.P., 291n.1
Monro, Gen. Sir Charles, 321
Mons, battle of, 160, 175, 179, 365
Montagu, Edwin S., M.P., 106,
205n.1, 241n.1 332, 349; joins
Cabinet, 240 and n.2; marries
Venetia Stanley, 254; Minister of
Munitions, 362–4 and 364n.1, 366,
380; and fall of H.H.A., 452n.1,
454, 457, 458, 460, 462, 466, 469–70;
reluctantly declines post, 491
Montenegro, 131
Montgomery, Field Marshal 1st
Viscount, quoted 286n.2
Morgan, David, quoted, 71
Morgan, J. P. & Co., 270
Morgan, Kenneth O., quoted, 178n.1
Morley, John, Viscount, 17, 139, 140,
142, 144
Morning Post, 358, 382, 383, 389, 390,
448, 458
Morocco, 129, 131, 132
Mortars, 269, 275–8
Mosses, William, 219n.1
Moulton, 1st Lord, 261, 281–2
Munitions, Ministry of, 183, 253, 254,
255, 372n.1, 395, 397, 398, 496; King
suggests appointment of Minister,
251; L.G. appointed, 251; his work
and achievements as Minister, 256–
307 *passim*; premises, 257 and n.2,
261, 307 and ·n.3, 407; personnel,
258–63, 270, 273, 278, 282–3, 293,
298, 307, 411; powers, 266, 284,
293, 296, 302; Anglo-French

collaboration, 268–9, 277, 282, 295,
322, 398n.1; American branch, 270;
organisation, 272–5; welfare, 301–5;
W.S.C.'s comment, 307; Montagu
appointed, 362; Addison appointed,
491
Munro, Robert, M.P. (later Lord
Alness), 491
Murray, Alexander, Master of Elibank,
M.P. (from spring 1912 Lord
Murray of Elibank), 15–16, 62n.1,
64, 65, 74, 95n.1; buys Marconi
shares for Lib. funds, 49; leaves
politics, 49–50; share purchase for
Party disclosed, 53–4; in S. America,
54, 56, 61; and Min. of Munitions,
298
Murray, Gen. Sir Archibald, 313 and
n.1
Murray, Capt. Arthur, 53, 64
Murray, Bruce K., quoted, 105 and n.1
Murray, Lt.-Gen. Sir James Wolfe,
198, 313n.1

Nash, Vaughan, 15, 17n.1
Nathan, Sir Matthew, 344–5, 347
National Farmers' Union, 102
National Labour Advisory Committee,
219, 265, 290
National Insurance, 16, 32–3, 34 and
n.1, 35, 40, 68–9, 92, 93, 151, 263,
296
National Register, 327, 329, 331
National Review, 18n.1, 51
National Service League, 329
National Union of Railwaymen, 478
Neue Freie Presse, of Vienna, 128, 129
Neuve Chapelle, battle of, 241, 242,
264, 312
Newman, Sir George, 302
New York Herald, 16
Nicholas II, Emperor of Russia ('The
Tsar'), 139, 310
Nicholson, Field Marshal Lord, 368
Nicholl, Sir William Robertson, 38n.1,
167, 186, 345n.1

make the proposal.'[1]

He was surely right to negotiate separately rather than to risk any repetition of the disastrous Buckingham Palace conference in 1914. His talks with the various Irish leaders took place at the Ministry of Munitions, and those involved were Redmond, Dillon, Devlin and T. P. O'Connor for the Nationalists, Carson and Craig for the Ulster Unionists. Agreement emerged with almost miraculous swiftness and the main points of it were published as a White Paper in mid-June. It was agreed that Home Rule should be put into effect immediately for the twenty-six counties of the south and west, while the six north-eastern counties should be excluded. The number of Westminster M.P.s from both parts of Ireland should remain unaltered. The Act incorporating the plan should remain in force until twelve months after the end of the War, but if Parliament had not by then 'made further and permanent provision for the Government of Ireland' the life of the Act should be extended by Order in Council for as long as might be necessary. It was also understood that an Imperial Conference would be held at the end of the War, with 'the permanent settlement of Ireland' one item on the agenda.

These terms were on balance remarkably favourable to the Nationalists, who stood to gain from them the immediate implementation of Home Rule for most of the country, without any loss of representation at Westminster. Some have objected that the cardinal Nationalist demand for a united Home Rule Ireland was not met; that the exclusion of the six counties was not explicitly stated to be temporary. Lloyd George has also been much criticised for giving Carson a written assurance that the six counties would not be coerced into joining the twenty-six under a Dublin government. But it was surely necessary for him to overcome Ulster Unionists' fears and suspicions if there was to be any agreement, and one may reasonably ask how he could have obtained their assent to any terms that went further to meet the Nationalists than those he negotiated? The wonder is not that the agreement failed to emphasise the temporary character of exclusion, but rather that it came so near to being explicit on the point.

After all, the agreement referred to action by Parliament in future to make permanent provision for the government of Ireland, which could only imply that the provision meanwhile would be temporary.

1. R.W.D., 27 May 1916, p. 184.

And it was also stated that a permanent settlement would be discussed at the post-war Imperial Conference – again in the future. Granted the strength of Unionist hostility to Home Rule in principle, and the proven determination of Protestant Ulster not to be coerced into submission to a Dublin government, there had at the very least to be a certain vagueness about the time factor. To Lloyd George the Nationalists were unrealistic to require a cast-iron commitment to Irish unity which would be meaningless in the absence of Ulster Protestant consent. His own desire for a self-governing united Ireland within the United Kingdom was as genuine as anybody's, but he could see, as most Nationalists could not, that the Ulstermen would have to be won over to it by a combination of time, wisdom and patience.

His fault was not in the agreement that he negotiated, which was a masterpiece, but in the tactics that he employed for putting it through. Here he showed much less than his usual adroitness, and in the end let the Nationalist leaders down very badly. Though he told Redmond that 'he had placed his life upon the table and would stand or fall by the agreement come to',[1] as things turned out it was Redmond's political life, not his, that was forfeit. Having won the support of Bonar Law, Balfour and F. E. Smith for the proposed deal – a remarkable feat, certainly, in view of their past records – he made the fatal mistake of assuming that somehow the remaining Conservative members of the Government, and the bulk of Conservative backbenchers, could be made to toe the line. He did not present the agreement to the Cabinet as a whole, or secure a formal Cabinet decision in its favour, before it was published and put by the Nationalist and Ulster Unionist leaders to their supporters. Thus it came to be accepted, with however many doubts and reservations, by the Irish parties, only to be repudiated by a section of the Cabinet and by a large number, probably a majority, of Conservative M.P.s.

All might still have been well if Asquith and Lloyd George had made the issue one of confidence, and had thrown everything into the task of giving effect to the agreement. But they allowed time to pass and so enabled the opposition to gather strength. Lloyd George blamed Asquith for not standing firm, and beyond question the Prime Minister was much to blame. The Tory dissidents within the Cabinet – Selborne (who resigned anyway), Lansdowne and Walter Long –

1. Stephen Gwynn, *Redmond*, p. 506.

were highly expendable. To have sacrificed an agreement of priceless value to the susceptibilities of such relatively unimportant figures, when the acknowledged leaders of Unionism were supporting it, was an appalling failure of judgment and nerve. And how unnecessary it may well have been is apparent from comments made by one of the wreckers, Long, when the project was being finally abandoned:

> He says that the P.M. is terribly lacking in decision, and that it is strange that a man with such a great intellect should be so indecisive. Long considers that the present unfortunate position of the Irish question is due in great measure to Mr A.'s failure to bring in the Bill without delay.[1]

It is hard to believe that, if he had done so, appealing for solidarity on the eve of great operations in France, the Conservative backbenchers and backwoodsmen would have pressed their opposition to the point of destroying the Government.

But Lloyd George has a heavy responsibility too. As the minister who had negotiated the agreement, at his colleagues' unanimous request, and who had given his word to Redmond that he would fight for it with his life, he should have been prepared to resign if the Cabinet turned it down or modified it in any significant way. He talked a lot about resigning, as he had done before, on other issues, without in the end acting on the threat. Now once again his bluff was called. On 27 July he joined a Cabinet committee consisting of himself, F. E. Smith and Robert Cecil to formulate any additions to the agreed proposals that might seem necessary. This was done to avert the resignations of Lansdowne and Long, but it failed to deter Lansdowne from stating publicly that the Cabinet was not bound by the agreement. On 5 July Redmond accepted a provision guaranteeing Imperial control of all matters relating to the war and public order in Ireland, but still Law felt unable to ask Conservative M.P.s to vote on the agreement, for fear that they would reject it. On 11 July Lansdowne struck his worst blow by insisting in the House of Lords that the deal, if enacted, would be 'permanent and enduring', to which Redmond soon inevitably replied that all parts of it would be 'temporary and provisional'. When, on the 22nd, Conservative M.P.s voted that the Southern Irish, after Home Rule, should no longer sit at Westminster, the deal was dead.

1. R.W.D., 21 July 1916, p. 205.

O'Connor told C. P. Scott that he thought Lloyd George had done his best,[1] but Frances Stevenson's first thoughts were different:

A large section of people think that D. should have resigned when he failed to carry those original terms in the Cabinet: he himself told me he would do so if the Unionists refused them. Now, however, he upholds the P.M. and says the Irish are unreasonable. I think he has done himself harm by his present attitude: he would have done himself less harm by leaving the Government. . . . I think he feels that he is in an awkward position, & I do not know what to say to him, as I don't agree with what he has done. I don't think he has quite played the game. . . . '

Two days later, though, she had come round to the view that it would have been a mistake for him to resign.[2]

Whatever the correct distribution of blame, the failure of his attempt was a tragedy. If it had succeeded there would have been a fair chance of a workable settlement in Ireland, of an end to conflict between Ireland and Great Britain, and even of a gradual reconciliation of Protestant Ulster to the idea of belonging to a Home Rule Ireland within the United Kingdom. Redmond, with all the prestige and patronage of government, might have been able to found a stable regime in Ireland, and moderation might have become fashionable there despite the recent turmoil in Dublin. As it was, he and the cause he represented were inexorably outbid by Sinn Fein. Constitutionalism was discredited and the belief that England would never 'keep faith' strikingly confirmed.

As for Lloyd George, his penance was to come after the war, when he had to handle an Irish situation altogether more deadly that that of Easter 1916, and to negotiate, in circumstances that were then far worse on both sides of the Irish Sea, a settlement which was necessarily less satisfactory than the one he failed to push through earlier. In 1921 his courage matched his skill, but the unique opportunity referred to by Asquith could not be recreated, and it was no longer possible to preserve the integrity of the United Kingdom. Home Rule was a thing of the past – except, ironically, for the six counties – and Lloyd George had then to concede Dominion Status (self-government under the Crown, on the Canadian model) to the rest of Ireland.

1. *The Political Diaries of C. P. Scott*, ed. Trevor Wilson, p. 224.
2. F.S.D., 26 July 1916 (p. 109) and 28 July 1916 (pp. 110–11).